Signature Derrida

Jacques Derrida

Edited with a Preface by
Jay Williams
Introduction by
Françoise Meltzer

The University of Chicago Press :: Chicago and London

Jacques Derrida (1930–2004) was director of studies at the École des hautes études en sciences sociales, Paris, and professor of humanities at the University of California, Irvine. He is the author of many books published by the University of Chicago Press. Jay Williams is senior managing editor of *Critical Inquiry*.

The University of Chicago Press, Chicago 60637
The University of Chicago Press, Ltd., London
© 2013 by The University of Chicago
All rights reserved. Published 2013.
Printed in the United States of America
22 21 20 19 18 17 16 15 14 13   1 2 3 4 5

ISBN-13: 978-0-226-92452-6 (cloth)
ISBN-13: 978-0-226-92454-0 (paper)
ISBN-13: 978-0-226-92455-7 (e-book)

Library of Congress Cataloging-in-Publication Data

Derrida, Jacques, author.
  [Essays. Selections. English]
  Signature Derrida / Jacques Derrida ; edited and with a preface by
Jay Williams ; introduction by Françoise Meltzer.
      pages cm.
  Essays previously published in the journal Critical inquiry.
  "A Critical inquiry book."
  ISBN 978-0-226-92452-6 (cloth : alkaline paper) — ISBN 978-0-226-
92454-0 (paperback : alkaline paper) — ISBN 978-0-226-92455-7 (e-book)
  I. Williams, Jay (James W.), editor, writer of added commentary.
II. Meltzer, Françoise, writer of added commentary. III. Critical inquiry.
IV. Title.
  B2430.D482E5 2013
  194—dc23
                      2012044796

♾ This paper meets the requirements of ANSI/NISO Z39.48–1992
(Permanence of Paper).

Signature Derrida

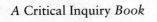

A Critical Inquiry *Book*

Contents

Preface vii

Acknowledgments xiii

Introduction xv

1 The Law of Genre 3
TRANSLATED BY AVITAL RONELL

2 The Linguistic Circle of Geneva 33
TRANSLATED BY ALAN BASS

3 Racism's Last Word 52
TRANSLATED BY PEGGY KAMUF

4 But, beyond . . . (Open Letter to Anne McClintock
and Rob Nixon) 63
TRANSLATED BY PEGGY KAMUF

5 Like the Sound of the Sea Deep within a Shell:
Paul de Man's War 81
TRANSLATED BY PEGGY KAMUF

6 Biodegradables: Seven Diary Fragments 152
TRANSLATED BY PEGGY KAMUF

7 Of Spirit 220
TRANSLATED BY GEOFFREY BENNINGTON AND RACHEL BOWLBY

8 Given Time: The Time of the King 240
TRANSLATED BY PEGGY KAMUF

9 "To Do Justice to Freud": The History of Madness
in the Age of Psychoanalysis 270
TRANSLATED BY PASCALE-ANNE BRAULT AND MICHAEL NAAS

10   Adieu   315
TRANSLATED BY PASCALE-ANNE BRAULT AND MICHAEL NAAS

11   By Force of Mourning   326
TRANSLATED BY PASCALE-ANNE BRAULT AND MICHAEL NAAS

12   What Is a "Relevant" Translation?   350
TRANSLATED BY LAWRENCE VENUTI

13   The Animal That Therefore I Am (More to Follow)   380
TRANSLATED BY DAVID WILLS

Preface

We are witnessing a new mode of attending to the work
of Jacques Derrida. I am tempted to say "era" instead of
"mode," but periodization does not work well with reception history; different modes operate coterminously, and
periodization too easily misleads us toward a supposed
telos. In summing up a complicated history of four past
modes of reception, though without assigning priority to
any one in particular, we can say that Derrida's work
has been required reading; that it has been considered
the instantiation of all that is wrong with the American
academy and the Left; that deconstruction and Derrida
together were declared dead and morally bankrupt; and
that selected works were considered fundamental to our
understanding of Marx, Freud, Foucault, and Husserl.
But now we are witnessing a new wave of primary and
secondary literature that is changing the general reception
of his work: the publication of his lectures, the first of
what will undoubtedly be a number of academic biog-
raphies, a journal entitled *Derrida Today*, and new critical work produced from a more serious intellectual topos
than that of the culture wars. It is a time of rereading
Derrida in order to more accurately assess his place, not
in the academy or the culture at large, but in the history
of philosophy and critical theory.

This volume collects major work from his entire career, a sampling made possible because of his friendship and intellectual relationship with the journal *Critical Inquiry* and its editors, especially W. J. T. Mitchell, Arnold I. Davidson, and Françoise Meltzer. There is an emphasis on his later writings, what Meltzer in her introduction calls the work of "the public intellectual who writes on a broad variety of topics." This shouldn't be surprising; after all, *Critical Inquiry* is not a specialized philosophical journal. We would like to think that this is why he found the journal compatible. A different genre in which he wrote specifically for *Critical Inquiry*, however, puts this issue of compatibility in a different light. Derrida wrote "But, beyond . . . (Open Letter to Anne McClintock and Rob Nixon)" and "Biodegradables: Seven Diary Fragments" at the invitation of the editors of *Critical Inquiry*, who had hoped he would respond to critiques, sometimes fierce, to essays he had first published in the journal's pages. (The critiques may be found at http://criticalinquiry.uchicago.edu/.) These two critical responses offer the clearest public record of Derrida's philosophical relationship to *Critical Inquiry*, one of his principal outlets in the Americas.

Time and again in these critical responses, Derrida refers to *Critical Inquiry*'s hospitality. But by calling the journal hospitable and inviting he is also calling attention to the problematic nature of being a host and of being a guest, the journal as host and the writer as guest. The host is inviting yet controlling, welcoming but exclusionary. The guest is grateful yet reluctant, proud to be selected yet suspicious of the reasons. In "Biodegradables," Derrida responds at great length yet insists that *Critical Inquiry* urged him to do so; he would not have come if he had not been invited. One must always insist on Derrida's graciousness and generosity, but his work reveals the aporias within the concepts of hospitality, the gift, and mourning (major themes that appear throughout this volume). *Critical Inquiry*, as host, invites critical responses to further dialogue, but it determines who responds and who has the last word. That Derrida chafes under these controls is quite obvious. But it is more than a merely personal reaction. It is the pressure he puts on the notion of hospitality that, for example, underlies the humor mixed with irritation in the following passage in "Biodegradables." In these journal fragments, he is deciding whether to respond to the six critical responses: "If one day I respond, could I make a bet? . . . A liberal journal [and the editors ask themselves, Are we really only 'liberal'? But this is the necessary defense of the guest in face of the host's rules.] has to accept that bets are made in its pages. All the more so since, with its liberal, pluralist concern to maintain public discussion without privileging any side (an irreproachable policy, especially if its principle could be rigorously and sincerely applied [here we have Derrida both accepting *Critical Inquiry*'s hospitality and questioning it]), this excellent publication is managed by wise men and women and responsible intellectuals [now of course the reader is wondering if indeed *CI* is 'excellent,' 'wise,' and 'responsible']. Thus they also know—it's the logic of debates, bets, auction bids, and bidding wars—that this can serve the prosperity of the institution, I mean the promotion of the journal that is urging me to respond at a single blow to six articles at once!"

Derrida goes on to consider the connection between hospitality and the archive. In "Biodegradables" Derrida plays with the ideas of the impermanence (one hopes) of bad thought—as represented by five of the six critical responses—the Heideggerian-inspired question of the remnant or remainder, and the content and nature of a written archive. As Peggy Kamuf, the translator of "Biodegradables," notes, Derrida is writing here in "a semiparodic or citational mode," so it is no small wonder that Derrida at one point discusses archive in the practical terms of the "problems of storage for American university libraries." Derrida imagines that if, in the future, in the interests of conserving space, all of *CI* had to be replaced by brief summations of its essays, what would remain of this debate about Paul de Man? And this questioning of the remainder leads him to a note to himself regarding the proper name function and the signature: "Try later to show how the proper name— the proper name function—finally corresponds to this function of non-biodegradability. The proper name belongs neither to language nor to the element of conceptual generality. In this regard, every work survives *like and as* a proper name." Derrida is led to conclude in this section of his response that "meaning," which is not "the measure of interest," also does not explain why one thing "wears away" and another does not. The question of the "nonbiodegradability" of the proper name and of its signature remains open.

This simultaneity of Derrida's multiple analyses—his ability in the short space of a critical response not only to refute his interlocutors but to step back and deconstruct the forum itself and its hosts and the concepts that guide the host's management of the forum in which he is a willing participant and then to indicate future philosophical work that needs to be done, all conducted in shifting yet appropriate rhetorical registers (comedy, seriousness, semiparody)—leads us to consider the signature of his work. *Signature Derrida*: We have first to think of *signature* in its most obvious sense. What was typical of Derrida's work? His essays often begin with a single interrogation, sometimes an interrogation of a single word: "what is a thing?" "Which war?" "How dare one

speak of translation?" "Whom would one be addressing" when one says
adieu? "Who could ever speak of the work of Louis Marin?" By beginning with a single word or phrase Derrida showed us the first step in the
long process of reading the inexhaustibility of a text and confronting the
impossibility of explicating the whole. A common misunderstanding of
Derrida's work is that he sought out opposed binaries in a word or larger
text. This was not the end of reading. Derrida did not have a signature
move or even a method, which is often labeled "deconstruction." His
suspicion of something called "deconstruction" is evident throughout
this volume. If he didn't use that word in quotation marks, then he often
pluralized it. In later work he found multiple ways to not say it at all.
What he did do was deploy various tactics of reading specifically called
for by the text at hand that would lead his own readers to often surprising and delightful revelations. He exposed what might have seemed
straightforward as ambiguous. The ambiguous might become contradictory. An author's meaning (even Paul de Man's) would usually be
exposed as out of his or her control. An author's intention disappeared,
and Derrida could signal the multiple (and sometimes outlandish) ways
in which a text wanted to mean. At his best, he never imposed his will
on a text.

This did not mean that the philosopher-theorist was off the hook,
and so Derrida used the word *signature* in another way: "to take responsibility" as an author. One must own up to one's words. Again, as I discussed above and as Meltzer points out, though Derrida greatly admired
Critical Inquiry he could strongly object to our policy of publishing critical responses. (He of course is not alone in making such an objection.)
For example, he sarcastically praised one of his interlocutors in the Paul
de Man debate. (And whether one thinks Derrida succeeds or fails in
this essay it still remains a valuable document about what deconstruction is and is not; Derrida was exceptionally clear about deconstruction
when he addressed someone whom he thought was wrong about it.) He
quotes from an inconspicuous passage in his interlocutor's essay (a common tactic for Derrida's writing), Jon Weiner's unnumbered footnote:
"'Mark Poster provided valuable comments on an earlier draft of this
paper; the errors that are present are the responsibility of the author.'"
What is an academic convention—to thank a colleague for help while
acknowledging the possibility of mistakes that the colleague missed—
becomes in Derrida's hands an admission of guilt for which Derrida has
respect: "The only concession one can make to him [Weiner] is that the
courageous use of this indicative is a responsible, honest, and prudent
signature." Weiner is "honest," says Derrida. He takes responsibility for

his writings. That is high praise, even if Weiner did not realize he was acknowledging the presence of errors that it took someone of Derrida's acuity to point out. Nothing was ever safe from Derrida's textual vision.

What an exacting responsibility it is to write, implies Derrida time and again. But what are the relationships among writing and the personal name of the author as manifested in the accompanying signature? Without pursuing this rabbit too far down the hole, I want to point to several issues that I hope are suggested by our title. The everyday sense is that to sign one's name is to commit to an identity. It is a self-acknowledgment: I am the person who wrote this. No other person wrote this, and I am no other person than the one who wrote this. But in "Signature Event Context," an essay that deals principally with theories of communication, the concept of the signature explodes beyond the ordinary meanings. Taking on an almost musicological significance (time signature), it now can indicate both the present and nowness, as if they were the numerator and denominator of the same fraction. The author's separation from both the time he wrote and from the text he wrote is marked by the linguistic sign of the signature. The signature marks time past as well as time present. This separation or detachment becomes in Derrida's later writings an opportunity to meditate on mortality. As Geoffrey Bennington writes in *Jacques Derrida*, a book cowritten with Derrida, "my proper name outlives me. After my death, it will still be possible to name me and speak of me. . . . My name marks my death." (This was written in 1991, thirteen years before Derrida's death in 2004.) In "Biodegradables," an essay that is as much a confrontation with his antagonists as it is a series of late-night journal musings on mortality, he touches on death and the proper name:

> Try later to show how the proper name—the proper name function—finally corresponds to this function of nonbiodegradability. The proper name belongs neither to language nor to the element of conceptual generality. In this regard, every work survives *like and as* a proper name. . . . Although more fragile, having an absolute vulnerability, as a singular proper name it appears less biodegradable than all the rest of culture that it resists.

This seriousness is in sharp contrast to the high-comedic effect in an essay like "Signature Event Context." In addition to the analysis above, we see how the signature takes on yet another level of meaning as a deconstructive coup de grace at the end of the essay. To cap his argument with Austin, Derrida deploys his own signature as a veritable yell (perhaps premature) of checkmate. That piece of artwork, "the most improbable signature," ends the essay as well as the book *Margins of Philosophy* with a typical Derridean flourish, offering in its moment of closure an opportunity for beginning new readings.

The connections among the concepts of signature, proper name, writing, and death serve Derrida as an impetus for new readings of the works of recently deceased colleagues and friends—Levinas, Marin, Foucault—thus bringing the concepts of gift and friendship into the same constellation, as Meltzer points out in her introduction. Derrida explores the significance of the proper names and the works they are attached to in the three eulogies that appear in this volume. Friendship, so much more than the mere adherence to a social code or obligation, becomes in the face of mortality a kind of salvation—if one practices true friendship, a constant worry for Derrida. This book, one hopes, is an instantiation of what he intended for his three friends. It is a prompting to continue and transform one's own thinking in the company of a philosopher to whom we are indebted. I would hope that Derrida would have recognized *Signature Derrida* as a gift of friendship from *Critical Inquiry* to one of its most acclaimed authors.

Jay Williams, Chicago, 2012

Acknowledgments

I want to thank W. J. T. Mitchell, Arnold I. Davidson, and Françoise Meltzer. Because of them, I became the editor of this volume. And their friendship has meant so much more. I also want to thank Patsy Williams and members of the staff of *Critical Inquiry* who helped edit these essays when they first appeared: Ellen Feldman, Dave Schabes, Mari Schindele, Ann Hobart, Kristin Cassady, Jeff Rufo, and Robert Huddleston, as well as Hank Scotch, the current manuscript editor. May we and all those who worked in WB 202 meet again at one more banquet and strike our unsplinterable glasses together.

: : :

"The Law of Genre" first appeared in *Glyph* VII, ed. Samuel Weber and John Michael (Spring 1980): 203–32, © 1980 Johns Hopkins University Press, and is reprinted here with permission of Johns Hopkins University Press. It appeared in *Critical Inquiry* 7 (Autumn 1980): 55–81.

"The Linguistic Circle of Geneva" first appeared in *Critical Inquiry* 8 (Summer 1982): 137–53, and was reprinted, with small changes, in Jacques Derrida's *Margins of Philosophy*, trans., with additional notes, by Alan Bass (Chicago: University of Chicago Press, 1982), 675–91.

"Racism's Last Word" first appeared in *Critical Inquiry* 12 (Autumn 1985): 290–99.

"But, beyond . . . (Open Letter to Anne McClintock and Rob Nixon)" first appeared in *Critical Inquiry* 13 (Autumn 1986): 155–70.

"Like the Sound of the Sea Deep within a Shell: Paul de Man's War" first appeared in *Critical Inquiry* 14 (Spring 1988): 590–652.

"Biodegradables: Seven Diary Fragments" first appeared in *Critical Inquiry* 15 (Summer 1989): 812–73.

"Of Spirit" first appeared in *Critical Inquiry* 15 (Winter 1989): 457–74, and was reprinted in *Of Spirit: Heidegger and the Question*, trans. Geoffrey Bennington and Rachel Bowlby (Chicago: University of Chicago Press, 1989).

"Given Time: The Time of the King" first appeared in *Critical Inquiry* 18 (Winter 1992): 161–87, and was reprinted, with small changes, in Jacques Derrida's *Given Time I: Counterfeit Money*, trans. Peggy Kamuf (Chicago: University of Chicago Press, 1992), 1–33.

"'To Do Justice to Freud': The History of Madness in the Age of Psychoanalysis" was originally given as a talk on 23 November 1991 at the Ninth Colloquium of the International Society for the History of Psychiatry and Psychoanalysis, a conference devoted to Michel Foucault and to mark the thirtieth anniversary of the publication of *Histoire de la folie*. The essay was then published in French in *Penser la folie: Essais sur Michel Foucault* (Paris: Éditions Galilée, 1992). It was first published in English in *Critical Inquiry* 20 (Winter 1994): 227–66.

"Adieu" was originally delivered as the oration at the funeral of Emmanuel Levinas on 28 December 1995, and was published simultaneously in *Philosophy Today* 40, no. 3 (Fall 1996): 334–40, and in *Critical Inquiry* 23 (Autumn 1996): 1–10. It is reprinted here by permission of Pascale-Anne Brault and Michael Naas. In an unnumbered note to the first page of the version of the essay in *Critical Inquiry* the cotranslators wrote: "We would like to thank the members of the 1996 Levinas Seminar at DePaul University for their generous help with the preparation of this translation. Unless otherwise noted, all translations, and all notes, are our own. . . . Many thanks to David Pellauer."

"By Force of Mourning" was originally delivered as a talk at the Centre Pompidou, Paris, on 28 January 1993, during a conference in honor of Louis Marin. It was later published in French in *Des pouvoirs de l'image: Gloses* (Paris: Éditions du Seuil, 1993). It first appeared in English in *Critical Inquiry* 22 (Winter 1996): 171–92.

"What Is a 'Relevant' Translation?" first appeared in *Critical Inquiry* 27 (Winter 2001): 174–200.

"The Animal That Therefore I Am (More to Follow)" first appeared in *Critical Inquiry* 28 (Winter 2002): 369–418.

Introduction

Question of context, as everyone knows, there is nothing but context, and therefore: there is no outside-the-text (used-up formula, yet unusable out of context).
—Jacques Derrida, "Biodegradables"

Jacques Derrida had a long-standing, intense relationship with *Critical Inquiry*, a relationship to which these collected essays attest. Published in the pages of *CI* between 1980 and 2002, these essays also manifest the evolution of Derrida's thought and development. Indeed, they mark out the three large periods that can be delineated in Derrida's writing: the (relatively) early, largely philosophical/ deconstructionist period; a middle stage—often autobiographical and frequently spent defending the principles of deconstruction; and the late period, in which Derrida becomes something of a public intellectual, writing about politics, the gift, animals, and religion (among many other things).[1] It will be noted that I am not giving dates to these three "periods"—mainly because they are rough outlines. Moreover, throughout his writings Derrida implies all of the questions to which he was to give more

1. See, for example, W. J. T. Mitchell, "Dead Again," *Critical Inquiry* 33 (Winter 2007): 222; reprinted in *The Late Derrida*, ed. W. J. T. Mitchell and Arnold I. Davidson (Chicago: University of Chicago Press, 2007), 4.

or less of his attention in other aspects of his work. No time frame, in other words, is innocent of other subjects that were to follow. So we cannot say that the early writing is somehow free of politics (in a 1971 interview, for example, he refers to ideology, Karl Marx, V. I. Lenin, materialism),[2] or unconcerned with the paradox that was to become the problem of the gift, or indifferent to religion, and so on. As Derrida himself notes, given the role played by contradiction in his thought, it is impossible to provide a linear, deductive representation of his writings; they do not "correspond to some 'logical order.'"[3] But there is an evolutionary arch, if only of focus, which can be traced in these essays.

Derrida seemed at times to be testing the journal. He knew that *CI* encouraged responses to his writing, and he seemed to relish the ensuing arguments and polemics, even if (particularly if?) he was at times quite angry with the journal for publishing essays that could infuriate him—for example, see his 1986 response to Anne McClintock and Rob Nixon after their own reaction to "Racism's Last Word," Derrida's essay on apartheid. "Racism's Last Word" had appeared in *CI*'s special issue on race.[4] McClintock and Nixon, two graduate students at the time, responded to the article in an essay that appeared the following year. They argued that capitalism works hand in glove with apartheid and that therefore Derrida's notion that the latter will be "brought to its knees" by a "liberalizing capitalism" is wrong. They further insinuated (rather strongly) that Derrida was ahistorical; his apartheid, they argued, is symptomatic of a severance from history.[5] Derrida replied with a cold corrective and outraged sarcasm. Deconstruction has never been merely a method, he writes; it is a series of political and institutional interventions. McClintock and Nixon are "less than honest," for they

2. See Jacques Derrida, "Positions," interview by Jean-Louis Houdebine and Guy Scarpetta, *Positions*, trans. Alan Bass (Chicago: University of Chicago Press, 1981), 37–96. The interview comes at a time when the journal *Tel Quel* broke with the French Communist Party and declared itself Maoist. In this interview with Derrida, Houdebine and Scarpetta more than once attempt to force him into an overtly political stance or at least declaration. Derrida largely elides these questions about "the Marxist concept of 'ideology'" (62); contradiction as Derrida articulates it and "its efficacy on the current ideological scene" (89); and "the question of *materialism*" (91). Derrida refuses yes or no responses, preferring the notion of "positions"; but, as he says himself, these interviews are readings in which he finds himself "*engaged*" (Derrida, "Notice," *Positions*, vii). The use of the Sartrean term is not without purpose.

3. Derrida, "Implications," interview by Henri Ronse, *Positions*, 4.

4. See Derrida, "Racism's Last Word," this volume, 52–62.

5. Anne McClintock and Rob Nixon, "No Names Apart: The Separation of Word and History in Derrida's 'Le Dernier Mot du Racisme,'" *Critical Inquiry* 13 (Autumn 1986): 153; see also 141.

are trying to turn deconstruction into a series of "monolithic menhirs." McClintock and Nixon want books to "stay in libraries," whereas, he continues, texts are not limited to books and paper; they are force fields that are without limit. McClintock and Nixon are guilty of "bad faith" for saddling Derrida with unbridled capitalism. "You have the nerve," he frequently fumes. As to the word *apartheid* itself, he adds, you don't stop using a word because the regime does; you don't confuse a word with history. Derrida thus turns the tables on McClintock and Nixon, arguing that he is the one who remembers history.[6]

If nothing else, "But, beyond . . ." demonstrates the extent to which Derrida firmly believed that deconstruction is not only far from ahistorical; it is a call to struggle—whether philosophical or political or both. Derrida's very difficult and problematic (for reasons I will suggest below) essay about Paul de Man's wartime writings, "Like the Sound of the Sea Deep within a Shell: Paul de Man's War," was the philosopher's first comment on the anti-Semitic texts that had been written by the young de Man, who was to become Derrida's friend and co-practitioner in deconstruction. Working from the famed logic of "on the one hand . . . on the other hand," Derrida erects, as is so often the case with him, contradictory logics and rhetorical oppositions that, he argues, undergird de Man's writings during the Second World War—especially, as we know, the articles written in Flemish.[7] In his response to the numerous attacks that "Paul de Man's War" motivated (many of which were published in the following issue of *CI*), Derrida—as he had with McClintock and Nixon—angrily defends deconstruction and his own previous essay. Here, too, he responds with a steely logic and angry sarcasm. Here, too, he says of various respondents that they "have the nerve"; "*I was invited*" to write this essay, he says; these attacks are "against me . . . against 'Deconstruction.'"[8] But deconstruction is always also "context," and as such it is "insulting" to suggest, continues Derrida, that he has forgotten history, or that the binary oppositions he uncovers elide politics ("B," 183, 184).

These essays spiral into self-defense and indignant justifications of the deconstructive project. They are not, in my opinion, Derrida's finest hour. It is worth repeating here, however, that for Derrida, decon-

6. Derrida, "But, beyond . . . (Open Letter to Anne McClintock and Rob Nixon)," this volume, 74, 71, hereafter abbreviated "BB."

7. See Derrida, "Like the Sound of the Sea Deep within a Shell: Paul de Man's War," this volume, 81–151, hereafter abbreviated "L."

8. Derrida, "Biodegradables: Seven Diary Fragments," 177, 218, 160, hereafter abbreviated "B," an essay to which I will be returning.

struction is always "context." But if context is history and a fortiori political, it has other valences in Derrida as well. De Man's fault during the war, writes Derrida, lay precisely in that he "accepted the context" ("L," 120). Resistance—political and intellectual—is always possible, at times (in de Man's case, as Derrida clearly suggests) necessary. To McClintock and Nixon, for example, he writes that his "Racism's Last Word" was not initially intended for *CI*; it had a different context—the catalog for an art exhibit against apartheid, which opened in Paris in 1983.[9] Derrida "agreed to its republication in *Critical Inquiry* . . . to engage a reflection or provoke a discussion about *apartheid* in a very visible and justly renowned place." McClintock and Nixon's reading, argues Derrida, ignores the "criterion of 'context'" ("BB," 64).

Thus, in "But, beyond . . . (Open Letter to Anne McClintock and Rob Nixon)," Derrida makes clear that the journal *Critical Inquiry* is itself a context. On the one hand (to use Derrida's own syntactical structure), while addressing the two authors he also thanks the journal: "I am also grateful to the editors of *Critical Inquiry*. By publishing your article and inviting me to respond to it, they have chosen to continue the debate that I began here in a modest way" (ibid.). On the other hand, Derrida harbors a suspicion with respect to McClintock and Nixon: "What if you had only pretended to find something to reproach me with in order to prolong the experience over several issues of this distinguished journal?" (ibid.). His suspicion, concludes Derrida, arose in part from the fact that he and the other two authors want apartheid talked about—the more the better. But only in part. We are not, as readers, entirely taken in here: well-known academic journals allow for more than making a case; they can also bring recognition, fame, and so on, to their authors—especially young ones (within, of course, the academic *context*). *Critical Inquiry*, writes Derrida, occupies "a very visible and justly renowned place." It is a place, however, "where, in general, people talk about other things" than apartheid (ibid.).

One senses, in these direct references to the journal, the growth of a different kind of suspicion on Derrida's part—and a profound one at that—regarding academe and "its" journals. *CI*, writes Derrida, has organized a discussion on a "violently political issue, one which has the appearance at least of being barely academic." But, first of all, talking about apartheid "is not enough" (ibid.). Secondly, in academic journals (here, *CI*), we have seen that "in general, people talk about other things." And it's high time they faced the facts of political oppression,

9. See the translator's note in Derrida, "Racism's Last Word," 52.

which, Derrida reminds us, he is doing. Thus, to those who accuse him of being ahistorical, Derrida again returns the compliment; he keeps the word *apartheid* "so that the history will not be forgotten" ("BB," 67). He scolds McClintock and Nixon, who seem now to stand in, not only for those who misunderstand deconstruction, not only for those scholars who want above all to be read in a well-known journal, but for those who—all the while arguing for political and intellectual probity—do not pay proper attention to Derrida's writing: "You quite simply *did not read* my text, in the most elementary and quasi-grammatical sense of what is called *reading*" ("BB," 65). Such academics, then, are not even capable of the first ability of the scholar: knowing how to read. Thus, in response to the accusation that he is monolithic, Derrida again turns the tables and tells the by-now hapless McClintock and Nixon: "You see, I fear you have a simple, homogeneistic, and mechanical vision of history and politics." Or again: "No more than logocentrism and the West, capitalism is not a monolith or a 'bulky homogeneity.' Have you ever heard of the contradictions of capitalism?" ("BB," 76). Derrida foregrounds this textual tactic of turning the tables and of beating a given writer at his or her own game in the de Man dispute.

Again and again, Derrida interweaves *Critical Inquiry* into his polemic with Nixon and McClintock. A serious response, he writes, would take hundreds and hundreds of pages, and "we mustn't abuse *Critical Inquiry*'s hospitality" (ibid.). He refers to the journal's "generous invitation" and says that he is "grateful to the editors of *Critical Inquiry*" ("BB," 75, 64). Such allusions to context and the journal particularly abound in the first de Man piece, "Paul de Man's War." When in December 1987, writes Derrida, he received "the telephone call from *Critical Inquiry* which proposed, singular generosity, that I be the first to speak, when a friendly voice said to me: 'it has to be you, we thought that it was up to you to do this before anyone else,' I believed I had to accept a warm invitation that also resonated like a summons" ("L," 88). Full disclosure: the "friendly voice" was mine, and I still feel oddly guilty that I got Derrida into this mess. But mine is also the only voice that is not named among the three phone calls he mentions in this text. For him, the "friendly voice" in question is that of the journal, and the request comes from the journal's collective "we thought." *Critical Inquiry* is a communal collaboration for Derrida. But, once again, there is a less than confident undercurrent with respect to context (it is worth repeating that the word is constant in his texts and of the first significance for him). A war has been waged against de Man by journalists, to be sure; but it has also been waged by "certain professors." Indeed, writes the philosopher, once one asks, "'What is the press in the culture and politics of this century,'" one ought to continue with "'What is Yale, for example, in American culture?'" ("L," 83). Yale is not only an elite institution in that culture; it is also, Derrida will note, itself less than innocent of past anti-Semitism (and not only Yale, of course). De Man's wartime journalism reveals as well the close connection between a newspaper (*le journal*), journals (also as in diaries), academic writing, and its "papers." Context continues here, and if the young de Man was guilty of anti-Semitic essays, the academy that now attacks him ("certain professors") engages in the hypocrisy of a certain moral superiority based on amnesia.

If it is unfortunate (and I believe it is) that in "Paul de Man's War" the usual rhetorical "on the one hand . . . on the other hand" falls short in facing the specific and serious charges against de Man, and if responsibility, of which Derrida makes (and will continue to make) much, is enlisted into countercharges, it is also the case that he nails the opposition with demonstrations of their own prejudice and totalitarianesque moves. Underwriting the attacks on de Man is the question of nationalism and of national character: French, Flemish, German. Why was de Man silent? Derrida is writing, in other words, in a context of a high-pitched return of the repressed: what were you doing during the war?

The context, to return to that word, was in this case an odd one. Victor Farías's *Heidegger and Nazism* (Philadelphia, PA: Temple University Press) was published in 1987—the same year as Derrida's first essay in *CI* on the de Man affair, and questions about Mircea Eliade's connection with the Iron Guard were growing ever louder. De Man, Heidegger, and Eliade are "certain professors" who elicit serious mistrust concerning their political pasts. Though they never denounced or killed, they are guilty of engaging in the expression, thought, and posture of collaboration—a very public one at that. But no better, for Derrida, are the "certain professors" who respond to "Paul de Man's War" by swooping to attack Derrida and deconstruction on the grounds of de Man's wartime anti-Semitic articles. Derrida responds, in the summer issue of 1989, with "Biodegradables: Seven Diary Fragments."

Written in the form of a diary as well as a rebuttal, "Biodegradables" is Derrida's outrage against his critics. He has decided, he writes, to respond: "I've made my decision. Telephone *CI*" ("B," 162). The title of the essay relates to "the common compost of a memory said to be living and organic" (ibid.). One of the questions this essay raises is, what lasts? What can be the future destiny of a document? What if "one day the complete collection of *Critical Inquiry* has to be destroyed or moved"? A "young librarian" will be given the task of summarizing "the two issues on Paul de Man in two sentences." He will do so in telegraphic, perplexed fashion. Is that what remains? Or perhaps there is too much: "I am going to stop. I have once again been too verbose and too elliptical. Someone, guess who, is perhaps going to reproach *Critical Inquiry* for publishing me too often and at too great a length" ("B," 164, 217). But he was invited to respond, says Derrida. Again, there is an undercurrent of suspicion—not only the "guess who" but also that "the last time, in *Critical Inquiry*, on the subject of my text against *apartheid*, only two authors were set up against me." This time, in reaction to his de Man essay, there are seven respondents. Is this to be an augmented sequence, he wonders: "thirty-six or forty-nine 'critical respondents'?" He is tired, writes Derrida, and furthermore he has never in his life "taken the initiative of a polemic." He has responded only when invited to do so. What others have seen as a "high-handed tone" is a response to aggression and mediocrity, of which he is the victim ("B," 218). In "Paul de Man's War," he had "merely proposed a narrative, some hypotheses, a call to responsibility" ("B," 194). Moreover, deconstruction is not, as some of the respondents have suggested, "in ruins or ruined" (ibid.). Derrida asks only, he says, "one read" ("B," 184).

" 'There is no outside-the-text' " means that "one never accedes to a text without some relation to its contextual opening." A context is not only text ("that is, the words of a book or the more or less biodegradable paper document in a library"). If one doesn't understand "this initial transformation of the concepts of text, trace, writing, signature, event, context," one understands nothing about "the aforesaid deconstruction." And that is "indeed the case here," he adds, with those seven (professors) who have responded to "Paul de Man's War" (ibid.). Surrounded as he is by hostile texts, did "we" at *CI* set Derrida up (should I *not* have made that phone call)? The "papers" (as academics call their lectures, he reminds us) contextualize the scene; and paper is biodegradable. But perhaps the trace that remains here is that of a wound on he-who-began-the-project, the project called deconstruction. Derrida's cold rage in "Biodegradables" cannot camouflage a certain fatigue, but also a sense of fair play being breached: "I give notice right now that I am tired of this scene and that I will not get back into the ring, at least not this ring" ("B," 218). It has, all of this, taken a toll on him—and on deconstruction itself, even as Derrida angrily defends it.

: : :

All that precedes here, all of the references (and there are many more) to *CI* and to the polemic that Derrida refuses even as he fights "in the ring," relate largely to what I earlier called the second period of his writing. Of the first period—the one that I have described as more focused on the philosophical deconstructionist, we have the two essays that open the present collection: "The Law of Genre" and "The Linguistic Circle of Geneva." The first of these, "The Law of Genre," was published in the autumn of 1980 as part of a special issue of *CI* on narrativity. From 26–28 October 1979, the University of Chicago hosted a symposium called "Narrative: The Illusion of Sequence." The symposium included, as well as Derrida, other famous theorists of narrative, such as Hayden White, Frank Kermode, Nelson Goodman, Victor Turner, and Paul Ricoeur. The conference ended with a wonderful talk by Ursula K. Le Guin, "It Was a Dark and Stormy Night: Or, Why Are We Huddling about the Campfire?" Why, asks Le Guin, "do we tell tales, or tales about tales—why do we bear witness, true or false?"[10]

"The Law of Genre" comes out of a time when there was great interest in what was called narratology, which generally required a particular focus on the brilliant textual taxonomies of Gerard Genette, to whom Derrida's essay turns to open the question of genre. "This much is certainly clear in Genette's propositions," writes Derrida, that the most advanced and "recent" work in critical theory has led to a "rereading of the entire history of genre-theory."[11] Rereading in itself was very much in vogue in the late seventies, Roland Barthes (to cite an obvious example) having famously declared that every reading is always a rereading. As against Le Guin, who asked why we huddle around the campfire to tell stories, Derrida's essay will question the boundaries of genre by way of a reading of Maurice Blanchot's short narrative, *La folie du jour* (The Madness of the Day). The law of genre itself, Derrida argues, is threatened in advance by a counterlaw that constitutes this very law. So "La folie du jour," argues Derrida, "makes the *récit* and the impossibility of the *récit* its theme" ("LG," 11). The word *récit* is in itself a dated one—both in the sense of "from a given period of time" and of (relatively) "passé." Blanchot uses the word to mean "short story," but also to mean "narrative," thus refusing a specific genre. (In the seventies, French publishers were still putting out works with the genre on the cover: "novel," "play," "poetry," and so on. Derrida notes this

---

10. Ursula K. Le Guin, "It Was a Dark and Stormy Night: Or Why Are We Huddling about the Campfire?" *Critical Inquiry* 7 (Autumn 1980): 198.

11. Derrida, "The Law of Genre," 8, hereafter abbreviated "LG."

absence from the cover of "La folie du jour.") And *récit* is also used in the Blanchot text to mean an account of events, which is demanded of the narrator.

But in "The Law of Genre," *récit* also elicits the influence of the Russian formalists on French theory and structuralism at the time. The difference between *histoire* (story) and *récit* (narrative or discourse) is based on the mechanistic aspects of the works of the formalists (who further distinguished, it will be remembered, between *fabula* or story, and *sjuzet* or plot). Barthes had written on this question as early as 1966,[12] and in the symposium the term remains central. Seymour Chatman, a narratologist who participated in the symposium, had written *Story and Discourse: Narrative Structure in Fiction and Film* (Ithaca, NY: Cornell University Press) a year before (1978). And Ricoeur was in the midst of writing *Temps et récit* (translated into English as *Time and Narrative*) (Paris: Seuil, 1991), the first volume of which was to appear a few years after the symposium, in 1983. The same year, Genette would publish *Nouveau Discours du récit* (Paris: Seuil, 1983). The term abounds, so that when Derrida asks what a *récit* finally is, or what the borders of a genre can be, or again how Blanchot's texts engage the place and borders (frames, edges, folds, hymen) of literature, he, Derrida, is making his well-known moves into the question of the text-as-text and of narrative (*récit*). The margins, borders, even punctuation marks of Blanchot's texts destabilize the notion of the law that names and controls genre. What Derrida produces here is not only a brilliant reading of "La folie du jour," but also a kind of narratology turned phenomenological. To what extent is consciousness engaged in the *récit* (the account, the telling of the story, the narrative)? And one smells—almost subliminally—the (unacknowledged) presence of Lacan: is the law of genre here perhaps akin to the law of sexual segregation that Jacques Lacan speaks of in relation to the sign? "The question of the literary genre is not a formal one," writes Derrida, "it covers the motif of the law in general, of generation in the natural and symbolic senses . . . of an identity and difference between the masculine and the feminine" ("LG," 24). It will return to the woman—or, rather, "'usually' to women" ("LG," 25). The law is in the feminine (grammatically, in French, *la loi*). The complications for what Lacan calls the "Symbolic" are raised (but again, not directly); the law is also mad: "but madness is not the predicate of the law" ("LG," 31). The Saussurean sign is assumed, of course (the signified made its

12. See Roland Barthes, "Introduction à l'analyse structurale des récits," *Communications*, no. 8 (1966): 1–27.

exit rather early, but it will be a long time before signifiers depart as well from critical theory). More importantly, in "The Law of Genre," the question of the subject comes back again and again: who is saying "I" in Blanchot's *récit*? Perhaps most importantly, "The Law of Genre" interrogates the space of literature (an echo of Blanchot's *L'espace littéraire*) (New York: French and European Publications, 1988) at the edge of which "I/we" kneel ("LG," 29). "The Law of Genre" is a tour de force.

At the end of the symposium, several people were complaining in the usual way about the uselessness of conferences in general, about the boring posturings and frequently unhelpful "papers" produced by many of the participants in this particular symposium. "I disagree," said Derrida. "I think that after this conference, no one will think of narrative in quite the same way. We have learned many things." Certainly, after "The Law of Genre," no one will ever think of genre—or the place of literature—in quite the same way. But Derrida's intellectual generosity and collegiality are also to be admired here. He was not willing to pose as blasé or superior; nor did he wish to dismiss—or belittle—the work of any other participant; nor, finally, had he lost the excitement of discovery or learning.

The second essay in this volume, "The Linguistic Circle of Geneva," is from 1982, three years after the symposium. Structuralism (vague a term though that was) still ruled, and the question of linguistics and the opposition of signs, that "most ancient fund of Western metaphysics," still prevailed.[13] Indeed, the linguistic sign in many ways propels this essay of Derrida's. The sign is clear in Jean-Jacques Rousseau (whom Derrida is here reading), and the essay also considers language in Noam Chomsky (*Cartesian Linguistics*) (Cambridge: Cambridge University Press, 2009) and Etienne Bonnot de Condillac. Tellingly, in the same issue of *Critical Inquiry* where "The Linguistic Circle of Geneva" appeared, there is also, a few pages later, an essay by de Man entitled "Sign and Symbol in Hegel's *Aesthetics*."[14] And though it was John Locke who coined the term *semiology*, it was that loose gathering of theorists interested in the linguistic sign who, starting in the sixties and well into the eighties, were lumped under the umbrella term *structuralist*.[15]

13. Derrida, "The Linguistic Circle of Geneva," 35.
14. See Paul de Man, "Sign and Symbol in Hegel's *Aesthetics*," *Critical Inquiry* 8 (Summer 1982): 761–76.
15. The most important instance of such categorizing was Richard Macksey and Eugenio Donato, eds., *The Languages of Criticisms and the Sciences of Man*, trans. Bernard Vannier and Gerald Kamber (Baltimore, MD: John Hopkins University Press, 1972), the second edition of which was called *The Structuralist Controversy* (Baltimore,

The circle in the title motivates the question of which comes first: language or thought or the social. Rousseau's concerns about the social as against the natural seem in obvious opposition to Condillac's about the theological. These opposing views on the origins of language are met in Derrida's essay by a classical deconstructive move: it could be shown, says Derrida, "that Condillac's procedure is not so far removed in its principles from Rousseau's."[16] But the circle is also suggestive of Georges Poulet, the phenomenological theorist associated with the Geneva school of criticism, who produced a major study entitled *Les Métamorphoses du cercle*.[17] Any French academic ear would hear in the words "the linguistic circle of Geneva" an allusion to Poulet as much as to Rousseau via his hometown in Switzerland. Moreover, Derrida often leapfrogs in his essays: the Geneva circle of linguistics is also an allusion to the Prague linguistic circle where, beginning around 1928, structural literary analyses, linguistics, and semiotics were so famously studied. Roman Jakobson was one of the major figures at the Prague school, and was to be of fundamental importance to Lacan and (to a lesser extent) to a student in one of his seminars, the young Derrida. In any case, "The Linguistic Circle of Geneva" is deconstruction at its best (one of a myriad of such examples); what is imagined as an epistemological break, Derrida will show, is more a closure of concepts and a repetition of that which is "most ancient."

: : :

The third period in Derrida's writing—the public intellectual who writes on a broad variety of topics—comprises the last seven essays in the present collection. The first of these, "Of Spirit," appeared as part of a small

---

MD: Johns Hopkins University Press, 2007) with the first title as subtitle. The book is based on a conference that took place in 1968 at Johns Hopkins University, with luminaries such as Barthes, Lacan, Derrida, Tzvetan Todorov, de Man, Georges Poulet, and Lucien Goldman. As the editors of the volume themselves note in the preface, "with the exception of Lévi-Strauss, all those whose names have come to be associated with structural theory—Foucault, Lacan, Derrida—have felt obliged programmatically to take their distance with relation to the term." (And I should add that near the end of his life Lévi-Strauss himself rejected the term *structuralism*.) The editors add that at the Hopkins conference there was still a "preoccupation with articulated sign-systems and the repudiation of the hermeneutic enterprises of the last century" (Macksey and Donato, "The Space Between—1971," in *Structuralist Controversy*, ix). This sentence serves as a good description of Derrida's text we have been considering.

    16. Derrida, "The Linguistic Circle of Geneva," 36.
    17. See Georges Poulet, *Les Métamorphoses du cercle* (Paris: Plon, 1961).

textual symposium in *CI* on Martin Heidegger and Nazism. Edited and introduced by Arnold Davidson, the essay was one among a lineup of stellar names: Hans-Georg Gadamer, Jürgen Habermas, Maurice Blanchot, Philippe Lacoue-Labarthe, and Emmanuel Levinas. These essays, excepting Derrida's, let me hasten to add, were not first published by *Critical Inquiry*; but by putting them together, Arnold Davidson was able to put pressure on the question of Heidegger's role in Nazism, his refusal to comment (not to mention apologize), and much of the ensuing controversies (Davidson's introduction should be read by anyone interested in this topic).[18] It is in this context then (to return to that word) that parts of Derrida's "Of Spirit" appeared in our pages. What are the "politics of spirit"? asks Derrida. In his 1933 "Rectorship Address," Heidegger "raises a hymn to spirit"; six years before, he had decided to avoid the word and to refer to it in scare quotes. What happened? Derrida asks. Spirit is involved in "the destiny of Europe" and in the legacy of Paul Valéry, Edmund Husserl, and others "whose 'politics' are less innocent than is often believed."[19]

"Given Time: The Time of the King" was a series of lectures given by Derrida at the University of Chicago in April 1991. The essay that appears here was the first in the series and was revised and augmented for *CI*. Derrida opens with a version of a sentence from Madame de Maintenon: "The King takes all my time; I give the rest to Saint-Cyr, to whom I would like to give all."[20] Circling in on Marcel Mauss's *The Gift* (New York: Norton, 2000), and Charles Baudelaire's prose poem "Counterfeit Money," the piece questions the very possibility of the gift—particularly the "gift" of time. The gift, argues Derrida, is aneconomic; it does not participate in the economy of the circle (exchanged goods, reciprocity, debt, credit, and so on). The gift is therefore *im*possible. Derrida's analysis is radical; the gift is another word for the impossible (one hears echoes of Levinas here). Hence, Baudelaire's prose poem on counterfeiting is central; to give a beggar a fake coin is the ultimate in *mauvaise foi* because you put the beggar in a position of

18. As Davidson explains, the essays by Gadamer, Blanchot, Lacoue-Labarthe, and Levinas originally appeared in *Le Nouvel Observateur*. Derrida's own essay, "Of Spirit," was here excerpted and edited by Davidson from the first five chapters of Derrida's book *Of Spirit: Heidegger and the Question* (Chicago: University of Chicago Press, 1991). See Davidson, "Questions Concerning Heidegger: Opening the Debate," *Critical Inquiry* 15 (Winter 1989): 407–26.

19. Derrida, "Of Spirit," 221.

20. Derrida, "Given Time: The Time of the King," 240. The translation should read "to which" (not "to whom"), since Saint-Cyr is a school.

apparent indebtedness to you even as he is placed in danger of being caught with a fake coin. Baudelaire's tale is the impossibility of the gift times two.

The next three essays are eulogies to do with intellectual legacies. Three major figures have died—Foucault, as extolled in "'To Do Justice to Freud': The History of Madness in the Age of Psychoanalysis"; Louis Marin in "By Force of Mourning"; and Levinas in "Adieu." Derrida's sorrow is palpable; at the same time, he uses the ideas of each of the three figures motivating the essays in order to push the implications of their thought—and his own. Thus the essay for Foucault "corrects" a previous essay (from 1963) of Derrida's by inserting Freud and psychoanalysis rather than René Descartes, who had motivated the earlier essay (the cogito, writes Derrida, excludes madness). Following Foucault, Derrida examines the place and role of psychoanalysis in Freud's project of the history of madness.[21] In "By Force of Mourning," Derrida examines the power of the image and its basis in death. "Louis Marin is outside and he is looking at me. . . . I am an image for the other and am looked at by the other." He wishes he could have told Marin how much he admired him. "Why wait for death?" asks Derrida. It has all been too fast; he is still "on the eve of reading" Marin's last book.[22] "Adieu," perhaps the most moving of the three eulogies/intellectual homages, turns to Levinas's ethics beyond ethics (purposely echoing Plato's "good beyond being"). We seem almost to escape the impossibility of the gift; the other is entrusted to me, writes Derrida following Levinas. The other is a duty beyond debt, and my relation to death is the death of the other who no longer responds. Here we arrive at a certain obsession in Derrida, one that is already in the de Man essay and continues in these three: the dead cannot respond to our call or judgments; we may not therefore judge or condemn them. We can only acknowledge. As with Marin, Derrida regrets that he did not tell Levinas his debt to him. Here debt is not the failure of the gift; it is rather the recognition of the grace of friendship, the significance of a mode of thinking, the insistence on the other "beyond being," the call to the other, the pun (and willed ambiguity) of *à Dieu*.[23]

Derrida is able to manifest a searing pain and generosity toward the dead, as if their absence allowed him to speak more freely and simply.

21. See Derrida, "'To Do Justice to Freud': The History of Madness in the Age of Psychoanalysis," 270–314.

22. Derrida, "By Force of Mourning," 345, 349.

23. See Derrida, "Adieu," 324.

So Lacan will appear, after his death, more and more frequently in Derrida who had otherwise passed him over in silence, or in rather irascible footnotes, or in an outright polemic ("The Purveyor of Truth").[24] All the more moving, then, that Derrida refused all orations and eulogies at his own funeral. "He knows from experience," wrote Derrida just before his own death, referring to himself in the third person as if death had already othered him, "what an ordeal it is for the friend who takes on this task."[25] These three essays that follow the thinking of three dead friends are heavy with regret and sorrow; but they also insist on the continuance of thought and the significance of legacy. Death opens up the space of force, which is in turn attached to the representation of fiction.

In the winter issue of 2001, *CI* published "What Is a 'Relevant' Translation?" The essay is from a conference of professional translators, whom Derrida addressed (in French) in 1998. He had been himself concerned with the stakes of translation as early as the first appearance of the English edition *Of Grammatology*.[26] He complained to me that the English translations of all of his early works were too heavily annotated; the Anglo reader had more "help" than the reader of Derrida in the original French. These subtexts that were the translators' footnotes annoyed him; they detracted, he said, from the original, and they changed the experience of reading him. And yet he was the first to remind us that translation cannot be transparent, that there is, in other words, no transcendent signified to which languages can confidently point. The essay in question here (superbly translated by Lawrence Venuti) revolves, as did "Given Time," around a single sentence—this time, from *The Merchant of Venice*: "When mercy seasons justice." Derrida proposes, he writes, to translate the phrase as "*Quand le pardon relève la justice.*"[27] There is somewhat of a *mise en abîme* here because Derrida translates Shakespeare's line from the English into French, which is then rerendered into English by Venuti. At issue, first, is the word *Aufhebung* in Hegel—that untranslatable term that means, it will be recalled, "to preserve," "lift up," and (contradictorily) "to abrogate." Generally translated in the English as "sublate," Derrida suggests *relever* for the French—which means "to lift up," but also "to season" (as in spice—hence a return to

24. See Derrida, "The Purveyor of Truth," trans. Willis Domingo et al., *Yale French Studies*, no. 52 (1975): 31–113.

25. Derrida, "Final Words," trans. Gila Walker, *Critical Inquiry* 33 (Winter 2007): 462.

26. See Derrida, *Of Grammatology*, trans. Gayatri Chakravorty Spivak (Baltimore: John Hopkins University Press, 1976).

27. Derrida, "What Is a 'Relevant' Translation?" 373, hereafter abbreviated "W."

Shakespeare's line). *The Merchant of Venice* is about debt, credit, payment, and Shylock's refusal to forgive and thus to show mercy; he will have his pound of flesh, as agreed. We are back inside the economy of the gift (reciprocity) and its difficulties. Moreover, we are also inside the logic of anti-Semitism. Shylock will not forgive the debt because he is a Jew; were he to convert to Christianity, he would learn the need for mercy and shun usury.

The power to pardon is inherently Christian. But Shakespeare's text is not itself anti-Semitic, Derrida argues; rather, it shows the anti-Semitism intrinsic to Christianity. A "relevant" translation (Derrida heavily underlines the double meaning, playing off the English) is also a transaction, a travail, a traveling. And it is a mourning within *Aufhebung*—sorrow for "the first body, the unique body that the translation thus elevates, preserves, and negates [*relève*]" ("W," 378). It marks the memory of Christ's passion and Shylock's forced conversion, "bound hand and foot" (ibid.), but also the memory haunted by the body that is lost (the lost original of which this is a translation and the dominant Christian context into which Shylock will be translated at the expense of his own Jewish identity). A memory "lost and yet preserved in its grave, the resurrection of the ghost or of the glorious body that rises, rises again [*se relève*]—and walks" ("W," 379). Hegel walks as one of the ghosts of Christianity: "one must never forget that [Hegel] was a very Lutheran thinker, undoubtedly like Heidegger" ("W," 378). Derrida is mourning the loss of that which is Jewish with the dominance of Christianity—in which Judaism is, after all, also a ghost that walks and occasionally returns. What mercy has been shown to Shylock? Perhaps prayer, Derrida says (in a footnote—that nonmarginalized place in his texts), which has "no place at all in the law," could offer some possibility for the gift; "prayer would be that which allows one to go beyond the law toward salvation or the hope of salvation; it would belong to the order of forgiveness, like benediction" ("W," 379n11). The "religious turn" taken by critical theory and philosophy in the last decades has Derrida as one of its heralds—not that he is "religious" (though Paul Ricoeur assured me once that his former assistant was very much so), but Derrida is clearly fascinated by the religious, by tradition, by the erasure of identity (such as Jewish) by a dominant religious discourse/ hegemony (such as Christianity).

Finally, there is "The Animal That I Therefore Am (More to Follow)." The play on the Cartesian cogito is obvious, and the original title is "L'animal que donc je suis (à suivre)," which puns on the verbs *to be* (*être*, thus I am—*je suis*) and *to follow* (*suivre*, which is also *suis*, the first-person singular). Thus I am an animal, and I follow the animal (in evolution and genealogy, but also in temperament, being). The question of the (human) subject is at issue. Long before the present obsession with (indeed, fad of) the question of the animal (Giorgio Agamben's bare life being one obvious example among many), Derrida asks how the human is an animal, to what extent the animal pushes the logic of the limit ("limitrophy"),[28] the edge between life and death, the privileging of a consciousness of mortality. The subject who says I, writes Derrida (that utterance being, after all, the definition of any subject according to linguistics), utters a *bêtise*—the pun in French meaning "stupidity" and, with the circumflex, "animal-ity." But what is the abyss between ipseity (the self) and the *I* of *I think*? Descartes is not enough here, nor is Aristotle with his insistence that the animal cannot speak, nor Friedrich Nietzsche with his reanimalization in *Ecce Homo*. What does his cat see, asks Derrida, when it sees him naked? There is a gaze in the cat that cannot be dismissed or circumscribed by the capacity of man for language. Derrida coins the term *animot*, punning on *word* (*mot*) and *animals* (*animaux*), thus producing a singular, chimerical word that, "though it contravened the laws of the French language," is not a species, a gender, or an individual. Rather, *animot* is "an irreducible living multiplicity of mortals," a "monstrous hybrid, a chimera." " 'But as for me,' " Derrida concludes, " 'whom am I (following)?' " (*Qui suis-je?*)[29] One hears the echo here of the famous French series about the various disciplines *Que sais-je* (Presses Universitaires de France), itself based on Michel de Montaigne's famous remark on the limits of knowledge: What do I know?

Underlying "The Animal That Therefore I Am," one of the last essays that Derrida was to publish before his death in 2004, is Jeremy Bentham's question: do animals suffer? It is a question that Derrida takes on as a question of animal rights and of human subjectivity, as we have noted. But it is also a question deeply philosophical: what does suffering mean in a life—and not just a human one? Suffering, as I have tried to suggest here, is an increasingly loud chord in Derrida's later work. The public intellectual took on the sorrow of loss (personal friends), the weight of mourning; the horrors of political oppressions (South Africa, Nazi Germany, Communist Czechoslovakia); the disturbing question of the fate of animals; the gift of and the hope for mercy; friendship and its risks; Judaism and its afflictions. And there is so much more. From the intense young philosopher who spawned the concept of logocentrism

28. Derrida, "The Animal That Therefore I Am (More to Follow)," 411.
29. Ibid., 424, 435.

and its assumptions, and of deconstruction, to the defensive thinker who refuted his detractors with scorn and outrage, we come to this later Derrida, motivated by a certain tenderness marked by sorrow. This collection of essays that *Critical Inquiry* was so fortunate to publish, and to collect here, is but a small piece of the singular and brilliant philosopher who was Jacques Derrida. On the one hand, he haunts us by his absence; on the other hand, from the beginning of his thought, he will have never left us.

Françoise Meltzer, Chicago, 2012

Signature Derrida

1

The Law of Genre

Translated by Avital Ronell

Genres are not to be mixed.

I will not mix genres.

I repeat: genres are not to be mixed. I will not mix them.

Now suppose I let these utterances resonate all by themselves.

Suppose: I abandon them to their fate, I set free their random virtualities and turn them over to my audience—or, rather, to *your* audience, to your auditory grasp, to whatever mobility they retain and you bestow upon them to engender effects of all kinds without my having to stand behind them.

I merely said, and then repeated: genres are not to be mixed; I will not mix them.

As long as I release these utterances (which others might call speech acts) in a form yet scarcely determined, given the open context out of which I have just let them be grasped from "my" language—as long as I do this, you may find it difficult to choose among several interpretative options. They are legion, as I could demonstrate. They form an open and essentially unpredictable series. But you may be tempted by *at least* two types of audience, two modes of interpretation, or, if you prefer to give these words more of a chance, then you may be tempted by two different genres of hypothesis. Which ones?

On the one hand, it could be a matter of a fragmentary discourse whose propositions would be of the descriptive, constative, and neutral genre. In such a case, I would have named the operation which consists of "genres are not to be mixed." I would have designated this operation in a neutral fashion without evaluating it, without recommending or advising against it, certainly without binding anyone to it. Without claiming to lay down the law or to make this an act of law, I merely would have summoned up, in a fragmentary utterance, the sense of a practice, an act or event, as you wish: which is what sometimes happens when we revert to "genres are not to be mixed." With reference to the same case, and to a hypothesis of the same type, same mode, same genre—or same order: when I said, "I will not mix genres," you may have discerned a foreshadowing description—I am not saying a prescription—the descriptive designation telling in advance what will transpire, predicting it in the constative mode or genre, that is, it will happen thus, I will not mix genres. The future tense describes, then, what will surely take place, as you yourselves can judge; but for my part it does not constitute a commitment. I am not making you a promise here, nor am I issuing myself an order or invoking the authority of some law to which I am resolved to submit myself. In this case, the future tense does not set the time of a performative speech act of a promising or ordering type.

But another hypothesis, another type of audience, and another interpretation would have been no less legitimate. "Genres are not to be mixed" could strike you as a sharp order. You might have heard it resound the elliptical but all the more authoritarian summons to a law of a "do" or "do not" which, as everyone knows, occupies the concept or constitutes the value of *genre*. As soon as the word "genre" is sounded, as soon as it is heard, as soon as one attempts to conceive it, a limit is drawn. And when a limit is established, norms and interdictions are not far behind: "Do," "Do not" says "genre," the word "genre," the figure, the voice, or the law of genre. And this can be said of genre in all genres, be it a question of a generic or a general determination of what one calls "nature" or *physis* (for example, a biological *genre* in the sense of *gender*, or the human *genre*, a genre of all that is in general), or be it a question of a typology designated as nonnatural and depending on laws or orders which were once held to be opposed to *physis* according to those values associated with *technè, thesis, nomos* (for example, an artistic, poetic, or literary genre). But the whole enigma of genre springs perhaps most closely from within this limit between the two genres of genre which, neither separable nor inseparable, form an odd couple of one without the other in which each evenly serves the other a citation to appear in the figure of the other, simultaneously and indiscernibly saying "I" and "we," me the genre, we genres, without it being possible to think that the "I" is a species of the genre "we." For who would have us believe that we, we two, for example, would form a genre or belong to one? Thus, as soon as genre announces itself, one must respect a norm, one must not cross a line of demarcation, one must not risk impurity, anomaly, or monstrosity. And so it goes in all cases, whether or not this law of genre be interpreted as a determination or perhaps even as a destination of *physis*, and regardless of the weight or range imputed to *physis*. If a genre is what it is, or if it is supposed to be what it is destined to be by virtue of its *telos*, then "genres are not to be mixed"; one should not mix genres, one owes it to oneself not to get mixed up in mixing genres. Or, more rigorously: genres should not intermix. And if it should happen that they do intermix, by accident or through transgression, by mistake or through a lapse, then this should confirm, since, after all, we are speaking of "mixing," the essential purity of their identity. This purity belongs to the typical axiom: it is a law of the law of genre, whether or not the law is, as one feels justified in saying, "natural." This normative position and this evaluation are inscribed and prescribed even at the threshold of the "thing itself," if something of the genre "genre" can be so named. And so it follows that you might have taken the second sentence in the first person, "I will not mix genres," as a vow of obedience, as a docile response to the injunction emanating from the law of genre. In place of a constative description, you would then hear a promise, an oath; you would grasp the following respectful commitment: I promise you that I will not mix genres, and, through this act of pledging utter faithfulness to my commitment, I will be faithful to the law of genre, since, by its very nature, the law invites and commits me in advance not to mix genres. By publishing my response to the imperious call of the law, I would correspondingly commit myself to be responsible.

Unless, of course, I were actually implicated in a wager, a challenge, an impossible bet—in short, a situation that would exceed the matter of merely engaging a commitment from me. And suppose for a moment that it were impossible not to mix genres. What if there were, lodged within the heart of the law itself, a law of impurity or a principle of contamination? And suppose the condition for the possibility of the law were the *a priori* of a counter-law, an axiom of impossibility that would confound its sense, order, and reason?

I have just proposed an alternative between two interpretations. I did not do so, as you can imagine, in order to check myself. The line or trait that seemed to separate the two bodies of interpretation is affected *straight away* by an essential disruption that, for the time being, I shall let you name or qualify in any way you care to: as internal division of the trait, impurity, corruption, contamination, decomposition, perversion, deformation, even cancerization, generous proliferation, or degenerescence. All these disruptive "anomalies" are engendered—and this is their common law, the lot or site they share—by *repetition*. One might even say by citation or re-citation (*ré-cit*), provided that the restricted use of these two words is not a call to strict generic order. A citation in the strict sense implies all sorts of contextual conventions, precautions, and protocols in the mode of reiteration, of coded signs, such as quotation marks or other typographical devices used for writing a citation. The same holds no doubt for the *récit* as a form, mode, or genre of discourse, even—and I shall return to this—as a literary type. And yet the law that protects the usage, in *stricto sensu*, of the words "citation" and "*récit*" is threatened intimately and in advance by a counter-law that constitutes this very law, renders it possible, conditions it and thereby renders it impossible—for reasons of edges on which we shall run aground in just a moment—to edge through, to edge away from, or to hedge around the counter-law itself. The law and the counter-law serve each other citations summoning each other to appear, and each recites the other in this proceeding (*procès*). There would be no cause for concern if one were rigorously assured of being able to distinguish with rigor between a citation and a non-citation, a *récit* and a non-*récit* or a repetition within the form of one or the other.

I shall not undertake to demonstrate, assuming it is still possible, why you were unable to decide whether the sentences with which I opened this presentation and marked this context were or were not repetitions of a citational type; or whether they were or were not of the performative type; or certainly whether they were, both of them, together—and each time together—the one or the other. For perhaps someone has noticed that, from one repetition to the next, a change had insinuated itself into the relationship between the two initial utterances. The punctuation had been slightly modified, as had the content of the second independent clause. Theoretically, this barely noticeable shift could have created a mutual independency between the interpretative alternatives that might have tempted you to opt for one or the other, or for one *and* the other of these two sentences. A particularly rich combinatory of possibilities would thus ensue, which, in order not to exceed my time limit and out of respect for the law of genre and of the audience, I shall abstain from recounting. I am simply going to assume a certain relationship between what has just now happened and the origin of literature, as well as its aborigine or its abortion, to quote Philippe Lacoue-Labarthe.

Provisionally claiming for myself the authority of such an assumption, I shall let our field of vision contract as I limit myself to a sort of species of the genre "genre." I shall focus on this genre of genre which is generally supposed, and always a bit too rashly, not to be part of nature, of *physis*, but rather of *technè*, of the arts, still more narrowly of poetry, and most particularly of literature. But at the same time, I take the liberty to think that, while limiting myself thus, I exclude nothing, at least in principle and *de jure*—the relationships here no longer being those of extension, from exemplary individual to species, from species to genre as genus or from the genre of genre to genre in general; rather, as we shall see, these relationships are a whole order apart. What is at stake, in effect, is exemplarity and its whole *enigma*—in other words, as the word "enigma" indicates, exemplarity and the *récit*—which works through the logic of the example.

Before going about putting a certain example to the test, I shall attempt to formulate, in a manner as elliptical, economical, and formal as possible, what I shall call the law of the law of genre. It is precisely a principle of contamination, a law of impurity, a parasitical economy. In the code of set theories, if I may use it at least figuratively, I would speak of a sort of participation without belonging—a taking part in without being part of, without having membership in a set. With the inevitable dividing of the trait that marks membership, the boundary of the set comes to form, by invagination, an internal pocket larger than the whole; and the outcome of this division and of this abounding remains as singular as it is limitless.

To demonstrate this, I shall hold to the leanest generalities. But I should like to justify this initial indigence or asceticism as well as possible. For example, I shall not enter into the passionate debate that poetics has brought forth on the theory and the history of genre-theory, on the critical history of the concept of genre from Plato to the present. My stance is motivated by these considerations: in the first place, we now have at our disposal some remarkable and, of late, handsomely enriched works dealing either with primary texts or critical analyses. I am thinking especially of the journal *Poétique*, of its issue entitled "Genres" (32) and of Genette's opening essay, "Genres, 'Types,' Modes." From yet another point of view, *L'Absolu littéraire* [The literary absolute] has already created quite a stir in this context, and everything that I shall risk here should perhaps resolve itself in a modest annotation on the margins of this magistral work which I assume some of you have already read. I could further justify my abstention or my abstinence here simply by acknowledging the terminological luxury or rapture as well as the taxonomic exuberance which debates of this kind, in a manner by no means fortuitous, have sparked: I feel completely powerless to contain this fertile proliferation—and not only because of time constraints. I shall put forth, instead, *two* principal *motives*, hoping thereby to justify my keeping to scant preliminary generalities at the edge of this problematic.

To what do these two motives essentially relate? In its most recent phase—and this much is certainly clear in Genette's propositions—the most advanced critical axis has led to a rereading of the entire history of genre-theory. This rereading has been inspired by the perception—and it must be said, despite the initial denial, by the correction—of two types of misconstruing or confusion. On the one hand, and this will be the first motive or ground for my abstention, Plato and Aristotle have been subjected to considerable deformation, as Genette reminds us, insofar as they have been viewed in terms alien to their thinking, and even in terms that they themselves would have rejected; but this deformation has usually taken on the form of *naturalization*. Following a classical precedent, one has deemed natural structures or typical forms whose history is hardly natural but, rather, quite to the contrary, complex and heterogeneous. These forms have been treated as natural—and let us bear in mind the entire semantic scale of this difficult word whose span is so far-ranging and open-ended that it extends as far as the expression "natural language," by which term everyone agrees tacitly to oppose natural language only to a formal or artificial language without thereby implying that this natural language is a simple physical or biological production. Genette insists at length on this naturalization of genres: "The history of genre-theory is strewn with these fascinating outlines that *inform and deform reality*, a reality often heterogenous to the literary field, and that claim to discover a natural 'system' wherein they construct a factitious symmetry heavily reinforced by fake windows" (p. 408, italics added). In its most efficacious and legitimate aspect, this critical reading of the history (and) of genre-theory is based on an opposition between nature and history and, more generally—as the allusion to an artificial construct indicates (". . . wherein they construct a factitious symmetry. . . .")—on an opposition between nature and what can be called the series of all its others. Such an opposition seems to go without saying; placed within this critical perspective, it is never questioned. Even if it has been tucked away discretely in some passage that has escaped my attention, this barely visible suspicion clearly had no effect on the general organization of the problematic. This does not diminish the relevance or fecundity of a reading such as Genette's. But a place remains open for some preliminary questions concerning his presuppositions, for some questions concerning the boundaries where it begins to take hold or take place. The form of these boundaries will contain me and rein me in. These general propositions whose number is always open and indeterminable for whatever critical interpretation will not be dealt with here. What however seems to me to require more urgent attention is the relationship of nature to history, of nature to its others, *precisely when genre is on the line.*

Let us consider the most general concept of genre, from the minimal trait or predicate delineating it permanently through the modulations of its types and the regimens of its history: it rends and defends itself by mustering all its energy against a simple opposition that arises from nature and from history, as from nature and the vast lineage of its others (*technè, nomos, thesis,* then *spirit, society, freedom, history,* etc.). Between *physis* and its others, *genos* certainly locates one of the privileged scenes of the process and, no doubt, sheds the greatest obscurity on it. One need not mobilize etymology to this end and could just as well equate *genos* with birth, and birth in turn with the generous force of engenderment or generation—*physis,* in fact—as with race, familial membership, classificatory genealogy or class, age class (generation), or social class; it comes as no surprise that, in nature and art, genre, a concept that is essentially classificatory and genealogico-taxonomic, itself engenders so many classificatory vertigines when it goes about classifying itself and situating the classificatory principle or instrument within a set. As with the class itself, the principle of genre is unclassifiable; it tolls the knell of the knell (*glas*), in other words, of classicum, of what permits one to call out (*calare*) orders and to order the manifold within a nomenclature. *Genos* thus indicates the place, the now or never of the most necessary meditation on the "fold" which is no more historical than natural in the classical sense of these two words, and which turns *phyein* over to itself across others that perhaps no longer relate to it according to that epoch-making logic which was decisory, critical, oppositional, even dialectical but rather according to the trait of an entirely different contract. *De jure,* this meditation acts as an absolute prerequisite without which any historical perspectivizing will always be difficult to legitimate. For example, the Romantic era—this powerful figure indicted by Genette (since it attempted to reinterpret the system of modes as a system of genres)—is no longer a simple era and can no longer be inscribed as a moment or a stage placeable within the trajectory of a "history" whose concept we could be certain of. Romanticism, if something of the sort can be thus identified, is also the general repetition of all the folds that in themselves gather, couple, divide *physis* as well as *genos* through the genre, and through all the genres of genre, through the mixing of genre that is "more than a genre," through the excess of genre in relation to itself, as to its abounding movement and its general assemblage which coincides, too, with its dissolution.[1] Such a "moment" is no longer a simple moment *in* the history and theory of literary genres. To treat it thus would in effect implicate one as tributary—whence the strange logic—of something that has in itself constituted a certain Romantic motif, namely, the teleological ordering of history. Romanticism simultaneously obeys naturalizing and historicizing logic, and it can be shown easily enough that we have not yet been delivered from the Romantic heritage—even though we might wish it so and assuming that such a deliverance would be of compelling interest to us—as long as we persist in drawing attention to historical concerns and the truth of historical production in order to militate against abuses or confusions of naturalization. The debate, it could be argued, remains itself a part or effect of Romanticism.

A second motive detains me at the threshold or on the edge of a possible problematic of genre (as) history and theory of history and of genre-theory—another genre, in fact. For the moment, I find it impossible to decide—impossible for reasons that I do not take to be accidental, and this, precisely, is what matters to me—I find it impossible to decide whether the possibly exemplary text which I intend to put to the test does or does not lend itself to the distinction drawn between *mode* and *genre*. Now, as you may recall, Genette demonstrates the stringent necessity of this distinction; and he rests his case on "the confusion of modes and genres" (p. 417). This implies a serious charge against Romanticism, even though "the romantic reinterpretation of the system of modes as a system of genres is neither *de facto* nor *de jure* the epilogue to this long history" (p. 415). This confusion, according to Genette, has aided and abetted the naturalization of genres by projecting onto them the "privilege of naturalness, which was *legitimately* . . . that of three modes . . ." (p. 421). Suddenly, this naturalization "makes these arch-genres into ideal or natural types which they neither are nor can be: there are no arch-genres that can totally escape historicity *while preserving a generic definition*. There are modes, for example: the

---

1. In this respect, the second footnote in *L'Absolu littéraire* (Paris, 1978), p. 271, seems to me, let us say, a bit too equitable in its rigorous and honest prudence.

récit. There are genres, for example: the novel; the relation of genres to modes is complex and perhaps not, as Aristotle suggests, one of simple inclusion."

If I am inclined to poise myself on *this* side of Genette's argument, it is not only because of his ready acceptance of the distinction between nature and history but also because of its implications with regard to mode and to the distinction between mode and genre. Genette's definition of mode contains this singular and interesting characteristic: it remains, in contradistinction to genre, purely formal. Reference to a content has no pertinence. This is not the case with genre. The generic criterion and the modal criterion, Genette says, are "absolutely heterogenous": "each genre defined itself essentially by a specification of content which was not prescribed by the definition of mode . . ." (p. 417). I do not believe that this recourse to the opposition of form and content, this distinction between mode and genre, need be contested, and my purpose is not to challenge isolated aspects of Genette's argument. One might just question the presuppositions for the legitimacy of such an argument. One might also question the extent to which his argument can help us read a given text when it behaves in a given way with regard to mode and genre, especially when the text does not seem to be written sensibly within their limits but rather about the very subject of those limits and with the aim of disrupting their order. The limits, for instance, of that mode which would be, according to Genette, the *récit* ("There are modes, for example: the *récit*"). Of the (possibly) exemplary text which I shall address shortly, I shall not hasten to add that it is a "*récit*," and you will soon understand why. In this text, the "*récit*" is not only a mode, and a mode put into practice or put to the test because it is deemed impossible; it is also the name of a theme. It is the nonthematizable thematic content of something of a textual form that *assumes* a point of view with respect to the genre, even though it perhaps does not come under the heading of any genre—and perhaps no longer even under the heading of literature, if it indeed wears itself out around genreless modalizations, and would confirm one of Genette's propositions: "Genres are, properly speaking, literary—or aesthetic—categories; modes are categories that pertain to linguistics or, more precisely, to an anthropology of verbal expression" (p. 418).

In a very singular manner, the very short text which I will discuss presently makes the *récit* and the impossibility of the *récit* its theme, its impossible theme or content at once inaccessible, indeterminable, interminable, and inexhaustible; and it makes the word "*récit*," under the aegis of a certain form, its titleless title, the mentionless mention of its genre. This text, as I shall try to demonstrate, seems to be made, among other things, to make light of all the tranquil categories of genre-theory and history in order to upset their taxonomic certainties, the distribution of their classes, and the presumed stability of their classical nomenclatures. It is a text destined, at the same time, to summon up these classes by conducting their proceeding, by proceeding from the proceeding to the law of genre. For if the juridical code has frequently thrust itself upon me in order to hear this case, it has done so to call as witness a (possible) exemplary text and because I am convinced fundamental rights are bound up in all of this: the law itself is at stake.

These are the two principal reasons why I shall keep to the liminal edge of (the) history (and) of genre-theory. Here now, very quickly, is the law of abounding, of *excess*, the law of participation without membership, of contamination, etc., which I mentioned earlier. It will seem meager to you, and even of staggering abstractness. It does not particularly concern either genres, or types, or modes, or any form in the strict sense of its concept. I therefore do not know under what title the field or object submitted to this law should be placed. It is perhaps the limitless field of general textuality. I can take each word of the series (genre, type, mode, form) and decide that it will hold for all the others (all genres of genres, types, modes, forms; all types of types, genres, modes, forms; all forms of forms, etc.). The trait common to these classes of classes is precisely the identifiable recurrence of a common trait by which one recognizes, or should recognize, a membership in a class. There should be a trait upon which one could rely in order to decide that a given textual event, a given "work," corresponds to a given class (genre, type, mode, form, etc.). And there should be a code enabling one to decide questions of class-membership on the basis of this trait. For example— a very humble axiom, but, by the same token, hardly contestable—if a genre exists (let us say the novel, since no one seems to contest its generic quality), then a code should provide an identifiable trait and one which is identical to itself, authorizing us to determine, to adjudicate whether a given text belongs to this genre or perhaps to that genre. Likewise, outside of literature or art, if one is bent on classifying, one should consult a set of identifiable and codifiable traits to determine whether this or that, such a thing or such an event belongs to this set or that class. This may seem trivial. Such a distinctive trait *qua* mark is however always *a priori* remarkable. It is always possible that a set—I have compelling reasons for calling this a text, whether it be written or oral—re-marks on this distinctive trait within itself. This can occur in texts that do not, at a given moment, assert themselves to be literary or poetic. A defense speech or newspaper editorial can indicate by means of a mark, even if it is not explicitly designated as such, "Voilà! I belong, as anyone may remark, to the type of text called a defense speech or an article of the genre newspaper-editorial." The possibility is always there. This does not constitute a text *ipso facto* as "literature," even though such a possibility, always left open and therefore eternally remarkable, situates perhaps in every text the possibility of its becoming literature. But this does not interest me at the moment. What interests me is that this re-mark—ever possible for every text, for every corpus of traces—is absolutely necessary for and constitutive of what we call art, poetry, or literature. It underwrites the eruption of *technè*, which is never long in coming. I submit this axiomatic question for your consideration: Can one identify a work of art, of whatever sort, but especially a work of discursive art, if it does not bear the mark of a genre, if it does not signal or mention it or make it remarkable in any way? Let me clarify two points on this subject. First, it is possible to have several genres, an intermixing of genres or a total genre, the genre "genre" or the poetic or literary genre as genre of genres. Second, this re-mark can take on a great number of forms and can itself pertain to highly diverse types. It need not be a designation or "mention" of the type found beneath the title of certain books (novel, *récit*, drama). The remark of belonging need not pass through the consciousness of the author or the reader, although it often does so. It can also refute this consciousness or render the explicit "mention" mendacious, false, inadequate, or ironic according to all sorts of overdetermined figures. Finally, this remarking-trait need be neither a theme nor a thematic component of the work—although of course this instance of belonging to one or several genres, not to mention all the traits that mark this belonging, often have been treated as theme, even before the advent of what we call "modernism." If I am not mistaken in saying that such a trait is remarkable, that is, noticeable, in every aesthetic, poetic, or literary corpus, then consider this paradox, consider the irony (which is irreducible to a consciousness or an attitude): this supplementary and distinctive trait, a mark of belonging or inclusion, does not properly pertain to any genre or class. The re-mark of belonging does not belong. It belongs without belonging, and the "without" (or the suffix "-less") which relates belonging to non-belonging appears only in the timeless time of the blink of an eye (*Augenblick*). The eyelid closes, but barely, an instant among instants, and what it closes is verily the eye, the view, the light of day.

But without such respite, nothing would come to light. To formulate it in the scantiest manner—the simplest but most apodictic—I submit for your consideration the following hypothesis: a text cannot belong to no genre, it cannot be without or less a genre. Every text participates in one or several genres, there is no genreless text; there is always a genre and genres, yet such participation never amounts to belonging. And not because of an abundant overflowing or a free, anarchic, and unclassifiable productivity, but because of the *trait* of participation itself, because of the effect of the code and of the generic mark. Making genre its mark, a text demarcates itself. If remarks of belonging belong without belonging, participate without belonging, then genre-designations cannot be simply part of the corpus. Let us take the designation "novel" as an example. This should be marked in one way or another, even if it does not appear, as it often does in French and German texts, in the explicit form of a subtitled designation, and even if it proves deceptive or ironic. This designation is not novelistic; it does not, in whole or in part, take part in the corpus whose denomination it nonetheless imparts. Nor is it simply extraneous to the corpus. But this singular topos places within and without the work, along its boundary, an inclusion and exclusion with regard to genre in general, as to an identifiable class in general. It gathers together the corpus and, at the same time, in the same blinking of an eye, keeps it from closing, from identifying itself with itself. This axiom of non-closure or non-fulfillment enfolds within itself the condition for the possibility and the impossibility of taxonomy. This inclusion and this exclusion do not remain exterior to one another; they do not exclude each other. But neither are they immanent or identical to each other. They are neither one nor two. They form what I shall call the *genre-clause*, a clause stating at once the juridical utterance, the precedent-making designation and the law-text, but also the closure, the closing that excludes itself from what it includes (one could also speak of a floodgate ["*écluse*"] of genre). The clause or floodgate of genre declasses what it allows to be classed. It tolls the knell of genealogy or of genericity, which it however also brings forth to the light of day. Putting to death the very thing that it engenders, it cuts a strange figure; a formless form, it remains nearly invisible, it neither sees the day nor brings itself to light. Without it, neither genre nor literature come to light, but as soon as there is this blinking of an eye, this clause or this floodgate of genre, at the very moment that a genre or a literature is broached, at that very moment, degenerescence has begun, the end begins.

The end begins, this is a citation. Maybe a citation. I might have taken it from the text which seems to me to bring itself forth as an example, as an example of this unfigurable figure of clusion.

What I shall try to convey to you now will not be called by its generic or modal name. I shall not say this drama, this epic, this novel, this novella or this *récit*—certainly not this *récit*. All of these generic or modal names would be equally valid or equally invalid for something which is not even quite a book, but which was published in 1973 in the editorial form of a small volume of thirty-two pages. It bears the title *La folie du jour* [approximately: The Madness of the Day]. The author's name: Maurice Blanchot. In order to speak about it, I shall call this thing La Folie du jour, its given name which it bears legally and which gives us the right, as of its publication date, to identify and classify it in our copyright records at the Bibliothèque Nationale. One could fashion a non-finite number of readings from *La folie du jour*. I have attempted a few myself, and shall do so again elsewhere, from another point of view. The *topos* of view, sight, blindness, *point of view* is, moreover, inscribed and traversed in *La folie du jour* according to a sort of permanent revolution that engenders and virtually brings to the light of day points of view, twists, versions, and reversions of which the sum remains necessarily uncountable and the account, impossible. The deductions, rationalizations, and warnings that I must inevitably propose will arise, then, from an act of unjustifiable violence. A brutal and mercilessly depleting selectivity will obtrude upon me, upon us, in the name of a law that *La folie du jour* has, in its turn, already reviewed, and with the foresight that a certain kind of police brutality is perhaps an inevitable accomplice to our concern for professional competence.

What will I ask of *La folie du jour*? To answer, to testify, to say what it has to say with respect to the law of mode or the law of genre and, more precisely, with respect to the law of the *récit*, which, as we have just been reminded, is a mode and not a genre.

On the cover, below the title, we find no mention of genre. In this most peculiar place that belongs neither to the title nor to the subtitle, nor even simply to the corpus of the work, the author did not affix, although he has often done so elsewhere, the designation "*récit*" or "novel," maybe (but only maybe) by erroneously subsuming both of them, Genette would say, under the unique category of the genre. About this designation which figures elsewhere and which appears to be absent here, I shall say only two things:

1. On the one hand it commits one to nothing. Neither reader nor

critic nor author are bound to believe that the text preceded by this designation conforms readily to the strict, normal, normed, or normative definition of the genre, to the law of the genre or of the mode. Confusion, irony, the shift in conventions toward a new definition (in what name should it be prohibited?), the search for a supplementary effect, any of these things could prompt one to entitle as *novel* or *récit* what in truth or according to yesterday's truth would be neither one nor the other. All the more so if the words "*récit*," "novel," "*ciné-roman*," "complete dramatic works" or, for all I know, "literature" are no longer in the place which conventionally mentions genre but, as has happened and will happen again (shortly), they are found to be holding the position and function of the title itself, of the work's given name.

2. Blanchot has often had occasion to modify the genre-designation from one version of his work to the next or from one edition to the next. Since I am unable to cover the entire spectrum of this problem, I shall simply cite the example of the "*récit-*" designation effaced between one version and the next of *Death Sentence* (trans. Lydia Davis [Barrytown, N.Y., 1978]) at the same time as a certain epilogue is removed from the end of a double *récit*, which, in a manner of speaking, constitutes this book. This effacement of "*récit*," leaving a trace that, inscribed and filed away, remains as an effect of supplementary relief which is not easily accounted for in all of its facets. I cannot arrest the course of my lecture here, no more than I can pause to consider the very scrupulous and minutely differentiated distribution of the designations "*récit*" and "novel" from one narrative work to the next, no more than I can question whether Blanchot distinguished the genre and mode designations, no more than I can discuss Blanchot's entire discourse on the difference between the narratorial voice and the narrative voice which is, to be sure, something other than a mode. I would point out only one thing: at the very moment the first version of *Death Sentence* appears, bearing mention as it does of "*récit*," the first version of *La folie du jour* is published with another title about which I shall momentarily speak.

La folie du jour, then, makes no mention of genre or mode. But the word "*récit*" appears at least four times in the last two pages in order to name the theme of *La folie du jour*, its sense or its story, its content or part of its content—in any case, its decisive proceedings and stakes. It is a *récit* without a theme and without a cause entering from the outside; yet it is without interiority. It is the *récit* of an impossible *récit* whose "production" occasions what happens or, rather, what remains, but which does not relate it, nor relate to it as to an outside reference, even if everything remains foreign to it and out of bounds. It is even less feasible for me to relate to you the story of *La folie du jour* which is staked precisely on the possibility and the impossibility of relating a story. Nonetheless, in order to create the greatest possible clarity, in the name of daylight itself, that is to say (as will become clear), in the name of the law, I shall take the calculated risk of flattening out the unfolding or coiling up of this text, its permanent revolution whose rounds are made to recoil from any kind of flattening. And this is why the one who says "I," and the one after all who speaks to us, who "recites" for us, this one who says "I" tells his inquisitors that he cannot manage to constitute himself as narrator (in the sense of the term that is not necessarily literary) and tells them that he cannot manage to identify with himself sufficiently or to remember himself well enough to gather the story and *récit* that are demanded of him—which the representatives of society and the law require of him. The one who says "I" (who does not manage to say "I") seems to relate what has happened to him or, rather, what has nearly happened to him after presenting himself in a mode that defies all norms of self-presentation: he nearly lost his sight (his facility for *viewing*) following a traumatic event—probably an assault. I say "probably" because *La folie du jour* wholly upsets, in a discrete but terribly efficient manner, all the certainties upon which so much of discourse is constructed: the value of an event, first of all, of reality, of fiction, of appearance and so on, all this being carried away by the disseminal and mad polysemy of "day," of the word "day," which, once again, I cannot dwell upon here. Having nearly lost his sight (*vue*), having been taken in by a kind of medico-social institution, he now resides under the watchful eye of doctors, handed over to the authority of these specialists who are representatives of the law as well, legist doctors who demand that he testify—and in his own interest, or so it seems at first—about what happened to him so that remedial justice may be dispensed. His faithful *récit*—(but let me borrow for the sake of simplicity, and because it conforms fairly well to this context, the English word "account")—hence, his faithful account of events should render justice unto the law. The law demands a narrative account.

Pronounced four times in the last three pages of *La folie du jour*, the word "account" does not seem to designate a literary genre but rather a certain type or mode of discourse. That is, in effect, the appearance of it. Everything seems to happen as if the account—the question of or rather the demand for the account, the response, and the nonresponse to the demand—found itself staged and figured as one of the themes, objects, stakes in a more bountiful text, *La folie du jour*, whose genre would be of another order and would in any case overstep the boundaries of the

account with all its generality and all its genericity. The account itself
would of course not cover this generic generality of the literary corpus
named *La folie du jour*. Now we might already feel inclined to consider
this appearance suspect, and we might be jolted from our certainties
by an allusion that "I" will make: the one who says "I," who is not by
force of necessity a narrator, nor necessarily always the same, notes that
the representatives of the law, those who demand of him an account in
the name of the law, consider and treat him, in his personal and civil
identity, not only as an "educated" man—and an educated man, they
often tell him, ought to be able to speak and recount; as a competent
subject, he ought to be able to know how to piece together a story by
saying "I" and "exactly" how things happened to him—they regard him
not only as an "educated" man, but also as a writer. He is writer and
reader, a creature of "libraries," *the* reader of this account. This is not
sufficient cause, but it is, in any case, a first clue and one whose impact
incites us to think that the required account does not simply remain in
a relationship that is extraneous to literature or even to a literary genre.
Lest we not be content with this suspicion, let us weigh the possibility of
the inclusion of a modal structure within a vaster, more general corpus,
whether literary or not and whether or not related to the genre. Such an
inclusion raises questions concerning edge, borderline, boundary, and
abounding which do not arise without a fold.

What sort of a fold? According to which fold and which figure of
enfoldment?

Here are the three final paragraphs; they are of unequal length, with
the last of these comprising approximately one line:

> They demanded: Tell us "exactly" how things happened.—An
> account? I began: I am neither learned nor ignorant. I have
> known some joy. This is saying too little. I related the story in its
> entirety, to which they listened, it seems, with great interest—at
> least initially. But the end was a surprise for them all. "After that
> beginning," they said, "you should proceed to the facts." How
> so? The account was over.
>
> I should have realized that I was incapable of composing
> an account of these events. I had lost the sense of the story;
> this happens in a good many illnesses. But this explanation only
> made them more demanding. Then I noticed, for the first time,
> that they were two and that this infringement on their tradi-
> tional method—even though it can be explained away by the
> fact that one of them was an eye doctor, the other a specialist in

mental illnesses—increasingly gave our conversation the character of an authoritarian interrogation, overseen and controlled
by a strict set of rules. To be sure, neither of them was the chief
of police. But being two, due to that, they were three, and this
third one remained firmly convinced, I am sure, that a writer, a
man who speaks and reasons with distinction, is always capable
of recounting the facts which he remembers.

An account? No, no account, nevermore.

In the first of the three paragraphs that I have just cited, he claims
that something is to begin after the word "account" punctuated by a
question mark (An account?—herein implied: they want an account,
is it then an account that they want? "I began . . ."). This something
is nothing other than the first line on the first page of *La folie du jour*.
These are the same words, in the same order, but this is not a citation
in the strict sense for, stripped of quotation marks, these words com-
mence or recommence a quasi-account that will engender anew the entire sequence comprising this new point of departure. In this way, the
first words ("I am neither learned nor ignorant . . .") that come after
the word "account" and its question mark, that broach the beginning
of the account extorted by the law's representatives—these first words
mark a collapse that is unthinkable, irrepresentable, unsituable within
a linear order of succession, within a spatial or temporal sequential-
ity, within an objectifiable topology or chronology. One sees, without
seeing, one reads the crumbling of an upper boundary or of the initial
edge in *La folie du jour*, uncoiled according to the "normal" order, the
one regulated by common law, editorial convention, positive law, the
regime of competency in our logo-alphabetical culture, etc. Suddenly,
this upper or initial boundary, which is commonly called the first line
of a book, is forming a pocket inside the corpus. It is taking the form
of an *invagination* through which the trait of the first line, the borderline, splits while remaining the same and traverses yet also bounds the
corpus. The "account" which he claims is beginning at the end and, by
legal requisition, is none other than the one that has begun from the
beginning of *La folie du jour* and in which, therefore, he gets around to
saying that he begins, etc. And it is without beginning or end, without
content and without edge. There is only content without edge—without boundary or frame—and there is only edge without content. The
inclusion (or occlusion, inocclusive invagination) is interminable: it is an
analysis of the account that can only turn in circles in an unarrestable,
inenarrable, and insatiably recurring manner—but one terrible for those

who, in the name of the law, require that order reign in the account, for those who want to know, with all the required competence, "exactly" how this happens. For if "I" or "he" continued to tell what he has told, he would end up endlessly returning to this point and beginning again to begin, that is to say, to begin with an end that precedes the beginning. And from the viewpoint of objective space and time, the point at which he stops is absolutely unascertainable ("I have told them the entire story . . ."), for there is no "entire" story except for the one that interrupts itself in this way.

A lower edge of invagination will, if one can say so, respond to this "first" invagination of the upper edge by intersecting it. The "final line" resumes the question posed *before* the "I began" (An account?) and bespeaks a resolution or promises it, tells of the commitment made no longer to give an account. As if he had already given one! And yet, yes (yes and no), an account has taken place. Hence the last word: "An account? No, no account, nevermore." It has been impossible to decide whether the recounted event and the event of the account itself ever took place. Impossible to decide whether there was an account, for the one who barely manages to say "I" and to constitute himself as narrator recounts that he has not been able to recount—but what, exactly? Well, everything, including the demand for an account. And if an assured and guaranteed decision is impossible, this is because there is nothing more to be done than to commit oneself, to perform, to wager, to allow chance its chance—to make a decision that is essentially edgeless, bordering perhaps only on madness.

Yet another impossible decision follows, one which involves the promise "No, no account, nevermore": Is this promise a part of or apart from the account? Legally speaking, it is party to *La folie du jour*, but not necessarily to the account or to the simulacrum of the account. Its trait splits again into an internal and external edge. It repeats—without citing—the question apparently posed above (An account?) of which it can be said that, in this permanent revolution of order, it follows, doubles, or reiterates it in advance. Thus another lip or invaginating loop takes shape here. This time the lower edge creates a pocket in order to come back into the corpus and to rise again on this side of the upper or initial line's line of invagination. This would form a double chiasmatic invagination of edges:

A. "I am neither learned nor ignorant . . ."
B. "An account? I began:"

A′. "I am neither learned nor ignorant . . ."
B′. "An account? No, no account, nevermore . . ."

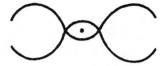

"I began . . ."

It is thus impossible to decide whether an event, account, account of event, or event of accounting took place. Impossible to settle upon the simple borderlines of this corpus, of this ellipse unremittingly repealing itself within its own expansion. When we fall back on the poetic consequences enfolded within this dilemma, we find that it becomes difficult indeed to speak here with conviction about an account as a determined mode included within a more general corpus or one simply related, in its determination, to other modes or, quite simply, to something other than itself. All is narrative account and nothing is; the account's outgate remains within the account in a non-inclusive mode, and this structure is itself related so remotely to a dialectical structure that it even inscribes dialectics in the account's ellipse. All is account, nothing is: and we shall not know whether the relationship between these two propositions— the strange conjunction of the account and the accountless—belongs to the account itself. What indeed happens when the edge pronounces a sentence?

Faced with this type of difficulty—the consequences or implications of which cannot be deployed here—one might be tempted to take recourse in the law or the rights which govern published texts. One might be tempted to argue as follows: all these insoluble problems of delimitation are raised "on the inside" of a book classified as a work of literature or literary fiction. Pursuant to these juridical norms, this book has a beginning and an end that leave no opening for indecision. This book has a determinable beginning and end, a title, an author, a publisher, its distinctive denomination is *La folie du jour*. At this place, where I am pointing, on this page, right here, you can see its first word; here, its final period, perfectly situable in objective space. And all the sophisticated transgressions, all the infinitesimal subversions that may captivate you are not possible except within this enclosure for which these transgressions and subversions moreover maintain an essential need in order to take place. Furthermore, on the inside of this normed space, the word "account" does not name a literary operation or genre, but a current mode of discourse, and it does so regardless of the formidable problems of structure, edge, set theory, the part and whole, etc., that it raises in this "literary" corpus.

That is all well and good. But in its very relevance, this objection cannot be sustained—for example, it cannot save the modal determination of the account—except by referring to extra-literary and even extra-linguistic juridical norms. The objection makes an appeal to the law and calls to mind the fact that the subversion of *La folie du jour* needs the law in order to take place. Whereby the objection reproduces and accomplishes its staging within *La folie du jour*: the account, mandated and prescribed by law but also, as we shall see, commanding, requiring, and producing law in turn. In short, the whole critical scene of competence in which we are engaged is *party* to and *part* of *La folie du jour*, in whole and in part, the whole is a part.

The whole does nothing but begin. I could have begun with what resembles the absolute beginning, with the juridico-historical order of this publication. What has been lightly termed the first version of *La folie du jour* was not a book. Published in the journal *Empédocle* (2 May 1949), it bore another title—indeed, several other titles. On the journal's cover, here it is, one reads:

> Maurice Blanchot
> *Un récit?*
> [*An Account?*]

Later, the question mark disappears twice. First, when the title is reproduced within the journal in the table of contents:

> Maurice Blanchot
> *Un récit*
> [*An Account*],

then below the first line:

Un récit	[*An Account*
par	by
Maurice Blanchot	M. B.]

Could you tell whether these titles, written earlier and filed away in the archives, make up a single title, titles of the same text, titles of the account (which of course figures as an impracticable mode in the book), or the title of a genre? Even if the latter were to cause some confusion, it would be of the sort that releases questions already implemented and enacted by *La folie du jour*. This enactment enables in turn the de-naturalization and deconstitution of the oppositions nature/history and mode/genre.

Now let us turn to some of these questions. First, to what could the words "An Account" refer in their manifold occurrences and diverse punctuations? And precisely how does reference function here? In one case, the question mark can *also* serve as a supplementary remark indicating the necessity of all these questions as the insolvent character of indecision: Is this an account? Is it an account that I entitle? asks the title in entitling. Is it an account that they want? What entitles them? Is it an account as discursive mode or as literary operation, or perhaps even as literary genre whose theme would be mode or genre? Likewise, the title could excerpt, as does a metonymy, a fragment of the account without an account (to wit, the words "an account" with and without a question mark), but such an iterative excepting is not citational. For the title, guaranteed and protected by law but also making law, retains a referential structure which differs radically from the one underlying other occurrences of the "same" words in the text. Whatever the issue—title, reference, or mode and genre—the case before us always involves the law and, in particular, the relations formed around and to law. All the questions which we have just addressed can be traced to an enormous matrix that generates the non-thematizable thematic power of a simulated account: it is this inexhaustible writing which recounts without telling, and which speaks without recounting.

Account of an accountless account, an account without edge or boundary, account all of whose visible space is but some border of itself without "self," consisting of the framing edge without content, without modal or generic boundaries—such is the law of this textual event, of this text that also speaks the law, its own and that of the other as reader of this text which, speaking the law, also imposes itself as a law text, as the text of the law. What, then, is the law of the genre of this singular text? It is law, it is the figure of the law which will also be the invisible center, the themeless theme of *La folie du jour* or, as I am now entitled to say, of "An Account?"

This law, however, as law of genre, is not exclusively binding on the genre *qua* category of art and literature. But, paradoxically, and just as impossibly, the law of genre also has a controlling influence and is binding on that which draws the genre into engendering, generations, genealogy, and degenerescence. You have already witnessed its approach often enough, with all the figures of this degenerescent self-engendering of an account, with this figure of the law which, like the day that it is, challenges the opposition between the law of nature and the law of symbolic history. The remarks that have just been made on the double chiasmatic invagination of edges should suffice to exclude any notion linking all these complications to pure form or one suggesting that they could be formalized outside the content. The question of the literary genre is not a formal one: it covers the motif of the law in general, of generation in the natural and symbolic senses, of birth in the natural and symbolic senses, of the generation difference, sexual difference between the feminine and masculine genre/gender, of the hymen between the two, of a relationless relation between the two, of an identity and difference between the feminine and masculine. The word "hymen" tells us several things. It not only points toward a paradoxical logic that is inscribed without however being formalized under this name; it should, in the first place, serve to remind the Anglo-American reader that, in French, the semantic scale of *genre* is much larger and more expansive than in English, and thus always includes within its reach the gender. Additionally, and with respect to the "hymen," let us not forget everything that Philippe Lacoue-Labarthe and Jean-Luc Nancy tell us in *L'Absolu littéraire* (especially on p. 276) about the relationship between genre (*Gattung*) and marriage, as well as about the intricate bonds of serial connections begotten by *gattieren* ("to mix," "to classify"), *gatten* ("to couple"), *Gatte/Gattin* ("husband/wife"), and so forth.

Once articulated within the precinct of Blanchot's entire discourse on the neuter, the most elliptical question would inevitably have to assume this form: What about a neutral genre/gender? Or one whose neutrality would not be *negative* (neither . . . nor), nor dialectical, but affirmative, and doubly affirmative (or . . . or)?

Here again, due to time limitations but also to more essential reasons concerning the structure of the text, I shall have to excerpt some abstract fragments. This will not occur without a supplement of violence and pain.

As first word and surely most impossible word of *La folie du jour*, "I" presents itself as self (*moi*), me, a man. Grammatical law leaves no doubt about this subject. The first sentence, phrased in French in the masculine ("Je ne suis ni savant ni ignorant" and not "Je ne suis ni savante ni ignorante"), says, with regard to knowledge, nothing but a double negation (neither . . . nor). Thus, no glint of self-presentation. But the double negation gives passage to a double affirmation (yes, yes) that enters into alignment or alliance with itself. Forging an alliance or marriage-bond ("hymen") with itself, this boundless double affirmation utters a measureless, excessive, immense *yes*: both to life and to death:

> I am neither learned nor ignorant. I have known some joy. This is saying too little: I am living, and this life gives me the greatest pleasure. And death? When I die (perhaps soon), I shall know an immense pleasure. I am not speaking of the foretaste of death, which is bland and often disagreeable. Suffering is debilitating. But this is the remarkable truth of which I am sure: I feel a boundless pleasure in living and shall be boundlessly content to die.

Now, seven paragraphs further along, the chance and probability of such an affirmation (one that is double and therefore boundless, limitless) is granted to woman. It returns to woman. Rather, not to woman or even to the feminine, to the female genre/gender, or to the generality of the feminine genre but—and this is why I spoke of chance and probability—"usually" to women. It is "usually" women who say yes, yes. To life to death. This "usually" avoids treating the feminine as a general and generic force; it makes an opening for the event, the performance, the uncertain contingencies, the encounter. And it is indeed from the contingent experience of the encounter that "I" will speak here. In the passage that I am about to cite, the expression "men" occurs twice. The second occurrence names the sexual genre, the sexual difference (*aner, vir*—but sexual difference does not occur between a species and a genre); in the first occurrence, "men" comes into play in an indecisive manner in order to name either the genre of human beings (the *genre humain*, named "species" in the text) or sexual difference:

> Men would like to escape death, bizarre *species* that they are. And some cry out, "die, die," because they would like to escape life. "What a life! I'll kill myself, I'll surrender!" This is pitiful and strange; it is in error.
>
>   But I have encountered *beings* who never told life to be quiet or death to go away—usually women, beautiful creatures. As for men, terror besieges them. . . . [Italics added]

What has thus far transpired in these seven paragraphs? Usually women, beautiful creatures, relates "I." As it happens, encounter, chance, affirmation of chance do not always manage to happen. There is no natural or symbolic law, universal law, or law of a genre/gender here. Only usually, usually women, (comma of apposition) beautiful creatures. Through its highly calculated logic, the comma of apposition leaves open the possibility of thinking that these women are not beautiful and then, on the other hand, as it happens, capable of saying yes, yes to life to death, of not saying be quiet, go away to life to death. The comma of apposition lets us think that they are beautiful, women and beauties, these creatures, insofar as they affirm both life and death. Beauty, the feminine beauty of these "beings," would be bound up with this double affirmation.

Now I myself, who "am neither learned nor ignorant," "I feel a boundless pleasure in living and shall be boundlessly content to die." In this random claim that links affirmation usually to women, beautiful ones, it is then more than probable that, as long as I say yes, yes, I am a woman and beautiful. *I am a woman, and beautiful.* Grammatical sex (or anatomical as well, in any case, sex submitted to the law of objectivity): the masculine genre is thus affected by the affirmation through a random drift that could always render it other. A sort of secret coupling would take place here, forming an odd marriage ("hymen"), an odd couple, for none of this can be regulated by objective, natural, or civil law. The "usually" is a mark of this secret and odd hymen, of this coupling that is also perhaps a mixing of genres. The genres pass into each other. And we will not be barred from thinking that this mixing of genres, viewed in light of the madness of sexual difference, may bear some relation to the mixing of literary genres.

"I," then, can keep alive the chance of being a fe-male or of changing sex. His transsexuality permits him, in a more than metaphorical and transferential way, to engender. He can give birth, and many other signs which I cannot mention here bear this out, among other things the fact that on several occasions he "brings something forth to the light of day." In the rhetoric of *La folie du jour*, the idiomatic expression "to bring forth to the light of day" ("donner le jour") is one of the players in an exceedingly powerful polysemic and disseminal game that I shall not attempt to reproduce here. I only retain its standard and dominant meaning which the spirit of linguistics gives it: *donner le jour* is to give birth—a verb whose subject is usually maternal, that is to say, generally female. At the center, closely hugging an invisible center, a primal scene could have alerted us, if we had had the time, to the *point of view* of *La folie du jour* and to *A Primal Scene*. This is also called a "short scene."

"I" can bring forth to light, can give birth. To what? Well, precisely to law or more exactly, to begin with, to the representatives of law, to those who wield authority—and let us also understand by this the authority of the author, the rights of authorship—simply by virtue of possessing an overseer's right, the right to see, the right to have everything in sight. This panoptic and this synopsis demand nothing else, but nothing less. Now herein lies the essential paradox: from where and from whom do they derive this power, this right-to-sight that permits them to have "me" at their disposal? Well, from "me," rather, from the subject who is subjected to them. It is the "I"-less "I" of the narrative voice, the I "stripped" of itself, the one that does not take place, it is he who brings them to light, who engenders these lawmen in giving them insight into what regards them and what should not regard them.

> I liked the doctors well enough. I did not feel belittled by their doubts. The bother was that their authority grew with every hour. One isn't initially aware of it, but these men are kings. Showing me my rooms they said: Everything here belongs to us. They threw themselves upon the parings of my mind: This is ours. They interpellated my story: Speak! and it placed itself at their service. In haste, I stripped myself of myself. I distributed my blood, my privacy among them, I offered them the universe, I brought them forth to the light of day. Under their unblinking gaze, I became a water drop, an ink blot. I was shrinking into them, I was held entirely in their view and when, finally, I no longer had anything but my perfect nullity present and no longer had anything to see, they, too, ceased to see me, most annoyed, they rose, shouting: Well, where are you? Where are you hiding? Hiding is prohibited, it is a misdeed, etc.

Law, day. One believes it generally possible to oppose law to affirmation, and particularly to unlimited affirmation, to the immensity of yes, yes. Law—we often figure it as an instance of the interdictory limit, of the binding obligation, as the negativity of a boundary not to be crossed. Now the mightiest and most divided trait of *La folie du jour* or of "An Account?" is the one relating birth to law, its genealogy, engenderment, generation, or genre—and here I ask you once more to be especially aware of gender—the one joining the very *genre* of the law to the process of the double affirmation. The excessiveness of *yes, yes* is no stranger to the genesis of law (nor to Genesis, as could be easily shown, for it also concerns an account of Genesis "in the light of seven days" [p. 20]). The double affirmation is not foreign to the genre, genius, or spirit of the law. No affirmation, and certainly no *double* affirmation without the law sighting the light of day and the daylight becoming law. Such is the madness of the day, such is an account in its "remarkable" truth, in its truthless truth.

Now the feminine, or generally affirmative gender/genre, is also the genre of this figure of law, not of its representatives, but of the law herself who, throughout an account, forms a couple with me, with the "I" of the narrative voice.

The law is in the feminine.

She is not a woman (it is only a figure, a "silhouette," and not a representative of the law) but she, *la loi*, is in the feminine, declined in the feminine; but not only as a grammatical gender/genre in my language (elsewhere Blanchot brought this genre into play for speech ["*la* parole"] and for thought ["*la* pensée"]). No, she is described as a "female element," which does not signify a female person. And the affirmative "I," the narrative voice, who has brought forth the representatives of the law to the light of day, claims to find the law seductive—sexually seductive. The law appeals to him: "The truth is that she appealed to me. In this milieu overpopulated with men, she was the only female element. One time she had me touch her knee: a bizarre impression. I declared to her: I am not the kind of man who contents himself with a knee. Her response: that would be revolting!" She pleases him and he would not like to content himself with the knee that she "had [him] touch." This contact with the knee (*genou*), as my student and friend Pierre-François Berger brought to my notice, recalls the inflectional contiguity of the I and the we, the *je* and the *nous*, of an I/we couple of whom we shall speak again in a moment.

The law's female element has thus always appealed to: me, I, he, we. The law is appealing: "The law appealed to me . . . In order to tempt her, I called softly to the law: 'Approach, so I can see you face to face' (I wanted to take her aside for a moment). Impudent appeal; what would I have done had she responded?"

He is perhaps subjected to law, but he neither attempts to escape her, nor does he shrink before her: he wishes to seduce the law to whom he gives birth (there is a hint of incest in this) and especially—this is one of the most striking and singular traits of this scene—he inspires fear in the law. He not only troubles the representatives of the law, the lawmen who are the legist doctors and the "psy-" who demand of him, but are unable to obtain, an organized account, a testimony oriented by a sense of history or his story, ordained and ordered by reason, and by the unity of an I think, or of an originally synthetic apperception accompanying all representations. That the "I" here does not always accompany itself

is by no means borne lightly by the lawmen; in fact, he alarms thus the lawmen, he radically persecutes them, and, in his manner, he conceals from them without altercation the truth they demand and without which they are nothing. But he not only alarms the lawmen, he alarms the law; one would be tempted to say the law herself, if she did not remain here a silhouette and an effect of the account. And what is more, this law whom the "I" frightens is none other than "me," than the "I," effect of his desire, child of his affirmation, of the genre "I" clasped in a specular couple with "me." They are inseparable (*je/nous* and *genou*, *je/toi* and *je/toit*), and so she tells him, once more, as truth: "The truth is that we can no longer be separated. I shall follow you everywhere, I shall dwell under your roof [*toit*], we shall have the same sleep." We see the law, whose silhouette stands behind her representatives, frightened by "me," by "him"; she is inclined toward and declined by *je/nous*, I/we, in front of "me," in front of him, her knees marking perhaps the articulation of a gait, the flexion of the couple and sexual difference, but also the continuity without contact of the hymen and the "mixing of genres."

> Behind their backs, I perceived the silhouette of the law. Not the familiar law, who is strict and not terribly agreeable: this one was different. Far from falling prey to her menace, I was the one who seemed to frighten her. According to her, my glance was lightning and my hands, grounds on which to perish. Moreover, she ridiculously attributed to me all kinds of power, she declared herself perpetually to be kneeling before me. But she let me demand nothing, and when she granted me the right to be in all places, that meant that I hadn't a place anywhere. [Elsewhere Blanchot designates the non-place and the atopical or hypertopical mobility of the narrative voice in this way.] When she placed me above the authorities, that meant: you are authorized to do nothing.

What game is the law, a law of this genre, playing? What is she playing up to when she has her knee touched? For if *La folie du jour* plays down the law, plays at law, plays with law, it is also because the law herself plays. The law, in its female element, is a silhouette that plays. At what? At being . . . born, at being born like anybody and no body. She plays upon her generation and displays her genre, she plays out her nature and her history, and she makes a plaything of an account. In mock-playing herself she takes into account the account: she recites; and her birth is accountable to the account, the *récit*, one could even say to her: (to *la voix* . . .) the narrative voice, *him, her, I, we,* the neuter genre that subjects and merges itself while giving birth to her, who lets himself be captivated by the law and escapes her, whom she escapes and whom she loves. She lets herself be put in motion, she lets herself be cited by him when, in the midst of her game, she says, pursuing an idiom that her disseminal polysemy conveys to the abyss, "I see day":

> Here is one of her games. [He has just recalled that she "once had (him) touch her knee."] She showed me a section of the space between the top of the window and the ceiling: "You are there," she said. I looked at this point with intensity. "Are you there?" I looked at it with all my power. "Well?" I felt the scars of my glaze leap, my sight became a wound, my head, a gap, a gutted bull. Suddenly she cried out: "Oh! I see day! Oh God!" etc. I protested that this game tired me enormously, but she was insatiable for my glory.

For the law to see the day is her madness, is what she loves madly like the glory, the emblazed illustration, the day of the writer, of the author who says "I," and who brings forth law to the light of day. He says that she is insaturable, insatiable for his glory—he, who is, too, author of the law to which he submits himself, he, who engenders her, he, her mother who no longer knows how to say "I" or to keep memory intact. I am the mother of law, behold my daughter's madness. It is also the Madness of the Day, for day, the word "day" in its disseminal abyss, is law, the law of the law. My daughter's madness is to want to be born—like anybody, whereas she remained a "silhouette," a shadow, a profile, her face never in view. He had said to her, to the law, in order to "tempt her": "Approach, so I can see you face to face."

Such would be the "remarkable truth" that clears an opening for the madness of day—and that appeals, like law, like madness, to the one who says "I" or I/we. Let us be attentive to this syntax of truth. She, the law, says: "The truth is that we can no longer be separated. I shall follow you everywhere, I shall live under your roof . . ." He: "The truth is that she appealed to me . . . ," she, law, but also—and this is always the principal theme of these sentences—she, *la vérité*, truth. One cannot conceive truth without the madness of the law.

I have let myself be commanded by the law of our encounter, by the convention of our subject, notably the genre, the law of genre. This law,

articulated as an I/we which is more or less autonomous in its movements, assigned us places and limits. Even though I have launched an
appeal against this law, it was she who turned my appeal into a confir-
mation of her own glory. But she also desires ours insatiably. Submitting
myself to the subject of our colloquium, as well as to its law, I sifted "An
Account," *La folie du jour.* I isolated a type, if not a genre, of reading
from an infinite series of trajectories or possible courses. I have pointed
out the generative principle of these courses, beginnings, and new beginnings in every sense: but from a certain point of view. Elsewhere—in
accordance with other subjects, other colloquia and lectures, other I/we
drawn together in one place—other trajectories could have, and have,
come to light.

Nonetheless, it would be folly to draw any sort of general conclusion
here. I could not say what exactly has happened in this scene, nor in my
discourse or my account. What was perhaps seen, in the blink of time's
eye, is a madness of law—and, therefore, of order, reason, sense, and
meaning, of day: "But often" (said "I"), "I was dying without saying a
thing. In time, I became convinced that I was seeing the madness of day
face to face; such was the truth: light became mad, clarity took leave of
her senses; she assailed me unreasonably, without a set of rules, without
a goal. This discovery was like jaws clutching at my life." I am woman,
and beautiful; my daughter, the law, is mad about me. I speculate on my
daughter. My daughter is mad about me; this is law.

The law is mad, she is mad about "me." And across the madness of
this day, I keep this in sight. There, this will have been my self-portrait
of the genre.

The law is mad. The law is mad, is madness; but madness is not the
predicate of law. There is no madness without the law; madness cannot be conceived before its relation to law. Madness is law, the law is
madness. There is a general trait here: the madness of the law mad for
me, the day madly in love with me, the silhouette of my daughter mad
about me, her mother, etc. But *La folie du jour, An* (accountless) *Account?*, carrying and miscarrying its titles, is not at all exemplary of this
general trait. Not at all, not wholly. This is not an example of a general
or generic whole. The whole, which begins by finishing and never fin-
ishes beginning apart from itself, the whole that stays at the edgeless
boundary of itself, the whole greater and less than a whole and nothing,
An Account? will not have been exemplary. Rather, with regard to the
whole, it will have been wholly counter-exemplary.

The genre has always in all genres been able to play the role of
order's principle: resemblance, analogy, identity and difference, taxo-

nomic classification, organization and genealogical tree, order of reason, order of reasons, sense of sense, truth of truth, natural light and sense of history. Now, the test of *An Account?* brought to light the madness of genre. Madness has given birth to and thrown light on the genre in the most dazzling, most blinding sense of the word. And in the writing of *An Account?*, in literature, satirically practicing all genres, imbibing them but never allowing herself to be saturated with a catalog of genres, she, madness, has started spinning Peterson's genre-disc like a demented sun. And she does not only do so *in* literature, for in concealing the boundaries that sunder mode and genre, she has also inundated and divided the borders between literature and its others.

There, that is the whole of it, it is only what "I," so they say, here kneeling at the edge of literature, can see. In sum, the law. The law summoning: what "I" can sight and what "I" can say that I sight in this site of a recitation where I/we is.

Une traduction?
par
M

2

The Linguistic Circle of Geneva

Translated by Alan Bass

Linguists are becoming more and more interested in the
genealogy of linguistics. And in reconstituting the history
or prehistory of their science, they are discovering numerous ancestors, sometimes with a certain astonished recognition. Interest in the origin of linguistics is awakened
when the problems of the origin of language cease to be
proscribed (as they had been from the end of the nineteenth century) and when a certain geneticism—or a certain generativism—comes back into its own. One could
show that this is not a chance encounter. This historical
activity is no longer elaborated solely at the margins of
scientific practice, and its results are already being felt. In
particular, we are no longer at the stage of the prejudice
according to which linguistics as a science was born of a
single "epistemological break"—a concept, called Bache-
lardian, much used or abused today—and of a break occurring in our immediate vicinity. We no longer think, as
does Maurice Grammont, that "everything prior to the
nineteenth century, which is not yet linguistics, can be expedited in several lines."[1] Noam Chomsky, in an article

1. Maurice Grammont, cited by Noam Chomsky, *Cartesian Linguistics* (New York, 1966), p. 1.

announcing his *Cartesian Linguistics*, which presents in its major lines
the concept of "generative grammar," states: "My aim here is not to justify the interest of this investigation, nor to describe summarily its procedure, but instead to underline that *by a curious detour* it takes us back to
a tradition of ancient thought, rather than constituting a new departure
or a radical innovation in the domain of linguistics and psychology."[2]

If we were to set ourselves down in the space of this "curious detour," we could not help encountering the "linguistics" of Jean-Jacques
Rousseau. We would have to ask ourselves, then, in what ways Rousseau's reflections on the sign, on language, on the origin of languages, on
the relations between speech and writing, and so on announce (but what
does "announce" mean here?) what we are so often tempted to consider
as the very modernity of linguistic science, that is, modernity *as* linguistic science, since so many other "human sciences" refer to linguistics as
their titular model. And we are all the more encouraged to practice this
detour in that Chomsky's major references, in *Cartesian Linguistics*, are
to the *Logic* and *General and Reasoned Grammar* of Port-Royal, works
that Rousseau knew well and held in high esteem.[3] For example, on several occasions Rousseau cites Duclos' commentary on the *General and
Reasoned Grammar*. The *Essay on the Origin of Languages* even closes
with one of these citations. Thus Rousseau acknowledges his debt.

There is only one allusion to Rousseau himself in *Cartesian Linguistics*, in a note which on the one hand compares him to Wilhelm von
Humboldt and on the other, while referring only to the most general
propositions of the second *Discourse*, presents him as strictly Cartesian,
at least as concerns the concepts of animality and humanity. Although
one might, in a certain sense, speak of Rousseau's fundamental Carte-
sianism in this regard, it seems that a more important and original place
must be reserved for him in such a history of philosophy and linguistics.
It is in this sense, under the heading of a very preliminary schema, that
I venture the following propositions.

One is authorized to speak of a linguistics of Rousseau only on two
conditions and in two senses:

2. Chomsky, "De quelques constantes de la théorie linguistique," *Diogène*, no. 51
(1965); my italics. See also Chomsky, *Current Issues in Linguistic Theory* (The Hague,
1964), pp. 15 ff. There is an analogous gesture in Jakobson, who refers not only to
Peirce and, as does Chomsky, to Humboldt but also to John of Salisbury, to the Sto-
ics, and to Plato's *Cratylus*: see Jakobson, "A la recherche de l'essence du langage,"
Diogène, no. 51 (1965).
3. "I began with some book of philosophy, like the Port-Royal *Logic*, Locke's *Essay*, Malebranch, Leibniz, Descartes, etc." (Jean-Jacques Rousseau, *Oeuvres complètes*,
vol. I, *Confessions* [Paris, 1959], p. 237).

1. On the condition and in the sense of a systematic formulation, one that defines the project of a theoretical science of language, in its method, its object, and its rigorously proper field. This might be accomplished by means of a gesture that for convenience's sake could be called an "epistemological break," there being no assurance that the stated intention to "break" has such an effect, nor that the so-called break is ever a—unique—datum in a work or an author. This first condition and first sense should always be implied by what we will entitle the *opening of the field*, it being understood that such an opening also amounts to a *delimitation* of the field.

2. On the condition and in the sense of what Chomsky calls the "constants of linguistic theory": in that the system of fundamental concepts, the exigencies and norms that govern the linguistics called modern, such as it is entitled and represented in its scientificity as in its modernity, is already at work, and discernible as such, in Rousseau's enterprise, in its very text; which, moreover, would not only be (and doubtless would not at all be) to interpret this text as the happy anticipation of a thinker who is to have predicted and preformed modern linguistics. On the contrary, is this not a question of a very general ground of possibilities, a ground on which might be raised all kinds of subordinate cross sections and secondary periodizations? Is it not a question of both Rousseau's project and modern linguistics belonging in common to a determined and finite system of conceptual possibilities, to a common language, to a reserve of oppositions of signs (signifiers/concepts) which first of all is none other than the most ancient fund of Western metaphysics? The latter is articulated, in its diverse epochs, according to schemas of implication that are not as easily mastered as is sometimes believed: whence the illusions of the break, the mirages of the new, the confusion or crushing of layers, the artifice of extractions and cross sections, the archeological lure. The *closure of concepts*: such would be the title that we might propose for this second condition and this second sense.

These two conditions seem to be fulfilled; and in these two senses it seems that one may legitimately speak of a linguistics of Rousseau. Here we can delineate it only through several indices.

I. The Opening of the Field

Rousseau states and wants, or in any case states that he wants, a break with every supernatural explication of the origin and functioning of language. If the theological hypothesis is not simply set aside, it never intervenes in its own name, de jure, in Rousseau's explication and description. This rupture is signified in at least two texts and at two points: in the second *Discourse* and in the *Essay on the Origin of Languages*.

Referring to Condillac, to whom he recognizes he owes a great deal, Rousseau clearly expresses his disagreement as concerns the procedure followed in the *Essay on the Origin of Human Knowledge*. Condillac, in effect, *seems* to take a constituted society, created by God, as given at the very moment when he asks the question of language, the question of the genesis and system of language, of the relations between natural and instituted signs, and so on. Now Rousseau wants to account for the very emergence of convention, that is, in his own words, to account simultaneously for society and language on the basis of a "pure state of nature." So he must put between parentheses everything that Condillac takes as given, and in effect this is what he allegedly does.

The concept of *nature*, therefore, bears the burden of scientificity here, as much in the requirement of a natural (nonsupernatural) explanation as in the ultimate reference to a purely (presocial, prehistoric, prelinguistic, etc.) natural state. The field of the analysis, the genealogical regression, and the explanation of functioning are all opened as such in the demand for naturality. We do not mean that Rousseau *himself* opened this field and this demand. We simply wish to recognize the signs that show him caught in this opening whose history and system remain to be constituted. The difficulty of the task and the theoretical or methodological innovations called for are such that to point out signs can only attribute, assign, and situate these signs as touchstones.

Before even asking whether natural naturality and originality are not still theological functions in Rousseau's discourse—and in general in every discourse—let us make specific the criticism addressed to Condillac. It could be shown—but this is not my aim here—that Condillac's procedure is not so far removed in its principles from Rousseau's and that the theological reference easily accommodates a concern for natural explanation:

> Adam and Eve did not owe to experience the exercise of the operations of their soul, and, emerging from the hands of God, by means of this extraordinary help, they were capable of reflection and of communicating their thoughts to each other. But I suppose that, some time after the deluge, two children, one of each sex, had been lost in the general desolation, before knowing the use of any sign. I am authorized to do so because of the fact I have reported. Who knows if a people does not exist somewhere

that owes its origin only to such an event? Permit me to make this supposition; the question is to know how this growing nation fashioned for itself a language.[4]

Further on, at the end of a note: "If I suppose two children in the necessity of imagining even the very first signs of language, it is because I have believed that it is not sufficient for a philosopher to say that a thing has been accomplished by extraordinary means; but that it was his duty to explain how it *could have* been done by natural means."[5] I underline the conditional tense, which supports the entire scientificity of the argument.

Thus, Condillac renounces neither a natural explanation nor the conjunction of the questions of the origin of languages and the origin of societies. Theological certitude is accommodated to a natural explanation according to a very classical framework in which the concepts of nature, experience, Creation, and Fall are strictly inseparable. (The most remarkable example of such a "system" is doubtless that of Nicolas Malebranche, which I am recalling here only because of its well-known influence on Rousseau.) Here the event of the Flood, whose analog will be found in Rousseau, liberates the functioning of the natural explanation.

This does not prevent Rousseau from taking his leave from Condillac precisely at the point at which he reproaches Condillac for taking as given that which is to be explained, that is, "a kind of already established society among the inventors of language." Rousseau reproaches Condillac less for rejecting every model of natural explanation—that would be untrue—than for not radicalizing his concept of nature: Condillac would not have descended to a pure state of nature to analyze the emergence of language:

> Permit me for a moment to consider all the confusions of the origin of Languages. I could content myself with citing or repeating here all of the Abbé de Condillac's investigations into this matter, which fully confirm my feeling, and which, perhaps, gave me my first ideas. But given the manner in which this Philosopher resolves the difficulties he creates for himself on the origin of in-

4. Etienne Bonnot de Condillac, *Essai sur l'origine des connaissances humaines* (Paris, 1973), p. 193.
5. Ibid., n. 1.

stitutionalized signs, that is, a kind of already established society
among the inventors of language, I believe that in referring to his
reflections I must add to them my own.[6]

Thus Condillac seems to have committed what Rousseau a little further
on calls "the fault of those who, reasoning on the State of Nature, transport into it ideas taken from Society."

The properly scientific concern, therefore, is indicated by the decision to refer only to purely natural causes. Such is the motif on which
the *Essay on the Origin of Languages* opens, from its very first paragraph: "In order to tell, it is necessary to go back to some principle
that belongs to the locality itself and antedates its customs, for speech,
being the first social institution, owes its form to natural causes alone."[7]
Now, without even entering into the content of the natural genealogy
of language that Rousseau proposes, let us note that the so-called epistemological break paradoxically corresponds to a kind of break in the
field of natural causality. If "speech," "the first social institution, owes
its form to natural causes alone," then the latter, themselves acting as
a force of break with nature, *naturally* inaugurate an order radically
heterogeneous to the natural order.[8] The two—apparently contradictory—conditions for the constitution of a scientific field and object, here

6. Rousseau, *Oeuvres complètes*, vol. 3, *Discours sur l'origine de l'inégalité* (second
Discourse), p. 146; all further references to the *Discourse* will be included in the text.
On all the problems of language in Rousseau, I refer most notably to the very valuable
notes of Jean Starobinski in this edition and of course to the other works on Rousseau
by this author, particularly *La Transparence et l'obstacle* (Paris, 1964).

7. Rousseau, *Essay on the Origin of Languages*, trans. John H. Moran (New York,
1966), p. 5; all further references to the *Essay* will be included in the text.

8. Attention must be paid to the word "form": natural causes must produce the
variety of forms *of* speech as the variety *of* languages. The *Essay* accounts for this by
means of physics, geography, and climatology. This distinction between speech itself and
languages underlies the notion of form at the beginning of the *Essay*:

> Speech distinguishes man among the animals; language distinguishes nations from
> each other; one does not know where a man comes from until he has spoken. Out
> of usage and necessity, each learns the language of his own country. But what deter-
> mines that this language is that of his country and not that of another? In order to
> tell, it is necessary to go back to some principle that belongs to the locality itself and
> antedates its customs, for speech, being the first social institution, owes its form to
> natural causes alone. [P. 5]

But the text that follows perhaps permits an extension of the variety of forms beyond
the diversity of oral languages to include the multiplicity of "substances of expressions,"
the means of communication. These natural means are the senses, and each sense has its
language. See section II below, "The Closure of Concepts."

language, would thus be fulfilled: a natural, a continuously natural, causality and a break designating the irreducible autonomy and originality of a domain. The question of the origin is in itself suspended in that it no longer calls for a continuous, real, and natural description, being but the index of an internal structural description.

Certainly all this is neither without difficulty nor without a certain apparent incoherence, for which Rousseau often has been reproached. And it has been that much easier to make this reproach because Rousseau himself on several occasions seems to renounce the natural explanation and to admit a kind of violent—catastrophic—interruption into the concatenation of natural causality: an arbitrary interruption, an interruption of the arbitrary, the decision which permits only the arbitrary and the conventional to be instituted. One comes back to the necessity of this question wherever the conceptuality organized around the opposition nature/arbitrary is accredited. Before defining the necessity of both the break and the at least apparent failure, before underlining the scientific and heuristic motivation that accommodates its opposite here, let us briefly recall its well-known points of apparition.

1. After attempting in the second *Discourse*, by means of a fiction, a derivation of languages on the basis of a primitive dispersion in the state of pure nature, on the basis of the biological nucleus uniting mother and child, Rousseau has to step back and suppose "this first difficulty overcome":

> Notice again that the Child having all his needs to explain, and consequently more things to say to the Mother than the Mother to the Child, it is he who must bear the burden of invention, and that the language he employs must in great part be his own handiwork; which multiplies Languages by as many individuals as there are to speak them, to which the wandering and vagabond life, which leaves no idiom the time to become consistent, contributes further still; for to say that the Mother dictates to the child words which he will have to use to ask her for such and such a thing well demonstrates how already formed Languages are taught, but teaches us nothing about how they are formed. *Let us suppose this first difficulty overcome: For a moment let us step across the immense space there had to be between the pure state of Nature and the need for Languages; and supposing them necessary, let us seek out how they might have begun to be established. A new difficulty, worse still than the preceding one;*

for if men had need of speech in order to learn to think, they had
even greater need of knowing how to think in order to find the
art of speech. [P. 147; my italics]

2. And later, when he has taken as given, by means of a *supposi-*
tion, both the "immense space there had to be between the pure state of
Nature and the need for Languages" and the solution of the circle that
demands speech before thought and thought before speech, Rousseau
must yet again, *a third time*, recoil before a *third difficulty*; he must even
feign giving up on a natural explanation in order to refer back to the
hypothesis of divine institution. It is true that in the interval between the
supposition and the apparent resignation he will have proposed an entire theory of language: a functional, systematic, and structural theory,
whose elaboration is occasioned by the pretext of a genetic question, a
fictitious problematic of the origin.

Rousseau's formulation of his apparent resignation, at the point
of the third difficulty in the *Discourse* ("As for myself, frightened by
the mounting difficulties, and convinced of the almost demonstrable
impossibility that Languages could have been born and established by
purely human means, I leave to whoever would like to undertake it
the discussion of this difficult problem: which was more necessary, an
already bound Society, for the institution of Languages, or already invented languages, for the establishment of Society" [p. 151]) is to be
juxtaposed with the following formulation from the *Essay*, in which
Rousseau, confronted by the necessity of acknowledging an unforeseen
and inexplicable irruption at the origin of languages (transition from
the inarticulate cry to articulation and convention), cites Father Lamy's
theological hypothesis without criticizing it, although without assuming
it, simply in order to illustrate the difficulty of natural explanation: "In
all tongues, the liveliest exclamations are inarticulate. Cries and groans
are simple sounds. Mutes, which is to say the deaf, can make only inarticulate sounds. Father Lamy thinks that if God had not taught men to
speak, they would never have learned by themselves" (p. 14).[9]

9. On Father Lamy, I refer to Genevieve Rodin-Lewis' study, "Un théoricien du langage au XVIIe siècle, Bernard Lamy," *Le Français moderne* (January 1968): 19–50. In
the *Confessions*, Rousseau recalls all that he owes to Father Lamy: "One of my favorite
Authors, whose works I still reread with pleasure" (p. 238). Earlier on: "The taste that
I had for him [M. Salomon] extended to the subjects of which he treated, and I began to
seek out books which could help me better to understand him. Those which mixed de-
voutness with the sciences suited me best; such, particularly, were those of the Oratoire
and of Port-Royal. I set myself to reading them, or rather to devouring them. Of these,
one fell into my hands by Father Lamy, entitled *Entretiens sur les sciences*. It was a kind

The three difficulties have the same form: the circle in which tradition (or transmission) and language, thought and language, society
and language each precede the other, postulate and produce each other
reciprocally. But these apparent, and apparently avowed, confusions
have a reverse side for which in a way they pay the price. The circle,
as a vicious circle, a logical circle, by the same token constitutes the
rigorously limited, closed, and original autonomy of a field. If there is
no entry into the circle, if it is closed, if one is always already set down
within it, if it has always already begun to carry us along in its movement, no matter where it is entered, it is because the circle forms a perfectly underivable figure and does so by means of a continuous causality,
something other than itself. It has been posited decisively by an absolute,
and absolutely irruptive, initiative, making it simultaneously open and
closed. Society, language, convention, history, and so on, together with
all the possibilities that go along with them, form a system, an organized
totality which, in its originality, can be the object of a theory. Beyond
its negative and sterilizing effects, beyond the question which it seems
incapable of answering logically, the "logical circle" positively delimits
an epistemological circle, a field whose objects will be specific. The condition for the study of this field as such is that the genetic and factual
derivation be interrupted. Ideal genealogy or structural description: such
is Rousseau's project. Let us cite the *Discourse* once more: "Let us begin
by setting aside all the facts, for they do not touch upon the question.
The Investigations one may enter into on this subject must not be taken
as historical truths, but only as hypothetical and conditional reasoning;
more apt to enlighten the Nature of things than to show their veritable
origin, and similar to the Investigations made every day by our Physi-
cians concerning the formation of the World" (pp. 132–33).

   3. This is what accounts for the absolutely unforeseeable intervention, in the *Essay*, of the "slight movement" of a finger which produces the birth of society and languages. Since the system of the state of
Nature could not depart *from itself*, could not itself depart from itself
(see the *Discourse*, p. 162), could not spontaneously interrupt itself,

---

of introduction to the knowledge of the books on this topic. I read and reread it a hundred times; I resolved to make it my guide" (p. 232). One might pick out more than one
correspondence between the two theories of language, notably as concerns the relations
between speech and writing. In Father Lamy's *Rhetoric* one may read: "Words on paper
are like a dead body laid out on the ground. In the mouth of whoever proffers them they
are efficacious; on paper they are without life, incapable of producing the same effects."
And "a written discourse is dead," "the tone, gestures, and air of the face of the speaker
support his words" (cited by Rodin-Lewis, "Théoricien du langage," p. 27).

some perfectly exterior causality had to come to provoke—*arbitrarily*—this departure, which is none other, precisely, than the *possibility of the arbitrary*. But this arbitrary and exterior causality will also have to act along natural or quasi-natural lines. The causality of the break will have to be both natural and exterior to the state of pure nature, and most notably to the state of nature, the state of the earth that corresponds to the state of nature. Only a *terrestrial revolution* or, rather, the catastrophe of terrestrial revolution, could furnish the model for this causality. This is the center of the *Essay*:

> Supposing eternal spring on the earth; supposing plenty of water, livestock, and pasture, and supposing that men, as they leave the hands of nature, were once spread out in the midst of all that, I cannot imagine how they would ever be induced to give up their primitive liberty, abandoning the isolated pastoral life so fitted to their natural indolence, to impose upon themselves unnecessarily the labors and the inevitable misery of a social mode of life.
>
> He who willed man to be social, by the touch of a finger shifted the globe's axis into line with the axis of the universe. I see such a slight movement changing the face of the earth and deciding the vocation of mankind: in the distance I hear the joyous cries of a naive multitude; I see the building of castles and cities; I see men leaving their homes, gathering to devour each other, and turning the rest of the world into a hideous desert: fitting monument to social union and the usefulness of the arts. [Pp. 38–39][10]

This fiction has the advantage of sketching out a model that explicates *nature's departure from itself*; this departure is simultaneously absolutely natural and absolutely artificial; it must simultaneously respect and violate natural legality. Nature *itself inverts itself*, which it can only do on the basis of a point absolutely exterior to itself, that is, on the basis of a force simultaneously void and infinite. By the same token, this model respects the heterogeneity of the two orders or the two moments (nature and society, nonlanguage and language, etc.) and coordinates the continuous with the discontinuous according to what

10. See also Rousseau's fragment on "L'Influence des climats sur la civilisation" (*Oeuvres complètes*, 3:531), and my *De la grammatologie* (Paris, 1967), pp. 360 ff.

we have analyzed elsewhere under the rubric of *supplementarity*.[11] For
the absolute irruption, the unforeseen revolution which made possible
language, institutions, articulation, the arbitrary, and so on, however,
has done nothing but develop the *virtualities* already present in the state
of pure nature. As is said in the *Discourse*, "*Perfectibility*, the social
virtues, and the other faculties that Natural man had received in abun-
dance, could never have been developed by themselves . . . ; they needed
for this the fortuitous concourse of several foreign causes which could
never be born, and without which he would have remained eternally in
his primitive condition" (p. 162).

The notion of virtuality, therefore, assures a cohering and joining
function between the two discontinuous orders, as between the two temporalities—imperceptible progression and definitive break—which scan
the passage from nature to society.[12] But despite the concepts of pure
nature and of virtuality, and even if the original movement of the finger
can still supplement the theological hypothesis, even if divine Providence
is called upon elsewhere, it remains that Rousseau, at a certain surface
of his discourse, can by all rights allege to do without any supernatural
explanation and, putting all history and all factual chronology between
parentheses, can propose a structural order of the origin and function
of language. In doing so, even while respecting the original order of
language and society, he correlates this order, and systematically maintains this correlation, with the order of nature, primarily with the geo-
logical or geographical order of this nature. Thereby the typology of
languages in the *Essay* will conform to a general topology, and "local
difference" will be taken into account in the origin of languages (see
chap. 8). Corresponding to the opposition south/north is the opposition
of languages of passion to languages of need, which are distinguished
by the predominance granted to accentuation in the one and articulation in the other, to the vowel in one and to the consonant in the other,
to metaphor in one and to exactness and correctness in the other. The
latter—the languages of the north—lend themselves more easily to writing; the former naturally reject it. Thus we have a series of correlations.
At the pole of the origin, at the point of greatest proximity to the birth

11. See Rousseau, "L'Influence," and my *Grammatologie*.
12. While marking the absolute break which—de jure and structurally—must separate nature and language or society, Rousseau alludes in the *Discourse* "to the inconceivable pains and infinite time that the first invention of Language must have cost," to the
"almost imperceptible progress of the beginnings"; "for the more that events were slow
to succeed one another, the quicker they are to describe" (pp. 146, 167).

of language, there is the chain origin-life-south-summer-heat-passion-accentuation-vowel-metaphor-song, and so on. At the other pole, to the extent that one departs from the origin: decadence-illness-death-north-winter-cold-reason-articulation-consonant-correctness-prose-writing. But by a strange motion, the more one departs from the origin, the more one tends to come back to what precedes it, to a nature which *has not yet* awakened to speech and to everything that is born along with speech. And between the two polar series are regulated relations of supplementarity: the second series is added to the first in order to be *substituted* for it, but in supplementing a lack in the first series, also to *add* something new, an addition, an *accident*, an excess that *should not have* overtaken the first series. In doing this, the second series will hollow out a new lack or will enlarge the original lack, which will call for a new supplement, and so forth. The same logic is at work in the historic and systematic classification of writings: corresponding to the three states of man in society (savage, barbaric, or policed peoples) are three types of writings (pictographic, ideographic, phonetic).[13] But although writing has a regular relation to the state of language ("Another way of comparing languages and determining their relative antiquity is to consider their script"), its system forms an independent totality in its internal organization and in its principle: "The art of writing does not at all depend upon that of speaking. It derives from needs of a different kind which develop earlier or later according to circumstances entirely independent of the duration of the people" (pp. 16, 19).

Reduced to their most impoverished, most general, most principal framework, such would be the motifs of an opening of the linguistic field. Did Rousseau *himself* and *himself alone* execute this opening, or is he already taken up and included in it? The question has not yet been elaborated fully enough, the terms are still too naive, the alternative is still too restricted for me to be tempted to offer an answer. No problematic, no methodology today seems to me to be capable of pitting itself effectively against the difficulties effectively announced in these questions. Thus without great risk and still in the form of a touchstone, I would say that despite the massive borrowings, despite the complicated

---

13. See the *Essay*: "These three ways of writing correspond almost exactly to three different stages according to which one can consider men gathered into a nation. The depicting of objects is appropriate to a savage people; signs of words and of propositions, to a barbaric people; and the alphabet to civilized peoples [*peuples policés*]." "To the preceding division there correspond the three conditions of man considered in relation to society. The savage is a hunter, the barbarian is a herdsman, and civil man is a tiller of the soil" (pp. 17, 38).

geography of sources, despite the passive situation in a milieu, what can be discerned empirically under the rubric of the "work of Jean-Jacques Rousseau" yields a reading of a relatively original and relatively systematic effort to delimit the field of a linguistic science. Today the poverty of these propositions will be more easily accepted, perhaps, if one thinks of the imprudent, that is, foolish, statements from which they protect us, at least provisionally.

Of course, it is not a matter of comparing the content of the linguistic knowledge discovered in a given field with the content of modern linguistic knowledge. But the disproportion that would make such a comparison derisory is a disproportion of content: it is massively reduced when theoretical intentions, lineaments, and fundamental concepts are in question.

II. The Closure of Concepts

It is tempting now to invert the procedure of verification and to bring to light, on the basis of certain exemplary projects in modern linguistics, the thread which leads back to Rousseau. Here I can only single out Saussurian linguistics and semiology, taking my justification both from the fact that this is the base of all the modern theories and from the self-evidence or number of the analogies it holds in store.

1. Rousseau and Saussure grant an ethical and metaphysical privilege to the voice. Both posit the inferiority and exteriority of writing in relation to the "internal system of language" (Saussure), and this gesture, whose consequences extend over the entirety of their discourses, is expressed in formulations whose literal resemblance is occasionally surprising. Thus:

> SAUSSURE: "Language and writing are two distinct systems of signs; the second exists for the sole purpose of representing the first."
>
> ROUSSEAU: "Languages are made to be spoken, writing serves only as a supplement of speech. . . . Writing is only the representation of speech."
>
> SAUSSURE: "Whoever says that a certain letter must be pronounced a certain way is mistaking the written image of a sound for the sound itself. . . . To attribute this oddity [*bizarrerie*] to an exceptional pronunciation is also misleading."
>
> ROUSSEAU: "Writing is only the representation of speech; it

is odd [*bizarre*] that more care is taken to determine the
image than the object."[14]

And one could continue to proliferate citations in order to show
that both fear the effects of writing on speech and thus condemn these
effects from a moral point of view. All of Rousseau's invectives against
a writing which "alters" and "enervates" language, obstructing liberty
and life (especially in the *Essay*, chaps. 5 and 20), find their echo in Saussure's warnings: "The linguistic object is not both the written and the
spoken forms of words; the spoken forms alone constitute the object."
"Writing obscures language; it is not a guise for language but a disguise"
(pp. 23–24, 30). The bond between writing and language is "fictitious,"
"superficial," and yet "writing acquires primary importance," and thus
"the natural sequence is reversed" (p. 25). Writing is therefore a "trap,"
and its actions are "vicious" and "tyrannical" (today we would say
despotic); its misdeeds are monstrosities, "teratological cases" that linguistics "should put . . . into a special compartment for observation"
(p. 32). Finally, both Rousseau and Saussure consider nonphonetic writing—for example, a universal characteristic of the Leibnizian type—as
evil itself.[15]

2. Both Rousseau and Saussure make linguistics a part of general
semiology, the latter itself being only a branch of the social psychology
which grows out of general psychology and general anthropology.

> SAUSSURE: "*A science that studies the life of signs within society*
> is conceivable; it should be a part of social psychology and
> consequently of general psychology; I shall call it *semiol-*
> *ogy* (from the Greek *sēmeion*, "sign"). Semiology should
> show what constitutes signs, what laws govern them. Since
> the science does not yet exist, no one can say what it would
> be; but it has a right to existence, a place staked out in
> advance. Linguistics is only a part of the general science
> of semiology; the laws discovered by semiology will be
> applicable to linguistics, and the latter will circumscribe a
> well-defined area within the mass of anthropological facts.

14. The quotations from Saussure are from his *Course in General Linguistics*, trans.
Wade Baskin (New York, 1959), pp. 23, 30; all further references to the *Course* will be
included in the text. The quotations from Rousseau are from the fragment on "Pronon-
ciation" (*Oeuvres complètes*, 2:1249–52).
15. See my *Grammatologie*, pp. 57 and 429.

To determine the exact place of semiology is the task of the psychologist" (p. 16).

From the very first chapter of the *Essay on the Origin of Languages* ("On the Various Means of Communicating Our Thoughts"), Rousseau also proposes a general theory of signs ordered according to the regions of sensibility that furnish the various signifying substances. This general semiology is part of a general sociology and anthropology. Speech is the "first social institution" and thus can be studied only by studying the origin and general structure of society, from within a general theory of the forms and substances of signification. This theory is inseparable from a psychology of the passions. For "the first invention of speech is due not to need but passion" (p. 11).

> As soon as one man was recognized by another as a sentient, thinking being similar to himself, the desire or need to communicate his feelings and thoughts made him seek the means to do so. Such means can be derived only from the senses, the only instruments through which one man can act upon another. Hence the institution of sensate signs for the expression of thought. The inventors of language did not proceed rationally in this way; rather their instinct suggested the consequence to them.
>
> Generally, the means by which we can act on the senses of others are restricted to two: that is, movement and voice. The action of movement is immediate through touching, or mediate through gesture. The first can function only within arm's length, while the other extends as far as the visual ray. Thus vision and hearing are the only passive organs of language among distinct individuals. [Pp. 5–6]

There follows a confrontation of the language of gesture and the language of voice: although both are "natural," they are unequally dependent upon convention. From this point of view, Rousseau certainly can vaunt the merits of mute signs, which are more natural and more immediately eloquent. But in linking society to passion and convention, he grants a privilege to speech within the general system of signs—and consequently to linguistics within semiology. This is the third point of a possible comparison of principles or program.

3. The privilege of speech is linked, in particular, in Saussure as in Rousseau, to the institutionalized, conventional, arbitrary character

of the sign. The verbal sign is more arbitrary, Rousseau and Saussure think, than other signs:

> SAUSSURE: "Signs that are wholly arbitrary realize better than the others the ideal of the semiological process; that is why language, the most complex and universal of all systems of expression, is also the most characteristic; in this sense linguistics can become the master-pattern for all branches of semiology although language is only one particular semiological system" (p. 67).
>
> ROUSSEAU: "Although the language of gesture and spoken language are equally natural, still the first is easier and depends less upon conventions" (*Essay*, p. 6).

And on the other hand, for Rousseau, only linguistics is an anthropological, social, and psychological science because "conventional language is characteristic of man alone" and because the origin of speech is in passion and not need: "It seems then that need dictated the first gestures, while the passions stimulated the first words" (pp. 10, 11). This explains the fact that language is originally metaphorical (see chap. 3). The originality of the linguistic field has to do with the break from natural need, a break which simultaneously initiates passion, convention, and speech.

4. For the same reason, and as Saussure will do later, Rousseau rejects any pertinence of the physiological point of view in the explication of language. The physiology of the phonic organs is not an intrinsic part of the discipline of linguistics. With the same organs, with no assignable physiological or anatomic difference, men speak and animals do not.

> SAUSSURE: "The question of the vocal apparatus obviously takes a secondary place in the problem of speech" (p. 10).
>
> ROUSSEAU: "Conventional language is characteristic of man alone. That is why man makes progress, whether for good or ill, and animals do not. That single distinction would seem to be far-reaching. It is said to be explicable by organic differences. I would be curious to witness this explanation" (p. 10).

(There are other analogous texts, due to the topicality and sharpness of the debate over this question at the time when Rousseau was editing the *Dictionnaire de musique*: most notably, see s.v. "Voice," and Dodart's critique, cited by Duclos, s.v. "Declamation of the Ancients.")

5. If animals do not speak, it is because they do not articulate. The possibility of human language, its emergence from animal calls, what makes possible the functioning of conventional language, is therefore *articulation*. The word and the concept of articulation play a central role in the *Essay*, despite the dream of a natural language, a language of unarticulated song, modeled after the neuma. In the *Course in General Linguistics*, immediately after noting that the "question of the vocal apparatus obviously takes a secondary place in the problem of speech," Saussure continues:

> One definition of *articulated speech* might confirm that conclusion. In Latin, *articulus* means a member, part, or subdivision of a sequence; applied to speech, articulation designates either the subdivision of a spoken chain into syllables or the subdivision of the chain of meanings into significant units; *gegliederte Sprache* is used in the second sense in German. Using the second definition, we can say that what is natural to mankind is not oral speech but the faculty of constructing a language, i.e. a system of distinct signs corresponding to distinct ideas. [P. 10]

One could push the inventory of analogies a long way, far beyond the programmatic and principal generalities. Since their interweaving is systematic, one may say a priori that no locus of the two discourses absolutely escapes it. For example, it suffices to accredit absolutely, here and there, the oppositions nature/convention, nature/arbitrary, animal/human or the concepts of sign (signifier/signified) or of representation (representer/represented) for the totality of the discourse to be affected systematically. The effects of such an opposition—which we know goes back further than Plato—can occasion an infinite analysis from which no element of the text escapes. By all rights, this analysis is assumed by any question, however legitimate and necessary, concerning the specificity of the effects of the same opposition in different texts. But the classical criteria of these differences ("language," "period," "author," "title and unity of the work," etc.) are even more derivative, and today have become profoundly problematical.

Within the system of the same fundamental conceptuality (fundamental, for example, at the point at which the opposition of *physis* to its others—*nomos, technē*—which opened the entire series of oppositions nature/law, nature/convention, nature/art, nature/society, nature/freedom, nature/history, nature/mind, nature/culture, and so on has governed, throughout the "history" of its modifications, the entire thinking

and language of the philosophy of science up to the twentieth century),
the play of structural implications, and the mobility and complication
of sedimentary layers are complex enough, and unlinear enough, for
the same constraint to occasion surprising transformations, partial exchanges, subtle discrepancies, turnings backward, and so forth. Thus,
for example, one may legitimately criticize certain elements of the Saussurian project only to rediscover pre-Saussurian motifs; or even criticize
Saussure on the basis of Saussure or even on the basis of Rousseau.
This does not prevent everything from "holding together" in a certain
way within "Saussure's" discourse and in the kinship that links him to
"Rousseau." Put simply, this unity of the totality must be differentiated otherwise than is usually done, if this play is to be accounted for.
It is only on this condition, for example, that one is able to explain the
presence in "Rousseau's" text of motifs that are indispensable to the
linguists who, despite their debt to Saussure in this regard, are no less
critical of his phonologism and psychologism (e.g., Louis Hjelmslev) or
of his taxinomism (Chomsky).[16] It is by attending to the subtlety of these
displacements that one may detect the conceptual premises of glossematics and of the theory of generative grammar in the second *Discourse*
and in the *Essay on the Origin of Languages.*

   One very quickly can see at work, beneath other names, the com-
bined oppositions of the notions of "substance" and "form," of "content" and "expressions," and each of the two former applied alternately,
as in glossematics, to each of the two latter. And how can we not give
credit to Rousseau for everything accredited to "Cartesian linguistics"?
Did not he who "began" with the Port-Royal *Logic* associate, from the
very beginning, the theme of the creativity of language with the theme
of a structural genesis of general grammaticality?[17]

   Once more, I am not concerned with comparing the content of doc-

---

16. See Louis Hjelmslev, "La Stratification du langage," in *Essais linguistiques,* Tra-
vaux du cercle linguistique de Copenhague, no. 12 (Copenhagen, 1959), p. 56, and
Prolégomènes à une théorie du langage (Paris, 1971); and Chomsky, e.g., *Current Issues
in Linguistic Theory* (London, 1964), pp. 23 ff.

17. For example, in the first part of the second *Discours,* when Rousseau describes
the order in which is produced the "Division of the Discourse into its constitutive parts,"
that is, the origin of the distinction between subject and attribute, verb and noun, on
the basis of a primitive indifferentiation: "They gave to each word the sense of an entire
proposition. . . . Substantives at first were but so many proper names," "the infinitive—
the present of the infinitive—was the only tense of the verbs, and as for adjectives, the
notion of them could only have developed with great difficulty, because every adjective is
an abstract word, and abstractions are painful Operations of the mind" (p. 149). Again,
it goes without saying that this is the description of an order rather than of a history,
although the latter distinction is no longer pertinent in a logic of supplementarity.

trines, the wealth of positive knowledge; I am concerned, rather, with discerning the repetition or permanence, at a profound level of discourse, of certain fundamental schemes and of certain directive concepts. And then, on this basis, of formulating questions. Questions, doubtless, about the possibility of given "anticipations," that some might ingenuously judge "astonishing." But questions too about a certain closure of concepts; about the metaphysics in linguistics or, if you will, about the linguistics in metaphysics.

3

Racism's Last Word

Translated by Peggy Kamuf

*Translator's Note.—"Racism's Last Word" is a transla-
tion of "Le Dernier Mot du racisme," which was written for the catalog of the exhibition Art contre/against
Apartheid. The exhibition was assembled by the Association of Artists of the World against Apartheid, headed
by Antonio Saura and Ernest Pignon-Ernest, in coopera-
tion with the United Nations Special Committee against
Apartheid. Eighty-five of the world's most celebrated artists contributed paintings and sculpture to the exhibition,
which opened in Paris in November 1983. In addition, a
number of writers and scholars were invited to contribute
texts for the catalog. "Le Dernier Mot du racisme" serves
in particular to introduce the project of the itinerant exhibition, which the organizers described briefly in their
preface to the catalog:*

> *The collection offered here will form the basis of a future
> museum against apartheid. But first, these works will be pre-
> sented in a traveling exhibition to be received by museums
> and other cultural facilities throughout the world. The day
> will come—and our efforts are joined to those of the interna-
> tional community aiming to hasten that day's arrival—when
> the museum thus constituted will be presented as a gift to*

*the first free and democratic government of South Africa to be
elected by universal suffrage. Until then, the Association of Artists of the World against Apartheid will assume, through the appropriate legal, institutional and financial structures, the trustee-
ship of the works.*

*A somewhat modified version of "Racism's Last Word" was origi-
nally published in the bilingual catalog of the exhibition.*

: : :

APARTHEID—may that remain the name from now on, the unique appellation for the ultimate racism in the world, the last of many.

May it thus remain, but may a day come when it will only be for the
memory of man.

A memory in advance: that, perhaps, is the time given for this exhibition. At once urgent and untimely, it exposes itself and takes a chance
with time, it wagers and affirms beyond the wager. Without counting on
any present moment, it offers only a foresight in painting, very close to
silence, and the rearview vision of a future for which apartheid will be
the name of something finally abolished. Confined and abandoned then
to this silence of memory, the name will resonate all by itself, reduced to
the state of a term in disuse. The thing it names today will no longer be.

But hasn't apartheid always been the archival record of the unnameable?

The exhibition, therefore, is not a presentation. Nothing is delivered
here in the present, nothing that would be presentable—only, in tomorrow's rearview mirror, the late, ultimate racism, the last of many.

I

THE LAST: or *le dernier* as one sometimes says in French in order
to signify "the worst." What one is doing in that case is situating the
extreme of baseness, just as, in English, one might say "the lowest of
the . . ." It is to the lowest degree, the last of a series, but also that which
comes along at the end of a history, or in the last analysis, to carry out
the law of some process and reveal the thing's truth, here finishing off
the essence of evil, the worst, the essence at its very worst—as if there
were something like a racism par excellence, the most racist of racisms.

THE LAST as one says also of the most recent, the last to date of
all the world's racisms, the oldest and the youngest. For one must not

forget that, although racial segregation didn't wait for the name apartheid to come along, that name became order's *watchword* and won its title in the political code of South Africa only at the end of the Second World War. At a time when *all* racisms on the face of the earth were condemned, it was in the world's face that the National party dared to campaign "*for the separate development of each race in the geographic zone assigned to it.*"

Since then, no tongue has ever translated this name—as if all the languages of the world were defending themselves, shutting their mouths against a sinister incorporation of the thing by means of the word, as if all tongues were refusing to give an equivalent, refusing to let themselves be contaminated through the contagious hospitality of the word-for-word. Here, then, is an immediate response to the obsessiveness of this racism, to the compulsive terror which, above all, forbids contact. The white must not let itself be touched by black, be it even at the remove of language or symbol. Blacks do not have the right to touch the flag of the republic. In 1964, South Africa's Ministry of Public Works sought to assure the cleanliness of national emblems by means of a regulation stipulating that it is "forbidden for non-Europeans to handle them."

APARTHEID: by itself the word occupies the terrain like a concentration camp. System of partition, barbed wire, crowds of mapped out solitudes. Within the limits of this untranslatable idiom, a violent arrest of the mark, the glaring harshness of abstract essence (*heid*) seems to speculate in another regime of abstraction, that of confined separation. The word concentrates separation, raises it to another power and sets separation itself *apart*: "apartitionality," something like that. By isolating being apart in some sort of essence or hypostasis, the word corrupts it into a quasi-ontological segregation. At every point, like all racisms, it tends to pass segregation off as natural—and as the very law of the origin. Such is the monstrosity of this political idiom. Surely, an idiom should never incline toward racism. It often does, however, and this is not altogether fortuitous: there's no racism without a language. The point is not that acts of racial violence are only words but rather that they have to have a word. Even though it offers the excuse of blood, color, birth—or, rather, *because* it uses this naturalist and sometimes creationist discourse—racism always betrays the perversion of a man, the "talking animal." It institutes, declares, writes, inscribes, prescribes. A system of marks, it outlines space in order to assign forced residence or to close off borders. It does not discern, it discriminates.

THE LAST, finally, since this last-born of many racisms is also the only one surviving in the world, at least the only one still parading itself in a political constitution. It remains the only one on the scene that dares to say its name and to present itself for what it is: a legal defiance taken on by *homo politicus*, a juridical racism and a state racism. Such is the ultimate imposture of a so-called state of law which doesn't hesitate to base itself on a would-be original hierarchy—of natural right or divine right, the two are never mutually exclusive.

This name apart will have, therefore, a unique, sinister renown. Apartheid is famous, in sum, for manifesting the lowest extreme of racism, its end and the narrow-minded self-sufficiency of its intention, its eschatology, the death rattle of what is already an interminable agony, something like the setting in the West of racism—but also, and this will have to be specified below, racism as a Western thing.

2

In order to respond to this singularity or, better yet, to fling back an answer, the singularity right here of another event takes its measure. Artists from all over the world are preparing to launch a new satellite, a vehicle whose dimensions can hardly be determined except as a satellite of humanity. Actually, it measures itself against apartheid only so as to remain in no measure comparable with that system, its power, its fantastic riches, its excessive armament, the worldwide network of its openly declared or shamefaced accomplices. This unarmed exhibition will have a force that is altogether other, just as its trajectory will be without example.

Its movement does not yet belong to any given time or space that might be measured today. Its flight rushes headlong, it commemorates in anticipation—not its own event but the one that it calls forth. Its flight, in sum, is as much that of a planet as of a satellite. A planet, as the name indicates, is first of all a body sent wandering on a migration which, in this case, has no certain end.

In all the world's cities whose momentary guest it will be, the exhibition will not, so to speak, take place, not yet, not *its* place. It will remain in exile in the sight of its proper residence, its place of destination to come—and to create. For such is here the *creation* and the work of which it is fitting to speak: South Africa beyond apartheid, South Africa in memory of apartheid.

While this might be the cape to be rounded, everything will have begun with exile. Born in exile, the exhibition already bears witness against the forced assignment to "natural" territory, the geography of birth. And if it never reaches its destination, having been condemned to an endless flight or immobilized far from an unshakable South Africa, it will not only keep the archival record of a failure or a despair but continue to *say* something, something that can be heard today, in the present.

This new satellite of humanity, then, will move from place to place, it too, like a mobile and stable habitat, "mobile" and "stabile," a place of observation, information, and witness. A satellite is a guard, it keeps watch and gives warning: Do not forget apartheid, save humanity from this evil, an evil that cannot be summed up in the principial and abstract iniquity of a system. It is also daily suffering, oppression, poverty, violence, torture inflicted by an arrogant white minority (16 percent of the population, controlling 60 to 65 percent of the national revenue) on the mass of the black population. The information that Amnesty International compiled on political imprisonment in South Africa and on the whole of the judicial and penal reality is appalling.[1]

Yet, what can be done so that this witness-satellite, in the truth it exposes, is not taken over and controlled, thus becoming another technical device, the antenna of some new politico-military strategy, a useful machinery for the exploitation of new resources, or the calculation in view of more comprehensive interests?

In order better to ask this question, which awaits an answer only from the future that remains inconceivable, let us return to immediate appearances. Here is an exhibition—as one continues to say in the old language of the West, "works of art," signed "creations," in the present case "pictures" or "paintings," "sculptures." In this collective and international exhibition (and there's nothing new about that either), pictural, sculptural idioms will be crossing, but they will be attempting to speak the other's language without renouncing their own. And in order to effect this translation, their common reference henceforth makes an appeal to a language that cannot be found, a language at once very old, older than Europe, but for that very reason to be invented once more.

3

Why mention the European age in this fashion? Why this reminder of such a trivial fact—that all these words are part of the old language of the West?

Because it seems to me that the aforementioned exhibition exposes

1. See *Political Imprisonment in South Africa: An Amnesty International Report* (London, 1978).

and commemorates, indicts and contradicts the whole of a Western history. That a certain white community of European descent imposes apartheid on four-fifths of South Africa's population and maintains (up until 1980!) the *official* lie of a white migration that preceded black migration is not the only reason that apartheid was a European "creation." Nor for any other such reason: the name of apartheid has managed to become a sinister swelling on the body of the world only in that place where *homo politicus europaeus* first put his signature on its tattoo. The primary reason, however, is that here it is a question of state racism. While all racisms have their basis in culture and in institutions, not all of them give rise to state-controlled structures. The judicial simulacrum and the political theater of this state racism have no meaning and would have had no chance outside a European "discourse" on the concept of race. That discourse belongs to a whole system of "phantasms," to a certain representation of nature, life, history, religion, and law, to the very culture which succeeded in giving rise to this state takeover. No doubt there is also here—and it bears repeating—a contradiction internal to the West and to the assertion of its rights. No doubt apartheid was instituted and maintained against the British Commonwealth, following a long adventure that began with England's abolition of slavery in 1834, at which time the impoverished Boers undertook the Long Trek toward the Orange Free State and the Transvaal. But this contradiction only confirms the occidental essence of the historical process—in its incoherences, its compromises, and its stabilization. Since the Second World War, at least if one accepts the givens of a certain kind of calculation, the stability of the Pretoria regime has been prerequisite to the political, economic, and strategic equilibrium of Europe. The survival of Western Europe depends on it. Whether one is talking about gold or what are called strategic ores, it is known to be the case that at least three-fourths of the world's share of them is divided between the USSR and South Africa. Direct or even indirect Soviet control of South Africa would provoke, or so think certain Western heads of state, a catastrophe beyond all comparison with the malediction (or the "bad image") of apartheid. And then there's the necessity of controlling the route around the cape, and then there's also the need for resources or jobs that can be provided by the exportation of arms and technological infrastructures— nuclear power plants, for example, even though Pretoria rejects international control and has not signed any nuclear nonproliferation treaty.

Apartheid constitutes, therefore, the first "delivery of arms," the first product of European exportation. Some might say that this is a diversion and a perversion, and no doubt it is. Yet somehow the thing had to be possible and, what is more, durable. Symbolic condemnations, even when they have been official, have never disrupted diplomatic, economic, or cultural exchanges, the deliveries of arms, and geopolitical solidarity. Since 1973, apartheid has been declared a "crime against humanity" by the General Assembly of the United Nations. Nevertheless, many member countries, including some of the most powerful, are not doing all that's required (that's the least one can say) to put the Pretoria regime in a difficult situation or to force it to abolish apartheid. This contradiction is sharpest no doubt in today's France, which has provided more support for this exhibition than anywhere else.

Supplementary contradictions for the whole of Europe: Certain Eastern European countries—Czechoslovakia and the USSR, for example—maintain their economic trade with South Africa (in phosphoric acids, arms, machinery, gold). As for the pressures applied to Pretoria to achieve the relaxation of certain forms of apartheid, in particular those that are called petty and that forbid, for instance, access to public buildings, one must admit that these pressures are not always inspired by respect for human rights. The fact is, apartheid *also* increases nonproductive expenditures (for example, each "homeland" must have its own policing and administrative machinery); segregation hurts the market economy, limits free enterprise by limiting domestic consumption and the mobility and training of labor. In a time of unprecedented economic crisis, South Africa has to reckon, both internally and externally, with the forces of a liberal current according to which "apartheid is notoriously inefficient from the point of view of economic rationality."[2] This too will have to remain in memory: if one day apartheid is abolished, its demise will not be credited only to the account of moral standards—because moral standards should not count or keep accounts, to be sure, but also because, on the scale which is that of a worldwide computer, the law of the marketplace will have imposed another standard of calculation.

2. Howard Schissel, "La Solution de rechange libérale: comment concilier défense des droits de l'homme et augmentation des profits" [The liberal alternative as solution: how to reconcile the defense of human rights with increase in profits], *Le Monde diplomatique*, Oct. 1979, p. 18. For the same tendency, cf. René Lefort, "Solidarités raciales et intérêts de classe: composer avec les impératifs de l'économie sans renoncer au 'développement séparé'" [Racial solidarity and class interests: meeting economic imperatives without renouncing "separate development"], *Le Monde diplomatique*, Oct. 1979, pp. 15–16. For the same "logic" from the labor-union point of view, see Brigitte Lachartre, "Un Système d'interdits devenu gênant" [A system of prohibitions become a nuisance], *Le Monde diplomatique*, Oct. 1979, pp. 16–17, and Marianne Cornevin, *La République sud-africaine* (Paris, 1972).

4

The theologico-political discourse of apartheid has difficulty keeping up sometimes, but it illustrates the same economy, the same intra-European contradiction.

It is not enough to invent the prohibition and to enrich every day the most repressive legal apparatus in the world: in a breathless frenzy of obsessive juridical activity, two hundred laws and amendments were enacted in twenty years (Prohibition of Mixed Marriage Act, 1949; Immorality Amendment Act [against interracial sexual relations], Group Areas Act, Population Registration Act, 1950; Reservation of Separate Amenities [segregation in movie houses, post offices, swimming pools, on beaches, and so forth], Motor Carrier Transportation Amendment Act, Extension of University Education Act [separate universities], 1955; segregation in athletic competition has already been widely publicized).

This law is also founded in a theology and these Acts in Scripture. Since political power originates in God, it remains indivisible. To accord individual rights "to immature social communities" and to those who "openly rebel against God, that is, the communists" would be a "revolt against God." This Calvinist reading of Scripture condemns democracy, that universalism "which seeks the root of humanity in a set of worldwide sovereign relations that includes humanity in a whole." It points out that "Scripture and History each demonstrate that God requires Christian States."[3]

The charter of the Institute for National Christian Education (1948) sets out the only regulations possible for a South African government. It prescribes an education

> in the light of God's word . . . on the basis of the applicable principles of Scripture.
>
> For each people and each nation is attached to its own native soil which has been allotted to it by the Creator. . . . God wanted nations and peoples to be separate, and he gave separately to each nation and to each people its particular vocation, its task and its gifts. . . . Christian doctrine and philosophy should be practiced. But we desire even more than this: the secular sciences should be taught from the Christian-National perspective on life. . . . Con-

---

3. *The Fundamental Principles of Calvinist Political Science*, quoted in Serge Thion, *Le Pouvoir pâle: Essai sur le système sud-africain* (Paris, 1969).

sequently, it is important that teaching personnel be made up
of scholars with Christian-National convictions. . . . Unless [the
professor] is Christian, he poses a danger to everyone. . . . This
guardianship imposes on the Afrikaner the duty of assuring that
the colored peoples are educated in accordance with Christian-
National principles. . . . We believe that the well-being and hap-
piness of the colored man resides in his recognition of the fact
that he belongs to a separate racial group.

It happens that this political theology inspires its militants with an
original form of anti-Semitism; thus the National party excluded Jews
up until 1951. This is because the "Hebrewistic" mythology of the Boer
people, coming out of its nomadic origins and the Long Trek, excludes
any other "Chosen People." None of which prevents (see above) all
sorts of worthwhile exchanges with Israel.

But let us never simplify matters. Among all the domestic contradictions thus exported, maintained, and capitalized upon by Europe,
there remains one which is not just any one among others: apartheid
is upheld, to be sure, but also condemned in the name of Christ. There
are many signs of this obvious fact. The white resistance movement in
South Africa deserves our praise. The Christian Institute, founded after
the slaughter in Sharpeville in 1961, considers apartheid incompatible
with the evangelical message, and it publicly supports the banned black
political movements. But it should be added that it is this same Christian Institute which was, in turn, banned in 1977, not the Institute for
National, Christian Education.

All of this, of course, is going on under a regime whose formal structures are those of a Western democracy, in the British style, with "universal suffrage" (except for the 72 percent of blacks "foreign" to the
republic and citizens of "Bantustans" that are being pushed "democrati-
cally" into the trap of formal independence), a relative freedom of the
press, the guarantee of individual rights and of the judicial system.

5

What is South Africa? We have perhaps isolated whatever it is that
has been concentrated in that enigma, but the outline of such analyses
has neither dissolved nor dissipated it in the least. Precisely because of
this concentration of world history, what resists analysis also calls for
another mode of thinking. If we could forget about the suffering, the
humiliation, the torture and the deaths, we might be tempted to look

at this region of the world as a giant tableau or painting, the screen for some geopolitical computer. Europe, in the enigmatic process of its globalization and of its paradoxical disappearance, seems to project onto this screen, point by point, the silhouette of its internal war, the bottom line of its profits and losses, the double-bind logic of its national and multinational interests. Their dialectical evaluation provides only a provisional stasis in a precarious equilibrium, one whose price today is apartheid. All states and all societies are still willing to pay this price, first of all by making someone else pay. At stake, advises the computer, are world peace, the general economy, the marketplace for European labor, and so on. Without minimizing the alleged "reasons of state," we must nevertheless say very loudly and in a single breath: If that's the way it is, then the declarations of the Western states denouncing apartheid from the height of international platforms and elsewhere are dialectics of denegation. With great fanfare, they are trying to make the world forget the 1973 verdict—"crime against humanity." If this verdict continues to have no effect, it is because the customary discourse on man, humanism and human rights, has encountered its effective and as yet unthought limit, the limit of the whole system in which it acquires meaning. Amnesty International: "As long as apartheid lasts, there can be no structure conforming to the generally recognized norms of human rights and able to guarantee their application."[4]

Beyond the global computer, the dialectic of strategic or economic calculations, beyond state-controlled, national, or international tribunals, beyond the juridico-political or theologico-political discourse, which any more serves only to maintain good conscience or denegation, it was, it will have to be, it is necessary to appeal unconditionally to the future of another law and another force lying beyond the totality of this present.

This, it seems to me, is what this exhibition affirms or summons forth, what it signs with a single stroke. Here also is what it must give one to read and to think, and thus to do, and to give yet again, beyond the present of the institutions supporting it or of the foundation that, in turn, it will itself become.

Will it succeed? Will it make of this very thing a work? Nothing can be guaranteed here, by definition.

But if one day the exhibition wins, yes, *wins* its place in South Africa, it will keep the memory of what will never have been, at the moment of these projected, painted, assembled works, the presentation of some present. Even the future perfect can no longer translate the tense, the

4. See *Political Imprisonment in South Africa.*

time of what is being written in this way—and what is doubtless no longer part of the *everyday current*, of the cursory sense of history.

Isn't this true of any "work"? Of that truth which is so difficult to put into words? Perhaps.

The exemplary history of "Guernica" (name of the town, name of a hell, name of the work) is not without analogy to the history of this exhibition, to be sure; it may even have inspired the idea for the exhibition. *Guernica* denounces civilized barbarism, and from out of the painting's exile, in its dead silence, one hears the cry of moaning or accusation. Brought forward by the painting, the cry joins with the children's screams and the bombers' din, until the last day of dictatorship when the work is repatriated to a place in which it has never dwelled.

To be sure: still it was the work, if one may say so, of a single individual, and also Picasso was addressing—not only but also and first of all—his own country. As for the lawful rule recently reestablished in Spain, it, like that of so many countries, continues to participate in the system which presently assures, as we have been saying, the survival of apartheid.

Things are not the same with this exhibition. Here the single work is multiple, it crosses all national, cultural, and political frontiers. It neither commemorates nor represents an event. Rather, it casts a continuous gaze (paintings are always gazing) at what I propose to name a continent. One may do whatever one wishes with all the senses of that word.

Beyond a continent whose limits they point to, the limits surrounding it or crossing through it, the paintings gaze and call out in silence.

And their silence is just. A discourse would once again compel us to reckon with the present state of force and law. It would draw up contracts, dialecticize itself, let itself be reappropriated again.

This silence calls out unconditionally; it keeps watch on that which is not, on that which is not yet, and on the chance of still remembering some faithful day.

4

But, beyond . . .
(Open Letter to Anne McClintock and Rob Nixon)

Translated by Peggy Kamuf

Dear Anne McClintock and Rob Nixon,

We have never met but, after reading your "response," I have a sense of something familiar, as if our paths had often crossed at colloquia or in some other academic place. So I hope you will not mind my addressing you directly—in order to tell you without delay how grateful I am to you and to avoid speaking of you in the third person. Whenever I take part in a debate or, which is not often, in a polemic, I make it a point to quote extensively from the text I am discussing, even though this is not standard practice. Since I am going to be doing that here, by addressing you directly I will save the space (and I'm thinking also of *Critical Inquiry*'s hospitality) otherwise needed for lengthy formulas such as: "Anne McClintock and Rob Nixon go so far as to write . . . ," "the authors of 'No Names Apart' claim that . . . ," "my interlocutors have not understood that . . . ," and so forth.

Yes, that's right, I am grateful. You have brought useful details to the attention of ill-informed readers. Many who want to fight *apartheid* in South Africa still know little of the history of this state racism. No doubt you will agree with me on this point: the better informed, the more lucid, and, I dare say, the more competent the fight, the better it will be able to adjust its strategies. I am also grateful to the editors of *Critical Inquiry*. By publishing your article and inviting me to respond to it, they have chosen to continue the debate that I began here in a modest way. Despite the duly celebrated liberalism and pluralism which open the pages of this excellent journal to the most diverse and opposed intellectual currents, it has in the main been devoted until now to theoretical research such as goes on for the most part in especially academic environments. Now, here is a case where this journal has organized and given free rein to a discussion on a violently political issue, one which has the appearance at least of being barely academic. I am very pleased with this development and even congratulate myself for having been the occasion for it. But I must add, to the credit of certain American colleagues and students, that apartheid is becoming a serious issue on several campuses [see "Postscript" below], and I regret that the same is not the case elsewhere, in other countries. Given this, academic journals have the obligation to speak about it; it is even in their best interest. Initially, my short text was not intended for *Critical Inquiry* (and in a moment I will come back to this criterion of "context" which your reading entirely neglects). Nevertheless, I agreed to its republication in *Critical Inquiry* with this in mind: to engage a reflection or provoke a discussion about apartheid in a very visible and justly renowned place—where, in general, people talk about other things.

Reading you, I very quickly realized that you had no serious objections to make to me, as I will try to demonstrate in a moment. So I began to have the following suspicion: what if you had only pretended to find something to reproach me with in order to prolong the experience over several issues of this distinguished journal? That way, the three of us could fill the space of another twenty or so pages. My suspicion arose since you obviously agree with me on this one point, at least: apartheid, the more it's talked about, the better.

But who will do the talking? And how? These are the questions.

Because talking about it is not enough. On such a grave subject, one must be serious and not say just anything. Well, you, alas, are not always as serious as the tone of your paper might lead one to think. In your impatient desire to dispense a history lesson, you sometimes say just anything. The effect you want to produce is quite determined, but in order to arrive at it, you are willing to put forward any kind of counter-truth, especially when, in your haste to *object*, you *project* into my text whatever will make your job easier. This is a very familiar scenario, as I will try to demonstrate as briefly as possible.

I

As you ought to have realized, I knew well before you did that an eight-page text accompanying an art exhibit couldn't be a historical or anthropological treatise. By reason of its context and its dimensions (which I was not free to choose), by reason also of its style, it could only be an *appeal*, an appeal to others and to other kinds of action. You're quite right when you say "such calls to action will remain of limited strategic worth" (p. 154). I had no illusions in this regard and I didn't need to be reminded of it by anyone. What I, on the other hand, must recall to your attention—and I will remind you of it more than once—is that the text of an *appeal* obeys certain rules; it has its grammar, its rhetoric, its pragmatics. I'll come back to this point in a moment, to wit: as you did not take these rules into account, you quite simply *did not read* my text, in the most elementary and quasi-grammatical sense of what is called *reading*.

As for the original context of "Racism's Last Word,"[1] the catalog of an exhibit, I regret that you didn't read the careful note placed in introduction to Peggy Kamuf's excellent translation. It's true, of course, that if you *had* taken it into account, you would not have written anything, this debate would not have taken place and that would have been too bad. On "limited strategic worth," we're in total agreement, alas. Yet you know, these things are always more complicated, more difficult to evaluate, more overdetermined than people think. My very modest contribution is part of a complex ensemble which I have neither the time nor the space to reconstitute. And even if I could, its limits are by definition not fixed and are in the process of shifting at the very moment I am writing to you. These overdeterminations should be of interest to historians, politologists, or activists who are eager to go beyond abstraction and partial perspectives, who, like you, are concerned not to dissociate words and history. If I had done nothing more than provoke the present debate in a place of high academic visibility, induce the article which I am now about to discuss, and get the attention of a certain number of

1. Translator's note.—I might acknowledge receipt here of Anne McClintock's and Rob Nixon's suggested revision to this translated title. In fact, however, I had already considered and rejected "The Last Word in Racism" for reasons which may now have become ironic. To me, the cliché "the last word in . . ." suggested pop fashions or fads. What is more, it is often used ironically to undercut the very finality it seems to announce. I wanted to avoid these associations in order not to undermine, however subliminally, the sense and force of Jacques Derrida's appeal: that apartheid remain the final name of racism.

influential and competent readers, the interest of "such calls to action" "will remain of limited strategic worth," no doubt about that, but it would be far from nil. As for its limits, they are no more restricted than those of a "response," yours, which not only *supposes* the appeal to which it responds in its own fashion but also, without appealing to any action, is content to chronicle the word "apartheid," while advising that, rather than making history, we all ought to become more like historians. I quote from your conclusion: "Instead," you say, "one would have to regard with an historical eye the uneven traffic between political interests and an array of cultural discourses" (p. 154). By the way, that's *also* what I did, as I will remind you in a moment, but without stopping there. In this domain, as in all domains, no one strategy is sufficient; there is, by definition, no ideal and absolute strategy. We have to multiply the approaches and conjugate efforts.

My "appeal" had to be launched according to a certain mode and in a determined context. You take no account of them. Isn't this a serious mistake on the part of those who constantly invoke the relations between words and history? If you had paid attention to the context and the mode of my text, you would not have fallen into the enormous blunder that led you to take a *prescriptive* utterance for a *descriptive* (theoretical and constative) one. You write for example (and I warned you that I was going to cite you often): "Because he views apartheid as a 'unique appellation,' Derrida has little to say about the politically persuasive function that successive racist lexicons have served in South Africa" (p. 141). But I never considered (or "viewed") apartheid as a "unique appellation." I wrote something altogether different, and it is even the first sentence of my text: "Apartheid—que cela reste le nom désormais, l'unique appellation au monde pour le dernier des racismes. Qu'il le demeure mais que vienne un jour . . . ," which Peggy Kamuf translates in the most rigorous fashion: "APARTHEID—may that remain . . . May it thus remain, but may a day come . . ." (p. 291). This translation is faithful because it respects (something you either could not or would not do) the grammatical, rhetorical, and pragmatic specificity of the utterance. The latter is not an historian's assertion concerning the lexicon of the South African racists or the past vicissitudes of the word apartheid. It is an appeal, a call to condemn, to stigmatize, to combat, to keep in memory; it is not a reasoned dictionary of the use of the word apartheid or its pseudonyms *in the discourse of the South African leaders.* One may think such an appeal is just too pathetic, one may judge its strategic force limited, but does one have the right to treat it as one would an historian's observation? To do so would be proof either that

one didn't know how to read (by which I mean how to distinguish a subjunctive, with the value of an imperative, from an indicative) or else that
one was ready to shortchange the ethics, to say nothing of the politics,
of reading or discussion. What is more, although it is not limited by the
form of descriptive observation, my "appeal" in no way contradicts the
historian's truth. Whatever may have been the vicissitudes of the word
apartheid and especially of the desperate efforts of the Pretoria regime's
propagandists and officials to rid themselves of it (to rid themselves
of the word, and not the thing, of *their* word and not *their* thing!), no
one can deny that apartheid designates today in the eyes of the whole
world, beyond all possible equivocation or pseudonymy, the last state
racism on the entire planet. I wanted therefore simply to formulate a
wish: may this word *become* and *remain* (subjunctive! optative or jussive mode!) "the unique appellation" destined to maintain the memory
of and stigmatize this state racism. It was not a thesis on the genealogy
of a word but an appeal, a call to action, as you put it, and first of all
an ethical appeal, as indicated by that which, in both ethics and politics,
passes by way of memory and promising, and thus by way of language
and denomination. Besides (and here I am speaking as a historian, that
is, in the *indicative*), whatever efforts the ideologues and official representatives of South Africa may have made to efface this embarrassing
word from *their* discourse, whatever efforts *you* may make to keep track
of their efforts, the failure is not in doubt and historians can attest to
it: the word apartheid remains and, as I hope or expect, it will remain
the "unique appellation" of this monstrous, unique, and unambiguous
thing. You say "Derrida is repelled by the word" (p. 141). No, what I
find repulsive is the thing that history has now linked to the word, which
is why I propose keeping the word so that the history will not be forgotten. Don't separate word and history! That's what you say to those
who apparently have not learned this lesson. It is the South African
racists, the National party, the Verwoerds and the Vorsters who ended
up being afraid of the word (*their* word!), to whom it began to appear
too repulsive because it had become so overseas. It's you, and not me,
who also seem to be frightened by this word because you propose that
we take seriously all the substitutes and pseudonyms, the periphrases
and metonymies that the official discourse in Pretoria keeps coming up
with: the tireless ruse of propaganda, the indefatigable but vain rhetoric of dissimulation. To counter it, I think the best strategy is to keep
the word, the "unique appellation" that the South African racists and
certain of their allies would like to make people forget. No doubt one
should also pay attention to the rhetorical contortions of the ideologues

and official politicians of apartheid. But should we, because they wish it, abandon the word apartheid and no longer consider it to be the most accurate word with which to designate this political reality, yesterday's and today's?

I could limit myself to this remark about grammar or pragmatics. In your haste, you took or pretended to take a subjunctive to be an indicative, a jussive or optative utterance to be an assertion, an appeal to be a thesis. At the same time, you took no account of what was nevertheless *realistic* in my appeal, you missed the way, even in my syntax, the performative was articulated with the constative (forgive me for using this language). In sum, I asked for a promise: let this "unique appellation" "remain," which means that it *already is* this unique appellation. Who can deny it? The official ideologues of South Africa can denegate it, but they cannot deny that they are now *alone* in no longer using this word. And if I ask that we keep the word, it is only for the future, for memory, in men's and women's memory, for when the thing will have disappeared. Thus, my appeal is indeed an appeal because it calls for something which is not yet, but it is still strategically realistic because it refers to a massively present reality, one which no historian could seriously put in question. It is a call to struggle but also to memory. I never separate promising from memory.

Here, then, is a first point. I could stop at this: you confused two verbal modes. Whether or not they are fighting against apartheid, whether or not they are activists, historians must be attentive to rhetoric, to the type and status of utterances, at the very least to their grammar. No good strategy otherwise. Yet, I don't regret your reading error, however elementary it might be. As everything in your paper follows from this misreading which begins with the first sentence—what am I saying? with the first two words ("APARTHEID—may . . .")—just a moment's lucidity would have prevented your bringing out these documents on South African policy, *Critical Inquiry* would not have opened its pages to this debate, and that would have been too bad.

So I could stop there, but to prolong the conversation, I will point out still some other mistakes, just the most serious and spectacular ones.

2

Another question of reading, still just as elementary and directly linked to the preceding one. You write: "The essay's opening analysis of the word apartheid is, then, symptomatic of a severance of word from history. When Derrida asks, 'hasn't apartheid always been the archival record of the unnameable?', the answer is a straightforward no. Despite its notoriety and currency overseas, the term apartheid has not always been the 'watchword' of the Nationalist regime" (p. 141). Once again you mistake the most evident meaning of my question. It did not concern the use of the word *by* the Nationalist regime but its *use value* in the world, "its notoriety and currency overseas," as you so rightly put it. The word "always" in my text referred to this notoriety and there is little matter here for disagreement. But I never said that apartheid had "always" been the *literal* "watchword" *within* the Nationalist regime. And I find the way you manage to slip the "always" out of *my* sentence ("but hasn't apartheid always been the archival record of the unnameable?") and into *yours* ("the term apartheid has not always been the 'watchword' of the Nationalist regime") to be less than honest. To be honest, you would have had to quote the whole sentence in which I myself speak of the "watchword" as such. I do so precisely in order to say that this "watchword" has a complex history, with its dates and places of emergence and disappearance. I knew this before reading you and I emphasized it despite the brevity of my text. Here, then, is *my* sentence—if you don't mind, I will quote myself whenever you have not done so or whenever you manipulate the quotations:

> For one must not forget that, although racial segregation didn't wait for the name apartheid to come along, the name became order's *watchword* and won its title in the political code of South Africa only at the end of the Second World War. At a time when *all* racisms on the face of the earth were condemned, it was in the world's face that the National party dared to campaign *"for the separate development of each race in the geographic zone assigned to it."* [Pp. 291–92]

This sentence, among others, gives a clear enough indication, I hope, of the historical concern with which I approached the question in general, and the question of the name apartheid in particular.

And while we're on the subject of this word, I would like to understand the meaning of a certain "but" in a passage I am going to cite at length. Its logic totally escapes me. You write:

> The word apartheid was coined by General Jan Smuts at the Savoy Hotel, London on 27 May 1917 [I knew it was in London, but I thought it was at the Lord Russell Hotel. Are you sure about the Savoy? Check it. This is one point of history on

which you would have taught me something.] but had barely
any currency until it rose to prominence as the rallying cry of
the Nationalist party's victorious electoral campaign of 1948.
[This is exactly² what I was recalling, incorrigible historian
that I am, in the sentence I just cited above. You might
have mentioned that.] Derrida has reflected on the word's
"sinister renown," *but* [my emphasis, J. D.] as far back
as the mid-fifties the South Africans themselves began to
recognize that the term apartheid had become sufficiently
stigmatized to be ostentatiously retired. [P. 141]

So what? [In English in the text.] Why this "but"? Has the word apartheid effaced its "sinister renown" because the South Africans wanted to
retire it from circulation and precisely because of its "sinister renown"?
It so happens that in spite of their efforts to "retire" this "sufficiently
stigmatized" term, the renown has not been effaced: it has gotten more
and more sinister. This is history, this is the relation between words and
history. It's the thing and the concept they should have retired, and not
just the word, if they had wanted to put an end to the "sinister renown."
So why this "but"? What objection is it making? Should I have said
nothing about the "sinister renown" because the South African National-
ists deemed it advisable to clean up their lexicon?

The unfortunate thing is that your entire text is organized around the
incredible "logic," if one can call it that, of this "but"; it is even oriented
by the stupefying politics of this "but." You are asking that we regulate
our vocabulary by the lexical strategies of the South African regime!
For, immediately after the passage just cited, you go on to write:

The developing history of South African racial policy and propaganda highlights the inaccuracy of Derrida's claim that South
African racism is "the only one on the scene that dares to say
its name and present itself for what it is." For in striving both
to win greater legitimacy for itself and to justify ideologically
the Nationalist bantustan policy, South African racism has
long since ceased to pronounce its own name: apartheid, the
term Derrida misleadingly calls "the order's *watchword*" (*mot*

2. Translator's note.—The exactness is still more striking when one recalls that Derrida's term *mot d'ordre*, translated as "watchword," could also have been rendered by
McClintock's and Nixon's term: "rallying cry."

d'*ordre*), was dismissed many years back from the lexical ranks
of the regime. [Pp. 141–42]

What do you want? That everyone stop *considering* that apartheid is—
and remains, as far as I know, still today—the watchword, the rallying
cry, the concept, and the reality of the South African regime? And even
that everyone stop *saying* it, on the pretext that the South African racists
deem it more prudent to utter it no more, this word which you yourselves
recognize to be the "proper name" of this racism, the word it has given
itself, "its own name" ("South African racism" you clearly say, "has
long since ceased to pronounce its own name: apartheid . . ." [p. 142])?
Come on, you're not being very serious, either as historians or as political strategists. Where would we be, where would all those struggling
against apartheid be if they had considered that apartheid ceased to be
the watchword of the South African regime on the day that, as you put
it so well, "the Nationalist party . . . radically rephrased its ideology"!
(p. 142). Because that happened in 1950, it would have been necessary
to stop talking about apartheid from then on! Thanks all the same for
your strategic advice and your reminder of historical reality! You speak
of a "quarantine from the historical process" but it's you, coming on
the heels of the Nationalist regime, who want to put the word apartheid
in quarantine! I, on the other hand, insist that we continue to use the
word, so that we may remember it, in spite of all the verbal denegations
and lexical stratagems of the South African racists. I, on the contrary,
insist that we remember this: whether or not the term is pronounced by
South African officials, apartheid remains the *effective* watchword of
power in South Africa. Still today. If *you* think, on the other hand, that
it's necessary to take account of the diplomatic prudence or the lexical
ruses of this power to the point of no longer speaking of apartheid as a
watchword, well, then you're going to have to ask the whole world to go
along with you and not just me. Historical reality, dear comrades, is that
in spite of all the lexicological contortions you point out, those in power
in South Africa have not managed to convince the world, and first of
all because, still today, they have refused to change the real, effective,
fundamental meaning of their watchword: apartheid. A watchword is
not just a name. This too history teaches us, as you should know since
you're so concerned with history. A watchword is also a concept and
a reality. The relation among the reality, the concept, and the word is
always more complex than you seem to suppose. The South Africans
in power wanted to keep the concept and the reality while effacing the

word, an evil word, *their* word. They have managed to do so in *their* official discourse, that's all. Everywhere else in the world, and first of all among black South Africans, people have continued to think that the word was indissolubly—and legitimately—welded to the concept and to the reality. And if you're going to struggle against this *historical* concept and this *historical* reality, well, then you've got to call a thing by its name. What would have happened if throughout the world—in Europe, in Africa, in Asia, or in the Americas—people had sworn off speaking of racism, anti-Semitism, or slavery on the pretext that the offenders never spoke of these things or did *not* use those words, better yet *no longer* used those words? In the best hypothesis and assuming one didn't want to accuse it of simple complicity with the adversary, such a strategy would have been both childish and disastrous.

So I stand by what I said. One must be attentive, and I was, to the word, to the watchword, and to their history. One must be attentive to what links words to concepts and to realities but also to what can dissociate them. Now if even as it kept the concept and the reality, the power in South Africa has tried to get rid of the word, nobody has been fooled. The concept and the reality persist, under other names, and South African racism, I repeat, "is the only one on the scene that dares to say its name and present itself for what it is," which is to say a state racism, the only one in the world today which does not hide its face. When I wrote that it "dares to say its name," I wanted to recall simply this: apartheid may have disappeared since 1950 from official speech or from the dispensaries of propaganda as if by magic, but this changes nothing in the fact ("facts are stubborn," you know) that the system of apartheid is not only practiced but *inscribed in the constitution* and in an impressive judicial apparatus. In other words, it is *declared, assumed, publicly approved.* To speak one's name, in politics (as history has shown over and over), is not simply to make use of a substantive but to present oneself as such, for what one is, in complex discourses, the texts of the law or of socioeconomic, even police and "physical" practices. In politics, as history should have taught you, a "watchword" is not limited to a lexicon. You confuse words and history. Or rather, you make poor distinctions between them.

What would have happened if I had followed your "strategic" advice? I would not have called for a fight against the state racism named apartheid (so named at the outset by its inventors!); instead I would have cautiously murmured as you do: "Careful, don't say apartheid anymore, you no longer have the right to use this word in order to name the watchword of South African racism because those who instituted the word, the concept, and the thing have not 'pronounced' the word since 1950"! Or maybe this: "Don't say apartheid anymore, but know that since 1948 there have been 'three phases' of racial policy in South Africa. Only the first of these (1948–58) would have been an 'ideological, doctrinaire, and negative' phase; the second (1958–66) is the one that 'mellowed into the homeland phase of separate development,' 'internal decolonisation'; the third, since 1966, would correspond to 'the unobtrusive dismantling of apartheid,' 'the movement away from discrimination,' 'the elimination of color as a determinant' and the introduction of 'democratic pluralism.' " Should I have said all that each time in place of the word apartheid? All that, which is to say what? Well, what you say by citing F. A. van Jaarsveld, "an apologist for the Nationalist regime," for the "periodizing changes in the *official discourse*" and for "the regime's justificatory ideology" (p. 142). Should I have been content to reproduce this official discourse? It is, in fact, the only one you cite at any length—the point of view of blacks being less represented in your text than that of apartheid's partisans, even if you must admit that their "ruse has failed politically" (p. 147).

I'm still trying to imagine what I should have written if I had been carefully following your "strategic" advice. Perhaps I should have said: You know, apartheid is no longer the right word, even *racism* is no longer the right word because ever since "the development of the bantustan policy," " 'the problem in South Africa is basically not one of race, but of nationalism, which is a world-wide problem. There is White nationalism, and there are several Black nationalisms' " (p. 144). Unfortunately, if I had done that, I would have been quoting you quoting Verwoerd or Vorster, or else at best I would have written a paper on the ideological strategies of state racism in South Africa. But I would not have said the essential thing, to wit: apartheid, as a state racism and under the name initially chosen by the Nationalist party, then in control in South Africa, has been and remains the effective and official practice, still today, in spite of all the denegations and certain softening touches to the facade (which, by the way, I also mentioned). And apartheid must be fought as such. Once again, it's a question of context and of "pragmatics": I wrote a brief text for an exhibit entitled "Art against Apartheid" and not a paper on Verwoerd's and Vorster's rhetoric, whatever interest there may be in knowing the resources of this discourse. And despite the constraints on the length of my text, I also spoke of the secondary transformations of apartheid (p. 295), of the discourse, the culture, what I call the "official lie," the "judicial simulacrum," and the "political theater" (p. 294) that organize the racist and nationalist ideology in

South Africa (see in particular parts 3 and 4). If *you* think apartheid has effectively given way to one nationalism among others, then you ought to have said so. If you don't think that's the case, well, then I don't see what objection you can have with me.

3

In spite of the brevity of my text, I never made do with what you call "such favored monoliths of post-structuralism as 'logocentrism' and 'Western metaphysics,' not to mention bulky homogeneities such as 'the occidental essence of the historical process' and a 'European "discourse" on the concept of race'" (p. 154). To be sure, I said, and I'll say it again, that the history of apartheid (its "discourse" and its "reality," the totality of its *text*) would have been impossible, unthinkable without the European concept and the European history of the state, without the European discourse on race—its scientific pseudoconcept and its religious roots, its modernity and its archaisms—without Judeo-Christian ideology, and so forth. Do you think the contrary? If so, I'd like to see the demonstration. That said, you would have shown a little more honesty if you had noted that, far from relying on "monoliths" or "bulky homogeneities," I constantly emphasized heterogeneity, contradictions, tensions, and uneven development. "Contradiction" is the most frequently occurring word in my text. You force me to quote myself again. I spoke of "a contradiction internal to the West and to the assertion of its rights" (p. 294). I even wrote that one is right to insist on these contradictions ("and it bears repeating" [p. 294]) and that one must never simplify ("but let us never simplify matters" [p. 297]). Is that what you call monolithism? In spite of the brevity of my text, I multiplied the examples of "contradiction" in the theologico-political discourse, of the strategic "contradiction" of the West, of economic contradiction (see pp. 296, 295). Is that a sign of monolithic thinking and a preference for homogeneity? This will surely have been the first time I have met with such a reproach, and I fear you deserve it more than I do.

4

To what level of bad faith must one stoop in order to palm off on me the credo of unbridled capitalism by implying that, in my view, it would suffice to let the law of the marketplace work to put an end to apartheid? You have the nerve, for example, to write the following: "The revisionists argue, against Derrida [!!!], that far from hurting the market

economy, 'racial policy is an historical product . . . designed primarily
to facilitate rapid capital accumulation, and has historically been used
thus by all classes with access to state power in South Africa'" (p. 148).
On the contrary, I have always thought that there was some truth—
it's stating the obvious—in this "revisionist" view. If, however, I *also*
said that, despite the apparent contradiction, "apartheid *also* increases
nonproductive expenditures (for example, each 'homeland' must have
its own policing and administrative machinery); segregation hurts the
market economy, limits free enterprise by limiting domestic consumption and the mobility and training of labor" (p. 295), I did so because
it's true and *especially* as a reminder that, if apartheid is abolished one
day, it will not be for purely moral reasons. You force me to quote
myself again, the passage immediately following the sentence you have
just read:

> In a time of unprecedented economic crisis, South Africa has
> to reckon, both internally and externally, with the forces of a
> liberal current according to which "apartheid is notoriously in-
> efficient from the point of view of economic rationality" [I'm
> not speaking here, this is a quote]. This too will have to remain
> in memory: if one day apartheid is abolished, its demise will not
> be credited only to the account of moral standards—because
> moral standards should not count or keep accounts, to be sure,
> but also because, on the scale which is that of a worldwide com-
> puter, the law of the marketplace will have imposed another
> standard of calculation. [Pp. 295–96]

After you had read that, it is quite simply indecent to make me out
to be pleading *for* capitalism or suggesting that laws of the marketplace
ought to be allowed free rein because *all by themselves* they would take
care of apartheid. You have the nerve nonetheless to do just that. Your
argument at this point reaches such a degree of bad faith that I even
wondered whether I ought to continue our dialogue in these conditions
and respond to *Critical Inquiry*'s generous invitation. You actually go
so far as to speak of "Derrida's optimistic vision of apartheid brought to
its knees by a liberalizing capitalism . . ." and you continue: "Indeed, if
Derrida takes to its logical conclusion his argument that apartheid may
be abolished by the imposition of the 'law of the market,' he will find
himself in the position of advocating accelerated international investment in order to hasten the collapse of the regime"! (p. 153). To be sure,
I defy you to find the least hint in my text of such an "optimistic vision"

(even supposing that it is optimistic!). Had I such a "vision," I would not have written anything "against apartheid." I would have thought: *laissons faire le capital*! That said, here again things are complex, heterogeneous, and contradictory, whether you like it or not. Apartheid can *at the same time* serve the interests of capitalist accumulation *and* get in the way of capitalist development. One has to distinguish here among different phases and *various* capitalisms or different, even contradictory sectors of capitalism. No more than logocentrism and the West, capitalism is not a monolith or a "bulky homogeneity." Have you ever heard of the contradictions of capitalism? Is it really that difficult for you to imagine how apartheid might serve capitalism in certain conditions and impede free enterprise at some other moment, in other conditions? You see, I fear you have a simple, homogeneistic, and mechanistic vision of history and politics.

5

One last point with which perhaps I should have begun. It's about your first paragraph, that little word "beyond" which you underline (*"beyond* the text") and what you call my "method." Once again, it's best that I quote you: "If, then, Derrida seeks not merely to prize open certain covert metaphysical assumptions but also to point to something *beyond* the text, in this case the abolition of a regime, then the strategic value of his method has to be considered seriously" (p. 140).

I am not sure I clearly understand the extent of what you mean by my "method." If you mean my "method" in this text against apartheid, in the appeal that I launch and in my treatment of the word apartheid, I have just answered you and told you what I think of *your* methods. But if you are suggesting that my "method" in this specific case reveals all that my "method" in general and elsewhere could learn from your lessons, well in that case, there are one or two more things I will have to add. I am led to think that you mean to contest, beyond the precise context of apartheid, the "strategic value" of my "method" *in general* by the allusions or insinuations tied to the word "text" (*"beyond* the text" is no doubt, and I'll come back to this in a moment, a clever, oh so clever nod in the direction of something I once said: there is nothing beyond the text), by the use of the word "post-structuralism" (which I myself have never used but which is commonly applied to me), or by words such as "logocentrism," "Western metaphysics," and so forth.

A serious response here would take hundreds and hundreds of pages, and we mustn't abuse *Critical Inquiry*'s hospitality. Know, however, that these pages are already written. If you wish to continue our correspondence privately, I will give you some exact references.

But one thing at least I can tell you now: an hour's reading, beginning on any page of any one of the texts I have published over the last twenty years, should suffice for you to realize that *text*, as I use the word, is not the book. No more than writing or trace, it is not limited to the *paper* which you cover with your graphism. It is precisely for strategic reasons (set forth at length elsewhere) that I found it necessary to recast the concept of text by generalizing it almost without limit, in any case without present or perceptible limit, without any limit that *is*. That's why there is nothing "*beyond* the text." That's why South Africa and apartheid are, like you and me, part of this general text, which is not to say that it can be read the way one reads a book. That's why the text is always a field of forces: heterogeneous, differential, open, and so on. That's why deconstructive readings and writings are concerned not only with library books, with discourses, with conceptual and semantic contents. They are not simply analyses of discourse such as, for example, the one you propose. They are also effective or active (as one says) interventions, in particular political and institutional interventions that transform contexts without limiting themselves to theoretical or constative utterances even though they must also produce such utterances. That's why I do not go "*beyond* the text," in this *new* sense of the word text, by fighting and calling for a fight against apartheid, for example. I say "for example" because it also happens that I become involved with institutional and academic politics or get myself imprisoned in Czechoslovakia for giving seminars prohibited by the authorities. Too bad if all this strikes you as strange or intolerable behavior on the part of someone whom you, like others, would like to believe remains enclosed in some "prison-house of language." Not only, then, do I not go "beyond the text," in this new sense of the word text (no more than anyone else can go beyond it, not even the most easy-to-recognize activists), but the strategic reevaluation of the concept of text allows me to bring together in a more consistent fashion, in the most consistent fashion possible, theoretico-philosophical necessities with the "practical," political, and other necessities of what is called deconstruction. The latter, by the way, has never presented itself as a method, for essential reasons that I explain elsewhere (once again, if you care to write to me, I'll send you the references).

This letter is too long. In order to hasten its conclusion, I will give you my opinion in two words:

1. Your "response" is typical. It reflects an incomprehension or

"misreading" that is widespread, and spread about, moreover, for very
determined ends, on the "Left" and the "Right," among those who
think they represent militantism and a progressivist commitment as
well as among neoconservatives. It is in the interest of one side and the
other to represent deconstruction as a turning inward and an enclosure by the limits of language, whereas in fact deconstruction *begins
by* deconstructing logocentrism, the linguistics of the word, and this
very enclosure itself. On one side and the other, people get impatient
when they see that deconstructive practices are also and first of all political and institutional practices. They get impatient when they see that
these practices are perhaps more radical and certainly less stereotyped
than others, less easy to decipher, less in keeping with well-used models whose wear and tear ends up by letting one see the abstraction, the
conventionalism, the academism, and everything that separates, as you
would say, words and history. In a word, verbalism. On one side and
the other, on one hand and on the other hand (but you see now how
the two hands join and maintain each other [comme les deux mains se
tiennent, maintenant]), there is an interest in believing, in pretending to
believe, or simply in making others believe that the "text" which concerns "deconstructionists" (this is the first time I use this word and I do
so, as others have done, to go quickly) can be found neatly in its place on
some library shelves. That being the case, in order to act (!) in the area
of *real* politics, in history (!), these poor "deconstructionists" should
go *"beyond* the text," into the field, to the front! As you do, I suppose.

Well, it so happens that the text which various deconstructions are
speaking of today is not at all the *paper* or the *paperback* with which
you would like to identify it. If there is nothing *"beyond* the text," in
this new sense, then that leaves room for the most open kinds of political
(but not just political) practice and pragmatics. It even makes them more
necessary than ever. But that is no reason—on the contrary—to give
up reading the books and writings still to be found in libraries. It is no
reason to read quickly or badly or to stop learning how to read otherwise other texts—especially if one wants to better adjust one's political
strategies. It is thus no reason to continue to spread the most uneducated
interpretations and the crudest prejudices about "deconstruction," the
"text," or "logocentrism." It is no reason to go on manipulating them
as you do, to keep rolling them along in a primitive fashion, after having
erected them into monolithic menhirs.

2. So, you share the impatience of those who would like texts to
remain in the libraries, who would like text to signify "book." And you
want this order maintained: let all those who concern themselves with

texts understood in this latter sense (the "deconstructionists"!) remain in their compartments, better yet in their departments! Let no "deconstructionists" concern themselves with politics since, as we all know, don't we, deconstruction, differance, writing, and all that are (in the best of cases) politically neutral, ahistorical! Those people are not to concern themselves with politics because we always believed that they never did, that they left such things to the qualified, conscious, and organized activists whom we clearly are according to that *good old tradition* [in English in the text] which anyone can easily recognize. Otherwise, you seem to be saying, what would be left for *us* to do? Let the theoreticians of literature concern themselves with literature, philosophers with philosophy, historians with history, Africanists with Africa, and we, the activists, with politics! There, that's the best strategy! When a "deconstructionist," as one says, concerns himself with apartheid, even if he is on the "good" side, his strategy is all wrong, he's getting mixed up with things that are none of his business because he's going "*beyond* the text"! He exceeds the limits of his competence, leaves his own territory! "The strategic value of his method has to be considered seriously"!

In short, you are for the division of labor and the disciplined respect of disciplines. Each must stick to his role and stay within the field of his competence, none may transgress the limits of his territory. Oh, you wouldn't go so far as to wish that some sort of apartheid remain or become the law of the land in the academy. Besides, you obviously don't like this word. You are among those who don't like this word and do not want it to remain the "unique appellation." No, in the homelands of academic culture or of "political action," you would favor instead reserved domains, the separate development of each community in the zone assigned to it.

Not me.

Cordially,

Jacques Derrida
6 February 1986

Postscript (April 1986): I am rereading the translation of this letter while in the United States, at several universities (Yale, Harvard, Columbia) which have seen an intensification of demonstrations against apartheid: the divestiture movement, "shantytowns," student arrests, and so on. I want to reiterate my admiration and solidarity. Such courageous demonstrations on campuses are also signs of strategic lucidity because the problem of apartheid is surely an *American problem*, as are so many others. *In a first sense*, this means that its evolution will depend from now on in large measure on American pressure. These signs of lucidity are carried by an energy and perseverance which cannot be explained *simply* by the economy of necessarily ambiguous motivations. Some might be tempted in effect to seek there the mechanism and dynamic of bad conscience. The latter is always quicker to arise among intellectuals and at the university, especially in universities obliged to manage their capital. For here again, and *in a second sense*, apartheid would be an *American problem*. According to this insufficient but necessary hypothesis, apartheid might have to be put at some remove, expulsed, objectified, held at a distance, prevented from returning (as a ghost returns), parted with, treated, and cured *over there*, in South Africa. Apartheid might bear too great a resemblance to a segregation whose image continues at the very least to haunt American society. No doubt, this segregation has become more urban, industrial, socioeconomic (the frightening percentage of young black unemployed, for example), less immediately racial in its phenomenon. But this might recall much more, by some of its features, the South African hell.

5

Like the Sound of the Sea Deep within a Shell: Paul de Man's War

Translated by Peggy Kamuf

Unable to respond to the questions, to all the questions, I will ask myself instead *whether responding is possible* and what that would mean in such a situation. And I will risk in turn several questions *prior to* the definition of a *responsibility*. But is it not an act to assume in theory the concept of a responsibility? Is that not already to take a responsibility? One's own as well as the responsibility to which one believes one ought to summon others?

The title names a war. Which war?

Do not think only of the war that broke out several months ago around some articles signed by a certain Paul de Man, in Belgium between 1940 and 1942. Later you will understand why it is important to situate the beginning of things *public*, that is the publications, early in 1940 at the latest, during the war but before the occupation of Belgium by the Nazis, and not in December 1940, the date of the first article that appeared in *Le Soir*, the major Brussels newspaper that was then controlled, more or less strictly, by the occupiers. For several months, in the United States, the phenomena of this war "around" Paul de Man have been limited to newspaper articles. War, a public act, is by rights something declared. So we will not count in the category of war the private phenomena—meetings, discussions, correspondences, or telephonic conclaves—however intense they may have been in recent days, and already well beyond the American academic milieu.

To my knowledge, at the moment I write, this war presents itself as such, it is *declared* in newspapers, *and nowhere else*, on the subject of arguments made in newspapers, *and nowhere else*, in the course of the last world war, during two years almost a half century ago. That is why my title alludes to the passage from Montherlant quoted by de Man in *Le Soir* in 1941. I will come back to it, but the double edge of its irony already seems cruel: "When I open the newspapers and journals of today, I hear the indifference of the future rolling over them, just as one hears the sound of the sea when one holds certain seashells up to the ear."

The future will not have been indifferent, not for long, just barely a half century, to what de Man wrote one day in the "newspapers and journals of today." One may draw from this many contradictory lessons. But in the several months to follow, the very young journalist that he will have been during less than two years will be read more intensely than the theoretician, the thinker, the writer, the professor, the author of great books that he was during forty years. Is this unfair? Yes, no. But what about later? Here is a prediction and a hope: without ever forgetting the journalist, people will relearn how to read "*all*" of the work (which is to say so many others as well) *toward that which opens itself up there*. People will learn to reread the books, and *once again* the newspapers, and *once again toward that which opens itself up there*. To do so, one will need in the first place, and more than ever *in the future*, the lessons of Paul de Man.

Elsewhere, having more time and more space, one will also analyze from every angle the significance of the press in the modernity of a history like this one, in the course of a war like this one: the one and the other would be impossible and inconceivable without journalism. Yet, whatever one may think of the ignorance, the simplism, the sensationalist flurry full of hatred which certain American newspapers displayed in this case, we will not engage in any negative evaluation of the press *in general*. Such an evaluation belongs to a code that one must always mistrust. It is not far removed from what we are going to talk about. What is more, I think it is only normal that the American press does not remain silent about the emotion aroused by, I quote, the "pro-Nazi articles" or the "anti-Semitic articles" published in a "pro-Nazi newspaper" by a "Yale scholar," a "revered" professor, "Sterling Professor of Humanities" who "died in 1983 while chairman of Yale's Comparative Literature Department." Incidentally, what would have happened if Paul de Man had not been a great American professor or if, as a professor, he had not been at Yale? And what if one also did a history of Yale, or of the great Eastern universities, a history of certain of their past (just barely, very recently) ideologico-institutional practices having to do with certain themes that we are going to talk about?[1] Well, after having had to set aside the question "What is the press in the culture and politics of this century?" I will also have to postpone this other question: "What is Yale, for example, in American culture?"

If newspapers have the duty to inform and the right to interpret, would it not have been better if they had done so with caution, rigor, honesty? There was little of that. And the press' most serious lapses from its elementary duties cannot be imputed to the newspapers or to the professional journalists themselves, but to certain academics.

The fact is there: at the point at which I take the risk of writing on this subject, I have the sense of being the first, thus so far the only one to do so, still too quickly to be sure, but without journalistic haste, which is to say without the excuses it sometimes gives the journalist but should never give the academic. It is a formidable privilege, one not designed to alleviate the feeling of my responsibility. For this deadly war (and fear, hatred, which is to say sometimes love, also dream of killing the dead in order to get at the living) has already recruited some combatants, while others are sharpening their weapons in preparation for it. In the evaluations of journalists or of certain professors, one can make out strategies or stratagems, movements of attack or defense, sometimes the two at once. Although this war no doubt began in the newspapers, it will be carried on for a long time elsewhere, in the most diverse forms. There will be many of us who will have to take their responsibilities and who, at the same time, will have to say, in the face of what is happening to us today, what *responding* and taking a *responsibility* can mean. For what is happening with these "revelations" (I am quoting the word from a newspaper) is happening *to us*.

It is *happening* to all those for whom this event ought to have a meaning, even if that meaning is difficult to decipher and even if, for

---

1. See Marcia Graham Synnott, *The Half-Opened Door: Discrimination and Admissions at Harvard, Yale, and Princeton, 1900–1970* (Westport, Conn., 1979), and Nitza Rosovsky, *The Jewish Experience at Harvard and Radcliffe* (Cambridge, Mass., 1986). I remember the indignation with which certain student newspapers at Yale, while I was teaching there, manifested surprise when learning of the anti-Semitism that had reigned in their university. I do not recall that there was any echo of this in the major press or among the majority of our colleagues.

many, the person and the work of de Man still remain not well known. Let those in this latter category be reassured or still more troubled: even for his admirers and his friends, especially for them, if I may be allowed to testify to this, the work and the person of Paul de Man were enigmatic. Perhaps they are becoming more enigmatic than ever. Do you believe friendship or admiration ought to reduce everything about this enigma? I believe just the opposite.

Why do I now underscore that expression: *"what is happening?"* Because for me this belongs to the order of the absolutely unforeseeable, which is always the condition of any event. Even when it seems to go back to a buried past, what comes about always comes from the future. And it is especially about the future that I will be talking. Something *happens* only on the condition that one is not expecting it. Here of course I am speaking the language of consciousness. But there would also be no event *identifiable as such* if some repetition did not come along to cushion the surprise by preparing its effect on the basis of some experience of the unconscious. If the word "unconscious" has any meaning, then it stems from this necessity.

With or without a *recognition of the unconscious*, today this is *happening to us*. I name thereby, in utter darkness, many people. But it is also the darkness of a blinding light: *us*, we are still the living and the survivors, however uncertain and incomprehensible such a phrase may remain. The said war, then, could only take place, if that is what certain people want, *among us*. For we must never forget this cold and pitiless light: Paul de Man *himself* is dead. If there are some who want to organize a trial in order to judge him, de Man, they must remember that he, de Man, is dead and will not answer in the present. This thing will always be difficult to think and perhaps it will become more and more difficult. He, *himself, he is dead*, and yet, through the specters of memory and of the text, he lives *among us* and, as one says in French, *il nous regarde*—he looks at us, but also he is our concern, we have concerns regarding him more than ever without his being here. He speaks (to) us among us. He makes us or allows us to speak of us, *to speak to us. He speaks (to) us [Il nous parle].* The equivocality of the French expression, because it is barely translatable, translates well the murkiness of the question. What do we mean, what do *us* and *among us* mean in this case?

However obscure this may remain, we have to register it: we still have responsibilities toward him, and they are more alive than ever, even as he is dead. That is, we have responsibilities regarding Paul de Man *himself* but *in us and for us*. Yes, it remains difficult to think that he is dead and what that can mean. How are we to know about what or whom one is speaking when there are some who venture to exploit *what is happening* against others and for ends that no longer concern Paul de Man *himself*, that in any case will never reach him, while others will still try to protect *themselves* by pretending to protect Paul de Man against *what is happening*?

Is it possible to assume here one's own responsibility without doing one or the other, without using *what happens to us* in order to attack or to protect oneself? Without war, therefore? I do not know yet, but I would like to try to get there, to say at least something about it, and, this I do know, no matter what may happen.

So we have to answer [*répondre*] for what is happening to us. It will not be a matter only of the responsibility of a writer, a theoretician, a professor, or an intellectual. The act of responding and the definition of what "responding" means carry our commitment well beyond, no doubt, what may look like a circumscribed example, well beyond the limits of the literary and artistic column that a very young man wrote for a newspaper, almost a half century ago, for less than two years, in very singular private and political circumstances many of which remain unclear to us, before leaving his country and undertaking, in another country and another language, the story that we know, the only one that we knew something about until a few months ago: that of a great professor whose teaching and influence spread well beyond the United States, a fact that no one denies, whose work as a philosopher and as a theoretician of literature is admired or put to work by many scholars and students throughout the world, discussed or attacked by others, but dismissed by no one; that also of a man whose many friends, colleagues, students recognized what they owe to his lucidity, his rigor, his tireless generosity. We will come back to this.

Which war, then? Paul de Man's war, in another sense, is also the Second World War. He began to publish during the war. As far as I know, none of the incriminated articles was written after 1942, that is, well before the end of the war and of the German occupation. The reconstitution and the analysis of what his experience was of that war and that occupation will require patient, careful, minute, and difficult research. Any conclusion that does not rely on such research would be unjust, abusive, and irresponsible—I would even say, given the gravity of these things, indecent. And will it ever be necessary to conclude? Is that what this is about? Is a measure, a fair measure, possible? We will come back to this.

Which war, then? Paul de Man's war is finally, in a third sense, the one that this man must have lived and endured *in himself*. He *was* this war. And for almost a half century, this ordeal was a war because it could not remain a merely private torment. It has to have marked his public gestures, his teaching and writing. It remains a secret, a hive of secrets, but no one can seriously imagine, today, that in the course of such a history, this man would not have been torn apart by the tragedies, ruptures, dissociations, "disjunctions" (here I am using one of his favorite words and a concept that plays a major role in his thought). How did he undergo or assume on the outside these internal conflicts? How did he live this unlivable discord between worlds, histories, memories, discourses, languages? Do we have the means to testify to this? Who has the right to judge it, to condemn or to absolve? We will come back to this as well.

If it is now a matter of *responding* and of taking *responsibilities*, then we do so necessarily, as always, in situations we neither choose nor control, by responding to *unforeseeable* appeals, that is, to appeals *from/of the other* that are addressed to us even before we decide on them. Permit me to say a few words about certain recent appeals to which I thought I ought to respond and without which I would not be writing what you are reading here.

Two of them took the allegorical form of the telephone call. One took me by surprise in August, the other in December.

So this time I will have to tell. "Have I anything *to tell*?" is a question I have often asked myself in English during these last months. Do I have anything to tell that those interested in these things do not already know, those who discovered these "early writings," as the newspapers put it, at the same time I did? Do I have anything to analyze in a pertinent fashion, to discern, to distinguish (to tell) in the tangled fabric of this enigma, in order to account for it? I am not sure, I still cannot tell. At least I will have been obliged to recall the first words of the *Mémoires* that I dedicated four years ago to the one who was and remains my friend. (May I be forgiven these "self-centered" references; I will not overdo them.) "I have never known how to tell a story"; those were its first words.[2] How could I then have imagined that it would be from the friend, from him alone, singularly from him, that would one day come the obligation to tell a story? And that this injunction would come to me from the one who always associated narrative structure with allegory,

2. Derrida, *Mémoires: for Paul de Man*, trans. Cecile Lindsay, Jonathan Culler, Eduardo Cadava (New York, 1986), p. 150; hereafter abbreviated *M*.

that discourse of the other that always says something still other than what it says?

Mémoires speak especially, and often, of the future, that is, of that which cannot be anticipated and which always marks the memory of the past as experience of the promise. I claimed to know what a future should be *in general*: the unforeseeable itself. But without foreseeing as yet, and precisely for that reason, *what* it would be, I named in effect a future that it was absolutely impossible for me to see coming. And what a future! And the future of what a past! A future and a past about which I have at least, consciously, this absolute certainty: I never shared them and will never share them with Paul de Man, *himself*, whether one is talking about what *he* might have written a long time before I knew him, or about what is happening *to us* after his death.

I have just quoted the first words of a book. I believed I was chancing them in utter darkness. The last words of the same book resonate no less strangely, uncannily for me today. Forgive me once again this last and long quotation:

> A promise has meaning and gravity only with the death of the other. When the friend is no longer *there*, the promise is still not tenable, it will not have been made, but as a trace of the future it can still be *renewed*. You could call this an act of memory or a given word, even an act of faith; I prefer to take the risk of a singular and more equivocal word. I prefer to call this an *act*, only an act, quite simply an act. An impossible act, therefore the only one worthy of its name, or rather which, in order to be worthy of its name, must be worthy of the name of the other, made in the name of the other. Try and translate, in all of its syntactical equivocity, a syntagm such as "donner au nom de l'autre" or "une parole donnée au nom de l'autre." In a single sentence, it could mean in French, or rather in English: "to give to the name of the other" and "to give in the name of the other." Who knows what we are doing when we *donnons au nom de l'autre*? [M, p. 150]

"*Who knows* . . . ?" Who can tell? Not only did I not know it myself, neither this nor the ordeal the future held in store for my bereaved friendship, for that promise that friendship always is—a promise and a grief which are never over. I also did not know *what* I was promising. Yet, what was I saying about this nonknowledge? That it is the very thing that makes of the promise to the other a true promise, the only true promise, if there is any, an excessive and unconditional promise, an impossible promise. One can never promise in a halfway fashion, one always has to promise too much, more than one can fulfill. I could not know that one day, the experience of such a wound would have to include responding for Paul de Man: not responding *in his place* or in his name, that will always be impossible and unjustifiable (the promise of friendship even supposes the respect of this impossibility or the irreplaceable singularity of the other). Nor do I mean judging, and certainly not approving of everything he did, but speaking once again, of-him-for-him, at a moment when his memory or his legacy risk being accused and he is no longer there to speak in his own name. To speak in one's own name, moreover, is that ever possible? Would he have done it, would he have been able to do it if he were alive? What would have happened? Would all this have happened if he were still alive today? What does that mean "to be alive today"? These are just so many questions that I will also have to leave unanswered, like that of a responsibility which would never be cancelled, but on the contrary provoked by the experience of prosopopeia, such as de Man seems to understand it.

Well, when I received, in December, the telephone call from *Critical Inquiry* which proposed, singular generosity, that I be the first to speak, when a friendly voice said to me: "it has to be you, we thought that it was up to you to do this before anyone else," I believed I had to accept a warm invitation that also resonated like a summons. Unable not to accept, I nevertheless wondered: why me? why me first? Why me who, by birth, history, inclination, philosophical, political, or ideological choice, have never had anything but a mistrustful relation to everything that is being incriminated with such haste about these texts? Why me, who did not even know of their existence until a few months ago? Why me, who knew nothing about the dark time spent between 1940–42 by the Paul de Man I later read, knew, admired, loved? I will have to try to explain the reasons for which I nevertheless accepted to respond *yes* to this appeal and thus to take such a responsibility.

But my account will begin with an earlier telephone call. In August, Samuel Weber calls me upon his return from Belgium. During a conference, he has met a young Belgian researcher, Ortwin de Graef, who informed him of a disturbing discovery: articles written by Paul de Man under the German Occupation, between 1941 and 1942, in two newspapers, the French language *Le Soir* and the Flemish language *Het Vlaamsche Land*. This research assistant of the Belgian National Fund for Scientific Research at the Katholieke Universiteit Leuven is preparing

a doctoral dissertation on Paul de Man. Sam Weber describes him over
the phone: an intelligent young man who admires and knows well the
work of Paul de Man. He can also foresee, therefore, what effects will
result, especially in the United States, from the publication of his discovery. That is why he talked to Sam Weber about it and also hopes, the
latter tells me, to get my advice. But—to an extent, under conditions,
and in a form that I still today do not know—he has already communicated, by that time, his research and discovery, as well as his desire
to make them public, to several persons in the United States, notably at
Yale. Likewise, he has already sent to the British journal *Textual Practice*, along with the translation of four Flemish texts published by Paul
de Man in 1942,[3] an introduction[4] that, he will subsequently tell me in a
letter, "is not really to his satisfaction" but "he does not have the time"
to write another text as he is about to begin his military service. All of
this gives me the sense that this young man, whom I have yet to meet, is
as worried about handling a dangerous and spectacular explosive as he
is careful, for this very reason of course, not to let it get out of his hands
(analysis interrupted).

After discussing it on the phone, we decide, Sam Weber and myself,
to ask Ortwin de Graef to send us, if possible, copies of the articles
published in French, which were the more numerous. Then we could
advise him from a more informed position. Sam Weber writes to him
to this effect on our behalf. A short while later, we receive copies of
twenty-five articles in French, accompanied by a bibliographical notice
concerning ninety-two articles published in *Le Soir* between February
1941 and June 1942. In a handwritten note, de Graef adds: "plus probably another 20–30 in the period July–December 1942."

I specify this point for two reasons. (1) First of all, I have still not
understood why and how this selection of twenty-five articles was made
from a set of about 125. But I have no reason to suspect the intention of
he who wrote the following to me, in a letter accompanying the package
and in order to forestall my anxiety: "Yesterday I received a letter from
Mr. Samuel Weber in which he tells me that you are prepared to give
me your opinion on the texts of Paul de Man that I have found. In this

3. The four articles in *Het Vlaamsche Land* translated by Ortwin de Graef are: "Art
as Mirror of the Essence of Nations: Considerations on *Geist der Nationen*, by A. E.
Brinckmann," 29–30 Mar. 1942; "Content of the European Idea," 31 May–1 June
1942; "Criticism and Literary History," 7–8 June 1942; "Literature and Sociology,"
27–28 Sept. 1942; hereafter abbreviated by title followed by *HVL*.
4. De Graef, "Paul de Man's Proleptic 'Nachlass': Bio-bibliographical Additions and
Translations," unpub. ms.

envelope, you will find a bibliographical list as well as a not altogether arbitrary selection of these texts (it is difficult, for practical reasons, to send you all the articles now, but if you wish to see them, I will try to find a way—in any case, the present selection can give an impression of the general content of the first writings of Paul de Man as concerns the events of the war)."[5] However neutral and honest the principle of this selection, however indispensable it may have seemed for technical reasons I know nothing about, it has perhaps privileged the texts that are politically and ideologically significant. Thus perhaps it has distorted a general configuration that would be better respected by an integral reading. It is for this reason, and I will come to this point later, that we decided to pursue systematically the research—which de Graef by that time had to abandon for reasons of military service—and to publish *all* the accessible articles. (2) For the same reason, at the moment of this writing, I have still been able to read, besides the twenty-five articles from *Le Soir*, only the four articles translated from Flemish into English and introduced by the translator. I cannot even evaluate the effects of this limitation on what I may say here, but I do not want to exclude them. The important thing is not only the limitation on my reading at the moment in which I must write, whatever meaning that may have, but the fact that all the sensationalist "information" delivered in great haste by the newspapers and by those who fed them their information remains marked by this same limitation that was generally *undeclared*, just as there was no mention made of the as yet very insufficient state of our most elementary knowledge concerning the essentials of this affair. I insist on heavily underscoring this point. To be sure, in the course of the research and debates that will undoubtedly continue, I will perhaps be led to complete or correct the first impressions that I am delivering here as such. I would have waited to do a more systematic job if the press had not pressed us to hurry.

What were these impressions after a first reading toward the end of August? As I said to Sam Weber, during the first phone call (and one may easily imagine this), I had first hoped to read less profoundly marked articles. I had hoped that the concessions to the occupier or the ideological contagion (which I already expected: one did not accept to publish in that context without paying the price, that is, without accepting what we know today to be unacceptable) would take minimal and some sort of negative forms: more those of omission or of abstention. This hope disappointed, I had to give in to this first appearance at least:

5. De Graef, letter to Derrida, 21 Aug. 1987.

things seemed serious and complicated. Paul de Man's discourse appeared to me right off to be clearly more engaged than I had hoped, but also more differentiated and no doubt more heterogeneous. The form of the engagement was even rather disconcerting. One could recognize very quickly in the writing, along with the traits of a certain juvenility, those of an extraordinary culture—a culture that was especially literary or artistic, already very international (French and German, especially, but also Anglo-American and Flemish), open to the great politico-philosophical problems that everything then made more dramatic and more pressing: the destiny of Europe, the essence and future of nations, the individual and democracy, war, science and technology, and most particularly the political meanings and importance of literature.

Rightly or wrongly, I believed I had to accept what could be in itself *contradictory* about this double impression. On the one hand, I perceived an intellectual maturity and a cultivation which were uncommon at that age, and thus an exceptional sense of historical, philosophical, political responsibilities. There can be no doubt about this; it forms, rather, the theme, so to speak, of all these texts. To a very great extent, Paul de Man knew what he was doing, as they say, and he constantly posed questions of responsibility, which does not mean that his response to his questions was ever simple. Nonetheless, on the other hand, this impressive precociousness was sometimes paid for (it is not so surprising) by some confusion, perhaps as well a certain haste. Especially when they go together, youth and journalism are not the best protections against such confusion. No doubt flattered to see himself entrusted with the literary and artistic column of a major newspaper, even if he owed this fortune (or misfortune) to his uncle Henri de Man, a young man of twenty-two did not resist the temptation. All the more so since, as we now know, this former student of the sciences dreamed of nothing but literature. I will also come back to what was no doubt the determining role of that uncommon man, Henri de Man, and to the question of age in this story.

I believed I could acknowledge something right away: the relative heterogeneity of these writings, due in part to the often careful articulation of the argument, to the skill, indeed the cunning of the ideologico-political rhetoric, was also to be explained, to an extent that I still cannot measure, by other factors. On the one hand, it was no doubt necessary to take into consideration a personal inability to give to the argument all its coherence, but there was also the structural impossibility that prevented this argument from attaining coherence. (I am talking about the fund of coded and stereotyped arguments from which Paul de Man had to draw.) On the other hand, how can one avoid taking into account the mobility of a situation that, during this beginning of the occupation and however brief may be the period we are talking about, must have made things evolve quickly from one day to the next? The diachronic overdetermination of the context demanded that one proceed carefully in the reading of this series of articles. I will later spell out other necessary precautions, but first of all I want to go on with a story.

From the first reading, I thought I recognized, alas, what I will call roughly an *ideological configuration*, discursive schemas, a logic and a stock of highly marked arguments. By my situation and by training, I had learned from childhood to detect them easily. A strange coincidence: it so happens, on top of it all, that these themes are the subject of seminars I have been giving for four years as well as of my last book, on Heidegger and Nazism.[6] My feelings were first of all that of a wound, a stupor, and a sadness that I want neither to dissimulate nor exhibit. They have not altogether gone away since, even if they are joined now by others, which I will talk about as well. To begin, a few words about what I thought I was able to identify at first glance but a glance that right away gave me to see, as one should always suspect, that a single glance will never suffice—nor even a brief series of glances.

And already, when I speak of a painful surprise, I must right away differentiate things.

A painful surprise, yes, of course, for *three reasons* at least: (1) some of these articles or certain phrases in them seemed to manifest, in a certain way, an alliance with what has always been for me the very worst; (2) for almost twenty years, I had never had the least reason to suspect my friend could be the author of such articles (I will come back again to this fact); (3) I had read, a short while earlier, the only text that was accessible to me up until then and that was written and signed by Paul de Man in Belgium during the war. Thomas Keenan, a young researcher and a friend from Yale who was preparing, among other things, a bibliography of de Man, had in fact communicated to me, as soon as he had found it in Belgium, the table of contents and the editorial of an issue from the fourth volume of a Brussels journal in which de Man had published his first writings. He had been a member of the editorial committee, then director of this journal, *Les Cahiers du Libre Examen, Revue du cercle d'étude de l'Université Libre de Bruxelles*, founded in 1937.

6. Derrida, *De l'esprit: Heidegger et la question* (Paris, 1987); forthcoming in a translation by Geoffrey Bennington and Rachel Bowlby (Chicago).

Now, what did this editorial say in February 1940, at the point at which
de Man had just taken over the editorship, *in the middle of the war but
right before the defeat*? Without equivocation, it took sides *against* Germany and *for* democracy, for "the victory of the democracies" in a war
defined as a "struggle . . . against barbarity." This journal, moreover,
had always presented itself as "democratic, anticlerical, antidogmatic,
and antifascist."[7] Here then are three reasons to be surprised by the texts
dating from the following year and that I discovered with consternation.

But I said that right away I had to complicate and differentiate
things, as I will have to do regularly. My surprise did not come all at
once. Even as I reassured myself ("good, during his Belgian youth that
I know nothing about, Paul was, in any case, on the 'right side' during
the war!"), what I had quickly read of this editorial left me with an
uneasy feeling and an aftertaste. In passing, but in a clearly thematic
fashion, I was able to identify their source. And here we approach the
heart of the problems we have to talk about. They are not only Paul de
Man's problems, but those of the equivocal structure of all the politico-
philosophical discourses at play in this story, the discourses from all
sides. Today, yesterday, and tomorrow—let the dispensers of justice
not forget that!

What, then, had already disturbed me in this editorial, in its opting
so resolutely for democracy, and in its call for a struggle against barbarity in 1940?

1. First of all, an insistent reference to the West and to "Western
civilization," a theme or lexicon whose careless manipulation has often slid over into rather undemocratic theses, as we know now from
experience, especially when it is a question of a "decadence" of the
said Western civilization. As soon as anyone talks about "decadence
of Western civilization," I am on my guard. We know that this kind of
talk can sometimes (not always) lead to restorations or installations of
an authoritarian, even totalitarian *order*. Now, the decadence of Western civilization was indeed the central theme of the editorial. It spoke
vigorously of the necessity of lucidly going beyond a "commonplace,"
not in order to overturn it but to clarify its presuppositions, to "render
account" of it and "to take account," with "lucidity," thus *to answer
for it [en répondre]*—not only as a "theoretician," but in practical, ethical, political terms.

7. "Editorial," *Les Cahiers du Libre Examen* 1 (Apr. 1937), as cited by de Graef in
his introduction.

But since it has become a *commonplace* to say that Western civilization is in a state of decadence and that it is crumbling everywhere, it is indispensable to take account of what exactly these values are that are being so directly threatened. And if one wishes to present oneself as champion ready to defend them, this lucidity no longer remains a pointless theoretician's game, but becomes a truly tactical necessity. (My emphasis; on which side is the *commonplace* to be found?)[8]

2. I was disturbed as well by a discreetly marked suspicion on the subject of the "individual" and the idea of the "liberation of the individual." We also know the constraints that this suspicion sometimes (not always) exercises whenever the program to which it belongs is not carefully engaged. Presenting the unity of this issue of *Les Cahiers*, the editorial of this resolutely democratic journal in effect said: "Western ethical principles seem, for almost all the authors, to come down in the final analysis to the idea of the liberation of the individual, thanks to which we are differentiated from neighboring civilizations. And if we think we are superior to them, we owe the belief to this concept." This was a way once again of problematizing a "commonplace" at the same time as one seemed to be assuming it. The strategy of this brief editorial is thus already overdetermined, distanced, gravely ironic. It sets out at once positions of value (democracy, individual, Western civilization that must be saved from decadence) and the necessity of not simplifying, of not giving in to *doxa*, to orthodox and conformist opinion, to the "commonplace," to the feeling of superiority, at least as long as it remains unjustified or unanalyzed: "if we think we are superior to them [neighboring civilizations], we owe the belief to this concept," that is, to this concept of the individual which must be analyzed and of which an account must be rendered, an account taken. The author of this editorial, then, has no taste for simplification or received ideas, for commonplaces and easy consensus. Good democratic conscience and the ideology of the "liberation of the individual" can sometimes give in to such facileness. Nothing permits us to imagine that the editorial was written by anyone other than the journal's editor, that is, by Paul de Man who, as editor, would in any case have to be the first to answer for it.

3. But that was not all. Aware of the manner in which, discreetly but surely (perhaps not yet surely enough), it desimplified consensus and

8. "Editorial," *Les Cahiers du Libre Examen* 4 (Feb. 1940), p. 1.

good conscience, I clearly saw already that, in order to avoid "simplifying dangerously," this calmly insolent editorial ran the risk of other dangers. It called for a new "order." This word is perhaps not diabolical in itself. No word means anything by itself, out of all context, and the same word appears sometimes in discourses that many, perhaps, would never think of suspecting today. But it was then, in 1940, known to be too often, too regularly associated with antidemocratic ideologies. An order to come, a new order is not necessarily the extreme right that we know under the name of "Ordre nouveau"[9] (an expression which, moreover, appears elsewhere), but the resemblance ought to have been cause for more vigilance. On the other hand, the paragraph that I am going to cite refuses, precisely in order not to "simplify dangerously," to draw a simple line there where the war was, nonetheless, simplifying it in fact. It is as if it were causing the fronts to proliferate and asking the reader not to forget that war could cross over "to the inside" onto other fronts. And that finally there were always several wars going on at once. The editorial suggests that decadence is not only on the side of the enemy, and that the expression "struggle of the West against barbarity" comes down precisely to "dangerously simplifying the question." Here then is the passage that left me perplexed and that explains why, a little while later, my surprise may have been painful, as I said a moment ago, but was not an absolute surprise. Up to a certain point, it had been prepared or cushioned; let us say rather it was divided by a kind of internal partition:

> It has not been explicitly a question of the war in this issue. One senses, however, that its presence guides the thinking of all our contributors and it is certainly not by chance that two of them have chosen France as a symbol of Western culture. But one could not say, *without dangerously simplifying the question*, *that the present war is a struggle of the West against barbarity. Factors of decadence are to be found in all nations, all individuals, and the victory of the democracies will be a victory of the West only to the extent it succeeds in establishing an order in*

9. *L'Ordre nouveau* was the title of a journal founded in 1933 by Robert Aron and Arnaud Dandieu. From the first, it proclaimed a broad sympathy with the National Socialist regime in Germany and was considered a principal forum of extreme right wing thought. Subsequently the phrase "ordre nouveau" became a favored means for certain political discourse in the occupied countries to indicate sympathy for the goal of a unified Europe under German rule without, however, naming Nazism. (Trans.)

which a civilization like the one we cherish can live again. (My emphasis)[10]

We can glimpse a certain "logic." It lies in wait for the calculation or the political consequence of political or rather any discourse. It is as if the possibility of its own overturning were ventriloquizing the discourse in advance, as if that possibility installed in it a quasi-internal war, or still more serious, an endless war, that is, both infinite and without boundaries, a war that can never be totally internalized nor externalized. It consists, in effect, of multiple fronts and frontiers. A finite strategy can never formalize them totally, still less master them. Whence the effect produced by the incessant passage of these fronts or frontiers. A paradoxical effect because the very possibility of the passage seems to forbid any advance, it seems aporetic *in itself.* Now, it is precisely in this place and at this moment, I will even go so far as to say on this condition, that all decisions, if there are any, must be taken, and that responsibilities *are taken.*

Halfway reassured by this editorial in the *Cahiers,* but my ears still tuned to the uneasy rumblings within me, it is then that I discovered, several months later in 1987, a series of articles also written several months later, after February 1940, in *Le Soir* and *Het Vlaamsche Land*: this time, therefore, after the defeat and under the occupation. What had happened in those few months? What was it I thought I could identify on a first reading, through the sadness and consternation I have mentioned? First of all, this massive and irreducible fact: whatever may be the overdetermination of the content or the internal strategy, a "literary and artistic column" had been regularly supplied between 1940 and 1942. A rather large number of texts had been published in newspapers accepted by the Nazi occupiers. If anyone still had any doubts about this, it sufficed, even before reading de Man's articles, to look at what surrounded them, sometimes framing them immediately on the same page. The subjection of this newspaper[11] cannot have escaped de Man

---

10. "Editorial," *Cahiers* 4 (Feb. 1940), p. 1.

11. In an article about the story as reported in the *New York Times* ("Yale Scholar's Articles Found in Pro-Nazi Paper," 1 Dec. 1987), *Le Soir* recalls that de Man was "neither arrested nor tried in Belgium" and then adds:

It should be noted that, as regards *Le Soir*, the *New York Times* article is far from a model of journalistic rigor. *Le Soir* is described as "an anti-Semitic Belgian newspaper that collaborated with the Nazis." What our American colleague obviously does not know is that *Le Soir* was stolen and controlled by the occupiers, the directors and editorial board of our newspaper having, on the contrary, decided not to

for very long, even if the latter, let us suppose hypothetically, had let him-self be blinded for several days or several weeks; even if, let us suppose hypothetically, he had thought he ought to benefit from the authority of a famous and influential uncle, Henri de Man, to whom he was very attached and whom he no doubt admired a lot;[12] and even if, let us also suppose hypothetically, de Man initially took advantage of things so as to see his unquestionable talent exercised and recognized—since the

---

collaborate. Likewise the *New York Times* is completely wrong when it states that Paul de Man's uncle, Henri, was "a minister in the collaborationist Belgian gov-ernment, trying to protect Belgian autonomy against Nazi domination." Need one recall that, except for the Vichy government in France, there was no collaborationist government in occupied Europe?

Le Soir is certainly correct to remind another newspaper of "journalistic rigor." But then what must be said of its own rigor when it blindly reproduces the nonsense published in certain American newspapers that are getting their information, in every case, from university professors? Here's what one may read in the same article: "Considered at Yale to be one of the most brilliant lights of the university, says the *New York Times*, he was the author of a controversial theory about language, some seeing in him one of the great-est thinkers of the age. This theory, 'deconstructionism,' sees in language an integrally false means of expression which always reflects the prejudices of the user." It is true that after reading such stupidities over and over again, one might end up believing them. ("Indignation aux États-Unis: un professor (belge) de Yale avait été un *collaborateur*: l'ahurissante équipée d'un *brilliant* opportuniste" [Indignation in the United States: A (Belgian) professor at Yale had been a *collaborator*: the astounding adventure of a *bril-liant* opportunist," *Le Soir*, 3 Dec. 1987.)

12. The influence of Henri de Man, Paul's uncle and godfather, was no doubt pow-erful and determining. One must approach this extraordinary European figure in order to understand anything of these dramatic events. During a half century, his reputation radiated through his actions and his writings. Among the latter, all of which are more or less autobiographical, two titles provide brief self-portraits, but also a prefiguration of Paul: *Cavalier seul* (Lone horseman) and *Gegen den Strom* (Against the current). Here, in a telegraphic style, are a few significant traits, for which I have relied on: *Au delà du marxisme* (French translation of Henri de Man's *Zur Psychologie des Sozialismus* [Jena, 1926]; reissued by Seuil in 1974 with a very useful preface by Michel Brelaz and Ivo Rens, the foreword of the first French edition [Paris, 1926], and a preface by the author denouncing the "nationalist imbecility" and the "prestige of race or nationality"); Henri de Man, *A Documentary Study of Hendrik de Man, Socialist Critic of Marxism*, comp., ed. and largely trans. Peter Dodge (Princeton, N.J., 1979); Dodge, *Beyond Marxism: The Faith and Works of Hendrik de Man* (The Hague, 1966); and Jules Gérard-Libois and José Gotovitch, *L'An 40: La Belgique occupée* (Brussels, 1971).

Freemason father, tolerant anticlerical: "one of the purest incarnations of stoic mo-rality," says his son of him. Henri was born in 1885, the year that the POB (Belgian Labor Party) was founded of which he will become vice-president in 1933. 1905: ex-pelled from the Ghent Polytechnic Institute for having demonstrated in support of the Russian revolutionaries of 1905. Moves to Germany, "the native and the chosen land of Marxism." Meets Bebel, Kautsky, Liebknecht, Rosa Luxemburg. Intense militant and theoretical activity in Germany. First Secretary of the Socialist Youth International. Dissertation on the woolen industry in Ghent in the Middle Ages. In London in 1910,

awarding of a prestigious literary and artistic column in a major newspaper cannot leave a young man of twenty-two indifferent, a young man who has things to say and who is longing to write once again, as he had already been doing in a brilliant way for several years, on all subjects: philosophy, sociology, politics, music, and especially literature.

Beyond this grave and undeniable fact, I would like to try to analyze now what I thought I was able to detect at the moment of that first, painful reading. It will be difficult, I prefer to say that right away, and for a number of reasons. The first has to do with the hypothesis of a general law that I believed I was able to form, then verify, at least in a first analysis. Like any law, this law supposes a sort of invariant that in this case takes the form of a recurrent alternation, according to the disjunctive partition of an "on the one hand . . . on the other hand." But one of the difficulties I announced arises from this: the said alternation (that, out of concern for clarity, I will be obliged to harden into an

joins the Social Democratic Federation (radical Marxist group). Returns to Belgium in 1911, provokes a crisis in the POB by criticizing its reformism.

First doubts about Marxism as the war begins, after having served as translator in talks between Jaurès and the future chancellor of the Weimar Republic to preserve the peace. Official mission to Russia after the Revolution in 1917. Publishes "La Révolution aux armées" in Emile Vandervelde's *Trois aspects de la révolution russe, 7 mai–25 juin 1917* (Three aspects of the Russian revolution). In "La Grande désillusion" (1919; The great disillusion): "It is not for this reason, it is not so that the Europe of tomorrow will resemble the Europe of yesterday that we fought. It is not for the destruction of the German and Russian nations, it was for the independence of all nations and in order to free Europe of militarism." Plans to immigrate to the U.S., two trips there (1918–20). Founds a system of worker education in Seattle. Professor of Social Psychology at University of Washington. Dismissed from his position after intervening in a local election campaign in favor of the Farmer-Labor Party. 1919: *The Remaking of a Mind: A Soldier's Thoughts on War and Reconstruction.* 1922–26: lives in Darmstadt and teaches at the Akademie der Arbeit in Frankfurt. 1926: publishes his best-known work, *The Psychology of Socialism* (trans. Eden and Cedar Paul [New York, 1928]. 1929–33: lives and teaches in Frankfurt (newly created chair in social psychology). 1933: publishes *Die sozialistische Idee*, confiscated by the Nazis. Director of the Office of Social Studies of the POB (1932) which issues the famous *Plan du travail* (Labor Plan) and the doctrine of planism (socialization of financial capital, credit, monopolies, and large landed property). Minister of Public Works and of Unemployment Reduction (1935), Finance Minister in 1936 in tripartite governments that reduce unemployment and fight back rexism (the extreme right). Appointed by the king to secret missions to preserve peace in 1938. Minister without portfolio for several months. Appointed to a post in the queen's service, during the final days before the defeat perhaps advises the king, who was already inclined in that direction, to share the fate of the army rather than to follow the government into exile. Like many others, believes the war is over. President of the POB, considers the political role of the party to be over and that the war "has led to the debacle of the parliamentary regime and of the capitalist plutocracy in the so-called

opposition through the rhetoric of an "on the one hand, on the other hand") will be only the phenomenon or the form of presentation, the logico-rhetorical scheme of this law—I will even say of the relation to the law in general. It would be necessary to go beyond the form of this schema and interrogate in its possibility that which thus sets limits on a complete binary formalization. No doubt I will only be able to sketch this movement with these examples and within the dimensions of an article. But I insist on showing the examples and on marking this necessity, even as I refer to other work, past or yet to come.

Let us say, then, "on the one hand . . . on the other hand," and what is more "on the one hand . . . on the other hand" on both hands. On both hands, both sides it would be necessary to pursue further the over-determining division.

On the one hand, the *massive, immediate, and dominant* effect of all these texts is that of a *relatively* coherent ideological ensemble which,

---

democracies. For the working classes and for socialism, this collapse of a decrepit world is, far from a disaster, a deliverance" ("The Manifesto," in *Hendrik de Man, Socialist Critic of Marxism*, p. 326). Dissolves the POB, creates a single central labor syndicate in 1940. His relations with the occupiers go downhill quickly. From June 1941, considers the pressures untenable, goes into exile in November 1941 in Savoie (France). Already in July 1940, his program had been considered by the German command, "because of its spirit and its origins" and despite elements that are "formally 'pseudo-fascist,'" to be incapable of ever "being really integrated into a European order, such as Germany conceives it" (quoted in Brelaz and Rens, *Au delà du marxisme*, p. 16). Writes his memoirs (*Après coup*). His *Réflexions sur la paix* (Reflections on peace) banned in Belgium in 1942. Maintains relations with Belgian "collaborationists," unorthodox Germans as well as French Resistants (Robert Lacoste). Informed of the conspiracy and the failed plot against Hitler. 1944: escapes to Switzerland where he is taken in by a Swiss socialist leader who helps him to win political asylum. At the time of the Liberation, severely condemned by a military tribunal "for having, while in the military, maliciously served the policy and the designs of the enemy." Third marriage. *Audelà du nationalisme* (1946). *Cavalier seul: Quarante-cinq années de socialisme européen* and *Gegen den Strom: Memoiren eines europäischen sozialisten* are two reworked versions of his 1941 autobiography. *Vermassung und Kulturverfall: Eine Diagnose unserer Zeit* (1951). On 20 June 1953, his car stops "for unknown reasons" on the railroad tracks at an unguarded crossing near his home. He dies with his wife when the train arrives. It was, they say, slightly behind schedule. (Suicides and allegories of reading: some day we will have to talk about suicide in this history.)

In 1973, in an article whose lucidity seems to me after the fact to be even more admirable and striking, Richard Klein was to my knowledge the first to take the figure of the uncle seriously into consideration. Paul de Man having pointed out to him that he (that is, Richard Klein!) had taken Henri de Man to be the former's father, Klein's postscript closes with the best possible question: "what, after all, is an uncle?" The rereading of this article, "The Blindness of Hyperboles, the Ellipses of Insight" (*Diacritics* 3 [Summer 1973]: 33–44), seems to me urgent for whoever is interested in these questions.

most often and in a preponderant fashion, conforms to official rhetoric, that of the occupation forces or of the milieux that, in Belgium, had accepted the defeat and, if not state and governmental collaboration as in France, then at least the perspective of a European unity under German hegemony. A rigorous description of the conditions in which is inscribed what I am *massively* calling here the *massive* effect would suppose taking into account the extraordinary tangle of the political, religious, and linguistic history of Belgium, at least at that critical turning point of the constitutional monarchy when Henri de Man, after having been a socialist minister, decides, as the government is going into exile, to stay with the king whose adviser he will remain until November 1941, the date at which he in turn leaves Belgium. I cannot undertake this description here, but I believe it will be indispensable, in the future, for any serious interpretation of these texts.

But *on the other hand* and within this frame, de Man's discourse is constantly split, disjointed, engaged in incessant conflicts. Whether in a calculated or a forced fashion, and no doubt beyond this distinction between calculation and passivity, all the propositions carry within themselves a counterproposition: sometimes virtual, sometimes very explicit, always readable, this counterproposition signals what I will call, in a regular and contradictory manner, a *double edge* and a *double bind*, the singular artefact of a blade and a knot. As a result, paradoxically, these articles and the attitude that seems to sustain them are not without a certain conformity to the editorial of the *Cahiers* that wanted to avoid "dangerously simplifying."

That is why, in the *three series of examples* with which my hypothesis will be put to the test, I will follow precisely the themes put into perspective by the journal editorial: the destiny of the West, Europe and its outside, the nation, democracy and the individual. *And literature*: if it occupies more than just one place among others in this network, the reason is not only that, as in the *Cahiers*, de Man had the responsibility, official and statutory, to treat of literature in a privileged way.

1. On the one hand . . . on the other hand, then (first series of examples)

On the one hand, everything takes place as if, the German victory leaving no doubt and no exit, it was more imperative than ever to pose the question of Europe's destiny by analyzing the past, the present, and especially the future. For that reason, de Man approves of those who attempt a "critical exposé" in order to "deduce the responsibilities for the defeat."[13] One must "direct one's thinking toward the new problems that have arisen" and not give in to clichés (once again the critique of the "commonplace"): "it is not by spreading the belief that we are inept cowards that we will plan for a better future." It is not enough to accuse "the decayed political climate that provoked the defeat since that climate was not much better in 1914." When it is a question of the defeat, a certain Belgian nationalism, sometimes more precisely Flemish nationalism, seems just as obvious, even if the discourse on the nation and nationalisms often remains more cautious than the praise of the Belgian army whose defeat would have been more "glorious" than that of its allies.[14] De Man judges this reflection on the war, that many others—but not everyone, and that is the question—might also think was over, to be just as necessary for France. He is already in a "postwar" period.[15] He praises the French who, by means of the "symptoms of what may be the future" "reveal the fruitful meditation of a people attempting to pull themselves together by understanding objectively how [the] blow that has been struck changes its historical destiny."[16] As in the editorial from the *Cahiers*, a big question cuts across all the articles: that of the future of Europe and of a European unity that, from now on, since the German victory seems irreversible and of profound importance, can only be accomplished around Germany.

Even if the form of his discourse is then more *descriptive* than *prescriptive*, even if it seems to call more for a realization and a knowledge than a commitment and an approbation, de Man permits himself no reservations (could he have done so in this newspaper?) when he defines, for example, what might "interest" the "visitors" on the occasion of an exhibition on the "history of Germany." One recognizes here the concern of someone who never ceased pointing to the necessity of posing the national problem, notably the German problem. And who can reproach him for that?

> This is the first element that may interest visitors: to have a
> clearer vision of the very complex history of a people whose im-
> portance is fundamental to the destiny of Europe. They will be

13. De Man, "Les livres sur la campagne de Belgique," *Le Soir*, 25 Feb. 1941.
14. Ibid.
15. De Man, "Le *Solstice de juin*, par Henri de Montherlant," *Le Soir*, 11 Nov. 1941; hereafter abbreviated "SjM."
16. De Man, "Témoignages sur la guerre en France," *Le Soir*, 25 Mar. 1941.

able to see that the historical evolution of Germany is governed by a fundamental factor: the will to unite the set of regions that have a like racial structure but that adversaries have incessantly endeavored to divide. The periods of weakness always coincide with a territorial parceling up. Each time there has been an attempt to react against a state of inferiority, it has taken the form of seeking to reconquer and assimilate the lost provinces.[17]

This paragraph echoes a concern whose traces may be found throughout the whole history and all the writings of Henri de Man. His nephew goes back to the treaties of Westphalia and Versailles, then he adds:

> There is another reason for which Germany's historical destiny both past and future cannot leave us indifferent: and that is because we depend on it directly . . . none can deny the fundamental importance of Germany for the life of the West as a whole. One must see this obstinacy that resists subjugation as more than a simple proof of national steadfastness. The whole continuity of Western civilization depends on the unity of the people who are its center.[18]

Likewise, although he assumes nothing directly to his own account, although his language is almost always that of a chronicler-commentator, de Man does not openly criticize those who, like Jacques Chardonne, dare "to look in the face of the situation born of the German victory" and form "the hope of finding that the victor has projects and intentions capable of reconstructing a Europe with better social and political conditions."[19] There seems to be no doubt in his eyes that Belgium and Europe are in the process of living a "revolution." That is his term. But this word is also borrowed: it is the rallying cry of all those who, notably in France, speak of "national revolution" in order to name the new Pétainist era. Revolution, which is to say, then, a social and national revolution of the right. It is, moreover, also in reference to France (which, as we shall see, he alternately praises and criticizes) that de Man speaks, as does his uncle during his Marxist and "beyond Marxism"

17. De Man, "L'exposition 'Histoire de l'Allemagne' au Cinquantenaire," *Le Soir*, 16 Mar. 1942.
18. Ibid.
19. De Man, "*Voir la figure*, de Jacques Chardonne," *Le Soir*, 28 Oct. 1941; hereafter abbreviated "VfC."

phase, of a "political and social revolution." What is more, he diagnoses a fatality rather than assigning a duty and we ought always to pay attention to the mode of his utterances. On the subject of *Notre avant-guerre* by Robert Brasillach: "I can imagine that, for a cultivated Frenchman, *Notre avant-guerre* still evokes a lost paradise. But he will have to resign himself to completing a political and social revolution before he can hope to regain a similar paradise, one that would have more solid and, consequently, less ephemeral foundations."[20] Thus the present moment is apprehended, in the then dominant code, as that of a "revolution": the "present revolution,"[21] the "maze of the present revolution,"[22] the "current revolution"[23] or the one to come (for Belgium that "has not yet had its revolution").[24] This "maze," who can seriously see its outcome, the topological design, the essential plan? No one or almost no one, in de Man's eyes, the eyes of someone who, knowing he cannot see in a labyrinth, pricks up his ears:

> For what must preoccupy the minds of those who wish to orient a reform or a revolution is not a search for the means of adapting themselves to new conditions. In the spiritual domain as much as in the political one, they find themselves confronted with new lines of conduct to be recast, with institutions to be recreated, with programs of organization to be elaborated. And one may remark that strictly none of the essays published in such great number in France and French-speaking Belgium since the war contain so much as a slight concern for tracing the givens of the different problems. ["SjM"]

One can see that de Man is defining a *labyrinthine* task, to be sure, but an altogether new one, that of a revolution in thinking. One has to think the revolution and do something other than "adapt to new conditions." Does he not feel that he alone, at the time, is up to defining or approaching this task? I have that impression. This labyrinthine

20. De Man, "*Notre avant-guerre*, de Robert Brasillach," *Le Soir*, 12 Aug. 1941; hereafter abbreviated "NaB."
21. De Man, "Content of the European Idea," *HVL*.
22. De Man, "*Sur les falaises de marbre*, de Ernst Jünger: deux ouvrages d'actualité," *Le Soir*, 31 Mar. 1942.
23. De Man, "Le Problème français; *Dieu est-il français*, de F. Sieburg," *Le Soir*, 28 Apr. 1942; hereafter abbreviated "PfS."
24. De Man, "La littérature française devant les évènements," *Le Soir*, 20 Jan. 1942.

task would be both theoretical (abstract) and more than theoretical. It resists its own theorization and the massiveness of the schema I have just outlined.

On the other hand . . .

For, *on the other hand*, the same article speaks of the need for an abstract theorization of problems that have not yet been elaborated—in particular on the subject of the "primordial question of European unity." De Man is politically cautious enough to specify that this theoretical elaboration must not be left to "technicians," even if caution can always (this is the double edge) be turned against itself (antitechnicism, demagogic populism—but this is not the dominant accent in the text):

> Which does not mean that only technicians can participate in the debate. The postwar period brings with it philosophical and psychological problems of a *purely abstract* nature just as much as it does difficulties having to do with tangible realities. More than that, one may even say that the most important questions are situated on a *purely abstract* plane. Thus, to take just this example, the primordial question of European unity can only be envisioned from a *quasi-theoretical* angle. ["SjM"; my emphasis]

Why is that? We have just gone from the "purely abstract" to the "quasi-theoretical." That is why, immediately afterward, the "spiritual givens" of the problem, which are taken to be essential, "cannot be treated in a general and theoretical form." In the rather awkward phrase I am going to cite (and where I do not exclude the possibility of a typo having slipped in, since this wartime newspaper contains many such mistakes), it is difficult to know whether language does or does not belong to these "spiritual givens." Language is defined as "material and direct," an interesting notation that probably also concerns national languages and their diversity, but which no doubt should not be overinterpreted retrospectively in the light of what de Man has since said about materiality:

> That which unites the European peoples are precisely those factors that escape all materialization: a similar political past, a common philosophical and religious thinking, an economic and social organization that has gone through an analogous evolution in all countries. On the contrary, that which is material and direct (such as language, habits, popular customs) appears as disparate and variable. One may thus see that, in this case, it is

> a matter of spiritual givens that cannot be treated in a general
> and theoretical form. ["SjM"][25]

What is still more interesting, through the convolution of this remark, is its final aim within the article. The article is about a book by
Montherlant. As far as I can judge at this point, the list of books, in particular of French books, reviewed by de Man can seem to speak loudly
all by itself (Jouvenel, Fabre-Luce, Benoist-Méchin, Chardonne, Drieu
La Rochelle, Giono, and so on). By what it retains as well as by what
it excludes, the filter seems to correspond to that of the legitimation
machine (thus the censorship machine) of the official Pétainist ideology.
Is de Man letting these choices be imposed totally from without? Is he
responding on his own to a demand? Does he assume responsibility for
it? Up to what point? Does he consider that these books, having just appeared (and being authorized to appear with authorized publishers—an
enormous French history that I have to leave aside here), were part of
the current events about which it is the chronicler's duty to speak, even
if, on the other hand, he has already indicated his interest in so many
other authors, from Joyce to Kafka, from Gide to Hemingway, and so
forth? As for me, I do not have the means to answer these questions.
But what I can say, from reading this article on Montherlant, for example, and taking responsibility for this reading, is that the argument I
mentioned a moment ago around "theory" seems destined, through de
Man's clever and not particularly docile strategy, to discredit Montherlant's political discourse at the point at which it proposes "a general
view." How does this text operate when we look at it closely?

It begins by quoting, as if in epigraph and in order to authorize itself,
a remark by Montherlant. Then it turns the remark against him with an
irony whose pitiless lucidity, alas (too much lucidity, not enough lucidity, blindly lucid), spares no one, not even de Man almost a half century
later. Writing by profession on current affairs, he deals with a current
affair in this domain and he announces the oblivion promised those
who devote their literature to current affairs. Do not these lines, that
name "the worst," become unforgettable from then on? It is frightening
to think that de Man might have handled so coldly the double-edged
blade, while perhaps expecting "the worst":

25. On "matter" in de Man, see *Mémoires*, chap. 2. On the lexicon of "spirit," that is
so manifest in these texts of 1940–42, as in the writings of so many others in the period
between the wars, see my *De l'esprit: Heidegger et la question*. I wish to make it clear,
however, that the number and nature of differences between Heidegger and de Man
would render any analogism more confused than ever.

In this collection of essays by Montherlant, there is a phrase that all those who have followed literary publication since August 1940 will approve. It is the passage that says: "To the writers who have given too much to current affairs for the last few months, I predict, for that part of their work, the most complete oblivion. When I open the newspapers and journals of today, I hear the indifference of the future rolling over them, just as one hears the sound of the sea when one holds certain seashells up to the ear." One could not have put it any better. And this just and severe sentence applies to all the books and essays in which writers offer us their reflections on war and its consequences, including *Solstice de juin* itself [the title of the book by Montherlant de Man is reviewing]. It is an odd distortion, belonging to our age, to demand from artists and writers, in particular, directives and judgments on political and historical circumstances. Because writers are capable of expressing commonplaces in an elegant way, they are made into oracles and one takes their words to be providential messages. And the credit they enjoy in this domain is considerable. Gide's quarrels with communism exercised more influence over people's minds than would have numerous documented and serious works treating the same question. And yet there is no reason whatsoever to grant men of letters such authority in an area of human behavior which, manifestly, lies outside their competence. It is surprising to discover the naïveté and nullity of some of their sentences once they have been stripped of the brilliant varnish that a careful style confers on them. A whole side of the question—the economic, social, technical side—is totally alien to them, so that when they venture onto this terrain, in that offhand way that only the ignorant are capable of, one may expect the worst. ["SjM"]

After that, one does not have to wait long for a condemnation of the individual and the individualist Montherlant "who likes to give lessons": his "meditations" are "conventional" and "insipid," "uninteresting" and "ineffective." By "practicing the political essay," Montherlant can only "echo official declarations" and "swell the ranks of those who talk to no useful purpose."

An analogous gesture, although more discreet, as regards Chardonne. After having quoted him ("Only Germany can organize the continent and that country provides us with the opportunity of an internal rebuilding that was necessary and that it is up to us to accomplish . . ."),

de Man adds: "After such sentences, one may perhaps *debate* Chardonne's ideas, but one certainly cannot reproach them for a lack of
sharpness [*netteté*]" ("VfC"). A double-edged sentence—on sharpness,
precisely, and on the cutting edge itself. One may suppose, without being sure, that de Man judges these ideas to be very debatable.

Likewise, although de Man often insists, and rightly so, on the riches
of German culture, on the complexity of the national problem in Germany, on the fundamental role that it always plays and ought still to play
in the destiny of Europe, at no point, to my knowledge, does he name
Nazism, a fortiori in order to praise it. In all the texts I have been able
to read and about which the least one can say is that they were turned
in the direction of politics and current affairs, the word "Nazi," "Nazi
party" appears only once or twice, if I am not mistaken, and then it does
so in a neutral or informative mode. What is more, on one occassion it
provides another opportunity to criticize a French writer who was then
one of the most "authorized" by collaborationist France: Brasillach and
his "lack of political sense"! "Brasillach's reaction faced with a spectacle
like that of the Nazi Party Congress in Nuremberg, when he manifests
a certain terror before the 'strange' nature of this demonstration, is that
of someone for whom the sudden importance of the political in the life
of a people is an inexplicable phenomenon" ("NaB").

However overdeterminable this remark may be, it indicates not just
a distance but a very critical step back when it comes to writers or
ideologues as marked as Montherlant, Chardonne, or Brasillach. As for
what remains neutral or suspended in his approach, one must, it seems
to me, find a supplementary explanation, and here again it will be a
question of "responsibility." In an article titled "Sur les possibilités de la
critique" (which will greatly interest those who would hasten toward a
recognition of prefigurations in these "early writings"), de Man defines
a certain autonomy of literature, but also of literary history. To be sure,
there is a responsibility to evaluate the literary object, but it is a specific
responsibility. It is not to be confused, he says, with that of a moral and
political judgment on the moral or political responsibilities of the writer.

> Literature is an independent domain having a life, laws, and
> obligations belonging only to it and which in no way depend
> on the philosophical or ethical contingencies stirring at its side.
> The least one can say is that the artistic values governing the
> world of letters do not merge with those of the Truth and the
> Good, and that whoever borrows his criteria from this region
> of human consciousness will be systematically mistaken in his

judgments. . . . One does not have the right to condemn Gide
as a novelist because his moral life was debatable. . . . A writer
can be attacked for the inadequacies of his style, for sins against
the laws of the genre he practices, but never for weaknesses
or lacks in his moral personality. The most beautiful pages in
the world's literatures are often those that express a failure, a
renunciation, a capitulation. And the worst platitudes have been
written to exalt the most noble sentiments. All of this is quite
obvious and it would be pointless to repeat it if we did not have
to listen to reassertions of criticism's duty to "derive from a set
of deductions, joined to a philosophy of broad humanism or
better yet to a moral responsibility linked to the supernatural
fidelity of man."[26]

This is not the place for a substantive debate about all these formulations and about literature as an "independent domain"—which,
moreover, de Man does not remove from history, any more than he
ever did. This is very clear in the rest of the same article which even
speaks of a "philosophy of literary history that is no less fruitful than the
philosophy of history as such." It is also "quite obvious" that literary
criticism, if it is *critical*, that is, if it is a judgment, an evaluation, an assignment of responsibility, could not be, insofar as it is *literary* criticism
of *works*, a moral or political criticism of authors. That being the case,
what does de Man do here?

   1. If the responsibility of the *criticized* works can be acute in literary
terms without that meaning it is a moral or political responsibility, then
this is also true for criticism, for *criticizing* criticism of works. Some will
be able to say, out of malevolence in my opinion, that de Man wants
to subtract his critical activity from any future moral and political trial,
even though some "capitulation" was readable there.

   2. More significant seems to me to be the example of Gide, the "accursed" author of the period. De Man disputes the validity of any moral
and political trial that one might bring against Gide's literary work.
He even formulates general principles invalidating such a judgment. He
puts forth reasons for a radical resistance to the organization of such
verdicts. He does it at a moment when moral and political trials, often
carried out in the name of, precisely, "humanism," were common and
had serious consequences. This seems to me to be a remarkable gesture.
For if literature remains neutral in de Man's eyes or at least independent

26. De Man, "Sur les possibilités de la critique," *Le Soir*, 2 Dec. 1941.

of morality and politics, it is not neutral, it is even an offensive and courageous gesture to recall this axiom and to resist the moralizing ortho-
doxy at a moment of great repression during which so many writers are
being condemned for their moral or political opinions (present or past).

3. The logic of this argument anticipates, up to a certain point, that
of Jean Paulhan (whom de Man was rediscovering during the last years
of his life, no doubt in reference to other themes, but it is still not insignificant). Writing after the Liberation in *De la paille et du grain* (On
the wheat and the chaff), this writer-resistant disputed the right of his
"friends" on the National Committee of Writers to conduct, as writers,
political trials of other writers known to have collaborated with the
enemy. If there were grounds for such a trial, then it was the province
of other tribunals competent to judge political acts: there ought to be
no literary "épuration" [purge], no writers' tribunals to judge other
writers *as writers*. Nor should there be "voluntary policemen," or "that
supplementary force of gendarmes that Charles Maurras cried out for—
and that you have invented."[27] My own thinking as regards Paulhan's
discourse cannot be summed up in a few lines. Yet, it is remarkable in
any case that an analogous logic was put to work several years earlier by
de Man *and this time in an opposite context*, so to speak, when it was
a matter of protesting against tribunals and purges on *the other side*.
Thus, once again do not "dangerously simplify the question"!

In a like manner, finally, although he grants a lot of attention to the
role that Germany or "German genius" has played or ought to play in
the destiny of Europe, although he recalls constantly the necessity of
understanding thoroughly the history of the German nation in order
to understand Hitlerism, although he is vigilantly opposed to the commonplace and the "lazy and widespread solution" that comes down to
"supposing an integral dualism between Germany, on the one hand,
and Hitlerism on the other . . . the latter considered to be a strange
phenomenon, having no relation to the historical evolution of the German people, but rather born of a momentary aberration and destined to
disappear like a morbid symptom that would have merely upset the normal life of the nation for a little while" ("VfC"), although his analysis
leads him to judge German "hegemony" in Europe to be ineluctable,
this diagnosis seems rather cold and rather far removed from exhortation. And when, in the same text, he describes the "innovations of

27. Jean Paulhan, *De la Paille et du grain* (Paris, 1948). The principal ideologue and
organizing force of the *Action Française*, Maurras was a prolific and much-admired
writer. (Trans.)

totalitarian regimes" and the "obligations" or "duties" taking the place
of "anarchy," he underscores that the "style that will result from this
process is far from being definitively consecrated. It may appear crude
and somewhat rudimentary" because of the "rigid and relatively narrow
mold that is the war." Then he concludes by noting that enriching these
possibilities may run the risk of "dangerous temptations" ("VfC). The
week before, in an article that was also, let us never forget, a commentary on Daniel Halévy, de Man recognized, admittedly, that in France
"immediate collaboration" seemed compelling to "any objective mind,"
but he warned against an attitude that would be content to "strike out
against the nearest guilty parties" or "to adopt the mystical beliefs from
which the victors have drawn their strength and power."[28] Here once
again, there is an appeal to historical, even the historian's, analysis of the
past so as to rediscover the strengths and the patrimony of the nation,
but also so as to draw "the lesson from events by means of theoretical
considerations."[29]

2. On the one hand . . . on the other hand (second series of examples)

On the one hand, the question of nations dominates all these texts. It is
approached in all its *theoretical* aspects (ethnic, historical, political, linguistic, religious, esthetic, literary). Nothing could be more legitimate,
one might say, especially at that moment, and I will add: still today. But
this interest is not only theoretical. In certain of its forms, it resembles
nationalist commitment: Belgian, sometimes Flemish. And there seems
to be evidence of a great respect, in a privileged fashion, with regard
to German nationalism. Most utterances of a "comparatist" style are
made to the benefit of Germany and to the detriment of conquered
France. This interest for the nation seems to dominate in two ways: it
outweighs interest for the state, notably in its democratic form, and still
more interest for the individual who constitutes the target of numerous
critiques.

We have already seen how this interest was resonating in a muffled
way in the editorial from the *Cahiers*. De Man, translator and commen-
tator of A. E. Brinckmann's *Geist der Nationen, Italiener-Franzosen-
Deutsche* (1938), speaks in this regard of "national grandeur." His commentary describes "a sober faith, a practical means to defend Western
culture against a decomposition from the inside out or a surprise attack

28. De Man, "*Trois épreuves*, par Daniel Halévy," *Le Soir*, 14 Oct. 1941.
29. Ibid.

by neighbouring civilizations."[30] Looked on more or less favorably by the Nazis, Brinckmann's book is concerned especially with the arts. But de Man recalls that it applies to all domains: "what is true in the domain of the history of arts holds true for all domains. Europe can only be strong, peaceful, and flourishing if it is governed by a state of mind which is deeply conscious of its national grandeur, but which keeps its eyes open for all experiments and problems that touch our continent" ("AM"). This Western nationalism must adapt itself to the "contemporary revolutions" we spoke of earlier. De Man emphasizes that the aims of the book he is reviewing are not only theoretical. They have value as practical engagement. Does he subscribe to them in his name? It seems that he does, but he does not say so:

> The aim of a work like this is not only to analyse the artistic activity from an aesthetic point of view, or to give an explanation of a practical nature. It originated out of an attempt to ensure the future of Western civilisation in all its aspects. As such it contains a lesson, which is indispensable for all those who, in the contemporary revolutions, try to find a firm guidance according to which they can direct their action and their thoughts. ["AM"]

Comparisons between the German and French cultures, notably as regards their literary manifestations, the one dominated by myth, metaphor, or symbol, the other by psychological analysis, the predilection for moderation, limit, and definition, thus for the finite (one thinks of many of Nietzsche's statements on this subject), seem often to be made to the benefit of the former. Does de Man assume to his own account what he says in commenting on Sieburg? It seems that he does, but he does not say so.

> Instead of an artificial and forced denationalization that leads to a considerable impoverishment—such as we have seen happen in Flanders and Walloon Belgium as a result of France's force of attraction—a free contact among peoples who know themselves to be different and who hold onto this difference, but who esteem each other reciprocally guarantees political peace and cultural stability. It is no doubt in this domain that France

---

30. De Man, "Art as Mirror of the Essence of Nations," *HVL*; hereafter abbreviated "AM."

must perform the most serious turnaround, or risk disappearing forever from the political scene.

As for the spiritual domain [*le domaine de l'esprit*], the forces that seem to have taken over the conduct of history are not very much in accordance with France's specific soul. To realize this, it suffices to examine the opposition pointed out by Sieburg between a certain form of French reason that everywhere seeks to fix limits and to establish the right measure, and the sense of grandeur and of the infinite that indeed seems to characterize present tendencies. We are entering a mystical age [let us not forget that elsewhere de Man speaks of his mistrust as regards the victor's mysticism], a period of faith and belief, along with everything that supposes in the way of suffering, exaltation, and intoxication. ["PfS"]

The Flemish nationalism is clearer, notably in "Le Destin de la Flandre," whose pretext was the "Germano-Flemish Cultural Convention." Paul de Man was born in Antwerp, and his family is Flemish. He recalls several times the "Flemish genius" and the struggle against "French influences that, through the intermediary of the complicitous Belgian state, were spreading rapidly." He supports a solution that would guarantee Flanders a certain autonomy in relation to Walloon Belgium and Germany, whether it is a matter of defense or of national, and first of all linguistic, patrimony: "that, of the language before all else and of that form of freedom that permits creators to work in accordance with their impulses and not as imitators of a neighbor whose spirit is dissimilar."[31] This attention to national language appears throughout these first texts which also form a short treatise on translation. Literature is often examined from the point of view of the problems of translation by someone who was also a polyglot, a very active translator (especially in his youth) and an original interpreter of Benjamin's "The Task of the Translator." Resistance to translation is how one recognizes national roots and the idiomatic character of a literary work. From this point of view, one should read the column devoted to German novels. It begins thus:

> There exists an excellent means that permits one to discover if a literary work either does or does not send its roots down into the depths of national feelings: it is to see whether it resists

31. De Man, "Le Destin de la Flandre," *Le Soir*, 1 Sept. 1941; hereafter abbreviated "F."

> translation. When a novel or a poem carries within itself these
> somewhat mysterious and undefinable virtues that make up the
> particular genius of a people, the most careful translation will
> never succeed in rendering the original.[32]

This problematic of translation is, moreover, in accordance with the
"comparatism" and the hierarchies (which, by the way, are very unstable) that we were evoking a moment ago. Notably, and in what is all
the same the most traditional fashion, between the Germanic spirit and
the Latin spirit. If "the most conscientious and most faithful translation cannot render the accent of the original work," it is in particular
because of

> the divergence between the rational and constructive French
> spirit and the German tendency toward the visionary, that does
> not stop at an objective consideration [of the sort de Man does
> not fail to call for elsewhere!], but penetrates regions where the
> laws of reason no longer hold. Thus, the virtues of clarity and
> harmony are lost. The novel [*Léonore Griebel*, by Hermann
> Stehr] is much less finished and less even than the work of Flau-
> bert. But one gains depth. . . . With the Latin, intelligence and
> rational reasoning prevail; with the Germanic, it is a stirring
> poetic intuition.[33]

Although it has to efface itself before the original text, the translation
ought not, therefore, to efface the fact that it is still a translation. One
ought to "feel that it is a translation." Hence the reproach addressed to
Betz, the translator of Rilke whom de Man already knew and appreci-
ated, when he translated Jünger (another of de Man's favorites) "too
well," to the point of making one forget that the original was written
in German, "which, especially when he recounts the story of a German
invading France, has something amazingly shocking about it."[34]

Between Germany and France, between these two "cultural blocks,"
Flemish nationalism should endeavor to save "that core that has given
humanity admirable products of an independent genius. The political
status of Flanders ought to be established in the new Europe in ac-

32. De Man, "Romans allemands," *Le Soir*, 10 Feb. 1942; hereafter abbreviated
"Ra."
33. Ibid.
34. De Man, "*Jardins et routes*, par Ernst Jünger," *Le Soir*, 23 June 1942.

cordance with this destiny" ("F"). Despite obvious affinities, this independent genius cannot be reduced to the German genius, and it is
clearly opposed to those ultra-French things that are "abstraction" and
"cerebralness" (remember this latter word; it occurs frequently and in
a moment we will see it applied to the Jew, not the Frenchman). Flemish genius manifests itself particularly in realist picturality, which does
not mean only painting but colorful plasticity even in literature, and
shows less interest in "abstract content." This is the "principal opposition between French and Flemish art." But the "attachment to external
forms rather than to cerebral analysis" has nothing "superficial" about
it. That is what Hegel says in his own way in the *Esthetics*. De Man
will later study that text closely, perhaps he already knows it when he
writes, in the service of Flemish genius—or any genius as it is tradition-
ally called: "This mentality has nothing superficial about it since the
external envelope of beings and objects, when it is seen by the careful
eye of genius that discovers all its resources, can reveal their deep meaning" ("F").

But *on the other hand*, already clearly enveloped, as we have indicated, by the cautious modality (more descriptive than prescriptive)
of the utterances, this nationalist demand is complicated, multiplied,
inverted in several ways. First of all, because, through the practice of
an abyssal logic of examplarity, the national affirmation *in general* is
caught up in the paradoxical necessity of respecting *the idiom in general*,
thus *all* idioms, all national differences. Next, because Flemish nationalism must resist both the French influence and the German influence.
Finally, because this young Fleming is also writing in French. If he is a
nationalist, his language, his training, and his literary preferences make
of him as much a nationalist of French culture as a Flemish nationalist.
This war and its fronts thus divide all the so-called early writings.

Because de Man *also* praises French individualism: it is "more analyst than organizer" and it "survives even if it no longer intends to play
an organizing role." It "remains a precious national character."[35] And
in the very text that speaks of the necessity for France to open itself to
"foreign influences" and to abandon "provincialism" [*l'esprit de clo-
cher*] (which are in themselves and out of context excellent recommen-
dations), praise of the "Latin spirit" compensates for and eloquently
overcodes the strategy of motifs that we quoted earlier, like the play
of forces that this strategy could serve. But let no one accuse me of
"dangerously simplifying": it is true that things can be reversed again,

35. De Man, "Littérature française."

a certain extreme right in France can also play the card of Latinity. Always the double edge. De Man has just spoken of "the lesson of a long humanist past that guards against any obscurantism" and he then continues, out of a concern, once again, not to "conform to the spirit of the day" and "the general orientation":

> It is on this last point that one sees the considerable role French genius may still be able to play. It cannot for a moment be a question of wanting to destroy or overlook, on the grounds that they do not conform to the spirit of the day, the virtues of clarity, logic, harmony that the great artistic and philosophic tradition of this country reflects. Maintaining the continuity of the French spirit is an inherent condition of Europe's grandeur. Particularly when the general orientation goes in the direction of profound, obscure, natural forces, the French mission, that consists in moderating excesses, maintaining indispensable links with the past, evening out erratic surges, is recognized to be of the utmost necessity. That is why it would be disastrous and stupid to destroy, by seeking to modify them by force, the constants of the Latin spirit. And it is also why we would be committing an unforgivable mistake if we cut our ties with the manifestations of this culture. ["PfS"]

Likewise, there are abundant warnings against narrow nationalism and jealous regionalism.[36] Will one say that these warnings can also serve German hegemony? Yet, in opposition to the latter, de Man defines a concept of an autonomous Flanders that will let itself be neither assimilated nor annexed by Germany as it was occasionally a question of doing. A moderate discourse, a differentiated position that rejects the "anti-Belgian spirit" of certain Flemish and sees the allegation of an "artificial and forced denationalization" of Flanders as a relic and a "myth." Once again from "The Destiny of Flanders":

> But the revisionist situation born of the present war causes various questions to bounce back again, questions that had been more or less skilfully settled before the conflict. And since the organizing force emanates from Germany, Flanders, for whom that country constitutes an eternal point of support, finds itself

36. "Art as Mirror" rejects "sentimental patriotism" and "narrow-minded regionalism."

placed in a peculiar situation. The memory of activism, when
Germany supported the Flemish in their legitimate claims, is still
too much alive not to provoke certain stirrings in an analogous
direction. Nevertheless, it should be pointed out that on this side
as well the danger of assimilation exists and all the more clearly
because affinities link the two races. As a result, the temptation
is even stronger for the Flemish to let themselves dissolve into a
Germanic community which risks effacing everything that constitutes their profound originality. It is for this reason that Mr.
Elias, burgomaster of Ghent, felt he had to react "against those
who wanted to extend the idea of the Germanic State to the re-
absorption of the Low Countries (Nederlanden) in an artificial
German community." ["F"]

It is true that the burgomaster's speech seems compelled to remain
within a contradiction, if I have understood it correctly, unless it is sig-
naling toward some confederation that, however, it does not name. As
for de Man, he merely quotes him:

> "Many no doubt fear that this would lead to the disappearance
> of the Flemish as a people and their leveling out as Germans. I
> have no hesitation about saying that such a conception could
> lead, in Flanders, to catastrophic results. . . . We can only be
> worthy members of a Germanic State as long as the State allows
> us to be worthy Netherlanders." ["F"]

3. On the one hand . . . on the other hand (third series of examples)

I will gather these examples around the article that appeared to me, as
to so many others, to be the most unbearable. I mean the article titled
"Les Juifs dans la littérature actuelle" (Jews in Present-day Literature).[37]
    Nothing in what I am about to say, analyzing the article as closely
as possible, will heal over the wound I right away felt when, my breath
taken away, I perceived in it what the newspapers have most frequently
singled out as recognized anti-Semitism, an anti-Semitism more serious than ever in such a situation, an anti-Semitism that would have
come close to urging exclusions, even the most sinister deportations.
Even if, in the texts already quoted, no pro-Nazism was ever declared,

---

37. De Man, "Les Juifs dans la littérature actuelle," *Le Soir,* 4 Mar. 1941; hereafter
abbreviated "Jla."

even if the disjunctions, the precautions, the complications seemed to protect against any simple allegiance, is not what we have here the most unquestionable manifestation of an anti-Semitism as violent as it is stereotyped? Does not this anti-Semitism take over from, so as to sharpen its coherence, the "racique" (rather than the racial) as it is frequently called in other texts? For example: the "historical, *racique*, and so forth, components that allow one to determine whether or not a people has a nationality worthy of being respected" ("F"), the "sensibility . . . intimately linked to the virtues of his race" ("Ra") (that of Hermann Stehr, author of *Léonore Griebel* that de Man is reviewing here). Does not the lack of vigilance regarding racism induce other articles to speak frequently of human "types," according to a familiar code which was not only that of Jünger (whom de Man admired and whom Heidegger criticized on this point in *Zur Seinsfrage*)? Whether or not he assumes it to his own account in the texts of commentaries, this vocabulary never seems to arouse suspicion when de Man speaks, rather pejoratively, of a "certain type of [French]man who was hearty and enterprising, sufficiently gifted to have been able to approach great problems without, however, being able to tolerate the intransigent demands made on true genius, a human type with an affection for friendship, irony" ("NaB"); or when he speaks, rather approvingly, of a "certain human type" or of a "personality-type" formed by "great renewals"; or the "creation of a new set of individual ideals" ("VfC"); or still again, paraphrasing Drieu La Rochelle, of "the creation of a radically new human type."[38] Even when he criticizes the individualist (French) conception of this "new type, human individual," de Man does not seem to distrust the constant reference to "type." Likewise, is not the logic of "The Jews in Present-day Literature," its praise for the "good health" and the "vitality" of a European literature that would keep its "intact originality" despite any "semitic interference" ("Jla"), coherent with the very frequent valorization of "vitality,"[39] of the "healthy" ("NaB"), of the "uncorrupted" ("Ra") as well as sometimes with the critique of abstraction and "cerebralness" here associated with Judaism? Is it not coherent with so many warnings against "outside influences" ("Ra")?

But let us now look more closely at an article that it will be better to quote *in extenso*.

On the one hand, it indeed seems to confirm the logic that we have

---

38. De Man, "*Notes pour comprendre le siècle*, par Drieu La Rochelle," *Le Soir*, 2 Dec. 1941.

39. Ibid.

just reconstituted. In effect, it describes the traits of what, according to some, are "degenerate and decadent, because *enjuivés* ['enjewished']" cultural phenomena, or yet again an "enjuivé" novel; he mentions the "important role" that the Jews have played in "the phony and disordered existence of Europe since 1920." He has recourse, following a well-known tradition, to the stereotypical description of the "Jewish spirit": "cerebralness," "capacity for assimilating doctrines while maintaining a certain coldness in the face of them." He notes that "Jewish writers have always remained in the second rank and, to speak only of France, the André Maurois's, the Francis de Croissets, the Henri Duvernois's, the Henri Bernsteins, Tristan Bernards, Julien Bendas, and so forth, are not among the most important figures, they are especially not those who have had any guiding influence on the literary genres" ("Jla"). And then, in a terrifying conclusion, the allusion to "a solution to the Jewish problem":

> The observation is, moreover, comforting for Western intellec-
> tuals. That they have been able to safeguard themselves from
> Jewish influence in a domain as representative of culture as lit-
> erature proves their vitality. If our civilization had let itself be
> invaded by a foreign force, then we would have to give up much
> hope for its future. By keeping, in spite of semitic interference in
> all aspects of European life, an intact originality and character,
> it has shown that its basic nature is healthy. What is more, one
> sees that a solution of the Jewish problem that would aim at
> the creation of a Jewish colony isolated from Europe would not
> entail, for the literary life of the West, deplorable consequences.
> The latter would lose, in all, a few personalities of mediocre
> value and would continue, as in the past, to develop according
> to its great evolutive laws. ["Jla"]

Will I dare to say "on the other hand" in the face of the *unpardonable* violence and confusion of these sentences? What could possibly attenuate the fault? And whatever may be the reasons or the complications of a text, whatever may be going on in the mind of its author, how can one deny that the effect of these conclusions went in the sense and the direction of the worst? In the *dominant* context in which they were read in 1941, did not their *dominant* effect go unquestionably in the direction of the worst? Of what we now know to have been the worst?

But one must have the courage to answer injustice with justice. And although one has to condemn these sentences, which I have just done, one ought not do it without examining everything that remains readable in a text one can judge to be disastrous. It is also necessary, when evaluating *this* act, *this* text (notice I do not say the life and work of its signatory which will never be reduced to this act, this text) to maintain a "certain coldness" and to take the trouble of that "work of lucid analysis" de Man associates with this "coldness" even as he attributes it, *in this very text*, to the Jews. As these traits are rules of intellectual responsibility rather than natural characteristics reserved to Jews and Frenchmen, does not the "work of analysis" have to be tirelessly pursued with "a certain coldness"? Therefore, I will dare to say, this time as before, "on the other hand."

Yes, *on the other hand* and *first of all*, the *whole* article is organized as an indictment of "vulgar antisemitism." It is, let us not forget, directed against that anti-Semitism, against its "lapidary judgment," against the "myth" it feeds or feeds on. In the first two paragraphs, which I am going to cite, de Man proceeds unquestionably toward a demystification, not without certain risks, of this vulgarity, of its "myth," of an "error" and a "very widespread opinion." Once again, as in the *Cahiers* and as he will always do, he takes on the "commonplace." Immediately after this critique, he continues with a "But . . ." ("But the reality is different.") This will then lead us to ask ourselves which reality interests him especially—and we will have to talk once again about literature. Here then is the uncompromising critique of "vulgar antisemitism" and of the contradiction, even of the boomerang effect to which the latter is exposed or which perhaps it already translates. I have just used the word "boomerang"; I could have said that de Man also designates the double edges of the said "vulgar antisemitism." These are the first two paragraphs, in which I hear some mockery:

> Vulgar antisemitism readily takes pleasure in considering postwar cultural phenomena (after the war of '14–18) as degenerate and decadent because they are *enjuivés*. Literature has not escaped this lapidary judgment: It has sufficed to discover a few Jewish writers behind Latinized pseudonyms for all of contemporary production to be considered polluted and harmful. This conception entails rather dangerous consequences. First of all, it condemns a priori a whole literature that in no way deserves this fate. What is more, from the moment one agrees that the

literature of our day has some merit, it would be a rather unflat-
tering appreciation of Western writers to reduce them to being
mere imitators of a Jewish culture that is foreign to them.

The Jews themselves have contributed to spreading this
myth. Often, they have glorified themselves as the leaders of literary movements that characterize our age. But the error has, in
fact, a deeper cause. At the origin of the thesis of a Jewish takeover is the very widespread belief according to which the modern
novel and modern poetry are nothing but a kind of monstrous
outgrowth of the world war. Since the Jews have, in fact, played
an important role in the phony and disordered existence of Europe since 1920, a novel born in this atmosphere would deserve,
up to a certain point, the qualification of *enjuivé*. ["Jla"]

Things are very serious. Rather than going too quickly, it would be better to run the risk of paraphrase and redundancy. What does this article
say? It is indeed a matter of criticizing vulgar anti-Semitism. That is the
primary, declared, and underscored intention. But to scoff at "vulgar
antisemitism," is that also to scoff at or mock the vulgarity of anti-
Semitism? This latter syntactic modulation leaves the door open to two
interpretations. To condemn vulgar anti-Semitism may leave one to understand that there is a distinguished anti-Semitism in whose name the
vulgar variety is put down. De Man never says such a thing, even though
one may condemn his silence. But the phrase can also mean something
else, and this reading can always contaminate the other in a clandestine
fashion: to condemn "vulgar anti-Semitism," *especially if one makes no
mention of the other kind*, is to condemn anti-Semitism itself *inasmuch
as* it is vulgar, always and essentially vulgar. De Man does not say that
either. If that is what he thought, a possibility I will never exclude, he
could not say so clearly in this context. One will say at this point: his
fault was to have accepted the context. Certainly, but what is that, to
accept a context? And what would one say if he claimed not to have
fully accepted it, and to have preferred to play the role there of the non-
conforming smuggler, as so many others did in so many different ways,
in France and in Belgium, at this or that moment, inside or outside the
Resistance? And I repeat, what is that, to *fully* accept a context? Because
this article, in any case, is nonconformist, as Paul de Man, as also his
uncle, always was. It is not particularly conformist to denounce anti-
Semitism, an anti-Semitism, whichever it may be, at that moment, in
that place, and to attribute to vulgar anti-Semitism the recognizable and
then widespread vocabulary of *all* anti-Semitism: "enjuivé," "degener-

ate," "decadent," "polluted," "harmful." At the very least, it is rather
anticonformist to add in the same breath, in the same sentences, that this
is a "lapidary judgment," that this anti-Semitism may have "dangerous
consequences," that what we have here is a "myth," an "error," that
these judgments turn back against the literature of those who pronounce
them and who from then on would give themselves away by talking,
finally, only about themselves. Already, in the second paragraph, the
argument that would consist in making the Jews coresponsible for this
antisemitic "myth" and this "error" is right away discredited. It was
evoked merely as a rhetorical ploy: "But the error has, in fact, a deeper
cause."

The logic of these first two paragraphs controls everything that follows: it is a matter of condemning anti-Semitism *inasmuch as it is vulgar*
(I leave this expression all its ambiguity, which is the ambiguity of the
article) and of condemning this anti-Semitism *as regards literature*: its
history, its own laws, its relations to history in general. It is as regards
literature that de Man wants to say something and obviously thinks he
has something original to say. He especially wants to talk about literature, here as elsewhere, and it is moreover literature that is his domain at
the newspaper. This is one of the early articles in *Le Soir*, where de Man
began writing about two months previously. I have yet to find any allusion to the Jewish problem or any declaration of anti-Semitism in any of
the other articles. Left to formulate hypotheses, I can imagine that, for a
page devoted to Judaism, he was asked to treat the subject from a literary point of view. What one can read on the same page surrounding this
article seems to me to support this hypothesis. One then notices that,
if de Man's article is necessarily contaminated by the forms of vulgar
anti-Semitism that frame it, *these coincide in a literal fashion, in their
vocabulary and logic, with the very thing that de Man accuses*, as if his
article were denouncing the neighboring articles, pointing to the "myth"
and the "errors," the "lapidary judgments," and the "very widespread
belief" that can be read just to one side, in another article in the same
issue ("Freudism"—and not Freud—as the product of a "particularly
keen Jewish intelligence," well received in "the intellectual and artistic
milieux of a decadent and *enjuivée* society"), as well as the declaration
no doubt falsely attributed to Benjamin Franklin: "A leopard cannot
change its spots. Jews are Asiatics; they are a threat to the country that
admits them and they should be excluded from the Constitution."

De Man wants especially to propose a thesis on literature that visibly interests him more here than either anti-Semitism or the Jews. But
before getting to that, a few points about vulgarity. It is a word and

a major motif in all the articles. An *ideology* dominated by a disdain for vulgarity can be evaluated in diverse and contradictory ways. We know these programs very well, so I may be spared further development. But one must be aware that de Man rejects all kinds of conformism of the period as so much "vulgarity" (the word was also a favorite of his uncle).[40] Once again the double edge. In his view, there can be no salvation for any "vulgarity." Read his "Propos sur la vulgarité artistique" (Remarks on artistic vulgarity). Behind the word vulgarity, and on almost every line, it is "our age" that is condemned, always in a fashion that cuts both ways: what "the radio, the cinema, publishing," even "the press" "undertake to unload on us"; and then there are "fake artists," "mechanized formulas that guarantee success with the masses," the "falseness of tone." That these are signs of aristocratism and estheticism is not at all in doubt, especially since de Man says so himself. Still one must be specific: this aristocratism is more esthetic than social, it is social *on the basis of* the esthetic, an esthetic determined *on the basis of* literature, even if music and painting play a considerable role. Although it intends "French letters" in particular, the conclusion of this article is eloquent in its every word: "Henri Pourrat represents something very pure and very precious within French letters: that regionalism of a noble attachment to the native soil which is the index of an authentic literary aristocracy."[41]

If his focus is on literature, what does de Man want to say about it? Why does he reproach vulgar anti-Semitism its mistake *as regards literature?* Why does he write "But the reality is different?" The following four paragraphs, which form the center and the thesis of the article, no longer contain the slightest allusion to Jews or to anti-Semitism. They speak only of literature, of its original historicity, and of the "very powerful laws" that govern "esthetic evolution." There is a history of art and of literature. It is essential and irreducible, but it maintains its

---

40. Henri de Man speaks, for example, of "pure Marxism and vulgar Marxism" in *The Psychology of Socialism*. The first is a "dead truth," the second is a "living error." Elsewhere, he writes:

> I despise all forms of vulgarization, of truth put within reach of those who prefer ersatz goods, radio and phonograph music, champagne for democratic banquets. . . . This confession might sound strange coming from the pen of a socialist, especially a former director of worker education programs. But socialism is not demagogy; and educating the people is not bringing science down to their level, but raising them to the level of science. Truths exist only for those who seek them.

(Henri de Man, foreword, *Au delà du marxisme* (Paris, 1926).

41. De Man, "Propos sur la vulgarité artistique," *Le Soir*, 6 Jan. 1942.

originality. It does not merge with sociopolitical history either in its rhythms or in its causal determinations. Historicism, and especially "vulgar" historicism, would consist in mapping one history onto the other, in ignoring the powerful structural constraints, the logics, forms, genres, methods, and especially the temporality proper to literary history, the duration of the waves within its depths that one must know how to listen for over and above the swirls and agitation of the immediate, to listen for the sounds coming from the "artistic life" there where it is "little swayed" by the waves of the present. Literary duration enfolds and unfolds itself otherwise, in a way that differs from the phenomena of sociopolitical history in the brief sequences of their events: it precedes them, sometimes succeeds them, in any case it exceeds them. This notion compromises all the ideologies of literature, even the opinions or the propaganda on the subject of literature whenever they would attempt to enclose themselves in a strictly determined context ("current affairs"). Whether they are revolutionary or not, on the left or the right, these ideological discourses speak of everything except literature itself. Sometimes, from "within" literature itself, manifest discourses of certain literary movements ("surrealism" or "futurism") are, precisely in the form of their "manifestos," ideological or doxical in this sense. They also mistake the historicity proper to literature, the ample rhythms of its tradition, the discreet convolutions of its "evolution": in sum, a "vulgar" approach to literature.[42]

There would be much to say in a closely argued discussion around this question: literature, history, and politics. Here I must restrict myself to *three points*.

1. Debatable or not, this interesting and consistent thesis concerns, then, first of all the historicity proper to literature and the arts. Forming the central body of the article which has no relation with any "Jewish question" whatsoever, it develops as a theoretical demonstration in three moments: (a) general propositions on art; (b) illustration using the privileged example of the novel; (c) "analogous demonstration" with the example of poetry.

2. In 1941, under the German occupation, and first of all in the context of this newspaper, the *presentation* of such a thesis (for pre-

42. This is a remarkably constant de Manian concern up until the final articles, and notably the article titled "Continuité de la poesie française: À propos de la revue 'Messages'" (Continuity of French poetry: On the journal "Messages"), *Le Soir*, 14 July 1942. The journal *Messages*, which was banned off and on in France, was published and made known in Belgium with Paul de Man's help. See below concerning the journal *Exercice du Silence*, which was apparently the title of the third issue of this journal.

cisely the reasons that some today would judge it to be "formalist" or "estheticist" or in any case too concerned about protecting "literarity," if not from all history, as we saw that is not the case, then at least from a sociopolitical history and against ideology) goes rather against the current. One can at least read it as an anticonformist attack. Its insolence can take aim at and strike all those who were then, in an active and properly punitive fashion, undertaking to judge literature and its history, indeed to administer, control, censor them in function of the dominant ideology of the war or, as de Man puts it, of a "profound upheaval in the political and economic world."

3. The examples chosen (Gide, Kafka, Lawrence, Hemingway, surrealism, futurism) are troubling in this context. They are visibly invoked as great canonic examples on the basis of which, beyond any possible question, one ought to be able to say what literature *is*, what writers and literary movements *do*. We know from many other signs, his articles in the *Cahiers* for example, that these writers were already important references for de Man. The examples chosen are already curious and insolent because there are no others, because there is no German example, because the French example is Gide, the American Hemingway, the English Lawrence, and because Kafka is Jewish, but especially because they represent everything that Nazism or the right wing revolutions would have liked to extirpate from history and the great tradition. Now, what does de Man say? That these writers and these movements were already canonical: they belong to tradition, they have "orthodox ancestors," whether one likes it or not, whether they recognize it themselves or not. Taking the risk of a certain traditionalism (always the double edge), de Manian genealogy reinscribes all of these "accursed ones" in the then protective legitimacy of the canon and in the great literary family. It lifts them out of repression's way and it does so in an exemplary fashion since, he says, "the list could be extended indefinitely." I have said why I will cite this article *in extenso*. Here are the central paragraphs, where I have underlined the "buts," "But the reality," "in reality":

> *But the reality* is different. It seems that esthetic evolution obeys very powerful laws that continue their action even when humanity is shaken by considerable events. The world war has brought about a profound upheaval in the political and economic world. *But* artistic life has been swayed relatively little, and the forms that we know at present are the logical and normal successors to what there had been before.
>
> This is particularly clear as concerns the novel. Stendhal's

definition, according to which "the novel is a mirror carried along a highway," contains within it the law that still today rules this literary genre. There was first the obligation to respect reality scrupulously. *But* by digging deeper, the novel has gotten around to exploring psychological reality. Stendhal's mirror no longer remains immobile the length of the road: it undertakes to search even the most secret corners of the souls of characters. And this domain has shown itself to be so fruitful in surprises and riches that it still constitutes the one and only terrain of investigation of the novelist.

Gide, Kafka, Hemingway, Lawrence—the list could be extended indefinitely—all do nothing but attempt to penetrate, according to methods proper to their personality, into the secrets of interior life. Through this characteristic, they show themselves to be, not innovators who have broken with all past traditions, *but* mere continuers who are only pursuing further the realist esthetic that is more than a century old.

An analogous demonstration could be made in the domain of poetry. The forms that seem to us most revolutionary, such as surrealism or futurism, *in reality* have orthodox ancestors from which they cannot be detached. ["Jla"]

Now let us look closely at what happens in the last paragraph of this central demonstration, that is in the conclusion of a sort of syllogism. No more than the central body of the article (the paragraphs just quoted), the *general* scope of the conclusion, I mean conclusion in its general and theoretical form, is not concerned with the Jews. It does not name them in this general formulation. This conclusion concerns—and contests—an "absurd" *general* theorem regarding current literature, an absurdity that is denounced, precisely, as the axiom of antisemitism inasmuch as it is vulgar. And this conclusion announces by means of a "Therefore . . ." what must be deduced from the preceding demonstration: "Therefore, one may see that to consider present-day literature as an isolated phenomenon created by the particular mentality of the 20s is absurd."

And so we arrive at the last paragraph of the article, the most serious and in fact the only one that can be suspected of anti-Semitism. There, the return to the question of "Jews in present-day literature" corresponds to the rhetoric of a supplementary or analogical example. It comes to the aid of a general thesis or antithesis opposed to vulgar anti-Semitism. The demonstration that matters is considered established.

De Man adds: "Likewise, the Jews. . . ." Next, and still without wanting to attenuate the violence of this paragraph that for me remains disastrous, let us remark this: even as he reminds us of the limits of "Jewish influence," of "semitic interference," even as, however, he seems to turn the discourse over to "Western intellectuals" by reconstituting their anxieties and then reassuring them, the manner in which he describes the "Jewish spirit" remains unquestionably positive. Even in its stereotyped, and therefore equivocal form, it is presented as a statement that no one is supposed to be able to question: a classical technique of contraband. For who, at that time, could dispense in public with *disputing* such praise? Who could publicly subscribe to it? Well, de Man does not dispute it; on the contrary, he assumes it. Even better, he himself underscores a *contradiction* that cannot go unnoticed and has to leave some trace in the consciousness or the unconscious of the reader:

> one might have expected that, given the specific characteristics of the Jewish spirit, the latter would have played a more brilliant role in this artistic production. Their cerebralness, their capacity to assimilate doctrines while maintaining a certain coldness in the face of them, would seem to be very precious qualities for the work of lucid analysis that the novel demands. ["Jla"]

One can hardly believe one's eyes: would this mean that what he prefers in the novel, "the work of lucid analysis," and in theory, a "certain coldness" of intelligence, correspond precisely to the qualities of the "Jewish spirit"? And that the "precious qualities" of the latter are indispensable to literature and theory? What is coiled up and resonating deep within this sentence? Did one hear that correctly? In any case, de Man does not say the contrary. And he clearly describes what were in his eyes "precious qualities." (Was he then recognizing the qualities of the enemy or those in which he would have liked to recognize himself? Later, these were the qualities his American enemies always attributed to him.)

The last lines, the most terrible, begin with another "But in spite of that. . . ." They are attacking once again, let us not forget, the anti-Semitic obsession that always needs, that has a compulsive and significant need, to *overevaluate* the Jewish influence on literature. Here is the final paragraph:

> Therefore, one may see that to consider present-day literature as an isolated phenomenon created by the particular mentality of the 20s is absurd. Likewise, the Jews cannot claim to have been

its creators, nor even to have exercised a preponderant influence over its development. On any somewhat close examination, this influence appears even to have extraordinarily little importance since one might have expected that, given the specific character-istics of the Jewish spirit, the latter would have played a more brilliant role in this artistic production. Their cerebralness, their capacity to assimilate doctrines while keeping a certain cold-ness in the face of them, seemed to be very precious qualities for the work of lucid analysis that the novel demands. But in spite of that, Jewish writers have always remained in the sec-ond rank and, to speak only of France, the André Maurois's, the Francis de Croissets, the Henri Duvernois's, the Henri Bern-steins, Tristan Bernards, Julien Bendas, and so forth, are not among the most important figures, they are especially not those who have had any guiding influence on the literary genres. The observation is, moreover, comforting for Western intellectuals. That they have been able to safeguard themselves from Jewish influence in a domain as representative of culture as literature proves their vitality. If our civilization had let itself be invaded by a foreign force, then we would have to give up much hope for its future. By keeping, in spite of semitic interference in all aspects of European life, an intact originality and character, that civilization has shown that its basic nature is healthy. What is more, one sees that a solution of the Jewish problem that would aim at the creation of a Jewish colony isolated from Europe would not entail, for the literary life of the West, deplorable consequences. The latter would lose, in all, a few personalities of mediocre value and would continue, as in the past, to develop according to its great evolutive laws. ["Jla"]

Through the indelible wound, one must still analyze and seek to understand. Any concession would betray, besides a complacent indul-gence and a lack of rigor, an infinitely culpable thoughtlessness with regard to past, present, or future victims of discourses that at least re-sembled this one. I have said why I am not speaking here as a judge, witness, prosecutor, or defender in some *trial of Paul de Man*. One will say: but you are constantly delivering judgments, you are evaluating, you did so just now. Indeed, and therefore I did not say that I would not do so at all. I said that in analyzing, judging, evaluating this or that discourse, this or that effect of these old fragments, I refused to extend these gestures to a general judgment, with no possibility of appeal, of

Paul de Man, of the totality of what he was, thought, wrote, taught, and so forth. I continue thus to ask myself questions. If I persist in wondering how, in what conditions he wrote this, it is because even in the sum total of the articles from that period that I have been able to read, I have found no remark analogous or identical to this one. I did not even find any allusion to the Jews or to some "Jewish problem." Or rather, yes: in May 1941, some remarkable and emphatic praise for Péguy the Dreyfusard.[43] How is one to explain that? Who will ever know how this text was written and published? Who can exclude what happens so often in newspapers, and especially during that period and in those conditions, when editors can always intervene at the last moment? If that was the case, Paul de Man is no longer here to testify to it. But at that point one can say: supposing this to have been the case, there was still a way of protesting which would have been to end his association with the newspaper. Yes, but he would have had to be certain that this rupture was a better idea than his ambiguous and sometimes anticonformist continuation on the job. He would also have had to evaluate the gravity of the last lines of this article as we are doing today. Now, in order to evaluate them correctly, we must understand what this allusion to "a Jewish colony isolated from Europe" meant at that moment. I admit that, in the present state of my information, I do not understand it. To which "solution," to which hypothesis that was perhaps current at the time was he making allusion? I do not know; perhaps to what was called the "Madagascar solution." As of that date (4 March 1941), the word "solution" could not be associated with what we now know to have been the project of the "final solution": the latter was conceived and put into effect later. At the end of 1942, Paul de Man stops contributing to the newspaper *Le Soir* (to my knowledge, he publishes nothing else during the war and he explains this in a letter that I will cite later). The same year, Henri de Man had left Belgium and given up all public responsibility.

Last September, then, this first reading and this first series of questions led me to an interpretation that is itself divided by what I have called "double bind," "disjunction," and especially "double edge," each term of this division never coming to rest in a monadic identity. The experi-

43. De Man, "Charles Péguy," *Le Soir*, 6 May 1941. The unmitigated praise for this "genius" who was "notoriously independent and undisciplined" is organized completely around the Dreyfus affair. In the portrait of Péguy the Dreyfusard, and in the history of (Péguy's) *Cahiers*, one cannot fail to remark all the quasi-autobiographical traits that de Man seems to take pleasure in proliferating.

ence of the double edge can be an ironic ruse on one side, a painful suffering on the other, and finally one and the other at every moment. But in what I have read of these texts, as in what I had learned to know earlier of Paul de Man and which it was difficult for me to abstract, nothing ever authorized me to translate this division into a hypocriti- cal, cynical, or opportunistic duplicity. First of all, because this kind of duplicity was, to a degree and with a clarity that I have rarely encoun- tered in my life, alien to Paul de Man. His irony and his anticonformist burst of laughter took instead the form of insolent provocation—one which was, precisely, cutting. One feels something of that in these "early writings." Second, because cynical opportunism is another form of ac- quiescence; it is profoundly conformist and comfortable, the opposite of the double edge. Finally because all of that would have continued after 1942. And this was not the case; the rupture was unquestionably a cut. I have the sense that de Man, in whom a certain analytical coldness always cohabited with passion, fervor, and enthusiasm, must have, like his uncle, obeyed his convictions—which were also those of his uncle: complicated, independent, mobile, in a situation that he thought, incor- rectly as did many others, offered no other way out after what seemed, up until 1942, like the end of the war.

So I will continue my story. For my own part, I was quickly con- vinced at the end of August that what had just been discovered could not and should not be kept secret. As quickly and as radically as possible, it was necessary to make these texts accessible to everyone. The neces- sary conditions had to be created so that everyone could read them and interpret them in total freedom. No limit should be set on the discussion. Everyone should be in a position to take his or her responsibilities. For one could imagine in advance the effect that these "revelations" were going to produce, at least in the American university. One did not have to have second sight to foresee even the whole specter of reactions to come. For the most part, they have been programmed for a long time— and the program is simple enough to leave little room for surprises. I was also conscious of the fact that the serious interpretation of these texts and their context would take a lot of time. All the more reason not to delay. I discuss it, once again in Paris, with Sam Weber. I suggest that we take advantage of a colloquium that is supposed to take place a few weeks later at the University of Alabama in Tuscaloosa in order to discuss the matter with about twenty colleagues. It is appropriately a colloquium dealing with academic institutions and politics ("Our Aca- demic Contract: The Conflict of the Faculties in America") and bringing together, *among others*, some former students and colleagues of Paul de

Man. Sam Weber agrees, as does Ortwin de Graef from whom I request authorization to distribute to all these colleagues photocopies of the articles I have just described. Richard Rand, the organizer of the colloquium, also agrees and makes the necessary arrangements. On 10 October, all the colloquium's participants having read these texts, we had a discussion that lasted more than three hours and touched on both the substance of things and the decisions to be made. I cannot summarize the discussion, all of which was tape-recorded.

Whatever may have been the remarks of the various people, no one, it seems to me, questioned the necessity of making these texts widely accessible and to do everything to permit a serious, minute, patient, honest study of them, as well as an open discussion. What remained to be decided was the best technical conditions in which to accomplish this. In the weeks that followed, broad exchanges led us to confide to Werner Hamacher, Neil Hertz, and Thomas Keenan the task of completing the collection of articles, of preparing their publication, as well as that of a volume in which as many as possible of those who wished to do so could communicate their reflections, whatever may have been their relation to Paul de Man and his work. A letter of invitation was addressed to this effect to numerous colleagues, known for their competence or for the interest they might have in the problem and, let me underscore this point, whatever may have been the extent, the form, or the premises of their agreement or their disagreement with the person or the work of de Man. These two volumes will appear soon. Even though they constitute merely the beginning of work that will have to be long term and opened to still more people, no one will doubt, I hope, the wish of those who took the initiative for it: to allow everyone to take his or her responsibilities in the clearest possible conditions. Nevertheless, as one could also foresee and as Werner Hamacher has since written to me, those who took this initiative have found themselves faced with a double accusation that is both typical and contradictory: on the one hand, of betraying Paul de Man, and, on the other hand, of protecting him; on the one hand, of exposing him in great haste to the violence of the most expeditious lapidary judgments, even to a symbolic lapidation and, on the other hand, of wanting to save his work and, at the same time, defend all those for whom, in one way or another, it is important. I can understand this double accusation and the indications it alleges in support. But it seems to me perverse and inevitably unjust. First of all because one cannot do both of these things at once. You could not succeed in doing both of them even if you tried. Second, because those who launch one or the other of these accusations are themselves, necessarily, doing one or the other by obeying one or the other of these motivations. So as to explain how, as I see it, neither one nor the other of these intentions should enter into things, I will quote now, in its literal and integral transcription, what I tried to say at the outset of the discussion in Tuscaloosa. After an account that corresponds, for the facts although not for the reading of the texts, to the one I have just given, I added this in French (which, because it is part of the archive, I think I have to include in my narration):

I insist on improvising. For the last two months, I have not stopped thinking in a quasi-obsessional fashion about this, but I preferred not to prepare what I am going to say. I think it is necessary this evening that everyone tell us, speaking personally and after a first analysis, what he or she thinks of these things. On the other hand, I wanted to tell you what my own feeling is. I have known Paul de Man since 1966. You know of the friendship that we shared since then. I knew that he had lived through some difficult times when he left Belgium for the United States. We never spoke of what happened during the war. We were very close, from a certain point of view, but because our friendship remained very discreet, I never felt indiscreet enough to ask him about what had happened then, even though, like many others, I knew that this had been a [singular? inaudible word] moment in his personal, private but also public (professional, et cetera) history. But I want to begin there: never in the course of these fifteen or sixteen years did I read anything of his nor hear anything from him that leaves the least suspicion in my memory as to any persistence of, let us say—how to name it?—a certain ideology, readable for me in the texts I read with you, in the texts published in French, the only ones I have been able to read directly. On the contrary, everything I can remember of the texts he published afterward and of conversations I had with him, of all the evaluations of different sorts (social, political, et cetera) leave me with the certainty that he had in any case broken in a radical, internal, rigorous way with anything whatsoever that one might suspect in the ideology of the texts we are going to talk about. I wanted thus to begin by setting temporal limits on the things we are going to talk about. I wanted to set out that everything indicates, in any case for me, that along with what there may be that is shocking in these texts (and I do not hide that), he had broken radically with all that and there was no trace to my knowledge either in his life or in his remarks or in his texts that allows one to think the opposite.

He broke with what happened when he was between twenty-one and twenty-three years old. I realize that we will now be able to read all his published texts, everyone will do so, us in particular, the texts we already know, while trying, some will do it with malevolence, with an unhealthy jubilation, others will do it otherwise, to find in the published texts signs referring back to that period.

Even as I improvise and in a somewhat confused way, I would like to say the following: I think there is a continuity and I would like to be specific. Paul de Man is someone who had that experience, who asked himself the questions that are asked in those texts, and who at twenty-one or twenty-three years old, brought to them the answers that are in these texts. He thus went through this experience which is not just any experience, he read the texts you know about, he wrote what you now know.

It is out of the question to imagine that the rupture means all of that is erased. All of it is part of his experience. In my opinion, he must have drawn a certain number of lessons from it: historical, political, rhetorical, of all sorts; and besides the rupture, this lesson must in effect be readable in his texts. It is one thing to read it as a lesson; it would be another to amalgamate everything, as some, I imagine, will perhaps be tempted to do, calling it a continuity, in which nothing happens without leaving traces, from these texts to those that followed. Our responsibility, in any case mine, would be to analyze all these texts, those from Le Soir. We do not have them all and some of them are much more convoluted, complicated, others are simple and unfortunately readable, but others are convoluted, complicated. Those who are seriously interested in the question will have to take the time to work on, analyze those texts, then the texts published in the U.S., with the greatest rigor and attention to detail. I have decided to improvise because I have taken as a rule to ally urgency with patience. It is urgent that we (perhaps I am forcing things by saying we, please excuse me), that some of us hasten to take their responsibilities as regards these texts, to be the first to show that there is no question of dissimulating them or of participating in any kind of camouflage operation. It is urgent that, in one mode or another, no doubt the mode of improvisation, we make the thing public, but it is also urgent that, while doing this, we call upon ourselves and those who are interested in the thing, the well-intentioned and the ill-intentioned, to look at them closely, to undertake a reflection on the substance of what made this possible, for Paul de Man and for others, and of what the rupture with that means for someone like Paul de Man, only a part of whose work (or life) we know. We have a lot of work before us if we are to know what actually happened, not only in the political, ideological fabric of Belgium at the time, but also in the life of Paul de Man.

Two more things, perhaps three. Rethinking about all of this in an obsessional way and with much, how to say, worry, consternation, the feeling that wins out over all the others in my bereaved friendship, bereaved once again, is, I have to say, first of all a feeling of immense compassion. Through these texts and through other things [inaudible] of what must have been Paul de Man's life during the ten years from 1940–50, through the ruptures, exile, the radical reconversion, what I begin to see clearly is, I imagine and I don't think I am wrong, an enormous suffering, an agony, that we cannot yet know the extent of. And I must say after having read these pages written by a young man of twenty-one or twenty-two (I do not mention his age in order to clear him or attenuate anything: at twenty-one or twenty-two, one takes responsibilities and, notably in that situation; people have pointed out, and they are right, that certain young men of twenty or twenty-one took adult responsibilities, in the Resistance, for example, or elsewhere. Thus, when I mention his age, it is not so as to say "he was a child.") Nevertheless, what appears clearly is that, in a situation that we will have to describe, that of occupied Europe from which hope seemed banished except for a few, through a reflection on what might be the spirit [inaudible] we were talking about earlier[44] and under the influence of his uncle (about whom we will certainly have much to say, perhaps not tonight but later), a young man with clearly an immense culture, gifted, brilliant, exceptional, became involved in all that, we'll talk about this some more, and then found that he had to break with it and turn everything almost upside down, through problems that were also personal problems, indissociable from this whole story. This man must have lived a real agony and I believe that what he wrote later, what he taught, what he lived through in the United States obviously carry the traces of this suffering. I want to say that whatever may be—how to say—the wound that these texts are for me, they have changed nothing in my friendship and admiration for Paul de Man.

One more thing: some of us might think that, having broken with what he said and did under his signature at that time, Paul de Man tried, in the United States at any rate, to hide the thing. The fact is that we did not speak about it and that to my knowledge he did not speak about it

---

44. This is an allusion to the lecture I had given the same afternoon on Heidegger (questions of spirit, of Nazism, of nationalism, of language, of the destiny of Europe, and so forth).

*very much. Perhaps he spoke to some people we do not know, but in any
case to most of those here he never spoke about these things. If he did,
then people will be able to say so.*

*But we do know, and Tom Keenan can confirm this in a moment,
that in 1955 while de Man was at Harvard, there was an anonymous
denunciation concerning his activity in Belgium during the war. And de
Man explained himself at that moment, in a letter of which we have at
least the draft, to the Head of the Society of Fellows.*[45] *This is a public
act with which he explained himself on these matters. It is a long letter
from which we can extract at least this: in effect during the German
occupation, in 1940–42, he maintained a literary column, but when the
pressure of German censorship became too much—Tom will read this
in a moment—he ceased writing and did what decency demanded that
he do. Naturally, we are not obliged to give credence to this presentation
of the thing, his version of the facts, in this letter. I don't know. We are,
for those who are interested in it, at the beginning of a long movement
of approach. But whatever the case may be, whether or not this letter
speaks the whole truth about what happened then, about the reasons
for which he wrote and then stopped writing, about these texts, what
they are or are not, that is less important for the moment and for what
I want to say, than the fact in any case (1) that he did explain himself
publicly; (2) that he indicated what his evaluation of the thing was, that
is, that he wished in 1955 never to have done anything that could be
suspected of Nazism or collaboration. He explains himself, he broke
with that and there can be no doubt about the kind of look he himself
casts at that time at least on the period in question and on the ideological implications that one may read in these texts. He explained himself
publicly and in my opinion that is a reason, whatever we might do from
now on, not to organize today a trial of Paul de Man. I would consider
it absolutely out of place, ridiculous, strictly ridiculous, to do something*

45. De Man, letter to Renato Poggioli, Director of the Harvard Society of Fellows,
25 Jan. 1955 (from a draft dated Sept. 1954). Here is an extract from this draft that no
doubt will be published: "In 1940 and 1941 I wrote some literary articles in the newspaper "Le Soir" and, I like most of the other contributors, stopped doing so when nazi
thought-control did no longer allow freedom of statement. During the rest of the occupation I did what was the duty of any decent person." According to Charles Dosogne, a
contemporary and friend of de Man, "beginning at the end of September 1940, preliminary censorship by the Propaganda Abteilung was limited to important political articles.
Literary columns were thus exempted from this, at least until August 1942—date at
which censorship was reestablished. It was at this moment that Paul de Man's activities
as a journalist ceased" (letter to Neil Hertz, 11 Jan. 1988). It seems, however, that they
continued a few months longer.

(I am not saying this for us but for others) that would look like a trial, after the death of Paul de Man, for texts that, whatever they may be (we will come back to this) he wrote when he was between twenty-one and twenty-three years old, in conditions with which he absolutely and radically broke afterward. I think that anything that would look like such a trial would be absolutely indecent and the jubilation with which some may hasten to play that game ought to be denounced. In any case, personally, I plan to denounce it in the most uncompromising manner.

These are the preliminary things that I wanted to say to you. On the texts you read, there will be much, very much to say, but I do not want to keep the floor any longer. I will take it again when the time comes on the subject of the texts. I already have an extremely complicated relation to these texts. There are things that are massively obvious to me and that seem to me to call for a denunciation whose protocols are rather clear. But these things are woven into a very complex fabric, one that deserves, not only this evening, but beyond this evening the most serious and careful analyses.

Before going to the end of my story, I want to be more specific about certain points touched on in this improvisation. First, about Paul de Man's silence. Although, as I mentioned, it was not absolute, although it was publicly broken on at least one occasion and thus cannot be understood in the sense of a dissimulation, although I have since learned that it was also broken on other occasions, in private, with certain colleagues and friends, I am left to meditate, endlessly, on all the reasons that induced him not to speak of it more, for example to *all* his friends. What could the ordeal of this mutism have been, for him? I can only imagine it. Having explained himself once publicly and believing he had demonstrated the absurdity of certain accusations in the Harvard letter, why would he himself have incited, spontaneously, a public debate on this subject?

Several reasons could both dissuade and discourage him from doing so. He was aware of having never collaborated or called for collaboration with a Nazism that he never even named in his texts, of having never engaged in any criminal activity or even any organized political activity, in the strict sense of the term, I mean in a public organization or in a political administration. Therefore, to provoke spontaneously an explanation on this subject was no longer an obligation. It would have been, moreover, an all the more distressing, pointlessly painful theatricalization in that he had not only broken with the political context of 1940–42, but had distanced himself from it with all his might, in his language, his country, his profession, his private life. His international notoriety having spread only during the last years of his life, to exhibit earlier such a distant past so as to call the public as a witness—would that not have been a pretentious, ridiculous, and infinitely complicated gesture? All of these articles, whose disconcerting structure we have glimpsed, would have had to be taken up again and analyzed under a microscope. He would have had himself to convoke the whole world to a great philologico-political symposium on his own "early writings," even though he was only recognized by a small university elite. I would understand that he might have found this to be indiscreet and indecent. And this modesty is more like him than a deliberate will to hide or to falsify. I even imagine him in the process of analyzing with an implacable irony the simulacrum of "confession" to which certain people would like to invite him after the fact, after his death, and the autojustification and auto-accusation quivering with pleasure which form the abyssal program of such a self-exhibition. He has said the essential on this subject and I invite those who wonder about his silence to read, among other texts, "Excuses (*Confessions*)" in *Allegories of Reading*. The first sentence announces what "political and autobiographical texts have in common"[46] and the conclusion explains again the relations between irony and allegory so as to render an account (without ever being able to account for it sufficiently) of this: "Just as the text can never stop apologizing for the suppression of guilt that it performs, there is never enough knowledge available to account for the delusion of knowing" (*A*, p. 300). In the interval, between the first and last sentences, at the heart of this text which is also the last word of *Allegories of Reading*, everything is said. Or at least almost everything one can say about the reasons for which a totalization is impossible: ironically, allegorically, and *en abyme*. Since I cannot quote everything, I will limit myself to recalling this citation of Rousseau, in a note. The note is to a phrase that names the "nameless avengers" (*A*, p. 288). Nameless? Minus the crime, (almost) everything is there, the count is there and it is almost correct, I mean almost the exact number of years: "'If this crime can be redeemed, as I hope it may, it must be by the many misfortunes that have darkened the later part of my life, by forty years of upright and honorable behavior under difficult circumstances'" (*A*, p. 288).

Even if sometimes a murmur of protest stirs in me, I prefer, upon reflection, that he chose not to take it on himself to provoke, during his

---

46. De Man, *Allegories of Reading: Figural Language in Rousseau, Nietzsche, Rilke, and Proust* (New Haven, Conn., 1979), p. 278; hereafter abbreviated *A*.

life, this spectacular and painful discussion. It would have consumed his time and energy. He did not have very much and that would have deprived us of a part of his work. Since it is at the moment of his greatest notoriety that this "demonstration" would have had some legitimacy, we do not know what price he would have had to pay for it. We do not know to what extent it would have weakened him or distracted him from his last works, which are among the most remarkable, when he was already ill. So he did the right thing, I say to myself, by leaving us also with this heavy and obscure part of the legacy. We owe it to him and we will owe him still more since what he leaves us is also the gift of an ordeal, the summons to a work of reading, historical interpretation, ethico-political reflection, an interminable analysis. Well beyond the sequence 1940–42. In the future and for the future, I mean also the future of philosophico-political reflection, this will not do anybody any harm. Especially not those who, if they want still to accuse or take revenge, will finally have to read de Man, from A to Z. Had they done so? Would they have done so otherwise? It is now unavoidable. You will have understood that I am speaking of transference and prosopopeia, of that which goes and returns only to the other, without any possible reappropriation, for anyone, of his own voice or his own face.

Permit me an ellipsis here since I do not have much more time or space. Transference and prosopopeia, like the experience of the undecidable, seem to make a responsibility impossible. It is for that very reason that they require it and perhaps subtract it from the calculable program: they give it a chance. Or, inversely: responsibility, if there is any, requires the experience of the undecidable as well as that irreducibility of the other, some of whose names are transference, prosopopeia, allegory. There are many others. And the double edge and the double bind, which are other phenomena of the undecidable. Before answering, responding for oneself, and *for* that purpose, in order to do so, one must respond, answer to the other, about the other, *for* the other, not in his place as if in the place of another "proper self," but *for* him. My ellipsis here, my economical aphorism, is a thought for all these "fors" that make responsibility *undeniable: there is some, one cannot deny it, one cannot/can only deny it [on ne peut (que) la dénier] precisely because it is impossible.*

Yes, to read him, that is the task. How shall one do that from now on? Everyone will go about it in his or her own way, the paths open are so many, the work is spreading and becoming more and more differentiated, and no one has any advice to give anyone. Therefore, at the moment of beginning to read or to reread Paul de Man, I will mention only a few of the rules that impose themselves on me today.

First of all, of course, to take account of what we have just discovered, to try to reconstitute this whole part of the corpus (I have mentioned only a few articles) without overlooking any of the "internal" or "contextual" overdeterminations ("public" and "private" situation, if possible—without forgetting what de Man has said about this distinction), in the direction, for example, of "Belgium during the war" and everything that can be transferred onto the uncle. But taking the 1940–42 articles into account does not mean giving them a disproportionate importance while minimizing the immensity of the rest, in a landscape that would look like those geographical maps of the Middle Ages or the territorial representations organized around a local, immediate, distorting perception. (I am thinking of those projections by Saul Steinberg where a New York street looks larger than the United States, not to mention the rest of the world.) How can one forget de Man's world, and first of all the United States? And the map of all his great voyages? The texts of 1940–42 can also be represented there as a minuscule point.

Next, without ever forgetting or overlooking these first articles (how could I?), I would try to *articulate* them with the work to come while avoiding, if possible, two more or less symmetrical errors.

One would consist in interpreting the rupture between the two moments of de Man's history and work as an interruption of any passage, an interdiction against any contamination, analogy, translation. In that case, one would be saying: no relation, sealed frontier between the two, absolute heterogeneity. One would also be saying: even if there were two moments, they do not belong to history, to the same history, to the history of the "work." There would have been a prehistory, some politico-journalistic accidents, then history and the work. This attitude would be giving in to defensive denegation, it would deprive itself of interpretive resources, including the political dimension of the work. Most important, by annuling the so-called prehistory, it would compound its own political frivolity by an injustice toward Paul de Man: what he lived through then was serious, probably decisive and traumatic in his life, and I will never feel I have the right, on the pretext of protecting him from those who would like to abuse it, of treating the experience of the war as a minor episode.

I would also try to avoid the opposite error: confusing everything while playing at being an authorized prosecutor or clever inquisitor.

We know from experience that these compulsive and confusionist practices—amalgam, continuism, analogism, teleologism, hasty totalization,
reduction, and derivation—are not limited to a few hurried journalists.

So I would make every effort to avoid giving in to the typical temptation of a discourse that seeks to shore up this shaky certainty: everything
is already there in the "early writings," everything derives from them
or comes down to them, the rest was nothing but their pacifying and
diplomatic translation (the pursuit of the same war by other means). As
if there were no more difference of level, no displacement, a fortiori no
fundamental rupture during these forty years of exile, reflection, teaching, reading, or writing! The crudeness of an enterprise guided by such
a principle (that, precisely, of the worst totalitarian police) can seek to
hide behind more or less honest tricks and take purely formal precautions on the subject of the too-obvious differences. But it cannot fool
anyone for long. It is not even necessary here to recall de Man's own
warnings against such foolishness or such trickery, against the models
of a certain historicism, or against the forms of causality, derivation, or
narration that still crowd these dogmatic somnambulisms. When one
is seeking, at all costs, to reconstruct in an artificial way genealogical
continuities or totalities, then one has to interpret discontinuity as a conscious or unconscious ruse meant to hide a persistence or a subsistence,
the stubborn repetition of an originary project (what this is is good old
existential psychoanalysis of the immediate postwar period!). Why is
this totalitarian logic essentially triumphant? Triumphalist? And made
strong by its very weakness? Why is it recognizable by its tone and its
affect? Because it authorizes itself to interpret everything that resists it in
every line, in Paul de Man's work or elsewhere, and resists it to the point
of disqualifying or ridiculing it, as the organization of a defensive resistance, precisely, in the face of its own inquisition. For example, when de
Man demonstrates theoretically (and more than just theoretically, but
beyond constative or cognitive logic, precisely) that a historical totalization is impossible and that a certain fragmentation is inevitable, even
in the presentation of his works, the detective or the chief prosecutor
would see there a maneuver to avoid assuming the totalizing anamnesis
of a shameful story. With a clever wink and while poking you each time
with his elbow, he would find damning evidence everywhere. He would
draw your attention to sentences as revealing, from this point of view,
as the following, among many others: "This apparent coherence *within*
each essay is not matched by a corresponding coherence *between* them.
Laid out diachronically in a roughly chronological sequence, they do not

evolve in a manner that easily allows for dialectical progression or, ultimately, for historical totalization."[47] This modest statement is relayed,
everywhere else, by a critical or deconstructive discourse with regard
to historical totalization in general. It would thus suffice to extend the
scope of these sentences through analogy to all de Man's writings and
to conclude confidently that this preface confesses what it hides while
declaring it inaccessible. The trap would be sprung, the amateur analyst
could rub his hands together and conclude: "de Man does not want to
sum up or assume the totality of his history and his writings. He declares
that it is impossible in principle in order to discourage in advance all
the policemen and to evade the necessary confession." Now, one could
find examples like this on every page. Before leaving this example, I
will quote only the end of this preface to *The Rhetoric of Romanticism*:
"The only place where I come close to facing some of these questions
about history and fragmentation is in the essay on Shelley's *The Triumph of Life*. How and where one goes on from there is far from clear,
but certainly no longer simply a matter of syntax and diction" (*R*, p. ix).

And from there, I would invite whoever wants to talk seriously about
de Man to read him, to read this essay on Shelley to its end or its final
interruption (*R*, pp. 121, 123). I do not have the room to quote the
pages where de Man speaks of "what we have done with the dead Shelley, and with all the other dead bodies . . . ," of the "suspicion that the
negation is a *Verneinung*, an intended exorcism," of what "always again
demands to be read," of "recuperative and nihilistic allegories of historicism" (*R*, pp. 121–22). Here is how the essay ends:

> Reading as disfiguration, to the very extent that it resists histori-
> cism, turns out to be historically more reliable than the products
> of historical archeology. To monumentalize this observation
> into a *method* of reading would be to regress from the rigor
> exhibited by Shelley which is exemplary precisely because it re-
> fuses to be generalized into a system. [*R*, p. 123]

If I give up playing the policeman's petty game, is it only because the
exercise is too easy? No, it is because its dogmatic naïveté will always
fail to render an account of this unquestionable fact: a statement can
never be taken as a presumption of guilt or evidence in a trial, even less
as proof, as long as one has not demonstrated that it has only an idiom-

---

47. De Man, *The Rhetoric of Romanticism* (New York, 1984), p. viii; hereafter abbreviated *R*.

atic value and that no one else, besides Paul de Man or a Paul de Man signatory of the 1940–42 texts, could have either produced the statement or subscribed to it. Or inversely, that all similar statements—their number is not finite and their contexts are highly diverse—could not be signed and approved by authors who shared nothing of Paul de Man's history or political experiences.

Even though I give up on this petty and mediocre game, I have at the disposal of those who would like to play it a whole cartography of false leads, beginning with what de Man wrote and gave us to think on the theme of memory, mourning, and autobiography. I have myself tried to meditate on this theme in *Mémoires*. Since Paul de Man speaks so much of memory and of mourning, since he extends the textual space of autobiography to this point, why not reapply his categories to his own texts? Why not read all these as autobiographical figures in which fiction and truth are indiscernible? And, as de Man himself shows, is not this latter problematic political through and through? Did I not underscore that myself in *Mémoires*, in a *certain way?* Yes, but in what way? Can one, ought one to take the reading possibilities that de Man himself offers us and manipulate them as arms, as a suspicion or an accusation against him in a "décision de justice," as we say in French, in a final judgment, authorizing oneself this time to decide in the absence of proof or knowledge? What would be the rule, if there is one, for avoiding abuse, injustice, the kind of violence that is sometimes merely stupidity? Before going any further into this question, here is the beginning of a list of themes that could become weapons in the arsenal of the investigators. The list is, by definition, incomplete, and, one may say it a priori, it links up with the "whole" de Manian text in a mode that never excludes "disjunction."

There is "Autobiography as De-Facement," an "autobiography [which] is not a genre or a mode, but a figure of reading or of understanding that occurs, to some degree, in all texts" (R, p. 70); then there is the autobiographical aspect, *that is, also the fictional* aspect of any text, even if one cannot remain within this undecidability ("the distinction between fiction and autobiography is not an either/or polarity but . . . it is undecidable" [R, p. 70]); or else, speaking of Lejeune's *Le Pacte autobiographique:* "From specular figure of the author, the reader becomes the judge, the policing power in charge of verifying the *authenticity* of the signature and the consistency of the signer's behavior, the extent to which he respects or fails to honor the contractual agreement he has signed" (R, pp. 71–72); or else, that about which I myself said it "precludes any anamnesic totalization of self" (M, p. 23):

> The specular moment that is part of all understanding reveals
> the tropological structure that underlies all cognitions, including
> knowledge of self. The interest of autobiography, then, is not
> that it reveals reliable self-knowledge—it does not—but that
> it demonstrates in a striking way the impossibility of closure
> and of totalization (that is the impossibility of coming into be-
> ing) of all textual systems made up of tropological substitutions.
> [R, p. 7]

Or yet again, the insistence on rhetoric and the irreducibility of the
tropological substitutions can always be interpreted, by "the reader" as
"judge" or "policing power," as a theoretical machine of the ruse meant
to lead him or her astray in advance and turn aside the police inquiry;
especially the insistence on the hallucinatory prosopopeia, about which I
said four years ago that it was "the sovereign, secret, discreet, and ideal
signature—and the most giving, the one which *knows how to efface
itself*" (M, p. 26). Is it not de Man who speaks to us "beyond the grave"
and from the flames of cremation? "The dominant figure of the epitaphic
or autobiographical discourse is, as we saw, the prosopopeia, the fiction
of the voice-from-beyond-the-grave; an unlettered stone would leave
the sun suspended in nothingness" (R, p. 77); and yet again, the motif
of "true mourning" and of the nostalgic resistance to the "materiality
of actual history"; and then there is the major motif of disjunction, as
well as what I called "an uncontrollable necessity, a *nonsubjectivizable*
law of thought beyond interiorization" (M, p. 37), the motif of thinking
memory (*Gedächtnis*) beyond interiorizing memory (*Erinnerung*); and
then the structure of allegory, even of memory itself, if not as amnesia,
then at least as relation to an "unreachable anteriority,"[48] a memory, in
sum, without a past in the standard sense of the term. Ah ha! someone
will say, is that not a maneuver meant to deny or dissimulate, even to
repress say the cleverest ones, an intolerable past? The problem is that
the maneuver being suspected, in other words, this *thought* of memory,
can be, has been, and will be once again, in this form or in a nearby
form, assumed by persons whose past has no relation with de Man's.
To the accusers falls the obligation of proving the contrary. I wish them
patience and courage.

So many false leads, then, for hurried detectives. The list is incomplete, as I said, the "whole" de Manian text is available as a booby-

---

48. De Man, *Blindness and Insight: Essays in the Rhetoric of Contemporary Criticism*, 2nd ed. (Minneapolis, 1983), p. 222.

trapped resource for symptomatologists in training. The latter could even begin by suspecting or denouncing the titles of "all" de Man's books! If they do not understand what I mean, they should write to me and I will point out a few tricks. Besides the pleasure (everyone gets it where he or she can), this exercise for late beginners may even procure a professional benefit for some. Especially if they take advantage of the opportunity to extend the trial, through contiguity or confusion, allusion, insinuation, or vociferation, to all those who are interested in de Man, to supposed groups or schools against whom it is advisable to wage war. I will come back to this in a moment.

As will have become clear, I see these two opposed errors as both intellectual and ethico-political errors, that is, both errors and falsifications. What would I do in the future so as to avoid them? Since it is a matter of nothing less than reading and rereading de Man without simplifying anything about the questions (general and particular, theoretical and exemplified) of the context, I cannot show here, in an article, what I would do at every step of a reading that ought to remain as open and as differentiated as possible. But I can try to advance a few hypotheses and, for the formation of these hypotheses themselves, one or two rules. Even if the hypotheses remain hypotheses, I assume as of now responsibility for the rules.

First rule: respect for the other, that is, for his right to difference, in his relation to others but also in his relation to himself. What are all these grand words saying here? Not only respect for the right to error, even to an aberration which, moreover, de Man never tired speaking of in a highly educated and educating manner; not only respect for the right to a history, a transformation of oneself and one's thought that can never be totalized or reduced to something homogeneous (and those who practice this reduction give a very grave ethico-political example for the future); it is also respect of that which, in *any* text, remains heterogeneous and can even, as is the case here, explain itself on the subject of this open heterogeneity while helping us to understand it. We are also the heirs and guardians of this heterogeneous text even if, precisely for this reason, we ought to maintain a differentiated, vigilant, and sometimes critical relation to it. Even those who would like to reject or burn de Man's work know very well and will have to resign themselves to the fact, that from now it is inscribed, at work, and radiating in the body or the corpus of our tradition. Not work but *works*: numerous, difficult, mobile, still obscure. Even in the hypothesis of the fiercest discussion, I would avoid the totalizing process and trial [procès]: of the work and the man. And the least sign of respect or fidelity will be this: to begin, precisely, by listening, to try to hear what he said to us, him, de Man, *already*, along with a few others, about totalizing violence, thus, to lend an ear, and an ear finely tuned enough to perceive, between the Atlantic and the Pacific, something other than monotonous noise and the rumbling [rumeur] of the waves.

The *second rule* is still more demanding, as inaccessible as what is called a "regulating ideal." But it is no less important to me and has been for a long time. Since we are talking at this moment about discourse that is totalitarian, fascist, Nazi, racist, anti-Semitic, and so forth, about all the gestures, either discursive or not, that could be suspected of complicity with it, I would like to do, and naturally I invite others to do, whatever possible to avoid reproducing, if only virtually, the *logic* of the discourse thus incriminated.

Do we have access to a complete formalization of this logic and an absolute exteriority with regard to its ensemble? Is there a systematic set of themes, concepts, philosophemes, forms of utterance, axioms, evaluations, hierarchies which, forming a closed and identifiable coherence of what we call totalitarianism, fascism, nazism, racism, anti-Semitism, never appear outside these formations and especially never on the opposite side? And is there a systematic coherence proper to each of them, since one must not confuse them too quickly with each other? Is there some property so closed and so pure that one may not find any element of these systems in discourses that are commonly opposed to them? To say that I do not believe that there is, not absolutely, means at least two things: (1) Such a formalizing, saturating totalization seems to me to be precisely the essential character of this logic whose project, at least, and whose ethico-political consequence can be terrifying. One of my rules is never to accept this project and consequence, whatever that may cost. (2) For this very reason, one must analyze as far as possible this process of formalization and its program so as to uncover the statements, the philosophical, ideological, or political behaviors that derive from it and wherever they may be found. The task seems to me to be both urgent and interminable. It has occurred to me on occasion to call this deconstruction; I will come back to that word in a moment.

I will give some concrete illustrations of these two abstractly formulated rules. In many of the discourses I have read or heard in the last few months (and I was expecting them in a very precise way), whether they attack or defend de Man, it was easy to recognize axioms and forms of behavior that confirm the logic one claims to have rid oneself of: purification, purge, totalization, reappropriation, homogenization, rapid objectification, good conscience, stereotyping and nonreading, *immediate* politicization or depoliticization (the two always go together), *immediate* historicization or dehistoricization (it is always the same thing), immediate ideologizing moralization (immorality itself) of all the texts and all the problems, expedited trial, condemnations, or acquittals, summary executions or sublimations. This is what must be deconstructed, these are a few points of reference (that is all I can do here) in the field open to this research and these responsibilities that have been called, for two decades, deconstructions (in the plural). I would not have pronounced this word here if all the newspaper articles and all the rumors that have reached me as of this day had not, in a way that is both so surprising and so unsurprising, associated deconstruction (in the singular) to this whole affair. By touching quickly on this problem, I will no doubt be able to go *from the rule to the hypothesis* and differentiate a little what I have meant since the beginning of this article by the word "rupture."

In spite of its discouraging effect, I have begun to get used to journalistic presentations of deconstruction and to the even more discouraging fact that the responsibility for them belongs most often not with professional journalists, but with professors whose training ought to require at least some attempt at reading. This time, finding as always its foothold in aggressivity, simplism has produced the most unbelievably stupid statements.[49] Some might smile with disabused indulgence at the highly transparent gesticulations of those who leap at the chance to exploit without delay an opportunity they think is propitious: at last, still without reading the texts, to take some cheap revenge on a "theory" that is all the more threatening to institutions and individuals because, visibly, they do not understand anything about it. One may also wonder, with the same smiling indulgence: but, after all, what does deconstruction (in the singular) have to do with what was written in 1940–42 by a very young man in a Belgian newspaper? Is it not ridiculous and dishonest to extend to a "theory," that has itself been simplified and homogenized, as well as to all those who are interested in it and develop it, the trial one would like to conduct of a man for texts written in Belgian newspapers forty-five years ago and that moreover, once again, one has not really read? Yes, this deserves perhaps hardly more than a smile and most often I manage to shrug it off.

But not always. Today I will speak of my indignation and my worry. (1) First, because the gestures of simplification and the expedited ver-

---

49. I will have neither the room nor the patience nor the cruelty to cite them all. I merely recall that they often appear in university campus newspapers and are generally passed along to the journalists by professors.

dicts have, yes, *in fact*, a relation to what happened around 1940–42, earlier and later, in Europe and elsewhere. When someone asking "not to be identified" sees himself quoted by an unscrupulous professor-journalist, when he says he is "shocked" by the fact that certain people are gathering, if only in order to *discuss* these problems (he would thus like to forbid the right to assembly and discussion? What does that remind you of?), and when he says he is "shocked" in the name of a "moral perspective,"[50] you can see why I am indignant and worried; and why it is necessary to remain vigilant; and why more than ever one must guard against reproducing the logic one claims to condemn. Precisely from a "moral perspective." Be on your guard for morality and thus the well-known immorality of so many moralisms.

2. Second, because, paradoxically, I think deconstructions *do have a relation*, but an altogether other relation, to the substance of the problems we are talking about here. To put it in a word, deconstructions have always represented, as I see it, the at least necessary condition for identifying and combating the totalitarian risk in all the forms already mentioned.

Not only can one not accuse deconstruction (in the singular) in the expeditious trial some are dreaming about today, but without deconstructive procedures, a vigilant political practice could not even get very far in the analysis of all these political discourses, philosophemes, ideologemes, events, or structures, in the reelaboration of all these questions on literature, history, politics, culture, and the university. I am not saying that, *inversely*, one must organize trials in the name of (singular) deconstruction! But rather that what I have practiced under that name has always seemed to me favorable, indeed destined (it is no doubt my principal motivation) to the analysis of the conditions of totalitarianism in all its forms, which cannot always be reduced to names of regimes.

50. Quoted in Jon Wiener, "Deconstructing de Man," *The Nation*, 9 Jan. 1988, p. 24. From its title to its final sentence, this spiteful and error-ridden article gathers within its pages more or less all the reading mistakes I have evoked up until now. It is frightening to think that its author teaches history at a university. Attempting to transfer onto deconstruction and its "politics" (such as he imagines them) a stream of calumny or slanderous insinuation, he has the nerve to speak of de Man as an "academic Waldheim," practices dogmatic summary without the least hesitation, attributes to me, for example, the foundation of deconstruction even as he also describes me as attributing its paternity to the "progenitor" Heidegger, about whom it would have been shown that his "commitment to Nazism was much stronger than has previously been realized." Now draw your own conclusion. Having explained myself at length elsewhere, again recently but for a long time already, on all these questions (notably on what the deconstruction that interests me receives but also deconstructs of Heidegger, on Heidegger and Nazism, and so on), I can here only refer the interested reader to these numerous publications.

And this in order to free oneself of totalitarianism as far as possible, because it is not enough to untie a knot through analysis (there is more than one knot and the twisted structure of the knot remains very resistant) or to uproot what is finally, perhaps, only the terrifying desire for roots and common roots. One does not free oneself of it effectively at a single blow by easy adherences to the dominant consensus, or by proclamations of the sort I could, after all, give in to without any great risk, since it is what is called the objective truth: "As for me, you know, no one can suspect me of anything: I am Jewish, I was persecuted as a child during the war, I have always been known for my leftist opinions, I fight as best I can, for example against racism (for instance, in France or in the United States where they are still rampant, would anyone like to forget that?), against *apartheid* or for the recognition of the rights of Palestinians. I have gotten myself arrested, interrogated, and imprisoned by totalitarian police, not long ago, so I know how they ask and resolve questions, and so forth." No, such declarations are insufficient. There can still be, and in spite of them, residual adherences to the discourse one is claiming to combat. And deconstruction is, in particular, the tireless analysis (both theoretical and practical) of these adherences. Now, today, from what I have read in newspapers and heard in conversation, I would say that these adherences are more numerous and more serious on the part of those who accuse de Man than in the latter's books or teaching. And this leads me to complicate or to differentiate still more (I warned that it would be long and difficult) what I have said so far about the "rupture."

By saying several times and repeating it again that de Man had radically *broken* with his past of 1940–42, I intend clearly an activity, convictions, direct or indirect relations with everything that then determined the context of his articles. In sum, a deep and deliberate uprooting. But after this decisive rupture, even as he never ceased reflecting on and interpreting this past, notably through his work and a historico-political experience that was ongoing, he must have proceeded with other *ruptures, divergences, displacements.* My hypothesis is that there were many of them. And that, with every step, it was indirectly at least a question of wondering: how was this possible and how can one guard oneself against it? What is it, in the ideologies of the right or the left, in this or that concept of literature, of history or of politics, in a particular protocol of reading, or a particular rhetorical trap which still contains, beneath one figure or another, the possibility of this return? And it is the "same man" who did that for forty years. My hypothesis is that this trajectory is in principle readable in what de Man was, in what he said, taught, published in the United States. The chain of consequences of these ruptures is even what is most interesting, in my view, in these texts, and whose lesson will be useful for everyone in the future, in particular for his enemies who would be well inspired to study it.

Those who would like to exploit the recent "revelations" against deconstruction (in the singular) ought to reflect on this fact. It is rather massive. "Deconstruction" took the forms in which it is now recognized more than twenty years after the war. Its relation to all its premises, notably Heideggerian premises, was from the start itself both critical and deconstructive, and has become so more and more. It was more than twenty years after the war that de Man discovered deconstruction. And when he began to talk about it, in the essays of *Blindness and Insight*, it was *first of all in a rather critical manner*, although complicated, as always. Many traits in this book show that the theoretical or ideologico-philosophical consequences of the "rupture" were not yet drawn out. I have tried to show elsewhere in *Mémoires*[51] what happens in his work when the word "deconstruction" appears (very late) and when, in *Allegories of Reading*, he elaborates what remains his original relation to deconstruction. Is it really necessary to recall once again so many differences, and to point out that this singular relation, however interesting it may seem to me, is not exactly mine? That little matters here. But since it is repeated everywhere, and for a long time now, that de Man is not interested in history and in politics, we can better take the measure today of the inanity of this belief. I am thinking in particular of the irony with which he one day responded, on the question of "ideology" and "politics": "I don't think I ever was away from these problems, they were always uppermost in my mind."[52] It is necessary to read the rest. Yes, they were "in [his] mind" and no doubt more than in the mind of those who, in the United States or in England, accused him of distraction in this regard. He had several reasons for that; experience had prepared him for it. He must have thought that well-tuned ears knew how to hear him, and that he did not even need to confide to anyone about the war in this regard. In fact, that is all he talked about. That is all he wrote about. At moments I say to myself: he supposed perhaps that I knew, if only from reading him, everything he never spoke to me about. And

---

51. See Derrida, *Mémoires*, pp. 120 and passim.

52. Stefano Rosso, "An Interview with Paul de Man," *The Resistance to Theory*, Theory and History of Literature, vol. 33 (Minneapolis, 1986), p. 121; rept. from *Critical Inquiry* 12 (Summer 1986): 788–95.

perhaps in effect I did know it in an obscure way. Today, thinking about him, about him himself, I say to myself two things, among others.

1. He must have lived this war, in himself, according to two temporalities or two histories that were at the same time disjoined and inextricably associated. On the one hand, youth and the years of Occupation appeared there as a sort of prehistoric prelude: more and more distant, derealized, abstract, foreign. The "real" history, the effective and fruitful history, was constituted slowly, laboriously, painfully after this rupture that was also a second birth. But, on the other hand and inversely, the "real" events (public and private), the grave, traumatic events, the effective and indelible history had already taken place, over there, during those terrible years. What happened next in America, for the one whom a French writer friend, he told me, had nicknamed in one of his texts "Hölderlin in America," would have been nothing more than a posthistoric afterlife, lighter, less serious, a day after with which one can play more easily, more ironically, without owing any explanations. These two lives, these two "histories" (prehistory and posthistory) are not totalizable. In that infinitely rapid oscillation he often spoke of in reference to irony and allegory, the one is as absolute, "absolved" as the other. Naturally these two nontotalizable dimensions are also equally true or illusory, equally aberrant, but the true and the false also do not go together. His "living present," as someone might put it, was the crossroads of these two incompatible and disjunctive temporalities, temporalities that nevertheless went together, articulated in history, in what was *his history*, the only one.

2. After the period of sadness and hurt, I believe that what has happened to us was doubly necessary. First as a fated happening: it had to happen one day or another and precisely because of the deserved and growing influence of a thinker who is fascinating enough that people always want to learn more—from him and about him. Second, it had to happen as a salutary ordeal. It will oblige all of us, some more than others, to reread, to understand better, to analyze the traps and the stakes—past, present, and especially future. Paul de Man's legacy is not poisoned, or in any case no more than the best legacies are if there is no such thing as a legacy without some venom. I think of our meeting, of the friendship and the confidence he showed me as a stroke of luck in my life. I am almost certain that the same is true for many, for those who can and will know how to make it known, and for many others, who perhaps do not even realize it or will never say so. I know that I am going to reread him and that there is still some future and promise

that await us there. He will always interest me more than those who are in a hurry to judge, thinking they know, and who, with the naïve assurance of good or bad conscience, have concluded in advance. Because one has in effect concluded when one already thinks of staging a trial by distributing the roles: judge, prosecutor, defense lawyer, witnesses, and, waiting in the wings, the instruments of execution. As for the accused himself, he is dead. He is in ashes, he has neither the grounds, nor the means, still less the choice or the desire to respond. We are alone with ourselves. We carry his memory and his name in us. We especially carry ethico-political responsibilities for the future. Our actions with regard to what remains to us of de Man will also have the value of an example, whether we like it or not. To judge, to condemn the work or the man on the basis of what was a brief episode, to call for closing, that is to say, at least figuratively, for censuring or burning his books is to reproduce the exterminating gesture which one accuses de Man of not having armed himself against sooner with the necessary vigilance. It is not even to draw a lesson that he, de Man, learned to draw from the war.

Having just reread my text, I imagine that for some it will seem I have tried, when all is said and done and despite all the protests or precautions, to protect, save, justify what does not deserve to be saved. I ask these readers, if they still have some concern for justice and rigor, to take the time to reread, as closely as possible.

The story I promised is more or less finished for the moment. As an epilogue, three more telephone calls, in December. The first is from Neil Hertz. He passes along the account of a certain Mr. Goriely, former Belgian resistant. He knew de Man well; they were friends during those dark years. Throughout the whole period of his clandestine activity, Mr. Goriely communicated in total confidence with de Man. He gives the same testimony to *Le Soir*, in an article dated 11 December 1987: according to this "university professor," de Man was "ideologically neither anti-Semitic nor even pro-Nazi . . . I have proof that de Man was not a fanatic from the fact that I saw him frequently during the war and he knew I was a clandestine, mixed up with the Resistance. I never feared a denunciation." The same professor has no memory of an anti-Semitic article, of that article that *Le Soir* claims it cannot find in its archives![53] And he adds: "What is more, I believe I know that our

53. I had already been intrigued by *Le Soir*'s remark in the article of 3 Dec. (see n. 11) that it could not find in its archives what was perhaps a separately printed special issue, and by Mr. Goriely's claim to have no memory of such an article. The same surprise is

man also gave texts to a Resistance publication: *Les Voix du silence*
[The voices of silence]!" Intrigued by this latter testimony and by the
Malraux title, Werner Hamacher calls me and asks me to try to learn
more from Georges Lambrichs, a Belgian writer who for a long time
was the director of the new NRF for Gallimard, and who, while in the
Resistance, would have had some part in this episode. De Man had
told me they knew each other well. I call him. His response is very firm,
without the least hesitation: "One must take into account the history
and the authority of the uncle. Even though de Man did not belong to an
organization of the Resistance, he was anything but a collaborator. Yes,
he helped French Resistants publish and distribute in Belgium a journal
that had been banned in France (with texts by Eluard, Aragon, and so
forth). The title of the journal was not *Les Voix du silence* but *Exercice
du silence*" (to be continued).

Although my ear is glued to the telephone, I am not sure I have heard
him clearly. Lambrichs repeats: "*Exercice du silence.*"

January 1988

---

marked by Charles Dosogne in his letter to Neil Hertz (see n. 45). Dosogne, who was the
first director of the *Cahiers du Libre Examen* (whose contributors included "a certain
number of Israelites"), recalls first of all that Paul de Man

> found himself at twenty years old, with a young wife and a baby, without a univer-
> sity degree, during a period of governmental disorganization, all of which did not
> permit him to aspire to a paying job. All he had going for him was his vast culture
> and his great intelligence, which he was able to take advantage of by accepting what
> some connections of his proposed to him: an association with "Le Soir" and the
> "Vlaamse Land."

Then, drawing from the experience of his long friendship (1938–47), Charles Dosogne
adds this:

> I can confirm that never, neither before nor after the war, did Paul de Man's remarks
> or attitudes permit one to suspect an antisemitic opinion—which, let me say in pass-
> ing, would have ended our relations. Racism was in fundamental contradiction with
> his profoundly human nature and the universal character of his mind. That is why
> I remain deeply skeptical concerning the remarks "with anti-Semitic resonances"
> cited by the *New York Times* that could be imputed to him. Is there not room to ask
> certain questions concerning a document that does not figure among "Le Soir"'s own
> collection, and, on the copy to be found at the Bibliothèque Albertine, is marked by
> three asterisks. Why??

6

Biodegradables
Seven Diary Fragments

Translated by Peggy Kamuf

Saturday, 24 December 1988, 5 A.M.

What is a thing?

What remains? What, after all, of the remains . . . ?
[*Quoi du reste . . . ?*]

Ergo je suis—the question of the thing. It is going to
be necessary once again to quibble [*ergoter*].

(This morning's decision: upon waking, take notes
on what remains of certain of my dreams, before they
sink back into oblivion. Retain in particular those—they
are finally rather rare—that already have a verbal consistency. This promises them an ideal identity, an autonomous existence of sorts, at the same time lighter and
more solid. For me, the duration of these words is like the
solitary persistence of a wreck. Its form run aground is
stabilized in the sand. One might see it surge up through
the morning fog in the manner of a damp ruin, jagged,
covered with algae and signs. A chance as well for the de-
ciphering to come when the thing resists. The promise of
work and reading, at least for a little while. On Saturday,
day of rest, distraction, or meditation, I will reassemble
these remains while reflecting them a little. Filtering and

ordering. We'll see what can be saved of them. But to float on the surface [*surnager*] does not necessarily mean to survive [*survivre*] . . .)

Longtemps je me suis, for a long time I have[1]—been interested in the "biodegradable." In the word or the thing? Difficult to distinguish, in any case in this case. It is a question of the case. The case: what falls, the fall [*la chute*], the falling due [*échéance*], or the waste [*déchet*]. In French, one also speaks of the "chute de papier."[2] *On the one hand*, this thing is not a thing, not—as one ordinarily believes things to be—a *natural* thing: in fact "biodegradable," on the contrary, is generally said of an artificial product, most often an industrial product, whenever it lets itself be decomposed by microorganisms. *On the other hand*, the "biodegradable" is hardly a thing since it remains a thing that does not remain, an essentially decomposable thing, destined to pass away, to lose its identity as a thing and to become again a non-thing. Preliminary question, this night or in the small hours of the morning, thinking again of the amnesia of which a culture is made: Can one say, figuratively, that a "publication" is biodegradable and distinguish here the degrees of degradation, the rhythms, the laws, the aleatory factors, the detours and the disguises, the transmutations, the cycles of recycling? Can one transpose onto "culture" the vocabulary of "natural waste treatment"—recycling, ecosystems, and so on—along with the whole legislative apparatus that regulates the "environment" in our societies? (Recall, but with vigilance—it's true I was just waking up—the "logic of the unconscious," censorship and repression, displacements and condensations. According to such a "logic," whose pertinence is, I believe, considerable but limited, nothing is destroyed and thus no "document"

1. Almost all the paragraphs on these two pages begin with a sentence that is playing, in a semiparodic or citational mode, with other texts. "What is a thing?" is a question that returns in numerous texts of Heidegger that have often been interpreted by Derrida, notably in *The Post Card: From Socrates to Freud and Beyond*, trans. Alan Bass (Chicago, 1987), and *The Truth in Painting*, trans. Geoff Bennington and Ian McLeod (Chicago, 1987). This question, in this very form, was both treated and parodied in *Glas*, trans. John P. Leavey, Jr. and Richard Rand (Lincoln, Nebr., 1986). A book constantly worked over by the motif of the remainder or of "remnance" [*restance*], as will be the present article, *Glas* began thus: "*Quoi du reste?*" On this subject, see as well Derrida's *Limited Inc*, ed. Gerald Graff (Evanston, Ill., 1988). As for the "Ergo je suis" and "Longtemps je me suis," these are more transparent allusions. The difficulty in translating the famous "Longtemps je me suis couché de bonne heure" from the *Recherche du temps perdu* is well known. There are at least three English versions. I cannot tell whether, with a smile or a groan, Derrida is here alluding to time lost. But, as we shall see, he often rises early to note down his dreams.—TRANS.

2. That is, the surplus or residue that falls or that overflows when large quantities of paper are cut (for books or newspapers, for example).—TRANS.

"biodegrades," even if it is, according to some criterion or other, the most degraded or the most degrading. As soon as the unconscious is in the picture, no law could regulate purification or reassure the ecologists. Those of "nature" and those of "culture." Unless the unconscious is already an ecosystem regulated by so many laws, and so on.) But can one say that, given this or that condition, one publication is more biodegradable, more quickly decomposed than another? Often, going from one to the other within the same hour and the same place, we read one thing that we know has resisted or will resist centuries of erosion and hermeneutic microorganisms, and then another thing that, from the very first page, we know we will forget on the plane even if it was nevertheless necessary to read and X-ray it while sighing all the way to the airport ("Why me again? Was it really necessary to read this? These lines are made to self-destruct, after a very brief passage; they poison themselves even before poisoning others, and carry within themselves their own microorganisms, and so on").

I wouldn't know how to qualify or delimit my interest in the question of the "biodegradable": scientific interest? philosophical? ethico-ecological? political? rhetorical? poetic? prag(ram)matological?[3] As for the word "biodegradable," which is not a thing and which in any case one cannot reduce to the state of the thing called "natural," no more than one can reduce its presumed "support" (paper, magnetic tape, diskette, and so on), how to define it?[4] Does it designate a rigorous concept? Does it have a proper meaning? And if it has a figurative meaning, which one? Must one prescribe "sound," nonpollutable rules for its use?

Tonight brought three other series of questions—but lacking for time, I will try to answer them some other Saturday.

---

3. This word was forged by Derrida to designate the internal and necessary link between two types of research, "at the intersection of a pragmatics and a grammatology," in "My Chances/*Mes Chances*: A Rendezvous with Some Epicurean Stereophonies," trans. Irene Harvey and Avital Ronell, in *Taking Chances: Derrida, Psychoanalysis, Literature*, ed. Joseph H. Smith and William Kerrigan (Baltimore, 1984), p. 27. There, the questions of the remainder, waste, the fall, and decay, which will come up often in this diary, are treated at length, as well as in the works cited in note 1, especially *Limited Inc.*—TRANS.

4. "Microbiological purification is generally associated with the assimilation of oxidizable organic wastes, which includes, for example, domestic sewage effluent and various industrial effluents such as those from paper manufacturing and food processing. The degradation of many hydrocarbons also proceeds to some extent by microbial action. A pollutant that is subject to decomposition by microorganisms is termed biodegradable" (Jay Benforado and Robert K. Bastian, "Natural Waste Treatment," in *McGraw-Hill Yearbook of Science and Technology, 1985* (New York, 1984), p. 38.

1. Is not the word "biodegradable" a recent artefact? All words in a so-called natural language are also, in their own way, artefacts, of course. But "biodegradable" overloads language with a supplement of artifice. It adds a prosthesis to it, a synthetic object, a modern and unstable graft of Greek and Latin in order to designate primarily that which is opposed to the structure of certain products of modern industry, products that are themselves artificial and synthetic, from plastic bags to nuclear waste. Is this synthetic object, the word "biodegradable," biodegradable? One might think that this very artificial word, this pluri-etymological, technoscientific, and synthetic composite is more decomposable than some other word. It would be called on to disappear or to let itself be replaced at the first opportunity. What is more, it barely belongs to a language. Is this foreigner, this graft—a little Greek, a little Latin, a little technoscience—first of all English, French? Will I have the time to look up the archive of the word? And what if it had decomposed itself, and so on? Well, precisely, it is perhaps this parasitic nonbelonging and this character of artificial synthesis that render the word less biodegradable than some other word; because it does not belong to the organic compost of a single natural language, this strange thing may be seen to float on the surface of culture like the wastes whose survival rivals that of the masterpieces of our culture and the monuments that we promise to eternity. A question is taking shape; I don't know what will remain of it: like biodegradable, nonbiodegradable can be said of the worst and the best.

2. Consequently, can one make a figure of the word "biodegradable"? Can one say, figuratively, "the biodegradable word"? Can one say of a word that it is biodegradable? And, along with the word, everything that is attached to words, everything that delivers itself over to words, everything that is delivered up by words? A *publication*, for example, a problematic but very strict notion that I am distinguishing provisionally from the text in general? In the publication, distinguish, if possible, the survival of the support (paper, magnetic tape, film, diskette, and so on) from the semantic content that also takes place, has a "place." Major question of the historicity of ideal objects (Husserl, the *Krisis*, the destruction of the archive,[5] the biodegradable, and so on).

3. Is not what we call rhetoric a large discourse, itself in a constant state of recycling, of that which in discourse submits to composition,

5. See Derrida, *Edmund Husserl's Origin of Geometry: An Introduction*, trans. Leavey, ed. David B. Allison (Stony Brook, N.Y., 1978).—Trans.

decomposition, recomposition? These processes could affect the very essence of language and the proper meaning of words. Can one speak nonfiguratively of biodegradability with regard to the identity attributed to a supposedly proper meaning? As a result of the action of certain bacteria (here, what are the "bacteria" of language? and the parasites and viruses that I've talked about at length elsewhere? Leave this connection for another occasion), the aforementioned proper meaning would decompose in order to pass, having become unrecognizable, into other forms, other figures. It would let itself be assimilated, circulating anonymously within the great organic body of culture, as would one of those metaphors called "dead."

Practice the most intractable vigilance, I said to myself last night in a half-sleep, with regard to all this bio-organicist rhetoric, if indeed a certain use of the word "biodegradable" gives in to that rhetoric. All the more so since, within its own physico-chemico-biological order, the concept of biodegradability is probably not fixed by definitive and rigorous limits. No doubt it is believed to be useful, pragmatic, provisional, and destined for recycling transformations.

One may also follow (I did it in *Mémoires*)[6] a certain itinerary of de Man as that of a progressively acute thinking of disjunction, that is, a progressively coherent critique of the "symbolist" and organicist totalization. Culler puts it well: "This political context gives a new dimension to de Man's attempt—from the early critiques of Heidegger to his late critiques of phenomenality—to undo totalizing metaphors, myths of immediacy, *organic unity*, and presence, and to combat their fascinations" ("'Paul de Man's War' and the Aesthetic Ideology," pp. 780–81; my emphasis).

"*Quoi du reste . . .*" Case and *chute de papier*, paper scraps.

More often than ever before, with the case of what has become a "case" in the newspapers—the "de Man case"—I have wondered: What will remain of all this in a few years, in ten years, in twenty years? How will the archive be filtered? Which texts will be reread? I have a few hypotheses, of course; I will not formulate all of them publicly, but at some later time I ought to say why, sometimes, I prefer to abstain.

I have never confused—indeed I have never stopped urging others not to confuse—traces or writing generally with what is said or written in books and newspapers, with archives and "publications." Thus the question "what will remain?" does not concern only, as I see it, librar-

6. See Derrida, *Mémoires for Paul de Man*, trans. Cecile Lindsay, Eduardo Cadava, and Jonathan Culler (New York, 1986).

ies and the academic world. It is, like the question of the remainder[7] in general, more vast, more reticent, more divisible, and thus more difficult. Even if one could draw a rigorous borderline around a particular journalistic-academic culture, which I do not believe is possible, the question "what will remain?" would still be of interest here. It has already been displaced, with great speed, in this limited sequence of history ("the de Man case") after scarcely more than a year, since the beginning of the "public" events, that is, since the moment when (must I recall this once again?) I myself believed (me, and none of those I am being urged to respond to in *Critical Inquiry*) I had to take the initiative to propose public discussion and, quite simply, publication of what is called today Paul de Man's *Wartime Journalism, 1939–1943* and *Responses* (about 1000 pages!).[8] Since then, people are beginning to forget the articles and the names of so many confused, hurried, and rancorous professor-journalists. Even if I wanted to recall here those articles and those names, I couldn't do it. What has saved a few of them from oblivion, according to a formidable paradox, a perverse law of cultural memory, have been the corrections, the responses, the calls to order and honesty—when, that is, certain newspapers have consented to publish them.

But if someone were tempted to conclude from this, judging by appearances and good sense, that these precipitous and compulsive publications were essentially "biodegradable" because destined in advance to oblivion, I would right away protest: the use of this figure demands many more precautions, as I would like to try to demonstrate. Conversely, the serious work of students, of young and not-so-young researchers on or in the wake of Paul de Man—and I am not the only one able to testify to this—has done nothing but grow in number and quality. This is even spectacular. One need not be a prophet to be able to predict that, like the books of Paul de Man (how many have been published since his death?), the articles and books that are proliferating on the subject of his work will have a longer and richer destiny—not an infinite one, of course, one cannot assert that about anything—but a much more interesting one in any case. (That is why, with the exception of Jonathan Culler's response, which reproaches me for a certain "exceedingly severe statement" to which I will return, the "critical re-

7. See above, notes 1 and 3; although the remainder, the remains, the rest are used here to translate "le reste," there is an untranslatable remainder: "reste" is also the form of the familiar imperative, "stay," as in "reste avec moi," stay with me.—TRANS.

8. See de Man, *Wartime Journalism, 1939–1943*, ed. Werner Hamacher, Neil Hertz, and Thomas Keenan (Lincoln, Nebr., 1988), and *Responses: On Paul de Man's Wartime Journalism*, ed. Hamacher, Hertz, and Keenan (Lincoln, Nebr., 1989).

sponses" to which I am urged to reply by *Critical Inquiry* appeared to me to be so behind the times and thus so tedious. They were behind the times from the beginning, if one can say that, but have become more and more so as of this date, and notably in relation to all the analyses and all the information we have at our disposal from now on.) Nonetheless, after some reflection, which, alas, does not mean that my decision is the right one, I have made it my duty to respond, to leave nothing without response. Yet, even as I force myself to face up to these attacks (half a dozen of them, what a disproportion!), I will advise the exacting reader to ignore this dossier, including my diary, and especially, especially to read, besides the work of Paul de Man (yes, again, again: the books published during his life and those that have been added since his death), the large quantity of research it has inspired, not only in the United States, as well as the two volumes I mentioned above.

The *difference in the predictable survival* of these texts is strange, for at least *three reasons*:

1. The richness, the rigor, and the fertility of Paul de Man's work. One may or may not agree with him, in general or on a particular point. The *two* things are possible and *both* have happened *to me*, be it a question of theory or politics, and concerning the most decisive stakes. This has not escaped the notice of those who have been willing to read each of us, with any lucidity and good faith, for more than twenty years. But it is not necessary to be in agreement with him *about anything* in order to recognize that the debates in which he participated, like the contribution he made to them, have an unquestionable—and moreover rarely questioned—*necessity*.

2. It is to the extent to which this original work is difficult to ignore that the articles from 1940–42 have resurfaced. People are not interested in *all* the writings of *all those* who pass as politically above suspicion, and simply for this latter reason. Fortunately. People are much less and too little interested, alas, in the writings and actions that are infinitely more serious and culpable, politically, than those of the young journalist Paul de Man. But the simple fact is their authors did nothing else or nothing better. A worrisome paradox, a disconcerting law of cultural memory: everything thus happens as if de Man, by his relentless work, by the richness of what he wrote or taught during almost forty years in the United States, had saved from immediate "biodegradation" some old newspaper articles that no one would have otherwise gone and exhumed (for this, there had to be an admirer of the succeeding generation, a whole generation of admirers and disciples; the ambivalence and resentment accumulated elsewhere, which had nothing to do

with the war, at least with *Le Soir* of 1940–42, will have done the rest). Perhaps even de Man wished this to happen, secretly or unconsciously. Perhaps he foresaw it even as he denied it. Until the end, he denigrated his own work as juvenilia and inadequate essays. And that is a little what I had meant to suggest by titling my article "Like the Sound of the Sea Deep within a Shell: Paul de Man's War" (trans. Peggy Kamuf, *Critical Inquiry* [Spring 1988]: 590–652). Montherlant's phrase quoted by de Man ventured something on the subject of the "biodegradability" of press publications. I was especially interested in the paradoxes or complications that were *overlooked* by this phrase and in particular by its citation. First of all, I was interested in the history of this phrase, in its possible survival, in the "nonbiodegradability" of this strange artefact, a sort of nuclear waste (I will have to come back to this next Saturday or later).

3. Those who have sought to exploit these revelations, those who have given in to the temptation to annihilate, along with the work of a whole life, all that which, from near or far, came to be associated with it ("Deconstruction," they say),[9] have produced, in spite of themselves, a premium of seduction. In spite of themselves? Perhaps, I am not sure of that. In any case, too bad for them. It is an effect that may be deemed perverse. One had to have a lot of ingenuousness and inexperience not to have foreseen it. Many of those who have taken part in this crusade against de Man and against "Deconstruction" are getting more and more irritated: now it turns out that, in part thanks to them, people are talking more and more about that which the crusaders wanted, without delay, to reduce to silence by denouncing the alleged hegemony that seems to cause them so much suffering. They should have thought of that. "Things" don't "biodegrade" as one might wish or believe. Some were saying that "Deconstruction" has been in the process, for the last twenty years, of extinguishing itself ("waning," as I read more than once) like the flame of a pilot light, in sum, the thing being almost all used up. Well, here they go and think they see, at the bottom of the little bit of oil remaining, a black stain (the specter of 1940–42, the diabolical de Man!). Certain this time that they will be able to get rid of it, without further delay and thus without any other precaution, they rush forward like children in order to wield the final blow and destroy the

9. Derrida writes "la déconstruction," thereby underscoring the singular and general sense conferred by the definite article. Since English drops the article altogether in this case, we have substituted a capital initial ("Deconstruction") to convey this sense and will do so wherever Derrida similarly calls attention to this misapprehension.—TRANS.

idol. And, of course, the flaming oil spreads everywhere, and now here they are crying even louder, angry with their own anger, frightened by their own fear and the fear they wanted to cause. Without them, would it have consumed itself; would the thing have been degraded on its own? False or useless question: too late, they were on the program, as was the unconscious.

Saturday, 31 December, 6 A.M.

Reread last night five of the six "critical responses." It's true, as I noted last week, these people are frightened. And so they want to frighten. A familiar scene. They are frightening sometimes, it's true. What I see of them frightens me, I won't hide the fact, and I will even say why. But—a distinction I hold to and always uphold, especially when I write—this fear does not intimidate me.

Those who have read me, in particular those who have read "Paul de Man's War," know very well that I would have quite easily accepted a genuine critique, the expression of an argued disagreement with my reading of de Man, with my evaluation (theoretical, moral, political) of these articles from 1940–42, and so on. After all, what I wrote on this subject was *complicated* enough, *divided*, tormented, most often hazarded as hypothesis, *open* enough to discussion, *itself* discussing *itself* enough in advance (on every page, indeed within every sentence, and from the very first sentence) for me to be able to welcome questions, suggestions, and objections. Provided this was done so as to demonstrate and not to intimidate or inflict wounds, to help the analysis progress and not to score points, to read and to reason and not to pronounce massive, magical, and immediately executory verdicts. Five of the six "responses" that I reread last night are written, as one used to say, with a pen dipped in venom. Less against the de Man of 1940–42, perhaps, than against me (I who said things that were nevertheless judged by Culler "exceedingly severe" against de Man and who have *nothing whatever to do* with everything that happened; I who, at the time, was rather on the side of the victims—shall I dare to recall this once again and will they forgive me for doing so?—struck by a *numerus clausus* that it will be necessary to talk about again). Less against me, in truth, than against "Deconstruction" (which at the time was at year minus twenty-five of its calendar! This suffices to shed light on this whole scene and its actual workings). How can the reader tell that these five "critical responses" are not "responses," critical texts or discussions, but rather the documents of a blinded compulsion? First of all, the fact that they are all *monolithic.* They take into account none of the complications of which my text, this is the very least one can say, is not at all sparing. They never seek to measure the possibility, the degree, or the form, as always happens in an honest discussion, of a partial agreement on this or that point. No, everything is rejected as a block; everything is a block and a block of hatred. Even when, here or there, someone makes a show of being moved by my sadness or my friendship for de Man, it is in order to get the better of me and suggest that I am inspired *only* by friendship, which will appear ridiculous to all those who have read me. Inspired by friendship means for those people misled by friendship. How foreign this experience must be to them!

Come on, am I going to waste time and paper (recyclable or not), spend the time and the money of my readers in commenting on someone who, for example, seriously wonders whether de Man knew that Kafka was Jewish ("How much did the young journalist really know about Kafka and his Jewishness?" ["Jacques Derrida's Apologia," p. 791]) and, in the same breath, cannot resist the urge to associate the names de Man and Göring? Is it still possible to correct a professional "historian" who, having once defined de Man as an "academic Waldheim," shows no regret for that and still today, apparently, has no idea of the enormity of a formula such as: "Only a small number of French and Belgian intellectuals cast their lot with the Nazis, as de Man did" (["The Responsibilities of Friendship: Jacques Derrida on Paul de Man's Collaboration," p. 800]!!! good God! He should do a little work, this guy. Such a show of ignorance appears all the more dismaying in that the best historians of this period are American and the best literature on this subject is in English, supposing, that is, that a historian reads only one language)? What's the point, on the other hand, of discussing with someone who, taking constant cover behind some history books, nevertheless compares de Man to Mengele, or at any rate gives in to the same compulsive desire to associate the two names in an analogy ("Response to Jacques Derrida," p. 775)? Or with still someone else who, in all seriousness, compares de Man to the author of Tintin ("in the case of Paul de Man, as in the similar case of Hergé" ["On Paul de Man's War," p. 766])?

It's really too much, too much confusion and dishonesty. Am I going to have to point out that (1) de Man could not not know that Kafka was Jewish (even if, for obvious reasons, he could not add a note saying "you know, I know, let's not forget it, Kafka is Jewish and his work is moreover on the index, as everyone knows"); (2) French or Belgian intellectuals collaborated *in very large numbers* and, alas, in much more serious ways; (3) de Man was neither Waldheim, nor Göring, nor Mengele, nor an author of comic books. These elementary reminders risk insulting my readers, even if, despite their impatience, they wanted for a moment to have a good laugh. And yet, it will indeed be necessary to respond and to do so, precisely, out of respect for the readers, and for the ethics of discussion, if anything can still be done on that score. So on these points and on *all* the others, I will respond. I've made my decision. Telephone *C.I.* [. . .]

5 P.M.

There are now so many examples of this! One of the most necessary gestures of a deconstructive understanding of history consists rather (this is its very style) in transforming things by exhibiting writings, genres, textual strata (which is also to say—since there is no outside-the-text, right—exhibiting institutional, economic, political, pulsive [and so on] "realities") that have been repulsed, repressed, devalorized, minoritized, delegitimated, occulted by hegemonic canons, in short, all that which certain forces have attempted to melt down into the anonymous mass of an unrecognizable culture, to "(bio)degrade" in the common compost of a memory said to be living and organic. From this point of view, deconstructive interpretation and writing would come along, without any soteriological mission, to "save," in some sense, lost heritages. This is not done without a counterevaluation, in particular a political one. One does not exhume just anything. And one transforms while exhuming. The presumed signatories of certain documents, for example, have no interest perhaps in seeing these documents assured of survival. Difficult to know how best to serve them, and what is true generosity. When someone writes a bad text or a nasty text [*un mauvais texte ou un texte mauvais*], is he or she asking to be saved or lost? And which response, in this case, is the most generous, the most friendly, the most salutary, the most just? The response or the nonresponse? It happens that people write bad things, libels or lampoons in which they know they are wrong or do wrong, but they do so, precisely, with the sole aim of provoking a response that will make them stand out and put them on stage, even if it is to their detriment and provided that a certain visibility is thus assured. And with public visibility comes the chance to endure. In this case, what to do? What would you be doing by responding "no" to someone who says to you "beat me so at least people see me or hear me crying and don't forget me"? No one gets out of such a situation unscathed, on one side or the other. I will have to return later to the relation between this scene, the proper name, and cultural "biodegradability." [. . .]

9 P.M.

Jonathan Culler contests and discusses certain remarks of mine in order to advance the understanding of things and shed light on those things that (I acknowledged it, said it, and said it again in "Like the Sound") sometimes remain enigmatic for me. In so doing, he does not seek to manipulate, inflict wounds, or denigrate. His procedure is honest. First of all because it is addressed to me. Not only to me, of course, but also to me, that is, to someone with whom one does not agree, to be sure, but with whom one discusses, and whom one is not trying from the outset to insult—in his intentions, his person, and his work. Even if he does not agree with me, he recognizes that I opened a debate (p. 783); he clearly condemns that which must be condemned in this or that article of 1941 (p. 779) without trying to mix everything up, without raging furiously [s'acharner] in the void in order to execute a dead young man, a dead old man, and a dead dead man, as others do who can no longer contain their violence against the name of a departed and only raise their heads above the funerary urn, their hands still shaking, so as to cry out for death and threaten again those who try to convince them and appease them, to reason with them by saying to them calmly, "I think you are wrong, but even if you are somewhat right, you ought to calm down a little. We'll talk about all this again when you will have regained your composure."

So in return I will address myself to Jonathan Culler, and later I will attempt, perhaps in an open letter, to explain to him why, on the contested point, I believe I must, with certain nuances, maintain what I wrote on the subject of de Man's wartime articles; that is, that "the *massive, immediate, and dominant* effect of all these texts is that of a *relatively* coherent ideological ensemble which, *most often and in a preponderant fashion*, conforms to official rhetoric, that of the occupation forces," which are lines that, along with so many others in a similar vein, the five other "respondents" seem not to have even read, that they cannot not have read, and thus they pretend *dishonestly and in bad faith* (I am weighing my words carefully) to know nothing about. It would be necessary to invent a new category here. "Bad faith" or "denegation" are insufficient. We're talking about something that falls between the "I-cannot-read" and "I-do-not-want-to-read" [*je-ne-peux-pas-lire et je-ne-veux-pas-lire*]. This new category, which has a relation to the question of the "remainder," naturally displaces the category of responsibility. How can one pronounce judgment against someone who can/will not read [*ne "pveut" pas lire*]? How could one bear him or her any ill will? [*Comment pourrait-on lui en vouloir?*]. Moreover, I bear these five no ill will; I have nothing against them; I would even like (if only in order to avoid this spectacle) to help them free themselves from this frightened, painful, and truly excessive hatred. What are they afraid of exactly, and what are they suffering from? Even if I happen to respond harshly to them, it will be with this concern, and especially the concern for the public, moral, and political consequences of this whole debate.

Was I "exceedingly severe" with de Man as Culler says? Or not? Culler on the one hand, the five others united on the other, thus seem to be saying, with regard to the same text—"Like the Sound"—*absolutely contradictory* things, at the extreme opposite from one another. Well, they can't all be right at the same time. So I wonder whether between the two, perhaps . . . (Get it? Will they see what I mean? No? Yes . . . yes, yes, they will see very well, nothing more to add, I could stop there, they will see very well that *the question is other and elsewhere*).

11 P.M.

So, none of them saw, none of them read that in "Like the Sound" the *question is other and elsewhere*, the question that preoccupies me, for example, the question of response and responsibility. At bottom and in the final analysis, I did not try to be either severe or indulgent. Or equitable in some *juste milieu* between two iniquitous judgments. Or to convince anyone that one must be severe or indulgent.

Midnight

Later, it will take time, people will understand that in this whole affair, and a few others, there are better things to do than to know whether one ought to be severe or indulgent. [. . .]

Since more room must be found in the "ecosystem" of an archive (the NEH is already concerning itself with these problems of storage for American university libraries, and the process will have to accelerate), let us suppose that one day the complete collection of *Critical Inquiry* has to be destroyed or moved. A young librarian is hastily given the task of indexing on computer the abstracts of the questions or the principal theses treated there. He comes across our dossier. Something of it has to be saved at all costs, since the journal received an award for "Best Special Issue of a Journal" (from the Conference of Editors of Learned Journals) for the Spring 1988 issue. So the young man has to summarize the two issues on Paul de Man in two sentences, preferably by citing some words in quotation marks (that looks more authentic). I see the sentences stretching across the green screen: "Seven authors accuse an

eighth of having engaged in an 'exceedingly severe' 'apology' on the
subject of a ninth author, apparently dead for six or forty-six years. The
eighth has as much trouble understanding as he does making himself
understood." [. . .]

Here is the most problematic thing in the "double binding" figure of the
"biodegradable": the worst but also the best that one could wish for a
piece of writing is that it be biodegradable. And thus that it not be so.
As biodegradable, it is on the side of life, assimilated, thanks to bacteria,
by a culture that it nourishes, enriches, irrigates, even fecundates but on
the condition that it lose its identity, its figure, or its singular signature,
its proper name. And yet, is not the best way to serve the said "culture,"
indeed the "agriculture," "the natural-culture-of nature" (these words
are no good. I keep them only in quotation marks; in fact I keep them
just long enough to wear them out and throw them away like useless
waste products, but ones that are perhaps very resistant, like the mutism
of the quotation marks) to oppose a certain resistance to living biodegradability? Is it not the case that, as "nonbiodegradable," the singularity of a work resists, does not let itself be assimilated, but stays on the
surface and survives like an indestructible artefact or in any case one
which is less destructible than another? Important question of *physis*
beyond the opposition nature/culture. I have never been convinced by
what Heidegger has said on this subject. And precisely because of the
remains that remain to be thought. Try later to show how the proper
name—the proper name function—finally corresponds to this function
of nonbiodegradability. The proper name belongs neither to language
nor to the element of conceptual generality. In this regard, every work
survives *like and as* a proper name. It shares the proper name *effect*
(because there is no *purely*, uncontaminable proper name and no absolute indestructibility) with all other proper names. It shares and divides
[*partage*] this effect in all its parts, even beyond its title and the name of
its presumed signatory. In the manner of a proper name, the work is singular; it does not function like an ordinary element of natural language
in its everyday usage. That is why it lets itself be assimilated less easily
by culture to whose institution it nevertheless contributes. Although
more fragile, having an absolute vulnerability, as a singular proper name
it appears less biodegradable than all the rest of culture that it resists, in
which it "rests" and remains, installing there a tradition, its tradition,
and inscribing itself there as inassimilable, indeed unreadable, at bottom
insignificant. A proper name is insignificant. But there are several ways

to be insignificant. More or less interesting. One might as well say that
meaning is not the measure of interest—or of wearing away [*usure*].[10]

Saturday, 7 January, 6 A.M.

In my response, I ought to set out from a fact that will have escaped no
reader's attention: like the fingers of the same hand, the five insulting
texts all take aim at the same principal target, that "deconstruction"
about which the authors visibly understand nothing, I mean really nothing, and this goes equally for all of them. What can I do? "Deconstruction" is for them *the* threat, the common and public enemy. *This* war is
the most urgent in their view. Since the five authors take no account of
that most massively obvious fact, which I clearly pointed out (p. 649),
to wit, that what happened in 1940–42 in Brussels cannot, by definition, have anything to do with deconstruction, their argument cannot be
taken seriously. Nor, therefore, can anything which follows from that
argument in the five "responses," which is to say just about everything.
I could stop here. It so happens, moreover, that deconstruction has no
more relation with what may have happened in a Belgian newspaper in
1940–42 than it does with the uninformed, uneducated, and grotesque
descriptions (I am weighing my words carefully) that these five "respondents" give of it. It goes without saying that I will not be able to dissipate such dense confusions about "Deconstruction" in a few sentences. I
give up trying in advance. I will merely point out that for all these people
the "de Man case" offers what they believe is a propitious occasion to
attack what they *believe to be "Deconstruction."*
Demonstration:
       1. One of them takes aim at the "standard deconstructionist prac-
tice" (p. 794) or what, according to him, would be "entirely typical":
"the failure to distinguish between existential and rhetorical categories
(and the tendency to reduce the former to the latter) is an earmark of
the mode of philosophizing that has been given currency by de Man
and Derrida" (p. 792). And, of course, so that it might be clear that my
case is more serious than de Man's, he adds: "I, for one, believe (and so
do many others) that there is a strongly mystifying element in de Man's
writings—sometimes almost (though never quite) as mystificatory as
Derrida's apologia for de Man" (p. 796). This definition of the "standard deconstructionist practice" and what would be "typical" within

---

10. See Derrida's "White Mythology: Metaphor in the Text of Philosophy," *Margins
of Philosophy*, trans. Bass (Chicago, 1982), pp. 209–71.—TRANS.

that "practice" is gratuitous, confused, perfectly irrelevant. I recognize nothing whatsoever in it, close up or from afar, and especially nothing of what I myself (since it is a question of me) may have ever thought or written. As for the sentence that begins "I, for one, believe (and so do many others)": what can it prove? Only this: someone believes that what he believes is true and interesting, and (classic technique but far too crude for anyone to be taken in by it) he wants to make others believe that he has an army of people behind him who believe as he does, who believe as he does that what they believe is true and even interesting. Everything, thus, still remains to be proved. And even if one could prove that "so do many others," that would not prove that they are doing anything more than believing or that their belief brings the least proof that their belief has the least value.

2. Another respondent concentrates his whole argumentation around what is derisively called "the prestige of deconstruction" ("Resetting the Agenda," p. 805) and announces clearly that if one fails to clear de Man (which, need I remind anyone, is something I never sought to do; see pp. 599, 600–610, 616–19, 621–23, 631, 633, and passim), deconstruction would be definitively compromised and "the wager will be lost" (!) (p. 805; I shall not fail to come back to this scene, one of the most comical ones in this whole corpus).

3. Another respondent lays into what he believes to be "the deconstructive method" (p. 799) and believing, since he has obviously never read me,[11] that it consists in taking no account of the "context" (!!!) and of "authorial intention," here he is ready to give me a lesson in deconstruction: "But of course Derrida's appeal to context and to authorial intention constitutes an abandonment of the deconstructive method" (p. 799). Then, by substituting "post-structuralist" for "deconstructive," he leaves me the choice only between "the unified subject" and "the post-structuralist critique of the unified subject." Ah, if only things could be that simple! Ah, if only one knew what a "subject" was and whether it could be only "unified" or "nonunified"! After having recalled the "post-structuralist critique of the unified subject," just so many words that have no meaning for me and that one would have a lot of trouble articulating with anything I have ever written, the same

---

11. Derrida has underscored on numerous occasions that deconstruction cannot be defined or practiced as a method. "*Point de méthode* [No method/point of method]," he writes in "The Double Session" (Derrida, *Dissemination*, trans. Barbara Johnson [Chicago, 1981], p. 271). See also Derrida, "Letter to a Japanese Friend," trans. David Wood and Andrew Benjamin, in *Derrida and "Différance,"* ed. Wood and Robert Bernasconi (Evanston, Ill., 1988), p. 3.—TRANS.

author calmly adds this, which has no meaning for me: "But Derrida apparently doesn't believe the critique of the unified subject applies to de Man" (p. 801). Come on, would anyone ever have talked or heard talk of deconstruction for more than ten minutes if it came down to such derisory dogmas or such stupid monoliths as these (of the sort: "I don't believe there is any context! There is no authorial intention! There is no subject! No unified subject! We have to stop paying attention to these things!"). One shows considerable contempt for many colleagues or students if one believes they are silly enough or credulous enough to interest themselves in such simple and pitiful discourses. Unless it is quite simply reading that is the object of one's contempt and one's fear. *On ne pveut pas lire.*

It is thus still a question, and at the cost of the crudest sort of maneuvers, of displacing the accusation and the verdict by making the attack converge on thought, theory, "Deconstruction" today and now. This is a program whose utterance was given its first (and also its most obscene) form by the same author already almost a year ago: "The important question about de Man, however, is not what he thought about Jews; the question concerns the relationship between his secrecy about his past and his literary theory."[12]

4. For another respondent, the stakes are even more precise. It is a question of nothing less, *in conclusion and to conclude*, than of handing down a verdict while pretending to deplore "the turn the deconstructive project, originally so liberating, is now taking" (p. 775). As if what happened to de Man in 1940–42 could constitute a "turn" or a "turning" of the "deconstructive project" in 1988!

5. For another, finally, the actual accused in this comic-book trial is once again, in conclusion, deconstruction. "What is indeed striking in deconstruction is that it escapes confrontation with historical development. That does not imply that it is linked to rightist thought [ah, good, at least there's that: *merci m'sieur*] (its technique [I have explained a hundred times why deconstruction was not essentially a "technique"] can be used either for 'fascist' [some proof, please, some arguments, some examples, at least one example!] or 'liberal' purposes), but it implies that this method [I have explained a hundred times why deconstruction was not essentially a "method"; see also above, note 10] rarely confronts historicity [I have explained a hundred times why deconstructive reading and writing took into account, more than any other, both "history" and the history of the concept of history; as for "Paul de Man's War," its

12. "Letters," *The Nation*, 9 Apr. 1988, p. 502.

historical content and its reference to historical referents is richer than
that of the five "critical responses" put together]. Because history reveals
the 'decidable' [who ever said the contrary?], which sometimes means
guilt" [did I not say just that, and precisely in the case of de Man? See
above; I am not going to reproduce this reference on every line] (p. 766).

What I find particularly tedious in this quintext is that, with very few
exceptions, it is composed and thus decomposed by *two motifs*:

1. There is, *on the one hand*, that which I already said myself and
that they repeat in a more or less confused way while claiming nevertheless to counter me thanks to forgetfulness or to denegation (or to *on ne
pveut pas lire*); for example (but I'll proliferate the examples and later
make a list of them), everything in my text that is, in Jonathan Culler's
words, "exceedingly severe" (p. 777) against de Man and that ought not
to have passed unnoticed by the six authors.

2. There is, *on the other hand*, the objections to which I had responded in advance, in an explicit fashion. I will redemonstrate this
later, and, out of concern for clarity, thoroughness, and economy, I
will propose *two tables*: a table of *concordances* or *redundancies*, of
concorredundancies (that which I already said and that it was useless—
redundant—to repeat, especially to use it against me with arrogant bad
faith) and a table of *discordances* (what I had already contested and
that, once again, they did not understand, read, try to read, or pretend
to read). Point of information: the recourse to the category of the *je ne
pveux pas lire* (I can/will not read), supposing that it can even be used in
the first person, would not exclude the old notions of lie, bad faith, denegation, in short, the philosophy of consciousness or the unconscious,
up to the point where both must also be exceeded. This would concern
as well whatever one may be tempted to say about "responsibility" or
the "biodegradable." [. . .]

Noon

Composition, decomposition. Everything that is "biodegradable" lets
itself be decomposed or returns to organic nature while losing there its
artificial identity. But everything that is "biodegradable" does not have
the same property or the same qualities (richness, fecundity, and so on).
In classical terms: the organic is not the living; natural life is not the
whole of life, and so on. If one still relies, provisionally, on this figure
transposed into the field of culture, then one may say: all writings and
all discourses, all forgotten works are not victims of an injustice and
have not become, to an equal extent, the ferments of the coming culture.
Moreover, today, our means of archiving are such that we keep almost

all published documents, even if we do not keep them in what used to be called living memory and even if libraries are obliged more and more often to destroy a part of their wealth. This is only an appearance: the originals or microfilms are elsewhere, kept safe for a long time, barring nuclear war or "natural" catastrophe. But there is an essential limit to this cultural transposition of the natural figure (I mean of this "return to nature" of a biodegradable artefact). What would an ecosystem be for discourses? An institution is also an attempt to calculate and control symbolic ecosystems, which is obviously impossible in a rigorous fashion. Come back to this next week.

These two tables may also be read as timetables or computer screens. Like those that are displayed in train stations or in airports, they announce delayed departures and arrivals: delay in relation to what I *already* said or in relation to what I *already* responded or said about my objection. But how to calculate such a delay? And once the delay is calculated, what would remain? That is a question I would have liked to treat, some Saturday when I had nothing to do. (Out of concern for space, I will limit myself to the points not directly addressed in the diary.)

TABLE OF CONCOR(REDUN)DANCES
(or, that which I *already* said and which, therefore, one should have avoided repeating, especially while claiming to oppose me with it)

"CRITICAL RESPONSES"	"PAUL DE MAN'S WAR"
p. 766, ll. 1–11	pp. 601–2, 604, 607–10, 621–23
p. 769, l. 30ff.	p. 604
p. 770, l. 4ff.	p. 606
p. 770, ll. 20–21	pp. 604–6
pp. 770–71	pp. 604–7
p. 771, ll. 32–45; p. 772, ll. 1–11	p. 604 and passim
p. 772, l. 16	p. 636, ll. 6–8
p. 775, ll. 6–10	pp. 604–5, 621–23, 631 and passim
p. 777, ll. 6–9	p. 598, ll. 18–40
p. 790, ll. 16–17	p. 604 and passim
p. 791, ll. 19–28	pp. 621–23
p. 793, ll. 9–11	passim

p. 802, l. 5ff.

pp. 599, ll. 11, 29–30; 600, l. 1

p. 805, l. 15

pp. 590, l. 1ff.; 593, ll. 2–5 and passim

pp. 806, l. 45; 807, ll. 1–8

pp. 604–10, 616–19, 621–23

TABLE OF DISCORDANCES
(or, the objections to which I had *already* responded)

"CRITICAL RESPONSES"	"PAUL DE MAN'S WAR"
pp. 765–811	pp. 590, ll. 1–3; 651, ll. 7–11
p. 766, ll. 1–11	pp. 599–652
p. 766, ll. 18–19	pp. 590–652 passim, especially 646–48
p. 773, ll. 11–12	p. 637, l. 4ff.
p. 773, ll. 19–21	p. 637, l. 4ff.
p. 773, l. 29	p. 637, l. 4ff.
p. 775, l. 26ff.	pp. 648–49
p. 784: title	pp. 590–652; in particular, 599, 600, 601, 604, 605, 607, 610, 616–19, 621–23, 631, 639
p. 785, ll. 23–25	pp. 590, l. 1ff.; 639, l. 38ff.
p. 786, ll. 3–5	pp. 593, 640, 646 and passim
p. 786, l. 13ff.	p. 602, l. 32ff.
p. 787, ll. 37–38	pp. 599–600, 605, 607–10, 616–19, 621–23, 631, 636
p. 788, ll. 30–31	pp. 599, 600, 604, 607–10, 616–19
p. 788, ll. 36–40	pp. 621–32
p. 789, l. 37	pp. 621–32
p. 789, l. 38ff.	pp. 621–23
p. 790, ll. 1–4	pp. 621–23, 626, notably ll. 14–15
p. 790, l. 5	pp. 621–23, 632
p. 790, l. 29	pp. 631–32
p. 791, ll. 19–28	pp. 621–23
p. 792, ll. 12–22	pp. 606–32
p. 793, ll. 5–8	pp. 604–10, 616–19, 621–23, 631, 638

p. 793, l. 24ff.	pp. 636–37, notably ll. 8–16; 639, l. 7
p. 794, l. 17	p. 631, ll. 17–18; 639
p. 795, ll. 17–19	p. 642
p. 796, ll. 20–23	p. 606
p. 796, ll. 41–42	pp. 648–49
p. 797: title	pp. 590, 592, 594, 595, 596, 597, 639 and passim
p. 797, ll. 12–13	pp. 604, ll. 18–19; 638 and passim
p. 798, ll. 19–22	pp. 599, 604–5, 607–10, 616–19, 621–23, 631
p. 799, ll. 3–4	p. 647
p. 799, ll. 12–30	pp. 637, 639, 647
p. 799, ll. 38–41 to p. 800, ll. 1–2	p. 647
p. 800, l. 10ff.	pp. 637, notably l. 8; 638–39
p. 800, l. 35ff.	pp. 635; 648, notably l. 14
p. 801, l. 34ff.	p. 624, l. 36ff.
p. 802, l. 5ff.	pp. 599, l. 11, ll. 29–30; 600, l. 1
p. 802, ll. 21–23	p. 647, n. 50, notably, l. 6ff.
p. 804–805	pp. 648–49 and passim
p. 804, ll. 11–12	pp. 635, 640, 648–49
p. 804, ll. 14–15	pp. 607–10, 616–19, 621–23
p. 805, l. 15 (a somewhat special case; I had averted, set aside, or voided the objection by saying the same thing; yet, since this happens more than once, there would have to be another table to take account of this rhetorical situation. I trust the reader to make the distinctions.)	pp. 591, l. 1ff.; 593, ll. 3–4; 596, l. 14ff.; 606ff.
p. 805, ll. 28–31	pp. 606–7ff.
p. 806, ll. 9–11	pp. 599–634
p. 806, ll. 34–42	pp. 604–5, 607–10, 616–19, 621–23
p. 806, l. 45 to p. 807, ll. 1–12	pp. 604–21
p. 807, l. 14	pp. 600, 605, 607, 623, 631, 635
p. 807, l. 40 to p. 808, l. 15	pp. 616–21

p. 808, ll. 29–30	pp. 624, l. 45; 625, l. 30
p. 809, ll. 10–14	pp. 623–31 and passim
p. 809, ll. 27–29	pp. 606–23
p. 810, l. 29	p. 646
p. 811, ll. 9–30	pp. 635, 648–49 and passim

Saturday, 14 January, 7 A.M.

A text, a verse, an aphorism, a *bonmot* (the Germans, Kant for example, used to write this as a single word, like biodegradable) can survive a long time, thus resisting the "biodegrading" erosion of culture, for all sorts of reasons not all of which are to be credited to them or to their author. They resist time just as do what in French are called "pearls." Durable because hard [*durs*]—and hard to digest.

The quintext numbers too many pearls for me to count. I bet that some of them will be passed on to posterity. If one day I respond, as I have the intention of doing, in *Critical Inquiry*, could I make a bet there? Can one make bets in such a serious journal? A liberal journal has to accept that bets are made in its pages. All the more so since, with its liberal, pluralist concern to maintain public discussion without privileging any side (an irreproachable policy, especially if its principle could be rigorously and sincerely applied), this excellent publication is managed by wise men and women and responsible intellectuals. Thus they also know—it's the logic of debates, bets, auction bids, and bidding wars—that this can serve the prosperity of the institution, I mean the promotion of the journal that is urging me to respond at a single blow to six articles at once! Six against one! The idea that an army has been mobilized against an article that was, moreover, also commissioned of me, does not displease me altogether, but all the same, what effrontery! What a number of fronts I must confront! I hope that all of this is pro-portional to the seriousness of the question, but I am not sure it is.

So I will make a bet. What is it? I bet that the longest life will be granted to a parenthesis. This one, let's read it and reread it: "at Har-vard and in the Boston area (where deconstruction and feminism were and continue to be a recurrent theme)" (p. 765). The article, fortunately very brief, a page and a half, begins in the mode of the autobiographical and autopromotional epos. Let's read, reread: "In 1982–83, I was pre-paring my volume on the Belgian cartoonist Hergé[1]" (the footnote refers the reader to *Les Métamorphoses de Tintin* [Paris, 1984]) (p. 765).

Let's imagine, in centuries to come, an enormous archive having been biodegraded or recycled, that a young reporter-journalist or an

archeologist-tourist (metempsychosis of Tintin) comes across some remains, for example this glorious incipit ("In 1982–83, I was preparing my volume . . . *Les Métamorphoses de Tintin* [Paris, 1984]"), and
next this parenthesis miraculously saved from the disaster: "at Harvard
and in the Boston area (where deconstruction and feminism were and
continue to be a recurrent theme)." Let's suppose that this journalist-
reporter-archeologist has in fact just found these debris of *Critical Inquiry* in very bad shape on a beach at Cape Cod or in the wreck of an
old boat, a kind of "Unicorn." (Will American readers have read, in the
Tintin series, *The Secret of "The Unicorn"* or *Red Rackham's Treasure*
by the same Hergé? I have just reread them, doing my homework; they
are really devoid of interest, very overdone out of a certain snobism, one
more difference between de Man and Hergé, which I mention for those
who may still be harboring the incongruous idea of comparing them.
As for their politico-ideological histories, there is simply no common
measure between them.) Tintin II would try to understand, to reconstitute the "context" and, as they will still be saying centuries from now,
"the authorial intention." What is more, he had earlier got his hands
on a fragment from an old debate in *Critical Inquiry* on the question of
beaches and authorial intention. Here's how Tintin's distant descendent
might imagine things for himself: "So this author meant that at this time
there was a place, two places at most (one or two? he says Harvard and
then Boston), in the United States I suppose, and nowhere else, where
one could locate a center, a double center of 'recurrence,' the recurrence
not of a disease, but of a 'theme,' of a 'recurrent theme': 'deconstruction and feminism.' In this region of a state of the United States and
nowhere else, in the United States and nowhere else. 'Deconstruction
and feminism' were thus a 'theme' at this time?" he asks himself. "What
is that? One theme or two? Are deconstruction and feminism the same
thing, or two symptoms of the same epidemic recurrence?" Our detective, who is getting more and more perplexed, may well continue to
wonder: "Unless deconstruction is to feminism as the Boston area is to
Harvard, if I am reading correctly ('at Harvard and in the Boston area
[where deconstruction and feminism were and continue to be a recurrent theme]'). This double theme, these two things, at any rate, 'were'
already recurrent in the past, which is *already* a lot. But there is worse
to come; it 'continues' to be, in those days, 'a recurrent theme.' To have
been recurrent, that's already a lot, but to continue to be recurrent, is
that not really too much? The trouble or problem or ill must have been
very serious. Apparently indestructible. Insufficiently energetic medi-

cine. Happily the pernicious theme seems to have been concentrated at that time in 'Harvard and the Boston area.' Verify that."

Intrigued, more and more fascinated by the glimmers of this cryptic notation, our clever sleuth tries to reconstitute the whole sentence and the whole paragraph, first in order to understand, but also out of honest respect for the authorial intention of the departed author of *Les Métamorphoses de Tintin*. From the first sentence of the paragraph, he believes he may conclude that between, on the one hand, this thing which is holding sway with such "recurrence" in "the Boston area," that is, deconstruction (which the author oddly calls a "theme") and, on the other hand, a certain de Man, there must have been a relation, to be sure, but also that this de Man must have been a feminist. Whether he knew it or not! Otherwise, what would this allusion to feminism, this other "theme," be doing here? Unless it was never possible, at this time and in this region of the world, to dissociate deconstruction and feminism, wonders now our disconcerted tourist-archeologist (Tintin couldn't do better). And so, whether he knew it or not, this de Man must have been a feminist because those "in the Boston area" were interested in him no doubt for reasons of "deconstruction and feminism." As soon as one has contracted a recurrent deconstructionism, one must have contracted a little feminism, at least by contagion, even if one doesn't know it. It's finally the same virus. Let's read:

> That is to say that, as far as I know, several people at Harvard and in the Boston area (where deconstruction and feminism were and continue to be a recurrent theme) were aware of de Man's former affiliation with rightist circles. One can ask why it took five more years for the "scandal" to appear: why this "sudden" revelation after several years of silence and dissimulation? Compared to the fact that Hergé had constantly been confronted with his political past, one can wonder how strongly Paul de Man's "secret" was kept. [P. 765]

Pulled up short, the little decrypter is plunged down a well of amazement since he must be amazed in his turn before this mark of amazement. He says to himself: "Here now is an author who is amazed. He is amazed that a 'secret' was kept for many years. He even seems to be accusing someone of it (who? he names no one), whereas for him and for 'several people' 'at Harvard and in the Boston area,' this 'secret' was not a secret. But then why did they not reveal it themselves? Whom is this author accusing exactly? By any chance would he be so bold as to accuse those who in fact made this 'secret' public, being in truth *the first ones to do so*? The first ones to do so: would it by any chance be these very ones whom the author seems to accuse? How strange, how strange."

More and more intrigued, but also convinced that this author, instead of accusing heaven only knows who (since he names no one), would have done better to take right away the initiative that he reproaches others for having taken too late, whereas he acknowledges that he was in a position to take it four years earlier, our little archivist reconstitutes the first paragraph of the text. The latter thus begins (we have not forgotten and will never forget) with: "In 1982–83, I was preparing my volume on the Belgian cartoonist Hergé[1]. . . . *Les Métamorphoses de Tintin*," and so on. This paragraph indeed confirms that the author of the aforesaid *Métamorphoses* flatters himself for having been aware, already at this time, of the articles by de Man in *Le Soir*, and even for having talked about them one "afternoon with a colleague from Boston University whose specialty is the hunting of presumed French fascist intellectuals" (p. 765). Monologue of the future little journalist-reporter-archeologist who is acquiring a taste for philology (I remember Tintin in *The Secret of "The Unicorn"*: "Look now! You'll see that the message of the parchments is right." Captain Haddock: "Thundering typhoons! The numbers and the letters are completed."): "Now who could this be, this professor at Boston University specialized in hunting? That won't be easy to discover, today, and I'm certainly not going to hunt down the hunters, especially in a university: 'a colleague from Boston University whose specialty is the hunting of presumed French fascist intellectuals.' I wonder who that could be. So there were intellectual hunters at this time, and intellectuals who made a profession of tracking other intellectuals? In sum, hunters specialized in the fanatical pursuit of a certain type of prey [*gibier*]? Intellectuals trained, equipped, motivated for the hunt (first of all fascinated by the said prey, as always, according to the well-known process of identification), intellectuals who finally were interested in nothing else? In any case, the hunter and the author of *Les Métamorphoses de Tintin* knew it all, according to the latter, but they never said anything about it publicly. And yet here is someone who accuses heaven knows who, since he names no one, for not having published the thing until five years later. But who published it exactly? And for the first time? In the most public way? Perchance, might it not be within the population afflicted by the 'recurrent theme' ('deconstruction and feminism') that one finds someone who, with no previous knowledge, would have decided that everything had to be published from the first moment he became aware of the 'secret'? So he is the one who would be within his rights to accuse the silence, the cowardice, the thoughtlessness, or the bad faith of those who, saying they had the newspapers in their hands and drawing from that fact not the least public consequence, having proposed neither republication, nor analysis, nor the most open discussion, now have the nerve to lecture those who *did* do all that."

Let's leave him there, our Tintin of centuries to come, with his hypotheses. If he had also found the last paragraph of the same author on the subject of "preferred ignorance," we can imagine his indignation. It would be necessary to invoke the energetic speech of Captain Haddock: "*Mille tonnerres de sabord, Zigomars, Gargarisme, Emplâtres;*[13] here's someone who claims he knew things that he did not talk about for years and still he dares to accuse those who, in the first place, made the thing absolutely public. He accuses them, says he with incredible cheek, of having 'preferred ignorance.'" "In the case of Hergé, whose work was banned in Belgium until 1947, he spent the rest of his life (he died in 1983 [that, along with his Belgian origins, is indeed the only thing he had in common with de Man]) rewriting the first adventures of Tintin in order to dissimulate his previous political mistakes [should de Man have done or could he have done the same? "Comparative" questions on the modes of circulation, duration, and degradability of the Tintin comic books and the different types of de Man's writings]. In the case of Paul de Man, who was still remembered in Belgium as a former rightist intellectual [a lie or a dishonest simplification; see on this subject the private and public attestations not only in "Paul de Man's War" but in *Responses*], ignorance was preferred in the American academic world— ignorance not only among his friends and disciples but also in theory" (p. 766). But who exactly preferred ignorance, I ask, if not the author of *Les Métamorphoses de Tintin*? It is difficult, moreover, to imagine what ignorance "in theory" of these articles could possibly mean. As far as I'm concerned, in any case, I took account of them and took my responsibilities as soon as I became aware of the said articles, that very

13. The English translation of *The Secret of "The Unicorn"* renders one such outburst of Captain Haddock's vivid epithets as follows: "Me, the culprit? You dare accuse me? . . . Miserable earthworms! . . . Sea-gherkins! . . . Slave-traders! . . . Sea-lice! . . . Black-beetles! . . . Baboons! . . . Artichokes! . . . Vermicellis! . . . Phylloxera! . . . Pyrographers! . . . Crab-apples! . . . Goosecaps! . . . Gogglers! . . . Jelly-fish!" At which point, Tintin interjects: "Captain! Captain! Calm yourself!" (Hergé, *The Secret of "The Unicorn*," trans. Leslie Lonsdale-Cooper and Michael Turner [1946, 1959; Boston, 1924], p. 29). See p. 61 for the moment when Tintin solves the message of the parchments.— TRANS.

week, something which the author of *Les Métamorphoses de Tintin* confesses he never did, no more than did his hunter colleague (now who can that be exactly?).

So I've made a bet: these pearls will be passed on to posterity, even if they are not destined to have the long life of nuclear wastes. But people will have understood very quickly that my interest in these pearls and this bet was only a pretext for advancing the following *nontheorem* on the subject of the figurative "biodegradability" of what are commonly called texts, or at least, let's put it more strictly, of publications. One cannot wager publicly on the survival of an archive without thereby giving it an extra chance. As if the wager on the survival itself contributed to the survival. Thus, the wager cannot take the form of a *theoretical* hypothesis on the subject of what will happen objectively in an autonomous field. That is why I spoke of a *nontheorem*. Like any discourse on the wager, a wager intervenes performatively in the field and partially determines it. It feigns "objective" and theoretical speculation while in fact it performs a practical transformation of its object. It is perhaps in part thanks to my wager, my public wager in the very place of its publication, that the phrase I have in effect just celebrated will become celebrated ("at Harvard and in the Boston area (where deconstruction and feminism . . .)"). I did nothing more than say it deserved it. But such an evaluation was already a chancy and violent intervention. Perhaps I exaggerated, on purpose or not on purpose. Perhaps none of this deserved so much attention. (Generalize again this nontheorem on the impossibility of any historical metatheorem, a fortiori of any foretelling. And recall as well, besides the original elaboration by de Man of the opposition performative/constative, his text on Pascal's wager.)[14] By definition, and this is why there is wagering and performative intervention of the wager, no calculation will ever be able to master the "biodegradability" to come of a document. All evaluations, in truth all texts, are war itself on the subject of this survival. Paul de Man's war means also that.

There is a moral question here, and even the example of one of those conflicts between obligations without which no decision and no responsibility would really have any meaning, I mean disquieting meaning, the

14. See de Man, "Pascal's Allegory of Persuasion," in *Allegory and Representation*, ed. Stephen Greenblatt (Baltimore, 1981), pp. 1–25. On de Man's reading of Pascal, allow me to recommend the admirable text by Geoffrey Bennington, "Aberrations: de Man (and) the Machine," in *Reading de Man Reading*, ed. Lindsay Waters and Wlad Godzich (Minneapolis, 1989), pp. 209–22. This vigilant, questioning, and inventive reading is exemplary in many respects, in particular those we are discussing here.

only meaning that it ought to have. A calm and assured responsibility is never a responsibility; it's good conscience. The moral question is at least double:

1. Is it necessary to respond to every interpellation, to everyone no matter who, to every question, and especially to every public attack? The answer is "yes," it seems, when time and energy permit, to the extent to which the response keeps open, in spite of everything, a space of discussion. Without such a space no democracy and no community deserving of the name would survive. But the answer is "no" if the said interpellations fail to respect certain elementary rules, if they so lack decency or interest that the response risks shoring them up with a guarantee, confirming in some way a perversion of the said democratic discussion. Yet, in that case, it would be necessary that the nonresponse be appropriately interpreted as a sign of respect for certain principles and not as contempt for the questioner or, especially, for the third party—reader or listener—whom one presumes should be the principal addressee of such an exchange, however difficult or improbable that exchange remains. It is rare that all these conditions come together and are clearly assured. It happens that a response may be a nonresponse, and nonresponse is sometimes the best response. An immediate degradability then annuls the archive of this response without response, which is thereby submitted to a kind of originary amnesia. We therefore see the latter at work at the very heart of the event, whatever it may be. The "organic" figure of biodegradability thus appears, already, to be of doubtful relevance. At least in the presumed literality of its point of origin.

2. Another question, another double bind. When the interpellation is disastrous (weak, ridiculous, violent, indecent, in bad faith, or whatever one wishes to imagine), does the most generous gesture consist in responding or not responding? Is it better to abandon the interpellation to its spontaneous degradability, which destines a discourse to rapid oblivion? Or rather to save it from that fate by pretending, at least, to take it seriously, thinking always of the responsibility one has with regard to the third party? But in this case, to save it means also to send it to its ruin, to confer a certain duration on that which one judges to be inept. To make a text last, that is, to contribute to assuring the conditions of public exhibition, may thus be also a perverse gesture, a sign of aggressivity toward the authors. Do everything to avoid that, if it is possible.

In their bottomless overdeterminability, these two questions are made still worse by the formidable ambiguity of the very concept of (bio)degradability. To be (bio)degradable means at least two things: on the one hand, the annihilation of identity; on the other hand, the chance to pass into the general milieu of culture, into the "life" of "culture" while enriching it with anonymous but nourishing substances. It will thus be necessary to come back to this concept and this figure, their analysis remaining up until now insufficient. (Is not the question finally that of the proper name, of what is called the proper name or at least the singular mark of the event, of the date? Come back to this.) [. . .]

10 P.M.
Feeling discouraged this evening. I will never manage to respond to this quintext. Since I have made the tally of the arguments and made clear, in the two tables, that there is nothing in these five diatribes which I have not already said (for example, as Culler points out, my "exceedingly severe statement" against the de Man of 1940–42), or to which I have not already responded in a detailed fashion, what remains? Very few rational arguments, the theater of petty passions, some of whose mechanisms and old rhetorical tricks I really must try to describe. But, all the same, I am not going to go back over everything and repeat myself in detail. I am not going to request that people reread what I wrote or, one more time, that they reread de Man. While I'm on the subject of rereading de Man, any careful reader will have noticed to what extent the things I said about the duty to read or reread de Man irritated my "critical respondents," with the exception of Culler. Three out of the five of them even said so. This request for reading (isn't this rather normal? what less could one ask for?) seems extraordinary to them, even exorbitant. What is more, I never said that *it was necessary at all costs to read* de Man or anybody else, but, and this is quite a different thing, that *if* at least one claims to speak about all this, it is a good idea to read, even better to reread, preferably everything one can. As we shall see, three of the critics *react* in an analogous fashion—I do not say identical—to this requirement, one that is nevertheless elementary. An intense and recurrent reaction (a "recurrent theme"?): it comes back three times in conclusion like a groan of protest ("Ah, so one would have to read, read de Man, and from A to Z?" "Hey, do you see that, he asks us, on top of everything else, to read de Man! and even to reread him!"). This single protest shows to what degree, whether one's talking about de Man or "Deconstruction" in general, the question is also that of a fierce resistance to reading, with all the forms that can be taken by "*pv*," the category of *on ne pveut pas lire*. I will thus cite *three examples:*

First example: "We must now reread de Man from A to Z: this is the recurrent theme [again! and in another "critical response"!] in the apologetic literature that has been appearing since late 1987" (p. 796). After having been associated with "deconstruction and feminism," the "recurrent theme" finds itself here associated, in its literality and by another of my censors, with the duty to read. Might it be a question of the same thing, in the three cases, and of the same "theme"? The two authors who have recourse to the same expression seem to be as amazed by the recurrence as by the theme. Here is someone, for example (a professor I am told), who is amazed that anyone would ask him to read or reread that which he, nevertheless, wants to talk about, and that he wants to condemn. And he makes yet another accusation: all the writing that appeals to reading de Man is "apologetic"! Or, if you prefer, all this apologetic literature is characterized by a strange obsession with reading, by this compulsion to read! There are those who go so far in their insolence as to try to infect us with, even impose on us their recurrent perversion, and to give us orders: so read! But we'll not let ourselves be talked into it. And, in fact, they don't.

These words ("apologetic," "apologia") almost always shock me. Sometimes they make me laugh. First of all because of their magical and visibly defensive repetition. They resonate from one end to the other of the same indictment, from its title ("Jacques Derrida's Apologia") to its final words ("Derrida's apologia for de Man"), as if it were enough to keep hammering away forcefully at the same nonsense in order to produce an effect of obvious fact. What I wrote was so far from an "apologia for Paul de Man" (it is enough to reread it or to consult the two tables to be convinced of this) that certain of my statements appeared "exceedingly severe." I repeated for tens of pages in a row, without the least indulgence, what I thought of certain "unpardonable" texts from *Le Soir* and of the collaboration with *Le Soir* as a whole. When I seem to "defend" de Man, and I never would have done it otherwise, it is always, as it is here once more, in the face of murderous caricatures, abusive simplifications, unjustified acts of violence by those (the most numerous, let's not forget, in truth *the only ones* during several months and while I was writing my article) who have spoken out loud their dream of destroying once and for all the memory of de Man, of his work, and of all that one can associate with him from near and from far. And later, when there appeared some letters or articles (still *in response* and largely in the minority, whenever, that is, newspapers consented to publish them!) that "defended" de Man against the iniquity and the dogmatism of these monolithic verdicts, there was, as far as I know, *not one of them* that did not pronounce a negative and "severe" judgment on certain articles from *Le Soir*, notably on one of them; we all know which one. I do *not* know of *one* of de Man's "friends," the so-called apologists, who has not publicly condemned what there was to condemn in these articles. I could stop there; that should suffice to disqualify all this uncontrolled agitation, this indecent and impatient trepidation. What exactly do they want, all these accusers? to condemn a priori, without even a trial? In a block and without opening the file? To condemn without listening to the accused or to those who claim to read and to listen? Would they also like to condemn the books of the accused? The friends of the accused? The readers of the accused? The readers of these readers? And why not their grandchildren? To condemn those who, without ever pleading Paul de Man's innocence and thus while pronouncing him guilty (within certain limits, of course, with restraint and precision, and this is the whole problem) still want to know what we are talking about? But what are people raging at? Where are we living? In which century? In which country?

It is thus grossly wrong and dishonest to speak of "apologetic literature." I am waiting for someone to show me a single text to have appeared up until now that does not recognize what I called—what *I* called, *before my detractors did*—"the most unbearable" (p. 621), "the *unpardonable* violence and confusion" (p. 623; read the rest of the paragraph, and passim; I am certainly not now going to re-cite and select, while isolating them, all my negative evaluations in order to reassure or embarrass my adversaries). I therefore assert that there was no apology, on any side, especially not on mine, unless one supposes apology to begin with this simple reminder: if you want to speak of someone, and especially if you want to condemn him in totality, without qualification and without appeal, read, read as much and as thoroughly as possible, with vigilance and honesty. Apparently this demand seems inordinate and intolerably apologetic to those who decidedly do not want to read or at least not de Man. That must be recognized as their right, but on the condition that they do not then claim to speak about what they refuse to read or, a still more intolerable obligation in their view, reread.

Second example. For another of my censors, the appeal to the duty of reading is not only the surprising "recurrent theme" of an "apologetic literature"; it is a "challenge." Reading, "a challenge"! Sigh of impatience: "a challenge we now hear regularly" (p. 775). Once again I will have to quote at length, a rule that should be more respected in every discussion and which I never fail to do.[15] For reasons of intellectual rigor and of ethics. Here, then:

> Derrida's own "exercice du silence" on such issues raises some hard questions, not only about this particular text but about the turn the deconstructive project, originally so liberating, is now taking. Is *context* always and only *verbal:* the judgment on the word by the word? "Those who, if they want still to accuse or take revenge," writes Derrida, "will finally have to read de Man, from A to Z" (p. 639). This is a challenge we now hear regularly, but its implication—that the issue is entirely *textual* (how do we read text X?) rather than *practical* (what choices did Paul de Man make?)—is deeply disturbing, suggesting as it does that Literature is All, that if de Man praised, say, Franz Kafka, he was somehow on the right side of history. Again, why is it imperative to read de Man from A to Z and not to read de Man's articles in the context of the related writings of the period? How indeed can these articles be understood without a knowledge of the events to which they were responding? In drawing a linguistic circle around such writings, aren't we once again worshipping at the shrine of the Sacred Text, this time the Sacred Text of the poet-substitute called "theorist"? [Pp. 775–76]

Faced with such a web of ignorance, confusion, and bad faith, it is my turn to sigh. Where to begin? Is it really necessary to waste all this time and so much paper, even if it is recyclable?

Yes, let's go *Aufklärer,* one more effort. Let's try to make things progress a little.

1. First of all, in order to attribute to the "deconstructive project" such a definition of context ("always and only *verbal*"), one would have to have never read (or in any case understood) a single line or the least letter of the texts that have defined this "project" (another inadequate word, but let's not bother). Since it is apparently a question of me in such a hallucination, I may be permitted to underscore that, for the last twenty-five years, I have not ceased to say and to recall exactly the contrary. No longer daring to ask that one read *me,* from A to Z, I ask

15. See in partricular my responses in *Limited Inc,* and "But, beyond, . . . (Open Letter to Anne McClintock and Rob Nixon)," trans. Peggy Kamuf, *Critical Inquiry* 13 (Autumn 1986): 155–70.

only that one read—if, that is, one still wants to talk about me—at least between A, B, and C.[16] There, one will discover that deconstruction begins by the deconstruction of the "verbal" limits set on the text and the context. This is, in particular, the meaning of a few of the words that this "critical respondent" may have overheard at a cocktail party: the deconstruction of phonocentrism, of logocentrism, and of phallogocentrism. Or again, "there is no outside-the-text" signifies that one never accedes to a text without some relation to its contextual opening and that a context is not made up of only what is so trivially called a text, that is, the words of a book or the more or less biodegradable paper document in a library. If one does not understand this initial transformation of the concepts of text, trace, writing, signature, event, context,[17] one understands nothing about nothing of the aforesaid deconstruction—and that is indeed the case here, even if one ventures to qualify deconstruction as "originally so liberating" (really???). One has to take the time to do a little more work. I would be insulting my other readers if I continued to recall such elementary things.

2. For these same reasons, the opposition between "textual" and "practical" has no meaning for me, and especially not the one attributed to it here. This is why, moreover, deconstruction is much more "practical" and political than so many people believe or pretend to believe. And that is exactly what they cannot bear. I have often explained myself on this subject, even in this very journal when already responding to a couple of "critical respondents."[18] I was already struggling, in vain apparently, against the most obstinate resistance to reading and to analysis.

16. See in particular Derrida, "Limited Inc, a b c," *Limited Inc*, pp. 29–110, and "But, beyond"; see also Derrida, "Living On: *Border Lines*," trans. James Hulbert, in *Deconstruction and Criticism*, ed. Harold Bloom et al. (New York, 1979), p. 81, where Derrida writes: "This is my starting point: no meaning can be determined out of context, but no context permits saturation. What I am referring to here is not richness of substance, semantic fertility, but rather structure: the structure of the remnant or of iteration."—TRANS.

17. These last three words correspond in effect to the title of one of Derrida's texts, "Signature Event Context," *Margins of Philosophy*, pp. 307–30. See also "Signature Event Context," trans. Samuel Weber and Jeffrey Mehlman, *Limited Inc*, pp. 1–23. —TRANS.

18. See Derrida, "But, beyond." An opposition analogous to that of "textual/practical," but just as crude and in this case irrelevant, plays a caricatural, which is to say totally misleading, role in the second article that *The Nation* has just devoted to the "affair," an affair that has become, in effect, good business [*une bonne affaire*]. After "Deconstructing de Man," a year ago, now it's "Debating de Man" (13 Feb. 1989; one has to admire at least the progress made in the titles. There is room for hope). With the same hastiness, in a confusion that has not abated in the last year or more, the same author organizes his whole article, well before the deadline (see below; he still wants

3. Who said "Literature is All"? Certainly not me, neither in "Paul de Man's War" nor anywhere else. I am sure Paul de Man never said it. And as for the way he had, which is, moreover, very interesting, of treating a certain irreducible specificity of literature (which does not come down to saying "Everything is Literature"), the disagreement between us was public and known to those who do us the honor of being interested in our publications and our debates of more than fifteen years (see notably *Mémoires*). I pointed this out several times in "Paul de Man's War" (at least on pp. 627, 649, and no doubt elsewhere as well).

4. Who ever said it sufficed to praise Kafka in order to be "on the right side of history"? Certainly not me, and the analysis I did of the reference to Kafka was, I hope, less stupid than that. Since those who have read me know that this analysis was rather nuanced, complicated, and meticulous (excessively so if I believe the apparent reproach made elsewhere), I will do no more than refer back to it.

5. I was the first to say, and to repeat with great insistence (see at least pp. 600, 635–37, 640, and in a more or less explicit fashion throughout), in particular for the reasons of principle I have just recalled (1 and 2), that it was necessary to read "de Man's articles in the context of the related writings of the period" and to have a "knowledge of the events to which they were responding." But I did not content myself

---

to be first), months before the publication of the 700-page book that he is claiming to review, around the well-known frontier that is supposed to separate "textualism" and "historicism" (! why doesn't this "historian" do any work? One has the urge to ask him a few very basic questions, such as: what is a "text" for you? And "history"? What have you read on this subject? Give us a few references). The result is sometimes outright laughable. By way of compensation, and since the author insists on having the right to the same "pardon" as others, I pardon this second series of errors and truncated quotations (of what I wrote on pp. 625, 637–39, for example), of obscene simplifications, of dishonest omissions, finally all these things that have now become familiar throughout the world, and still the same disdain for the most elementary forms of probity. This disdain now calmly authorizes itself, indeed ennobles itself with a quotation from Lindsay Waters (speaking of Paul de Man!) that the journalist from *The Nation* misuses by turning aside its destination. He seems to be saying that anything is allowed (to him) since, according to Waters, "for him [de Man in the 1960s who wrote for *The New York Review of Books*] it was part of the intellectual's job to try to convey complex ideas for as general an audience as would receive them, despite the risks of distortion [and] the need to make deadlines." In "Paul de Man's War," I indicated (for example, p. 591, ll. 30–31) the respect due the functions of the press and thus to the journalists who have a sense of the immense and difficult responsibility that is theirs—which Waters also recalls. It is even in the name of this respect and this responsibility that the violent simplifications, the deformations ("distortions"), and everything that is sacrificed to the "deadline" must be evaluated. And that one does not have the right to say anything one pleases. It is because of my respect for what journalism should be, no less than what the university should be, that I am shocked by these two articles in *The Nation*.

with *saying* that this *was necessary* (although that is already a big step and one which I like to think was not without consequences); *I did so*, right away, as best I could, in the limits of a sixty-page article that, on the subject of the writings and the events of this period, contains more historical information, more references ("textual" and "practical" references, to take up this very primitive but convenient distinction) than in the harangues of *all* my censors put together. I leave it to them to count the references, if they can. Whoever read "Paul de Man's War" cannot say without bad faith that I traced a "linguistic circle" around a "Sacred Text," a ridiculous formula that has had a place for the last quarter century in the largely degraded dictionary of all the antideconstructionist stereotypes. (For the quickest summary—I am thinking of the time of those who *ne veulent pas lire*—allow me to refer once again to "Signature Event Context," which is only twenty pages long.)

Third example. Here the scene is a little different, first of all more disarming, no doubt, but also more crude. The author seems to accept the rule of "rereading de Man" but only if it is in order to recognize de Man's "errors." And the recognition of the right to error seems to him in effect "reasonable," but only if one consents to extend it first of all to the journalist-professors who have written whatever they wanted about de Man (pp. 802–3). I found this gesture rather sympathetic and, especially, amusing. Here at least is someone, I said to myself, who is profiting from the occasion (better late than never) in order to ask to be forgiven the "reading mistakes" he accumulated and, what is still more serious, indirectly propagated in the world press. Here is the final paragraph of a text that, right away, beginning with its title ("The Responsibilities of Friendship"), took a wrong turn by suggesting that everything I had written in this context, like the responsibilities I took or defined, were controlled by my friendship for de Man. That adds a "reading mistake" to an already impressive list (I will return to this). Let us reread this conclusion:

> Derrida suggests "rules" for "rereading de Man," the first of which is "respect for the right to error." That's a reasonable suggestion, but for Derrida it applies only to de Man, not to his critics. The conclusion one is left with is that what de Man did—collaborate with the Nazi occupiers of Belgium—should be understood and forgiven, but what de Man's critics have done—commit "reading mistakes"—should be condemned as unforgivable. Outside the circle of de Man's most committed defenders, few readers will find this argument persuasive. [Pp. 802–3]

I do not know if I am part of the "circle" in question, but I do not find this argument "persuasive" for this initial reason: I have not come across it anywhere and thus never formulated it myself. I find it touching that a professor-journalist asks forgiveness for his "reading mistakes" as soon as, so he believes, other "errors" have been pardoned. But all of this is incongruous and beside the question, not to say out of the question. First of all, contrary to the assertion of the same professor-journalist, who decidedly still refuses to read, I never put myself in the situation of pardoning or of asking others to pardon de Man for anything whatsoever. I explain this at length in the vicinity of a passage that speaks of "the unpardonable violence and confusion of these sentences" (p. 623; the reference is to the article "Jews in Present-day Literature"). I even underlined the word "unpardonable," and I could cite many other passages that go in the same direction (pp. 621–31 and passim). Is this clear enough? Did I not insist enough on the reasons for which I did not feel I had the right to pardon this or that writing, this or that act, no more than I had the right to condemn the *whole* discourse, the *whole* life, the *whole* work of de Man? And on the reasons for which such a totalization seemed to me unjust, summary, confused, and politically dangerous (see in particular p. 631, but also in numerous other places)?

I not only signed and underlined the word "unpardonable" (is it pardonable to lie by acting as if one had not read that? Is it pardonable not to have read it? Is it pardonable to accuse me of not having written it?), I also explained why I did not feel I had the right to pardon. Not because I have set myself up in the position of judge, but because this would be to talk in the place of victims. I will ask the one who accuses others, even as he demands pardon for his numerous errors, to reread the whole page (and a little beyond) in my article that begins thus: "Through the indelible wound, one must still analyze and seek to understand. Any concession would betray, besides a complacent indulgence and a lack of rigor, an infinitely culpable thoughtlessness with regard to past, present, or future victims of discourses that at least resembled this one" (p. 631). To finish on this point, I do not know whether the enormities published in *The Nation* (9 January 1988) were only "reading mistakes." For many reasons, I never sought to compare them with anything whatsoever of Paul de Man's, really. I do not know if they are "unforgivable." I do not have the power to decide this in the face of the whole world. If I may be permitted a confidence, I would say this: While I continue to pay the greatest attention to the *possibility* and the *significance* of such violent journalistic acts, I had already begun to forget the fact and the literality of *these particular ones*. Their author would have done better not to recall them. Apparently, he prefers to expose himself to criticism rather than let himself be forgotten. [. . .]

On forgetting and forgiving, a huge question. To be added to the file of the "biodegradable." [. . .]

Why is the *figure of the biodegradable* so provocative? Both useful, from a heuristic point of view, but essentially limited in its relevance? In the most general and novel sense of this term, a *text* must be "(bio)degradable" in order to nourish the "living" culture, memory, tradition. To the extent to which it has some sense, makes sense, then its "content" irrigates the milieu of this tradition and its "formal" identity is dissolved. And by formal identity, one may understand here all the "signifiers," including the title and the name of one or more presumed signatories. And yet, to enrich the "organic" soil of the said culture, it must also resist it, contest it, question and criticize it enough (dare I say deconstruct it?) and thus it must not be assimilable ([bio]degradable, if you like). Or at least, it must be assimilated as inassimilable, kept in reserve, unforgettable because irreceivable, capable of inducing meaning without being exhausted by meaning, incomprehensibly elliptical, secret. What is it in a "great" work, let's say of Plato, Shakespeare, Hugo, Mallarmé, James, Joyce, Kafka, Heidegger, Benjamin, Blanchot, Celan, that resists erosion? What is it that, far from being exhausted in amnesia, increases its reserve to the very extent to which one draws from it, as if expenditure augmented the capital? This very thing [*cela même*], this singular event that, enriching the meaning and accumulating memory, is nevertheless not to be reduced to a totality or that always exceeds interpretation. What resists immediate degradation is this very thing, the text or in the text, which is no longer on the order of meaning and which joins the universal wealth of the "message" to unintelligible singularity, finally unreadable (if reading means to understand and to learn to know), of a trace or a signature. The irreplaceable singularity, the event of signature, is not to be summed up in a patronymic name, because it is the work itself. The "proper name" in question—which has no meaning and is not a concept—is not to be reduced to the appellation of civil status. What is more, it is proper to nothing and to no one, reappropriable by nothing and by no one, not even by the presumed bearer. It is this singular impropriety that permits it to resist degradation—never forever, but for a long time. Enigmatic kinship between waste, for example nuclear waste, and the "masterpiece."

Yet, one cannot say that the best way to escape cultural "(bio)degradability" is to be irreceivable, inassimilable, to exceed meaning. For then one would have to say that absurdities, logical errors, bad readings, the worst ineptitudes, symptoms of confusion or of belatedness are, by that very fact, assured of survival. Even if there are those who hope this is true, we know that, most often, nothing of the sort is the case. That which has no meaning, purely and simply, is almost immediately "(bio) degradable." That which has little meaning does not last long. What is "bad" does not resist (this is at least what one would like to believe, the story I tell myself when I wake up tired, but in a good mood.) So, in order to "remain" a little while, the meaning has to link up *in a certain way* with that which exceeds it. Sign itself in a certain way. [. . .]

Here one would have to make a long detour (but I won't have time today) through music, the memory of the musical work, to explain what I mean here by proper name. Not that music does not have meaning, but I am interested here in what it is in music that surpasses discursive meaning, exceeds a certain kind of translatable intelligibility into "good sense" sentences. Music has nothing in common with what some call music when, understanding nothing of certain discourses that they *ne pveulent pas* [can/will not] read, they believe or want to make others believe that these latter have no meaning. Anyone who does not under-stand can always complain or accuse: All I am given to hear or under-stand is unintelligible sounds, I am not convinced, I am being subjected to the musical apparatus of seduction. [. . .]

What I tried to say about "responsibility" in "Paul de Man's War" is difficult, I realize. What I am trying to think about responsibility in general is obscure, even perilous; other texts could attest to this and I do not hide it. But the thing itself is obscure, and my discourse is always highly argued, even if it cannot be a question of reproducing this argu-mentation here, for lack of time and space. All the more so since this argument claims to move beyond the usual stereotypes of the concept of responsibility. That is why, I grant you, this argument does not fol-low in my text (and I wanted it this way) that "clear-cut line" (p. 785) demanded by someone who seems to like to read the way one drives on the interstate, perhaps even while driving on the interstate.

Can one speak of responsibility or assume a responsibility without difficulty and without anguish? I don't believe so. To speak of it calmly and as if there were some obvious, commonsense facts available on this subject, *as if one knew* what were and ought to be the "ethical categories," is irresponsibility itself—moral, political, philosophical, intellectual irresponsibility in general. Here is someone who, certain that he knows what responsibility and "ethical categories" are, ironizes about my "tour de force" ("To write about responsibility with so little

reference to ethical categories is something of a tour de force" [p. 785]).
With or without the irony, the same author had just been amazed to
see "responsibility" associated with "responding," with the categories
of "rhetoric" and "psychoanalysis." I suppose that for him, when one
treats of responsibility or of "ethical categories," it is not necessary to
speak of either "response," or language, or rhetoric, or transference, or
the unconscious (I would really like to see him demonstrate this). These
would be digressions toward the inessential, avoidances. What can you
respond to that?

And what is one doing when, understanding neither the sense nor
the form of a discourse on responsibility (because one deems it to be
"impenetrably elliptic" (p. 785; I will come back to this marvelous treatment of ellipsis), one compares it to a music that has no meaning, to
some "variations on a theme"? I think I have already said that when one
doesn't understand something, one can always resort to decreeing: This
is not a discourse, these are only meaningless sonorities. I will not be
so cruel as to illustrate this practice with examples that always amount
to taking a discourse or a language (for example, a foreign language)
for meaningless music. This is, in sum, the definition that certain people
would give of analphabetism. Out of respect for nonalphabetic writings,
I would say instead illiteracy in the broad sense. And in the case that
concerns us, the diagnosis that may be summed up as "it is unintelligent
or unintelligible like music" seeming still too generous, the diagnostician
preferred to insinuate, wound, add a clever little wink: like Wagnerian
music ("a Wagnerian leitmotiv"). By which I believe I understand, without being certain of this, pre-Nazi, as is only proper. "In fact these
'variations' are more musical than analytic: 'responsibility' comes close
to being a Wagnerian leitmotiv" (p. 785).

One can imagine the musical culture that dictates such sinister "bon-
mots." It presents a hardly more cheering aspect than that which one
perceives behind the "I-do-not-understand-therefore-it's-irrational-
non-analytic-magical-illogical-perverse-seductive-diabolical" that has
always signed the triumph of the old obscurantism. Some may think
that the latter has disappeared, at least in the university; well, it hasn't. It
resists, it survives, it lingers on, and, if you want to know my prognosis,
it is almost indestructible.

Saturday, 21 January, 5 A.M.

Music can also, in certain situations, resist effacement to the extent to
which, by its very form, it does not let itself be so easily dissolved in the

common element of discursive sense. From this point of view, at any rate, music would be less "(bio)degradable" than discourse and even than the art of discourse.

[When I rewrite these fragments in view of publication, I hope that the reader will pardon me for having constantly mixed up reflexions on the biodegradable with certain reading impressions with which I neither wanted to close myself up nor closet the reader for too long. Thus, for essential and fundamental reasons (because these questions are indissociable, as I hope to have demonstrated), but also in order not to die of boredom.]

There are also verbal harassments that, without producing what was so unforgettably called a "clear-cut line of argument," procure for you no musical experience. In this category, I class a sort of rhetorical trance that consists in repeating often enough, in the most mechanical, automatic way possible, one or two words so as to produce after a while, in the other or in oneself, a kind of hallucination: If this word is proffered so often, there must indeed be a corresponding thing, the thing one is talking about. I sense this intoxication or this compulsion when the words "fascism," "fascist," and "Nazi" are hammered at with such frequency and such an imperturbable authority (pp. 804–11) that the hypnotized reader would end up consenting: Yes, since they say it so often, and moreover since there are two of them saying it at the same time, with such force and assurance; and I would even go further: since they believe it so firmly, both of them, and so unanimously, one has to believe them, the words must correspond to something, yes, there was indeed a "fascist ideology" (p. 804) of de Man, yes, there were indeed "de Man's fascist sympathies"; I will even go further: "a fascist de Man," yes, his "practices" were indeed those of a "fascist intellectual" (p. 805), and yes, in fact, there was indeed a "fascist intellectual's practice" (p. 805) in de Man, and even a "fascist project" (p. 811) by de Man, yes, there was indeed on his part a "commitment to fascism" (p. 806); and I will even say further (as Dupont or Dupond would say),[19] an "ideological

19. Besides Tintin and Captain Haddock, the detectives Dupont and Dupond are inevitable and indiscernable characters in this series of comic books. In the English version they are called Thompson and Thomson. They resemble twins who are constantly lost, running to catch up, beside the question, always on the wrong trail. They are especially noted for the way in which each one repeats literally the discourse of the other, introducing the echo of this pure repetition by a phrase that ups the ante, such as "I will even say further," or "I would even add," expressions whose frequency may be noticed in the passage we are here translating. For example, in *Red Rackham's Treasure*, Dupont, unless it is Dupond, says: "A real gang of thugs!" and Dupond, unless it is Dupont, adds: "I would even say further: A real gang of thugs!"—TRANS.

commitment to fascism" (p. 807), and even an "intellectual engagement with fascism" (p. 806); yes, in fact, we can now conclude that there indeed were "fascist tendencies" in de Man (p. 807). Worn down to the point of hypnosis, even knocked out, the reader may very well no longer wonder if, perchance, the two are not repeating these words so often, like a litany, in order to believe something they can't quite manage to believe, still less to demonstrate. And when they pronounce, in the form of an incantatory verdict, the words "the most obvious," it is in order to thrust forward the least obvious, to wit: "on the one hand, de Man was a Nazi collaborator; on the other hand, he was a Belgian fascist" (p. 808). This is indeed what the two authors would like to inculcate in us rather than prove.

Because all of this is false. So as to demonstrate it in an economical fashion and so as not to oblige anyone to reread "Paul de Man's War" from A to Z, without even citing the many attestations and analyses that are now available, I will recall only one point (that I had, moreover, already underscored [p. 604] when quoting from the article in *Le Soir* of 3 December 1987; how much longer will it be necessary to repeat this?). These young men, who are giving everybody history lessons, seem as yet unaware that, after the war, there were judges in Belgium far more vigilant than they: better informed, more severe, and more seriously motivated. There was as well a still more ruthless law that was enforced without flinching in the cases of those suspected of the least collaboration. *No charges were filed against de Man.* There was not even the beginning of a trial. "*Paul de Man was not the object of proceedings before the War Council for his attitude or his activity during the war* [Paul De Man n'a pas fait l'objet de poursuites devant le Conseil de guerre pour son attitude ou son activité pendant la guerre]."[20]

Here then are two young Americans, probably born after the war, who would like to reinstate the Purge, to purge, purge, purge. Decontextualizing with a fury the whole dossier, they demand a new investigation; they are ready to begin a second prosecution and to call a new meeting of the War Council, indeed to reinstitute it themselves because the other one was undoubtedly too indulgent. And now, almost a half century later, they insist on a guilty verdict without appeal regarding that which the Belgian tribunals, who were on the spot and were, we

---

20. Representative of the Auditor General, letter to the Director of the Center for Research and Historical Study of the Second World War, 23 June 1988. This letter is cited *in extenso* in Thomas Keenan's remarkable compilation, "Documents: Public Criticisms," in *Responses*, p. 475.—Trans.

should not forget, the most implacable in Europe, did not judge to be guilty and, truth to tell, did not even accuse! Since they obviously do not have the means to institute this New War Council, they reproach *me* for not having done it. They still have not understood that that goes counter to my principles as well as my tastes. On the other hand, if in view of establishing this NWC, they have to begin by acquiring the assistance of a new Academic Bureau of Investigation and of some professional detectives, why don't they get in contact with the other "critical respondents"? One of them offers an apology of the "detective" whose "task is to discover the truth" (p. 794), while another knows a colleague who is a connoisseur of intellectual prey [*gibier*] and "whose specialty is the hunting of presumed French fascist intellectuals" (p. 765; I really wonder who that could be). Will they be clever enough to disqualify the War Council, I mean the true one, the first, the real, the tough one, over there, in Belgium after the war, with all the documents and all the witnesses it examined? I still have a few doubts about that, but good luck anyway for this other bidding war. As for me, I am not going to lose any more time on such a comedy of justice nor waste any more paper, even if it is recyclable, in describing the spectacle created by this juvenile hysteria, nor the political judgment it calls up in me.

No; nevertheless, just a word about the spectacle in order to indicate clearly that, once again, the actual stakes, the enemy to be destroyed in these simulacra of trial proceedings, is doubtless not only and not principally the de Man of 1940–42, but "the Deconstruction" of 1989. The two coauthors of this masquerade are not content to dismiss the Belgian purge of 1945 as too indulgent. They are not dreaming only of hunting and purging; they are not dreaming only of erecting a New War Council. They project the ridiculous scene of a struggle for "prestige" and a game of "double or nothing" in which "Deconstruction," no more no less, would risk its whole fortune on a single throw. We leave the scene of the New War Council. Now we are in an academic casino. Standing behind the gaming table, holding the card of deconstruction (there is only one card, obviously, "Paul de Man's War"), I alone represent "Deconstruction" all gathered into one for this last throw, this last chance. Oh yes, I almost forgot: it must be the last chance, at the last moment, at dawn. And if I lose, the croupiers will declare "Deconstruction" in ruins, bankrupt. Exit "Deconstruction." I am going to quote a hallucinating paragraph that first made me think of a mini-imitation-potlatch improvised during a morning panel at the MLA (the title of the session: "The Prestige of Deconstruction on the Line"). Then I said to myself that there is no potlatch without risk, gift, and countergift, destruction of goods *on both sides*. I look in vain for the other side. No, two umpire-croupiers presenting themselves as the representatives of society, two notary publics, in sum, or two court bailiffs, would like to decide in all equanimity whether the "coup" is won or lost; they would even be content just to register the results as impartial observers. Here is this Monte Carlo of political theory from the 1930s: "With these claims Derrida puts the prestige of deconstruction on the line: its political significance, its power to explain political and cultural conjunctures, and its capacity for self-understanding. If these remain staked on the procedures and outcomes of his account of 'Paul de Man's War,' the wager will be lost" (p. 805).

If there are any readers who still find this staging credible, I refer them not to the gaming table, but to the tables of concor(redun)dance and discordance. They will be able to observe that there is nothing around this just-quoted paragraph, before or after it, which I have not already said (in another mode, or so I like to believe) or to which I have not already responded. As for the "prestige of deconstruction" (!!! within this same atmosphere and this same mundanity, one might think of an advertisement for tax-free luxury perfumes), supposing that I understand what is being given such a clownish title, the two croupier-notaries cannot imagine to what extent I don't give a damn, nor everything that I am able—and even make it my duty, an ethical and political duty—to prefer to their "prestige." No, really, someone has to wake up these sleepyheads: Despite their naïve desire that it be true, despite the mad hope that all of "deconstruction" be on the line in an article that they dream of making into a bad card, things, yes, *things*—real, resistant, historical, political things, in other words, referents—will not be reduced to this pathetic, ridiculous "agenda." I recall once again that "Paul de Man's War" presents itself also as a sort of first reflection on my part. Beginning modestly by "Unable to respond to the questions, to all the questions" (which once again distinguishes me from the six "critical respondents" who have an answer for everything in advance), I had merely proposed a narrative, some hypotheses, a call to responsibility (and first of all to reflect on responsibility), an invitation to work and to discussion, and not a card to be played, a "coup," certainly not a dogmatic apparatus, or a sum of settled conclusions. Even if, *concesso non dato*, my article was vulnerable to this or that criticism (a hypothesis I can easily accept but whose demonstration I am awaiting with interest), one would never be reasonably within one's rights to conclude that "Deconstruction" is in ruins or ruined, in the sense that could allow one to say, while rubbing one's hands together: that's it, it's over, whew! "the wager is lost." This ruin is all the more improbable in that deconstruction is neither a system nor an edification, nor, like five of the "critical responses," an edifying discourse. It is a very differentiated movement that passes by way of so many other texts; it has many other places, many other resources than mine and than those that are put to work in an article written for *Critical Inquiry* in great haste and at its request. One more thing: the secret without secret of resistance, for deconstruction, is perhaps a certain connivance with ruin. But I am not going to begin here another discourse on ruin (perhaps on the basis of but also beyond what Benjamin says about it, for example). That is too difficult. Let's stay with the "(bio)degradable." [. . .]

(Draft of a letter)

Dear Jonathan Culler,

I thank you for the courtesy with which you discussed my article and formulated firmly your disagreement. You addressed yourself to me, in any case to the one who wrote "Paul de Man's War," a difficult text to write for thousands of reasons that I hope are respectable, and a text that you began by troubling yourself to read. Taking into account the complexity of things, you avoided summary globalizations. You never confused objection with insult. That goes without saying, you will reply. To be sure, but I insist on thanking you all the same because such rules are neglected by the six other "critical respondents" to whom I am asked to respond (I will try to do it, but it is difficult to address myself directly—and I think I ought not do so—to persons who are only seeking to inflict wounds and to hurl abuse, who, when they are not dreaming about a New War Council, confuse discussion with a manhunt [a man who is, more than ever, oh yes, "wanted"], a scalp dance, or with upping the ante in a casino. The six other "critical respondents" no more address me than they have read me). For the example that you set, allow me to thank you in the name of those who still have a sense of the gravity of all these stakes, whether it is a question of what happened a half-century ago or of the future of discussion, that is, of a certain number of other things inside and outside the university. No doubt, nothing authorizes me to speak otherwise than in my own name. But I like to imagine that others will share my gratitude. The clarifications, the information, the new historical sources with which you enrich the debate will be useful. I find them very valuable from two points of view: (1) You take into account the historical context much more rigorously than do, for example, the other "critical respondents" who often

believe it suffices to parade around with the banner "historical context"
leading the parade to authorize them then to say anything whatsoever
about that context and to "decontextualize" with all their might [à tour
de bras] *or, as one says in French, "à* bras raccourcis" *[with brutal ag-*
gression]. I have rarely read more abstract and logocentered texts, more
enclosed within the prison house of language, than these. The fact that
they present themselves as historicist and concerned with the real refer-
ent has always been part of the logocentric picture. (2) I subscribe to the
essential part of your analysis of the criticism of aesthetic ideology by
de Man. I will not go back over the light this sheds on the debate. My
agreement on this subject was predictable. Like Mémoires, *my* Critical
Inquiry *article was cleary oriented in this direction.*

So I will limit myself to the point of disagreement. I have read all
the articles now available in Wartime Journalism. *One must in fact ac-*
knowledge their diversity and, for a large majority of them, their less
directly political character. I would nevertheless be tempted to uphold,
in the main, the judgment that you found to be "exceedingly severe." I
grant you that the assertion you cite can be seen as, precisely, too massive
(I re-cite it in my turn since none of my detractors seems to have read
it, no more than they read so many other sentences that go in the same
direction: "the massive, immediate, and dominant *effect of all these texts*
is that of a relatively *coherent ideological ensemble which,* most often
and in a preponderant fashion, *conforms to official rhetoric, that of*
the occupation forces"). Yes, despite the prudence of certain underlined
words ("relatively," "most often," and so on), this assertion itself has
something massive about it. But I deliberately designated the "effect"
(which I distinguish here from intention) that, in certain situations, must
also be analyzed in a global and macroscopic fashion. That does not
prevent one, elsewhere and later, from looking at it more closely. News-
paper articles are most often read, alas, very quickly and are crudely
contextualized. They let themselves be dominated, up to a certain point,
by their framing. Political responsibility consists in trying to take ac-
count of this framing, even if this is not always easy. That is what I tried
to do. Yes, the measure of "up to a certain point" is very difficult to
evaluate, just as it is difficult to control. There will always be a margin
of the uncontrollable. Decisive things can be produced in that margin,
according to more or less long, more or less conscious trajectories. But
how can one deny that the simple fact of publishing so many articles,
whatever they were and whatever they said, in those newspapers, at that
moment, *the simple fact of writing* acceptable *things, was to run the risk*
of alliance with that which I several times called "the worst" (p. 623

and passim)? This is what I massively called the massive. In traditional language, let's say that it is here the structure of the thing that is first of all massive and not the judgment that relates to it. Massively, the least one can say is that the de Man of this period was not a resistant and his articles in Le Soir *tended to go* rather *towards the other side. It seems to me that you yourself acknowledge this when you speak of a "global effect" (p. 778).*

This massive thing was admitted from the beginning of my text, and I did not stop recalling it. But, of course, one must next take a rigorous and minute account of all the complications. And then, without even speaking of the majority of the articles, there remains the one that you judge, as I do, to be "unpardonable" (p. 779); yet another word that the six authors in search of a character did not read or pretended not to have read) and of which, without the least equivocation, you judge de Man "guilty" (p. 780). Whatever may be the complexity of this terrible article, whatever we are compelled by honesty to read there, as I tried to do, one cannot deny, as I said, that it also, in its own way, made a contribution that was at the very least equivocal to the massively anti-Semitic operation undertaken by this newspaper and to the politics that it was then supporting. You knew I would agree that to acknowledge this obviously does not authorize one to reduce all the other articles (almost 200) to this one, even less to extend the condemnation to the work of a whole life, especially if this work, as you have demonstrated well, permits one to criticize, dare I say to deconstruct, the very axiomatics of fascist or Nazi ideology.

That said, I grant you that one of the words in the sentence you quote lends itself to ambiguity. It would no doubt deserve to be corrected or clarified in a later edition. I should not have said "all" of these texts because I had not read them all at the time. I was only referring then to those that were politically the most significant. In my mind, "all" concerned all the texts that were then available to me, the most "political" among them, and I should have emphasized this clearly. Or, rather, more clearly since I did also indicate it (p. 598). Without thinking that my conclusion about the "massive" or the "dominant" is thereby effected, I concede that, having read the 200 texts, I now see the landscape as even more differentiated and politically even more complicated than I thought at the time.

Your analysis thus allows one to make some progress toward understanding and toward an honest reading of de Man's texts. Numerous signs let one think that other work of the same type will be coming along to enrich and clarify this debate still further. That is precisely what we hoped would happen by publishing very quickly this whole archive and by immediately taking the initiative for a large and open discussion. Once again, thank you, and so on. Sincerely [. . .]

Ellipses. There are several ways not to name. Or to silence proper names. Of these, one may be dictated by respect for people. To avoid hurting them by the harshness of a criticism, a necessary harshness (ethical and political duty: we are not in a duel; there are third parties and stakes that surpass us). The name may be silenced in order to save the name. There is a long tradition of this, isn't there? [. . .]

The biodegradable: don't speak of it lightly, without "fear and trembling." How not to think of the death camps, the mass graves, the recycling of corpses, the fabrication of "soap," for example, from animal fat, everything that was endured, as I said (p. 631 and passim) by the "victims of discourses that at least resembled" the discourse of "Jews in Present-day Literature"?[21] How not to think of ashes in general, the ashes of Auschwitz in particular? Of what I several times called "the worst" in "Paul de Man's War"? Of trace and ashes.[22] All that managed to survive, survival itself, are some names, in the large black archives or on the somber wall plaques in a museum in Jerusalem. Even so they are not all there. Even names can be incinerated. Not repressed or censured, held in reserve in another place, but forever incinerated. [. . .]

The "non(bio)degradable" is always finite. But since this can be said of the worst and of the best, one must either give up this figure or overlook

---

21. "Through the indelible wound, we must still analyze and seek to understand. Any concession would betray, besides a complacent indulgence and a lack of rigor, an infinitely culpable thoughtlessness with regard to past, present, or future victims of discourses that at least resembled this one" (p. 631).

22. On the conjoined motifs of the singular event, the date, the proper name, and ashes [*cendres*], as well as on that which, in general, links the problems of trace, remains, and ashes, see notably Derrida, *Schibboleth, pour Paul Celan* (Paris, 1986); a partial translation by Joshua Wilner appears under the title "Shibboleth" in *Midrash and Literature*, ed. Geoffrey H. Hartman and Sanford Budick (New Haven, Conn., 1986), pp. 307–47; see also Derrida, *Feu la cendre* (Paris, 1987). This latter book, in the form of a polylogue, reconstitutes everything that, in the problematics of the trace which Derrida has been elaborating since 1965, calls for and names the figure without figure of ashes, notably in *Dissemination, Glas,* and *The Post Card.* The reference to the "burn-everything" [*brûle-tout*] and to the Holocaust directs, of course, all these meditations ("You were saying a moment ago that there could be no phrase of 'today' for the word of ash. Yes there is, there is perhaps only one whose publication is worthy; it would say the burn-everything, in other words the Holocaust and the cremation oven, in German in all the Jewish tongues of the world" [*Feu la cendre,* p. 41]).—TRANS.

nothing in order to make the fine blade of discernment pass between the worst and the best. It is so risky. What is a proper name? What is meant by "survival" here, now? How to translate survival (living on, *Fortleben*, or *Überleben;* see Benjamin on translation, the [after]life of the spirit, and organic life, and so on).[23] [. . .]

9 P.M.

Will I have been right to respond? Would it not have been better to put my trust in honest and intelligent readers? One will never know; the calculation will be, by definition, impossible. Ought I to respond briefly? At length? In the one case, I will be accused of being too "elliptic" (p. 785) (forgetting that I myself began by excusing myself for this ellipsis on the fiftieth page of my article: "Permit me an ellipsis here since I do not have much more time or space. Transference and prosopopeia . . ." [p. 639]). In the other case, I will be accused of giving in to "verbosity" (p. 785). What choice does he leave me, the one who associates these two accusations in a constant and indissoluble fashion? He manifestly does not want to leave me any chance: I will always say too much *and* too little.

A few remarks on this subject. Apparently, someone is suffering.

1. He suffers first of all by my writing too much, always too much, "as usual," he says. (Why does he suffer from it? Who obliges him, what obliges him to read me? Who obliges anyone to read me and even to publish me?) "Derrida's lack of haste [so one should make haste?] expresses itself, *as usual* [my emphasis], in the form of impressive dimensions (sixty-two pages!), so that manageability requires a subdivision into sections" (p. 785).

I wonder if the author of these lines has ever read articles and books, if the distinction between parts, which seems to bother him so much, is something he has so rarely encountered or practiced in his life. And since he is apparently a professor, I wonder if he takes the responsibility to advise his students not to subdivide their texts into parts or into moments that are distinct and articulated among themselves. I said to myself that, at the first chance, I will try to read what this lesson-giver has himself published. Everything leads me to hope that his publications do not have "impressive dimensions"—I am sure at least that that is not what he suffers from, because he is in favor of brevity—and I especially hope that he has ordered things a little by distinguishing among sections, chapters, paragraphs, sentences, and so on. This man suffers so much from seeing

23. See Derrida, "Des Tours de Babel" [on Walter Benjamin], trans. Joseph F. Graham, in *Difference in Translation*, ed. Graham (Ithaca, N.Y., 1985).—TRANS.

me write and speak—and no doubt also publish—too much, that his complaint becomes inexhaustible. He repeats over and over again the same protest for pages on end and takes up as much space as possible denouncing the space that I usurp and that I will usurp here yet again (will one ever know whether he wished for or dreaded my response?).

In effect: after the *first paragraph* that I have just quoted abundantly ("as usual"), the *second paragraph* repeats the same diagnostic, hammering away at it: "the dimensions of verbality are distinctly Derridean." Really? So I am the only one? There would thus be "dimensions of verbality" that are proper to me? What is this exactly, how does one measure this thing? I have the vague impression that this man who suffers would like to wound me in turn or at least hurt me, but I do not know exactly where. And in case the poor reader's intelligence and memory might be totally lacking, this man who suffers and who is decidedly not economical with his words adds, in a *third paragraph*, what he hopes is a really deadly sentence about my "extreme verbosity." The *fourth paragraph* is still hounding my "rhetorical ratiocinations," and so on (pp. 784, 785).

2. The snarling grimace of this suffering is not a rare or unintelligible phenomenon. I have read or heard the same complaint more than once. In substance, it goes like this: "these people [the 'deconstructionists,' of course, not only me] talk, write, and especially publish too much." Not that they "work, analyze, research, and find too much" but "they chatter too much," meaning: "they occupy too much space in our ecosystem. There should be a good housecleaning."

3. This man who suffers does not relent because, after having ironized elegantly about the "distinctly Derridean" "dimensions of verbality," he mocks, just as subtly, my "art": "Derrida possesses the unique art of combining extreme ellipsis with extreme verbosity" (p. 785). I am blushing, it's true, but I don't know if it is with shame or with pleasure. In any case, here is someone who knows what's what, who knows the measure of the too-much and the too-little. I suppose, then, that this man, who is not laughing and who, I am told, is interested in literature as well as interpretation, only reads, teaches, and recommends to his students works to his taste: without "ellipsis" and without verb: without "verbality" or "verbosity." While wishing him good luck, I would be curious to know what his canonical bibliography is, the titles of the works without ellipsis or verbality that he recommends to his students, on which, I suppose, he works or teaches. I only ask for one or two titles, no more, in two lines, via the next "Letters to the Editor" section of *Critical Inquiry*.

If such a remark were not indecent or immodest on my part, after the reproaches made against me in this way, I would dare to say that, in my view, the works that best resist time are those which are simultaneously eloquent and enigmatic, generously abundant and inexhaustibly elliptical. It is on this condition that they are the least—or if you prefer, the most—"(bio)degradable." Having already said too much about this, I will not be so impudent as to cite a few examples. But what would exegesis, hermeneutics, poetics, or just simply teaching of literature or philosophy be without this *double condition*? Not even to mention art and masterpieces. Has there ever been a single sentence in the world that escapes from this double "excess," ellipsis and overabundance? The fascinating rarification that hollows out the economy of what the old rhetoric praised under the name of *copia verborum*?

4. This man suffers not only from my elliptical verbosity; he suffers from the "centrifugal impetus" that, it seems, I never resist. I leave the reader to judge the restraint with which, for his part, he ironizes about my "repetitive, often coquettishly long-winded rhetorical disquisition, complete with puns and digressions, marked at times by a centrifugal impetus that seems hard to resist" (p. 784). What is one supposed to understand here by "puns"? I have no memory of any pun in my article. Once again I would need an example and a demonstration. Like a certain number of others, the concept of pun remains here, let us put it euphemistically, rather hospitable.[24] Fortunately, on the other hand, there are two examples of what is meant by "digressions" and "centrifugal impetus," and thus I am going to be able to proceed with the required "elucidation" or "analysis."

The *first example* of centrifugal digression on my part, it seems, is the interest shown in "'the significance of the press in the modernity of a history like this one'" (p. 784). I will not respond at length. To judge this interest to be "centrifugal" today, in any context whatsoever and in particular in this one, is eccentricity itself. To put it in the most neutral way possible: I see here a striking manifestation of intellectual and political distraction. Thoughtless and dizzying [*étourdie et étourdissante*] decontextualization. Ought I then to have spoken about de Man's writings in 1940–42 and of the "de Man case" in 1987 without attending to the "significance of the press"? Without even posing the problem? Now that is what I would call a digression, and even a stupid avoidance, ahistorical abstraction, and irresponsibility itself. The fact is, if I had not spoken about the press in this context, then there would have

24. See the excellent collection *On Puns: The Foundation of Letters*, ed. Culler (Oxford, 1988).

been nothing left for me to do but be silent (this is no doubt the demand
that is being addressed to me and I get the message). What I regret is, on
the contrary, having had to, for lack of time and space, "renounce the
temptation" (this is acknowledged to be to my credit with a wry condescendence) to treat such a problem as fully as it deserves.

The *second example* is still more odd. It concerns anti-Semitism
at Yale. With the same condescendence, I am given credit for having
elected to "postpone" such a history, but apparently I ought not even
to have mentioned it. Why? Let's listen once again; it is a question of
suffering.

> He does manage to remind us of the relatively recent *numerus
> clausus* practices in Ivy League schools. Although I am myself
> a Yale alumnus who might once upon a time conceivably have
> suffered from such procedures, I fail to understand their rela-
> tionship to de Man's institutional affiliation, or to see how the
> atmosphere in the New Haven of 1930, or even 1940, can be
> compared, even at its worst (if indeed such a farfetched com-
> parison was intended) with the situation in the Brussels of 1942.
> [P. 785]

Responses:
1. Of course, I *never* dreamed of or left the least room for such a
"comparison." I deem it to be so "farfetched" that I find even its hypothesis incongruous and indecent. Yet the fact remains that anti-Semitism
is anti-Semitism, a *numerus clausus* is a *numerus clausus*, wherever they
occur in the world. I will never denounce them *here* without doing the
same *there*, under the pretext that the conditions are not exactly the
same or, worse still, that although some suffered from it *here*, I myself
might only have suffered from it *there* ("might have suffered" but fortunately he seems not to have suffered from it, even though he knew that
he could have suffered from it). With such an opportunistic caution, I
might never have been able, personally, to condemn anti-Semitism in
general, not even French anti-Semitism, only the *numerus clausus* in
force during the Occupation in Algeria, and from which I, along with a
few others, did effectively suffer.

If one wants to know what I meant to say with this allusion to Yale,
one can reread the half-paragraph and the note I devote to it (p. 592). It
is very clear. Two questions are asked. They are distinct from each other.
On the one hand: What is the link between the stir created by the case of
de Man, a Yale professor, and what Yale is "for example, in American

culture"? On the other hand: Why are so many American intellectuals (but, fortunately, not all of them) so quick to investigate, denounce, condemn what is going on far away, to dream of New War Councils and Academic Bureaus of Investigation while their vigilance is lulled to sleep easily in good conscience when it is a question of more domestic things, things closer to home in time and space? On the more general subject of, let's call it, segregation, I could have chosen graver examples of this bad-good-conscience.

2. Someone declares "I am myself a Yale alumnus" and reproaches me for not letting all these ancient histories "(bio)degrade" by themselves. Ancient histories? So ancient as all that? The research in one of the books I cite goes up to 1970. But this "Yale alumnus" seems to have been aware of these practices of *numerus clausus*. Has he spoken about them before? Publicly? If so, please forgive me and show me the references. If he did nothing, is it only because he did not suffer from them? But what is it finally he is suffering from today? Visibly he is not happy that I permitted myself a digression, even if it was "postponed," on Yale, whether the question is that of the *numerus clausus* or of what he calls "de Man's institutional affiliation." He does not see the relation. But there isn't any, of course; I never said there was! Moreover, he himself did not suffer from the *numerus clausus* at Yale (is he really sure of that?), neither he himself, nor for others (there are those who suffer for others; I have met such people), and the periods are quite distinct, right? De Man arrived at Yale after 1972, if I am not mistaken. No relation, therefore. The author of "Jacques Derrida's Apologia" knows the whole story quite well. He was in a position to know it since he was, as I learn from another of my critical respondents in "The Responsibilities of Friendship," heavy responsibilities, "de Man's successor at Cornell" (p. 802). But he is going to find that I am once again too "verbal" and "elliptic" at the same time. That never happens to him? He is going to think that I am too interested in rhetoric and psychoanalysis. I think he is too little interested in them. And that is not good for ethics.

This "Yale alumnus," who was also, I quote again, "de Man's successor" (at Cornell, it should be added; I hope he did not suffer too much from this but he "might . . . conceivably have suffered"), thus seems certain that he knows what responsibility is. More certain than I am in any case, I easily grant him that. He is just as sure he knows what "ethical categories" ought to be. He reproaches me for not knowing this and for mixing in psychoanalytic categories. He also regrets, because it would not be relevant and would not even have any relation to the serious things we are talking about, that I mention the *numerus clausus* and the anti-Semitism at Yale (at least before 1970). And why you ask? Well, because this "Yale alumnus," it seems, did not suffer from it, personally. He recognizes that he "might . . . conceivably have suffered from such procedures," but fortunately he did not. He does not say that he even suffered for others (and yet, without understanding a whole lot about ethical categories and responsibility, as everyone knows, I believe there are people who suffer for others. I know people like that, I've met them, very close to me. There is even one of them who sees in this experience the beginning, indeed the condition, of ethics).

For the rest of my response to this article, no doubt the most pained and painful as well as the most venomous of them all, I refer to the two tables (will he say of these tables of figures that they are elliptical or verbose?). Naturally I will not respond to the usual ineptitudes on the subject of a presumed "usual Derridean practice": "And indeed the sequel of Derrida's essay will be radically at odds with usual Derridean practice, as a straightforward piece of exposition that could almost make us believe for a moment that meanings are possibly determinable. Further, it will lean on biographical and historical contexts that one would expect to be foreign to the author and anathema to the one for whom he speaks" (p. 786), which, let it be said in passing, contradicts once more the reproach of decontextualization that is later made against me.

Here once again, if one relies on this ignorant and aberrant reading of "Deconstruction" or of my "practice," I have no way out. Whenever such a reader cannot deny my attention to context, to history, to biography, and so on, then he reproaches me for not being faithful to what he believes to be my "practice" or my "theory" (anticontextualist, right, everyone knows that, see above!). When he believes that I am faithful to what he *believes* or wants others to believe deconstruction means to say or to do, then I am reproached for decontextualizing, making meaning indeterminate and neglecting history. I will not respond on these points; I have done so a thousand times over the last twenty-five years, and once again here just a few pages ago. Faced with those who do not want or do not know how to read, I confess I am powerless. Powerless before the obtuse petty-mindedness that consists in counting the presumed pages "for" and the presumed pages "against" de Man, as if rhetoric were an arithmetic, as if the meaning of a discourse could be measured chronometrically, as if the brevity of plain and clear utterances were not enough to recall the things that are *massively* evident when that is what they are (which I never failed to do), while the complexity of other texts requires more attention and more time. I feel just as powerless before the fury that impels someone to want to suppress even a rhetorical question mark in a sentence as simple and as clear as this one:

> "How can one deny," Derrida closes his account, "that the effect of these conclusions went in the sense and the direction of the worst? In the *dominant* context in which they were read in 1941, did not their *dominant* effect go unquestionably in the direction of the worst? Of what we now know to have been the worst?" (p. 623). It is important to note the built-in attenuations; the interrogative mode; the emphasis on the dominant (and not the whole) effect; the stress on the context of 1941 (suggesting that it may be unduly limited). [P. 788]

But what would this man want? That there not even be a rhetorical question mark? I emphasize that the interrogation does not bear on the content but, on the contrary, on the possibility of scandalously "denying" this content, to wit, an effect regarding which the same sentence says clearly and in the most affirmative way in the world that it goes "unquestionably in the direction of the worst." What more would he like? That instead of "How can one deny" I write "One cannot deny"? That would have really reassured, satisfied, fully convinced him that de Man was not going to get out of it thanks to a question mark. Since there is no difference, I confirm for him that in my view "How can one deny?" was perfectly equivalent to "One cannot deny." What would this man want? That instead of "dominant," underlined twice, I say "whole" and that in the total confusion I leave no more room for the least fold, the least nuance, the least differentiation? What these people want is not only that one say "unpardonable," which I clearly did, but that one stop there, without even completing the sentence, that one repeat this word indefinitely like an exorcism or rather an insult, and that one condemn the dead man to death, with immediate execution (firing squad or electric chair, instantaneous reincineration), without even sifting among the ashes, without stopping to read and to analyze the remains, without even keeping anything in memory, because to remember is already to *analyze*, thus to complicate things. [. . .]

Yes, to condemn the dead man to death: they would like him *not to be dead* yet so they could put him to death (preferably along with a few of the most intolerable among the living). To put him to death this time without remainder. Since that is difficult, they would want him to be *already dead without remainder*, so that they can put him to death without remainder. Well, the fact is he is dead (they will no longer be able to do anything in order to kill him), and there are remains, something surviving that bears his name. Difficult to decipher, translate, assimilate. Not only can they do nothing against that which survives, but they cannot keep themselves from taking the noisiest part in that survival. Plus there are other survivors, aren't there, who are interested in survival, who talk, respond, discuss, *analyze* endlessly. We'll never have done with it. It's as if something nonbiodegradable had been submerged at the bottom of the sea. It irradiates. [. . .]

Another word about *analysis*. We are abruptly going to change the scene and go back, and now we are shown into a kind of butcher shop. Each time I try to analyze and progress by minute stages and distinctions, I am accused of resorting to "the age-old salami technique, which consists in cutting off slice after slice until the sausage has totally disappeared" (p. 789). I persist in thinking, on the contrary, that a text is not exactly a sausage. In any case, I do not share such a phantasm on this subject. I wonder what would happen if this reproach were extended to all those who try to analyze anything. I do not know what texts this professor explicates in class, but I can imagine the look on the faces of his students if he said to them, in all seriousness, each time he encountered an analytic procedure: "Aha! The age-old salami technique!" I won't be so cruel or so presumptuous as to give some great examples and to describe the scene: "Aha, look at this text (I let you choose the example—there are plenty of them—of an author who has a taste for analysis); Aha, the age-old salami technique!" Let's be serious. I remark first of all that this is the same author who elsewhere reproaches me for being too *and* too little elliptical, for contextualizing *and* decontextualizing, here for analyzing *too much* and elsewhere (p. 785) of *not* being "analytic" enough. What is one to respond to such contradictory accusations? Perhaps simply this: By trying to analyze honestly and to differentiate as best as I could, without erasing the folds and complications, I never sought to skirt the global, massive, or *dominant* effects of the texts I was interrogating in this way in their context. On the contrary, I underscored them, as I did the words "massive," "dominant," and so on (which is precisely what Culler reproaches me for), in order to distinguish *again* between analysis, in the good sense, and the effect of the "salami technique." So I myself indeed discerned the two. The same professor should have acknowledged it, all the more so since I make this distinction in the sentences *he himself quoted* above ("How can one deny that the effect of these conclusions went in the sense and the direction of the worst? In the *dominant* context in which they were read in 1941, did not their *dominant* effect go unquestionably in the direction of the worst?"). There were analogous ones on nearly every page of my article.

If I had to choose the most enlightening phrase for elucidating the text titled "Jacques Derrida's Apologia," it would perhaps be this one, a veritable lighthouse in the silence of the night: "de Man's tone as the expression of a powerful urge for cultural authority, which makes the young man already speak like the oracular gray eminence he would succeed in becoming forty years later" (p. 787). What does "succeed" mean here? To what is allusion being made here? "De Man's successor" (at Cornell) seems to know what he is talking about, but doesn't breathe a word of it. Too bad. How many silences, how much suffering! Could he name anyone who does not seek to attain for himself some "cultural authority"? It is true that some succeed in doing so. But just as every eminence is not gray, not all grayness [*grisaille*; colorlessness, dullness] is eminent. [. . .]

Someone—the same one—finds the "discretion" between de Man and myself "rather odd" (p. 793). Not me. He does not say why he finds "this discretion rather odd," so I can't answer him, at least not with anything new. I explained myself on this subject. Likewise, when he writes two pages later in all tranquillity: "The fact that others, with different backgrounds, may have made statements similar to de Man's is totally beside the point" (p. 795), he does not give the least reason. So I cannot answer. Why would it be "beside the point"? As for me, I tried at least to explain why it was not. [. . .]

I noted last Saturday, I think, that one can only extend the use of this figure, the "(bio)degradable," by taking into account the logic of the unconscious. But that is not enough. It is also necessary to go beyond economy and topical relations, censorship and repression, condensation (ellipsis) and displacement. These keep what they cause to disappear. They simply cause it to change places. Now, there is also the possibility of a radical destruction without displacement, of a forgetting without remainder. I have called this ashes [*cendres*]. No trace as such without this possibility, which also lies in wait for the (bio)degradable and the non(bio)degradable, at least in their figure. But in what is called the literal or strict sense, is there some absolute non(bio)degradable? For example, the nuclear waste that is deeply immerged so as to neutralize its physical effects, if not the accumulated anguish that will always resonate deep within our unconscious? If there were a limit here between the (bio)degradable and the non(bio)degradable, as between the literal and the figurative meaning, this is where it would lie. But I am not sure it does in all strictness. Take up everything again: *physis*, earth, world, man, life, survival, spirit, OK, OK. . . . [. . .]

One of the very many things my six judges did not read (not even "de Man's successor," who is amazed to hear talk of the "psychoanalytic" category or of "transference" [p. 785] with regard to response and responsibility) is the way a logic or a time of the unconscious in this whole history is taken into account: (1) in the "personal" history of de Man, which is never totally and rigorously separated from that of his work and writings; (2) in the history of the relation his readers, students, friends, and enemies have maintained with him and with his work, including the relation to his silences, which one sees more than ever now in the compulsive outbursts of certain of his former disciples who today are publicly repudiating a debt that was publicly declared but no doubt always intolerable to them; (3) in the history (memory, disappearance, reapparition, survival, and so on) of the whole archive—oral and written, journalistic and epistolary. In all of this, the problematic of biodegradability is at stake, and this example of it remains fascinating whatever else one may think of it. As regards all these events, I venture to recall that I warned against the "language of consciousness" which I had to adopt at points. Then I referred, and very carefully, to "some experience of the unconscious," while adding and underscoring the following: "If the word 'unconscious' has any meaning, then it stems from this necessity. With or without a *recognition of the unconscious*, . . . ," and so on (p. 593). A double necessity advised caution: to take seriously the unconscious in all these "histories" but not to rely dogmatically on the ordinary axioms of psychoanalysis, neither from the ethico-political point of view nor as regards their determinism, economism, topologism (according to which nothing is lost, everything is held in reserve under the watch of repression simply by changing places). It is as if everything were at once integrally (bio)degradable (by conserving itself in other forms in an organic compost that would draw nourishment from everything, including transformed, unrecognizable, and recycled wastes) and non(bio)degradable, that is, indestructible, leaving no resource other than metamorphosis or displacement.

I will go so far as to claim that, from the title to the last word of my article, everything was set in motion by this question: What remains? What is "*survivre*" (living on, surviving, *Fortleben, Überleben*)? How did these newspaper articles and everything they record resist time? From what distance and by means of what detours? Why are they reappearing and how do we hear and understand what perhaps we have never stopped hearing, from afar, telephonically, through so many layers of apparent amnesia—this transoceanic rumor and rumbling "deep within a shell"? By quoting de Man quoting what is, in sum, Montherlant's wager ("'"To the writers who have given too much to current affairs for the last few months, I predict, for that part of their work, the most complete oblivion. When I open the newspapers and journals of today, I hear the indifference of the future rolling over them, just as one hears the sound of the sea when one holds certain seashells up to the ear"'"), I called attention to the paradoxical and cruel survival of an error or a lost wager (p. 612). What interested me most consistently in this article was the transmission at a distance, the teleprogrammatrix, the delays, detours, halts, the play of mediation, of the media, and of the immediacy in the storing and routing of a still readable or audible archive (whence my "telephonic" title and the recurrence, which was real moreover, of telephone calls: that transatlantic cabling [*cablure*] that was both literal and figurative and that my judges paid no attention to or understood not at all).[25]

What interested me above all was the *structure of this event* in the enormous mass of that which it conditions or in which it participates: first an error of appraisal (Montherlant's then de Man's quoting Montherlant on the subject of the disappearance of the newspapers and the indifferent amnesia that awaits them). This error sees itself cruelly belied by history, which takes charge of its own survival, the archived survival of this very error, of this utterance and of this quotation that I again quoted and have just requoted once more here. In a newspaper, someone quotes an error while making in his turn an error on the subject of the nonsurvival of newspapers and assures *in that very way, in determined conditions*, the survival of the newspaper article, of the quotation, and of the requotation of these very errors. As such! It is as if I were

25. See, for example, p. 774. I am crazy about sentences that begin with "Which is to say, of course." You can bet, five to one, that a lie or a stupidity will quickly follow therefrom, in any case a countertruth, or at least, in the best-case scenario, something that is not self-evident ("of course"). Otherwise, why say "in other words" or "which is to say, of course"? When one teaches, which is to say, of course, when one's job is reading, can one, without laughing or wincing, begin a sentence with "Which is to say, of course"? Here is the example. Reread the paragraph in which this occurs: "'Lambrichs repeats: "Exercice du silence."'" Which is to say, of course (and Derrida's essay ends on this note), that it is time for us to exercise silence, to put an end to the pernicious journalistic 'war' on Paul de Man." Of course not. But I cannot explain it, of course; one would have to reread everything, begin everything again. See below: "Close, subtle reading" required. Thus, exercise of silence.

assuring the survival of a text by mistakenly saying of it: "I bet this will
not survive." I said (temporary) "survival," thinking of proper names,
of the literality of the formula, which is in itself just about insignificant,
of the singularity of textual events, but I could have said the contrary
("[bio]degradability") while referring to the meaning and to everything
that lets itself be anonymously assimilated into the tradition of a more
or less common memory, into what is confusedly called "culture." [. . .]

When one speaks of the destruction of an archive, do not limit oneself
to the meaning, to the theme, or to consciousness. To be sure, take
into account an economy of the unconscious, even if only to exceed it
once again. But it is also necessary to take into consideration the "supports," the subjectiles[26] of the signifier—the paper, for example, but
this example is more and more insufficient. There is this diskette, and
so on. Differences here among newspapers, journals, books, perhaps,
the modes of storage, of reproduction and of circulation, the "ecosystems" (libraries, bookstores, photocopies, computers, and so on). I am
also thinking of everything that is happening today to libraries. Official
institutions are calculating the choices to be made in the destruction of
nonstorable copies or the salvaging of works whose paper is deteriorat-
ing: displacement, restructuring of the archive, and so on. What would
have happened if people had been able—yesterday or ten years ago—to
consult on a screen the whole "de Man" archive in a minute, from one
library to another? In short, telematically? Difference between the war
articles and certain of his last seminars whose "voice" we still have, the
audio archive that students pass among themselves from one university
to another, even in Europe, and certain of which are already *published
on the basis of* this recording. I risk annoying any number of people, for
example "de Man's successor," if I say once more that I must "postpone"
two short treatises that are indispensable here. Possible titles: (1) On the
support and the insupportable (keep the ellipsis and the pun in French);
(2) On the impossible distinction between public and private, in general
and in particular, in a modern problematic of the archive. [. . .]

Repetition, wear [*usure*], and biodegradability: In certain cases, quotation, the rhythmic return of the same wears down the mark; it is boring,
provokes disgust, pushes toward oblivion. In other cases, it is the contrary. Intellectual modes are born and die from this repetition. What is

---

26. See Derrida, "Forcener le subjectile," in Derrida and Paule Thévenin, *Antonin
Artaud: Dessins et portraits* (Paris, 1986), pp. 55–108.—TRANS.

the rule? The determination of the rule is part of the process; it does not dominate that process. [. . .]

People will wonder: Since he doesn't believe in the pertinence of this figure, the "biodegradable," when it is applied to discourses, to discursive texts, to culture in general, why, then, does he devote so much space to it? Why is he writing so publicly and at such length on this subject, and so on? Response: Well, for no reason, just to see, to reflect and see what remains of it, perhaps to take the measure of the "(bio)degradability" of this text here, precisely, beyond its meaning, to test its conditions of translation, publication, and conservation. To see what passes and what happens beyond its content, its theme, or the interest of the debate in which it must take part, no doubt a very minor interest. Since this text here (private and public) does not come down to the content of its meaning, I abandon it more or less like an empty form, a mere container, one of those plastic packages that float (for how long?) on one of our beautiful rivers (why do I say "our"?). A minuscule simulacrum of nucleo-literary waste. And then I am also thinking somewhat about diverting certain readers who, concerned about the essential gravity of these questions, might be a little tired of the vain polemics that are turning around it. [. . .]

Brief exchange Thursday night with I. and D. They had just read the "critical responses":

  I.—What relentless fury! [*Quel acharnement!* from a verb that formerly had the sense to give the pack the scent of the prey's flesh, *chair*]. Yet one wonders where is the flesh. They don't go into detail, the six of them. Real executioners! I don't know what they do love, but you, well, you're not held in any fondness in their thoughts.

  D.—Don't be so sure. As for me, I think deep down they love you. I mean, they don't want to let you go. This is a good opportunity; they want *to stay with you* [rester avec toi]. As long as possible. At all costs.

  I.—What does that mean, "to stay" [*rester*] and "at all costs"? Who fixes the prices and the deadlines? [After a burst of laughter and while patting me on the shoulder:] At any rate, if they love you, they don't seem to suspect it, they don't have the foggiest idea that they do. . . .

  Me—On the contrary, I think two of them suspect it (all it would take is a bit of analysis or attention to rhetoric). Guess which ones. [I then spent a certain amount of time pointing out to them the signs of this. It was necessary to reread, from A to Z.] What is less clear for me, more complicated, is the case of Jonathan Culler.

Saturday, 28 January, 8 A.M.

For the last two minutes, I have been observing attentively the little word "most" in a declaration such as "Derrida ignores most of this history" (p. 771). The point is to produce an effect; guess which one. What does "most" mean? I have not read certain books that, since my article appeared, the author of this verdict has had the conscientiousness to read. I noted the references, thank you. There are still many books, particularly dealing with this history, that neither one nor the other of us has read, and that is regrettable. I have read some others. But that is not the question. In the reference thus made to sources unknown to me, *I found not a single fact, even a factual detail*[27] that completes or contradicts in a *pertinent* fashion the description of the historical context that I proposed (I point this out, as well as a certain number of other things, in the two "tables"). So I knew "most of this history." I took account of it. I was even *the first*, in this academic debate around de Man, to put it forward—and in a more precise and more abundant fashion than anyone since. I would have liked it if someone had at least had the honesty

---

27. *Mea culpa.* Here I must confess an error, the only one, even though, as you will see, it is not a detail. I formally acknowledge to my "critical respondent" who, tending more toward "'hard information'" than toward "close, subtle reading," reproaches me for not having specified the first name of Mr. Goriely ("whose first name is not provided"; pp. 768, 767, 774). In effect, I should not have silenced this first name. I will mention it in the next edition: Georges. Thus, since there might be another Goriely, and since this homonym might also be Jewish, a "former Belgian resistant," a "university professor," quoted by *Le Soir*, and since, one never knows, he might not agree with his double, I mean Georges, about de Man (Paul), all confusion would be avoided and this "hard information" would run no risk of being compromised. We would leave the "textual" in order finally to enter into the "practical" (p. 775). There is undoubtedly much I still have to learn from these historians and their exemplary demands. So, *mea culpa.* But for the moment I see nothing else to confess to in the way of "hard information." And I maintain that there is more of that in my article than in the whole set of those that are set up against me. As for what is said about my lack of interest in "hard information," this is but one more confusion. I leave here in the state of ellipsis a long discourse on history and what is "hard," on reading what is "hard" and what resists reading, on what is "hard" to read, on the distinction between "hard" and a certain sort of unreadability (only a certain sort), and on the relations between "hard," "soft," and "non(bio)degradable." On the subject of mea culpa, an excellent article by J. Hillis Miller (" 'Reading' Part of a Paragraph in *Allegories of Reading*," in *Reading de Man Reading*, pp. 155–70) reminds me of a sentence of de Man's. It warns in advance all those who demanded that he do his *mea culpa* before dying: "We never lie as much as when we want to do full justice to ourselves, especially in self-accusation" (de Man, *Allegories of Reading: Figural Language in Rousseau, Nietzsche, Rilke, and Proust* [New Haven, Conn., 1979], pp. 269–70).

to acknowledge this. I was the first to demand with some insistence that this work of the historian be pursued.

To write next in the same paragraph, with just as much bad faith, "Derrida pays little attention to this disclaimer," is to make a use of "little" that is as abusive as the use of "most" (p. 771). What is the measure here for "most" and for "little"? The accusation is all the more arrogant in that it is a question of the attention paid to a text *that I myself cite* on the subject of the "*Soir* volé"! What would they have said if I had not quoted it? By calling the reader's attention to the, finally, decisive role that, by means of crude and childish rhetorical strategies, one wants to assign to words as big or as petty as "most" and "little," am I abusing what the same author calls "close, subtle, . . . reading" (specifying right away that such "reading" is "quintessentially Derridean") (p. 767)? One will have quickly figured out that the compliment was meant to be poisoned. But I wonder on the basis of what norms of reading one can ironize in this way. Such "close, subtle reading" is not a good thing then? Should one avoid *teaching*, inculcating, or propagating this vice? Must one recognize it as the property, the originality, or the eccentricity of this or that individual ("close, subtle, indeed quintessentially Derridean reading")? I underlined "teaching" because I am thinking first of all of the students who read this sort of thing, of the undergraduates who are perhaps more vulnerable than we are (I hope not, all the same, not *all of them*, not all of them more vulnerable than *all* of us) to the consequences of "jokes" as sinister as this one. If they were vulnerable to it, the risk is that they might say to themselves: "Oh, I get it, 'close, subtle reading' is not good therefore; it's perhaps a style, a perversion, maybe even a European fashion; would that by any chance be what people call deconstruction? Yecch!" and so on. So the real question becomes: What is happening in a university (let's leave aside the personal case of the professor who indulges in this operation and takes such a responsibility) when one of its members can permit herself or himself to be sarcastic on the subject of what she or he calls "close, subtle reading"? When she or he expects to derive a benefit from these sarcasms and be given credit for them by the community? What is the *politics* of this sarcasm? And since we are talking about history, doesn't this accusation launched against the refinement of reading, against the taste for analysis remind you of anything? You would have a short memory.

But this warning by a professor against "close, subtle reading" sets up even more troubling acts of violence. I refer to the manner of treating witnesses' testimony. First of all, one means to discredit living witnesses on the pretext that their names are not in some book or other recently consulted in the United States. So what? I quote: "Goriely and Dosogne (neither of whose names I have been able to find in any of the books on the Belgian Resistance I have consulted) provide de Man with little more ["little" once again; how much more, exactly?] than the 'some of my best friends are Jews' alibi" (pp. 774–75). Illusionism, confusion, or manipulation? I will not decide among them, but I will first remark that such "alibis" are generally alleged by non-Jews who want to clear themselves of the accusation of anti-Semitism. In the present case, this argument might perhaps have "a little" worth, just a little, if de Man himself had said "some of my best friends are Jews." Well, he is dead and never said such a thing. And the suspicion of an alibi becomes ridiculous when it is the friends themselves who take the initiative of the testimony. What is more, to my knowledge, only Goriely (Georges) is Jewish and presents himself as such. The testimonies that I quoted have, moreover, been confirmed, developed, enriched by many others in the same vein. They will have been published by the time this appears.

But there is something still worse and more confused. With a jubilating snicker that doesn't even try to disguise itself anymore, the author of this "response" reports (Georges) Goriely's attacks against de Man. I cite them in turn for more clarity: "Goriely informed the audience that de Man was 'completely, almost pathologically, dishonest,' a man to whom 'swindling, forging, lying were, at least at the time, second nature'" (p. 774 n.8). A cause for exultation. This time renouncing any suspicion, the author puts the two parts of the testimony on the same level. Since this respondent has little patience, as was clearly stated from the first lines, for "close, subtle reading," there is no more time wasted looking at things more closely or asking a single question. One doesn't wonder whether the very form and the logic of the judgments thus reported might not correspond better to some evening of a score or to some resentment that would have nothing to do with politics or racism. Well, it seems to me on the contrary that, all political matters once again set aside, "portraits" of this type disqualify themselves. What is more, they appear extravagant to those who knew de Man well or from a distance, for several decades, in Belgium before and during the war, and in the United States. On the other hand, I can attest that all those who have met Mr. (Georges) Goriely these last months and have spoken to me of him charged this violence to the account of personal rancor that has nothing to do with what we are discussing here. Because for what we are discussing here, here is what counts: a man, Mr. (Georges) Goriely, so brimming over with hatred as regards de Man (almost as much as those

who quote him with gratitude and delight), declares loudly and clearly
that the accusations of pro-Nazism and anti-Semitism against the same
de Man are absurd and ridiculous. He is only *therefore all the more
credible on this point*. In the testimony of such a violent and relentless
"prosecutor," the part favorable to the accused, the public concession
seems more convincing than ever. Everything leads one to suppose that
if he had been able to condemn de Man on yet another count, Mr.
(Georges) Goriely would not have let the chance slip away. Here is
someone who had no desire to let de Man off lightly. At any rate, finally,
as important as it may be, the recourse to testimony, in particular to this
one, was far from being the only argument determining my analysis.

By spewing such venomous insults, did Mr. (Georges) Goriely ever
suspect that they were going to turn up intact (still "nonbiodegraded")
in the mouths of all those who would like to savor them in their turn,
chew them over again, or spit them out like so much chewing gum?
Of all those who are ready to pass the precious poison from mouth to
mouth without wondering whether the motivations and ruminations of
this man don't justify some caution? And in fact, I find the same substance again, cited, countersigned, I should say spread out in the conclusion of another one of the six authors. Manifestly, for these people, it is
imperative to cite it as often as possible so that its archive does not get
lost. But don't count on it; the laws of conservation and wear are more
paradoxical than one thinks. Once again, therefore, I cite this quotation
in my turn, persuaded on the contrary that the frequent and careful rereading of these words will better allow one to evaluate their credibility,
supposing things were not clear at first reading:

> Defending de Man's character, Derrida quotes Georges Goriely,
> a "former Belgian resistant" who "knew de Man well," as saying
> that de Man was not "'ideologically . . . antisemitic.'" Goriely,
> who today is professor emeritus of sociology at the Free Univer-
> sity of Brussels, subsequently described de Man as "completely,
> almost pathologically, dishonest," declaring that "swindling,
> forging, lying were, at least at the time, second nature to him."
> [P. 802]

I note without further comment that this latter phrase is thus calmly
cited and accredited by an expert, an expert specialized in the de Man
affair, the now-famous author of "Deconstructing de Man" (*The Nation*, 9 January 1988).

My intention was no more (may I spell this out once more in passing?) to "defend de Man's character" than to "fulfill the responsibilities of friendship." The author of "The Responsibilities of Friendship," formerly the author of "Deconstructing de Man," believes or affects to believe that my article was essentially inspired by friendship. For him, de Man is only and before all else my friend ("his friend") (p. 801). And here he has the audacity, I can't believe my eyes, to give me a lesson in an "honorable way to fulfill the responsibilities of friendship" (p. 797). If I needed someone to teach me honor, and how to distinguish the honorable from the dishonoring, really, I would look for another teacher in the future. Second, concerning friendship and the responsibility for what I write, especially on such subjects, my idea is a little more complicated. Finally, my friendship for Paul de Man did not for a moment forbid me to judge "unpardonable" what seemed to me to be so (it is true that, as I said above, the same preacher had forgotten, as is his wont, to read or to mention this judgment, and the same could be said for so many other analogous remarks). In conditions where it was rather difficult, where it would have been so easy, on the contrary, to join the pack or to be silent, I did indeed reaffirm my friendship (that's the way I am). But that never prevented me, I will say on the contrary, from proposing each time that it seemed just and honest, and almost on every page, conclusions that have also been found to be "exceedingly severe." What idea do these people have of friendship? The most suspect one, in my view, the one that implies blind approbation, projection, or identification.

If one wants to authorize oneself to give advice on what is "honorable" or not, it would be better to begin by recognizing publicly one's own errors or falsifications, especially when they are as numerous and serious as those published under the title "Deconstructing de Man" (*The Nation* 9 January 1988). I was surprised (really? was I so surprised?) to see the author of this article claim to direct criticisms at me without thinking for a moment about first responding to those that I, like so many others, formulated indignantly in note 50 of "Paul de Man's War." He turns aside the questions and the focus in the direction of a *New York Times* article. He accuses me of having attacked the "messenger" of "bad news" or those who "reported the news" (p. 801). No, the messenger was first of all me, long before any journalist. And those who "reported the news," months earlier, *on my proposal*, he forgets this as well, were some colleagues *and myself*. The journalists mentioned by this journalist came after, long after; they have not "reported"; they have simplified and deformed "the news." And they would have done nothing, known nothing, seen nothing for a long time if *we, on my pro-*

posal, had not organized the meeting in Tuscaloosa and taken the decisions that are now public knowledge and that I recalled in my article.[28]

I cannot enumerate all the signs of such a lack of probity; it would take us too long. I'll just mention one more. How can a professional "historian" write this: "*Le Soir* in those years was thus a Nazi publication, and the official postwar tribunal—the *Conseil de Guerre*—considered those who published in its pages to be collaborators" (p. 798) while holding it against de Man even as he must specify in a note that, as Jonathan Culler appropriately reminds him, *de Man was never condemned, was not even tried by such a War Council* (see what I say about this above, p. 849)? His note says that "de Man was questioned by the Auditeur Général in 1945 but not formally charged" (p. 798 n.1), thereby insinuating once again that he could have been informally charged, which is dishonest and gratuitous. When one acts like this, how can one inscribe the word "responsibility" in a title ("The Responsibilities of Friendship")? How can one dare to give advice about what is or is not "honorable" (p. 797)?

The only lesson the author of "Deconstructing de Man" draws from his past "errors," but it is the least he can do, is to release *in advance* a colleague from any responsibility for the errors that he, the author, did not fail to make, *yet again, right here* and to which he seems willing to get accustomed more quickly than his readers: "Mark Poster provided valuable comments on an earlier draft of this paper; the errors that are present are the responsibility of the author" (p. 797). The only concession one can make to him is that the courageous use of this indicative is a responsible, honest, and prudent signature.

I am going to stop. I have once again been too verbose and too elliptical. Someone, guess who, is perhaps going to reproach *Critical Inquiry* for publishing me too often and at too great a length. I will point out that I myself never asked for anything and would have gladly done without all this extra work whose usefulness is doubtful. I like to think that I have better things to do at the moment. If only to read, for example, much

---

28. See Derrida, "Paul de Man's War," pp. 633–37. I will take advantage of the present opportunity to make clear that the planning for this colloquium, titled "Our Academic Contract: The Conflict of the Faculties in America," had begun two years earlier. The three-day program in no way concerned the "de Man affair" about which, with the exception of the colloquium organizer, Richard Rand, and myself, the participants knew nothing until then. It was only at the end of the last session that the discussion took place which I recounted in "Paul de Man's War."

better and newer responses in the volume of that name, or *Reading de Man Reading*, or those texts of de Man recently assembled in *Critical Writings (1953–1978)*, not all of which I knew, far from it.[29] As to the length (completely relative) of my responses, is it not justified by the fact that six texts and seven authors were mobilized against my single article? The last time, in *Critical Inquiry*, on the subject of my text against *apartheid*, only two authors were set up against me. At the progressive rhythm of this capitalization, is the present response going to lead *Critical Inquiry* to call on thirty-six or forty-nine "critical respondents"? I give notice right now that I am tired of this scene and that I will not get back into the ring, at least not this ring, even if others still want to be seen there or have their photographs taken there. I have never in my life taken the initiative of a polemic. Three or four times, and *always in response, and always because I was invited to do so*, I have simply tried to confront some manipulations that were too serious to ignore. I have always limited myself in these cases to stakes that are not personal, but philosophical, moral, and political. [. . .]

Of those who might regret the harshness or the high-handedness of certain of my remarks, right here, I ask—isn't it only fair?—to reread one more time the critical responses. Then they will have a better measure of the aggression—its violence and its mediocrity—that has me as its victim, in five of the six cases. It is not possible for me to respond on that level. And it is my duty not to accept it. One does not always decide by oneself on a high-handed tone.

Saturday, 4 February, 10 P.M.

This paper is "biodegradable." Note the very extended use of "paper" in English, even in the university (every speech is a "paper"). The word "paper" recalls the name of "journal," in the sense of newspaper and not of diary. [. . .] Only in English? And the French word *journal*—in a certain way the homonym of the English word, but the latter is what we call a *revue*—works equally well as a translation of *newspaper* and of *diary*. This is naturally only a pretext for asking two questions: (1) Is what resists translation more or less (bio)degradable (see above on the proper name)? (2) Isn't it striking that, according to some extraordinary destiny, Paul de Man's articles ("Wartime Journalism") have been reproduced in facsimile, the book thereby preserving the appearance of the paper-journal? (I am reminded that those who can/will not read

29. See de Man, *Critical Writings (1953–1978)*, ed. Waters (Minneapolis, 1989).

[*ne pveulent pas lire*] had the audacity to accuse us of publishing in the original so as to prevent them from reading it. Alas, they do not need our strategies for that. I am dreaming of other strategies: to *make* them read instead!) How to translate the valuable and economical French expression *papier-journal?* It designates the least noble species of paper— newsprint. It is thought that, since it lends itself to all uses, it is better suited than any other to biodegradation.

Here, now, the word "biodegradable" is waste matter [*un déchet*]. Already partly biodegraded. Will I have used it up enough? [. . .]

An "internal" reading will always be insufficient. And moreover impossible. Question of context, as everyone knows, there is nothing but context, and therefore: there is no outside-the-text [*il n'y a pas de hors-texte*] (used-up formula, yet unusable out of context, a formula that, at once used up and unusable, might appear to be impossible to wear out [*inusable*]. I don't believe that in the least, but the time involved is difficult to calculate). [. . .]

For example, what can be the future destiny of a document that would now give one to read, like right here, this sole phrase: "Forget it, drop it, *all of this is biodegradable*"?

7 Of Spirit

Translated by Geoffrey Bennington and Rachel Bowlby

In order better to present the context of our excerpt from *De l'esprit*, Jacques Derrida has asked us to include the following remarks, which originally appeared on the back cover of his book—ED.

"I shall speak of ghost, of flame and of ashes." These are the first words of a lecture on Heidegger. It attempts a new crossing: neither an "internal" commentary nor an indictment on the basis of "external" documents, however necessary they remain within their limits.

It again has to do with Nazism—of what remains to be thought of Nazism in general and of Heidegger's Nazism. But also with "politics of spirit," declarations on the "crisis of spirit" and on "freedom of spirit," which people thought then, and still want today, to oppose to the inhuman (Nazism, fascism, totalitarianism, materialism, nihilism, and so on). It is starting with the "Rectorship Address" (1933) that Heidegger raises a hymn to spirit. Six years earlier, he had decided to "avoid" this word, and then surrounded it with quotation marks. What happened? Why has no one ever noticed? Just like today, the invocation of spirit wanted to be a meditation on the des-

tiny of Europe. This was the echo from the eloquence of the great Euro-
pean "spirits": of Valéry, Husserl, or others—whose "politics" are less
innocent than is often believed.

At the very heart of their tradition, European philosophies, systems
of morals and religions share their discourse, exchange it with that of
Heidegger when he names spirit. What are we to do with this sharing
and this exchange? Can we interrupt them? Should we? At stake here
are Good and Evil, Enlightenment and Flame, spirit in its fiery tongue:
Geist is Flame, says Heidegger.

This book has two focal points. If, in 1933, Heidegger celebrates
the spirit whose name he had wanted to "avoid" until then, this first
inflection does not have the form of the "turn" [Kehre] that fascinates
the commentators. It is nonetheless decisive. Later, a second inflection
displaces the privilege of the question held until then to be "the piety
of thought." The question of the question remains suspended, held to
the gauge of an acquiescence that must precede it. Yes, the gauge, the
engagement or the wager before the abyss. What happens when this be-
comes "ethical" or "political"? To what and to whom does one say yes?

I shall speak of ghost [revenant], of flame and of ashes.

And of what, for Heidegger, *avoiding* means.

What is avoiding? Heidegger on several occasions uses the common
word *Vermeiden*: to avoid, to flee, to dodge. What might he have meant
when it comes to "spirit" or the "spiritual"? I specify immediately: not
spirit or the spiritual but *Geist, geistig, geistlich*, for this question will
be, through and through, that of language. Do these German words allow themselves to be translated? In another sense: are they avoidable?

Sein und Zeit (1927): what does Heidegger say at that time? He
announces and he prescribes. He *warns* [avertit]: a certain number of
terms will have to be avoided (*vermeiden*). Among them, spirit (*Geist*).
In 1953, more than twenty-five years later—and this was not just any
quarter-century—in the great text devoted to Georg Trakl, Heidegger
notes that Trakl always took care to avoid (*vermeiden* again) the word
geistig. And, visibly, Heidegger approves him in this; he thinks the same.
But this time, it is not *Geist* nor even *geistlich* that is to be avoided, but
geistig.

How are we to delimit the difference, and what has happened? What
of this meantime? How are we to explain that in twenty-five years,
between these two *warning* signals ("avoid," "avoid using"), Heidegger
made a frequent, regular, marked (if not remarked) use of all this vo-

cabulary, including the adjective *geistig*? And that he often spoke not only of the word "spirit" but, sometimes yielding to the emphatic mode, in the name of spirit?

Could it be that he failed to avoid what he knew he ought to avoid? What he in some sense had promised himself to avoid? Could it be that he forgot to avoid? Or else, as one might suspect, are things tortuous and more entangled than this? . . .

I will not rely for the essential justification of my topic on an introduction or preface. Here, nonetheless, are *three* preliminary arguments.

There is first the necessity of this essential *explanation*, the quarrel between languages, German *and* Rome, German *and* Latin, and even German *and* Greek, the *Übersetzung* as *Auseinandersetzung* between *pneuma, spiritus,* and *Geist*. At a certain point, this last no longer allows of translation into the first two. "Tell me what you think about translation and I will tell you who you are," recalls Heidegger on the subject of Sophocles' *Antigone*.[1] In this title, *De l'esprit*, the Franco-Latin *de* also announces that, in the classical form of the inquiry, and even of the dissertation, I wish to begin to treat *of spirit*—the word and the concept, the terms *Geist, geistig, geistlich*—in Heidegger. I shall begin to follow modestly the itineraries, the functions, the formations and regulated transformations, the presuppositions and the destinations. This preliminary work has not yet been systematically undertaken—perhaps not even, to my knowledge, envisaged. Such a silence is not without significance. It does not derive only from the fact that although the lexicon of spirit is more copious in Heidegger than is thought, he never made it the title or the principal theme of an extended meditation, a book, a seminar, or even a lecture. And yet—I will attempt to show this—what thereby remains unquestioned in the invocation of *Geist* by Heidegger is, more than a *coup de force*, force *itself* in its most out-of-the-ordinary manifestation. This motif of spirit or of the spiritual acquires an extraordinary authority *in its German language*. To the precise extent that it does not appear at the forefront of the scene, it seems to withdraw itself

---

1. "Sage mir, was du vom Übersetzen hältst, und ich sage dir, wer du bist." Immediately afterward the matter is raised of the translation, which is itself "deinon," of the deinon: "Furchtbare," "Gewaltige," "Ungewöhnliche," and, in less "correct" but "more true" fashion, says Heidegger, "unheimlich." See Martin Heidegger, "Die Bedeutung des δεινόν [deinon]. (Erläuterung des Anfangs des Chorliedes)," *Hölderlins Hymne "Der Ister,"* ed. Walter Biemel, vol. 53 of *Gesamtausgabe* (Frankfurt am Main, 1984), pp. 77–78. I invoke this passage because the *deinon* leaves its mark on all the texts we shall have to approach.

from any destruction or deconstruction, as if it did not belong to a history of ontology—and the problem will be just that.

On the other hand, and this is a second argument, this motif is regularly inscribed in contexts that are highly charged politically, in the moments when thought lets itself be preoccupied more than ever by what is called history, language, the nation, *Geschlecht*, Greek or German. On this lexicon, which we are not justified in calling spiritualist or even spiritual—can I risk saying *spirituelle*?—Heidegger draws abundantly in the years 1933–35, above all in the "Rectorship Address" and *An Introduction to Metaphysics*, and also in a different way in *Nietzsche*. But during the following twenty years, and except for one inflection that I will try to analyze, this same lexicon gives direction, for example, to the seminars and writings on Schelling, Hölderlin, and especially Trakl. It even takes on a thematic value in them, which is not without a certain novelty.

Here, finally, is my third preliminary argument: if the thinking of *Geist* and of the difference between *geistig* and *geistlich* is neither thematic nor athematic, and if its modality thus requires another category, then it is not only inscribed in contexts with a high political content, as I have just said rapidly and rather conventionally. It perhaps decides the very meaning of the political as such. In any case it would situate the place of such a decision, if it were possible. Whence its privilege, still scarcely visible, for what are called the questions of the political or of politics that are stimulating so many debates around Heidegger today—doubtless in renewed form in France, thanks notably to Philippe Lacoue-Labarthe—at the point at which they tie up with the great questions of Being and truth, of history, of the *Ereignis*, of the thought and unthought or, for I always prefer to say this in the plural, the thoughts and the unthoughts of Heidegger.

∴ ∴ ∴

To my knowledge, Heidegger never asked himself, "What is spirit?" At least, he never did so in the mode, or in the form, or with the developments that he grants to questions such as: "Why is there something rather than nothing?"; "What is Being?"; "What is technology?"; "What is called thinking?"; and so on. No more did he make of spirit one of those grand poles that metaphysics is supposed to have opposed to Being, in a sort of limitation (*Beschränkung*) of Being, such as is contested by *An Introduction to Metaphysics*: Being and becoming, Being and appearance, Being and thinking, Being and duty, or Being and value. No more did he oppose spirit to nature, even dialectically, according to the most forceful and permanent of metaphysical demands.

What is called spirit? What does spirit call up? *Was heisst der Geist?*—so that is the title of a book Heidegger never wrote. When they have to do with spirit, Heidegger's statements *rarely* take the form of a definition of essence. Rarely, that is to say, exceptionally, and we are interested in these exceptions, which are in fact very different and even opposed to each other. Most often, Heidegger will have *inscribed* the noun (*Geist*) or the adjective (*geistig, geistlich*): say in a linked group of concepts or philosophemes belonging to a deconstructible ontology, and most often in a sequence going from Descartes to Hegel, in other words, in propositions I will again risk calling axiomatic, axiological, or axiopoetic. The spiritual, then, no longer belongs to the order of these metaphysical or ontotheological meanings. Rather than a value, spirit seems to designate, beyond a deconstruction, the very resource for any deconstruction and the possibility of any evaluation.

What then does he call spirit, *Geist*?

In *Sein und Zeit*, it is first of all a word whose meaning remains steeped in a sort of ontological obscurity. Heidegger recalls this and asks for the greatest possible vigilance on this point. The word relates back to a series of meanings that have a common feature: to be opposed to the thing, to the metaphysical determination of thingness, and above all to the thingification of the subject, of the subjectivity of the subject as supposed by Descartes. This is the series of soul, consciousness, spirit, person. Spirit is not the thing, spirit is not the body. Of course, it is from this *subjective* determination of spirit that a delimitation (*Abgrenzung*) must disengage, one could say liberate, the existential analytic of *Dasein*. *Dasein* finds itself given the task of preparing a philosophical treatise of the question "What is man?" It should be remembered that it *precedes* (*liegt* vor; Heidegger's emphasis) all biology, all anthropology, all psychology. One could say all *pneumatology*, this being the other name Hegel gives to *rational psychology*, which, further, he also criticizes as an "abstract metaphysics of understanding."[2] . . .

Now who are we? Here, let us not forget, we are first and only deter-

---

2. G. W. F. Hegel, "Introduction" to *The Philosophy of Spirit* in the *Encyclopedia*, sect. 378. In the same introduction, Hegel defines the essence of spirit as *liberty* and as the capacity, in its formal determination, to support *infinite suffering*. I think I must quote this paragraph to anticipate what will be said later about spirit, liberty, and evil for Heidegger: "This is why the essence of spirit is formally *liberty*, the absolute negativity of the concept as self-identity. According to this formal determination, it can abstract

mined from the opening to the *question of Being*. Even if Being must be given to us for that to be the case, we are only at this point, and know of "us" only this: the power or rather the possibility of questioning, the experience of questioning.

We were speaking a moment ago of the question. Now precisely this entity which we are, this "we," which, at the beginning of the existential analytic, must have no name other than *Dasein*, is chosen for the position of exemplary entity only from *the experience of the question*, the possibility of the *Fragen*, as it is inscribed in the network of the *Gefragte* (Being), the *Erfragte* (the meaning of Being), of the *Befragte der Seinsfrage*, that is, the entity which we are and which thus becomes the exemplary or privileged entity for a *reading*—Heidegger's word—of the meaning of Being. The point of departure in the existential analytic is legitimated first of all and only from the possibility, experience, structure, and regulated modifications of the *Fragen*. Such is the exemplarity of the entity which we are, of the *ourselves* in this discursive situation of *Mitsein* in which we can, to ourselves and to others, say *we*. This exemplarity can become or remain problematical. But this ought not to dissimulate a still less apparent problematicity—which is, precisely, perhaps no longer even a *problematicity*. It could not even be determined as question or problem. For it depends on this point of departure in a reflection on the question (it's better to say the *Fragen*) and its structural components. How, without confirming it a priori and circularly, can we *question* this inscription in the structure of the *Fragen* from which *Dasein* will have received, along with its privilege (*Vorrang*), its first, minimal, and most secure determination? Even supposing that this structure is described properly by Heidegger (which is not certain, but I leave that to one side for the moment), any worry as to the legitimacy or axiomatic necessity of such a point of departure in a reflection on the Being-able-to-question would leave intact neither the principle, nor the order, nor finally the interest of the existential analytic: in three words, of *Sein und Zeit*. One would then turn against it what Heidegger himself says: however provisional the analysis, it always and already demands the assurance of a correct point of departure (*Sein und Zeit*, sect. 9).

I insist on this point of departure in the possibility of the *Fragen* not only for the reasons I pointed out at the start. A few years later, when

---

all that is exterior and its own exteriority, its own presence: it can support the negation of its individual immediacy, infinite *sufferance*: that is, conserve itself affirmative in this negation and be identical for itself. This possibility is in itself the abstract universality of spirit, universality which-is-for-itself" (sect. 382).

the references to spirit are no longer held in the discourse of *Destruktion* and in the analytic of *Dasein*, when the words *Geist* and *geistig* are no longer avoided but rather *celebrated*, spirit itself will be defined by this manifestation and this force of the question. And therefore of the question *in the name of which* the same words are avoided in *Sein und Zeit*. When he says he must avoid them, Heidegger is right to emphasize that he does so not out of caprice, stubbornness, or concern for terminological oddness (sect. 10). The terms of this series: spirit, but also soul or *psyché*, consciousness, ego, reason, subject—and Heidegger adds on life and man too—block any interrogation on the Being of *Dasein*. They are all linked, as the unconscious would be as well, to the Cartesian position of the *subjectum*. And even when they inspire the modernity of eloquent discourses on the nonthingification or nonreification of the subject, they—and in particular the terms life and man—mark a lack of interest, an indifference, a remarkable "lack of need" (*Bedürfnislosigkeit*) for the question of the Being of the entity which we are.

:   :   :

Should we close *Sein und Zeit* at this point? Do the many developments devoted to the heritage of the Cartesian graft add nothing to these premises? Is this the book's last word on the theme of spirit?

Yes and no.

Yes, insofar as the premises and the deconstruction will *never* be called into question again. Neither in *Sein und Zeit* nor later.

No, because the rhetorical strategy is displaced when a step is taken, already, in the direction of this analytic of *Gemüt*. As early as *Sein und Zeit*, Heidegger takes up the value and the word "spirit," simply *in quotation marks*. He thus assumes it without assuming it, he avoids it in no longer avoiding it. To be sure, this un-avoidance now supposes and will henceforth maintain the earlier delimitation. It does not contradict but confirms and renews the necessity of avoiding (*vermeiden*), and it will always do so. And yet, along with the word, even surrounded by quotation marks, something of spirit—doubtless what signals toward *Gemüt*—allows itself to be withdrawn from the Cartesian-Hegelian metaphysics of subjectity. Something that the word "spirit" still names between quotation marks thus allows itself to be salvaged. Spirit returns. The word "spirit" starts to become acceptable again. The catharsis of the quotation marks frees it from its vulgar, *uneigentlich*, in a word, Latino-Cartesian marks. There then begins, at the other end of the same book, the slow work of reappropriation that will merge, as I should like to demonstrate, with a re-Germanization.

: : :

It's the law of quotation marks. Two by two they stand guard: at the frontier or before the door, assigned to the threshold in any case, and these places are always dramatic. The apparatus lends itself to theatricalization and also to the hallucination of the stage and its machinery: two pairs of pegs hold in suspension a sort of drape, a veil or a curtain. Not closed, just slightly open. There is the time this suspension lasts: six years, the suspense of the spectator and the tension that follows the credits. Then, suddenly, with a single blow and not three, the lifting [levée] of the quotation marks marks the raising [lever] of the curtain. And there's a *coup de théâtre* immediately, with the overture: the entry on stage of spirit itself, unless it's delegating its ghost, its *Geist*, again.

Six years later, 1933, and here we have the "Rectorship Address": the curtain-raising is also the spectacle of academic solemnity, the splendor of the staging celebrating the quotation marks' disappearance. In the wings, spirit was waiting for its moment. And here it makes its appearance. It presents itself. Spirit *itself*, spirit in its spirit and in its letter, *Geist* affirms itself through the self-affirmation of the German university. Spirit's affirmation inflamed. Yes, *inflamed*: I say this not only to evoke the pathos of the "Rectorship Address" when it celebrates spirit, not only because of what a reference to flame can illuminate of the terrifying moment that is deploying its specters around this theater, but because twenty years later, exactly twenty years, Heidegger will say of *Geist*, without which it is impossible to think Evil, that *in the first place* it is neither *pneuma* nor *spiritus*, thus allowing us to conclude that *Geist* is no more heard in the Greece of the philosophers than in that of the Gospels, to say nothing of Roman deafness: *Geist* is flame. Which would then be said, and thus thought, only in German.

How are we to explain this sudden inflammation and inflation of *Geist*? *Sein und Zeit* was all tortuous prudence, the severe economy of a writing holding declaration within the discipline of severely observed marks. So how does Heidegger get from this to the eloquent fervor and the sometimes rather edifying proclamation dedicated to the self-affirmation of the German university? What is the leap from the one to the other? And what in spite of this is confirmed and continued from the one to the other?

Each word of the title, *Die Selbstbehauptung der deutschen Universität*, is traversed, steeped, illuminated, determined (*bestimmt*)—I mean both defined and destined—called for by spirit. Self-affirmation, first of all, would be impossible, would not be heard, would not be what it is if it were not of the order of spirit, spirit's very order. The [English] word "order" designating both the value of command, of duction or conduction, the *Führung*, and the value of mission: sending, order given. Self-affirmation *wants* to be (we must emphasize this willing) the affirmation of spirit through *Führung*. This is a spiritual conducting, of course, but the *Führer*, the guide—here the Rector—says he can only lead if he is himself led by the inflexibility of an order, the rigor or even the *directive* rigidity of a mission (*Auftrag*). This is also already spiritual. Consequently, conducted from guide to guide, the self-affirmation of the German university will be possible only through those who lead while themselves being led, directors directed by the affirmation of this spiritual mission. Later we shall have to recognize a passage between this *affirmation* and a certain thinking of consent, of commitment in the form of a reply, of a responsible acquiescence, of agreement or confidence (*Zusage*), a sort of word given in return. Before any question and to make possible the question itself.

The *German* character of this university is not a secondary or contingent predicate, it cannot be dissociated from this affirmation of spirit. As the highest agency of the institution thus erected, of this "high school" (*hohe Schule*), directed upward from the heights, spirit can do nothing other than affirm itself—and this, as we shall hear, in the movement of an authentification or identification, which would *want themselves to be properly German.*

Right from the opening of the "Address," Heidegger himself emphasizes the adjective "spiritual" (*geistig*). It is thus the first thing he stresses. I shall emphasize it in my turn, reading Gérard Granel's [French] translation: not only because it is the first word to be stressed by Heidegger, but because this adjective, *geistig*, is the word that twenty years later will be opposed to *geistlich*. The latter would no longer have anything platonico-metaphysical or christo-metaphysical about it, whereas *geistig*, Heidegger will say then, in his own name and not in a commentary on Trakl, remains caught in the metaphysico-platonico-christian oppositions of the below and the beyond, of the low and the high, of the sensible and the intelligible. And yet, in the "Rectorship Address," the *Geistigkeit* to which Heidegger appeals is already opposed to "the christo-theological interpretation of the world which came after"

(*Die nachkommende christlich-theologische Weltdeutung*).[3] But there is
no *Geistlichkeit* yet. Is this simply a terminological incoherence, a verbal
adjustment that takes a certain time? Up to a point, without doubt, but
I do not think that things can be reduced to that.

Here, then, is the first paragraph of the "Rectorship Address," the
lifting of the quotation marks that are carried off, the raising of the curtain on the first act, the inaugural celebration of spirit: cortege, academic
procession—spirit is at the head, and in the highest, since it leads the
very leaders. It precedes, anticipates [*prévient*], and gives the direction
to be followed—to the *spiritus rector* (whose directives we know better
today) and to those who follow him:

> To take over the rectorship is to oblige oneself to guide this
> high school *spiritually* (*die Verpflichtung zur* geistigen *Führung
> dieser hohen Schule*). Those who follow, masters and pupils,
> owe their existence and their strength only to a true common
> rootedness in the essence of the German University. But this
> essence comes to the clarity, the rank and the power which are
> its own, only if first of all and at all times the guiders [*guideurs*]
> [*Führer*: I prefer "guide" to "guider," a rather rare and perhaps
> neologistic word, which runs the risk of making us forget that
> *Führer* was at that time very common in Germany.] are them-
> selves guided—guided by the inflexibility of this spiritual mis-
> sion (*jenes geistigen Auftrags*), the constraining nature of which
> imprints the destiny of the German people with its specific his-
> torical character. [*S*, p. 9; "A," p. 5]

This final sentence speaks, then, of the imprint (*Gepräge*) marked in
the destiny of the German people. A typographical motif, and even an
ontotypological motif, as Lacoue-Labarthe would put it. Its recurrence

3. Heidegger, *Die Selbstbehauptung der deutschen Universität. Rede, gehalten bei
der feierlichen Übernahme des Rektorats der Universität Freiburg i. Br. am 27. 5. 1933*
(1933; Frankfurt am Main, 1983), p. 12; hereafter abbreviated *S*. As Jacques Derrida
indicates, his reading of Heidegger's address proceeds by way of Gérard Granel's French
translation. In order to reproduce, as closely as possible, the details of this reading, we
have translated directly from the French text: "L'Auto affirmation de l'université alle-
mande," *Editions Trans-Europ-Repress* (Toulouse, 1982), p. 10; hereafter abbreviated
"A." An English translation by Karsten Harries is also available: "The Self-Assertion of
the German University: Address, Delivered on the Solemn Assumption of the Rectorate
of the University Freiburg" and "The Rectorate 1933/34: Facts and Thoughts," *Review
of Metaphysics* 38 (Mar. 1985): 467–502.

in the "Rectorship Address" must be interrogated retrospectively in light of the letter to Ernst Jünger (*Zur Seinsfrage*) and what relates there to the modern accomplishment of subjectity. Without being able to enter into this problem, I would point out that the figure of the imprint is associated here, regularly and essentially, with that of force. Heidegger sometimes says *Prägekraft* (*S*, p. 9) or *prägenden Kraft* (*S*, p. 18). Now force is just as regularly, just as essentially, associated with spirit in the sense that it is celebrated thereafter without quotation marks.

At the center of the "Address," for the first time to my knowledge (subsequently he does so only twice, in texts on Schelling and on Trakl), Heidegger offers a definition of spirit. It is certainly presented in the form of a definition: S is P. And without any possible doubt, Heidegger takes it up for himself. He is no longer mentioning the discourse of the other. No longer speaking of spirit as in Descartes, Hegel, or later Schelling or Hölderlin, he links this predicative determination to a series of headings whose importance there is no need for me to stress. I will name *four* of them to prepare for the reading of this definition.

1. First there is *questioning, Fragen*, which manifests here—and manifests *itself*—as will: will to know and will to essence. Even before the definition of spirit, which reaffirms it, this will had been affirmed earlier in the "Address":

> To will the essence of the German university is to will science, in the sense of willing the spiritual historical mission of the German people (*Wille zum geschlechtlichen geistigen Auftrag des deutschen Volkes*) as a people that knows itself to be in its State. Science and German destiny must, in this will to essence, achieve power (*Macht*) at the same time. [*S*, p. 10; "A," p. 7]

2. Next there is the *world*, a central theme of *Sein und Zeit*. Like the renewed quest of *Fragen*, it marks the profound continuity between *Sein und Zeit* and the "Address."

3. Further, and still linked to force, there is the theme of *earth and blood*: "erd- und bluthaften Kräfte als Macht" (*S*, p. 14).

4. Finally, and above all, still in essential and internal continuity with *Sein und Zeit*, there is *Entschlossenheit: resolution*, determination, the decision that gives its possibility of opening to *Eigentlichkeit*, the authentic property of *Dasein*.

Here now is this key paragraph, with these *four determinations of spirit*:

If we want the essence of science in the sense of *this manner of holding firm, questioning (fragenden) and exposed, in
the middle of the uncertainty of entities in their totality,* then
this will to essence creates for our people its most intimate
and extreme world of danger, in other words its true *spiritual*
world (*seine wahrhaft* geistige *Welt* [*geistige* is underlined]). For
"spirit" [in quotation marks, but this time to recall in a still negative definition the spirit others talk of] is neither empty sagacity
nor the gratuitous game of joking [*Spiel des Witzes*: this distinction between spirit and the *mot d'esprit*, between *Geist* and
Witz, recalls the Kant of the *Anthropology*, noting that a feature
of the French spirit was marked by the fact that French has only
one word, the word *esprit*, to designate *Witz* and *Geist*], nor
the unlimited work of analysis of the understanding, nor even
the reason of the world [probably an allusion to Hegel], but
spirit is the being-resolved to the essence of Being (*ursprünglich
gestimmte, wissende Entschlossenheit zum Wesen des Seins*),
of a resolution which accords with the tone of the origin and
which is knowledge [*savoir*]. And the *spiritual world* (geistige
Welt [underlined]) of a people is not the superstructure of a culture, and no more is it an arsenal of bits of knowledge [*connaissances*] and usable values, but the deepest power of conservation
of its forces of earth and blood, as the most intimate power of
emotion (*Macht der innersten Erregung*) and the vastest power
of disturbance of its existence (*Dasein*). Only a spiritual world
(*Eine geistige Welt allein*) guarantees the people its grandeur, for
it imposes the constraint that the constant decision between the
will to grandeur on the one hand, and on the other the *laisser-
faire* of decadence (*des Verfalls*), give its rhythm to the march
our people has begun toward its future history. [*S*, p. 14; "A,"
pp. 13–14]

The celebration corresponds properly, literally, to an *exaltation*
of the spiritual. It is an elevation. This is not only a question of the
kerygmatic tone, of proclamation or declaration, but of an exaltation in
which is declared and erected the most high. As always, the profound
and the haughty are allied in the most high: the highest of what guides
the spiritual guides of *die hohe Schule* and the depth of forces of earth
and blood. For it is precisely in them that consists the spiritual world.
As to what is clear in this exaltation, spirit has here no longer the sense

of metaphysical subjectity. There is no contradiction with *Sein und Zeit* in this regard. Spirit does not belong to subjectity, *at least* in its psychical or egological form, for it is not certain that the massive voluntarism of this "Address" is not still caught up in the said epoch of subjectity.

One other thing seems as clear: in a sense that would, to be sure, *like* to think itself not Hegelian, historicity is immediately and essentially determined as spiritual. And what is true of history is true of the world. On several occasions, Heidegger associates, with a hyphen, the adjectives *geistig* and *geschichtlich*: *geistig-geschichtlich* is *Dasein* (*S*, p. 16; "A," p. 17); *geschichtlich-geistig* is the world (*S*, p. 17; "A," p. 18). This association will be constant, two years later, in *An Introduction to Metaphysics*. But still in the "Address," and still in order to follow this trace of the question and its privilege, I shall insist on the following point: the union, the hyphen [*trait d'union*] between spirit and history plays a very significant role in a passage that makes of the *Fragen* the very assignment of spirit. The question is *of spirit* or it is not:

> Such an original concept of science carries the obligation not only of "objectivity" ("*Sachlichkeit*"), but again and above all of the essentiality and simplicity of interrogation (*des Fragens*) at the center of the spiritual world, which is, historially, that of the people (*inmitten der geschichtlich-geistigen Welt des Volkes*). And even, it is solely from this that objectivity can receive its true foundation, in other words, find its genre and its limits. [*S*, p. 17; "A," p. 18]

The Self-Affirmation of the German University: every word of the title is, as we said, steeped in the exalting celebration of this spirit. We have just seen how the force of its imprint marks the self-affirmation, signing in the *same stroke* the being-German of the people and of their world, that is its university as will to know and will to essence. It remains to confirm that the same spiritual imprint is inscribed in the academic organization, in the legislation of faculties and departments, in the community (*Gemeinschaft*) of masters and pupils:

> The faculty is a faculty only if it deploys itself in a capacity for spiritual legislation (*geistiger Gesetzgebung*) rooted in the essence of science, so as to give to the powers of existence (*Mächte des Daseins*), which form its urgency, the form of the people's unique spiritual world (*die* eine *geistige Welt des Volkes*). [*S*, p. 17; "A," p. 18]

As for what is commanded or recommended *of spirit* in it, this "Address" calls for *at least* three readings, three evaluations, or rather three protocols of interpretation.

1. To the extent that he countersigns the assignment of spirit, the author of this "Address," as such, cannot withdraw from any responsibility.

His discourse is first of all that of response and responsibility. Responsibility properly assumed, or even claimed before different authorities. These latter are always associated among themselves inasmuch as they are united with spirit. Spirit writes their hyphen, the hyphen between the world, history, the people, the will to essence, the will to know, the existence of *Dasein* in the experience of the question.

2. This responsibility is nonetheless exercised according to a strategy. Tortuous, at least double, the strategy can always hold an extra surprise in reserve for whomever thinks he controls it.

On the one hand, Heidegger thus confers the most reassuring and elevated *spiritual* dignity on everything in which and on all before whom he commits himself, on everything he thus sanctions and consecrates at such a height. One could say that he spiritualizes National Socialism. And one could reproach him for this, as he will later reproach Nietzsche for having exalted the spirit of vengeance into a "spirit of vengeance spiritualized to the highest point" (*ein höchst vergeistigter Geist der Rache*).[4]

But, on the other hand, by taking the risk of spiritualizing Nazism, he might have been trying to absolve or save it by marking it with this affirmation (spirituality, science, questioning, and so on). By the same

---

4. Heidegger, "Wer ist Nietzsches Zarathustra?" *Vorträge und Aufsätze*, 2d ed. (Pfullingen, 1959), p. 121; hereafter abbreviated *VA*. This lecture has been published as "Who Is Nietzsche's Zarathustra?" in *Nietzsche*, ed. and trans. David Farrell Krell, 4 vols. (San Francisco, 1979–82), 2:228; hereafter abbreviated *N*. [We have sometimes slightly altered the translation.] Of course, this is not a "reproach" nor even a refutation. Heidegger always denies doing this. He never criticizes nor refutes. This is, according to him, the "game of the small-minded" (*Kleingeisterei*), as he explains precisely after the passage I have just quoted and the question he asks in it (*VA*, p. 121; *N*, 2:229). He had first of all applauded Nietzsche for thinking revenge "metaphysically"—the dimension of revenge not being primarily "moral" or "psychological" (*VA*, p. 112; *N*, 2:221). Then he sketches the movement leading to the limit of Nietzsche's thought as the accomplishment of metaphysics, to the place where something appears in Nietzsche's thought that it can no longer think. And it is precisely the spirit of revenge (*Geist der Rache*), which would perhaps not be overcome (merely "spiritualized to the highest point") by this discourse on the imprint (*Aufprägen*) that Nietzsche talks about: "'*Dem Werden den Charakter des Seins* aufzuprägen—*das ist der* höchste Wille zur Macht'" (*VA*, p. 120; *N*, 2:228).

token, this sets apart [*démarque*] Heidegger's commitment and breaks an affiliation. This address *seems* no longer to belong simply to the "ideological" camp in which one appeals to obscure forces—forces that would not be spiritual, but natural, biological, racial, according to an anything but spiritual interpretation of "earth and blood."

3. The force to which Heidegger appeals, and again in conclusion when he speaks of the destiny of the West, is thus a "spiritual force" (*geistige Kraft*). And we will find this theme of spirit and of the West again, though displaced, in the text on Trakl.

What is the price of this strategy? Why does it fatally turn back against its "subject"—if one can use this word, as one must, in fact? Because one cannot demarcate oneself off from biologism, from naturalism, from racism in its genetic form; one cannot be *opposed* to them except by reinscribing spirit in an oppositional determination, by once again making it a unilaterality of subjectity, even if in its voluntarist form. The constraint of this program remains very strong, it reigns over the majority of discourses that, today and for a long time to come, state their opposition to racism, to totalitarianism, to Nazism, to fascism, and so on, and do this in the name of spirit, and even of the freedom of (the) spirit,[5] in the name of an axiomatic—for example, that of democracy or "human rights"—which, directly or not, comes back to this metaphysics of *subjectité*. All the pitfalls of the strategy of establishing demarcations belong to this program, whatever place one occupies in it. The only choice is the choice between the terrifying contaminations it assigns. Even if all forms of complicity are not equivalent, they are *irreducible*. The question of knowing which is the least grave of these forms of complicity is always there, its urgency and its seriousness could not be overstressed, but it will never dissolve the irreducibility of this fact. This "fact" [*fait*], of course, is not simply a fact. First, and at least, because it is not yet *done* [*fait*], not altogether [*pas tout à fait*]: it calls more than ever, as for what in it remains to come after the disasters that have happened, for absolutely unprecedented responsibilities of "thought" and "action." This is what we should have to try to designate, if not to name, and begin to analyze here.

In the "Rectorship Address," this risk is not just a risk run. If its program seems diabolical, it is because, *without there being anything fortuitous in this*, it capitalizes on the worst, that is, on both evils at once: the sanctioning of Nazism and the gesture that is still metaphysical. Behind

5. This liberty of spirit always runs the risk rigorously determined by the Hegel text quoted above (in footnote 2): that of a merely formal liberty of an abstract universality.

the ruse of quotation marks, of which there is never the right amount (always too many or too few of them), this equivocation has to do with the fact that *Geist* is always haunted by its *Geist*: a spirit, or in other words, in French [and English] as in German, a phantom, always surprises by returning to be the other's ventriloquist. Metaphysics always returns, I mean in the sense of a *revenant* [ghost], and *Geist* is the most fatal figure of this *revenance* [returning]. Of the double that can never be separated from the single.

Is this not what Heidegger will never finally be able to avoid (*vermeiden*), the unavoidable itself—spirit's double, *Geist* as the *Geist* of *Geist*, spirit as spirit of the spirit, which always comes with its double? Spirit is its double.

However we interpret this awesome equivocality, for Heidegger it is inscribed *in spirit*. It is *of spirit*. He will say so in speaking of spiritual evil in the text on Trakl. But he already notes it, in another mode, at the beginning of *An Introduction to Metaphysics*, two years after the "Rectorship Address."

In the same way that, in spite of the *coup de théâtre*, the raising of the curtain or the lifting of the quotation marks, the "Address" relaunches and confirms the essential elements of *Sein und Zeit*, so the *Einführung in die Metaphysik* (1935) repeats the invocation of spirit launched in the "Address." It even relaunches it, explains it, extends it, justifies it, specifies it, surrounds it with unprecedented precautions.

The rhetoric is no longer, to be sure, that of a treatise, as in *Sein und Zeit*, nor that of an inaugural and emphatic speech, as in the "Rectorship Address." Here we have a teaching language, which partakes of both genres simultaneously. No more than in 1933 does it rehabilitate the concept of spirit deconstructed in *Sein und Zeit*. But it is still in the name of spirit, the spirit which guides in resolution toward the question, the will to know and the will to essence, that the other spirit, its bad double, the phantom of subjectity turns out to be warded off by means of *Destruktion*.

Is this duplicity the same as the equivocality or the ambiguity that Heidegger recalls right at the beginning of *An Introduction to Metaphysics*, when he speaks of the *Zweideutigkeit* in which "every essential form of spiritual life" stands?[6] The more singular a figure of spirit, the

6. Heidegger, *An Introduction to Metaphysics*, trans. Ralph Manheim (New Haven, Conn., 1959), p. 9. The German sentence is: "Jade wesentliche Gestalt des Geistes steht in des Zweideutigkeit" (Heidegger, *Einführung in die Metaphysik*, ed. Petra Jaeger, vol. 40 of *Gesamtausgabe* [Frankfurt am Main, 1983], p. 11; hereafter abbreviated *E*).

more tempted one is to be mistaken about it through comparison and confusion. Now philosophy is one of the essential forms of spirit: independent, creative, rare among the possibilities and the necessities of human *Dasein* in its historiality. Precisely because of its essential rarity, a singularity always inspires mistakes, just as *Zweideutigkeit* inspires *Missdeutung*. The first misinterpretation consists in demanding first of all—we are still very familiar with this program today—that philosophy procure for the *Dasein* and the age of a people the foundations of a culture, and then denigrate philosophy when it is useless from this point of view and is useless for that culture. Second expectation, second mistake: this figure of spirit, philosophy, ought at the very least to procure a system, synopsis, world-picture (*Weltbild*), map of the world (*Weltkarte*), a sort of compass for universal orientation. If philosophy cannot ground culture, then it should at least alleviate and facilitate the technicopractical functioning of cultural activities, and lighten the burden on science by taking off its hands epistemological reflection on its presuppositions, its concepts, and its fundamental principles (*Grundbegriffe, Grundsätze*). What is expected of the philosopher? That he be the functionary of the fundamental. These misunderstandings, more full of life today than ever, are sustained, notes Heidegger (and who will argue with him?), by teachers of philosophy.

Self-affirmation or self-presentation of spirit: all that the "Rectorship Address" announces in these terms is renamed in the *Einführung in die Metaphysik*. One could say from the title and name of *Einführung*. The assignment of the question is here immediately associated with that of the *Führung* said to be *spiritual*. The *Einführung* opens a meditation on the question, or more precisely, on the *introduction to the question*, on what introduces, induces, and conducts to within the question, the *Hineinführen in das Fragen der Grundfrage* (E, p. 22).

There is no questioning except in the *experience* of the question. Questions are not things, like water, stone, shoes, clothes, or books. The *Hineinführen* into the question does not conduct or induct *something*, it guides, conducts toward the experience, the awakening, or the production of the question. But as nothing ought to dictate the question nor precede it in its *freedom*, the *Führen* is *already* questioning. It comes before, it is an already questioning fore-coming of the question (*ein fragendes Vorangehen*), a prequestioning, *ein Vor-fragen*. In this way, if nothing precedes the question in its freedom, not even the introduction to questioning, then the spirit of spiritual conduction (*geistige Führung*)—spoken of in both the "Rectorship Address" and *An Introduction to Metaphysics*—can be interpreted, through and through, as the possibility of questioning. It responds and corresponds to this possibility. Unless this latter already responds or corresponds to it, in the ties and obligations or even the alliances of such a correspondence, as also in the experience of this coresponsibility. This discourse on spirit is also a discourse on the freedom of spirit.

Given that nothing precedes it, spiritual duction remains itself unconducted, and thus breaks the circle of empty reflection that threatened the question of being in its fundamental form: "Why are there entities and not nothing?" That was the first sentence of the book. There was a risk that the reflective machine would make it circle ad infinitum in the question of the question: why "why"? and so on. Heidegger speaks rather of a leap (*Sprung*) of the question. The leap makes the originary upsurge (*Ursprung*) surge, liberates it without having to introduce the question from anything other than an *already* questioning conduction: *and this is spirit itself.* Spirit wakes, awakens rather [*plutôt*]—earlier [*plus tôt*]—from the *Vor-fragen* of the *Führung*. Nothing anticipates this power of awakening in its freedom and its resolution (*Entschlossenheit*). What comes *before* and *in front*, what anticipates and questions before all else (*vor*), is spirit, the freedom of spirit. As *Führer*, it goes or comes on the way, in front, up in front, before any politics, any psychagogy, any pedagogy.

For in all honesty we must make clear the fact that at the very moment at which he runs the risk of placing this thematics of the *Führung* in the service of a determinate politics, Heidegger gives it to be understood that he is breaking in advance with any such service. In its spiritual essence, this free conduction should not give rise to any camp-following [*suivisme*], one should not accord it any following, any follower, any *Gefolgschaft*, any aggregation of disciples or partisans. One can naturally extend to the party what Heidegger says, to exclude them, of the school as academic study, technical apprenticeship, or professional training. Undoubtedly it will be difficult to understand what can be meant by a *Führung* that mandates, demands, or commands without being followed, obeyed, or listened to in any way. However spiritual it may be, one will say, it must surely guide. Certainly, Heidegger would say here, but if one finds it difficult to understand, that means that one remains imprisoned in a logic of the understanding and does not accede to this freedom of listening, to this fidelity or modality of following, which would have no relationship to the mindless following of *Gefolgschaft*. Perhaps. But it is also the case that, on the other hand, if it is not further reduced to its discursive modalities or to interrogative utterances, this questioning belongs through and through, that is to say,

essentially, to will and to will as the will to know. "Fragen ist Wissen-
wollen" (*E*, p. 23).

All this conducts the *Einführung* back to the "Rectorship Address,"
and again to the thematics of resolution (*Entschlossenheit*). This last
plays a decisive role, in fact, the role of decision itself in *Sein und Zeit*.
The paragraph defining questioning as will to know (sect. 74) also reminds us that will itself is a being-resolved (*Entschlossensein*).

Although at least in appearance—the appearance of a less emphatic
tone—the *Einführung* begins to mark a political retreat in relation to
the "Rectorship Address"; in fact it proposes a kind of *geopolitical* diagnosis, of which all the resources and all the references return to spirit,
to spiritual historiality, with its already tried and tested concepts: the fall
or decadence (*Verfall*) are *spiritual*, so too force is *spiritual*.

Geopolitical, then: Europe, Russia, and America are named here,
which still no doubt means just Europe. But the dimension remains
properly geopolitical. Thinking the world is determined as thinking the
earth or the planet.

Heidegger denounces, then, a "spiritual decadence" (*geistiger Verfall*). Peoples are in the process of losing their last "spiritual forces"
because of this. This last expression returns often. The *Verfall* of spirit
cannot allow itself to be thought other than in its relation to the destiny of being. If, in questioning, the experience of spirit appears pro-
portional to "danger," the German people, "our people," this "metaphysical people" (*das metaphysische Volk*) par excellence, is at once
the most spiritual (Heidegger specifies this clearly later on in speaking
of language) and the most exposed to danger. For it is caught in a vice,
in the middle (*in der Mitte*) (*E*, p. 41) between its European neighbors,
Russia and America.[7] On it devolves the "great decision" (*die grosse
Entscheidung*), which will engage the destiny of Europe, the deployment
of "new *spiritual* forces from this middle place" (*neuer geschichtlich
geistiger Kräfte aus der Mitte*). Emphasis, *emphase*: the word "spiritual"
is again *underlined* both to mark that the fundamental determination
of the relation to being occurs there, and to ward off the possibility of
a politics other than *of spirit*. A new commencement is called for. It is
called for by the question: "Wie steht es um das Sein?" What about Being? And this commencement, which is first a recommencement, consists

7. The indictment of America, its "pseudo-philosophy" and its "patent psychol-
ogy," continues for a long time, no doubt reaching its apogee in 1941. See Heidegger,
Die Grundbegriffe der Metaphysik, ed. Freidrich-Wilhelm von Herrmann, vol. 29/30 of
Gesamtaugabe (Frankfurt am Main, 1983).

in repeating (*wieder-holen*) our historially spiritual existence (*Anfang unseres geschichtlich-geistigen Daseins*) (*E*, p. 42). The "we" of this "our" . . . is the German people. I referred overhastily to a geopolitical *diagnosis*, at the point where the discourse is neither that of knowledge nor clinical or therapeutic. But geopolitics conducts us back again from the earth and the planet to the world, and to the world as a world *of spirit*. Geopolitics is none other than a *Weltpolitik of spirit*. The world is not the earth. On the earth arrives an obscuring of the world (*Welt-verdüsterung*) (*E*, p. 48): the flight of the gods, the destruction of the earth, the massification of man, the preeminence of the mediocre.

8

Given Time: The Time of the King

Translated by Peggy Kamuf

Epigraph

> *The King takes all my time; I give the rest to Saint-Cyr, to whom I would like to give all.*

It is a woman who signs.

For this is a letter, and from a woman to a woman. Madame de Maintenon is writing to Madame Brinon. This woman says, in sum, that to the King she gives all. For in giving all one's time, one gives all or the all, if all one gives is in time and one gives all one's time.

It is true that she who is known to have been the influential mistress and even the morganatic wife of the Sun

Given Time [*Donner le temps*] was the general title of the series of the Frederick Ives Carpenter Lectures that Jacques Derrida gave at the University of Chicago in April 1991. What follows is a translation of the first lecture, which has been revised and augmented. It puts in place several of the works (Marcel Mauss's *The Gift* and Charles Baudelaire's "Counterfeit Money" among others) that will be the object of detailed readings in the subsequent lectures. The complete text of *Donner le temps* has just been published in French and is forthcoming in English translation.

King[1] (the Sun and the King, the Sun-King will be the subjects of these lectures), Madame de Maintenon, then, did not say, in her letter, literally, that she was *giving* all her time but rather that the King *was taking* it from her ("the King takes all my time"). Even if that means the same thing, in her mind, one word does not equal the other. What she *gives*, for her part, is not time but the *rest*, the rest of the time: "I give the rest to Saint-Cyr, to whom I would like to give all." But as the King *takes* all her time, then the rest, by all good logic and good economics, is nothing. She can no longer *take* her time. She has no more time. And yet she gives it. Lacan says speaking of love: It gives what it does not have, a formula whose variations are ordered by the *Écrits* according to the final and transcendental modality of the woman inasmuch as she is, supposedly, deprived of the phallus.[2]

Here Madame de Maintenon *is writing*, and she says *in writing*, that she gives the rest. What is the rest? *Is* it, the rest? She gives the rest which is nothing, since it is the rest of a time concerning which she

1. Madame de Maintenon's sentence is remarkable enough to have attracted the attention of the editors of the *Littré*. It is their version that I cite. There are those who will be surprised, perhaps, to see me evoke the secret wife of a great king at the beginning of such a lecture. However, Madame de Maintenon seems to me to be exemplary not only because, from her position as woman and "grande dame," she poses the question of the gift, of time, and of the rest. She who played the role of Louis XIV's "sultan of conscience" was at the same time—and this configuration is rarely fortuitous—an outlaw and the very figure of the law. Before she became, upon the death of the Queen, the morganatic wife of the King (and thus excluded from all noble titles and rights; the word *morganatic* says something of the gift and the gift of the origin: it is from low Latin *morganegiba*, gift of the morning), she had led the Sun King back to his duties as husband (by estranging him from Madame de Montespan whose protégée she had been) and as Catholic king (by restoring austerity to the court, by encouraging the persecution of the Protestants—even though she herself was raised a Calvinist—and by supporting the revocation of the Edict of Nantes). She who took so much trouble over what was to be given and taken, over the law, over the name of the King, over legitimacy in general was also the governess of the royal bastards, a promotion she no doubt owed to the protection of Madame de Montespan. Let us stop there where we should have begun: When she was a child, she experienced exile in Martinique and her father, Constant, was arrested as a counterfeiter. Everything in her life seems to bear the most austere, the most rigorous, and the most authentic stamp of counterfeit money.

2. "For if love is to give what one does not have . . ." (Jacques Lacan, *Écrits* [Paris, 1966], p. 618); "What is thus given to the Other to fill and which is properly what he/she does not have, since for him/her as well Being is lacking, is what is called love, but it is also hatred and ignorance" (p. 627); "This privilege of the Other thus outlines the radical form of the gift of what he/she does not have, that is, what is called his/her love" (p. 691). The symmetry of these formulae, which seem to concern love *in general*, is interrupted when the truth of this "not-having-it" appears, namely, the woman *quoad matrem* and the man *quoad castrationem* (Lacan, *Encore*, vol. 20 of *Le Séminaire de*

has just informed her correspondent she has nothing of it left since the King takes it all from her. And yet, we must underscore this paradox, even though the King takes all *her* time, she seems to have some left, as if she could return the change. "The King takes all *my* time," she says, a time that belongs to her therefore. But how can a time belong? What is it *to have time*? If a time belongs, it is because the word *time* designates metonymically less time itself than the things with which one fills it, with which one fills the form of time, time *as form*. It is a matter, then, of the things one does *in the meantime* [cependant] or the things one has at one's disposal *during* [pendant] this time. Therefore, as time does not belong to anyone as such, one can no more *take* it, itself, than *give* it. Time already begins to appear as that which undoes this distinction between taking and giving, therefore also between receiving and giving, perhaps between receptivity and activity, or even between being-affected and the affecting of any affection. Apparently and according to common logic or economics, one can only exchange, by way of metonymy, one can only take or give what is *in* time. That is indeed what Madame de Maintenon seems to *want to say* on a certain surface of her letter. And yet, even though the King takes it all from her, altogether, this time or whatever fills up the time, she has some left, a

---

Jacques Lacan, ed. Jacques-Alain Miller [Paris, 1975], p. 36), to use a later formula but one which draws together very well this whole economy. Returning, then, to the *Écrits*:

> If it is the case that man manages to satisfy his demand for love in his relationship to the woman to the extent that the signifier of the phallus constitutes her precisely as giving in love what she does not have—conversely, his own desire for the phallus will throw up its signifier in the form of a persistent divergence towards "another woman" who can signify this phallus on several counts, whether as a virgin or a prostitute. . . . We should not, however, think that the type of infidelity which then appears to be constitutive of the masculine function is exclusive to the man. For if one looks more closely, the same redoubling is to be found in the woman, the only difference being that in her case, the Other of Love as such, that is to say, the Other as deprived of that which it gives, is difficult to perceive in the withdrawal whereby it is substituted for the being of the same man whose attributes she cherishes.

The difference of "the only difference being" organizes all the dissymmetries analyzed on this page, which, let us remember, concludes as follows: "Correlatively, one can glimpse the reason for a feature which has never been elucidated and which again gives a measure of the depth of Freud's intuition: namely, why he advances the view that there is only one libido, his text clearly indicating that he conceives of it as masculine in nature" (Lacan and the *école freudienne*, "The Meaning of the Phallus," in *Feminine Sexuality*, trans. Jacqueline Rose, ed. Rose and Juliet Mitchell [New York, 1985], pp. 84–85).

The expression "to give what one does not have" is found in Heidegger (in particular in "The Anaximander Fragment" ["Der Spruch das Anaximander," in *Holzwege*] but also elsewhere). [This conjunction of Lacan and Heidegger is discussed more fully in a later chapter.—TRANS.]

remainder that is not nothing since it is beyond everything, a remainder that is nothing but that *there is* since she *gives it*. And it is even essentially what she gives, *that very thing*. The King takes all, she gives the rest. The rest is not, there is the rest that is given or that gives itself. It does not give itself to someone, because, as everyone knows, Saint-Cyr is not her lover, and it is above all not masculine. Saint-Cyr is a—very feminine—place, a charity, an institution, more exactly a *foundation* of Madame de Maintenon's. Saint-Cyr is the name of a charity for the education of impoverished young ladies of good families. Its founder retired there and no doubt was able to devote all her time to it, in accordance with her declared wish, after the death of the King in 1715. Would we say, then, that the question of the rest, and of the rest of given time, is secretly linked to the death of some king?

Thus the rest, which *is* nothing but that *there is* nevertheless, does not give itself to someone but to a foundation of young virgins. *And it never gives itself enough, the rest*: "I give the rest to Saint-Cyr, to whom I would like to give it all." She never gets enough of giving this rest that she does not have. And when she writes, Madame de Maintenon, that she would like to give it all, one must pay attention to the *literal* writing of her *letter, to the letter of her letter*. This letter is almost untranslatable; it defies exchange from language to language. I insist on the fact that it is a question of a letter since things would not be said in the same way in a different context. So when she writes that she would like to give *all* [*elle voudrait* le tout *donner*], she allows two equivocations to be installed: *le* can be a personal pronoun (in an inverted position: *je voudrais tout le donner*, I would like to give it all), or it can be an *article* (before the word *tout*, which is thus nominalized: I would like to give *all*, that is everything). That would be the first equivocation. The second equivocation: *tout* or *le tout* can be understood to refer to *time* (all of which the King takes from her) as well as to the *rest* of time, of the time and of what presents itself there, occupying it thus, or of the rest and of what presents itself there, likewise occupying it. This phrase lets one hear the infinite sigh of unsatisfied desire. Madame de Maintenon says to her correspondent that everything leaves her something to be desired. Her wish is not fulfilled or attained either by what she allows herself to take from the King nor even by the rest that she gives—in order to *make a present* of it, if you will, to her young virgins.

Her desire would be there where she *would like*, in the conditional, to give what she cannot give, the all, that rest of the rest of which she cannot make a present. Nobody takes it all from her, neither the King nor Saint-Cyr. This rest of the rest of time of which she cannot make a present, that is what Madame de Maintenant (as I wish to call her) desires, that is in truth what she would desire, not for herself but to be able to give it [*pour le pouvoir donner*]. For the power of giving [*pour le pouvoir de donner*], perhaps, in order to give herself this power of giving. She lacks not lacking time, she lacks not giving enough. She lacks this leftover time that is left to her and that she cannot give—that she doesn't know what to do with. But this rest of the rest of time, of a time that moreover is nothing and that belongs properly to no one, this rest of the rest of time, that is the whole of her desire. Desire and the desire to give would be the same thing, a sort of tautology. But maybe as well the tautological designation of the impossible. Maybe the impossible. The impossible may be—if giving and taking are also the same—the same, the same thing which would certainly not be a thing.

One could accuse me here of making a big deal and a whole *history* out of words and gestures that remain very clear. When Madame de Maintenon says that the King takes her time, it is because she is glad to give it to him and takes pleasure from it: the King takes nothing from her and gives her as much as he takes. And when she says, "I give the rest to Saint-Cyr, to whom I would like to give all," she is confiding in her correspondent about a *daily* economy concerning the leisures and charities, the works and days of a "grande dame" somewhat overwhelmed by her obligations. None of the words she writes has the sense of the unthinkable and the impossible toward which my reading would have pulled them, in the direction of giving-taking, of time and the rest. She did not mean to say that, you will say.

What if . . . yes she did [*Et si*].

And if what she wrote meant to say that, then what would that suppose? How, where, on the basis of what and when can we read this letter fragment as I have done? How could we even hijack it as I have done, while still respecting its literality and its language? End of the epigraph.

Let us begin by the impossible.

To join together, in a title, time and the gift may seem to be a laborious artifice. What can time have to do with the gift? We mean: What would there be to see in that? What would they have to do with each other, or more literally to see together; *qu'est-ce qu'ils auraient à voir ensemble*, one would say in French. Of course, they have nothing to *see* together and first of all because both of them have a singular relation to the visible. Time, in any case, gives nothing to see. It is at the very least the element of invisibility itself. It withdraws whatever could give itself to be seen. It itself withdraws itself from visibility. One can only be blind to time, to the essential *disappearance* of time even as, nevertheless, in a certain manner nothing *appears* that does not require and take time. Nothing sees the light of day, no phenomenon, which is not on the order of the day, in other words, of the *revolution* that is the rhythm of a sun's course. And that orients this course from its endpoint: from the rising in the east to the setting in the west. The works and days as we said a moment ago.

We will let ourselves be carried away by this word *revolution*. At stake is a certain *circle* whose figure precipitates both time and the gift toward the possibility of their impossibility.

To join together, in a title, both time and the gift may seem to be a laborious artifice, as if, in order to economize, one sought to treat two subjects at once. And that is in fact the case, for reasons of economy. But economy is here the subject. What is economy? Among its irreducible semantic predicates or values, economy no doubt includes the values of law (*nomos*) and of home (*oikos*, home, property, family, the hearth, the fire within). *Nomos* does not only signify the law in general, but also the law of distribution (*nemein*), the law of sharing or partition [*partage*], the law as partition, *moira*, the given or assigned part, participation. Another sort of tautology already implicates the economic within the nomic as such. As soon as there is law, there is partition: as soon as there is *nomy*, there is economy. Besides the values of law and home, of distribution and partition, economy implies the idea of exchange, of circulation, of return. The figure of the circle is obviously *at the center*, if that can still be said of a circle. It stands at the center of any problematic of *oikonomia*, as it does of any economic field: circular exchange, circulation of goods, products, monetary signs or merchandise, amortization of expenditures, return on investment, substitution of use-values and exchange-values. This motif of circulation can lead one to think that the law of economy is the—circular—return to the point of departure, to the origin, also to the home. So one would have to follow the *odyssean* structure of the economic narrative. *Oikonomia* would always follow the path of Ulysses. The latter returns to the side of his loved ones and to himself, and he only goes away in view of *repatriating* himself, in order to return to the home from which [*à partir duquel*] the signal for departure is given and the part assigned, the side chosen [*le parti pris*], the lot divided, destiny commanded (*moira*). The being-next-to-self of the Idea in Absolute Knowledge would be odyssean in this sense, that of an *economy* and a *nostalgia*, a "homesickness," a provisional exile longing for reappropriation.

Now the gift, *if there is any*, would no doubt be related to economy. One cannot treat the gift without treating this relation to economy, that goes without saying, even to the money economy. But is not the gift, if there is any, that which interrupts economy? That which, in suspending economic calculation, no longer gives rise to exchange? That which opens the circle so as to defy reciprocity or symmetry, the common measure, and so as to turn aside the return in view of the no-return? If there is gift, the *given* of the gift (*that which* one gives, *that which* is given, the gift as given thing or as act of donation) must not come back to the giving (let us not already say to the subject, to the donor). It must not circulate, it must not be exchanged, it must not in any case be exhausted, as a gift, by the process of exchange, by the movement of circulation of the circle in the form of return to the point of departure. If the figure of the circle is essential to the economic, the gift must remain *aneconomic*. Not that it remains foreign to the circle, but it must *keep* a relation of foreignness to the circle, a relation without relation of familiar foreignness. It is perhaps in this sense that the gift is the impossible.

Not impossible but *the* impossible. The very figure of the impossible. It announces itself, gives itself to be thought as the impossible. It is proposed that we begin by this.

And we will do so. We will begin later. By the impossible.

The motif of the circle will obsess us throughout this cycle of lectures. Let us provisionally set aside the question of whether it is a matter of a geometric figure, a metaphorical representation or a great symbol, the symbol of the symbolic itself. We have learned from Hegel to treat this problem. Saying that the circle will obsess us is another manner of saying that it will encircle us. It will besiege us all the while that we will be regularly attempting to exit [*la sortie*]. But why exactly would one desire, along with the gift, if there is any, the exit? Why desire the gift and why desire to interrupt the circulation of the circle? Why wish to get out of it [*en sortir*]? Why wish to get through it [*s'en sortir*]?

The circle has already put us onto the trail of time and of that which, by way of the circle, circulates between the gift and time. One of the most powerful and ineluctable representations, at least in the history of metaphysics, is the representation of time as a circle. Time would always be a process or a movement in the form of the circle or the sphere. Of this privilege of the circular movement in the representation of time, let us take only one index for the moment. It is a note by Heidegger, the last and the longest one in *Sein und Zeit*. Some time ago I attempted a reading of it in "*Ousia* and *Grammē*: Note on a Note from *Being and Time.*"[3] Since this Note and this note on a note will be part of our premises, it will help to recall at least the part concerning the absolute insistence of this figure of the circle in the metaphysical interpretation of time. Heidegger writes:

> The priority which Hegel has given to the 'now' which has been levelled off, makes it plain that in defining the concept of time he is under the sway of the manner in which time is *ordinarily* understood; and this means that he is likewise under the sway of the *traditional* conception of it. It can even be shown that his conception of time has been drawn *directly* from the 'physics' of Aristotle. . . . Aristotle sees the essence of time in the *nun*, Hegel in the 'now' (*jetzt*). Aristotle takes the *nun* as *oros*; Hegel takes the 'now' as 'boundary' (*Grenze*). Aristotle understands the *nun* as *stigmē*; Hegel interprets the 'now' as a point. Aristotle describes the *nun* as *tode ti*; Hegel calls the 'now' the 'absolute this' (*das 'absolute Dieses'*). Aristotle follows tradition in connecting *khronos* with *sphaira*; Hegel stresses the 'circular course' (*Kreislauf*) of time. . . . In suggesting a direct connection between Hegel's conception of time and Aristotle's analysis, we are not accusing Hegel of any 'dependence' on Aristotle, but are calling attention to the *ontological import which this filiation has in principle* for the Hegelian logic.[4]

There would be more to say on the figure of the circle in Heidegger. His treatment is not simple. It also implies a certain assumed affirmation of the circle. One should not necessarily flee or condemn circularity as one would a bad repetition, a vicious circle, a regressive or sterile process. One must, in a *certain way* of course, inhabit the circle, turn around in it, live there a celebration of thinking, and the gift, the gift of thinking would not be a stranger there. That is what *Der Ursprung des Kunstwerks* [*The Origin of the Work of Art*] suggests. But this motif, which is not a stranger to that of the hermeneutic circle either, coexists with what we might call a de-limitation of the circle: the latter is but a particular figure, the "particular case" of a structure of *nodal* coiling

---

3. See Jacques Derrida, "*Ousia* and *Grammē*: Note on a Note from *Being and Time*," *Margins of Philosophy*, trans. Alan Bass (Chicago, 1982), pp. 29–67.

4. Martin Heidegger, *Being and Time*, trans. John Macquarrie and Edward Robinson (New York, 1962), p. 500 n. 30; quoted in Derrida, *Margins of Philosophy*, pp. 36–38.

up or interlacing that Heidegger names the *Geflecht* in *Unterwegs zur Sprache*.

If one were to stop here with this first somewhat simplifying representation or with these hastily formulated premises, what could one already say? That wherever there is time, wherever time predominates or conditions experience in general, wherever *time as circle* (a "vulgar" concept, Heidegger would therefore say) is predominant, the gift is impossible. A gift could only be possible, there can only be a gift at the instant an effraction in the circle will have taken place, at the instant all circulation will have been interrupted and *on the condition* of this instant. Moreover, this instant of effraction (of the temporal circle) must no longer be part of time. That is why we said "on the condition of this instant." This condition concerns time but does not *pertain* to it, is not a *part* of it without being for all that more logical than chronological. There would be a gift only at the instant when the *paradoxical* instant (in the sense in which Kierkegaard says of the paradoxical instant of decision that it is madness) tears time apart. In this sense one would never have the time of a gift. In any case, time, the "present" of the gift, is no longer thinkable as a now, that is, as a present bound up in the temporal synthesis.

The relation of the gift to the "present," in all the senses of this term, also to the presence of the present, will form one of the essential knots in the interlace of this discourse, in its *Geflecht*, in the knot of that *Geflecht* of which Heidegger says precisely that the circle is perhaps only one figure or a particular case, an inscribed possibility. That a gift is called a present, that "to give" may also be said "to make a present," "to give a present" (in French as well as in English, for example), this will not be for us just a verbal clue, a linguistic chance or *aléa*.

We said a moment ago: "Let us begin by the impossible." By the impossible, what ought one to have understood?

If we must speak of it, we will have to name something. Not to present the thing, here the impossible, but to try with its name, or with some name, to give an understanding of or to think this impossible thing, this impossible itself. To say we are going to "name" is perhaps already or still to say too much. For it is no doubt the name of name that is going to find itself put in question. If, for example, the gift were impossible, the name or noun "gift," what the linguist or the grammarian believes he recognizes to be a name, would not be a name. At least, it would not name what one thinks it names, to wit, the unity of a meaning that would be that of the gift. Unless the gift were the impossible but not the unnameable or the unthinkable, and unless in this gap between the impossible and the thinkable the dimension opens up where *there is* gift—and even where *there is* period, for example time, where *it gives* being and time (*es gibt das Sein* or *es gibt die Zeit*, to say it in a way that anticipates excessively what would be precisely a certain essential excess of the gift, indeed an excess of the gift beyond the essence itself).

Why and how *can I think that the gift is the impossible*? And why is it here a matter precisely of *thinking*, as if thinking, the word *thinking*, conformed itself only to this disproportion of the impossible, even as if it announced itself—as thought irreducible to intuition, irreducible also to perception, judgment, experience, science, faith—only on the basis of *this* figure of the impossible, on the basis of the impossible *in the figure of the gift*?

Let us suppose that someone wants or desires to give to someone. In our logic and our language we say it thus: someone wants or desires, someone *intends-to-give* something to someone. The complexity of the formula appears already formidable. It supposes a subject and a verb, a constituted subject, which can also be collective—for example, a group, a community, a nation, a clan, a tribe—in any case, a subject identical to itself and conscious of its identity, indeed seeking by the gesture of the gift to constitute its own unity and, precisely, to get its own identity recognized so that that identity comes back to it, so that it can reappropriate its identity: as its property.

Let us suppose, then, an intention-to-give: Some "one" wants or desires to give. Our common language or logic will cause us to hear the interlace of this already complex formula as incomplete. We would tend to complete it by saying "some 'one'" (A) intends-to-give B to C, some "one" intends to give or gives "something" to "someone other." This "something" may not be a thing in the common sense of the term but rather a symbolic object; the donee may be a collective subject, likewise the donor, but in any case A gives B to C. These three elements, identical to themselves or on the way to an identification with themselves, look like what is presupposed by every gift event. For the gift to be possible, for there to be gift event, it seems, according to our common language and logic, that this compound structure is indispensable. Notice that in order to say this, I must already suppose a certain precomprehension of what *gift* means. I suppose that I know and that you know what "to give," "gift," "donor," "donee" mean in our common language. As well as "to want," "to desire," "to intend." This is an unsigned but effective contract between us, indispensable to what is happening here, namely, that you accord, lend, or give some attention and some meaning to what I myself am doing by giving, for example, a lecture. This whole presupposition will remain indispensable at least for the *credit* that we accord each other, the faith or good faith that we lend each other, even if in a little while we were to argue and disagree about everything. It is by making this precomprehension (credit or faith) explicit that one can authorize oneself to state the following axiom: In order for there to be gift, gift event, some "one" has to give some "thing" to someone other, without which "giving" would mean nothing. In other words, if giving indeed means what, in speaking of it among ourselves, we think it means, then it is necessary, in a certain situation, that some "one" give some "thing" to some "one other," and so forth. This appears tautological, it goes without saying and seems to imply the defined term in the definition, which is to say it defines nothing at all. Unless the discreet introduction of "one" and of "thing" and especially of "other" ("someone other") does not portend some perturbation in the tautology of a gift that cannot be satisfied with giving or with giving (to) *itself* [se *donner*] without giving something (other) to someone (other).

For this is the impossible that seems to give itself to be thought here. It is that these conditions of possibility of the gift (that some "one" gives some "thing" to some "one other") designate simultaneously the conditions of the impossibility of the gift. And already we could translate this in other terms: These conditions of possibility define or produce the annulment, the annihilation, the destruction of the gift.

Once again, let us set out in fact from what is the simplest level and let us still entrust ourselves to this semantic precomprehension of the word *gift* in our language or in a few familiar languages. For there to be a gift, there must be no reciprocity, return, exchange, countergift, or debt. If the other gives me back or owes me or ought to give me back what I give him or her, there will not have been a gift, whether this restitution is immediate or whether it is programmed by a complex calculation of a long-term deferral or, if you like, *différance*. This is all too obvious if the other, the donee, gives me back *immediately* the same thing. It may, moreover, be a matter of a good thing or a bad thing. Here we are anticipating another dimension of the problem, namely, that if giving is spontaneously evaluated as *good* (it is *well* and *good* to give and what one gives, the present, the *cadeau*, the gift, is a good), it remains the case that this "good" can easily be reversed. We know that as good, it can also be bad, poisonous (*Gift, gift*), and this is true from the moment the gift puts the other in debt, so that giving comes down to hurting, to doing bad; here one need hardly mention the fact that in certain languages, for example in French, one may say as readily "to give a gift" as "to give a blow" [*donner un coup*], "to give life" as "to give death" [*donner la mort*], thereby either dissociating and opposing them or identifying them. So we were saying that, quite obviously, if the donee gives back the same thing, for example an invitation to lunch (and the example of food or of what are called consumer goods will never be just one example among others), the gift is annulled. It is annulled each time there is restitution or countergift. Each time, according to the same circular ring that leads to "giving back" ["*rendre*"], there is payment and discharge of a debt. In this logic of the debt, the circulation of a good or of goods is not only the circulation of the "things" that we will have offered to each other but even of the values or the symbols that are engaged there and the intentions to give, whether they are conscious or unconscious. Even though all the anthropologies, indeed the metaphysics of the gift have, *quite rightly and justifiably*, treated *together*, as a system, the gift and the debt, the gift and the cycle of restitution, the gift and the loan, the gift and credit, the gift and the countergift, we are here *departing*, in a peremptory and distinct fashion, from this tradition. That is to say, from tradition itself. We will take our point of departure in the dissociation, in the overwhelming evidence of this other axiom: There is gift, if there is any, only in what interrupts the system as well as the symbol, in a partition without return and without division [*répartition*], without being-with-self of the gift-countergift.

For there to be a gift, *it is necessary* [il faut] that the donee not give back, amortize, reimburse, acquit himself, enter into a contract, and that he never have contracted a debt. (This "it is necessary" is already the mark of a duty, of a debt owed, the duty-not-to-be [*le devoir de-ne-pas*]: The donee owes it *to himself* even not to give back; he has the *duty* not to *owe* [*il a le* devoir *de ne pas* devoir], and the donor not to count on restitution.) It is necessary, at the limit, that he not *recognize* the gift as gift. If he recognizes it *as* a gift, if the gift *appears to him as such*, if the present is present to him *as present*, this simple recognition suffices to annul the gift. Why? Because it gives back, in the place, let us say, of the thing itself, a symbolic equivalent. Here one cannot even say that the symbolic *re*constitutes the exchange and annuls the gift in the debt. It does not reconstitute an exchange, which, because it no longer takes place as exchange of things or of goods, would be transfigured into a symbolic exchange. The symbolic opens and constitutes the order of exchange and of the debt, the law or the order of circulation in which the gift is annulled. It suffices therefore for the other to *perceive the gift*— not only to perceive it in the sense in which, as one says in French, *on perçoit*, that is, receives, for example, merchandise, payment, or compensation—but to perceive its nature of gift, the meaning or intention, the *intentional meaning* of the gift, in order for this simple *recognition* of the gift *as* gift, *as such*, to annul the gift as gift even before *recognition* becomes *gratitude*. The simple identification of the gift seems to destroy it. The simple identification of the passage of a gift as such, that is of an identifiable thing among some identifiable "ones," would be nothing other than the process of the destruction of the gift. It is as if, between the event or the institution of the gift *as such* and its destruction, the difference were destined to be constantly annulled. *At the limit, the gift as gift* should not *appear as gift: either to the donee or to the donor.* It cannot be gift as gift except by not being present as gift. Neither to the "one" nor to the "other." If the other perceives or receives it, if he or she keeps it as gift, the gift is annulled. But the one who gives it must not see it or know it either; otherwise he begins, at the threshold, as soon as he intends to give, to pay himself with a symbolic recognition, to praise himself, to approve of himself, to gratify himself, to congratulate himself, to give back to himself symbolically the value of what he thinks he has given or of what he is preparing to give. The temporalization of time (memory, present, anticipation; retention, protention, imminence of the future; "ecstasies," and so forth) always sets in motion the process of a destruction of the gift: through keeping, restitution, reproduction, the anticipatory expectation or apprehension that grasps or comprehends in advance.

In all these cases, the gift can certainly keep its phenomenality or, if one prefers, its appearance as gift. But its very appearance, the simple phenomenon of the gift annuls it as gift, transforming the apparition into a phantom and the operation into a simulacrum. It suffices that the other perceive and *keep*, not even the object of the gift, the object given, the thing, but the meaning or the quality, the gift property of the gift, its intentional meaning, for the gift to be annulled. We expressly say: It suffices that the gift *keep* its phenomenality. But *keeping* begins by *taking*. As soon as the other accepts, as soon as he or she takes, there is no more gift. For this destruction to occur, it suffices that the movement of acceptance (of prehension, of reception) last a little, however little that may be, more than an instant, an instant already caught up in the temporalizing synthesis, in the *syn* or the *cum* or the being-with-self of time. There is no more gift as soon as the other *receives*—and even if she refuses the gift that she has perceived or recognized as gift. As soon as she keeps for the gift the signification of gift, she loses it, there is no more *gift*. Consequently, if there is no gift, there is no gift, but if there is gift held or beheld *as* gift by the other, once again there is no gift; in any case the gift does not *exist* and does not *present* itself. If it presents itself, it no longer presents itself.

We can imagine a first objection. It concerns the at least implicit recourse that we have just had to the values of subject, self, consciousness, even intentional meaning and phenomenon, a little as if we were limiting ourselves to a phenomenology of the gift even as we declared the gift to be irreducible to its phenomenon or to its meaning and said precisely that it was destroyed by its own meaning and its own phenomenality. The objection would concern the way in which we are describing the intentionality of the intention, the reception, the perception, the keeping, the recognition—in sum, everything by means of which one or the other, donee and donor, *take part* in the symbolic and thus annul the gift in the debt. It will be objected that this description is still given in terms of the self, of the subject that says I, *ego*, of intentional or intuitive perception-consciousness or even of the conscious or unconscious ego (for Freud the ego or a part of the ego can be unconscious). One may be tempted to oppose this description to another that would substitute for the economy of perception-consciousness an economy of the unconscious: Across the forgetting, the nonkeeping, and the nonconsciousness called up by the gift, the debt and the symbolic would reconstitute themselves for the subject of the Unconscious or the unconscious subject. As donee or donor, the Other would keep, bind himself, obligate himself, endebt himself according to the law and the order of the symbolic, according to the figure of circulation,[5] even as the conditions of the gift—forgetfulness, nonappearance, nonphenomenality, nonperception, nonkeeping—would have been fulfilled. Here we are pointing out only the principle of a problematic displacement that we would have to go into more carefully.

The necessity of such a displacement is of the greatest interest. It offers us new resources of analysis; it alerts us to the traps of the would-be *gift* without debt; it activates our critical or ethical vigilance. It permits us always to say: "Careful, you think there is gift, dissymmetry, generosity, expenditure or loss, but the circle of the debt, of exchange or of symbolic equilibrium reconstitutes itself according to the laws of the Unconscious; the 'generous' or 'grateful' consciousness is only the

---

5. On this subject, see Lacan's "Seminar on 'The Purloined Letter'" and the reading I proposed of it in "Le Facteur de la vérité," *The Post Card: From Socrates to Freud and Beyond*, trans. Bass (Chicago, 1987), p. 436ff., especially around the circle of reappropriation of the gift in the debt.

phenomenon of a calculation and the ruse of an economy. Calculation and ruse, in truth economy, would be the truth of these phenomena."

But such a displacement does not affect the paradox with which we are struggling, namely, the impossibility or the double bind of the gift: For there to be gift, it is necessary that the gift not even appear, that it not be perceived or received as gift. For if we added "not even *taken* or *kept*," it was precisely so that the generality of these notions (of *taking* and especially of *keeping*) could cover a wider reception, acceptance, and acceptation than that of consciousness or of the perception-consciousness system. We had in mind also the keeping in the Unconscious, memory, the putting into reserve or temporalization as effect of repression. For there to be gift, not only must the donor or donee not perceive the gift as such, have no consciousness of it, no memory, no recognition; he or she must also forget it right away [*à l'instant*], and moreover this forgetting must be so radical that it exceeds even the psychoanalytic categoriality of forgetting. This forgetting of the gift must even no longer be forgetting in the sense of repression; it must not give rise to any of the repressions (originary or secondary) that reconstitute the debt and the exchange when they put in reserve, when they keep or save up what is forgotten, repressed, or censured. Repression does not destroy or annul anything; it keeps by displacing. Its operation is systemic or topological; it always consists of keeping by exchanging places. And, by keeping the meaning of the gift, repression annuls it in symbolic recognition. However unconscious this recognition may be, it is effective and can be verified in no better fashion than by its effects or by the symptoms it yields up [*qu'elle donne*] for decoding.

So we are speaking of an absolute forgetting—a forgetting that also absolves, that unbinds absolutely and infinitely more, therefore, than excuse, forgiveness, or acquittal. As condition of a gift event, condition for the advent of a gift, absolute forgetting should no longer have any relation with either the psycho-philosophical category of forgetting or even with the psychoanalytic category that links forgetting to meaning or to the logic of the signifier, to the economy of repression and to the symbolic order. The thought of this radical forgetting as thought of the gift should accord with a certain experience of the *trace* as *cinder* or *ashes* in the sense in which we have tried to approach it elsewhere.[6]

And yet we say "forgetting" and not nothing. Even though it must

6. For example, in *Feu la cendre* (Paris, 1987) and the other texts intersecting with it at the point where, precisely, a certain "il y a là" ["there is there"] intersects with the giving of the gift (pp. 57, 60ff.).

leave nothing behind it, even though it must efface everything, including the traces of repression, this forgetting, this *forgetting of the gift* cannot be a simple nonexperience, a simple nonappearance, a self-effacement that is carried off with what it effaces. For there to be gift event (we say event and not act), something must come about or happen, in an instant, in an instant that no doubt does not belong to the economy of time, in a time without time, in such a way that the forgetting forgets, that it forgets *itself*, but also in such a way that this forgetting, without being something present, presentable, determinable, sensible, or meaningful, is not nothing. What this forgetting and this forgetting of forgetting would therefore give us to think is something other than a philosophical, psychological, or psychoanalytic category. It does not give us to think the possibility of the gift; on the contrary, it is on the basis of what takes shape in the name *gift* that one could *hope* thus to think forgetting. For there to be forgetting in this sense, there must be gift. The gift would be the *condition* of forgetting. By condition, let us not understand merely "condition of possibility," system of premises or even of causes, but a set of traits defining a given situation in which something, or "that" ["*ça*"], is established (as one says "the human condition," "the social condition," and so forth). We are not talking therefore about conditions in the sense of conditions posed (since forgetting and gift, if there is any, are in this sense unconditional),[7] but in the sense in which forgetting would be in the *condition of the gift* and the gift in the *condition of forgetting*; one might say on the mode of being of forgetting, if "mode" and "mode of being" did not belong to an ontological grammar that is exceeded by what we are trying to talk about here, that is, the gift and forgetting. But such is the condition of all the words that we will be

---

7. Of course, this unconditionality must be absolute and uncircumscribed. It must not be simply declared and in fact dependent in its turn on the condition of some context, or some proximity or family tie, be it general or specific (among human beings, for example, to the exclusion of, for example, "animals"). Can there be any gift *within the family*? But has the gift ever been thought *without the family*? As for the unconditionality evoked by Lewis Hyde, it is explicitly limited to gifts among close friends, relatives, and most often close relatives. Which is to say that it is not what it is or claims to be: unconditional. This is what the literature on "organ donation" brings out. One of these studies records that the son who donates a kidney to his mother does not want any gratitude from her because she had borne him in the first place. Another who donates to his brother insists that the latter should not feel either endebted or grateful: "those who prize their closeness to the recipient are careful to make it clear that the gift is not conditional." Earlier, it had been pointed out that if, in fact, something comes back, after the gift, if a restitution takes place, the gift would nevertheless cease to be a gift from the moment this return would be its "explicit condition" (Lewis Hyde, *The Gift: Imagination and the Erotic Life of Property* [New York, 1983], pp. 69, 9; hereafter abbreviated *TG*).

using here, of all the words given in our language—and this linguistic problem, let us say rather this problem of language before linguistics, will naturally be our obsession here.

Forgetting and the gift would therefore be each in the condition of the other. This already puts us on the path to be followed. Not a particular path leading here or there, but on *the* path, on the *Weg* or *Bewegen* (path, to move along a path, to cut a path) which, leading nowhere, marks the step that Heidegger does not distinguish from thought. The thought on whose path we are, the thought as path or as movement along a path is precisely what is related to that *forgetting* that Heidegger does not name as a psychological or psychoanalytic category but as the condition of Being and of the truth of Being. This truth of Being or of the meaning of Being was foreshadowed, for Heidegger, on the basis of a question of Being posed, beginning with the first part of *Sein und Zeit*, in the transcendental horizon of the question of time. The explicitation of time thus forms the horizon of the question of Being as question of presence. The first line of *Sein und Zeit* says of this question that it "has today fallen into oblivion [*in Vergessenheit*]. Even though in our time [*unsere Zeit*] we deem it progressive to give our approval to 'metaphysics' again. . . ."

Here we must be content with the most preliminary and minimal selection within the Heideggerian trajectory, and we will limit ourselves to situating that which links the question of time to the question of the gift, and then both of them to a singular thinking of forgetting. In fact, forgetting plays an essential role that aligns it with the very movement of history and of the truth of Being (*Sein*) which is nothing since it is not, since it is not being (*Seiendes*), that is, being present or present being. Metaphysics would have interpreted Being (*Sein*) as being present/present being only on the basis of, precisely, a preinterpretation of time, which preinterpretation grants an absolute privilege to the now-present, to the temporal ecstasy named present. That is why the transcendental question of time (and within it a new existential analysis of the temporality of *Dasein*) was the privileged horizon for a reelaboration of the question of Being. Now, as we know, this movement that consisted in interrogating the question of Being within the transcendental horizon of time was not interrupted (even though *Sein und Zeit* was halted after the first half and even though Heidegger attributed this interruption to certain difficulties linked to the language and the grammar of metaphysics), but led off toward another turn or turning (*Kehre*). After this turning, it will not be a matter of subordinating the question of Being to the question of the *Ereignis*, a difficult word to translate (event or propriation that is inseparable from a movement of dispropriation, *Enteignen*). This word *Ereignis*, which commonly signifies event, signals toward a thinking of appropriation or of depropriation that cannot be unrelated to that of the gift. So from now on it will not be a matter of subordinating, through a purely logical inversion, the question of Being to that of *Ereignis*, but of conditioning them otherwise one by the other, one with the other. Heidegger sometimes says that Being (*das Seyn* in an archaic spelling that attempts to recall the word to a more thinking—*denker-isch*—mode) is *Er-eignis*.[8] And it is in the course of this movement that Being (*Sein*)—which is not, which does not exist as being present, present being—is signalled on the basis of the gift.

This is played out around the German expression *es gibt*, which, moreover, in *Sein und Zeit* (1928) had made a first, discreet appearance that was already obeying the same necessity.[9] We translate the idiomatic locution *es gibt Sein* and *es gibt Zeit* by "il y a l'être" in French and in English "there is Being" (Being is not but there is Being), "il y a le temps," "there is time" (time is not but there is time). Heidegger tries to get us to hear in this [*nous donner à y entendre*] the "it gives," or as one might say in French, in a more neutral but not negative fashion, "ça donne," an "it gives" that would not form an utterance in the propositional structure of Greco-Latin grammar, that is, bearing on present being and in the subject-predicate relation (S/P). The enigma is concentrated both in the "it" or rather the "es," the "ça" of "ça donne," which is not a thing, and in this giving that gives but without giving anything and without anyone giving anything—nothing but Being and time (which are nothing). In *Zeit und Sein* (1952), Heidegger's attention bears down on the giving (*Geben*) or the gift (*Gabe*) implied by the *es gibt*. From the beginning of the meditation, Heidegger recalls, if one can put it this way, that in itself time is nothing temporal, since it is nothing, since it is not a thing (*kein Ding*). The temporality of time is not temporal, no more than proximity is proximate or treeness is woody. He also recalls that Being is not (being present/present being), being that it is not something (*kein Ding*), and that therefore one cannot say either "time is" or "Being

8. See for example Heidegger, *Beiträge zur Philosophie (Vom Ereignis)*, vol. 65 of *Gesamtausgabe*, ed. Friedrich-Wilhelm von Herrmann (Frankfurt am Main, 1989). A French translation of §267 has recently been proposed by Jean Greisch, in *Rue Descartes*, no. 1, an issue titled "Des Grecs" (Apr. 1991): 213ff. Beginning with the first pages of the *Vorblick*, a certain *Ereignis* is defined as the truth of Being [*die Wahrheit des Seyns*]. "L'être est l'Ereignis [*Das Seyn ist das Er-eignis*]" (§267; p. 470); or again: "L'être est (este, s'essencie) comme l'Ereignis [*Das Seyn west als Ereignis*]" (§10; p. 30).

9. We will come back to this point much later, in the second volume of *Donner le temps*, when we approach a reading of *Time and Being* and other related texts.

is," but "es gibt Sein" and "es gibt Zeit." It would thus be necessary to
think a thing, something (*Sache* and not *Ding*, a *Sache* that would not be
a *being*) that would be Being and time but would not be either a being
or a temporal thing: "Sein—eine Sache, aber nichts Seiendes. Zeit—eine
Sache, aber nichts Zeitliches" ["Being—a thing in question, but not a
being. Time—a thing in question, but nothing temporal"]. He then adds
this, which we read in translation for better or worse:

> In order to get beyond the idiom and back to the matter [*Sache*],
> we must show how this "there is" ["*es gibt*"] can be experienced
> [*erfahren*] and seen [*erblicken*]. The appropriate way [*der geeig-
> nete Weg*] to get there is to explain [elucidate, localize: *erörten*]
> what is given [*gegeben*] in the "It gives" ["*Es gibt*"], what "Be-
> ing" means, which—It gives [*das—Es gibt*]; what "time" means,
> which—It gives [*das—Es gibt*]. Accordingly, we try to look
> ahead [*vorblicken*] to the It [*Es*] which—gives [*gibt*] Being [*Sein*]
> and time [*Zeit*]. Thus looking ahead, we become foresighted in
> still another sense. We try to bring the It [*Es*] and its giving [*Ge-
> ben*] into view, and capitalize the "It" ["*Es*"].[10]

And after having thus written the "It gives Being" and "It gives time,"
"there is Being" and "there is time," Heidegger in a certain way asks
the question of what it is in this gift or in this "there is" that relates
time to Being, conditions them, we would now say, one to the other.
And he writes:

> First, we shall think [in the trace of: *nach*] Being in order to
> think It itself into its own element [*um es selbst in sein Eigenes
> zu denken*].
> Then, we shall think [in the trace of: *nach*] time in order to
> think it itself into its own element.
> In this way, the manner must become clear how there is, It
> gives [*Es gibt*] Being and how there is, It gives [*Es gibt*] time. In
> this giving [*Geben*; in this "*y avoir*" *qui donne*, says the French
> translation; in this "there Being" that gives, one might say in En-
> glish], it becomes apparent [*ersichtlich*] how that giving [*Geben*]
> is to be determined which, as a relation [*Verhältnis*], first holds
> [*hält*] the two toward each other and brings them into being
> [*und sie er-gibt*; by producing them or obtaining them as the

10. Heidegger, *On Time and Being*, trans. Joan Stambaugh (New York, 1972), p. 5.

result of a donation, in some sort: the *es* gives Being and gives time by giving them one to the other insofar as it holds (*hält*) them together in a relation (*Verhältnis*) one to the other].[11]

In the very position of this question, in the formulation of the project or the design of thinking, namely, the "in order to" (we think "in order to" [*um . . . zu*] think Being and time in their "own element" [*in sein Eigenes, in ihr Eigenes*]), the desire to accede to the proper is already, we could say, surreptitiously ordered by Heidegger according to the dimension of "giving." And reciprocally. What would it mean to think the gift, Being, and time *properly* in that which is most proper to them or in that which is properly their own, that is, what they can give and give over to the movements of propriation, expropriation, de-propriation, or appropriation? Can one ask these questions without anticipating a thought, even a desire of the proper? A desire to accede to the property of the proper? Is this a circle? Is there any other definition of desire? In that case, how to enter into such a circle or how to get out of it? Are the entrance and the exit the only two modalities of our inscription in the circle? Is this circle itself inscribed in the interlacing of a *Geflecht* of which it forms but one figure? These are so many threads to be pursued.

The only thread that we will retain here, for the moment, is that of *play*. Whether it is a matter of Being, of time, or of their deployment in presence (*Anwesen*), the *es gibt* plays (*spielt*), says Heidegger, in the movement of the *Entbergen*, in that which frees from the withdrawal [*retrait*], the withdrawal of the withdrawal, when what is hidden shows itself or what is sheltered appears. The *play* (*Zuspiel*) also marks, works on, manifests the unity of the three dimensions of time, which is to say a fourth dimension: The "giving" of the *es gibt Zeit* belongs to the play of this "quadridimensionality," to this *properness* of time that would thus be quadridimensional. "True time [authentic time: *die eigentliche Zeit*]," says Heidegger, "is four-dimensional [*vierdimensional*]." This fourth dimension, as Heidegger makes clear, is not a figure, it is not a manner of speaking or of counting; it is said of the thing itself, on the basis of the thing itself (*aus der Sache*) and not only "so to speak." This thing itself of time implies the play of the four and the play of the gift.

Faced with this play of *fours*, of the four, as play of the gift, one thinks of the hand dealt by this game [*la donne de ce jeu*], of the locution "ça donne" (it gives), of the French imperative "donne" that, given by grammar to be an imperative, perhaps says something other than

11. Ibid.

an order, a desire, or a demand. And then one thinks of *la dona*, of the woman who has been soliciting us since the epigraph, of all the questions of language that are crossing, in German and in French, in the locutions *es gibt* and *ça donne*. Thinking of all that and the rest, we will also evoke a very fine book by Lucette Finas[12] which interlaces all these motifs: the *aléa*, the play of the four [*quatre*] and of cards [*cartes*], the verb *give*, the locution *ça donne* (for example, when it is said in French of a purulent body). All these motifs and a few others find themselves woven into a narration, into a narration of narration or into a passion of narration. Later, we will have to recognize that the question of *récit* and of literature is at the heart of all those we are talking about now. Finas's novel knots all these threads into the absolute idiom, the effect of the absolute idiom, which is a proper name (*Donne* is a proper name in the novel), a proper name without which perhaps there would never be either a narration effect or a gift effect. Even though we do not meet Heidegger in person in this novel, it is hard to resist the impression that he is hiding behind a series of men's proper names whose initial, with its German assonance, is H.

This detour was meant first of all to remind us that the forgetting we are talking about, if it is constitutive of the gift, is no longer a category of the *psyche*. It cannot be unrelated to the forgetting of Being, in the sense in which Blanchot also says, more or less, that forgetting is another name of Being.

As the condition for a gift to be given, this forgetting must be radical not only on the part of the donee but first of all, if one can say here first of all, on the part of the donor. It is also on the part of the donor "subject" that the gift not only must not be repaid but must not be kept in memory, retained as symbol of a sacrifice, as symbolic in general. For the symbol immediately engages one in restitution. To tell the truth, the gift must not even appear or signify, consciously or unconsciously, *as* gift for the donors, whether individual or collective subjects. From the moment the gift appeared as gift, as such, as what it is, in its phenomenon, its sense and its essence, it would be engaged in a symbolic, sacrificial, or economic structure that would annul the gift in the ritual circle of the debt. The simple intention to give, insofar as it carries the intentional meaning of the gift, suffices to make a return payment to oneself. The simple consciousness of the gift right away sends itself back the gratifying image of goodness or generosity, of the giving-being who,

12. See Lucette Finas, *Donne* (Paris, 1976).

knowing itself to be such, recognizes itself in a circular, specular fashion, in a sort of auto-recognition, self-approval, and narcissistic gratitude.

And this is produced as soon as there is a subject, as soon as donor and donee are constituted as identical, identifiable subjects, capable of identifying themselves by keeping and naming themselves. It is even a matter there, in this circle, of the movement of subjectivization, of the constitutive retention of the subject that identifies with itself. The becoming subject then reckons with itself; it enters into the realm of the calculable as subject. That is why if there is gift, the gift cannot take place between two subjects exchanging objects, things, or symbols. The question of the gift should therefore seek its place before any relation to the subject, before any conscious or unconscious relation to self of the subject—and that is indeed what happens with Heidegger when he goes back before the determinations of Being as substantial being, subject or object. One would even be tempted to say that a subject as such never gives or receives a gift. It is constituted, on the contrary, in view of dominating, through calculation and exchange, the mastery of this *hubris* or of this impossibility that is announced in the promise of the gift. There where there is subject and object, the gift would be excluded. A subject will never give an object to another subject. But the subject and the object are arrested effects of the gift: arrests of the gift. At the zero or infinite speed of the circle.

If the gift is annulled in the economic odyssey of the circle as soon as it appears *as* gift or as soon as it signifies *itself as* gift, there is no longer any "logic of the gift," and one may safely say that a consistent discourse on the gift becomes impossible: It misses its object and always speaks, finally, of something else. One could go so far as to say that a book as monumental as Marcel Mauss's *The Gift* speaks of everything but the gift: It deals with economy, exchange, contract (*do ut des*), of raising the stakes, of sacrifice, of gift *and* of countergift—in short, of everything that in the thing itself impels the gift *and* the annulment of the gift. All the gift supplements (potlatch, transgressions and excesses, surplus values, the necessity to give or give back more, returns with interest, in short, the whole sacrificial bidding war) are destined to bring about once again the circle in which they are annulled. Moreover, this figure of the circle is evoked *literally* by Mauss (literally in French since I am for the moment setting aside an essential problem of translation to which we will return). On the subject of the Kula, a kind of "great potlatch" practiced in the Trobriand Islands and the "vehicle of a great inter-tribal trade extending over all the Trobriands," Mauss writes:

Malinowski does not give a translation of the word, which
probably means "circle"; and in fact it seems as if all these
tribes, these marine expeditions, these precious objects and objects of ordinary use, this food and these feasts, these services of
all sorts, ritual and sexual, these men and women, were caught
in a *circle** around which they kept up a *regular movement* in
time and space. *Note: M. Malinowski has a fondness for the
expression "*kula ring.*"[13]

Let us take this first reference to Mauss as a pretext for indicating
right away the two types of questions that will be guiding our reading.
    1. The question of language or rather of languages. How is one to
legitimate the translations thanks to which Mauss circulates and travels,
identifying from one culture to another what he understands by gift,
what he calls *gift*? He does this essentially on the basis of the Latin
language and of Roman law. The latter plays a singular role throughout
the essay, but Mauss also takes into account German law, which is the
occasion for him to remark that the "serious study of the extensive German vocabulary of words derived from *geben* and *gaben* [has] yet to be
undertaken" (*G*, p. 251). This question of the idiom, as we shall see,
is in itself a question of gift in a rather unusual sense that amounts to
neither the gift of languages nor the gift of language.
    2. The second type of question cannot be separated from the first,
in its widest generality. It would come down to asking oneself in effect:
what and who Mauss is talking about in the end? What is the seman-

---

13. Marcel Mauss, *The Gift: Forms and Functions of Exchange in Archaic Societies*,
trans. Ian Cunnison (New York, 1967), p. 20; italics added; hereafter abbreviated *G*.
[As this translation is throughout at best approximate and incomplete, I have modified
it considerably.—TRANS.] This circle of the Kula Ring is evoked at length by Hyde at the
beginning of a chapter that is itself titled "The Circle" and that opens with these words
from Whitman: "The gift is to the giver, and comes back most to him—it cannot fail"
(quoted in *TG*, p. 11). In a later chapter, we will evoke once again the scene of the gift
and the debt, not as it is studied scientifically, but rather as it is first of all lived, acted
out, assumed, or denied by French sociologists. Let us note here, at the point of citing
the work of Americans who are themselves "indebted" to Mauss, that they extend this
chain of the debt in a manner that is just as necessary and as paradoxical. Hyde notes
that Mauss's essay was the "point of departure" for all the research on exchange over
the last half-century. Citing as well Raymond Firth and Claude Lévi-Strauss, he recognizes a particular debt to Marshall Sahlins, notably to the chapter titled "The Spirit of
the Gift" in Sahlins's *Stone Age Economics* (Chicago, 1972), which "applies a rigorous
explication de texte" to Mauss's sources and situates "Mauss's ideas in the history of
political philosophy. It was through Sahlins's writings that I first began to see the possibility of my own work, and I am much indebted to him" (*TG*, p. xv).

tic horizon of anticipation that authorizes him to gather together or
compare so many phenomena of diverse sorts, belonging to different
cultures, manifesting themselves in heterogeneous languages, under the
unique and supposedly identifiable category of gift, under the sign of
"gift"? What remains problematic is not only the *unity* of this semantic
horizon, that is, the presumed identity of a meaning that operates as
general translator or equivalent, but the very existence of something
like *the* gift, that is, the common referent of this sign, which is itself
uncertain. If what Mauss demonstrates, one way or the other, is indeed
that every gift is caught in the round or the contract of usury, then not
only the unity of the meaning "gift" remains doubtful but, on the hypothesis that giving would have a *meaning* and *one* meaning, it is still
the possibility of an effective existence, of an effectuation or an event
of the gift that seems excluded. Now, this problematic of the difference (in the sense that we evoked earlier) between "the gift exists" and
"there is gift" is never, as we know, deployed or even approached by
Mauss, no more than it seems to be, at least to my knowledge, by the
anthropologists who come after him or refer to him. Questions of this
type should be articulated with other questions that concern the meta-
linguistic or meta-ethnological conceptuality orienting this discourse,
the category of totality ("total social fact"), the political, economic, and
juridical ideology organizing the classification and the evaluation, for
example, the one that permits Mauss, at the end (it is especially at the
end that these evaluations are openly declared) to say that "segmented"
societies—Indo-European societies, Roman society before the Twelve
Tables, Germanic societies up to the writing of the *Edda,* Irish society up
to the writing of its "chief literature"—were ones in which individuals
were "less morose, less serious, less avaricious and selfish than we are;
externally at least they were or are more generous and more giving than
we are" (*G,* p. 79).

Everything thus seems to lead us back toward the paradox or the
aporia of a nuclear proposition in the form of the "if . . . then": If the
gift appears or signifies itself, if it exists or if it is presently *as gift,* as
what it is, then it is not, it annuls itself. Let us go to the limit: The truth
of the gift (its being or its appearing such, its *as such* insofar as it guides
the intentional signification or the meaning) suffices to annul the gift.
The truth of the gift is equivalent to the nongift or to the nontruth of the
gift. This proposition obviously defies common sense. That is why it is
caught in the impossible of a very singular double bind, the bond without bond of a bind and a nonbind. On the one hand, Mauss reminds
us that there is no gift without bond, without bind, without border,

without obligation or ligature; but, on the other hand, there is no gift that does not have to untie itself from obligation, from debt, contract, exchange, and thus from the bind.

But, after all, what would be a gift that fulfills the condition of the gift, namely, that it not appear as gift, that it not be, exist, signify, want-to-say as gift? A gift without wanting, without wanting-to-say, an insignificant gift, a gift without intention to give? Why would we still call that a gift? That, which is to say what?

In other words, what are we thinking when we require simultaneously of the gift that it appear and that it not appear in its essence, in what it has to be, in what it is to be, in what it will have had to be (in its *to ti en einai* or in its *quidditas*)? That it obligate and not obligate? That it be and not be that for which it is given? What does "to give" mean to say? And what does language give one to think with this word? And what does "to give" mean to say *in the case* of language, of thinking and of meaning-to-say?

It so happens (but this "it so happens" does not name the fortuitous) that the structure of this impossible of the *gift* is also that of Being—which gives itself to be thought on the condition of being nothing (no present being, no being present)—and of time that, even in what is called its "vulgar" determination, from Aristotle to Heidegger, is always defined in the paradoxia or rather the aporia of what is without being, of what is never present or what is only scarcely and dimly. Once again let us refer to all the texts, notably those of Aristotle, that are cited in "*Ousia* and *Grammē*," beginning with the Fourth Book of the *Physics* which says, in the exoteric phase of its discourse, *dia tōn exoterikōn logōn*, that time "is not at all or only scarcely and dimly is [*holōs ouk estin ē molis kai amudrōs*]." Such is the aporetic effect—the "what does not pass" or "what does not happen"—of time defined on the basis of the *nun*, of the now, as *peras*, limite, and as *stigmē*, the point of the instant. "Some of it has been and is not [*gegone kai ouk esti*], some of it is to be and is not yet [*mellei kai oupō estin*]. From these both infinite time [*apeiros*] and any arbitrary time [time in its incessant return; *aei lambanomenos*] are composed. But it would seem to be impossible that what is composed of things that are not should participate in being [*ousia*]."[14]

We will not analyze here the context and the situation of this proposition called exoteric. Let us take it simply as a marker in the history of

14. Aristotle, *Physics* 4.10.217b–18a, in *A New Aristotle Reader*, ed. J. L. Ackrill (Princeton, N.J., 1989), p. 122.

an aporetics that will become law and tradition: From the moment time is apprehended on the basis of the *present* now as general form and only modifiable or modalizable in such a way that the past and the future are still presents-past and presents-to-come, this predetermination entails the aporetics of a time that is not, of a time that is what it is *without being (it)* [sans l'être], that is not what it is and that is what it is not: which is to be it *without being (it)*.

If it shares this aporetic paralysis with the gift, if neither the gift nor time exist as such, then the gift that *there can be* [*qu'il peut y avoir*] cannot in any case *give time*, since it is nothing. If there is something that can in no case be given, it is time, since it is nothing and since in any case it does not properly belong to anyone; if certain persons or certain social classes have more time than others—and this is finally the most serious stake of political economy—it is certainly not *time itself* that they possess. But inversely, if giving implies in all rigor that one gives nothing that is and that appears as such—determined thing, object, symbol—if the gift is the gift of the giving itself and nothing else, then how to give time? This idiomatic locution, "to give time," seems to mean in common usage "leave time for something, leave time to do something, to fill time with this or that." As usual, it intends less time itself and properly speaking than the temporal or what there is in time. "To give time" in this sense commonly means to give something other than time but something other that is measured by time as by its element. Beyond this historical hardening or sedimentation, perhaps the idiomatic locution "to give time" gives one at least to think—to think the singular or double condition both of the gift and of time.

What there is to give, uniquely, would be called time.

*What there is *to give*, uniquely, would be called time.

What there is to give, uniquely, *would be called time*.

For finally, if the gift is another name of the impossible, we still think it, we name it, we desire it. We intend it. And this even if—or because or to the extent that—we *never* encounter it, we never know it, we never verify it, we never experience it in its present existence or in its phenomenon. The gift *itself*—we dare not say the gift *in itself*—will never be confused with the presence of its phenomenon. Perhaps there is nomination, language, thought, desire, or intention only there where there is this movement still for thinking, desiring, naming that which gives itself neither to be known, experienced, nor lived—in the sense in which presence, existence, determination regulate the economy of knowing, experiencing, and living. In this sense one can think, desire, and say only the impossible, according to the measureless measure of the impossible.[15] If one wants to recapture the proper element of thinking, naming, desiring, it is perhaps according to the measureless measure of this limit that it is possible, possible as relation without relation to the impossible. One can desire, name, think in the proper sense of these words, if there is one, *only* to the *immeasuring* extent [*dans la mesure* démesurante] that one desires, names, thinks *still* or *already*, that one still lets announce itself what nevertheless cannot *present itself* as such to experience, to knowing: in short, here *a gift that cannot make itself (a) present* [un don qui ne peut pas se faire présent]. This gap between, on the one hand, thought, language, and desire and, on the other hand, knowledge, philosophy, science, and the order of presence is also a gap between the gift and economy. This gap is not present anywhere; it resembles an empty word or a transcendental illusion. But it also gives to this structure or to this logic a form analogous to Kant's transcendental dialectic, as relation between thinking and knowing, the noumenal and the phenomenal. Perhaps this analogy will help us and perhaps it has an essential relation to the problem of "giving-time."

We are going to give ourselves over to and engage in the effort of thinking or rethinking a sort of transcendental illusion of the gift. For in order to think the gift, a *theory of the gift* is powerless by its very essence. One must engage oneself in this thinking, commit oneself to it, give it tokens of faith [*gages*], and with one's person, risk entering into the destructive circle. One must promise and swear. The effort of thinking or rethinking a sort of transcendental illusion of the gift should not be a simple reproduction of Kant's critical machinery (according to the opposition between thinking and knowing, and so forth). But neither is it a matter of rejecting that machinery as old-fashioned. In any case, we are implicated in it, in particular because of that which communicates, in this dialectic, with the problem of time on one side, that of the moral law and of practical reason on the other side. But the effort to think the groundless ground of this quasi-"transcendental illusion" should not be either—if it is going to be a matter of *thinking*—a sort of adoring and faithful abdication, a simple movement of faith in the face of that which exceeds the limits of experience, knowledge, science, economy—and even philosophy. On the contrary—desire beyond desire—it is a matter of responding faithfully but as rigorously as possible both to the injunc-

15. On the singular modality, of this "impossible," permit me to refer to my *Psyché: Inventions de l'autre* (Paris, 1987), pp. 26–59; *Mémoires: for Paul de Man*, trans. Cecile Lindsay, Jonathan Culler, and Eduardo Cadava (New York, 1986), p. 35ff.; and *L'Autre Cap* (Paris, 1991), p. 46ff.

tion or the order of the *gift* ("give" ["*donne*"]) as well as to the injunction or the order of meaning (presence, science, knowledge): *Know* still what giving *wants to say, know how to give,* know what you want and want to say when you give, know what you intend to give, know how the gift annuls itself, commit yourself even if commitment is the destruction of the gift by the gift, give economy its chance.

For finally, the overrunning of the circle by the gift, if there is any, does not lead to a simple, ineffable exteriority that would be transcendent and without relation. It is this exteriority that sets the circle going; it is this exteriority that puts the economy in motion. It is this exteriority that *engages* in the circle and makes it turn. If one must *render an account* (to science, to reason, to philosophy, to the economy of meaning) of the circle effects in which a gift gets annulled, this account-rendering requires that one take into account that which, while not simply belonging to the circle, engages in it and sets off its motion. What is the gift as the first mover of the circle? And how does it contract itself into a circular contract? And from what place? Since when? From whom?

That is the contract, between us, for this cycle of lectures. (Recall that Mauss's *The Gift* has its premises in his work and that of Georges Davy on the contract and on sworn faith.)[16]

Even if the gift were never anything but a simulacrum, one must still *render an account* of the possibility of this simulacrum and of the desire that impels toward this simulacrum. And one must also render an account of the desire to render an account. This cannot be done against or without the *principle of reason* (*principium reddendae rationis*), even if the latter finds there its limit as well as its resource. Otherwise, why would I commit myself—making it an obligation for myself—to speak and to render an account? Whence comes the law that obligates one to give even as one renders an account of the gift? In other words, to *answer* [répondre] still for a gift that calls one beyond all responsibility? And that forbids one to forgive whoever *does not know how to give*?

"I will never forgive him the ineptitude of his calculation," concludes the narrator of "Counterfeit Money," the brief story by Baudelaire that we will read together. Was he reproaching his friend in sum for not having *known how to give*? That is one of the questions waiting for us. Here is "Counterfeit Money":

16. See Georges Davy, *La Foi jurée: Étude sociologique du problème du contrat, la formation du lien contractuel* (Paris, 1922), and Mauss, "Une Forme ancienne de contrat chez les Thraces," *Revue des études grecques*, no. 24 (1921): 388–97.

As we were leaving the tobacconist's, my friend carefully separated his change; in the left pocket of his waistcoat he slipped small gold pieces; in the right, small silver pieces; in his left trouser pocket, a handful of pennies and, finally, in the right he put a silver two-franc piece that he had scrutinized with particular care.

"What a singularly minute distribution!" I said to myself.

We encountered a poor man who held out his cap with a trembling hand.—I know nothing more disquieting than the mute eloquence of those supplicating eyes that contain at once, for the sensitive man who knows how to read them, so much humility and so much reproach. He finds there something close to the depth of complicated feeling one sees in the tear-filled eyes of a dog being beaten.

My friend's offering was considerably larger than mine, and I said to him: "You are right; next to the pleasure of feeling surprise, there is none greater than to cause a surprise." "It was the counterfeit coin," he calmly replied as though to justify himself for his prodigality.

But into my miserable brain, always concerned with looking for noon at two o'clock (what an exhausting faculty is nature's gift to me), there suddenly came the idea that such conduct on my friend's part was excusable only by the desire to create an event in this poor devil's life, perhaps even to learn the varied consequences, disastrous or otherwise, that a counterfeit coin in the hands of a beggar might engender. Might it not multiply into real coins? Could it not also lead him to prison? A tavern keeper, a baker, for example, was perhaps going to have him arrested as a counterfeiter or for passing counterfeit money. The counterfeit coin could just as well, perhaps, be the germ of several days' wealth for a poor little speculator. And so my fancy went its course, lending wings to my friend's mind and drawing all possible deductions from all possible hypotheses.

But the latter suddenly shattered my reverie by repeating my own words: "Yes, you are right; there is no sweeter pleasure than to surprise a man by giving him more than he hopes for."

I looked him squarely in the eyes and I was appalled to see that his eyes shone with unquestionable candor. I then saw clearly that his aim had been to do a good deed while at the same time making a good deal; to earn forty cents and the heart of God; to win paradise economically; in short, to pick up gratis the certificate of a charitable man. I could have almost forgiven him the desire for the criminal enjoyment of which a moment before I assumed him capable; I would have found something bizarre, singular in his amusing himself by compromising the poor; but I will never forgive him the ineptitude of his calculation. To be mean is never excusable, but there is some merit in knowing that one is; the most irreparable of vices is to do evil out of stupidity.[17]

17. Charles Baudelaire, *Paris Spleen*, trans. Louise Varèse (New York, 1970), pp. 58–59; translation modified.

9   "To Do Justice to Freud": The History of Madness in the Age of Psychoanalysis

Translated by Pascale-Anne Brault and Michael Naas

When Elisabeth Roudinesco and René Major did me the honor and kindness of inviting me to a commemoration that would also be a reflection, to one of these genuine tributes where thought is plied to fidelity and fidelity honed by thought, I did not hesitate for one moment.

First of all, because I love memory. This is nothing original, of course, and yet how else can one love? Indeed, thirty years ago, this great book of Foucault was an event whose repercussions were so intense and multiple that I will not even try to identify much less measure them deep down inside me. Next, because I love friendship, and the trusting affection that Foucault showed me thirty years ago, and that was to last for many years, was all the more precious in that, being shared, it corresponded to my professed admiration. Then, after 1972, what came to obscure this friendship, without, however, affecting my admiration, was not, in fact, alien to this book, and to a certain debate that ensued—or at least to its distant, delayed, and indirect effects. There was in all of this a sort of dramatic chain of events, a compulsive and repeated precipitation that I do not wish to describe here because I do not wish to be alone, to be the only one to speak of this after the death of Michel Foucault—except to say that this shadow that made us invisible to one another, that made us not associate with one another for close to ten years (until 1 January 1982 when I returned from a Czech prison), is still part of a story that I also love like life itself. It is part of a story or history that is related, and that thus relates me by the same token, to the book whose great event we are commemorating here, to something like its postface, one of its postfaces, since the drama I just alluded to also arose out of a certain postface, and even out of a sort of postscript added by Foucault to a postface in 1972.

While accepting wholeheartedly this generous invitation, I nonetheless declined the suggestion that came along with it to return to the discussion that began some twenty-eight years ago. I declined for numerous reasons, the first being the one I just mentioned: one does not carry on a stormy discussion after the other has departed. Second, because this whole thing is more than just overdetermined (so many difficult and intersecting texts, Descartes's, Foucault's, so many objections and responses, from me but also from all those, in France and elsewhere, who later came to act as arbiters); it has become too distant from me, and perhaps because of the drama just alluded to I no longer wished to return to it. In the end, the debate is archived and those who might be interested in it can analyze as much as they want and decide for themselves. By rereading all the texts of this discussion, right up to the last word, and especially the last word, one will be better able to understand, I imagine, why I prefer not to give it a new impetus today. There is no privileged witness for such a situation—which, moreover, only ever has the chance of forming, and this from the very origin, with the possible disappearance of the witness. This is perhaps one of the meanings of any history of madness, one of the problems for any project or discourse concerning a history of madness, or even a history of sexuality: is there any witnessing to madness? Who can witness? Does witnessing mean seeing? Is it to provide a reason [*rendre raison*]? Does it have an object? Is there any object? Is there a possible third that might provide a reason without objectifying, or even identifying, that is to say, without examining [*arraisoner*]?

Though I have decided not to return to what was debated close to thirty years ago, it would nevertheless be absurd, obsessional to the point of pathological, to say nothing of impossible, to give in to a sort of fetishistic denial and to think that I can protect myself from any contact with the place or meaning of this discussion. Although I intend to speak today of something else altogether, starting from a very recent rereading of *The History of Madness in the Classical Age*, I am not surprised, and you will probably not be either, to see the silhouette of certain questions reemerge: not their content, of course, to which I will in no way return, but their abstract type, the schema or specter of an analogous problematic. For example, if I speak not of Descartes but of Freud, if I thus avoid a figure who seems central to this book and who, because he is decisive as far as its center or centering of perspective is concerned, emerges right from the early pages on, right from the first border or approach,[1] if I thus avoid this Cartesian reference in order to move toward another (psychoanalysis, Freudian or some other) that is evoked only on the edges of the book and is named only right near the end, or ends, on the other border, this will perhaps be once again in order to pose a question that will resemble the one that imposed itself upon me thirty years ago, namely, that of the very possibility of a history of madness. The question will be, in the end, just about the same, though it will be posed from another border, and it still imposes itself upon me as the first tribute owed such a book. If this book was possible, if it had from the beginning and retains today a certain monumental value, the presence and undeniable necessity of a *monument*, that is, of what imposes itself by recalling and cautioning, it must tell us, teach us, or ask us something about its own possibility.

About its own possibility *today*: yes, we are saying *today*, a certain today. Whatever else one may think of this book, whatever questions or reservations it might inspire in those who come at it from some other point of view, its pathbreaking force seems incontestable. Just as

---

1. See Michel Foucault, *Folie et déraison: Histoire de la folie à l'âge classique* (Paris, 1961), pp. 53–57; hereafter abbreviated *F*. Derrida refers here and throughout to the original edition of this work. The book was reprinted with different pagination in 1972 and included as an appendix "Mon corps, ce papier, ce feu," Foucault's response to Derrida's "Cogito et histoire de la folie," a lecture first given in 1963 and reprinted in 1967 in Derrida, *L'Écriture et la différence* (Paris, 1967). A much abridged version of *Histoire de la folie* was published in 1964 and was translated into English by Richard Howard under the title *Madness and Civilization: A History of Insanity in the Age of Reason* (New York, 1965); hereafter abbreviated *M*.

Since Derrida refers to the unabridged text of 1961 and works with the original title throughout, we have referred to this work as *The History of Madness* (or in some cases, *The History of Madness in the Classical Age*). This is in keeping with "Cogito and the History of Madness," *Writing and Difference*, trans. Alan Bass (Chicago, 1978), pp. 31–63. For the reader who wishes to follow Derrida's itinerary through *Folie et déraison: Histoire de la folie à l'âge classique*, we have given all references to the 1961 French version along with references to the English translation when they exist in the abridged version. Since all the other texts of Foucault cited by Derrida have been translated in their entirety, we have in each case given the French followed by the English page references. Translations have been slightly modified in several instances to fit the context of Derrida's argument.—TRANS.

incontestable, in fact, as the law according to which all pathbreaking opens the way only at a certain price, that is, by bolting shut other passages, by ligaturing, stitching up, or compressing, indeed repressing, at least provisionally, other veins. And so today, like yesterday, I mean in March of 1963, it is this question of the *today* that is important to me, the question such as I had tried to formulate it yesterday. I ask you to pardon me this once, then, since I will not make a habit of it, for citing a few lines that then defined, in its general form, a task that seems to me still necessary, on the side of [*du côté de*] Freud this time rather than on the side of Descartes. By saying "on the side of Freud" rather than "on the side of Descartes," let us not give in too quickly to the naivete that would precipitate us into believing that we are closer to a today with Freud than with Descartes, though this is the opinion of most historians.

Here, then, is the question of yesterday, of the today of yesterday, such as I would like to translate it today, on the side of Freud, transporting it in this way into the today of today:

> Therefore, if Foucault's book, despite all the acknowledged impossibilities and difficulties [acknowledged by him, of course], was capable of being written, we have the right to ask what, in the last resort, supports this language without recourse or support ["without recourse" and "without support" are expressions of Foucault that I had just cited]: who enunciates the possibility of nonrecourse? Who wrote and who is to understand, in what language and from what historical situation of logos, who wrote and who is to understand this history of madness? For it is not by chance that such a project could take shape today. Without forgetting, *quite to the contrary*, the audacity of Foucault's act in the *History of Madness*, we must assume that a certain liberation of madness has gotten underway, that psychiatry has opened itself up, however minimally [and, in the end, I would be tempted simply to replace *psychiatry* by *psychoanalysis* in order to translate the today of yesterday into the today of my question of today], and that the concept of madness as unreason, if it ever had a unity, has been dislocated. And that a project such as Foucault's can find its historical origin and passageway in the opening produced by this dislocation.
>
> If Foucault, more than anyone else, is attentive and sensitive to these kinds of questions, it nevertheless appears that he

does not acknowledge their quality of being prerequisite methodological or philosophical considerations.[2]

If this type of question made any sense or had any legitimacy, if the point was then to question that which, today, in this time that is ours, this time in which Foucault's *History of Madness* was written, made possible the event of such a discourse, it would have been more appropriate for me to elaborate this problematic on the side of modernity, *a parte subjecti*, in some sense, on the side where the book was written, thus on the side, for example, of what must have happened to the modern psychiatry mentioned in the passage I just read. To modern psychiatry or, indeed, to psychoanalysis or rather to psychoanalyses or psychoanalysts, since the passage to the plural will be precisely what is at stake in this discussion. It would have thus been more imperative to insist on modern psychiatry or psychoanalysis than to direct the same question toward Descartes. To study the place and role of psychoanalysis in the Foucauldian project of a history of madness, as I am now going to try to do, might thus consist in correcting an oversight or in confronting more directly a problematic that I had left in a preliminary stage, as a general, programmatic frame, in the introduction to my lecture of 1963. That lecture made only one allusion to psychoanalysis. It is true, however, that it inscribed it from the very opening. In a protocol that laid out certain reading positions, I spoke of the way in which philosophical language is rooted in nonphilosophical language, and I recalled a rule of hermeneutical method that still seems to me valid for the historian of philosophy as well as for the psychoanalyst, namely, the necessity of first ascertaining a surface or manifest meaning and, thus, of speaking the language of the patient to whom one is listening: the necessity of gaining a good understanding, in a quasi-scholastic way, philologically and grammatically, by taking into account the dominant and stable conventions, of what Descartes *meant* on the already so difficult surface of his text, such as it is interpretable according to classical norms of reading; the necessity of gaining this understanding *before* submitting the first reading to a symptomatic and historical interpretation regulated by other axioms or protocols, *before and in order to* destabilize, wherever this is possible and if it is necessary, the authority of canonical interpretations. Whatever one ends up doing with it, one must begin by listening to the canon. It is in this context that I recalled

2. Derrida, "Cogito et histoire de la folie," p. 61; "Cogito and the History of Madness," p. 38.

Ferenczi's remark cited by Freud in *The Interpretation of Dreams* ("Every language has its own dream language") and Lagache's observations concerning polyglotism in analysis.[3]

In its general and historical form, my question concerned the *site* that *today* gives rise to a history of madness and thereby makes it possible. Such a question should have led me, it is true, toward the situation of psychiatry and psychoanalysis rather than toward a questioning of a reading of Descartes. This logic would have seemed more natural and the consequence more immediate. But if, in so strictly delimiting the field, I substituted Descartes for Freud, it was perhaps not only because of the significant and strategic place that Foucault confers upon the Cartesian moment in the interpretation of the *Great Confinement* and of the *Classical Age*, that is to say, in the layout of the very object of the book; it was already, at least implicitly, because of the role that the reference to a certain Descartes played in the thought of that time, in the early sixties, as close as possible to psychoanalysis, in the very element, in truth, of a certain psychoanalysis and Lacanian theory. This theory developed around the question of the subject and the subject of science. Whether it was a question of anticipated certainty and logical time (1945, in *Écrits*) or, some years later (1965–1966), of the role of the cogito and—precisely—of the deceitful God in "La Science et la vérité," Lacan returned time and again to a certain unsurpassability of Descartes.[4] In 1945, Lacan associated Descartes with Freud in his "Propos sur la causalité psychique" and concluded by saying that "neither Socrates, nor Descartes, nor Marx, nor Freud, can be 'surpassed' insofar as they led their research with this passion for unveiling whose object is the truth."[5]

The title I have proposed for the few reflections I will risk today, "The History of Madness in the Age of Psychoanalysis," clearly indicates a change—a change in tense, in mode or in voice. It is no longer a question of the age *described* by a *History of Madness*. It is no longer a question of an epoch or period, such as the classical age, that would, inasmuch as it is its very object, stand before the history of madness such as Foucault writes it. It is a question today of the age to which the book itself belongs, the age from out of which it takes place, the age

---

3. See ibid., p. 53; p. 307.—TRANS.

4. See Jacques Lacan, "Propos sur la causalité psychique" and "La Science et la vérité," *Écrits* (Paris, 1966), p. 209, pp. 219–44. The latter was translated by Bruce Fink under the title "Science and Truth," *Newsletter of the Freudian Field* 3, nos. 1–2 (1989):4–29.—TRANS.

5. Lacan, "Propos sur la causalité psychique," p. 193.

that provides it its situation; it is a question of the age that is *describing* rather than the age that is *described*. In my title, it would be necessary to put "the history of madness" in quotation marks since the title designates the age of the book, *The History (historia rerum gestarum) of Madness*—as a book—in the age of psychoanalysis and not the history (*res gestae*) of madness, of madness itself, in the age of psychoanalysis, even though, as we will see, Foucault regularly attempts to objectify psychoanalysis and to reduce it to that of which he speaks rather than to that from out of which he speaks. What will interest me will thus be rather the time and historical conditions in which the book is rooted, those that it takes as its point of departure, and not so much the time or historical conditions that it recounts and tries in a certain sense to objectify. Were one to trust too readily in the opposition between subject and object, as well as in the category of objectification (something that I here believe to be neither possible nor just, and hardly faithful to Foucault's own intention), one would say for the sake of convenience that it is a question of considering the history of madness *a parte subjecti*, that is, from the side where it is written or inscribed and not from the side of what it describes.

Now, from the side where this history is written, there is, of course, a certain state of psychiatry—as well as psychoanalysis. Would Foucault's project have been possible without psychoanalysis, with which it is contemporary and of which it speaks little and in such an equivocal or ambivalent manner in the book? Does the project owe psychoanalysis anything? What? Would the debt, if it had been contracted, be essential? Or would it, on the contrary, define the very thing from which the project had to detach itself, and in a critical fashion, in order to take shape? In a word, what is the situation of psychoanalysis at the moment of, and with respect to, Foucault's book? And how does this book situate its project with respect to psychoanalysis?

Let us put our trust for a moment in this common name, psychoanalysis. And let us delay a bit the arrival of proper names, for example Freud or Lacan, and provisionally assume that there is indeed a psychoanalysis that is a single whole: as if it were not, already in Freud, sufficiently divided to make its localization and identification more than problematic. Yet the very thing whose coming due we are here trying to delay will no doubt form the very horizon, in any case the provisional conclusion, of this talk.

As you well know, Foucault speaks rather little of Freud in this book. This may seem justified, on the whole, by the very delimitation that a historian of madness in the classical age must impose upon himself. If one accepts the great caesura of this layout (even though this raises a question, or swarm of questions, that I prudently, and by economy, decide not to approach in order to get a better grasp on what Foucault *means* by Freud, situating myself, therefore, within the thesis or hypothesis of the partition between a classical and a postclassical age), then Freud does not have to be treated. He can and must be located at the very most on the borderline. The borderline is never a secure place, it never forms an indivisible line, and it is always on the border that the most disconcerting problems of topology get posed. Where, in fact, would a problem of topology get posed if not *on the border*? Would one ever have to worry about the border if it formed an indivisible line? A borderline is, moreover, not a place per se. It is always risky, particularly for the historian, to assign to whatever happens on the borderline, to whatever happens between sites, the taking-place of a determinable event.

Now, Foucault *does and does not want* to situate Freud in a historical place that is stabilizable, identifiable, and open to a univocal understanding. The interpretation or topography that he presents us of the Freudian moment is always uncertain, divided, mobile, some would say ambiguous, others ambivalent, confused, or contradictory. Sometimes he wants to credit Freud, sometimes discredit him, unless he is actually doing both indiscernibly and at the same time. One will always have the choice of attributing this ambivalence to either Foucault or Freud; it can characterize a motivation, the gesture of the interpreter and a certain state of his work, but it can also, or in the first place, refer simply to the interpreter or historian's taking account of a structural duplicity that his work reflects from the thing itself, namely, from the event of psychoanalysis. The motivation would thus be *justly* motivated, it would be *just that*—motivated; it would be called for and justified by the very thing that is in question. For the ambiguity of which we are going to speak could indeed be on the side of psychoanalysis, on the side of the event of this invention named psychoanalysis.

To begin, let us indicate a few telling signs. If most of the explicit references to Freud are grouped in the conclusions of the book (at the end of "The Birth of the Asylum" and in the beginning of "The Anthropological Circle"),[6] what I would here call a *charnière*, a *hinge*, comes earlier on, right in the middle of the volume, to divide at once the book and the book's relation to Freud.

---

6. This final chapter of *Histoire de la folie* is not included in *Madness and Civilization*.—TRANS.

Why a *charnière*? This word can be taken in the technical or anatomical sense of a central or cardinal articulation, a hinge pin (*cardo*) or pivot. A *charnière* or hinge is an axial device that enables the circuit, the trope, or the movement of rotation. But one might also dream a bit in the vicinity of its homonym, that is, in line with this other *artifact* that the code of falconry also calles a *charnière*, the place where the hunter attracts the bird by laying out the flesh of a lure.

This double articulation, this double movement or alternation between opening and closing that is assured by the workings of a hinge, this coming and going, indeed this *fort/da* of a pendulum [*pendule*] or balance [*balancier*]—that is what Freud means to Foucault. And this technico-historical hinge also remains the place of a possible simulacrum or lure—for both the body and the flesh. Taken at this level of generality, things will never change for Foucault. There will always be this interminable alternating movement that successively opens and closes, draws near and distances, rejects and accepts, excludes and includes, disqualifies and legitimates, masters and liberates. The Freudian place is not only the technico-historical apparatus, the *artifact* called *charnière* or hinge. Freud himself will in fact take on the ambiguous figure of a doorman or doorkeeper [*huissier*]. Ushering in a new epoch of madness, our epoch, the one out of which is written *The History of Madness* (the book bearing this title), Freud also represents the best guardian of an epoch that comes to a close with him, the history of madness such as it is recounted by the book bearing this title.

Freud as the doorman of the today, the holder of the keys, of those that open as well as those that close the door, that is, the *huis*: onto the today [*l'aujourd'hui*] or onto madness. He [*Lui*], Freud, is the double figure of the door and the doorkeeper. He stands guard and ushers in. Alternatively or simultaneously, he closes one epoch and opens another. And as we will see, this double possibility is not alien to an institution, to what is called the analytic situation as a scene behind closed doors [*huis clos*]. That is why—and this would be the paradox of a serial law—Freud does and does not belong to the different series in which Foucault inscribes him. What is outstanding, outside the series [*hors-série*], turns out to be regularly reinscribed within different series. I am not now going to get involved in formal questions concerning a quasi-transcendental law of seriality that could be illustrated in an analogous way by so many other examples, each time, in fact, that the transcendental condition of a series is also, paradoxically, a part of that series, creating aporias for the constitution of any set or whole [*ensemble*], particularly, of any historical configuration (age, *episteme*, paradigm, *themata*, epoch, and so on). These aporias are anything but accidental impasses that one should try to force at all costs into received theoretical models. The putting to the test of these aporias is also the chance of thinking.

To keep to the contract of this conference, I will restrict myself to a single example.

The first sign comes right in the middle of the book (*F*, pp. 410–11; *M*, pp. 197–98). It comes at the end of the second part, in the chapter entitled "Doctors and Patients." We have there a sort of epilogue, less than a page and a half long. Separated from the conclusion by asterisks,[7] the epilogue also signals the truth of a transition and the meaning of a passage. It seems to be firmly structured by two unequivocal statements:

1. Psychology does not exist in the classical age. It does *not yet* exist. Foucault says this without hesitation right at the beginning of the epilogue: "In the classical age, it is futile to try to distinguish physical therapeutics from psychological medications, for the simple reason that psychology did not exist."

2. But as for the psychology that was to be born after the classical age, psychoanalysis would not be a part, it would *no longer* be a part. Foucault writes: "It is not psychology that is involved in psychoanalysis."

In other words, if in the classical age there is *not yet* psychology, there is, in psychoanalysis, *already no more* psychology. But in order to affirm this, it is necessary, *on the one hand*, to resist a prejudice or a temptation, to resist that which continues to urge so many interpreters of good sense (and sometimes, in part, Foucault among them) to take psychoanalysis for a psychology (however original or new it may be). Foucault is going to show signs of this resistance, as we will see. But it is also necessary, *on the other hand*, to accept, within this historical schema, the hypothesis of a return: not the *return to Freud* but the *return of Freud* to—.

What return? Return to what? *Return* is Foucault's word, an underscored word. If psychoanalysis is already *no longer* a psychology, does it not, at least in this respect, seem to suggest a certain return to the time when psychology was *not yet*? Beyond eighteenth-century psychology and, very broadly, beyond the psychologistic modernity of the nineteenth century, beyond the positivist institution of psychology, does it not seem as if Freud were joining back up with a certain classical age or, at least, with whatever in this age does not determine madness

---

7. This is the case for the French versions but not for the English.—TRANS.

as a psychical illness but as unreason, that is, as something that has to do with reason? In the classical age, if such a thing exists (an hypothesis of Foucault that I take here, in this context, as such, as if it were not debatable), unreason is no doubt reduced to silence; one does not speak with it. One interrupts or forbids dialogue; and this suspension or interdiction would have received from the Cartesian cogito the violent form of a sentence. For Freud *too* madness would be unreason (and in this sense, at least, there would be a neo-Cartesian logic at work in psychoanalysis). But this time one should resume speaking with it: one would reestablish a dialogue with unreason and lift the Cartesian interdiction. Like the word *return*, the expression "dialogue with unreason" is a quotation. The two expressions scan a final paragraph of this epilogue, in the middle of the book, that begins with the phrase with which I entitled this talk: "We must do justice to Freud" (*F*, p. 411; *M*, p. 198).

When one says, "one must do justice," "one has to be fair" ["*il faut être juste*"], it is often with the intention of correcting an impulse or reversing the direction of a tendency; one is also recommending resisting a temptation. Foucault had to have felt this temptation, the temptation to do an injustice to Freud, to be unfair to him, that is, in this case, to write him into the age of the psychopathological institution (which we will define in a moment). He must have felt it outside or within himself. Indeed, such a temptation must still be threatening and liable to reemerge since it is still necessary to call for vigilance and greater justice.

Here, then, is the paragraph, which I read in extenso, since its internal tension determines, it seems to me, the matrix of all future statements about psychoanalysis; it determines them in the very oscillation of their movement back and forth. It is like scales of justice [*la balance d'une justice*] that not even the death sentence [*arrêt de mort*] would ever be able to stop [*arrêterait*] in their even or just [*juste*] stability. It is as if justice were to remain its own movement:

> This is why we must do justice to Freud. Between Freud's *Five Case Histories* and Janet's scrupulous investigations of *Psychological Healing*, there is more than the density of a *discovery*; there is the sovereign violence of a *return*. Janet enumerated the elements of a division, drew up his inventory, annexed here and there, perhaps conquered. Freud went back to madness at the level of its *language*, reconstituted one of the essential elements of an experience reduced to silence by positivism; he did not make a major addition to the list of psychological treatments for madness; he restored, in medical thought, the possibility of

a dialogue with unreason. Let us not be surprised that the most "psychological" of medications has so quickly encountered its converse and its organic confirmations. It is not psychology that is involved in psychoanalysis: but precisely an experience of unreason that it has been psychology's meaning, in the modern world, to mask. [*F*, p. 411; *M*, p. 198][8]

"To mask": positivist psychology would thus have masked the experience of unreason: an imposition of the mask, a violent dissimulation of the face, of truth or of visibility. Such violence would have consisted in disrupting a certain unity, that which corresponded precisely [*justement*] to the presumed unity of the classical age: from then on, there would be, on the one hand, illness of an organic nature and, on the other, unreason, an unreason often tempered by this modernity under its "epithetic" form: the *unreasonable*, whose discursive manifestations will become the object of a psychology.[9] This psychology then loses all relation to a certain truth of madness, that is, to a certain truth of unreason. Psychoanalysis, on the contrary, breaks with psychology *by speaking with the Unreason* that speaks within madness and, thus, by returning through this exchange of words not to the classical age itself—which also determined madness as unreason, but, unlike psychology, did so only in order to exclude or confine it—but toward this eve of the classical age that still haunted it.

While this schema is firmly established by the page just cited, I was struck in rereading *The History of Madness* by a paradox in the form of

---

8. One will note in passing that we have here, along with very brief allusions to the *Three Essays on the Theory of Sexuality, Introductory Lectures on Psycho-Analysis*, and a couple of individual cases in *Mental Illness and Psychology*, and a reference just as brief to *Totem and Taboo* in *The Order of Things*, one of the few times that Foucault mentions a work of Freud; beyond this, he does not, to my knowledge, cite or analyze any text of Freud, or of any other psychoanalyst, not even those of contemporary French psychoanalysts. Each time, only the proper name is pronounced—Freud, or the common name—psychoanalysis. See Michel Foucault, *Maladie mentale et psychologie* (Paris, 1962), hereafter abbreviated *MM*, trans. Alan Sheridan, under the title *Mental Illness and Psychology* (Berkeley, 1987), p. 31, hereafter abbreviated *MI*; and *Les Mots et les choses: Une Archéologie des sciences humaines* (Paris, 1966), hereafter abbreviated *MC*, trans. pub., under the title *The Order of Things: An Archaeology of the Human Sciences* (New York, 1973), p. 379, hereafter abbreviated *OT*.

Discovery is underscored by Foucault, along with *return* and *language*. Freud is the event of a *discovery*—the unconscious and psychoanalysis as a movement of *return*—and what relates the discovery to the return is language, the possibility of speaking with madness, "the possibility of a dialogue with unreason."

9. Foucault had earlier noted this in *F*, p. 195.

a chiasm. I had not, in my first reading, given it the attention it deserves. What is the schema of this paradox? By reason of what we have just heard, in order to do "justice" to Freud we ought to give him credit— and this is what happens—for finding a place in the gallery of all those who, from one end of the book to the other, announce, like heralds of good tidings, the very possibility of the book: Nietzsche above all and, most frequently, Nietzsche and Artaud, who are often associated in the same sentence, Nietzsche, Artaud, Van Gogh, sometimes Nerval, and Hölderlin from time to time. Their excess, "the madness in which the work of art is engulfed," is the gulf or abyss out of which opens "the space of our enterprise" (F, p. 643; M, p. 288).

It is *before* this madness, in the fleeting moment when it is joined to the work, that we are *responsible*. We are far from being able to arraign it or make it appear, for it is we who must appear *before* it. Let us recognize, then, that we are responsible before it rather than being authorized to examine it [*arraisonner*], to objectify and demand an explanation from it. At the end of the last page, after having spent a good deal of time speaking of Nietzsche and after having mentioned Van Gogh, Foucault writes: "The moment when, together, the work of art and madness are born and fulfilled is the beginning of the time when the world finds itself arraigned by that work of art and responsible before it for what it is" (F, p. 643; M, p. 289). This is what *The History of Madness*, in responding to the summons, takes note of and assumes responsibility for. It assumes responsibility before that which is named by the names of Nietzsche and all these others who, as everyone knows, were deemed crazy by society (Artaud, and before him Van Gogh, and before him Nerval, and before him Hölderlin).

But what about Freud? Why is he, in the same book, sometimes associated with and sometimes opposed to these great witnesses of madness and excess, these great witnesses who are also great judges, our judges, those who judge us? Must we be arraigned before Freud? And why do things then get complicated?

I would see the chiasm of which I just spoke appearing in a place where Freud is in fact found near Nietzsche, on the same side as he, that is, on our side, on the side of what Foucault calls "contemporary man": this enigmatic "we" for whom a history of madness opens today, for whom the door of today [*l'huis d'aujourd'hui*] is cracked open so that its possibility may be glimpsed. Foucault has just described the loss of unreason, the background against which the classical age determined madness. It is the moment when unreason degenerates or disappears into the unreasonable; it is the tendency to pathologize, so to speak, madness. And there again, it is through a return to unreason, this time without exclusion, that Nietzsche and Freud reopen the dialogue with madness *itself* (assuming, along with Foucault, that one can here say "itself"). This dialogue had, in a sense, been *broken off* twice, and in two different ways: the second time, by a psychological positivism that no longer conceived of madness as unreason, and the first time, already by the classical age, which, while excluding madness and breaking off the dialogue with it, still determined it as unreason, and excluded it precisely because of this—but excluded it as close as possible to itself, as its other and its adversary: this is the Cartesian moment, such as it is determined, at least, in the three pages that were the object of our debate nearly thirty years ago.

I will underscore everything that marks the today, the present, the now, the contemporary, this time that is proper and common to us, the time of this fragile and divided "we" from which is decided the possibility of a book like *The History of Madness*, decided while scarcely being sketched out, while promising itself, in short, rather than giving itself over. Nietzsche *and* Freud are here conjoined, conjugated, like a couple, Nietzsche *and* Freud, and the conjunction of their coupling is also the copula-hinge or, if you prefer, the middle term of the modern proposition:

> If *contemporary* man, since Nietzsche and Freud, finds deep within himself the site for contesting all truth, being able to read, in what he *now* knows of himself, the signs of fragility through which unreason threatens, seventeenth-century man, on the contrary, discovers, in the immediate presence of his thought to itself, the certainty in which reason in its pure form is announced. [F, pp. 195–96]

Why did I speak of a chiasm? And why would we be fascinated by the multiple chiasm that organizes this entire interpretative scene?

It is because, in the three pages devoted to Descartes at the beginning of the second chapter "The Great Confinement," Foucault spoke of an *exclusion*. He described it, posed it, declared it unequivocally and firmly ("madness is excluded by the subject who doubts"). This exclusion was the result of a "decision," the result (and these are all his words) of a "strange act of force" that was going to "reduce to silence" the excluded madness and trace a very strict "line of division." In the part of the *Meditations* that he cited and focused on, Foucault left out all mention of the Evil Genius. It was thus in recalling the hyperbolic raising of the stakes in the fiction of the Evil Genius that I had then confessed my perplexity and proposed other questions. When Foucault responds to me nine years later in the afterward to the 1972 Gallimard edition of *The History of Madness*, he still firmly contests the way I used this Cartesian fiction of the Evil Genius and this hyperbolic moment of doubt. He accuses me of erasing "everything that shows that the episode of the evil genius is an exercise that is voluntary, controlled, mastered and carried out from start to finish by a meditating subject who never lets himself be surprised";[10] (*F*, p. 601; such a reproach was indeed unfair, unjust, since I had stressed that this methodical mastery of the voluntary subject is "almost always" at work and that Foucault, therefore, like Descartes, is "almost always right [*a . . . raison*]," and almost always wins out over [*a raison de*] the Evil Genius.[11] But that is not what is at issue here, and I said that I would not reopen the debate.) And by accusing me of erasing this methodical neutralization of the Evil Genius, Foucault—once again in his response of 1972—confirms the claims of the three pages in question and maintains that "if the evil genius again takes on the powers of *madness*, this is only after the exercise of meditation has excluded the risk of *being mad*."[12] One might be tempted to respond that if the Evil Genius can *again take on* these powers of madness, if he once "again takes them on" afterwards, after the fact, it is because the exclusion of the risk of being mad makes way for an *after*. The narrative is thus not interrupted during the exclusion alleged by Foucault, an exclusion that is, up to a certain point at least, attested to and incontestable (and I never in fact contested this exclusion in this regard, quite the contrary); neither the narrative nor the exercise of the meditation that it retraces are any more interrupted than the order of reasons is definitively stopped by this same exclusion. But let us move on. As I said earlier, I am not invoking this difficulty in order to return to an old discussion. I am doing it because Freud is going to be, as I will try to show, doubly situated, *twice* implicated in the chiasm that interests me: *on the one hand*, in the sentence that I cited a moment ago (where Freud was immediately associated with Nietzsche, the only one to be associated with him, on the "good" side, so to speak, on the side where

10. Foucault, "My Body, This Paper, This Fire," trans. Geoff Bennington, *Oxford Literary Review* 4 (Autumn 1979): 26; trans. mod.; "Mon corps, ce papier, ce feu" was first published in *Paideia* (Sept. 1971) and was reissued as the appendix to the 1972 edition of *Histoire de la folie*.

11. Derrida, "Cogito et histoire de la folie," p. 91; "Cogito and the History of Madness," p. 58.

12. Foucault, "My Body, This Paper, This Fire," p. 26.

"we" contemporaries reopen the dialogue with unreason that was twice interrupted); this sentence is followed by a few references to the Evil Genius that complicate, as I myself had tried to do, the reading of the scene of Cartesian doubt as the moment of the great confinement; but also, and *on the other hand*, since I will later try, in a more indirect way—and this would be in the end the essence of my talk today—to recall the necessity of taking into account a certain Evil Genius *of* Freud, namely, the presence of the demonic, the devil, the devil's advocate, the limping devil, and so on in *Beyond the Pleasure Principle*, where psychoanalysis finds, it seems to me, its greatest speculative power but also the place of greatest resistance to psychoanalysis (death drive, repetition compulsion, and so on, and *fort/da!*).

Thus, just after having spoken of "contemporary man, since Nietzsche and Freud," Foucault offers a development *on the subject of the Evil Genius*. The logic of this sequence seems to me guided by a "One must not forget" that I would be tempted to relate to the "One must do justice" of a moment ago. What must one not forget? The Evil Genius, of course [*justement*]. And especially, I emphasize, the fact that the Evil Genius is *anterior* to the cogito, such that its threat remains *perpetual*.

This might contradict (as I had attempted to do) the thesis argued 150 pages earlier on the subject of the Cartesian cogito as the simple exclusion of madness. This could have, as a result, indeed this should have, spared us a long and dramatic debate. But it is too late now. Foucault reaffirms all the same, despite the recognized anteriority of the Evil Genius, that the cogito is the absolute beginning, even if, in this absolute beginning, "one must not forget" what has, in short, been forgotten or omitted in the discourse on the exclusion of madness by the cogito. The question thus still remains what a methodically absolute beginning would be that does not let us forget this anterior—and moreover perpetual—threat, nor the haunting backdrop that first lets it appear. As always, I prefer to cite, even though it is a long passage. Here is what Foucault says immediately after having evoked the "contemporary man" who, "since Nietzsche and Freud," meets in "what he now knows of himself" that "through which unreason threatens." He says, in effect, that what is called contemporary had already begun in the classical age and with the Evil Genius, which clearly, to my eyes at least, cannot leave intact the historical categories of reference and the presumed identity of something like the classical age (for example).

> But this does not mean that classical man was, in his experience of the truth, more distanced from unreason than we ourselves

might be. It is true that the cogito is the absolute beginning [this statement thus confirms the thesis of *F*, pp. 54–57] *but one must not forget* [my emphasis] that the evil genius is anterior to it. And the evil genius is not the symbol in which are summed up and systematized all the dangers of such psychological events as dream images and sensory errors. Between God and man, the evil genius has an absolute meaning: he is in all his rigor the possibility of unreason and the totality of its powers. He is more than the refraction of human finitude; well beyond man, he signals the danger that could prevent man once and for all from gaining access to the truth: he is the main obstacle, not of such a spirit but of such reason. And it is not because the truth that gets illuminated in the cogito ends up entirely masking the shadow of the evil genius that one *ought to forget* its perpetually threatening power [my emphasis: Foucault had earlier said that *one must not forget* that the evil genius is anterior to the cogito, and he now says that *one must not forget* its perpetually threatening power, even after the passage, the moment, the experience, the certainty of the cogito, and the exclusion of madness that this brings about]: this danger will hover over Descartes' reflections right up until the establishment of the existence and truth of the external world. [*F*, p. 196]

One would have to ask, though we will not have the time and this is not the place, about the effects that the category of the "perpetual threat" (and this is Foucault's term) can have on indications of presence, positive markings, the determinations made by means of signs or statements, in short, the whole criteriology and symptomatology that can give assurance to a historical knowledge concerning a figure, an *episteme*, an age, an epoch, a paradigm, once all these determinations are found to be in effect [*justement*] threatened by a perpetual haunting. For, in principle, all these determinations are, for the historian, either presences or absences; as such, they thus exclude haunting; they allow themselves to be located by means of signs, one would almost say on a table of absences and presences; they come out of the logic of opposition, in this case, the logic of inclusion *or* exclusion, of the alternative between the inside and the outside, and so on. The perpetual threat, that is, the shadow of haunting (and haunting is, like the phantom or fiction of an Evil Genius, neither present nor absent, neither positive nor negative, neither inside nor outside) does not challenge only one thing or another; it threatens the logic that distinguishes between one thing and another, the very logic of exclusion or foreclosure, as well as the history that is founded upon this logic and its alternatives. What is excluded is, of course, never simply excluded, not by the cogito nor by anything else, without this eventually returning—and that is what a certain psychoanalysis will have also helped us to understand. Let me leave undeveloped this general problem, however, in order to return to a certain regulated functioning in the references to psychoanalysis and to the name of Freud in *The History of Madness in the Classical Age*.

Let us consider the couple Nietzsche/Freud, this *odd couple* about which there is so much else to say (I have attempted this elsewhere, especially in *The Post Card*, and precisely [*justement*] in relationship to *Beyond the Pleasure Principle*). The affiliation or filiation of this couple reappears elsewhere. It is again at a filial limit, in the introduction to the third and final part, when the "delirium" of *Rameau's Nephew* sets the tone or gives the key, just as the Cartesian cogito had, for a new arrangement or division [*partition*]. For the "delirium" of *Rameau's Nephew* "announces Freud and Nietzsche." Let us set aside all the questions that the concept of "announcing" might pose for the historian. It is not by accident that they resemble those raised a moment ago by the concept of *haunting*. As soon as that which *announces* already no longer completely belongs to a present configuration and already belongs to the future of another, its place, the taking-place of its event, calls for another logic; it disrupts, in any case, the axiomatics of a history that places too much trust in the opposition between absence and presence, outside and inside, inclusion and exclusion. Let us read, then, this sentence and note the recurring and thus all the more striking association of this *announcement* with the figure of the Evil Genius, but, this time, with the figure of "another evil genius":

> The delirium of Rameau's Nephew is a tragic confrontation of need and illusion in an oneiric mode, one that announces Freud and Nietzsche [the order of names is this time reversed]; it is also the ironic repetition of the world, its destructive reconstitution in the theater of illusion. [*F*, p. 422]

An Evil Genius then immediately reappears. And who will see this inevitable repetition as a coincidence? But it is not the same Evil Genius. It is another figure of the evil genius. There would thus be a recurring function of the Evil Genius, a function that, in making reference to a Platonic *hyperbole*, I had called hyperbolic in "Cogito and the History of Madness." This function had been fulfilled by the Evil Genius, under

the guise as well as under the name that it takes on in Descartes. But
another Evil Genius, which is also the same one, can reappear without
this name and under a different guise, for example, in the vicinity or lineage of Rameau's Nephew: a different Evil Genius, certainly, but bearing enough of a resemblance because of its recurring function that the
historian, here Foucault, allows himself a metonymy that is legitimate
enough in his eyes to continue calling it Evil Genius. This reappearance
occurs after the second passage of Freud-and-Nietzsche, as they are
furtively announced by *Rameau's Nephew*, whose laugh "prefigures in
advance and reduces the whole movement of nineteenth-century anthropology" (*F*, p. 424). This time of prefiguration and announcement,
this delay between the anticipatory lightning flash and the event of what
is foreseen, is explained by the very structure of an experience of unreason, if there is any, namely, an experience in which one cannot maintain
oneself and out of which one cannot but fall after having approached
it. All this thus forbids us from making this history into a properly successive and sequential history of events. This is formulated in Foucault's
question: "Why is it not possible to maintain oneself in the difference of
unreason?" (*F*, p. 425).

> But in this vertigo where the truth of the world is maintained
> only on the inside of an absolute void, man also encounters
> the ironic perversion of his own truth, at the moment when it
> moves from the dreams of interiority to the forms of exchange.
> Unreason then takes on the figure of *another evil genius* [my
> emphasis]—no longer the one who exiles man from the truth of
> the world, but the one who at once mystifies and demystifies, en-
> chants to the point of extreme disenchantment, this truth of man
> that man had entrusted to his hands, to his face, to his speech;
> an evil genius who no longer operates when man wants to ac-
> cede to the truth but when he wants to restitute to the world a
> truth that is his own, when, thrown into the intoxication of the
> sensible realm where he is lost, he finally remains "immobile,
> stupid, astonished." It is no longer in *perception* that the pos-
> sibility of the evil genius resides [that is, as in Descartes] but in
> *expression.* [*F*, p. 423]

But immediately after this appearance or arraignment of Freud next
to Nietzsche and all the Evil Geniuses, the pendulum of the *fort/da* is
put back in motion; from this point on, it will not cease to convoke and
dismiss Freud from the two sides of the dividing line, both inside and

outside of the series from out of which the history of madness is signed. For it is here, in the following pages, that we find Freud separated from the lineage in which are gathered all those worthy heirs of Rameau's Nephew. The name of the one who was not crazy, not crazy enough in any case, the name of Freud, is dissociated from that of Nietzsche. It is regularly passed over in silence when, according to another filiation, Höderlin, Nerval, Nietzsche, Van Gogh, Roussel, and Artaud are at several reprieves named and renamed—renowned—within the same "family."

From this point on, things are going to deteriorate. "To do justice to Freud" will more and more come to mean putting on trial a psychoanalysis that will have participated, in its own way, however original that may be, in the order of the immemorial figures of the Father and the Judge, of Family and Law, in the order of Order, of Authority and Punishment, whose immemorial figures must, as Philippe Pinel had noted, be brought into play by the doctor, in order to cure (see *F*, p. 607; *M*, p. 272). There was already a disturbing sign of this long before the chapter on "The Birth of the Asylum" that will so strictly inscribe psychoanalysis into the tradition of Tuke and Pinel and will go so far as to say that "all nineteenth-century psychiatry really converges on Freud" (*F*, p. 611; *M*, p. 277). For the latter had already appeared in another chain, the chain of those who, since the nineteenth century, know that madness, like its counterpart reason, has a history. These will have been led astray by a sort of historicism of reason and madness, a risk that is avoided by those who, "from Sade to Hölderlin, to Nerval and to Nietzsche," are given over to a "repeated poetic and philosophical experience" and plunge into a language "that abolishes history." As a cultural historian of madness, like others are of reason, Freud thus appears between Janet and Brunschvicg (*F*, p. 456).

While accumulating the two errors, the rationalist historian of this cultural phenomenon called madness nonetheless continues to pay tribute to myth, magic, and thaumaturgy. Indeed *thaumaturgy* will be the word chosen by Foucault himself for the verdict. There is nothing surprising in this collusion of reason and a certain occultism. Montaigne and Pascal would have perhaps called it mystical authority; the history of reason and reason within history would exercise essentially the same violence, the same obscure, irrational, dictatorial violence, serving the same interests in the name of the same fictional allegation, as psychoanalysis does when it confers all powers to the doctor's speech. Freud would free the patient interned in the asylum only in order to reconstitute him "in his essential character" at the heart of the analytic situation. There is a continuity from Pinel and Tuke to psychoanalysis. There is an inevitable movement, right up to Freud, a persistence of what Foucault calls "the myth of Pinel, like that of Tuke" (*F*, p. 577). This same insistence is always concentrated in the figure of the doctor; it is, in the eyes of the patient who is always an accomplice, the becoming-thaumaturge of the doctor, of a doctor who is not even supposed to know. *Homo medicus* does not exercise his authority in the name of science but, as Pinel himself seems to recognize and to claim, in the name of order, law, and morality, specifically, by "relying upon that prestige that envelops the *secrets* of the Family, of Authority, of Punishment, and of Love; . . . by wearing the mask of Father and of Judge" (*F*, pp. 607–8; *M*, p. 273; my emphasis).

And when the walls of the asylum give way to psychoanalysis, it is in effect a certain concept of the *secret* that assures the tradition from Pinel to Freud. It would be necessary to follow throughout these pages all the ins and outs of the value—itself barely visible—of a secret, of a certain secrecy value. This value would come down, in the end, to a *technique* of the secret, and of the secret without knowledge. Wherever knowledge can only be supposed, wherever, as a result, one knows that supposition cannot give rise to knowledge, wherever no knowledge could ever be disputed, there is the production of a *secrecy effect*, of what we might be able to call a *speculation on the capital secret or on the capital of the secret*. The calculated and yet finally incalculable production of this secrecy effect relies on a simulacrum. This simulacrum recalls, from another point of view, the situation described at the opening of *Raymond Roussel*: the risk of "being deceived less by a secret than by the awareness that there is a secret."[13]

What persists from Pinel to Freud, in spite of all the differences, is the figure of the doctor as a man not of knowledge but of order. In this figure all *secret, magic, esoteric, thaumaturgical* powers are brought together—and these are all Foucault's words. The scientific objectivity that is claimed by this tradition is only a magical reification:

> If we wanted to analyze the profound structures of objectivity in the knowledge and practice of nineteenth-century psychiatry from Pinel to Freud [this is the definitive divorce between Nietzsche and Freud, the second coupling for the latter], we should have to show in fact that such objectivity was from the start

13. Foucault, *Raymond Roussel* (Paris, 1963), p. 10; trans. Charles Ruas, under the title *Death and the Labyrinth: The World of Raymond Roussel* (New York, 1986), p. 3.

a reification of a magical nature, which could only be accomplished with the complicity of the patient himself, and beginning from a transparent and clear moral practice, gradually forgotten as positivism imposed its myths of scientific objectivity. [*F*, p. 610; *M*, p. 276]

In the name of Freud, one can read the call for a note. At the bottom of the page, Foucault persists, dates and signs, but the note introduces a slight precaution; it is indeed a note of prudence, but Foucault insists nonetheless and speaks of persistence: "These structures still persist in non-psychoanalytic psychiatry, and in many aspects or on many sides [*par bien des côtés*] of psychoanalysis itself" (*F*, p. 610; *M*, p. 299).

Though too discreetly marked, there is indeed a limit to what persists "on many sides." The always divisible line of this limit situates, in its form, the totality of the stakes. More precisely, the stakes are nothing other than those of totality, and of the procedures of totalization: what does it mean to say psychoanalysis "itself"? What does one thereby identify in such a global way? Is it psychoanalysis "*itself*," as Foucault says, that inherits from Pinel? What is psychoanalysis *itself*? And are the aspects or sides through which it inherits the essential and irreducible aspects or sides of psychoanalysis itself or the residual "asides" that it can win out over [*avoir raison de*]? or even, that it must, that it should, win out over?

If the answer to this last question still seems up in the air in this note, it is soon going to come in a more determined and less equivocal form: no, psychoanalysis will never free itself of the psychiatric heritage. Its essential historical situation is linked to what is called the "*analytic situation*," that is, to the thaumaturgical mystification of the couple doctor-patient, regulated this time by institutional protocols. Before citing word for word a conclusion that will remain, I believe, without appeal not only in *The History of Madness* but in Foucault's entire oeuvre—and right up to its awful interruption—I will once again risk wearing out your patience in order to look for a moment at the way in which Foucault describes the thaumaturgical play whose *techne* Pinel would have passed down to Freud, a *techne* that would be at once art and technique, the secret, the secret of the secret, the secret that consists in knowing how to make one suppose knowledge and believe in the secret. It is worth pausing here in order to point out another paradoxical effect of the chiasm—one of the most significant for what concerns us here, namely, a certain diabolical repetition and the recurrence of the various figures of the Evil Genius. What does Foucault say? That in the couple doctor-patient "the doctor becomes a thaumaturge" (*F*, p. 609; *M*, p. 275). Now, to describe this thaumaturgy, Foucault does not hesitate to speak of the demonic and satanic, as if the Evil Genius resided this time not on the side of unreason, of absolute disorder and madness (to say it quickly and with a bit of a smile, using all the necessary quotation marks, "on the good side"), but on the side of order, on the side of a subtly authoritative violence, the side of the Father, the Judge, the Law, and so on:

> It was thought, and by the patient first of all, that it was in the esotericism of his knowledge, in some *almost* daemonic secret of knowledge [I emphasize "almost": Foucault will later say— his relation to Freud surely being anything but simple—that the philistine representation of mental illness in the nineteenth century would last "right up to Freud—or almost"] that the doctor had found the power to unravel insanity; and increasingly the patient would accept this self-surrender to a doctor both divine and satanic, beyond human measure in any case. [*F*, p. 609; *M*, p. 275]

Two pages later, it is said that Freud "amplified the thaumaturgical virtues" of the "medical personage," "preparing for his omnipotence a quasi-divine status." And Foucault continues:

> He focussed upon this single presence—concealed behind the patient and above him, in an absence that is also a total presence—all the powers that had been distributed in the collective existence of the asylum; he transformed this into an absolute Observation, a pure and circumspect Silence, a Judge who punishes and rewards in a judgment that does not even condescend to language; he made it the mirror in which madness, in an almost motionless movement, clings to and casts off itself.
>
> To the doctor, Freud transferred all the structures Pinel and Tuke had set up within confinement. [*F*, p. 611; *M*, pp. 277–78]

Fictive omnipotence and a divine, or rather "quasi-divine," power, divine by simulacrum, at once divine and satanic—these are the very traits of an Evil Genius that are now being attributed to the figure of the doctor. The doctor suddenly begins to resemble in a troubling way the figure of unreason that continued to haunt what is called the classical age after the *act of force* [*coup de force*] of the *cogito*. And like the authority of the laws whose "mystical foundation" is recalled by Montaigne and Pascal,[14] the authority of the psychoanalyst-doctor is the result of a fiction; it is the result, by transfer, of the credit given to a fiction; and this fiction appears analogous to that which provisionally confers all powers—and even more than knowledge—to the Evil Genius.

At the conclusion of "The Birth of the Asylum," Foucault is going to dismiss without appeal this bad genius of the thaumaturgical doctor in the figure of the psychoanalyst; he is going to do this—I believe one can say without stretching the paradox—*against Descartes*, against a certain Cartesian subject still represented in the filiation that runs from Descartes to Pinel to Freud. But he is also going to do this, more or less willingly, *as Descartes*, or, at least, as the Descartes whom he had accused of excluding madness by excluding, mastering, or dismissing— since these all come down to the same thing—the powers of the Evil Genius. Against Freud, this descendant of Descartes, against Descartes, it is still the Cartesian exclusion that is repeated in a deadly and devilish way, like a heritage inscribed within a diabolical and almost all-powerful program that one should admit one never gets rid of or frees oneself from without remainder.

To substantiate what I have just said, I will cite the conclusion of this chapter. It describes the transfer from Pinel to Freud (stroke of genius, "masterful short-circuit"—it is a question of Freud's genius, the good like the bad, the good as bad)—and it implacably judges psychoanalysis *in the past, in the present, and even in the future.* For psychoanalysis is condemned in advance. No future is promised that might allow it to

---

14. "And so laws keep up their good standing, not because they are just, but because they are laws: that is the mystical foundation of their authority, they have no other. . . . Anyone who obeys them because they are just is not obeying them the way he ought to" (quoted in Derrida, "Force of Law: The 'Mystical Foundation of Authority,'" trans. Mary Quaintance, *Cardozo Law Review* 11 [July/Aug. 1990]: 939; Derrida's French text appears on facing pages). Elsewhere, Montaigne had mentioned the "legitimate fictions" on which "our law" "founds the truth of its justice" (ibid.). And Pascal cites Montaigne without naming him when he recalls both the principle of justice and the fact that it should not be traced back to its source unless one wants to ruin it. What is he himself doing, then, when he speaks of "the mystical foundation of its authority," adding in the same breath, "Whoever traces it to its source annihilates it" (ibid.)? Is he re-founding or ruining that of which he speaks? Will one ever know? Must one know?

Power, authority, knowledge and non-knowledge, law, judgment, fiction, good standing or credit, transfer: from Montaigne to Pascal onto others, we recognize the same network of a critical problematic, an active, vigilant, hypercritical problematization. It is difficult to be sure that the "classical age" did not thematize, reflect, and also deploy the concepts of its symptoms: the concepts that one will later direct toward the symptoms that it will one day be believed can be assigned to it.

CHAPTER NINE 294

escape its destiny once it has been determined both within the institutional (and supposedly inflexible) structure of what is called the *analytic situation* and in the figure of the doctor as *subject*:

> To the doctor, Freud transferred all the structures Pinel and Tuke had set up within confinement. He did deliver the patient from the existence of the asylum within which his "liberators" had alienated him; but he did not deliver him from what was essential in this existence; he regrouped its powers, extended them to the maximum by uniting them in the doctor's hands; he created the psychoanalytical situation where, by a masterful short-circuit [*court-circuit génial*; I underscore this allusion to the stroke of genius (*coup de génie*), which, as soon as it confirms the evil of confinement and of the interior asylum, is diabolical and properly evil (*malin*); and as we will see, for more than twenty years Foucault never stopped seeing in Freud—and quite literally so—sometimes a good and sometimes a bad or evil (*mauvais*) genius], alienation becomes disalienating because, in the doctor, it becomes a subject.
>
> The doctor, as an alienating figure, remains the key to psychoanalysis. It is perhaps because it did not suppress this ultimate structure, and because it referred all the others to it, that psychoanalysis has not been able, *will not be able* [I thus emphasize this future; it announces the invariability of this verdict in Foucault's subsequent work], to hear the voices of unreason, nor to decipher in themselves the signs of the madman. Psychoanalysis can unravel some of the forms of madness; it remains a stranger to the sovereign enterprise of unreason. It can neither liberate nor transcribe, nor most certainly explain, what is essential in this enterprise. [*F*, pp. 611–12; *M*, p. 278]

And here, just after, are the very last lines of the chapter; we are far from the couple Nietzsche/Freud. They are now separated on both sides of what Foucault calls "moral imprisonment," and it will be difficult to say, in certain situations, who is to be found on the *inside* and who on the *outside*—and sometimes outside but inside. As opposed to Nietzsche and a few other great madmen, Freud no longer belongs to the space *from out of* which *The History of Madness* could be written. He belongs, rather, to this history of madness that the book in turn makes its *object*:

> Since the end of the eighteenth century, the life of unreason no longer manifests itself except in the lightning-flash of works such as those of Hölderlin, of Nerval, of Nietzsche, or of Artaud—forever irreducible to those alienations that can be cured, resisting by their own strength that gigantic moral imprisonment which we are in the habit of calling, doubtless by antiphrasis, the liberation of the insane [*aliénés*] by Pinel and Tuke. [*F*, p. 612; *M*, p. 278]

This diagnosis, which is also a verdict, is confirmed in the last chapter of the book, "The Anthropological Circle." This chapter fixes the new distribution of names and places into the great series that form the grid of the book. When it is a question of showing that since the end of the eighteenth century the liberation of the mad has been replaced by an objectification of the concept of their freedom (within such categories as desire and will, determinism and responsibility, the automatic and the spontaneous) and that "one will now untiringly recount the trials and tribulations of freedom," which is also to say, of a certain humanization as anthropologization, Freud is then regularly included among the exemplary figures of this anthropologism of freedom. Foucault says, page after page: "From Esquirol to Janet, as from Reil to Freud or from Tuke to Jackson" (*F*, p. 616), or again, "From Esquirol to Freud" (*F*, p. 617), or again "since Esquirol and Broussais right up to Janet, Bleuler, and Freud" (*F*, p. 624). A slight yet troubling reservation comes just after to mitigate all these regroupings. Concerning general paralysis and neurosyphilis, philistinism is everywhere, "right up to Freud—or almost" (*F*, p. 626)

The chiasmatic effects multiply. Some two hundred pages earlier, what had inscribed both Freud *and* Nietzsche, like two accomplices of the same age, was the reopening of the dialogue with unreason, the lifting of the interdiction against *language*, the *return* to a proximity with madness. Yet it is precisely this or, rather, the silent double and hypocritical simulacrum of this, the mask of this language, the same freedom now objectified, that separates Freud from Nietzsche. It is this that now makes them unable to associate or to be associated with one another from the two sides of a wall that is all the more unsurmountable insofar as it consists of an asylum's partition, an invisible, interior, but eloquent partition, that of truth itself as the truth of man and his alienation. Foucault was able, much earlier, to say that Freudian psychoanalysis, to which one must be fair or "*do justice*," is not a psychology as soon as it takes language into account. Now it is language itself that brings psychoanalysis back down to the status of a psycho-anthropology of alienation, "this language wherein man appears in madness as being other than himself," this "alterity," "a dialectic that is always begun anew between the *Same* and the *Other*," revealing to man his truth "in the babbling movement of *alienation* or *madness*" (*F*, p. 631).

Concerning dialectic and alienation or madness—concerning everything, in fact, that happens in the circulation of this "anthropological circle" wherein psychoanalysis is caught up or held—one should, and I myself would have liked to have done this given more time, pause a bit longer than Foucault did on a passage from Hegel's *Encyclopedia*. I am referring to the Remark of §408 in which Hegel situates and deduces madness as a contradiction of the subject between the particular determination of self-feeling and the network of mediations that is called consciousness. Hegel makes in passing a spirited praise of Pinel (I do not understand why Foucault, in quickly citing this passage, replaces this praise for Pinel by an ellipsis). More important, perhaps, is the fact that Hegel also interprets madness as the taking control of a certain Evil Genius (*der böse Genius*) in man. Foucault elliptically cites a short phrase in translation ("méchant génie") without remarking on it and without linking these few extraordinary pages of Hegel to the great dramaturgy of the Evil Genius that concerns us here.

Let me be absolutely clear about this: my intention here is not at all to accuse or criticize Foucault, to say, for example, that he was wrong to confine *Freud himself* (*in general*) or *psychoanalysis itself* (*in general*) to this role and place; on the subject of Freud or psychoanalysis *themselves and in general*, I have in this form and place almost nothing to say or think, except perhaps that Foucault has some good arguments and that others would have some pretty good ones as well to oppose to his. It is also not my intention, in spite of what it may look like, to suggest that Foucault contradicts himself when he so firmly places the same Freud (in general) or the same psychoanalysis (in general) sometimes on one side and sometimes on the other of the dividing line, *and always on the side of the Evil Genius*—who is found sometimes on the side of madness, sometimes on the side of its exclusion-reappropriation, on the side of its confinement to the outside or the inside, with or without asylum walls. The contradiction is no doubt in the things themselves, so to speak. And we are in a region where the wrong (the *being-wrong* or the *doing-someone-wrong*) would want to be more than ever on the side of a certain reason, on the side of what is called *raison garder*—that is, on the side of keeping one's cool, keeping one's head—on the side, precisely, where one is right [*a raison*], and where *being right* [*avoir raison*] is to *win out over* or *prove someone wrong* [*avoir raison de*], with a violence whose subtlety, whose hyperdialectic and hyperchiasmatic resources, cannot be completely formalized, that is, can no longer be dominated by a metalanguage. Which means that we are always caught in the knots that are woven, before us and beyond us, by this powerful—all too powerful—logic. The history of reason embedded in all these turbulent idioms (*to prove someone wrong* [*donner tort*] or *to prove them right* [*donner raison*], *to be right* [*avoir raison*], *to be wrong* [*avoir tort*], *to win out over* [*avoir raison de*], *to do someone wrong* [*faire tort*], and so on) is also the history of madness that Foucault wished to recount to us. The fact that he was caught up, caught up even before setting out, in the snares of this logic—which he sometimes thematizes as having to do with a "system of contradictions" and "antinomies" whose "coherence" remains "hidden"—cannot be reduced to a fault or wrong on his part (*F*, p. 624). This does not mean, however, that we, without ever finding him to be radically wrong or at fault, have to subscribe a priori to all his statements. One would be able to master this entire problematic, assuming this were possible, only after having satisfactorily answered a few questions, questions as innocent—or as hardly innocent—as, What is reason? for example, or more narrowly, What is the principle of reason? What does it mean to be right [*avoir raison*]? What does it mean to be right or to prove someone right [*avoir ou donner raison*]? To be wrong, to prove someone wrong, or to do them wrong [*avoir, donner ou faire tort*]? You will forgive me here, I hope, for leaving these enigmas as they are.

I will restrict myself to a modest and more accessible question. The distribution of statements, such as it appears to be set out before us, should lead us to think two apparently incompatible things: the book entitled *The History of Madness*, as the history of madness itself, is and is not the same age as Freudian psychoanalysis. The project of this book thus does and does not belong to the age of psychoanalysis; it already belongs to it and already no longer belongs to it. This division without division would put us back on the track of another logic of division, one that would urge us to think the internal partitions of wholes, partitions that would make such things as madness, reason, history, and age—especially the whole we call age—but also psychoanalysis, Freud, and so on, into rather dubious identities, sufficiently divided from within to threaten in advance all our statements and all our references with parasitism: it would be a bit as if a virus were introduced into the matrix of language, the way such things are today introduced into computer software, the difference being that we are—and for a very good reason—very far from having at our disposal any of these diagnostic and remedial antiviral programs that are available on the market today, even though these same programs—and for a very good reason—have a hard time keeping pace with the industrial production of these viruses, which are themselves sometimes produced by those who produce the intercepting programs. A maddening situation for any discourse, certainly, but a certain mad panic is not necessarily the worst thing that can happen to a discourse on madness as soon as it does not go all out to confine or exclude its object, that is, in the sense Foucault gives to this word, to *objectify* it.

Does one have the right to stop here and be content with this as an internal reading of Foucault's great book? Is an *internal* reading possible? Is it legitimate to privilege to this extent its relation to something like an "age" of psychoanalysis "itself"? The reservations that such presumptions of identity might arouse (the unity of an "age," the indivisibility of psychoanalysis "itself," and so on—and I've made more than one allusion to them—would be enough to make us question this.

One would be able to justify a response to this question, in any case, only by continuing to read and to analyze, by continuing to take into account particularly Foucault's corpus, his archive, what this archive says on the subject of the archive. Without limiting ourselves to this, think in particular of the problems posed some five to eight years later: (1) by *The Order of Things* concerning something that has always seemed enigmatic to me and that Foucault calls for a time *episteme* (there where it is said, "We think in that place" [*MC*, p. 396; *DT*, p. 384]); a place that, and I will return to this in a moment, encompasses or comprehends the psychoanalysis that does not comprehend it, or more precisely, that comprehends it without comprehending it and without acceding to it; (2) by *The Archaeology of Knowledge* concerning "The Historical *a priori* and the Archive" (this is the title of the central chapter) and archaeology in its relation to the history of ideas.

It is out of the question to get involved here, in so short a time, in such difficult readings. I will thus be content to conclude, if you will still allow me, with a few indications (two at the most) along one of the paths I would have wanted to follow on the basis of these readings.

1. On the one hand, I would have tried to identify the signs of an imperturbable constancy in this movement of the pendulum or balance. The oscillation *regularly* leads from one topological assignation to the other: as if psychoanalysis had *two places* or took place *two times*. Yet

it seems to me that the law of this displacement operates without the structural possibility of an event or a place being analyzed for itself, and without the consequences being drawn with regard to the identity of all the concepts at work in this history that does not want to be a history of ideas and representations.

This constancy in the oscillation of the pendulum is first marked, of course, in books that are more or less contemporary with *The History of Madness*. *Maladie mentale et psychologie* [*Mental Illness and Psychology*] (1962) intersects and coincides at many points with *The History of Madness*. In the history of mental illness, Freud appears as "the first to open up once again the possibility for reason and unreason to communicate in the danger of a common language, ever ready to break down and disintegrate into the inaccessible" (*MM*, p. 82; *MI*, p. 69). In truth, though profoundly in accord with the movement and logic of *The History of Madness*, this book of 1962 is, in the end, a bit more precise and differentiated in its references to Freud, although *Beyond the Pleasure Principle* is never mentioned. Foucault speaks both of Freud's "stroke of genius" (and this is indeed his word) and of the dividing line that runs down his work. Freud's "stroke of genius" was to have escaped the evolutionist horizon of John Hughlings Jackson (*MM*, p. 37; *MI*, p. 31), whose model can nevertheless be found in the description of the evolutive forms of neurosis and the history of libidinal stages,[15] the

---

15. Insofar as, and to the extent that, it follows Jackson's model (for the "stroke of genius" also consists in escaping from this), psychoanalysis is *credulous*, it *will have been* credulous, for it is in this that it is outdated, a credulous presumption: "it believed that it could," "Freud believed." After having cited Jackson's *The Factors of Insanities*, Foucault in fact adds (I emphasize the verb and tense of *to believe*):

> Jackson's entire work tended to give right of place to evolutionism in neuro- and psycho-pathology. Since the *Croonian Lectures* (1874), it has no longer been possible to omit the regressive aspects of illness; evolution is now one of the dimensions by which one gains access to the pathological fact.
>
> A whole side of Freud's work consists of a commentary on the evolutive forms of neurosis. The history of the libido, of its development, of its successive fixations, resembles a collection of the pathological possibilities of the individual: each type of neurosis is a return to a libidinal stage of evolution. And psychoanalysis *believed that it could* write a psychology of the child by carrying out a pathology of the adult. . . . This is the celebrated Oedipus complex, in which Freud *believed* that he could read the enigma of man and the key to his destiny, in which one must find the most comprehensive analysis of the conflicts experienced by the child in his relations with his parents and the point at which many neuroses became fixated.
>
> In short, every libidinal stage is a potential pathological structure. Neurosis is a spontaneous archeology of the libido. [*MM*, pp. 23–26; *MI*, pp. 19–21]

libido being mythological (a myth to destroy, often a biopsychological myth that is abandoned, Foucault then thinks, by psychoanalysts), just as mythological as Janet's "'psychic force,'" with which Foucault associates it more than once (*MM*, p. 29; *MI*, p. 24).[16]

If the assignation of Freud is thus double, it is because his work is divided: "In psychoanalysis, it is always possible," says Foucault, "to separate that which pertains to a psychology of evolution (as in *Three Essays on the Theory of Sexuality*) and that which belongs to a psychology of individual history (as in *Five Psychoanalyses* and the accompanying texts)" (*MM*, p. 37; *MI*, p. 31).

Despite this consideration for the "stroke of genius," Foucault is indeed speaking here of an analytic psychology. This is what he calls it. Insofar as it remains a psychology, it remains speechless before the language of madness. Indeed, "there is a very good reason why psychology can never master madness; it is because psychology became possible in our world only when madness had already been mastered and excluded from the drama" (*MM*, p. 104; *MI*, p. 87—a few lines before the end of the book).

In other words, the logic at work in this conclusion, the consequences—the ruinous consequences—of which one would ceaselessly have to take into account, is that what has already been mastered can no longer be mastered, and that too much mastery (in the form of exclusion but also of objectification) deprives one of mastery (in the form of access, knowledge, competence). The concept of mastery is an impossible concept to manipulate, as we know: the more there is, the less there is, and vice versa. The conclusion drawn in the few lines I just cited thus excludes *both* Freud's "stroke of genius" *and* psychology, be it analytic or some other. Freudian man remains a *homo psychologicus*. Freud is once again passed over in silence, cut out of both the lineage and the work of mad geniuses. He is given over to a forgetfulness where one can then accuse him of silence and forgetting.

> And when, in lightning flashes and cries, madness reappears, as in Nerval or Artaud, Nietzsche or Roussel, it is psychology that remains silent, *speechless*, before this language that borrows a meaning of its own from that *tragic split* [I emphasize

16. For example: "It is not a question of invalidating the analyses of pathological regression; all that is required is to free them of the myths that neither Janet nor Freud succeeded in separating from them" (*MM*, p. 31; *MI*, p. 26).

this phrase; this is a tragic and romantic discourse on the essence
of madness and the birth of tragedy, a discourse just as close,
literally, to that of a certain Novalis as to that of Hölderlin],
from that freedom, that, for contemporary man, only the existence of "psychologists" allows him to forget. [*MM*, p. 104; *MI*,
pp. 87–88][17]

And yet. Still according to the interminable and inexhaustible *fort/da*
that we have been following for some time now, the same *Freudian man*
is reinscribed into the noble lineage at the end of *Naissance de la clinique*
[*The Birth of the Clinic*] (a book published in 1963 but clearly written
during the same creative period). Why single out this occurrence of the
reinscription rather than another? Because it might give us (and this is,
in fact, the hypothesis that interests me) a rule for reading this *fort/da*; it
might provide us with a criterion for interpreting this untiring exclusion/
inclusion. It is a question of another divide, within psychoanalysis, or, in
any case, a divide that seems somewhat different than the one I spoke of
a moment ago between Freud, the psychologist of evolution, and Freud,
the psychologist of individual history. I say "seems somewhat different"
because the one perhaps leads back to the other.

The line of this second divide is, quite simply—if one can say this—
death. The Freud who breaks with psychology, with evolutionism and
biologism, the tragic Freud, really, who shows himself *hospitable* to
madness (and I take the risk of this word) because he is foreign to the
space of the hospital, the tragic Freud who deserves hospitality in the
great lineage of mad geniuses, is the Freud who talks it out with death.
This would especially be the Freud, then, of *Beyond the Pleasure Principle*, although Foucault never, to my knowledge, mentions this work
and makes only a very ambiguous allusion in *Mental Illness and Psychology* to what he calls a death instinct, the one by which Freud wished
to explain the war, although "it was war that was dreamed in this shift
in Freud's thinking" (*MM*, p. 99; *MI*, p. 83).

Death alone, along with war, introduces the power of the negative
into psychology and into its evolutionist optimism. On the basis of this

---

17. A literally identical schema was at work a few pages earlier: "Psychology can
never tell the truth about madness because it is madness that holds the truth of psychology." It is again a tragic vision, a tragic discourse on the tragic. Hölderlin, Nerval,
Roussel, and Artaud are again named through their works as witnesses of a "tragic
confrontation with madness" free of all psychology (*MM*, p. 89; *MI*, pp. 74, 75). No
reconciliation is possible between psychology, even if analytic, and tragedy.

experience of death, on the basis of what is called in the final pages of
The Birth of the Clinic "originary finitude"[18] (a vocabulary and theme
that then take over Foucault's text and that always seemed to me difficult to dissociate from Heidegger, who as you know is practically never
evoked, nor even named, by Foucault),[19] Freud is reintegrated into this
modernity from out of which *The History of Madness* is written and
from which he had been banished at regular intervals. It is by taking
account of death as "the concrete a priori of medical experience" that
"the beginning of that fundamental relation that binds modern man to
his originary finitude" comes about (*N*, pp. 198, 199; *B*, pp. 196, 197).
This modern man is also a "Freudian man":

> the experience of individuality in modern culture is bound up
> with that of death: from Hölderlin's Empedocles to Nietzsche's
> Zarathustra, and on to Freudian man, an obstinate relation to
> death prescribes to the universal its singular face, and lends to
> each individual the power of being heard forever. [*N*, p. 199;
> *B*, p. 197]

Originary finitude is a finitude that no longer arises out of the infinity of
a divine presence. It now unfolds "in the void left by the absence of the
gods" (*N*, p. 200; *B*, p. 198). What we have here, then, is, in the name
of death, so to speak, a reinscription of Freudian man into a "modern"
grouping or whole from which he was sometimes excluded.

One can then follow *two* new but equally ambiguous consequences.
On the one hand, the grouping in question is going to be restructured.
One should not be surprised to see reappear, as on the very last page of

18. Foucault, *Naissance de la clinique: Une Archéologie du regard médical* (Paris,
1963), p. 199; hereafter abbreviated *N*; trans. A. M. Sheridan Smith, under the title *The
Birth of the Clinic: An Archeology of Medical Perception* (New York, 1975), p. 197;
hereafter abbreviated *B*.

19. Except perhaps in passing in *Les Mots et les choses*: "the experience of Hölderlin,
Nietzsche, and Heidegger, in which the return is posited only in the extreme recession of
the origin" (*MC*, p. 345; *OT*, p. 334).

This ponderous silence would last, I believe, right up until an interview that he gave
not long before his death. Faithful to the Foucauldian style of interpretation, one might
say that the spacing of this omission, of this blank silence—like the silence that reigns
over the name of Lacan, whom one can associate with Heidegger up to a certain point,
and thus with a few others who never stopped, in France and elsewhere, to dialogue with
these two—is anything but the empty and inoperative sign of an absence. It *gives rise*
or *gives the place* [*donne lieu*], on the contrary, it marks out the place and the age. The
dotted lines of a suspended writing *situate* with a formidable precision. No attention to
the age or to the problem of the age should lose sight of this.

The Birth of the Clinic, the name of Jackson—and, before him, Bichat, whose *Traité des membranes* (1827) and *Recherches physiologiques* would have allowed death to be seen and thought. This vitalism would have arisen against the backdrop of "'mortalism'" (*N*, p. 147; *B*, p. 145). It would be a characteristic of the entire European nineteenth century, and it could be attested to just as well by Goya, Géricault, Delacroix, or Baudelaire, to name just a few: "The importance of Bichat, Jackson, and Freud in European culture does not prove that they were philosophers as well as doctors, but that, in this culture, medical thought is fully engaged in the philosophical status of man" (*N*, p. 200; *B*, p. 198).

But there is a second ambiguous consequence of this relation to death as originary finitude. And so, *on the other hand*, the figure or face that is then fixed, and in which one believes one recognizes the traits of "Freudian man," comes to occupy a rather singular place with respect to what Foucault calls the analytic of finitude and the modern *episteme* at the end of *Les Mots et les choses* [*The Order of Things*] (1966). From the standpoint of a certain epistemological trihedron (life, work, and language, or biology, economy, and philology), the human sciences are seen to be at once *inclusive* and *exclusive*; these are Foucault's words (see *MC*, p. 358; *OT*, p. 347).

As for this inclusive exclusion, Freud's work, to which Foucault unwaveringly assigns a model that is more philological than biological, still occupies the place of the *hinge*; Foucault in fact speaks about the place and workings of a "*pivot*": "all this knowledge, within which Western culture had given itself in one century a certain image of man, pivots on the work of Freud, though without, for all that, leaving its fundamental arrangement" (*MC*, p. 372; *OT*, p. 361).

"Though without, for all that, leaving its fundamental arrangement": that is how everything turns round the event or the invention of psychoanalysis. It turns in circles and in place, endlessly returning to the same. It is a revolution that changes nothing. Hence this is not, as Foucault adds at this point, "the most decisive importance of psychoanalysis."

In what, then, does this "most decisive importance of psychoanalysis" consist? In exceeding both consciousness and representation—and, as a result, the human sciences, which do not go beyond the realm of the representable. It is in this respect that psychoanalysis, like ethnology in fact, does not belong to the field of the human sciences. It "relates the knowledge of man to the finitude that gives man its foundation" (*MC*, p. 392; *OT*, p. 381). We are far from its earlier determination as an analytic psychology. And this same excessive character leads psychoanalysis toward the very forms of finitude that Foucault writes in capital letters, that is, toward Death, Desire, Law or Law-Language (see *MC*, p. 386; *OT*, p. 375). It would be necessary to devote a more detailed and more probing reading to these few pages, something I cannot do here. To keep to the surest schema, let us simply say that, from this point of view and to this degree at least, psychoanalysis, as an analytic of finitude, is now granted an intimacy with the madness that it had sometimes been conceded but had most often been emphatically denied in *The History of Madness*. And this intimacy is a sort of complicity with the madness of the day, the madness of today, "madness in its present form, madness as it is posited in the modern experience, as its truth and its alterity" (*MC*, p. 387; *OT*, p. 375).

But let us not oversimplify things. What Foucault generously grants psychoanalytic experience is now nothing other than what is denied it; more precisely, it is the being able to see what is denied it. Indeed, the only privilege that is here granted to psychoanalysis is that of the experience *that accedes to that to which it can never accede*. If Foucault here mentions, under the name of madness, only schizophrenia and psychosis, it is because psychoanalysis most often approaches these only in order to acknowledge its own limit: a forbidden or impossible access. *This limit defines psychoanalysis*. Its intimacy with madness par excellence is an intimacy with the least intimate, a nonintimacy that relates it to what is most heterogenous, to that which in no way lets itself be interiorized, nor even subjectified: neither alienated, I would say, nor inalienable.

> This is why psychoanalysis finds in that madness *par excellence* ["madness *par excellence*" is also the title given by Blanchot many years earlier to a text on Hölderlin, and Foucault is no doubt echoing this without saying so]—which psychiatrists term schizophrenia—its intimate, its most invincible torture: for, given in this form of madness, in an absolutely manifest and absolutely withdrawn form [this absolute identity of the manifest and the withdrawn, of the open and the secret, is no doubt the key to this double gesture of interpretation and evaluation], are the forms of finitude towards which it usually advances unceasingly (and interminably) from the starting-point of that which is voluntarily-involuntarily offered to it in the patient's language. So psychoanalysis 'recognizes itself' when it is confronted with those very psychoses to which, nevertheless (or rather, for that very reason), it has scarcely any means of access: as if the psychosis were displaying in a savage illumination, and offering in a mode not too distant but precisely too close,

that towards which analysis must make its laborious way. [*MC*,
p. 387; *OT*, pp. 375–76]

This displacement, as ambiguous as it is, leads Foucault to adopt the
exact opposite position of certain theses of *The History of Madness* and
Mental Illness and Psychology concerning the couple patient-doctor,
concerning transference or alienation. This time, psychoanalysis not
only has nothing to do with a psychology but it constitutes neither a
general theory of man—since it is above all else a knowledge linked to
a practice—nor an anthropology (see *MC*, pp. 388, 390; *OT*, pp. 376,
378–79). Even better: in the movement where he clearly affirms this,
Foucault challenges the very thing of which he had unequivocally accused psychoanalysis, namely, of being a mythology and a thaumaturgy.
He now wants to explain why psychologists and philosophers were so
quick, and so naive, to denounce a Freudian mythology there where that
which exceeds representation and consciousness must have in fact *resembled*, but only resembled, something mythological (see *MC*, p. 386;
OT, p. 374). As for the thaumaturgy of transference, the logic of alienation, and the subtly or sublimely asylumlike violence of the analytic
situation, they are no longer, Foucault now says, essential to psychoanalysis, no longer "constitutive" of it. It is not that all violence is absent
from this rehabilitated psychoanalysis, but it is, I hardly dare say it, a
good violence, or in any case what Foucault calls a "calm" violence,
one that, in the singular experience of singularity, allows access to "the
concrete figures of finitude":

> neither hypnosis, nor the patient's alienation within the fan-
> tasmatic character of the doctor, is constitutive of psychoanal-
> ysis; . . . the latter can be deployed only in the calm violence of
> a particular relationship and the transference it produces. . . .
> Psychoanalysis makes use of the particular relation of the trans-
> ference in order to reveal, on the outer confines of representa-
> tion, Desire, Law, and Death, which outline, at the extremity of
> analytic language and practice, the concrete figures of finitude.
> [*MC*, pp. 388–89; *OT*, pp. 377–78]

Things have indeed changed—or so it appears—between *The History of Madness* and *The Order of Things*.

From where does the theme of finitude that seems to govern this new
displacement of the pendulum come? To what philosophical event is this
analytic of finitude to be attributed—this analytic in which is inscribed

the trihedron of knowledges or models of the modern *episteme*, with its nonsciences, the "'human sciences,'" according to Foucault (*MC*, p. 378; *OT*, p. 366), and its "'counter-sciences,'" which Foucault says psychoanalysis and ethnology also are (*MC*, p. 391; *OT*, p. 379)?

As a project, the analytic of finitude would belong to the tradition of the Kantian critique. Foucault insists on this Kantian filiation by specifying, to cite it once again: "We think in that place." Here is again and for a time, according to Foucault, *our* age, *our* contemporaneity. It is true that if originary finitude obviously makes us think of Kant, it would be unable to do so alone, that is—to summarize an enormous venture in a word, in a name—without the active interpretation of the Heideggerian repetition and all its repercussions, particularly, since this is our topic today, in the discourse of French philosophy and psychoanalysis, and especially, Lacanian psychoanalysis; and when I say Lacanian, I am also referring to all the debates *with* Lacan during the past few decades. This would have perhaps deserved some mention here on the part of Foucault, especially when he speaks of originary finitude. For Kantian finitude is precisely not "originary," as is, on the contrary, the one to which the Heideggerian interpretation leads. Finitude in Kant's sense is instead derived, as is the intuition bearing the same name. But let us leave all this aside, since it would, as we say, take us a bit too far afield.

The "we" who is saying "we think in that place" is evidently, tautologically, the "we" from out of which the signatory of these lines, the author of *The History of Madness* and *The Order of Things*, speaks, writes, and thinks. But this "we" never stops dividing, and the places of its signature are displaced in being divided up. A certain untimeliness always disturbs the contemporary who reassures him or herself in a "we." This "we," our "we," is not its own contemporary. The self-identity of its age, or of any age, appears as divided, and thus problematic, *problematizable* (I underscore this word for a reason that will perhaps become apparent in a moment), as the age of madness or an age of psychoanalysis—as well as, in fact, all the historical or archeological categories that promise us the determinable stability of a configurable whole. In fact, from the moment a couple separates, from the moment, for example, just to locate here a symptom or a simple indication, the couple Freud/Nietzsche forms and then unforms, this decoupling fissures the identity of the epoch, of the age, of the *episteme* or the paradigm of which one or the other, or both together, might have been the significant representatives. This is even more true when this decoupling comes to fissure the self-identity of some individual, or some presumed individuality, for example, of Freud. What allows one to presume the non–self-difference of Freud, for example? And of psycho-analysis? These decouplings and self-differences no doubt introduce a good deal of disorder into the unity of any configuration, whole, epoch, or historical age. Such disturbances make the historians' work rather difficult, even and especially the work of the most original and refined among them. This self-difference, this difference *to self* [*à soi*], and not simply *with self*, makes life hard if not impossible for historical science. But inversely, would there be any history, would anything ever *happen*, without this principle of disturbance? Would there ever be any event without this disturbance of the principality?

At the point where we are, the age of finitude is being de-identified for at least one reason, from which I can here abstract only the general schema: the thought of finitude, as the thought of finite man, speaks *both* of the tradition, the memory of the Kantian critique or of the knowledges rooted in it, *and* of the end [*fin*] of this finite man, this man who is "nearing its end," as Foucault's most famous sentence would have it in this final wager, placed on the edge of a promise that has yet to take shape, in the final lines of *The Order of Things*: "then one can certainly wager that man would be effaced, like a face drawn in sand at the edge or limit of the sea" (*MC*, p. 398; *OT*, p. 387). The *trait* (the trait of the face, the line or the limit) that then runs the risk of being effaced in the sand would perhaps also be the one that separates an end from itself, thereby multiplying it endlessly and making it, once again, into a limit: the self-relation of a limit at once erases and multiplies the limit; it cannot but divide it in inventing it. The limit only comes to be effaced—it only comes to efface itself—as soon as it is inscribed.

2. I'm finished with this point, and so I should really finish it up right here. Assuming that I haven't already worn out your patience, I will conclude with a second indication as a sort of *postscript*—and even more schematically—in order to point once again in the direction of psychoanalysis and to put these hypotheses to the test of *The History of Sexuality* (1976–1984).[20]

If one is still willing to follow this figure of the pendulum [*balancier*] making a scene before psychoanalysis, then one will observe that

---

20. *Histoire de la sexualité* is the name given by Foucault to his entire project on sexuality, of which three volumes have now been published: *La Volonté de savoir* (Paris, 1976), hereafter abbreviated *VS*, trans. Robert Hurley, under the title *The History of Sexuality: An Introduction* (New York, 1978), hereafter abbreviated *HS*; *L'Usage des plaisirs* (Paris, 1984), trans. Hurley, under the title *The Use of Pleasure* (New York, 1985); and *Le Souci de soi* (Paris, 1984), trans. Hurley, under the title *The Care of the Self* (New York, 1986).

the *fort/da* here gives a new impetus to the movement, a movement with the same rhythm but with a greater amplitude and range than ever before. Psychoanalysis is here reduced, more than it ever was, to a very circumscribed and dependent moment in a history of the "strategies of knowledge and power" (juridical, familial, psychiatric) (*VS*, p. 210; *HS*, p. 159). Psychoanalysis is taken by and interested in these strategies, but it does not think them through. The praises of Freud fall decisively and irreversibly: one hears, for example, of "how wonderfully effective he was—worthy of the greatest spiritual fathers and directors of the classical period—in giving a new impetus to the secular injunction to study sex and transform it into discourse" (*VS*, p. 210; *HS*, p. 159). This time, in other words, in reinscribing the invention of psychoanalysis into the history of a disciplinary dynamic, one no longer indicts only the ruses of objectivization and psychiatric alienation, as in *The History of Madness*, and no longer only the stratagems that would have allowed the *confinement without confinement* of the patient in the invisible asylum of the analytic situation. This time, it is a question of going much further back, and more radically than the "repressive hypothesis" ever did, towards the harsh ruses of the monarchy of sex and the agencies of power that support it. These latter invest in and take charge of sexuality, so that there is no need to oppose, as one so often and naively believes, power and pleasure.

And since we have been following for so long now the obsessive avatars of the Evil Genius, the irresistible, demonic, and metamorphic returns of this quasi-God, of God's second in command, this metempsychotic Satan, we here find Freud himself once again, Freud, to whom Foucault leaves a choice between only two roles: the bad genius and the good one. And what we have here is another chiasm: in the rhetoric of the few lines that I will read in a moment, one will not be surprised to see that the accused, the one who is the most directly targeted by the indictment—for no amount of denying will make us forget that we are dealing here with a trial and a verdict—is the "good genius of Freud" and not his "bad genius." Why so? In the final pages of the first volume of *The History of Sexuality*, the accusation of pansexualism that was often leveled against psychoanalysis naturally comes up. Those most blind in this regard, says Foucault, were not those who denounced pansexualism out of prudishness. Their only error was to have attributed "solely to the *bad genius* [*mauvais génie*] of Freud what had already gone through a long stage of preparation" (*VS*, p. 210; *HS*, p. 159; my emphasis). The opposite error, the symmetrical lure, corresponds to a more serious mystification. It is the illusion that could be called emancipatory, the aberration of the Enlightenment, the misguided notion on the part of those who believed that Freud, the *"good genius"* of Freud, had finally freed sex from its repression by power. These

> were mistaken concerning the nature of the process; they be-
> lieved that Freud had at last, through a sudden reversal, restored
> to sex the rightful share which it had been denied for so long;
> they had not seen how the *good genius* of Freud had placed it at
> one of the critical points marked out for it since the eighteenth
> century by the strategies of knowledge and power, how wonder-
> fully effective he was . . . in giving a new impetus to the secular
> injunction to study sex and transform it into discourse. [*VS*,
> p. 210; *HS*, p. 159; my emphasis][21]

The "good genius" of Freud would thus be worse than the bad one. It would have consisted in getting itself well placed, in spotting the best place in an old strategy of knowledge and power.

21. It is perhaps appropriate to recall here the lines immediately following this, the last in the first volume of *The History of Sexuality*. They unequivocally describe this sort of Christian teleology or, more precisely, modern Christianity (as opposed to "an old Christianity") whose completion would, in some sense, be marked by psychoanalysis:

> the secular injunction to study sex and transform it into discourse. We are often reminded of the countless procedures which an old Christianity once employed to make us detest the body; but let us ponder all the ruses that were employed for cen- turies to make us love sex, to make the knowledge of it desirable and everything said about it precious. Let us consider the stratagems by which we were induced to apply all our skills to discovering its secrets, by which we were attached to the obligation to draw out its truth, and made guilty for having failed to recognize it for so long. These devices are what ought to make us wonder today. Moreover, we need to consider the possibility that one day, perhaps, in a different economy of bodies and pleasures, people will no longer quite understand how the ruses of sexuality, and the power that sustains its organization, were able to subject us to that austere monarchy of sex, so that we became dedicated to the endless task of forcing its secret, of exacting the truest of confessions from a shadow.
> The irony of this deployment is in having us believe that our "liberation" is in the balance. [*VS*, pp. 210–11; *HS*, p. 159]

Some might be tempted to relate this conclusion to that of *The Order of Things*, to everything that is said there about the *end* and about its *tomorrow*, about man "nearing his end" right up to this "day" when, as *The History of Sexuality* says, "in a different economy of bodies and pleasures, people will no longer quite understand how," and so on. It is difficult not to hear in the rhetoric and tonality of such a call, in the apocalyptic and eschatological tone of this promise (even if "we can at the moment do no more than sense the possibility [of this event]—without knowing either what its form will be or what it promises" [*MC*, p. 398; *OT*, p. 387]), a certain resonance with the Christianity and Christian humanism whose end is being announced.

Whatever questions it might leave unanswered—and I will speak in just a moment of one of those it suscitates in me—this project appears nonetheless exciting, necessary, and courageous. And I would not want any particular reservation on my part to be too quickly classified among the reactions of those who hastened to defend the threatened privilege of the pure invention of psychoanalysis, that is, of an invention that would be *pure*, of a psychoanalysis that one might still dream would have inno-cently sprung forth already outfitted, helmeted, armed, in short, outside all history, after the epistemological cutting of the cord, as one used to say, indeed, after the unraveling of the navel of the dream. Foucault himself during an interview seemed to be ready for some sort of com-promise on this issue, readily and good-spiritedly acknowledging the "impasses" (this was his word) of his concept of *episteme* and the dif-ficulties into which this new project had led him.[22] But only those who work, only those who take risks in working, encounter difficulties. One only ever thinks and takes responsibility—if indeed one ever does—in the testing of the aporia; without this, one is content to follow an incli-nation or apply a program. And it would not be very generous, indeed it would be especially naive and imprudent, to take advantage of these avowals, to take them literally, and to forget what Foucault himself tells us about the confessional scene.

The question that I would have liked to formulate would thus not aim to protect psychoanalysis against some new attack, nor even to cast the slightest doubt upon the importance, necessity, and legitimacy of Foucault's extremely interesting project concerning this great history of sexuality. My question would only seek—and this would be, in sum, a sort of modest contribution—to complicate somewhat an axiomatic and, on the basis of this perhaps, certain discursive or conceptual proce-dures, particularly regarding the way in which this axiomatic is inscribed in its age, in the historical field that serves as a point of departure, and in its reference to psychoanalysis. In a word, without compromising in the least the necessity of reinscribing almost "all" psychoanalysis (as-suming one could seriously say such a thing, which I do not believe one can: psychoanalysis *itself*, *all* psychoanalysis, *the whole truth about all* psychoanalysis) into a history that precedes and exceeds it, it would be

22. See "Le Jeu de Michel Foucault," *Ornicar?* 10 (July 1977): 62–93; ed. Alain Grosrichard, under the title "The Confessions of the Flesh," *Power/Knowledge: Selected Interviews and Other Writings, 1972–77*, trans. Colin Gordon et al., ed. Gordon (New York, 1980), esp. pp. 196–97.

a question of becoming interested in certain gestures, in certain works, in certain moments of certain works of psychoanalysis, Freudian and post-Freudian (for one cannot, especially in France, seriously treat this subject by limiting oneself to a strictly Freudian discourse and apparatus), in certain traits of a consequently nonglobalizable psychoanalysis, one that is divided and multiple (like the powers that Foucault ceaselessly reminds us are essentially dispersed). It would then be a question of admitting that these necessarily fragmentary or disjointed movements say and do, provide resources for saying and doing, what *The History of Sexuality* (*The Will to Knowledge*) wishes to say, what it *means* [*veut dire*], and what it wishes to do (to know and to make known) with regard to psychoanalysis. In other words, if one still wanted to speak in terms of age—something that I would only ever do in the form of citation—at this point, here on this line, concerning some trait that is on the side from out of which the history of sexuality is written rather than on the side of what it describes or objectifies, one would have to say that Foucault's project belongs too much to "the age of psychoanalysis" in its possibility for it, when claiming to thematize psychoanalysis, to do anything other than let psychoanalysis continue to speak obliquely of itself and to mark one of its folds in a scene that I will not call self-referential or specular but whose structural complication I will not here try to describe (I have tried to do this elsewhere). This is not only because of what withdraws this history from the regime of representation (because of what already inscribes the possibility of this history in and since the age of Freud and Heidegger—to use these names as mere indications for the sake of convenience). It is also for a reason that interests us here more directly: what Foucault announces and denounces about the relation between pleasure and power, in what he calls the "double impetus: pleasure and power" (*VS*, p. 62; *HS*, p. 45), would find, already in Freud, to say nothing of those who followed, discussed, transformed, and displaced him, the very resources for the objection leveled against the "good genius," the so very bad "good genius," of the father of psychoanalysis. I will situate this with just a word in order to conclude.

Foucault had clearly cautioned us: this history of sexuality was not to be a historian's history. A "genealogy of desiring man" was to be neither a history of representations nor a history of behaviors or sexual practices. This would lead one to think that sexuality cannot become an object of history without seriously affecting the historian's practice and the concept of history. Moreover, Foucault puts quotation marks

around the word *sexuality*: "the quotation marks have a certain importance," he adds.[23] We are thus also dealing here with the history of a
word, with its usages starting in the nineteenth century and the reformu-
lation of the vocabulary in relation to a large number of other phenomena, from biological mechanisms to traditional and new norms, to the
institutions that support these, be they religious, juridical, pedagogical,
or medical (for example, psychoanalytic). This history of the uses of a
word is neither nominalist nor essentialist. It concerns procedures and,
more precisely, zones of "problematization." It is a "history of truth"
as a history of *problematizations*, and even as an "archeology of problematizations," "through which being offers itself as something that can
and must be thought."[24] The point is to analyze not simply behaviors,
ideas, or ideologies but, first of all, these *problematizations* in which a
thought of being intersects "practices" and "practices of the self," a "genealogy of practices of the self" through which these problematizations
are formed. With its reflexive vigilance and care in thinking itself in its
rigorous specificity, such an analysis thus calls for the *problematization
of its own problematization*. This latter must *itself* also question itself,
and with the same archaeological and genealogical care, the same care
that it itself methodically prescribes.

When confronted with a historical problematization of such scope
and thematic richness, one should not be satisfied with a mere survey,
nor with asking in just a few minutes an overarching question so as
to insure some sort of synoptic mastery. What we can and must try to
do in such a situation is to pay tribute to a work that is this great and
this uncertain by means of a question that it itself raises, by means of a
question that it carries within itself, that it keeps in reserve in its unlimited potential, one of the questions that can thus be deciphered within
it, a question that keeps it in suspense, holding its breath [*tient . . . en
haleine*]—and, thus, keeps it alive.

One of these questions, for me, for example, would be the one I had
tried to formulate a few years ago during a conference honoring Foucault at New York University.[25] It was developed by means of a problematization of the concept of power and of the theme of what Foucault
calls the *spiral* in the duality power/pleasure. Leaving aside the huge
question of the concept of power and of what gives it its alleged unity

23. Foucault, *L'Usage des plaisirs*, p. 9; *The Use of Pleasure*, p. 3.
24. Ibid., pp. 17–19; pp. 11–13.
25. The following analysis thus intersects a much longer treatment of the subject in
an unpublished paper entitled "Beyond the Power Principle" that I presented during
this conference at New York University, organized by Thomas Bishop, in April 1986.

under the essential dispersion rightly recalled by Foucault himself, I will put out only a thread: it would lead to that which, in a certain Freud and at the center of a certain—let's say for the sake of convenience—French heritage of Freud, would not only not let itself be objectified by the Foucauldian problematization but would actually contribute to it in the most determinate and efficient way, thereby deserving to be inscribed on the thematizing rather than on the thematized border of this history of sexuality. I thus have to wonder what Foucault would have said, in this perspective and were he to have taken this into account, not of "Freud" or of psychoanalysis "itself" *in general*—which does not exist any more than power does as one big central and homogeneous corpus—but, for example, since this is only one example, about an undertaking like *Beyond the Pleasure Principle*, about something in its lineage or between its filial connections—along with everything that has been inherited, repeated, or discussed from it since then. In following one of these threads or filial connections, one of the most discreet, in following the abyssal, unassignable, and unmasterable strategy of this text, a strategy that is finally without strategy, one begins to see that this text not only opens up the horizon of a beyond of the pleasure principle (the hypothesis of such a beyond never really seeming to be of interest to Foucault) against which the whole economy of pleasure needs to be rethought, complicated, pursued in its most unrecognizable ruses and detours. By means of one of these filiations—another one unwinding the spool of the *fort/da* that continues to interest us—this text also problematizes, in its greatest radicality, the agency of power and mastery. In a discreet and difficult passage, an original drive for power or drive for mastery (*Bemächtigungstrieb*) is mentioned. It is very difficult to know if this drive for power is still dependent upon the pleasure principle, indeed, upon sexuality as such, upon the austere monarchy of sex that Foucault speaks of on the last page of his book.

How would Foucault have situated this drive for mastery in his discourse on power or on irreducibly plural powers? How would he have read this drive, had he read it, in this extremely enigmatic text of Freud? How would he have interpreted the recurring references to the demonic from someone who then makes himself, according to his own terms, the "devil's advocate" and who becomes interested in the hypothesis of a late or derived appearance of sex and sexual pleasure? In the whole problematization whose history he describes, how would Foucault have inscribed this passage from *Beyond the Pleasure Principle*, and this concept and these questions (with all the debates to which this book of Freud either directly or indirectly gave rise, in a sort of critical capitalization, particularly in the France of our age, beginning with everything in Lacan that takes its point of departure in the repetition compulsion [*Wiederholungszwang*])? Would he have inscribed this problematic matrix *within* the whole whose history he describes? Or would he have put it on the other side, on the side of what allows one on the contrary to delimit the whole, indeed to problematize it? And thus on a side that no longer belongs to the whole, nor, as I would be tempted to think, to any whole, such that the very idea of a gathering of problematization or procedure, to say nothing any longer of age, *episteme*, paradigm, or epoch, would make for so many problematic names, just as problematic as the very idea of problematization?

This is one of the questions that I would have liked to ask him. I am trying, since this is, unfortunately, the only recourse left us in the solitude of questioning, to imagine the principle of the reply. It would perhaps be something like this: what one must stop believing in is principality or principleness, in the problematic of the principle, in the principled unity of pleasure and power, or of some drive that is thought to be more originary than the other. The theme of the *spiral* would be that of a drive duality (power/pleasure) that is *without principle*.

It is *the spirit of this spiral* that keeps one in suspense, holding one's breath—and, thus, keeps one alive.

The question would thus once again be given a new impetus: is not the duality in question, this spiralled duality, what Freud tried to oppose to all monisms by speaking of a dual drive and of a death drive, of a death drive that was no doubt not alien to the drive for mastery? And, thus, to what is most alive in life, to its very living on [*survivance*]?

I am still trying to imagine Foucault's response. I can't quite do it. I would need him to take it on himself.

But in this place where no one can answer for him, in the absolute silence where we remain nonetheless turned toward him, I would venture to bet that, in a sentence that I will not construct for him, he would have associated and yet also dissociated, he would have placed back to back, mastery and death, that is, the same—death *and* the master, death *as* the master.

10 Adieu

Translated by Pascale-Anne Brault and Michael Naas

For a long time, for a very long time, I've feared having to say *adieu* to Emmanuel Levinas. I knew that my voice would tremble at the moment of saying it, and especially saying it aloud, right here, before him, so close to him, pronouncing this word of *adieu*, this word "*à-Dieu*," which in a certain sense I get from him, a word that he will have taught me to think or to pronounce otherwise. By meditating upon what Emmanuel Levinas wrote about the French word "*adieu*"—which I will recall in a few moments—I hope to find a sort of encouragement to speak here. And I would like to do so with unadorned, naked words, words as childlike and disarmed as my sorrow.

Yet whom would one be addressing at such a moment? And in whose name would one allow oneself to do so? Oftentimes, those who come forward to speak, to speak publicly, thereby interrupting the animated whispering, the secret or intimate exchange that always links one deep down inside to the dead friend or master, those who can be heard in a cemetery, end up addressing *directly, straight on*, the one who, as we say, is no longer, is no longer living, no longer there, who will no longer respond; with tears in their voice, they sometimes speak

familiarly [*tutoient*] to the other who keeps silent, calling upon him
without detour or mediation, apostrophizing him, greeting him even or
confiding in him. This is not necessarily out of respect for convention,
not always simply part of the rhetoric of oration. It is rather so as to traverse speech at the very point where we find ourselves lacking the words,
and because all language that would return to the self, to us, would seem
indecent, a sort of reflexive discourse that would end up coming back
to the stricken community, to its consolation or its mourning, to what
is called, in this confused and terrible expression, "the work of mourning." Concerned only with itself, such speech would, in this return, run
the risk of turning away from what is here our law—and the law as
straightforwardness or *uprightness* [*droiture*]: to speak straight on, to
address oneself directly *to* the other, and to speak *for* the other whom
one loves and admires, before speaking *of* him. To say to him *adieu*, to
him, Emmanuel, and not merely to recall what he will have first taught
us about a certain *Adieu*.

This word *droiture*—"straightforwardness" or "uprightness"—is
another word that I began to hear otherwise and to learn when it came
to me from Emmanuel Levinas. Of all the places where he speaks of
uprightness, what comes to mind first is one of his *Four Talmudic Readings*, since it is there that uprightness names that which is, as he says,
"stronger than death."

But let us also keep from trying to find in everything that is said to
be "stronger than death" a refuge or an alibi, yet another consolation.
To define uprightness, Emmanuel Levinas says in his commentary on the
"Tractate *Shabbath*" that consciousness is the "urgency of a destination
leading to the Other and not an eternal return to self,"

> an innocence without naivete, an uprightness without stupid-
> ity, an absolute uprightness which is also absolute self-criticism,
> read in the eyes of the one who is the goal of my uprightness
> and whose look calls me into question. It is a movement toward
> the other that does not come back to its point of origin the way
> diversion comes back, incapable as it is of transcendence—a
> movement beyond anxiety and stronger than death. This up-
> rightness is called *Temimut*, the essence of Jacob.[1]

1. Emmanuel Levinas, *Quatre Lectures Talmudiques* (Paris, 1968), p. 105; trans.
Annette Aronowicz, under the title "Four Talmudic Readings," *Nine Talmudic Readings*
(Bloomington, Ind., 1990), p. 48.

This same meditation also set to work—as each meditation did, though each in a singular way—all the great themes to which the thought of Emmanuel Levinas has awakened us, that of responsibility first of all, but of an "unlimited" responsibility that exceeds and precedes my freedom, that of an "unconditional yes," as this text says, of a "*yes* older than that of naive spontaneity," a *yes* in accord with this uprightness that is "original fidelity to an indissoluble alliance."[2] And the final words of this Lesson return, of course, to death, but they do so precisely so as not to let death have the last word, or the first one. They remind us of a recurrent theme in what was a long and incessant meditation upon death, but one that set out on a path that ran counter to the philosophical tradition running from Plato to Heidegger. Elsewhere, before saying what the *à-Dieu* must be, another text speaks of the "extreme uprightness of the face of my neighbor" as the "uprightness of an exposure to death, without any defense."[3]

I cannot find, and would not even want to try to find, a few words to size up the oeuvre of Emmanuel Levinas. It is so large that one can no longer even see its edges. And one would have to begin by learning once again from him and from *Totality and Infinity*, for example, how to think what an "oeuvre" or "work" is—as well as fecundity. Moreover, one can predict with a certain confidence that centuries of readings will set this as their task. Already, well beyond France and Europe—and we see innumerable signs of this every day in so many works and in so many languages, in all the translations, courses, seminars, conferences, and so on—the reverberations of this thought will have changed the course of the philosophical reflection of our time, and of the reflection *on* philosophy, on that which orders it according to ethics, according to another thought of ethics, responsibility, justice, the state, and so on, another thought of the other, a thought that is newer than so many novelties because it is ordered to the absolute anteriority of the face of the Other.

Yes, ethics before and beyond ontology, the state, or politics, but also ethics beyond ethics. One day, on the rue Michel Ange, during one of those conversations whose memory I hold so dear, one of those conversations illuminated by the radiance of his thought, the goodness of his smile, the gracious humor of his ellipses, he said to me: "You know, one often speaks of ethics to describe what I do, but what really interests

2. Ibid., pp. 106–8; pp. 49–50.
3. Levinas, "La Conscience non-intentionnelle," *Entre nous: Essais sur le penser-à-l'autre* (Paris, 1991), p. 149; hereafter abbreviated "C."

me in the end is not ethics, not ethics alone, but the holy, the holiness of the holy." And I then thought of a singular separation, the unique separation of the curtain or veil that is given, ordered and ordained [*donné, ordonné*], by God, the veil entrusted by Moses to an inventor or an artist rather than to an embroiderer, the veil that would *separate* the holy of holies in the sanctuary. And I also thought of how other *Talmudic Lessons* sharpen the necessary distinction between sacredness and holiness, that is, the holiness of the other, the holiness of the person, who is, as Emmanuel Levinas said elsewhere, "more holy than a land, even a holy land, since, faced with an affront made to a person, this holy land appears in its nakedness to be but stone and wood."[4]

This meditation on ethics, on the transcendence of the holy with regard to the sacred, that is, with regard to the paganism of roots and the idolatry of place, was, of course, indissociable from an incessant reflection upon the destiny and thought of Israel, yesterday, today, and tomorrow. Such reflection consisted in a requestioning and reaffirmation of the legacies of not only the biblical and talmudic tradition but of the terrifying memory of our time. This memory dictates each of these sentences, whether from close or from afar, even if Levinas would sometimes protest against certain self-justifying abuses to which such a memory and the reference to the Holocaust might give rise.

But refraining from commentaries and questions, I would simply like to give thanks to someone whose thought, friendship, trust, and "goodness" (and I ascribe to this word *goodness* all the significance it is given in the final pages of *Totality and Infinity*) will have been for me, as for so many others, a living source, so living, so constant, that I am unable to think what is happening to him or happening to me today, namely, this interruption or a certain nonresponse in a response that will never come to an end for me as long as I live.

The nonresponse: you will no doubt recall that in the remarkable course he gave in 1975–76 (exactly twenty years ago) on *Death and Time*, there where he defines death as the patience of time, and where he engages in a grand and noble critical encounter with Plato as much as with Hegel, but especially with Heidegger, Emmanuel Levinas there often defines death, the death that "we meet" "in the face of the Other," as *nonresponse*; "it is the without-response," he says. And elsewhere: "There is here an end that always has the ambiguity of a departure with-

---

4. Schlomo Malka, interview with Levinas, *Les Nouveaux Cahiers* 18 (1982–83): 1–8; trans. Jonathan Romney, in *The Levinas Reader*, ed. Seán Hand (Cambridge, Mass., 1989), p. 297.

out return, of a passing away but also of a scandal ('is it really possible that he's dead?') of non-response and of my responsibility."[5]

Death: not first of all annihilation, nonbeing, or nothingness, but a certain experience for the survivor of the "without-response." Already *Totality and Infinity* called into question the traditional "philosophical and religious" interpretation of death as either "a passage to nothingness" or "a passage to some other existence."[6] To identify death with nothingness is what the murderer would like to do, Cain for example, who, says Emmanuel Levinas, must have had such a knowledge of death. But even this nothingness presents itself as a "sort of impossibility" or, more precisely, an interdiction. The face of the Other forbids me from killing; it says to me "you shall not kill," even if this possibility remains presupposed by the interdiction that makes it impossible. This question without response, this question of the without-response, would thus be underivable, primordial, like the interdiction against killing, more originary than the alternative of "to be or not to be," which is thus neither the first nor the last question. "To be or not to be," another essay concludes, "is probably not the question par excellence" ("C," p. 151).

I draw from all this today that our infinite sadness must shy away from everything in mourning that would turn toward nothingness, that is, toward that which still—even potentially—links guilt to murder. Levinas indeed speaks of the guilt of the survivor, but it is a guilt without fault and without debt; it is, in truth, an *entrusted responsibility*, entrusted in a moment of unparalleled emotion, at the moment when death remains the absolute ex-ception. To express this unprecedented emotion, the one I feel here and share with you, the one that our sense of propriety forbids us from exhibiting, and so as to make clear without personal avowal or exhibition how this singular emotion is related to this entrusted responsibility, entrusted as legacy, allow me once again to let Emmanuel Levinas speak, he whose voice I would so much love to hear today when it says that the "death of the other" is the "first death," and that "I am responsible for the other insofar as he is mortal." Or else the following, from this same course of 1975–76:

> The death of someone is not, in spite of what it appeared to be at first glance, an empirical facticity (death as an empirical fact

---

5. Levinas, *La Mort et le temps* (Paris, 1991), pp. 10, 13, 41–42; hereafter abbreviated *MT*.

6. Levinas, *Totalité et infini* (The Hague, 1961), pp. 208–9; trans. Alphonso Lingis, under the title *Totality and Infinity* (Pittsburgh, 1969), p. 232.

whose induction alone could suggest its universality); it is not exhausted in such an appearance. Someone who expresses himself in his nakedness—the face—is in fact one to the extent that he calls upon me, to the extent that he places himself under my responsibility: I must already answer for him, be responsible for him. Every gesture of the Other was a sign addressed to me. To return to the classification sketched out above: to show oneself, to express oneself, to associate oneself, *to be entrusted to me.* The Other who expresses himself is entrusted to me (and there is no debt with regard to the Other—for that which is due cannot be paid: one will never be even) [further on it will be a question of a "duty beyond all debt" for the I who is what it is, singular and identifiable, only through the impossibility of being able to be replaced, even though it is precisely here that the "responsibility for the Other," the "responsibility of the hostage," is an experience of substitution and sacrifice]. The Other individuates me in that responsibility that I have for him. The death of the Other who dies affects me in my very identity as a responsible I . . . made up of unspeakable responsibility. This is how I am affected by the death of the Other, this is my relation with his death. It is, in my relation, my deference toward someone who no longer responds, already a guilt of the survivor. [*MT*, pp. 14–15; quotation in brackets, p. 25]

And a bit further on:

> The relation to death in its ex-ception—and, regardless of its signification in relation to being and nothingness, it is an exception—while conferring upon death its depth, is neither a seeing nor even an aiming towards (neither a seeing of being as in Plato nor an aiming towards nothingness as in Heidegger), a purely emotional relation, moving with an emotion that is not made up of the repercussions of a prior knowledge upon our sensibility and our intellect. It is an emotion, a movement, an uneasiness with regard to the *unknown*. [*MT*, pp. 18–19]

The unknown is here emphasized. The unknown is not the negative limit of some knowledge. This nonknowledge is the element of friendship or hospitality for the transcendence of the stranger, the infinite distance of the other. "Unknown" is the word chosen by Maurice Blanchot for the title of an essay, "Knowledge of the Unknown," which he devoted to the one who had been, from the time of their meeting in Strasbourg in 1923, the friend, the very friendship of the friend. For many among us, no doubt, for myself certainly, the absolute fidelity, the exemplary friendship of thought, the *friendship* between Maurice Blanchot and Emmanuel Levinas was a grace, a gift; it remains as a benediction of this time, and, for more than one reason, the good fortune that is also a blessing for all those who have had the great privilege of being the friend of either one of them. In order to hear once again today, right here, Blanchot speak for Levinas, and with Levinas, as I had the good fortune to do when in their company one day in 1968, I will cite a couple of lines. After having named that which in the other "ravishes" us, after having spoken of a certain "rapture" (the word often used by Levinas to speak of death), Blanchot says:

> But we must not despair of philosophy. In Emmanuel Levinas's book [*Totality and Infinity*]—where, it seems to me, philosophy in our time has never spoken in a more sober manner, putting back into question, as we must, our ways of thinking and even our facile reverence for ontology—we are called upon to become responsible for what philosophy essentially is, by welcoming, in all the radiance and infinite exigency proper to it, the idea of the Other, that is to say, the relation with *autrui*. It is as though there were here a new departure in philosophy and a leap that it, and we ourselves, were urged to accomplish.[7]

If the relation to the other presupposes an infinite separation, an infinite interruption where the face appears, what happens, where and to whom does it happen, when another interruption comes at death to hollow out with even more infinity this prior separation, a rending interruption at the heart of interruption itself? I cannot speak of the interruption without recalling, like many among you no doubt, the anxiety of interruption that I could feel in Emmanuel Levinas when, on the telephone for example, he seemed at each moment to fear being cut off, to fear the silence or disappearance, the "without-response," of the other whom he tried to call out to and hold on to with an "allo, allo" between each sentence, and sometimes even in midsentence.

7. Maurice Blanchot, *L'Entretien infini* (Paris, 1969), pp. 73–74; trans. Susan Hanson, under the title *The Infinite Conversation* (Minneapolis, 1993), pp. 51–52.

What happens when a great thinker becomes silent, one whom we knew living, whom we read and reread, and also heard, one from whom we were still awaiting a response, as if such a response would help us not only to think otherwise but also to read what we thought we had already read under his signature, a response that held everything in reserve, and so much more than what we thought we had already recognized in that signature? This is an experience that, I have learned, would remain for me interminable with Emmanuel Levinas, as with all thoughts that are sources, for I will never stop beginning or beginning anew to think with them on the basis of the new beginning they give me, and I will begin again and again to rediscover them on just about any subject. Each time I read or reread Emmanuel Levinas, I am overwhelmed with gratitude and admiration, overwhelmed by this necessity, which is not a constraint but an extremely gentle force that obligates and obligates us not to bend or curve otherwise the space of thought in its respect for the other but to yield to this other heteronomous curvature that relates us to the completely other (that is, to justice, as he says somewhere in a powerful and formidable ellipsis: the relation to the other, that is to say, justice), according to the law that thus calls us to yield to the other infinite precedence of the completely other. It will have come, like this call, to disturb, discreetly but irreversibly, the most powerful and established thoughts of the end of this millennium, beginning with those of Husserl and Heidegger whom Levinas in fact introduced into France some sixty-five years ago! Indeed, this country whose hospitality he so much loved (and *Totality and Infinity* shows not only that "the essence of language is goodness" but that "the essence of language is friendship and hospitality"),[8] this hospitable France, owes him, among so many other things, among so many other significant contributions, at least two irruptive events of thought, two inaugural acts that are difficult to measure today because they have been so much incorporated into the very element of our philosophical culture after having transformed its landscape.

There was first, to say it all too quickly, beginning in 1930 with translations and interpretative readings, the initial introduction to Husserlian phenomenology, which would in turn irrigate and fecundate so many French philosophical currents. Then, and in truth simultaneously, there was the introduction to Heideggerian thought, which was no less important in the genealogy of so many French philosophers, professors, and students. Husserl and Heidegger at the same time, beginning

8. Levinas, *Totalité et infini*, p. 282; Levinas, *Totality and Infinity*, p. 305.

in 1930. I wanted last night to reread a few pages from this prodigious book that was for me, as for many others before me, the first and best guide. I picked out a few sentences that have made their mark in time and that allow us to measure the distance he will have helped us cover. In 1930, a young man of twenty-three said in the preface that I reread, and reread smiling, smiling at him: "The fact that in France phenomenology is not a doctrine known to everyone has been a constant problem in the writing of this book." Or again, speaking of the so very "powerful and original philosophy" of "Mr. Martin Heidegger, whose influence on this book will often be felt," the same book also recalls that "the problem raised here by transcendental phenomenology is an ontological problem in the very precise sense that Heidegger gives to this term."[9]

The second event, the second philosophical tremor, I would even say the happy traumatism that we owe him (in the sense of the word *traumatism* that he liked to recall, the "traumatism of the other" that comes from the Other), is that, while closely reading and reinterpreting the thinkers I just mentioned, but so many others as well, both philosophers such as Descartes, Kant, and Kierkegaard, and writers such as Dostoyevsky, Kafka, Proust, and so on—all the while disseminating his words through publications, courses, and lectures (at the École Normale Israélite Orientale, at the Collège Philosophique, and at the Universities of Poitiers, Nanterre, and the Sorbonne)—Emmanuel Levinas slowly displaced, but so as to bend them according to an inflexible and simple exigency, the axis, trajectory, and even the order of phenomenology or ontology that he had introduced into France beginning in 1930. Once again, he completely changed the landscape without landscape of thought; he did so in a dignified way, without polemic, at once from within, faithfully, and from very far away, from the attestation of a completely other place. And I believe that what occurred there, in this second sailing, in this second time that leads us even further back than the first, is a discreet but irreversible mutation, one of those very powerful, very singular, and very rare provocations within history that, for over two thousand years now, will have ineffaceably marked the space and body of what is more or less, or in any case something different than, a simple dialogue between Jewish thought and its others, the phi-

---

9. Levinas, *Théorie de l'intuition dans la phénoménologie de Husserl* (1930; Paris, 1970), pp. 7, 14–15; trans. André Orianne, under the title *The Theory of Intuition in Husserl's Phenomenology*, (Evanston, Ill., 1973), pp. xxxiv. As the translator notes, Levinas's short preface, or "Avant-Propos," was omitted from the translation and replaced by the translator's foreword so as to include a series of "historical remarks more specifically directed to today's English reader" (p. xxvii).

losophies of Greek origin or, in the tradition of a certain "here I am," the other Abrahamic monotheisms. This happened, this mutation happened, *through him*, through Emmanuel Levinas, who was conscious of this immense responsibility in a way that was, I believe, at once clear, confident, calm, and modest, like that of a prophet.

One of the indications of this historical shock wave is the influence of this thought well beyond philosophy, and well beyond Jewish thought, in various circles of Christian theology, for example. I cannot help but recall the day when, during a meeting of the Congrès des Intellectuels Juifs, as we were both listening to a lecture by André Neher, Emmanuel Levinas turned to me and said with the gentle irony so familiar to us: "You see, he's the Jewish Protestant and I'm the Catholic"—a quip that would call for long and serious reflection.

Everything that has happened here has happened through him, thanks to him, and we have had the good fortune not only of receiving it while living, from him living, as a responsibility entrusted by the living to the living, but also the good fortune of owing it to him with a light and innocent debt. One day, speaking of his research on death and of what it owed Heidegger at the very moment when it was moving away from him, Levinas wrote: "It distinguishes itself from Heidegger's thought, and it does so in spite of the debt that every contemporary thinker owes to Heidegger—a debt that one often regrets" (*MT*, p. 8). Now, the good fortune of our debt toward Levinas is that we can, thanks to him, assume it and affirm it without regret, in the joyous innocence of admiration. It is of the order of this unconditional *yes* of which I spoke earlier and to which it responds "yes." The regret, my regret, is not having said this to him enough, not having shown him this enough in the course of these thirty years, during which, in the modesty of silences, through brief or discreet conversations, writings that were too indirect or reserved, we often addressed to one another what I would call neither questions nor answers but, perhaps, to use another one of his words, a sort of "question, prayer," a question-prayer that, as he says, would be anterior even to the dialogue. This question-prayer that turned me toward him perhaps already shared in this experience of the *à-Dieu* with which I began earlier. The greeting of the *à-Dieu* does not signal the end. "The *à-Dieu* is not a finality," he says, thus challenging this "alternative between being and nothingness," which "is not ultimate." The *à-Dieu* greets the other beyond being, in "what signifies, beyond being, the word glory." "The *à-Dieu* is not a process of being; in the call, I am referred back to the other human being through whom this call signifies, to the neighbor for whom I am to fear" ("C," p. 150).

But I said that I did not want simply to recall what he entrusted to us of the *à-Dieu* but first of all to say *adieu* to him, to call him by his name, to call his name, his first name, such as he is called at the moment when, if he no longer responds, it is because he responds in us, from the bottom of our hearts, in us but before us, in us right before us—in calling us, in recalling to us: "à-Dieu."

Adieu, Emmanuel.

11

By Force of Mourning

Translated by Pascale-Anne Brault and Michael Naas

Who could ever speak of the work of Louis Marin?

Who would already know how to speak of the works of Louis Marin and of all the work that bore them, a work without measure?

Work: that which makes for a work, for an *oeuvre*, indeed that which works—and works to open: *opus* and *opening*, *oeuvre* and *overture*: the work or labor of the *oeuvre* insofar as it engenders, produces, and brings to light, but also labor or travail as suffering, as the enduring of force, as the pain of the one who gives. Of the one who gives birth, who brings to the light of day and gives something to be seen, who enables or empowers, who gives the force to know and to be able to see—and all these are powers of the image, the pain of what is given and of the one who takes the pains to help us see, read, and think.

Who could ever speak of all the work and works of Louis Marin?

As for this work—but what does one do when one works?

When one works *on* work, on the work of mourning, when one works at the work of mourning, one is already, yes, already, *doing* such work, enduring this work of mourning from the very start, letting it work within oneself, and thus authorizing oneself to do it, according it to oneself, according it within oneself, and giving oneself this liberty of finitude, the most worthy and the freest possible.

One cannot hold a discourse *on* the "work of mourning" without taking part in it, without announcing or partaking in [*se faire part de*] death, and first of all in one's own death. In the announcement of one's own death, which says, in short, "I am dead," "I died"—such as this book lets it be heard—one should be able to say, and I have tried to say this in the past, that all work is also the work of mourning. All work in general works *at mourning*. In and of itself. Even when it has the power to give birth, even and especially when it plans to bring something to light and let it be seen. The work of mourning is not one kind of work among other possible kinds; an activity of the kind "work" is by no means a specific figure for production in general.

There is thus no metalanguage for the language in which a work of mourning is at work. This is also why one should not be able to say anything about the work of mourning, anything about this subject, since it cannot become a theme, only another experience of mourning that comes to work over the one who intends to speak. To speak of mourning or of anything else. And that is why whoever thus works *at* the work of mourning learns the impossible—and that mourning is interminable. Inconsolable. Irreconcilable. Right up until death—that is what whoever works at mourning knows, working at mourning as both their object and their resource, working *at mourning* as one would speak of a painter working *at a painting* but also of a machine working *at such and such an energy level*, the theme of work thus becoming their very force, and their term, a principle.

What might be this principle of mourning? And what was its force? What is, what will have been, what will still be tomorrow, the energy of Louis Marin?

Let us begin by letting him speak. Here are a few words, his words, that say something difficult to understand. They advance a truth, advance toward a singular aporia that Louis Marin states or rather announces precisely on the subject of "mourning."

It says, and for the moment I cite just part of a sentence, as if it were all of a sudden suspended, an interruption coming to take its breath away:

the modalities of a work of mourning of the absolute of "force."[1]

This fragment of a long sentence by Louis Marin names—and we thus repeat it—"the modalities of a work of mourning of the absolute of 'force.'"

Five nouns linked together, which can be read as the scanned filiation of a single genitive in the preface of his last book. And never before had I paid attention to the terrible ambiguity of this expression "the last book" of Louis Marin. It makes it impossible to decide between the final book and simply the most recent one, the last one to have come out. For there will be others. This one will simply be the last to have come out, though we know that those that will come out later will have been completed before this one, which will thus remain in the end, and forever, the last one. Forever. From now on the final one.

The preface to *Des pouvoirs de l'image: Gloses* thus announces and pronounces that it will address the "modalities of a work of mourning of the absolute of 'force.'" The slow and cautious procession, the vigilant theory of these complements of the noun leave no determination exempt from analysis. If the word "force" is here in quotation marks, it is for a good reason; it is because the mourning in question and the so-called work of mourning are not self-evident; they go beyond understanding in some way, they go past the usual understanding of this word "force," indeed, they just don't quite go. It is a question, in truth, of the impossible itself. And that is why I took the risk of speaking a moment ago of an aporia. You will also understand, for this is the law, the law of mourning, and the law of the law, always in mourning, that it would have to fail in order to succeed. In order to succeed, it would well have to *fail*, to fail *well*. It would well have to fail, for this is what has to be so, in failing *well*. That is what would have to be. And while it is always promised, it will never be assured.

In the era of psychoanalysis, we all of course speak, and we can always go on speaking, about the "successful" work of mourning—or, inversely, as if it were precisely the contrary, about a "melancholia" that would signal the failure of such work. But if we are to follow Louis Marin, here comes a work without force, a work that would have to work at renouncing force, its own force, a work that would have to work at failure, and thus at mourning and getting over force, a work working at its own unproductivity, absolutely, working to absolve or

1. Louis Marin, *Des pouvoirs de l'image: Gloses* (Paris, 1993), pp. 16–17; hereafter abbreviated *P*.

to absolve itself of whatever might be absolute about "force," and thus of something like "force" itself: "a work of mourning of the absolute of 'force,'" says Louis Marin, keeping the word "force" between quotation marks that just won't let go. It is a question of the absolute renunciation of the absolute of force, of the absolute of force in its impossibility and unavoidability; both at once, as inaccessible as it is ineluctable.

What then is force, absolutely? But also: what is this "without force," this state of being drained, without any force, where death, where the death of a friend, leaves us, when we also have to work at mourning force? Is the "without force," the mourning of force, possible? In the end this is the question Marin leaves us. It is with this question that he leaves us, like rich and powerless heirs, that is, both provided for and at a loss, given over to being forlorn and distraught, full of and fortified by him, responsible and voiceless.

If he leaves us with this question, at least he will have reformulated it in a singular and new way, indicating another path, another way to engage or to be engaged with it, with this proliferating thought that buzzes like a hive. (What is force? force itself, absolute force, if there is any? where does it come from? how does one recognize it? how does one measure it? What is the greatest force? the invulnerable force? And if this infallible force were the place of the greatest weakness, for example, the place of the "defenselessness" of death, of the dead's "defenselessness," of their helplessness, of their "without force," and of the "defenselessness" and thus the "without-force of the survivors faced with death"? what is meant by "force," in quotation marks? what is that?)

Let us look for another way to engage this aporetic question to which there are however so many different points of entry. They all come down to asking in the end what *is* that which is called "force." In the quotation marks that suspend even the assurance of a term of reference, the question would seem to mark out a strange path. Which one? Force itself—by preceding and thus violating in advance, in some sense, the possibility of a question concerning it—force itself would trouble, disturb, dislocate the very form of the question "what is?," the imperturbable "what is?," the authority of what is called the ontological question.

For the powers of the image lead back perhaps in the last resort to this power, to the force of an image that must be protected from every ontology. It would have to be protected from such ontologies because it itself, in truth, protects itself from them; it begins, and this is precisely the force of its force, by tearing itself away from an ontological tradition of the question "what is?" Marin recalls already in the introduction to his book that this tradition itself tended to consider the image as a lesser being, that is, as a being without power, or as a weaker and inferior being, a being of little power, of little force. To submit the image to the question "what is?" would thus already be to miss the image and its force, the image in its force, which has to do perhaps not with what it is or is not, with the fact that it is not or does not have much being, but with the fact that its logic or rather its dynamic, its *dynamis*, the dynasty of its force, will not submit to an onto-logic: its dynamo-logic would no longer be, it would have never been, a logic of being, an ontology. Or rather, to come at it from the other direction, which actually makes more sense: the ontological order (that is, philosophy) would have been constituted as such for not knowing the powers of the image: *for* not knowing or denying them, in the double sense of this "for," that is, *because* it did not take them into account, but also *for* mistaking them, *with a view to* doing so, so as to oppose them, in this most veiled and clandestine war, to the unavowed counterpower of a denial intended to assure an ontological power *over* the image, over the power of the image, over its *dynamis*.

Dynamis: the word seems indispensable. If I emphasize it so forcefully, while Louis Marin uses it only once in his preface as an apposition to the words "force" and "virtue," *virtù* ("the force in the image and of the image, the *virtù*, the virtue, the *dynamis* that 'propels' it to vision" [*P*, p. 18]), it is because this concept plays, it seems to me, a decisive role as soon as it is protected or withdrawn from the traditional ontology that generally dominates it. We will later see that this *dynamis* here links in a most original way the ideas it has always associated, namely, force, power, and *virtù*, with the possible or the virtual *as such*, that is to say, with a virtual that has no vocation to go into action, or rather, whose going into action or whose enactment does not destroy its virtual power.

With what does this have to do (if one can say this, since the logic of the act and of acting, of doing, is precisely what is at stake here)? It would have to do with a possible that is in potential of being only on the condition of remaining possible as possible, and of marking within itself—the scar of a wound and the potentialization of force—the interruption of this going into action, this enactment, an absolute interruption that bears no other seal here than that of death: whence a thought of the *virtual work*, one might also say of a virtual space, of an *opus*, an *opus operatum*, that would accomplish the possible *as such* without effacing it or even enacting it in reality. The thought of a spectral power of the virtual work. One that envelops or develops within itself a thought of death. Only death, which is not, or rather mourning, which takes its place in advance, can open up this space of absolute *dynamis*: force, virtue, the possible as such, without which one understands nothing of the power of the image. And this "understands nothing," this ontological denial, would be nothing other than philosophy itself, which thus cannot be considered to be one conjuring practice among others. For trying to reduce, weaken, and wear out a power of the image so as to subject it to itself, this philosophical exorcism of such powerful scope would—and this would be my hypothesis—in some way *regard* death.

It would regard that which should not be seen, and so denied, namely death. This clandestine war of denial would thus be waged in the shadows, in that twilight space of what is called mourning: the mourning that follows death but also the mourning that is prepared and that we expect from the very beginning to follow upon the death of those we love. Love or friendship would be nothing other than the passion, the endurance, and the patience of this work.

Whence this paradox: when Marin puts a question mark after the being of the image ("The being of the image?" [*P*, p. 10]) and later answers: "The being of the image, in a word, would be its force: but how are we to think this 'force'?," and when he once again puts the word *force* into quotation marks—this would amount to substituting force for being. But the logic of this substitution—and this is the reason for the conditional ("*would be* its force")—itself calls for the quotation marks. *For this force owes it to itself not to be.* It owes it to itself not to be a being. It must thus now be on intimate terms with what is not force, with its opposite, with the "without-force," a domestic and paradoxically necessary commerce being established between them. The greatest force is to be seen in the infinite renunciation of force, in the absolute interruption of force by the without-force. Death, or rather mourning, the mourning of the absolute of force: that is the name, or one of the names, of this affect that unites force to the without-force, thereby relating the manifestation of force, as image, to the being without force of *that which* it manifests or lets be seen, right before our very eyes and according to our mourning.

For what appears most striking from the very opening of this last book, *Des pouvoirs de l'image*, is that it brings about in an irresistible way a double conversion, I dare not say a double reversal. There is first of all the turn or move by which Marin protects the question of the image from the authority of ontology, and this is already a question of force and of power. Then there is the other turn or move whereby this first move finds its truth or its law in—if we can now put it in a non-ontological way—what I would be tempted to call, using a code that would have precisely nothing Heideggerian about it, the being-towards-death of the image. Or, let us say to avoid ambiguity, the *being-to-death* of an image that *has* the force, that *is nothing other than* the force, to *resist, to consist and to exist* in death, precisely there where it does not insist in being or in the presence of being. This *being-to-death* would oblige us to think the image not as the weakened reproduction of what it would imitate, not as a *mimēme*, a simple image, idol, or icon, at least as they are conventionally understood (for it is a question of moving away from this convention), but as the increase of power, the origin, in truth, of authority, the image itself becoming the author, the author and the augmentation of the *auctoritas* insofar as it finds its paradigm, which is also its *enargeia*, in the image of the dead.

In other words, we would not have *images*, a *typology of images* among which a particular class representing the dead or death might be identified. For it would be from death, from what might be called the *point of view of death*, or more precisely, of the dead, the dead man or woman, or more precisely still, from the point of view of the *face* of the dead in their portraiture, that an image would give seeing: not only would give *itself* to be seen but would give insofar as it sees, as if it were seeing as much as seen.

A displacement of the point of view, therefore, which quite obviously inscribes all the essays of this book into the ongoing tradition of work undertaken by Marin for many years concerning that which founds the foundation and institutes the institution of power in a certain logic of representation. And this work, as we all know, allowed him in the course of so many innovative, fertile, and brilliant analyses, to articulate a thought of the theologico-political and a certain icono-semiological theory of representation.

But it seems to me (and this is a reading hypothesis that regards, if I may say this, only me and indicates only a moment of my mournful reading) that in these important developments of earlier research an inflection or break comes to inscribe a paradox. This paradox complicates and in turn illuminates, it seems to me, the earlier trajectory. It concerns the mourning of force or the force of mourning, that is to say, a law according to which the greatest force does not consist in continually expanding ad infinitum but develops its maximal intensity, so to speak, only at the mad moment of decision, at the point of its absolute interruption, there where *dynamis* remains virtuality, namely, a virtual work as such. A moment of infinite renunciation as the potentialization of the virtual work. But the virtual work is not one category of work or image among others; it is the essence of the work, a nonessential essence, since it is an essence that remains possible *as such*. And this is death (or at least that's what this word here signifies—and there where there is no death in itself that would ever be possible as such there is only the experience of mourning without death: mourning is the phenomenon of death and it is the only phenomenon behind which there is nothing; the *phainesthai* of this phenomenon is the only possible access to an original thought of the image, and so on). Here is death, then, there where the image annuls its representative presence, there where, more precisely, the non *re*productive intensity of the *re-* of representation gains in power what the present that it represents loses in presence. And this point, which also punctuates an entire way of thinking the temporalization of time, is evidently the point, not of death itself, but of mourning, and of the mourning of the absolute of force.

If, therefore, the first examples Marin proposes in order to make this power of the image visible and energetic, in order to *illustrate* it, are images of the dead, one should not see here a simply fortuitous occurrence. It is in the *re*-presentation of the dead that the power of the image is exemplary. When Marin asks about this *re-* of representation, about the substitutive value that this *re-* indicates at the moment when that which was present is no longer present and comes to be *re*-presented, and when he then takes the example of the disappearance of the present as death, it is in order not only to track a re-presentation or an absolute substitution of representation for presence but also to detect within it an increase, a re-gaining of force or a supplement of intensity in presence, and thus a sort of potency or potentialization of power for which the schema of substitutive value, of mere replacement, can give no account. Representation is here no longer a simple reproductive re-presentation; it is such a regaining of presence, such a recrudescence or resurgence of presence thereby intensified, that it gives to be thought the lack, the default of presence or the mourning that had hollowed out in advance the so-called primitive or originary presence, the presence that is represented, the so-called living presence.

Here, in a word, is the question of the image, the image put into question, not the question "What is the image?" but "image?" Let us read Marin (*P*, p. 11):

> The prefix *re-* brings into this term the value of substitution. Something that *was* present and *is* no longer is *now* represented. In place of something that is present *elsewhere*, there is here a present, a *given* . . .

[I underscore *elsewhere* here, though we are going to see in a moment that the radical example of death makes of this *elsewhere*, which refers to a Gospel, the metonymy of a possible *nowhere*, or at least of an elsewhere without locality, without a home in presentable space, in the given space of presentation.]

> . . . there is here a present, a *given*: image? . . .

[This single-word question—"image?"—is going to come up more than once. But is it really a question of an image? Can one still speak of an image when representation seems to do more than represent, when it actually gains in intensity and force, when it seems to have even more power than that of which it is said to be the image or the imitation? Marin's response will necessarily be double, *no and yes: no*, it is not simply an image if we are to accept the ontological concept of the image as the mimetic and weakened double of the thing itself; *yes*, for it is the very essence, the proper power, the *dynamis* of the image, if one thinks the image on the basis of death, that is, in truth, on the basis of the mourning that will confer upon it its power and an increase in intensive force. Let us continue this reading.]

> . . . image? Instead of representation, then, there is an absence
> in time or space, or rather an other . . .

[The replacement of "absence" by "other" here no doubt indicates that the substitutive value is no longer operative in the couple "absence/presence" but in the couple "same/other" that introduces the dimension of mourning.]

> . . . an other, and a substitution takes place from an other to
> this other, in its place. Thus in this primitive (or originary) scene
> of the Christian West, the angel at the tomb on the morning of
> the resurrection—"he is not here, he is elsewhere, in Galilee,
> as he had said"—which substitutes a message for this thing,
> for this dead body and its inertia, which makes appear the
> "force" [again in quotation marks, and we will later see why]
> of an utterance whose content is, nonetheless, limited to re-
> marking upon an absence, "he is not here . . . ," the absence of
> the "same" in the heterogeneity of another semiotic potential,
> language.

Let us pause for a moment at this allusion to "the heterogeneity of another semiotic potential, language" in the presentation of the image. It explains and justifies in advance the very form of Marin's book, namely, the necessity of a textual weaving of words and images, the imbrication of glosses sewn upon the iconic tissue: glosses upon glosses that are, in truth, just as originary as the image, as an image that language will have made possible, and glosses of glosses that we here can only gloss in turn, on one side or the other of the image. Marin immediately goes on to repeat this question in a word ("image?"). He links it this time to the theme of resurrection and transfiguration:

> Here—look here, listen here—in place of a cadaver, removed from the agency of signification, from the ritual gesturality of the funeral unction, a message: this exchange between the cadaver and language, the gap of this exchange, is precisely the resurrection of the body, and the traversing of this gap, the ontological transfiguration of the body: image?

[The question is repeated: "image?" This elliptical question without verb or copula suggests that the image is more than an image, stronger or *more forceful* than the image defined and weakened by ontology. The same ellipsis also lets something else be thought: outside the evangelical, doctrinal, or dogmatic space of the resurrection, before it, more originary than it, but in an originarity of which Christianity makes an event, there would be the very possibility, the power, the force of resurrection and of transfiguration that will be treated so magnificently in Gloss 8 of the book to which I will return in a moment; this force would here stem from the semiotic heterogeneity, from the power of language, and from the power of alterity that works over the being-to-death of every image.]

> Between dead cadaver [a strange redundancy, "dead cadaver," which leaves no chance for illusion or hallucination] and enunciated message, the enunciation so *powerful* of/by an absence [*puissante d'une absence*]— . . .

[I underscore *powerful*, the key word in this expression "the enunciation so powerful of/by an absence," because the adjective "powerful" matters more than both the subject, "enunciation," and the complement of the attributive noun, "of/by an absence."]

> . . . and it is in this that its pragmatic and historical force resides,
> its foundational efficacity—the absence of the founding body.

[The logic of these propositions is dictated by a thought of the foundation itself as the power of the image: the body is not first founding and then, once dead or absent, confirmed in its founding power. No, this power comes to it from the imaginal transfiguration. This founding power advenes thanks to and as the result of the imaginal transfiguration. The foundation is first of all imaginal; it is from the very start fantastic or phantasmatic: under certain conditions, of course, and this is the central problem of the pragmatic conditions of such efficacity; all of history is at issue here, and, first of all, the enigma of all the examples taken in such an exemplary way, that is, at once invariant and (yet) indifferent, open to variation, from the Gospels. In any case, it will be said that this founding power of the image or of the portrait (of the king, for example), with all the political dimensions that Marin never ceased to analyze, did not exist before death. It comes to it from this imaginal representation, from the "exchange between the cadaver and language," from the "ontological transfiguration of the body."

But what might this mean? Why did the founding power of the image not exist before death? What might it mean in general for something not to exist before death, when the anticipation of death comes so indisputably to hollow out the living present that precedes it, and when mourning is at work, as we know, before death?

It means perhaps that the power of the image as the power of death does not wait for death, but is marked out in everything—and for everything—that awaits death: the death of the king gets its efficacity from the portrait made before the death of the king, and every image enacts its efficacity only by signifying the death from which it draws all its power.]

> It is this ["the absence of the founding body"] that will constantly require throughout the ages that the body be covered over, buried, and in a way monumentalized by and in its representations. Such would be the first effect of representation *in general*.

[I underscore *in general*. Such generality affects the Christian example with the sign of a possible imaginary variation, as if the privilege of Christian culture were, in a sort of phenomenological eidetic reduction, but the imaginary basis for an intuition of a general essence concerning the nature of a representation or an imagination in general, beyond the Christic space. When Marin here names the "first effect," he is not pointing out a simple consequence, something that would follow upon the operation of the image: interested as always—as the great Pascalian that he was—in the logic of the effect, in the reason of effects, he knows that the image is nothing, that it does not exist before or outside the effect, the word "effect" designating at once the change brought about and that which *has an effect*, namely, the energy of the aspect, of the manifestation, of visibility, of *phainesthai*. The reason of effects thus comes not so much from the principle of reason or causality as from the fact that it reveals the power of representation, an essence of representation that effectuates more than its so-called ontological essence. If I gloss things in my own way, all the while trying not to be unfaithful to Marin's intention, if I oppose the "reason of effects," which Marin does not invoke directly here, to the "principle of reason" and, implicitly, to the interpretation of it given by Heidegger, whom Marin, it seems to me, if I am not speaking too hastily here, never evokes in this work (except indirectly, in a note concerning a reference by Panofsky to Heidegger [see *P*, p. 205]), it is to try to make sense of the underlying reason for this silence and to try implicitly or obliquely to justify it, assuming that a silence can ever be justified. For Heidegger always associates the predominance and the closure of a certain accentuation of the Principle of reason (that is, of the *Satz vom Grund* as principle of causality or of final causality, the *Grund* or the foundation here being the cause), especially since the seventeenth century, with a certain authority of representation. In so doing he perhaps misses out on understanding how the authority or power, and particularly the theologico-political power of representation, even if aesthetic, might come to it, even in its very founding agency, precisely from its lack or absence of *Grund*, from the *Abgrund* on the basis of which it founds: for it founds precisely there where the founding body, the founding agency or existence, comes to disappear in death, to act as the one who has disappeared or passed away. All these are problems or dimensions of the foundation, and first of all of the political foundation—in and through representation—that, as such, never interested Heidegger, if I am not mistaken, at least not in *The Principle of Reason*, which is *also*, however, a meditation upon that which happens to representation, and through representation, in the seventeenth century.]

> Such would be the "primitive" of representation as effect: to presentify, to make the absent present, as if that which returned were the same . . .

[There is here, then, an acute thought of mourning and of the phantom that returns, of haunting and spectrality: beyond the alternative between presence and absence, beyond negative or positive perception even, the effect of the image would stem from the fantastic force of the specter, and from a supplement of force; and the increase becomes fantastic at the very heart of lack, for Marin immediately raises the stakes, this capital raising of the stakes concerning a capital surplus value of the image, concerning, in sum, the *interest* of the image and of the desire for the image:]

> Such would be the "primitive" of representation as effect: to presentify, to make the absent present, as if that which returned were the same and sometimes better, *more* intense, *more* forceful than if it were the same [my emphasis].

The "more" here seems affected by an "as if" ("as if it were the same"), but the more intensity or force, far from being lessened or attenuated by the fiction of the "as if," draws from it, on the contrary, all its *dynamis*, at once its power and its increase of potential being, of being in potential. There is also here, I would be tempted to say, a theory of the capital and of the capitalization of energy, there where capital is represented from its heraldic depths [*abîme*], both in the chief or head (of state, for example) and in the capital portrait. For this is also a book on the decapitation of the king (look at *Entreglose* 8 entitled "The Severed Head" on Corneille's *The Death of Pompey*) and on the fate of this capital punishment that turns regicide into an event whose possibility is inscribed right on the effect called "portrait of the king."

To reinforce this demonstration of force and of what links power to death, Marin goes on to cite an extraordinary text by Alberti. In book 11 of his treatise *On Painting*, Alberti speaks of death and of friendship. I could not help but recall a certain moment during a seminar we taught together three years ago when we asked about what links friendship to the testamentary experience, particularly in a certain text of Montaigne, of whom Marin was also a marvelous reader. What does Alberti say here? If painting has within itself a force that is absolutely divine (*vim divinam*) it is because it makes the absent present: "as friendship is said to do," Alberti then adds, thinking perhaps of a certain text of Aristotle, the very one that Montaigne evokes and that we had discussed in this seminar.[2] Alberti then moves on—right to the limit of death. Death is

2. Leon Battista Alberti, *On Painting*, trans. John R. Spencer (1956; New Haven, Conn., 1966), p. 63.

not one example of absence among others; it speaks to us of absence itself by naming the most absent of absences, the one that is given by death. Henceforth death, which is expressed, in sum, by all the other absences as absences, is what gives painting its greatest force, for "divine force" also means "the greatest force." But because it bears death, so to speak, this greatest force is also the "without-force," the mourning of the absolute of "force." And to suggest, as I have just done, that "divine force" means "the greatest force" is not simply to call divine that which is the greatest, that in relation to which nothing greater can be thought, as Saint Anselm would say, or to think it according to a schema of ordinary meaning that would unite the idea of God to the superlative; it is also to approach the divinity of the divine on the basis of death, or rather as the mourning-bearing power that makes the greatest force equal to the without-force, to the mourning of the absolute of "force." And under these conditions, the schemas of the eucharistic transubstantiation, of the transfiguration, or of the resurrection, even if taken outside the context of pure Christian dogmatism, retain an exemplary value for Marin's works, in the most enigmatic sense of this Christian exemplarity. This exemplarity does not suggest one occurrence among others but the occurrence of the unique and irreplaceable historical advent that allows one to give an account of all the effects of the "portrait of the king." By allowing them to take place, by giving them their proper place, it determines Marin's so necessary and so rigorous analyses on this subject—be it in the book that bears this title (*Portrait of the King*)[3] or in the second part of this last book, "The Genealogical and Political Powers of the Image."

What do all these analyses, each one emanating beauty and truth, show? To put it all too poorly in a word, they demonstrate and display what, in the course of history, allows one to say, following Pascal, that "the portrait of the king is the king" and that it is the "'portrait effect,' the mimetic effect, the effect of representation, that *makes* the king" (*P*, p. 187).

This logic presupposes that a sort of death of the king comes *in advance* to divide the king's body in two: the individual or real body on the one hand, the fictive—ideal or representative—body of dignity on the other. (The politico-juridical history of the two bodies of the king in Christian Europe, such as it is analyzed by Ernst Kantorowicz, plays an organizing role in these texts of Marin; it runs through them, as we know, as the continuous thread of an axiomatic—so indispensable and

3. See Marin, *Portrait of the King*, trans. Martha M. Houle (Minneapolis, 1988).

obvious that Kantorowicz hardly has to be mentioned.) Now, as we know, this dividing or this redoubling of the king's body, this functional death of the physical body in the body of dignity, what Marin elsewhere calls the "caesura of the royal body,"[4] could be written into the rights of absolute and hereditary monarchy only on the basis of a Christian doctrine. I'll cite just one sentence, at the end of Gloss 6 ("The Portrait of the King, Shipwrecked"), which would here have to be read extremely closely: "The king in his portrait, the king as image, the king-representation, is thus in the 'parable' a parody of the eucharistic mystery of the mystic body and of real presence" (*P*, p. 194).

One could readily show, in fact, that this logic remains at work wherever there is a monarchy in a Christian country, even in a Christian democracy, I mean in a democratic regime with a Christian culture, as soon as the unity or the independence of the nation-state is represented in the body of a monarch or president, no matter the length of the term or the forms of inheritance by election (filiation or succession), indeed, no matter the mode of election.

But let's return to Alberti: "painting," he writes, "contains an absolutely divine force [*in se vim admodum divinam habet*] that not only makes absent men present, as friendship is said to do, but shows the dead to the living so that even after many centuries [*defunctus long post saecula viventibus exhibeat*] they may be recognized by them with great pleasure and with great admiration for the painter" (quoted in *P*, p. 11). In Alberti's description we see pleasure and admiration becoming inextricably linked to mourning, the force of the three affects increasing from their combination.

Yet it is necessary here to underscore an obvious fact. It could easily be forgotten because it is so obvious, like the nose in the middle of one's face. It is that the image and representation are treated by Alberti—and by Marin citing Alberti—*on the basis of the portrait*. The portrait is not just any painting. It thus has to be recalled why it is the history of the image *as portrait* that must be investigated in order to analyze power, particularly the theologico-political power of representation. The portrait is not one fiction or figure, one face of the figure, among others. Not only because it represents *at once* the gaze that gazes at us *and* the head that governs the body *and* the chief or head who governs the social body. (In his political analyses Marx is always interested just as much in the head of those who govern as in the logic of capital.) But especially because, like the photographic portrait, its relation to the ref-

4. See Marin, *Lectures traversières* (Paris, 1992), pp. 179–93.

erent appears (and it is this appearance that counts even if one must not trust it) irreducible. This fiction of the figure, of the face, is given as essentially nonfictive, and it claims to give us—and Barthes relied a good deal, perhaps a bit too much, on this claim—what once was and could not not have been present before the gaze or before the lens. What the portrait says, the *title* "portrait" (and it is because a title is of the order of discourse that we are here in a gloss), is that what is shown, portraitured, is what was (supposed to have been) real, really present. This is obviously not the case of every other pictorial figure or fiction, which do not then strictly speaking deserve the name of representation, or even, in the end, that of image. The portrait is here the capital representation insofar as it represents the capital element in a power of the image. Forcing things only a bit, one could say that, *at least* from the point of view of the theologico-political power guaranteed by the portrait of the king, and based on Marin's analysis, there is no difference between painting and photography, for the photographic portrait continues to guarantee, and sometimes even accentuates, the function of the painted portrait. The photographic technique fulfills even more powerfully the pictorial vocation, namely, to seize the dead and transfigure them—to resuscitate as *having been* the one who (singularly, he or she) will have been. The presidential portraits that can be seen today in all places of public authority (government agencies, town halls, departmental and municipal buildings, police stations) express the origin, identity, and place of the capital gathering of legitimate power insofar as it holds us in its gaze and looks at us looking at it by recalling us to what looks at and regards us, that is, to our responsibility before it and in its eyes. It is also true that photography at the same time goes against the very vocation it fulfills or continues since it makes the portrait available to everyone. Through this technical democratization, photography tends to destroy the aura and rarity of the painting that restricts the commissioning of the painted portrait, which sometimes turns out to be a masterpiece, to certain privileged places, of which the court is at the very least the metonymic figure. In any case, one should not be surprised to see Marin, just after having spoken of what is "most intense" and "most forceful" about the effect of representation, and just before citing Alberti, make reference in a single sentence to photography, and more precisely to the photograph of someone who, as we say, has disappeared or "passed away," the photograph, like the portrait, having the virtue of making appear the one who has disappeared, of making them re-appear with greater clarity or *enargeia*. Before citing Alberti, Marin makes as if he were giving an example just in passing, a few words of pedagogic illustration: "Thus the photograph of someone who has passed away displayed on the mantel" (*P*, p. 11).

I am going to have to break this off, for there is not enough time; but before saying in a few words in what direction I would have liked to share with you the reading of this great book, I would especially like to convey to you, trying not to take advantage of the emotion, how difficult and painful it is for me to speak here of this book. This difficulty or pain has nothing to do with the time we do or do not have this evening; we and, alas, we alone, will later have more time. A bit more time.

Such difficulty or pain has to do with the strange time of reading that the time of the writing of this book will have, as if in advance, imprinted in us, the friends of Louis.

I imagine him writing these lines, citing and glossing Alberti in his preface not long before his death, for a book he did not know whether he would see, whether he would, while still living, see it come out. The book, as *you* will see, multiplies these analyses, these examples, these images of what I would call the survival effect, the effect of living on. Louis not only saw death coming, as we all see it coming without seeing it, as we all expect it without expecting it. He approached death, which approached him, more and more quickly; he approached it in preceding it, and anticipated it with these images and glosses, for which the grammar of the future anterior no doubt does not suffice to convey their force and time, their tense. The future anterior is still a simplistic modalization of a fundamental present or representation; simplistic because still too simple to be able to translate the strange temporality that here gives its force to the mourning affect of which we are speaking. It would likewise be too simple, though true in an oblique way, to say that Louis Marin, citing Alberti and speaking of the portrait of others, of death and of friendship, painted himself in advance, painting at the same time his grieving friends, pointing us out to ourselves in advance with a finger, and signing the extraordinary utterance, which he comments upon elsewhere, that allows one to say "I died" (this incredible grammar, this impossible time or tense that he analyzes in *La Voix excommuniée*).[5]

To say "I died," "I am dead," is not simply a future anterior. It is the strange time of his writing, the strange time of reading that looks at and regards us in advance this evening, that will have regarded us, that will regard us long after us. The "I died" is not a phenomenologico-grammatical monstrosity, a scandal of common sense or an impossible sentence with no meaning. It is the time or tense, the grapho-logical

5. See Marin, *La Voix excommuniée: Essais de mémoire* (Paris, 1981), p. 64.

time, the implicit tempo of all writing, all painting, of every trace, and
even of the presumed present of every *cogito ergo sum* (which, as I tried
to show a long time ago elsewhere, necessarily implies an "I am dead."
For in Descartes one cannot separate these words and the system of their
enunciation from what is considered to be one of Descartes's minor
discourses, namely, what he says of the Eucharist when he dares, more
or less clandestinely, to enter into the debate among theologians on this
subject. I later tried to show this again in a seminar where I referred, of
course, to the works of Marin on the Eucharist and added to them this
Cartesian gloss.).

During the past few weeks spent admiring *Des pouvoirs de l'image* I
kept saying to myself that I have never known such an emotion in reading a book. It was not only the emotion of mourning that we all know
and recognize, even if it hits us each time in a new and singular way, like
the end of the world, an emotion that overwhelms us each time we come
across the surviving testimonies of the lost friend, across all the "images" that the one who has "passed away" has left or passed on to us.

There was, this time, something more, something else as well. There
was another emotion that came to overwhelm this first mourning, this
common mourning, coming to make it turn upon itself, I would almost
want to say to reflect it to the point of vertigo, another emotion, another quality and intensity of emotion, at once too painful and strangely
peaceful, which had to do, I believe, with a certain time of reading.

Without even trying to say something more, however minimal, about
this magnificent book and about the strange time of reading by which
I was overwhelmed, I would like to venture a few words on the subject
of mourning, and on the time of an interminable mourning, so as not to
rush ahead—something I would deem intolerable—to speak this evening of the last book of Marin as I might have spoken in another time
and in more conventional circumstances of his most recent book. In
returning regularly to common places, I mean to the places that were
common to us, sitting in the office I shared with him for so long on Bou-
levard Raspail, walking around the Maison des Sciences de l'Homme,
taking part just recently in a discussion during the seminar he led for
many years with certain among you whom I see in this room, I have said
to myself that, ever since psychoanalysis came to mark this discourse,
the image commonly used to characterize mourning is that of an interiorization (an idealizing incorporation, introjection, consumption of
the other, in effect, an experience that would have received one of its
essential aspects from the Eucharist, which was, for Louis, the great
Thing, the great mourning-object, both his object and the object of his

mourning, to which he will have devoted a work so original and all-consuming, a work that unrelentingly pursues the eucharistic body from every side—exegetical, philosophical, historical, logical, linguistic—as if it were necessary before dying to come to know what mourning is, to know how to come to terms with death, and how to transfigure the work of death into a work that gives and gives something to be seen). Now, if the modes of interiorization or of subjectification that psycho-analysis talks about are in some respects undeniable in the work of mourning where the death of the friend leaves us, that is, leaves us alone, I told myself the following, which is certainly not original but which I feel with a singular acuteness and, indeed, an increased intensity: if this interiorization is not possible, if it must not—and this is the unbearable paradox of fidelity—be possible and completed, it would not be because of a limit, because of a border that cannot be crossed, because of a frontier that comes to enclose a given space, organizing finitude into an inside and an outside that would be, in effect, homogeneous with one another, symmetrical and commensurable on each side of an indivisible line. It would be, rather, because of another organization of space and of visibility, of the gazing and the gazed upon. Whatever the truth, alas, of this inevitable interiorization (the friend can no longer be but *in us*, and whatever we may believe about the after-life, about living-on, according to all the possible forms of faith, it is *in us* that these movements might appear), this being-in-us reveals a truth *to and at death*, at the moment of death and even before death by everything in us that prepares itself for and awaits death, that is, in the undeniable anticipation of mourning that constitutes friendship. It reveals the truth of its topology and tropology. When we say "in us," when we speak so easily and so painfully of inside and outside, we are naming space, we are speaking of a visibility of the body, a geometry of gazes, an orientation of perspectives. *We are speaking of images.* What is only *in us* seems to be reducible to images, which might be memories or monuments, but which are reducible in any case to a memory that consists of *visible* scenes that are no longer anything but *images*, since the other of whom they are the images appears only as the one who has disappeared or passed away, as the one who, having passed away, leaves "in us" only images. He is no more, he whom we see in images or in recollection, he of whom we speak, whom we cite, to whom we attempt to give back words, to let speak—he is no more, he is no longer here, no longer there. And nothing can begin to dissipate the terrifying and chilling light of this certainty. As if respect for this certainty were still a debt, the last one, owed to the friend.

What this rhetoric of space, this topology and this tropology miss, what this description of lack lacks, is that the force of the image has to do less with the fact that one sees something in it than with the fact that one is seen there in it. The image sees more than it is seen. The image looks at us. (Indeed, some of you here this evening, Hubert Damisch in particular, work on this inversion of the gaze that comes from painting and on the dissymmetry and demastering brought about by such an inversion; and everything Marin tells us of the portrait has to do, in the end, with this inversion of dissymmetry that can be interiorized only by exceeding, fracturing, wounding, injuring, traumatizing the interiority that it inhabits or that welcomes it through hospitality, love, or friendship. This dissymmetry also inscribes—unless it actually depends on it—an essential anachrony in our being exposed to the other; it dislocates all contemporaneity at the very heart of what we have our sights on at the same time.)

Louis Marin is outside and he is looking at me, he himself, and I am an image for him. At this very moment. There where I can say *cogito, sum,* I know that I am an image for the other and am looked at by the other, even and especially by the mortal other. I move right before his eyes, and the force of this image is irreversible (because of the reversion, the conversion, of force into weakness and vice versa). Louis Marin is looking at me, and it is for this, for him, that I am here this evening. He is my law, the law, and I appear before him, before his word and his gaze. In my relationship to myself, he is here in me before me, stronger or more forceful than me. It might be said that I came because other witnesses asked me to, because I appear also before those close to him, Françoise, Anne, Frédérique, and Judith, before his friends and the friends we had in common. This is surely true, but I would not have felt this imperative before them had I not known that what unites us is at once common and outside us, and that we are all looked at (each one of us singularly) by the one who, with each page, will have providentially deciphered and prescribed, arranged in advance, a reading of what is happening here, of what makes the present scene possible, foreseeing and watching over it with the benevolent regard (since it is he who watches out to watch over us) and with all the love of someone who can say, at the moment of dying, even if he is not Christ or even Christian, *hoc est meum corpus, which is given for you. Do this in remembrance of me* (Luke 22:19).

We are all looked at, I said, and each one singularly, by Louis Marin. He looks at us. *In us.* He looks in us. This witness sees in us. And from now on more than ever. But what might this indicate that would not be a mere rhetorical commonplace? It would indicate an *absolute* excess and dissymmetry in the space of what relates us to ourselves and constitutes the "being-in-us," the "being-us," in something completely other than a mere subjective interiority: in a place open to an infinite transcendence. The one who looks at us in us—and *for whom* we are—is no longer; he is completely other, infinitely other, as he has always been, and death has more than ever entrusted him, given him over, distanced him, in this infinite alterity. However narcissistic it may be, our subjective speculation can no longer seize and appropriate this gaze before which we appear at the moment when, bearing it in us, bearing it along with every movement of our bearing or comportment, we can get over our mourning *of him* only by getting over *our* mourning, by getting over, by ourselves, the mourning of ourselves, I mean the mourning of our autonomy, of everything that would make us the measure of ourselves. That is the excess and the dissymmetry: we bear *in ourselves* the gaze that Louis Marin bears *on us*. Powers of the image. This gaze is his, and it will always remain his, infinitely; it comes from him singularly, from him alone, alone as always, more alone than ever, over there, outside, far away. Far away in us. In us, there where this power of the image comes to open the being-far-away. This excess also brings about the limitless enlargement of the image. Its power of dilation gives it its greatest force in the mourning of the absolute of "force."

It was, in the end, the experience of this time of reading that I discovered. Louis Marin described this scene on each page of his book, all the while mobilizing a corpus at once extremely diverse and singularly rich. I was thus read, I said to myself, and staged by what I read; I found myself caught up in the time of his time, inscribed, situated by this other present that was still his this summer. And my sadness, while trying to distinguish itself from his, could never really dissociate itself from it. It still resonates in the very scope and score of his time. He remained the master of it, as one would say of a subject or a disciple.

It would be necessary to accede or do justice to this torsion of the time of reading. At once painful and fascinated, it calls or recalls in advance a sort of living present, or what is assumed to be so, that is, our own living present, toward the present of Louis Marin, toward the other fractured present of the one who, having written this book in a more or less continuous fashion over several years, developing still further premises elaborated for more than twenty years, wrote or reviewed a few months ago, I imagine, the preface, and reread—the ultimate test or proof—as the editors tell us, almost all the proofs, almost, or just about, the final proofs, the final test.

In doing this, he will have brought to term, that is, right up to the final interruption, the ordeal or the putting to the test of this default of force wherein is marked the "mourning of the absolute of 'force.'"

For, in the end, what does this book tell us, in its at once paradoxical and prudent thesis, I would even say in its fantastic aporia, or, if you prefer, its ontological fiction? That this power whose effects it analyzes does not exist. It never attains existence, that is, the presence of the present. *There is* power, there are *effects* of power, but power does not exist. It is nothing. It *is attached to death*, which is not. There is only "force," the quotation marks reminding us that the effect of force is attached to the representative fiction. This fiction counts only on the death of the one who is thought to hold power, from whom it then withdraws power by feigning to confer it upon him in the portrait. The trait of the portrait, its infinite attraction, is that it subtracts or withdraws: it withdraws or takes back all the power that it confers, because it requires already in advance the death of the subject, the death of the king as subject and of the subject of the subject in question, that is, of everything related to its reference:

> In the representation that is power, in the power that is representation, the real—provided one understands by "real" the always deferred fulfillment of this desire—is nothing other than the fantastic image in which the subject would contemplate itself as absolute.
>
> If it is of the essence of all forces to tend towards the absolute, it is part of the "reality" of its subject never to be content with not being so. The representation-effects that constitute powers and that powers in turn permit and authorize would be the modalities (historical, anthropological, sociological . . .) of a work—though infinite in space and time—of the mourning of the absolute of "force." [*P*, pp. 16–17]

All this is worked out, demonstrated, and will live on in the pages that will be read and reread on "The Severed Head," concerning *The Death of Pompey* by Corneille where the "deadly mirror"—analyzed earlier in the chapters on the idol, narcissism, and the "position of the I"—lets us see, in some sense, the very origin of the political and shows how the "great politician then converts the phantasmatic object, the head of the Medusa, emblem of the violent origins of the State, the severed head of Pompey, into its own face, the disquieting and cold mask of political power" (*P*, p. 157).

But the reading of *The Tempest* exceeds this purely political dimension. For it shows how the recognition that the king discovers in the gaze that representation turns toward him is also *cosmic* (see *P*, p. 175). Had I the time, I would have tried to venture into the current space of this *cosmopolitics*. But the pages that, while just as convincing and force-ful as all the others, nonetheless moved me the most, I would even say overwhelmed me, are those that—in a reading of whiteness that is quite properly dazzling, in the writing of white light, in what one might want to call the photography of certain Gospels—speak about the *potestas filiationis*, about the son in the bosom of the father, the son as the sight of the image of the father. Of the father *in view* of the son, of the father looked upon, judged, made possible by the son. An abyssal thought of inheritance. It would be necessary to cite here the entire Gloss 7 on "the son in the bosom of the father" and reread what is said "in the light of the stained-glass window." Marin speaks of this in a dazzling fashion, for he is himself no doubt bedazzled by bedazzlement, by the knowl-edge "through bedazzlement," through the blindness that comes from an excess of vision. Here again is the theme of what Abbot Suger refers to as a "force renewed" through the very renunciation of all restitution, all reconstitution, all *post mortem* retribution: the gift itself (*P*, p. 213). And as for the Transfiguration, the event of the absolute visual that constitutes the ground without ground of the foundation of power, the bedazzlement of whiteness is there associated with this anticipation of death that also marks the time of this book, "as if," says Marin, "the extreme, final, image, that of the absolutely white figure or face, could only anticipate the taste of an exquisite death" (*P*, p. 239).

We will never have the time.

Had I the time, had I been able to treat the last six pages of this book, which speak in Gloss 9 of "The Reversion of Shadow and Light" and of a certain structural link between "genealogical power" and a supple-ment of force or "intensification" based on a passage from Nietzsche's *The Birth of Tragedy*, I would have tried to situate a bit better what is, to my eyes, Marin's singular place within a hidden tradition, at the heart of a secret lineage, one that is inadmissible to every church or chapel. I am speaking of this heretical filiation that runs from Pascal to Nietzsche, who was also the thinker of force and of the reciprocal convertibility of the strongest or most forceful and the weakest. These two thinkers have often been associated, especially during the heydays of existentialism. But I do not know of anyone before Louis Marin who has given to this intolerable genealogy, to this heretical heritage, such a force of evidence, such titles, I would even say such a force of law. If this tradition was possible, virtual, dynamic, it did not exist, it never had such an incontestable actuality before the work of Marin, and singularly so in *Des pouvoirs de l'image*. That this actuality remains a potentiality without limit—that is what I would have wanted to show.

And that is what secretly links the gift to death.

Why does one give and what can one give to a dead friend? And what does one give oneself with this liberty, when one knows that the relation to oneself, that Narcissus himself, gazes at himself only from the gaze of the other, and precedes himself, answering then only for himself, only from the resonance of Echo, when this latter speaks freely of herself, for herself, by seeming to repeat the last syllables of the other and thus to give in to the jealous dictates of divine law.

Louis knew what I thought of him, he was aware of my admiration and my gratitude; he had countless indications of this in everything that was woven between our gestures, our various itineraries, our respective works as well, and in everything that went unspoken, which did not fail, as always, alas, to resound and resonate in all of this. But while he was aware of this admiration, I never really declared it to him to the extent that I am this evening. I am not saying this only, not only, to confess a mistake, a regret, or an inconsolable sadness. This situation is, in the end, rather common; it is what links me to more than one friend, no doubt to all those one calls "best friends."

But then why? Why wait for death? Tell me why we wait for death? Marin's last book will have again helped me to think this, to think that which in fact regards each of us so singularly, namely, the law of what does not return or come back, of what comes back to us only there where it can no longer come back to us, and so all comes down, like mastery, that is, like the fiction of force, to the incontestable authority of death, to the very inexistence of the image, to its fantastic power, to the impresence of a trace.

Louis Marin knew that this authority begins before death, and that death begins its work before death. Death's watch [*veille*], the time of this book, had begun long ago for Louis Marin, well before the eve [*veille*] of his death.

This is also why this book cannot be closed, why it interrupts itself interminably. And however prepared I might have been for it, I read it too quickly. In a sort of haste that no mourning will be able to diminish or console. It happened to me too quickly, like Louis's death. I feel as if I'm still on the eve of reading it.

12   What Is a "Relevant" Translation?

Translated by Lawrence Venuti

Then must the Jew be merciful.
(I leave untranslated this sentence from Portia in *The Merchant of Venice*.)
Portia will also say, *When mercy seasons justice*, which I shall later propose to translate as *Quand le pardon relève la justice . . .*

How dare one speak of translation before you who, in your vigilant awareness of the immense stakes—and not only of the fate of literature—make this sublime and impossible task your desire, your anxiety, your travail, your knowledge, and your knowing skill?

How dare I proceed before you, knowing myself to be at once rude and inexperienced in this domain, as someone who, from the very first moment, from his very first attempts (which I could recount to you, as the English saying goes, off the record), shunned the translator's métier, his beautiful and terrifying responsibility, his insolvent duty and debt, without ceasing to tell himself "never ever again": "no, precisely, I would *never* dare, I should *never*, could *never*, would *never* manage to pull it off"?

If I dare approach this subject before you, it is because this very discouragement, this premature renunciation of which I speak and from which I set out, this declaration of insolvency before translation was always, in me, the other face of a jealous and admiring love, a passion for what summons, loves, provokes, and defies translation while running up an infinite debt in its service, an admiration for those men and women who, to my mind, are the only ones who know how to read and write—translators. Which is another way of recognizing a summons to translation at the very threshold of all reading-writing. Hence the infinity of the loss, the insolvent debt. Much like what is owed to Shylock, insolvency itself. Speaking, teaching, writing (which I also consider my profession and which, after all, like many here among you, engages me body and soul almost constantly)—I know that these activities are meaningful in my eyes only in the proof of translation, through an experience that I will never distinguish from experimentation. As for the word (for the word will be my theme)—neither grammar nor lexicon hold an interest for me—I believe I can say that if I love the word, it is only in the body of its idiomatic singularity, that is, where a passion for translation comes to lick it as a flame or an amorous tongue might: approaching as closely as possible while refusing at the last moment to threaten or to reduce, to consume or to consummate, leaving the other body intact but not without causing the other to appear—on the very brink of this refusal or withdrawal— and after having aroused or excited a desire for the idiom, for the unique body of the other, in the flame's flicker or through a tongue's caress. I don't know how, or in how many languages, you can translate this word *lécher* when you wish to say that one language licks another, like a flame or a caress.

But I won't put off any longer saying "merci" to you, in a word, addressing this *mercy* to you in more than (and no longer) one language.

For no sooner will I have thanked you for the hospitality with which you honor me than I will need to ask your forgiveness and, in expressing my gratitude [*grâce*] to you, beg your pardon [*grâce*], ask you to be *merciful* to me. For your part, forgive me from the outset for availing myself of this word *merciful* as if it were a citation. I'm *mentioning* it as much as I'm *using* it, as a speech act theorist might say, a bit too confident in the now canonical distinction between *mention* and *use*.

In other words, I certainly won't delay in thanking you for the signal honor you have accorded me, but also, via this word of gratitude and *mercy*, in asking your forgiveness for all the limits, starting with my own inadequacies, which hinder me from measuring up to it. As for my inadequacies, I will no doubt make a vain effort to dissemble them with contrivances more or less naively perverse.

Before these thanks rendered, this pardon begged, I must first acknowledge a defect of language that could well be a breach in the laws of hospitality. In effect, is it not the first duty of the *guest* [*hôte*] that I am to speak a language that is intelligible and transparent, hence without equivocation? And therefore to speak a single language, namely that of the addressee, here of the *host* [*hôte*], a language especially designed for whoever must and can understand it, a language that is shared, like the very language of the other, that of the other to whom one addresses it, or at the very least a language that the listener or reader can make his or her own? A language that is, in a word, translatable?

Now, here is one of the admissions that I owe you on several scores. First, on the score of my title and on the score of speaking about my title, as I shall do in a moment, in an entirely untranslatable manner. Admitting more than one failure, I confess this double inadequacy that is all the more impossible to avoid because it bears a self-contradiction: if I need to address you in a single language, French (thereby recognizing that every so-called discourse *on* translation, every metalanguage or metatheorem on the topic of translation is fated to inscribe itself within the limits and possibilities of a single idiom), I am nevertheless always already inclined to leap over this language, my own, and I shall do it again, thus leaving undecided the question of a simple choice between language and metalanguage, between one language and another. At the word go we are within the multiplicity of languages and the impurity of the limit.

Why would my title remain forever untranslatable? In the first place, because one can't decide the source language to which it is answerable [*relève*]; nor, therefore, in what sense it travails, *travels*, between *hôte* and *hôte*, *guest* and *host*.

It is impossible to decide the source language to which, for example, the word "relevante" answers [*relève*], a word that I leave within quotation marks for now. Nor the language to which it belongs at the moment when I use it, in the syntagms or the phrases where I move to reinscribe it. Does this word speak one and the same language, *in* one and the same language? At the same time, we don't even know if it is really one word, a single word with a single meaning, or if, homonym or homophone of itself, it constitutes more than one word in one.

What I shall propose to you under this title ("What Is a 'Relevant' Translation?"), undoubtedly short of any reflection worthy of this word about the word, about the unity of the word in general, will perhaps be a more modest and *laborious* approach, on the basis of a single word, the word "relevant." I underline *laborious* to announce several words in *tr.* and to indicate that the motif of *labor* [*travail*], the *tra*vail of childbirth, but also the *transferential* and *tra*nsformational *tra*vail, in all possible codes and not only that of psychoanalysis, will enter into competition with the apparently more neutral motif of *tra*nslation, as *tra*nsaction and as *tra*nsfer. We shall then wind up revolving around a single example, a punning example, if there is such a thing, and if the word "relevant" may be one, unique, solitary, at once an adjectival and verbal form, a sort of present participle that becomes an epithet or predicate.

What of this vocable "relevant"? It possesses all the traits of the linguistic unity that one familiarly calls a word, a verbal body. We often forget, in this same familiarity, how the unity or identity, the independence of the word remains a mysterious thing, precarious, not quite natural, that is to say historical, institutional, and conventional. There is no such thing as a word in nature. Well, this word "relevant" carries in its body an ongoing process of translation, as I will try to show; as a translative body, it endures or exhibits translation as the memory or stigmata of suffering [*passion*] or, hovering above it, as an aura or halo. This translative body is in the process of being imported into the French language, in the act of crossing borders and being checked at several intra-European customs points that are not only Franco-English, as one might infer from the fact that this word of Latin origin is now rather English (*relevant/irrelevant*) in its current usage, in its use-value, in its circulation or its *currency*, even though it is also in the process of Frenchification. This acculturation, this Frenchification is not *strictu senso* a translation. The word is not only *in* translation, as one would say in the works or in transit, *traveling, travailing*, in *labor*. In my proposed title, it serves, through a supplementary fold [*pli*], to qualify translation and to indicate what a translation might be *obliged* to be, namely *relevant*.

Those of you who are familiar with English perhaps already understand the word as a domestication, an implicit Frenchification [*francisation*] or—dare I say?—a more or less tacit and clandestine enfranchisement [*l'affranchissement*] of the English adjective *relevant*, which would have thus passed into our language with bag and baggage, with its predicates of denotation and connotation. The French feminine of this word ("*une traduction relevante*") sounds even more English and takes us back to the signature and the sexual difference at stake wherever translation or translators (in the masculine or feminine) are involved.

What is most often called "relevant"? Well, whatever feels right, whatever seems pertinent, apropos, welcome, appropriate, opportune, justified, well-suited or adjusted, coming right at the moment when you expect it—or corresponding as is necessary to the object to which the so-called relevant action relates: the relevant discourse, the relevant proposition, the relevant decision, the relevant translation. A relevant translation would therefore be, quite simply, a "good" translation, a translation that does what one expects of it, in short, a version that performs its mission, honors its debt and does its job or its duty while inscribing in the receiving language the most *relevant* equivalent for an original, the language that is *the most* right, appropriate, pertinent, adequate, opportune, pointed, univocal, idiomatic, and so on. *The most* possible, and this superlative puts us on the trail of an "economy" with which we shall have to reckon.

The verb *relever* brings me back to a modest but effective experiment in translation in which I have found myself engaged for more than thirty years, almost continuously, first between German and French, then more recently between English and French. That this same French word (the very same word, assuming that it is the very same word, and that henceforth it is French through and through), that this same word could have thus operated, in a single language, between three languages, so as to "translate," or in any case to put to *work* different words belonging to apparently different contexts in at least two other source languages (German and English)—this fact seems an incalculable stroke of luck, an invention or necessity for which I wonder who can bear the responsibility, even if it was apparently mine at first and mine to sign. I harbor no illusion or pretension in this respect: if I took the initiative in these quasi-translations, I could do so only to hear, in order to record, various possibilities or laws—semantic and formal—already inscribed in this family of languages and, first and foremost, in "my" language. In any case, because the happy coincidence in question has since then become somewhat more familiar to me, because I feel less exposed—in my incompetence—to the risk of saying highly irrelevant things about translation in general before the expert scholars and accomplished professionals that you are, I have therefore preferred to suggest that we prowl around a small word and follow it like a "go-between" rather than engage anew, on the level of generality, in theoretical or more obviously philosophical or speculative reflections that I have elsewhere ventured on various universal problems of Translation, in the wake of Walter Benjamin, James Joyce, and several others.

And perhaps I should then confess under this very heading, thus pleading guilty without extenuating circumstances, that I chose my title precisely because of its untranslatability, premeditating my crime in this way, conspiring to insure the apparent untranslatability of my title through a single word, a word wherein I sign, in an idiom that is something like my signature, the theme of this lecture, which will therefore resemble a seal that, cowardice or arrogance, would abridge itself into my initials.

What remains is that—trust me—I don't transgress a code of decency or modesty through a provocative challenge, but through a trial, by submitting the experience of translation to the trial of the untranslatable.

As a matter of fact, I don't believe that anything can ever be untranslatable—or, moreover, translatable.

How can one dare say that nothing is translatable and, by the same token, that nothing is untranslatable? To what concept of translation must one appeal to prevent this axiom from seeming simply unintelligible and contradictory: "nothing is translatable; nothing is untranslatable"? To the condition of a certain *economy* that relates the translatable to the untranslatable, not as the same to the other, but as same to same or other to other. Here "economy" signifies two things, *property* and *quantity*: *on the one hand*, what concerns the law of *property* (*oikonomia*, the law—*nomos*—of the *oikos*, of what is proper, appropriate to itself, at home—and translation is always an attempt at appropriation that aims to transport home, in its language, in the most appropriate way possible, in the most relevant way possible, the most proper meaning of the original text, even if this is the proper meaning of a figure, metaphor, metonymy, catachresis, or undecidable impropriety) and, *on the other hand*, a law of *quantity*—when one speaks of economy, one always speaks of calculable quantity. *On compte et on rend compte*, one counts and accounts for. A relevant translation is a translation whose economy, in these two senses, is the best possible, the most appropriating and the most appropriate possible.

How does a *principle of economy* permit one to say two apparently contradictory things at the same time (1. "Nothing is translatable"; 2. "Everything is translatable") while confirming the experience that I suppose is so common to us as to be beyond any possible dispute, namely, that any given translation, whether the best or the worst, actually stands between the two, between absolute relevance, the most appropriate, adequate, univocal transparency, and the most aberrant and opaque irrelevance? To understand what this economy of inbetweenness signifies, it is necessary to imagine two extreme hypotheses, the following two hyperboles: if to a translator who is fully competent in at least two languages and two cultures, two cultural memories with the sociohistorical knowledge embodied in them, you give all the time in the world, as well as the words needed to explicate, clarify, and teach the semantic content and forms of the text to be translated, there is no reason for him to encounter the untranslatable or a remainder in his work. If you give someone who is competent an entire book, filled with *translator's notes*, in order to explain everything that a phrase of two or three words can mean in its particular form (for example, the *he war* from *Finnegans Wake*, which has occupied me in another place,[1] or else *mercy seasons justice* from *The Merchant of Venice*, which we shall discuss below), there is really no reason, in principle, for him to fail to render—without any remainder—the intentions, meaning, denotations, connotations and semantic overdeterminations, the formal effects of what is called the original. Of course, this operation, which occurs daily in the university and in literary criticism, is not what is called a translation, a translation worthy of the name, translation in the strict sense, the translation of a *work*. To make legitimate use of the word *translation* (*traduction, Übersetzung, traducción, translaciôn,* and so forth), in the rigorous sense conferred on it over several centuries by a long and complex history in a given cultural situation (more precisely, more narrowly, in Abrahamic and post-Lutheran Europe), the translation must be *quantitatively* equivalent to the original, apart from any paraphrase, explication, explicitation, analysis, and the like. Here I am not speaking of quantity in general or of quantity in the prosodic sense (meter, rhythm, cæsura, rhyme—all the classic constraints and limits that are in principle and in fact insurmountable by translation). I also deliberately set aside all sorts of phenomena—quite interesting, as a matter of fact—due to which this form of quantitative equivalence is never rigorously approachable. It has been recognized that certain languages with a tendency toward excessively long constructions take them much farther in translation. No translation will ever reduce this quantitative or, in a Kantian sense, this aesthetic difference, since it concerns the spatial and temporal forms of sensibility. But this will not be my point. No, what matters to me more and today in particular, in this quantitative law, in this economy, is the unit of measurement that governs at once the classic concept of translation and the calculus that informs it. This quantitative unit of measurement is not in itself quantitative; it is rather qualitative in a certain sense. It is not a question of measuring a homogeneous space

1. See Jacques Derrida, *Ulysse Gramophone, deux mots pour Joyce* (Paris, 1987). [An English translation of Derrida's text is available in *Post-structuralist Joyce: Essays from the French*, ed. Derek Attridge and Daniel Ferrer (Cambridge, 1984)—TRANS.]

or the weight of a book, nor even of yielding to an arithmetic of signs and letters; it is not a question of counting the number of signs, signifiers or signifieds, but of counting the *number of words*, of lexical units called words. The unit of measurement is the unit of the word. The philosophy of translation, the ethics of translation—if translation does in fact have these things—*today* aspires to be a philosophy of the word, a linguistics or ethics of the word. At the beginning of translation is the word. Nothing is less innocent, pleonastic and natural, nothing is more historical than this proposition, even if it seems too obvious. This has not always been the case, as you well know. As it was formulated, among others, by Cicero, I believe, to watch impassively over subsequent developments, to watch over a turbulent and differentiated history of translation, of its practices and its norms, the first imperative of translation was most certainly not the command of "word-to-word." In *De optimo genere oratorum*, Cicero freed translation from its obligation to the *verbum*, its debt to word-for-word. The operation that consists of converting, turning (*convertere, vertere, transvertere*) doesn't have to take a text at its word or to take the word literally. It suffices to transmit the idea, the figure, the force. And the slogan of St. Jerome, who with Luther was one of the fathers of a certain translation ethics, an ethics that survives even if it is contested in our modernity, is *non verbum e verbo, sed sensum exprimere de sensu* [to express not word by word, but sense by sense]. He was speaking just as much of translating the Greeks as of translating the Holy Scriptures, even if he had been tempted to make an exception for the "mysterious order of words" (*verborum ordo mysterium*) in the Bible.[2] In recent times, for scarcely a few centuries, a so-called literal translation that aims to attain the greatest possible relevance hasn't been a translation that renders letters or even only what is placidly termed the sense, but rather a translation that, while rendering the so-called proper meaning of a word, its literal meaning (which is to say a meaning that is determinable and not figural) establishes as the law or ideal—even if it remains inaccessible—a kind of translating that is not *word-to-word*, certainly, or *word-for-word*, but nonetheless stays as close as possible to the equivalence of "one word *by* one word" and thereby respects verbal quantity as a quantity of words, each of which is an irreducible body, the indivisible unity of an acoustic form that incorporates or signifies the indivisible unity of a meaning or concept. This is why, whenever several

2. See Cicero, *Liber de optimo genere interpretandi* (*Epistula 57*). For this reference I am indebted to the admirable recent work (still unpublished) of Andrès Claro, *Les Vases brisés: Quatre variations sur la tâche du traducteur.*

words occur in one or the same acoustic or graphic form, whenever a *homophonic* or *homonymic effect* occurs, translation in the strict, traditional, and dominant sense of the term encounters an insurmountable limit—and the beginning of its end, the figure of its ruin (but perhaps a translation is devoted to ruin, to that form of memory or commemoration that is called a ruin; ruin is perhaps its vocation and a destiny that it accepts from the very outset). A homonym or homophone is never translatable word-to-word. It is necessary either to resign oneself to losing the effect, the economy, the strategy (and this loss can be enormous) or to add a gloss, of the translator's note sort, which always, even in the best of cases, the case of the greatest relevance, confesses the impotence or failure of the translation. While indicating that the meaning and formal effects of the text haven't escaped the translator and can therefore be brought to the reader's attention, the translator's note breaks with what I call the economic law of the word, which defines the essence of translation in the strict sense, the normal, normalized, pertinent, or relevant translation. Wherever the unity of the word is threatened or put into question, it is not only the operation of translation that finds itself compromised; it is also the concept, the definition, and the very axiomatics, the idea of translation that must be reconsidered.

In saying these things, I have gotten ahead of myself, formalized too quickly, proceeded to an unintelligible economy. What I have just said undoubtedly remains untranslatable. I shall slow down, then, and start over.

You might ask to what language the word *relevante* belongs. It is one of those English words that, in a confused and irregular way, is in the process of winning both use-value and exchange-value in French without ever having been, to my knowledge, officially sanctioned through the institutional channels of any academy. On this score, it represents one of those words whose use floats between several languages (there are more and more examples of them) and that merits an analysis that is at once linguistic and sociological, political and especially historical, wherever the phenomena of hegemony thus come to inscribe their signature on the body of a kind of idiom that is European or indeed universal in character (that it may in the first place be European, moreover, far from excludes the fact that it is spreading universally, and that it involves a vast question of translation without translators, if I can put it this way, although I must set it aside, like so many previous questions, for want of time).

This word "relevant," this present participle that functions as a predicate, is here entrusted with an exorbitant task. Not the task of the translator, but the task of defining—nothing less—the essence of translation. This word, whose relation to French or English is not very certain or decidable and that—I hope to show shortly—also retains an obscure Germanic filiation, thus comes to occupy a position that is *doubly* eminent and exposed.

On the one hand, it extends and announces the accomplishment of an ambitious response to the question of the essence of translation. (What is a translation?) To know what a relevant translation can mean and be, it is necessary to know what the essence of translation, its mission, its ultimate goal, its vocation is.

On the other hand, a relevant translation is assumed, rightly or wrongly, to be better than a translation that is not relevant. A relevant translation is held, rightly or wrongly, to be the best translation possible. The teleological definition of translation, the definition of the essence that is realized in translation, is therefore implicated in the definition of a relevant translation. The question, What is a relevant translation? would return to the question, What is translation? or, What should a translation be? And the question, What should a translation be? implies, as if synonymously, What should the best possible translation be?

Put another way (and put another way, the expression "put another way," "in other terms," "in other words," "en d'autres mots" is the phrase that silently announces every translation, at least when it designates itself as a translation and tells you, in an autodeictic manner, look, I am a translation, you are reading a translation, not an interlinguistic translation, to make use of Roman Jakobson's distinction, but an intralinguistic one[3]—and I am not sure whether or not this autodeixis accompanies the word "relevante" in my title), put another way, if the question, What is a relevant translation? signifies nothing other than the question, What is a translation? or What should the best possible translation be? then one should jettison the word "relevant" and forget it, dropping it without delay.

3. If one reflects on Jakobson's classification, only *interlinguistic* translation (the operation that transfers from one language to another and to which one most often refers as translation in the proper or strict sense) is governed by the economy I have described and, within it, by the unit of the word. Neither *intralinguistic* translation nor *intersemiotic* translation is governed by a principle of economy or above all by the unit of the word. [Derrida is referring to Roman Jakobson's famous essay, "On Linguistic Aspects of Translation," *On Translation*, ed. Reuben Brower (Cambridge, Mass., 1959), pp. 232–39, rpt. in *The Translation Studies Reader*, ed. Lawrence Venuti (London, 2000), pp. 113–18—TRANS.]

And yet I have kept it. Why? Perhaps to try to convince you of two things: on the one hand, this word of Latin origin, even though I no longer know to what language it belongs, whether French or English, has become indispensable to me, in its uniqueness, in translating several words originating in several languages, starting with German (as if it in turn contained more than one word in a single one); on the other hand, this translative word has become in turn untranslatable for the same reason. And when I say that this has happened to me, as I try to relate it, I don't mean at all that it is empirically personal because what has happened to me, or what has passed through me coming from languages and returning to them, was also a project of institutional accreditation and canonization in the public sphere. My first concern, then, has never been to appropriate this translation for myself, but to legitimate it, to make it known as the most relevant translation possible and therefore, on the contrary, to expropriate it from myself, to dispossess myself of it, while putting it on the market—even if I could still dream of leaving my likeness on this common currency and, like Shylock, expect an IOU for it.

How can I try to justify, or in any case submit for your discussion, the reasons for which, several times over the space of thirty years, I have judged relevant my use of one and the same verb, *relever*, to translate first a German word, then an English one?

The English word—let us start at the end—can be found in *The Merchant of Venice*. The privilege that I assign here to Shakespeare's play does not only depend on the presence of this word to be translated. In addition, by virtue of connotation, everything in the play can be re-translated into the code of translation and as a problem of translation; and this can be done according to the three senses that Jakobson distinguishes: interlinguistic, intralinguistic, and intersemiotic—as, for example, between a pound of flesh and a sum of money. At every moment, translation is as necessary as it is impossible. It is the law; it even speaks the language of the law beyond the law, of the impossible law, represented by a woman who is disguised, transfigured, converted, travestied, read *translated*, into a man of the law. As if the subject of this play were, in short, the task of the translator, his impossible task, his duty, his debt, as inflexible as it is unpayable. At least for three or four reasons:

1. First there is an *oath*, an untenable promise, with the risk of perjury, a debt and an obligation that constitute the very impetus for the intrigue, for the *plot*, for the conspiracy [*complot*]. Now it would be easy to show (and I have tried to do so elsewhere) that all translation

implies an insolvent indebtedness and an oath of fidelity to a given original—with all the paradoxes of such a law and such a promise, of a *bond* and a contract, of a promise that is, moreover, impossible and asymmetrical, transferential and countertransferential, like an oath doomed to treason or perjury.

2. Then there is the theme of economy, calculation, capital, and interest, the unpayable debt to Shylock: what I said above about the unit of the word clearly set up a certain economy as the law of translation.

3. In *The Merchant of Venice*, as in every translation, there is also, at the very heart of the obligation and the debt, an incalculable equivalence, an impossible but incessantly alleged correspondence between the pound of flesh and money, a required but impractical translation between the unique literalness of a proper body and the arbitrariness of a general, monetary, or fiduciary sign.

4. This impossible translation, this conversion (and all translation is a conversion: *vertere, transvertere, convertere*, as Cicero said) between the original, literal flesh and the monetary sign is not unrelated to the Jew Shylock's forced conversion to Christianity, since the traditional figure of the Jew is often and conventionally situated on the side of the body and the letter (from bodily circumcision or Pharisaism, from ritual compliance to literal exteriority), whereas St. Paul the Christian is on the side of the spirit or sense, of interiority, of spiritual circumcision. This relation of the letter to the spirit, of the body of literalness to the ideal interiority of sense is also the site of the passage of translation, of this conversion that is called translation. As if the business of translation were first of all an Abrahamic matter between the Jew, the Christian, and the Muslim. And the *relève*, like the relevance I am prepared to discuss with you, will be precisely what happens to the flesh of the text, the body, the spoken body and the translated body—when the letter is mourned to save the sense.

Shylock recalls that he promised *under oath* to respect the original text of the contract, the IOU. What is owed to him refers, literally, to the pound of flesh. This oath binds him to heaven, he recalls, he can't break it without perjuring himself, that is to say, without betraying it by translating its terms into monetary signs. In the name of the letter of the contract, Shylock refuses the translation or transaction (translation is a transaction). Portia proceeds to offer him three times the sum of money he is owed in exchange for the pound of flesh. If you translate the pound of flesh into money, she essentially proposes to him, you will have three times the sum owed. Shylock then exclaims:

> An oath, an oath, I have an oath in heaven,—
> Shall I lay perjury upon my soul?
> No not for Venice.[4]

Portia pretends to take note of this refusal and to recognize that "this bond is forfeit." With the contract, the bond, the IOU falling due, the Jew has the right to claim a pound of flesh that he must literally cut out very close to the merchant's heart:

> Why this bond is forfeit,
> And lawfully by this the Jew may claim
> A pound of flesh, to be by him cut off
> Nearest the merchant's heart.
> [*MV*, 4.1.226–29]

Portia will press Shylock one last time to pardon while cancelling the debt, remitting it, forgiving it. "Be merciful," she asks, "Take thrice the money, bid me tear the bond," the promissory note, the contract. Shylock again refuses; he swears truly on his soul that he cannot perjure himself and retract his oath. Countersigning his act of faith, swearing on what he has already sworn, he refers to language, to a tongue of man incapable of being measured, in its relative economy, in the proposed translation or transaction, against the absolute oath that binds his soul, unconditionally, before God:

> by my soul I swear,
> There is no power in the tongue of man
> To alter me,—I stay here on my bond.
> [*MV*, 4.1.236–38]

Thus the oath is, *in* the human tongue, a promise that human language, however, cannot itself undo, control, obliterate, subject by loosening it. An oath is a bond *in* human language that the human tongue,

---

4. This abstract arithmetic, this apparently arbitrary economy of multiplication by three—three times more than the monetary signs—points us to the scene of Portia's three suitors at the end of the play and the entire problematic of the three caskets, from *The Merchant of Venice* to *King Lear*. Read through a Freud who has been mobilized and interrogated, this will also be a great scene of transfer, metaphor, and translation. [See William Shakespeare, *The Merchant of Venice*, ed. John Russell Brown, vol. 23 of *The Arden Edition of the Works of William Shakespeare*, ed. Una Ellis-Fermor (London, 1951), 4.1.224–26; hereafter abbreviated *MV*—TRANS.]

as such, insofar as it is human, cannot loosen. *In* human language is a *bond* stronger than human language. More than man in man. In human language, the element of translation is an inflexible law that at once prohibits the translation of the transaction but commands respect for the original literalness or the given word. It is a law that presides over translation while commanding absolute respect, without any transaction, for the word given in its original letter. The oath, the sworn faith, the act of swearing is transcendence itself, the experience of passing beyond man, the origin of the divine or, if one prefers, the divine origin of the oath. This seems true of the law of translation in general. No sin is more serious than perjury, and Shylock repeats, while swearing, that he cannot perjure himself; he therefore confirms the first oath by a second oath in the time of a repetition. This is called fidelity, which is the very essence and vocation of an oath. When I swear, I swear in a language that no human language has the power to make me abjure, to disrupt, that is to say, to make me perjure myself. The oath passes *through* language, but it passes beyond human language. This would be the truth of translation.

In this fabulous tale of the oath, of the contractual *bond*, at issue is an indebtedness in which the exchange-values are incommensurable and thus each is untranslatable into the other (money/pound of flesh). In 4.1 Portia, disguised as a lawyer, first addresses herself to Antonio to ask him to acknowledge, to confess his unpaid or unpayable debt: "Do you confess the bond?" Do you confess, do you recognize the contract, the promise, the bond? "Reconnais-tu le billet?" ["Do you recognize the note?"] is the flat rendering by François-Victor Hugo, whose translation I have followed, at times modifying it. Do you acknowledge the acknowledgement of the debt, the IOU? Do you confirm the signed pledge, the bond, that which you owe, that because of which you are in debt or in default, indeed at fault (hence the word "confess")? Antonio's response: "I do" (a performative). Yes, I confess, I acknowledge, I recognize, I confirm and sign or countersign. *I do*: a sentence as extraordinary as a "yes." The economy and brevity of the response: as simple and bare as possible, the utterance implies not only an "I," an "I" who *does* what it says while saying it, confirming that he himself is the very person who has already heard, understood, memorized in its entirety the meaning of the question posed and integrated in turn into the response that signs the identity between the *I* who has heard and the *I* who utters the "yes" or the "I do." But it is also, given this understanding and the memory of the question, the same person as the one posing the question: I say *yes, I do*, precisely in response to what you mean by asking me this or posing this question to me. We think and mean the same thing (intralinguistic translation), we are the same person in the mirror of this measure. This mirrored or transparent univocity, this ideal translation, is supposed to be at work in all performative utterances of the type "I pardon."

After Antonio's confession, the response falls like a verdict. "Then must the Jew be merciful." Six brief words name *the Jew* and *mercy* in the same breath. This short sentence simultaneously signs both the economy and the incomparable genius of Shakespeare. It deserves to rise above this text as an immense allegory; it perhaps recapitulates the entire history of forgiveness, the entire history between the Jew and the Christian, the entire history of economics (*merces*, market, merchandise, *merci*, mercenary, wage, reward, literal or sublime) as a history of translation: "Then must the Jew be merciful."

Then (hence, consequently, *igitur*) the Jew must be *merciful*. He must be *clément, indulgent*, say certain French translations. Obviously, this means *here*: therefore, *igitur, then*, since you acknowledge the debt or the fault, the Jew (*this* Jew, Shylock, in this precise context) must free you from it. But the elliptical force of the verdict tends to take on a colossal symbolic and metonymic value on the scale of every historical period: "the Jew" also represents every Jew, the Jew in general in his *différend* with his Christian counterpart, Christian power, the Christian State. The Jew must forgive.

(Permit me a parenthesis here: while rereading this extraordinary verdict whose ruse we shall analyze in a moment—namely, the phrase that says "then the Jew must forgive," implying that "it is the Jew who must forgive," "it is up to the Jew in general to forgive"—I can't avoid recalling the Pope's extraordinary sigh at the end of the second millennium. Several months ago, as he was about to board a plane for one of his transcontinental journeys, he was asked what he thought of the French episcopate's declaration of repentence, and after sighing, after feeling a bit sorry for himself, after feeling a bit sorry for Christianity and Catholicism, he said: "I notice that it is always we who are asking for forgiveness." Well! The implication: forgiveness from the Jews [even if some people legitimately think of certain American Indians, too, as well as various other victims of the Inquisition whom the Pope has since put on the list as an another duty of commemoration, as it is called—or of repentence]. It is always we, Christians or Catholics, who are asking for forgiveness, but why? Yes, why? Is it that forgiveness is a Christian thing and Christians should set an example because Christ's Passion consisted of assuming sin on the cross? Or indeed because, under the circumstances, a certain Church, if not Christianity, will always have reproached itself a great deal, while asking for forgiveness, and first of all from the Jew, whom it has asked for forgiveness—and to be *merciful*? "Then must the Jew be merciful.")

Portia thus addresses herself to Antonio, her accomplice, and while referring to the Jew as a third party, she hears what the Jew hears: faced with your recognition, your acknowledgement, your confession, the Jew must be *merciful*, compassionate, forbearing, capable of forgiving, of remitting your pain or your payment, of erasing the debt, and so on. But the Jew doesn't understand Portia's deductive reasoning, he entirely refuses to understand this logic. She would like him to grant forgiveness and absolve the debt simply because it is recognized. The Jew then grows indignant:

"In virtue of what obligation, what constraint, what law must I be *merciful*?" The word that is translated by "obligation" or "constraint" or "law" is an interesting one: it is *compulsion*, which signifies an irresistable impulse or constraining power. "In virtue of what compulsion should I show myself *merciful*?"

> On what compulsion must I? Tell me that.
> [*MV*, 4.1.179]

In response to the Jew's question, Portia launches into a grand panegyric of the power of forgiveness. This superb speech defines *mercy*, forgiveness, as the supreme power. Without constraint, without obligation, gratuitous, an act of grace, a power above power, a sovereignty above sovereignty, a superlative might, mightier than might since it is a might without might, a respite within might, this transcendent might of *mercy* rises above might, above the economy of might and therefore above sanction as well as transaction. This is why mercy is the king's attribute, the right of grace, the absolute privilege of the monarch (or, in this case, of the doge). Yet it is also an infinite extravagance, another tread or trade in an infinite ascent, and just as this power is above power, a might mightier than might, so the monarch's attribute is at the same time above him and his sceptre. This might passes beyond humanity even as it passes through humanity, just as language does (as we mentioned earlier): it is only in God's keeping. Grace is divine, in earthly power it recalls what most resembles divine power, it is the superhuman within the human. The two discourses here echo or mirror one another, that of Shylock the Jew and Portia the Christian or the Christian in the guise of the law. Both place something (the oath, forgiveness) above human language *in* human language, beyond the human order *in* the human order, beyond human rights and duties *in* human law.

The strength of forgiveness, if you listen to Portia, is *more than* just, more just than justice or the law. It rises above the law or above what in justice is only law; it is, beyond human law, the very thing that invokes prayer. And what is, finally, a discourse on translation (possible/impossible) is also a discourse of *prayer on prayer*. Forgiveness is prayer; it belongs to the order of benediction and prayer on two sides: that of the person who requests it and that of the person who grants it. The essence of prayer has to do with forgiveness, not with power and law. Between the elevation of prayer or benediction—above human power, above even royal power insofar as it is human, above the law, above the penal code—and the elevation of forgiveness above human power, royal power and the law, there exists a sort of essential affinity. Prayer and forgiveness have the same provenance and the same essence, the same eminence that is more eminent than eminence, the eminence of the Most High.

Shylock is frightened by this exorbitant exhortation to forgive beyond the law, to renounce his right and his due. He is being asked to do more than he can and more than he even has the right to grant, given the *bond* (one is tempted to say the *Bund*) that obliges him beyond every human link. Shylock also senses that it is an attempt to steer his ship in circles, if I can speak this way about a story that involves a ship and a shipwreck. He who is presented as a diabolical figure ("the devil . . . in the likeness of a Jew" [*MV*, 3.1.20]) senses that he is in the process of being had, of being diabolically possessed in the name of the sublime transcendence of grace. There is a pretense of elevating him above everything, with this tale of divine and sublime forgiveness, but it is a ruse to empty his pockets while distracting him, to make him forget what he is owed and to punish him cruelly. So he protests, he grumbles, he complains, he clamors for the law, his right, his penalty. In any case, he is not deceived. In the name of this sublime panegyric of forgiveness, an economic ruse, a calculation, a stratagem is being plotted, the upshot of which (you know it well: the challenge to cut flesh without shedding one drop of blood) will be that Shylock loses everything in this translation of transaction, the monetary signs of his money as well as the literal pound of flesh—and even his religion, since when the situation takes a bad turn at his expense he will have to convert to Christianity, to translate himself *(convertere)* into a Christian, into a Christian language, after having been in turn forced, through a scandalous reversal—he who was entreated to be *merciful*—to implore the doge for mercy on his knees ("Down therefore," Portia will tell him, "and beg mercy from the duke"). The doge of Venice pretends to grant him this pardon so as to show how superior his generosity as a Christian and a monarch is to that of the Jew:

> That thou shalt see the difference of our spirit
> I pardon thee thy life before thou ask it:
> For half thy wealth, it is Antonio's,
> The other half comes to the general state,
> Which humbleness may drive unto a fine.
> [*MV*, 4.1.364–69]

The sovereignty of the doge, in its crafty manifestation, mimics absolute forgiveness, the pardon that is granted even where it is not requested, yet it is the pardon of a life. As for the rest, Shylock is totally expropriated, half of his fortune going to a private subject, Antonio, half to the State. And then—another economic ruse—in order to receive a reduction of the penalty and avoid total confiscation, the doge adds a condition, which is that Shylock repent ("repentir" is Hugo's translation for "humbleness"): if you give proof of humility while repenting, your penalty will be reduced and you will have only a fine to pay instead of total expropriation. As for the absolute pardon, the doge wields such sovereign power over it that he threatens to withdraw it:

> He shall do this, or else I do recant
> The pardon that I late pronounced here.
> [*MV*, 4.1.387–88]

Portia had protested against the offer to reduce the total confiscation to a fine on the condition of repentence. She says, "Ay for the state, not for Antonio" (which means that the penalty of confiscation is reduced for what Shylock owes the State, but not for what he owes Antonio). Then Shylock rebels and refuses the pardon. He refuses to pardon, for sure, to be *merciful*, but he reciprocally refuses to be pardoned at this price. He therefore refuses both to grant and to ask for forgiveness. He calls himself a foreigner, in short, to this entire phantasmic tale of forgiveness, to this entire unsavory plot of forgiveness, to all the Christian and theologico-political preaching that tries to pass off the moon as green cheese. He prefers to die than to be pardoned at this price because he understands or in any case senses that he would actually have to pay very dearly for the absolute and merciful pardon, and that an economy always hides behind this theatre of absolute forgiveness. Shylock then says, in a sort of countercalculation: Well, keep your pardon, take my life, kill me, for in taking from me everything that I have and all that I am, you in effect kill me.

> Nay, take my life and all, pardon not that,—
> You take my house, when you do take the prop
> That doth sustain my house: you take my life
> When you do take the means whereby I live.
> [*MV*, 4.1.370–73]

You know how things turn out: the extraordinary economy of rings and oaths. Regardless of whether Shylock is implicated in it, he finally loses everything. Once the doge has threatened to withdraw his pardon, he must agree to sign a complete remission of the debt and to undergo a forced conversion to Christianity.

Gratiano tells him:

> In christ'ning shalt thou have two godfathers,—
> Had I been judge, thou shouldst have had ten more,
> To bring thee to the gallows, not to the font.
> [*MV*, 4.1.394–96]

Exit Shylock.

Immediately after the scene I have just evoked, when Shylock has lost everything and left the stage (no more Jew on stage, no more Jew in the story), the profits are split, and the doge beseeches, implores, entreats (which is rendered into French as *conjure*) Portia to dine with him. She refuses, humbly begging his pardon: "I humbly do desire your grace of pardon" (the fact that great people are often called Your Grace or Your Gracious Majesty clearly underscores the power we are discussing here). She begs His Grace's pardon because she must travel out of town. The doge orders that *she*, or *he*, be remunerated ("gratify"), that she/he be paid or rewarded for her/his services:

> Antonio, gratify this gentleman,
> For in my mind you are much bound to him.
> [*MV*, 4.1.402–3]

This gratuity, this reward, is a wage. Portia knows it and she recognizes it, she knows and says that she has been paid for performing well in a scene of forgiveness and pardon as an able and cunning man of law; she admits, this woman in the guise of a man, that she has in some way been paid as a mercenary of gratitude [*le merci*], or mercy [*la merci*]:

> He is well paid that is well satisfied,
> And I delivering you, am satisfied,
> And therein do account myself well paid,—
> My mind was never yet more mercenary.
> [*MV*, 4.1.411–14]

No one could better express the "mercenary" dimension of "merci" in every sense of this word. And no one could ever express it better than Shakespeare, who has been charged with anti-Semitism for a work that stages with an unequalled power all the great motives of Christian anti-Judaism.

Finally, again in the same scene, Bassanio's response to Portia passes once more through a logic of forgiveness:

> Take some remembrance of us as a tribute,
> Not as a fee: grant me two things I pray you,—
> Not to deny me, and to pardon me.
> [*MV*, 4.1.418–20]

Such is the context in which Portia displays the eloquence for which she is paid as a mercenary man of the law.

Now here is the main dish, the plat de résistance. I have left the spiciest [*relevé*] taste for the end. Just after saying, "Then must the Jew be merciful," and after Shylock protests by asking, "On what compulsion must I?" Portia begins to speak again. I cite her speech in English, then translate or rather paraphrase it, step by step. It raises the stakes in admirable rhythms:

> First movement:
> The quality of mercy is not strain'd,
> It droppeth as the gentle rain from heaven
> Upon the place beneath: it is twice blest,
> It blesseth him that gives, and him that takes,
> [*MV*, 4.1.180–83]

The quality of mercy is not forced, constrained: mercy is not commanded, it is free, gratuitous; grace is gratuitous. Mercy falls from
heaven like a gentle shower. It can't be scheduled, calculated; it arrives
or doesn't, no one decides on it, nor does any human law; like rain, it
happens or it doesn't, but it's a good rain, a gentle rain; forgiveness isn't
ordered up, it isn't calculated, it is foreign to calculation, to economics,
to the transaction and the law, but it is good, like a gift, because mercy
gives by forgiving, and it fecundates; it is good, it is *bene*ficient, *bene*vo-
lent like a *bene*fit as opposed to a *male*faction, a good deed as opposed
to a misdeed. It falls, like rain, from above to below ("it droppeth . . .
upon the place beneath"): the person who forgives is, like forgiveness
itself, on high, very high, above the person who asks for or obtains
forgiveness. There is a hierarchy, and this is why the metaphor of rain
is not only that of a phenomenon that is not ordered up, but also that
of a vertical descending movement: forgiveness is given from above to
below. "It is twice blest; /It blesseth him that gives, and him that takes":
thus there is already a sharing of the good, of the good deed, a sharing
of the benediction, a performative event and a mirroring between two
benefits of the benediction, a mutual exchange, a translation between
giving and taking.

> Second movement:
> 'Tis the mightiest in the mightiest, it becomes
> The throned monarch better than his crown.
> His sceptre shows the force of temporal power,
> The attribute to awe and majesty,
> Wherein doth sit the dread and fear of kings:
> But mercy is above this sceptred sway,
> It is enthroned in the hearts of kings,
> It is an attribute to God himself;
> And earthly power doth then show likest God's
> When mercy seasons justice.
> [*MV*, 4.1.184–93]

Forgiving mercy is the mightiest or the almighty *in* the almighty:
"'Tis the mightiest in the mightiest," the omnipotence of omnipotence, the omnipotence in omnipotence or the almighty among all the
almighty, absolute greatness, absolute eminence, absolute might in absolute might, the hyperbolic superlative of might. The omnipotence of
omnipotence is at once the essence of power, the essence of might, the
essence of the possible, but also what, like the essence and superlative

of might, is at once the mightiest *of* might and more *than* might, *beyond* omnipotence. This limit of power, of might and of the possible obliges us to ask ourselves if the experience of forgiveness is an experience of "power," of the "power-to-forgive," the affirmation of power through forgiveness at the conjunction of all the orders of "I can," and not only of political power, or even the beyond of all power. What is always at issue here—another problem of translation—is the status of *more* as *the most* and as *more than*, of the mightiest as *more mighty than*—and as *more than* mighty, and therefore as another order than might, power, or the possible: the impossible that is *more than impossible and therefore possible.*[5]

In the same way, if forgiveness, if "mercy" or "the quality of mercy" is "the mightiest in the mightiest," this situates both the apex of omnipotence and something more and other than absolute power in "the mightiest in the mightiest." We should be able to follow, accordingly, the wavering of this limit between power and absolute powerlessness, powerlessness or the absolute impossible as unlimited power—which is not unrelated to the im-possible possible of translation.

Mercy becomes the throned monarch, Portia says, but even better than his crown. It is higher than the crown on a head; it *suits* the monarch, it becomes him, but it *suits* higher than his head and the head [*la tête et le chef*], than the attribute or sign of power that is the royal crown. Like the sceptre, the crown manifests temporal power, whereas forgiveness is a supratemporal, spiritual power. Above the authority of the sceptre, it is enthroned in the heart of kings. This omnipotence is

---

5. This structure is analogous to what Angelus Silesius, in *The Cherubic Pilgrim* (which I cite and analyze in *Sauf le nom* [Paris, 1993], p. 33), calls *Überunmöglichste* and describes as possible—this is God: *das Überunmöglichste ist möglich*—which can be translated, depending on how *über* is understood, as "*the most* impossible, the absolute impossible, the impossible par excellence is possible" or as "the more *than* impossible, the beyond of impossible is possible." These renderings are very different yet amount to the same thing, because in the two cases (the one comparative, the other superlative) they wind up saying that the tip of the summit (the peak) belongs to another order than that of the summit; the highest is therefore contrary to or other than what it surpasses; it is higher than the height of the most high: the most impossible and the more *than* impossible belong to another order than the impossible in general and can therefore be possible. The meaning of "possible," the significance of the concept of possibility, meanwhile, has undergone a mutation at the point and limit of the im-possible—if I can put it this way—and this mutation indicates what is at stake in our reflection on the impossible possibility of translation: there is no longer any possible contradiction between possible and impossible since they belong to two heterogeneous orders. [See Derrida's commentary on Angelus Silesius in *On the Name*, trans. David Wood and John P. Leavey Jr., ed. Thomas Dutoit (Stanford, Calif., 1995)—TRANS.]

different from temporal might, and to be different from might that is temporal and therefore earthly and political, it must be interior, spiritual, ideal, situated in the king's heart and not in his exterior attributes. The passage across the limit clearly follows the trajectory of an interiorization that passes from the visible to the invisible by becoming a thing of the heart: forgiveness as *pity* [*miséricorde*], if you wish, pity being the sensitivity of the heart to the misfortune of the guilty, which motivates forgiveness. This interior pity is divine in essence, but it also says something about the essence of translation. Portia obviously speaks as a Christian, she is already trying to convert or to pretend that she is preaching to a convert. In her effort to persuade Shylock to forgive, she is already attempting to convert him to Christianity; by feigning the supposition that he is already a Christian so that he will listen to what she has to say, she turns him toward Christianity by means of her logic and her rhetoric; she predisposes him to Christianity, as Pascal said, she preconverts him, she converts him inwardly, something that he will soon be forced to do physically, under constraint. She tries to convert him to Christianity by persuading him of the supposedly Christian interpretation that consists of interiorizing, spiritualizing, idealizing what among Jews (it is often said, at least, that this is a very powerful stereotype) will remain physical, external, literal, devoted to a respect for the letter. As with the difference between the circumcision of the flesh and the Pauline circumcision of the heart—there will certainly be a need to look for a translation, in the broad sense, with regard to this problematic of circumcision (literal circumcision of the flesh versus ideal and interior circumcision of the heart, Jewish circumcision versus Christian circumcision, the whole debate surrounding Paul). What happens between the Jew Shylock and the legislation of the Christian State in this wager of a pound of flesh before the law, the oath, the sworn faith, the question of literalness, and so on? If forgiveness dwells within the king's heart and not in his throne, his sceptre, or his crown, that is, in the temporal, earthly, visible, and political attributes of his power, a leap has been made toward God. The power to pardon interiorized in mankind, in human power, in royal power as human power, is what Portia calls divine: it will be God-*like*. This *like*, this analogy or resemblance, supports a logic or analogic of theologico-political translation, of the translation of the theological into political.

> It is enthroned in the hearts of kings,
> It is an attribute to God himself;

And earthly power doth then show likest God's
When mercy seasons justice.

The earthly power that most resembles God is that which "seasons justice," which "tempers" justice with forgiveness.

"Tempère" [tempers] is Hugo's translation for "seasons." It isn't an erroneous choice; it in fact means "to season" [*assaisonner*], to mix, to cause to change, to modify, to temper, to dress food or to affect a climate, a sense of taste or quality. Let's not forget that this speech began by trying to describe "the quality of mercy."

Yet I am tempted to replace Hugo's translation, "tempère," which is not bad, with another. It will not be a true translation, above all not a relevant translation. It will not respond to the name *translation*. It will not *render*, it will not pay its dues, it will not make a full restitution, it will not pay off all its debt, first and foremost its debt to an assumed concept, that is, to the self-identity of meaning alleged by the word *translation*. It will not be answerable to [*relever de*] what is currently called a translation, a *relevant* translation. But apart from the fact that the most relevant translation (that which presents itself as the transfer of an intact signified through the inconsequential vehicle of any signifier whatsoever) is the least relevant possible, the one I offer will allow me to attempt at least *three gestures* at once, to tie together, in the same economy, three necessities that will all be linked to the history of a translation that I took the somewhat rash initiative in proposing, over thirty years ago, and that is now publicly canonized in French—all the while naturally remaining untranslatable into any other language. I shall therefore translate "seasons" as "relève": "when mercy seasons justice," "quand le pardon relève la justice (ou le droit)" [*when mercy elevates and interiorizes, thereby preserving and negating, justice (or the law)*].

1. *First justification*: an immediate guarantee in the play of the idiom. *Relever* first conveys the sense of cooking suggested here, like *assaisonner*. It is a question of giving taste, a different taste that is blended with the first taste, now dulled, remaining the same while altering it, while changing it, while undoubtedly removing something of its native, original, idiomatic taste, but also while adding to it, and in the very process, *more* taste, while cultivating its natural taste, while giving it *still more of its own taste*, its own, natural flavor—this is what we call "relever" in French cooking. And this is precisely what Portia says: mercy seasons [*relève*] justice, the quality of mercy seasons the taste of justice. Mercy keeps the taste of justice while affecting it, refining it, cultivating it;

mercy resembles justice, but it comes from somewhere else, it belongs to a different order, at the same time it modifies justice, it at once tempers and strengthens justice, changes it without changing it, converts it without converting it, yet while improving it, while exalting it. Here is the first reason to translate *seasons* with "relève," which effectively preserves the gustatory code and the culinary reference of *to season*, "assaisonner": *to season with spice*, to spice. *A seasoned dish* is, according to the translation in the *Robert* dictionary, "un plat relevé."[6] Justice preserves its own taste, its own meaning, but this very taste is better when it is *seasoned* or "relevé" by mercy. Without considering that *mercy* can redeem, deliver, ease, indemnify, indeed cure (this is the chain *heal, heilen, holy, heilig*) justice which, thus eased, lightened, delivered (*relieved*), redeems itself with a view to sacrosanct salvation.

2. *Second justification*: "relever" effectively expresses elevation. Mercy elevates justice, it pulls and inspires justice toward highness, toward a height higher than the crown, the sceptre, and power that is royal, human, earthly, and so on. Sublimation, elevation, exaltation, ascension toward a celestial height, the highest or the most high, higher than height. Thanks to forgiveness, thanks to mercy, justice is even more just, it transcends itself, it is spiritualized by rising and thus lifting itself [*se relevant*] above itself. Mercy sublimates justice.

3. There is, finally, a *third justification* for the verb *relever*. I use this word *justification* to reconcile what would render this translation relevant to the conjoined motif of justice ("Mercy seasons justice") and justness or appropriateness [*justesse*], to what must be the appropriate word, the most appropriate possible, more appropriate than appropriate. This last justification would then give a philosophical meaning and coherence to the economy, accumulation, capitalization of good grounds. In 1967, to translate a crucial German word with a double meaning (*Aufheben, Aufhebung*), a word that signifies at once to suppress and to elevate, a word that Hegel says represents the speculative risk of the German language, and that the entire world had until then agreed was untranslatable—or, if you prefer, a word for which no one had agreed with anyone on a stable, satisfying translation into any lan-

6. The rich entry in the *Oxford English Dictionary* gives some splendid uses for such diverse meanings as "to render more palatable by the addition of some savoury ingredient," "to adapt," "to accommodate to a particular taste," "to moderate, to alleviate, to temper, to embalm; to ripen, to fortify." A more rare and more archaic (sixteenth century) use: "to impregnate, to copulate," as in "when a male hath once seasoned the female, he never after touches her."

guage—for this word, I had proposed the noun *relève* and the verb *relever*. This allowed me to retain, joining them in a single word, the double motif of the elevation and the replacement that preserves what it denies or destroys, preserving what it causes to disappear, quite like—in a perfect example—what is called in the armed forces, in the navy, say, the relief [*relève*] of the guard. This usage is also possible in English, *to relieve.*[7] Was my operation a translation?[8] I am not sure that it deserves this term. The fact is that it has become irreplaceable and nearly canonized, even in the university, occasionally in other languages where the French word is used as if it were quoted from a translation, even where its origin is no longer known, or when its place of origin—I mean "me"—or its taste is disliked. Without plunging us very deeply into the issues, I must at least recall that the movement of *Aufhebung*, the process of establishing relevance, is always in Hegel a dialectical movement of interiorization, interiorizing memory *(Erinnerung)* and sublimating spiritualization. It is also a translation. Such a *relève* is precisely at issue here, in Portia's mouth (mercy *relève*, it elevates, replaces and interiorizes the justice that it seasons). Above all, we find the same need for the *Aufhebung*, the *relève*, at the very heart of the Hegelian interpretation of mercy, particularly in *The Phenomenology of Mind*: the movement toward philosophy and absolute knowledge as the truth of the Christian religion passes through the experience of mercy.[9] Mercy is a *relève*, it is in its essence an *Aufhebung*. It is translation as well. In the horizon of expiation, redemption, reconciliation, and salvation.

When Portia says that mercy, above the sceptre, seated on the inte-

---

7. I have just alluded to the navy. Well, then, Joseph Conrad, for example, writes in "The Secret Sharer": "I would get the second mate to relieve me at that hour"; then "I . . . returned on deck for my relief." [Joseph Conrad, "The Secret Sharer," (1910; New York, 1981), pp. 139, 149.]

8. Curiously, the first time that the word *relève* seemed to me indispensable for translating (without translating) the word *Aufhebung* was on the occasion of an analysis of the sign. (See *Le Puits et la pyramide: Introduction à la semiologie de Hegel*, a lecture delivered at the Collège de France in Jean Hyppolite's seminar during January 1968, reprinted in *Marges de la philosophie* (Paris, 1972), p. 102 [See Derrida, "The Pit and the Pyramid: An Introduction to Hegel's Semiology," *Margins of Philosophy*, trans. Alan Bass (Chicago, 1982)—TRANS.].) Most of the so-called undecidable words that have interested me ever since are also, by no means accidentally, untranslatable into a single word (*pharmakon*, supplément, différance, hymen, and so on). This list cannot, by definition, be given any closure.

9. In *The Phenomenology of Mind*, at the end of *Die offenbare Religion*, just before *Das absolute Wissen*, therefore at the transition between absolute religion and absolute knowledge—as the truth of religion.

rior throne in the king's heart, is an attribute of God himself, and that therefore, as an earthly power, mercy *resembles* a divine power at the moment when it elevates, preserves, and negates [*relève*] justice (that is, the law), what counts is the resemblance, the analogy, the figuration, the maximal analogy, a sort of human translation of divinity: in human power mercy is what most resembles, what most is and reveals itself *as*, a divine power ("then show likest God's"):

> But mercy is above the sceptred sway,
> It is enthroned in the hearts of kings,
> It is an attribute to God himself;
> And earthly power doth then show likest God's
> When mercy seasons justice.

This doesn't mean, necessarily, that mercy comes only from one person, up there, who is called God, from a pitying Father who lets his mercy descend upon us. No, that can also mean that as soon as there is mercy, if in fact there is any, the so-called human experience reaches a zone of divinity: mercy is the genesis of the divine, of the holy or the sacred, but also the site of pure translation. (A risky interpretation. It could, let us note too quickly, efface the need for the singular person, for the pardoning or pardoned person, the "who" irreducible to the essential quality of a divinity, and so forth.)

This *analogy* is the very site of the theologico-political, the hyphen or translation between the theological and the political; it is also what underwrites political sovereignty, the Christian incarnation of the body of God (or Christ) in the king's body, the king's two bodies. This analogical—and Christian—articulation between two powers (divine and royal, heavenly and earthly), insofar as it passes here through the sovereignty of mercy and the right of grace, is also the sublime greatness that authorizes or enables the authorization of every ruse and vile action that permit the lawyer Portia, mouthpiece of all Shylock's Christian adversaries from the merchant Antonio to the doge, to get the better of the Jew, to cause him to lose everything, his pound of flesh, his money, even his religion. In expressing all the evil that can be thought of the Christian ruse as a discourse of mercy, I am not about to praise Shylock when he raises a hue and cry for his pound of flesh and insists on the literalness of the *bond*. I analyze only the historical and allegorical cards that have been dealt in this situation and all the discursive, logical, theological, political, and economic resources of the concept of mercy, the legacy (our legacy) of this semantics of mercy—precisely inasmuch as it is indissociable from a certain European interpretation of translation.

After thus proposing three justifications for my translation of *seasons* and *Aufhebung* as *relève* (verb and noun), I have gathered too many reasons to dissemble the fact that my choice aimed for the best transaction possible, the most economic, since it allows me to use a single word to translate so many other words, even languages, with their denotations and connotations. I am not sure that this transaction, even if it is the most economic possible, merits the name of *translation*, in the strict and pure sense of this word. It rather seems one of those other things in *tr.*, a transaction, transformation, travail, *travel*—and a treasure trove [*trouvaille*] (since this invention, if it also seemed to take up [*relever*] a challenge, as another saying goes, consisted only in discovering what was waiting, or in waking what was sleeping, in the language). The treasure trove amounts to a travail; it puts to work the languages, first of all, without adequation or transparency, here assuming the shape of a new writing or rewriting that is performative or poetic, not only in French, where a new use for the word emerges, but also in German and English. Perhaps this operation perhaps still participates in the travail of the negative in which Hegel saw a relève *(Aufhebung)*. If I supposed, then, that the quasi-translation, the transaction of the word *relève* is indeed "relevant" (an English word in the process of Frenchification), that would perhaps qualify the effectiveness of this travail and its supposed right to be legitimated, accredited, quoted at an official market price. But its principal interest, if I can evaluate it in terms of usury and the market, lies in what it might say about the economy of every interlinguistic translation, this time in the strict and pure sense of the word. Undoubtedly, in taking up a challenge [*en relevant un défi*], a word is added to the French language, a word in a word. The use that I have just made of the word *relever*, "en relevant un défi," also becomes a challenge, a challenge, moreover, to every translation that would like to welcome into another language all the connotations that have accumulated in this word. These remain innumerable in themselves, perhaps unnameable: more than one word in a word, more than one language in a single language, beyond every possible compatibility of homonyms. What the translation with the word "relevant" also demonstrates, in an exemplary fashion, is that every translation should be relevant by vocation. It would thus guarantee the *survival* of the body of the original (*survival* in the double sense that Benjamin gives it in "The Task of the

Translator," *fortleben* and *überleben*: prolonged life, continuous life, *living on*, but also life after death).[10]

Isn't this what a translation does? Doesn't it guarantee these *two* survivals by losing the flesh during a process of conversion [*change*]? By elevating the signifier to its meaning or value, all the while preserving the mournful and debt-laden memory of the singular body, the first body, the unique body that the translation thus elevates, preserves, and negates [*relève*]? Since it is a question of a travail—indeed, as we noted, a travail of the negative—this relevance is a travail of mourning, in the most enigmatic sense of this word, which merits a re-elaboration that I have attempted elsewhere but cannot undertake here. The measure of the *relève* or relevance, the price of a translation, is always what is called meaning, that is, value, preservation, truth as preservation *(Wahrheit, bewahren)* or the value of meaning, namely, what, in being freed from the body, is elevated above it, interiorizes it, spiritualizes it, preserves it in memory. A faithful and mournful memory. One doesn't even have to say that translation preserves the value of meaning or must raise [*relever*] the body to it: the very concept, the value of meaning, the meaning of meaning, the value of the preserved value originates in the mournful experience of translation, of its very possibility. By resisting this transcription, this transaction which is a translation, this *relève*, Shylock delivers himself into the grasp of the Christian strategy, bound hand and foot. (The cost of a wager between Judaism and Christianity, blow for blow: they translate themselves, although not into one another.)

I insist on the Christian dimension. Apart from all the traces that Christianity has left on the history of translation and the normative concept of translation, apart from the fact that the relève, Hegel's *Aufhebung* (one must never forget that he was a very Lutheran thinker, undoubtedly like Heidegger), is explicitly a speculative *relève* of the Passion and Good Friday into absolute knowledge, the travail of mourning also describes, through the Passion, through a memory haunted by the

---

10. [See Walter Benjamin, "The Task of the Translator," *Illuminations*, trans. Harry Zohn, ed. Hannah Arendt (New York, 1968), pp. 69–82, esp. pp. 71–73. For Derrida's commentary on Benjamin's concepts, see "Des Tours de Babel," (trans. Joseph Graham) in *Difference in Translation*, ed. Graham (Ithaca, N.Y., 1985). Zohn's translation contains significant errors that have been described by Steven Rendall in his "Notes on Zohn's translation of Benjamin's 'Die Aufgabe des Übersetzers,'" *TTR: Traduction Terminologie Rédaction*, no. 10 (1997): 191–206. Rendall offers an alternative translation of the essay in the same issue (pp. 151–65). The German text appears in Benjamin, *Gesammelte Schriften*, ed. Rolf Tiedemann and Hermann Schweppenhäuser, 7 vols. in 14 (Frankfurt am Main, 1974–89) 4:1:7–21—TRANS.]

WHAT IS A "RELEVANT" TRANSLATION

body lost yet preserved in its grave, the resurrection of the ghost or of the glorious body that rises, rises again [*se relève*]—and walks.

Without wishing to cause any grief to Hegel's ghost, I leave aside the third movement that I had announced in Portia's speech (which would have dealt with translation as prayer and benediction).[11]

Merci for the time you have given me, pardon, *mercy*, forgive the time I have taken from you.

11. This would be a matter, without speaking further about the doge and the State, of examining and weighing justice on one side (and justice here must be understood as the law, the justice that is calculable and *enforced*, applied, applicable, and not the justice that I distinguish elsewhere from the law; here justice means the juridical, the judiciary, positive, indeed penal law). To examine and weigh justice on one side with salvation on the other, it seems necessary to choose between them and to renounce law so as to attain salvation. This would be like giving an essential dignity simultaneously to the word and the value of *prayer*; prayer would be that which allows one to go beyond the law toward salvation or the hope of salvation; it would belong to the order of forgiveness, like benediction, which was considered at the beginning (forgiveness is a *double benediction*: for the person who grants it and for the person who receives it, for whoever gives and for whoever takes). Now if prayer belongs to the order of forgiveness (whether requested or granted), it has no place at all in the law. Nor in philosophy (in onto-theology, says Heidegger). But before suggesting that a calculation is an economy again lurking in this logic, I read these lines from Portia's speech. Just after saying "when mercy seasons justice," she (or he) continues:

> Therefore, Jew
> Though justice be thy plea, consider this,
> That in the course of justice, none of us
> Should see salvation. We do pray for mercy,
> And that same prayer, doth teach us all to render
> The deeds of mercy. I have spoke thus much
> To mitigate the justice of thy plea,
> Which if thou follow, this strict court of Venice
> Must needs give sentence 'gainst the merchant there.
> [*MV*, 4.1.193–201]

Paraphrase: "Thus, Jew, although justice (the good law) may be your argument (*plea*: your allegation, what you plead, that in the name of which you plead, your cause but also your plea), consider this: that with the simple process of the law (the simple juridical procedure) none of us would attain salvation: we pray, in truth, for forgiveness (mercy) (*we do pray for mercy*), and this is the prayer, this prayer, this very prayer (*that same prayer*) that teaches us to do merciful acts (to forgive) to everyone. Everything I have just said is to mitigate the justice of your cause; if you persist, if you continue to pursue this cause, the strict tribunal of Venice will necessarily have to order the arrest of the merchant present here."

13   The Animal That Therefore I Am (More to Follow)

Translated by David Wills

To begin with, I would like to entrust myself to words that, were it possible, would be naked.

Naked in the first place—but this is in order to announce already that I plan to speak endlessly of nudity and of the nude in philosophy. Starting from Genesis. I

This article represents the first part of a ten-hour address Derrida gave at the third Cerisy-la-Salle conference devoted to his work, in July 1997. The title of the conference was "L'Animal autobiographique"; see *L'Animal autobiographique: Autour de Jacques Derrida*, ed. Marie-Louise Mallet (Paris, 1999); Derrida's essay appears on pp. 251–301. Later segments of the address dealt with Descartes, Kant, Heidegger, Lacan, and Lévinas, as note 4 explains and as other allusions made by Derrida suggest. The Lacan segment will appear in *Zoo-Ontologies: The Question of the Animal in Contemporary Theory and Culture*, ed. Cary Wolfe (Minneapolis, 2002).

The French title of Derrida's article is *"L'Animal que donc je suis (à suivre)."* An obvious play on Descartes's definition of consciousness (of the thinking animal as human), it also takes advantage of the shared first-person singular present form of *être* (to be) and *suivre* (to follow) in order to suggest a displacement of that priority, also reading as "the animal that therefore I follow after." Throughout the translation "I am" has, very often, to be read also as "I follow," and vice versa. I have adopted the formula "I am (following)," except where the context, or demands of fluency, dictate a choice of one or the other possibility.—TRANS.

would like to choose words that are, to begin with, naked, quite simply, words from the heart.

And to utter these words without repeating myself, without beginning again what I have already said here, more than once. It is said that one must avoid repeating oneself, in order not to give the appearance of training [*dressage*], already, of a habit or a convention that would in the long term program the very act of thanking.

Some of you, and the thought of it moves me to tears, were already here in 1980, or again in 1992, at the time of the previous two conferences. Some even, among my dearest and most faithful friends (Philippe Lacoue-Labarthe and Marie-Louise Mallet), had already inspired, conceived of, and brought to fruition those two occasions, with the smiling genius that Marie-Louise radiates once again. Jean-Luc Nancy promised us he would be here again. With Philippe he opened the 1980 conference. I think of him constantly, and he must know that his friends and admirers send him their very best wishes from here.

To those I have just named I owe so much that the language of gratitude is insufficient. What I owe them remains infinite and indelible.

Without forgetting that, I wish, if you'll forgive me, to go back in time, back to an earlier moment still, to a time before that time.

And to speak from that point in time, so long ago [*depuis le temps*] as one says,[1] a time that for me becomes fabulous or mythical.

Some of you here, Maurice de Gandillac first of all, whom I wish to greet and thank in pride of place, know that about forty years ago, in 1959, our wonderful hosts here at Cerisy were already offering me their hospitality—and it was the moment of my very first lecture, in fact the first time I spoke in public. If already I were to give in to what others might call the instinct of the autobiographical animal, I might recall that in 1959, as today, the theme was, in short, Genesis. The title of the conference was "Structure and Genesis," and it was my first ten-day Cerisy event. Following that I have greatly enjoyed returning for "Nietzsche" in 1972, "Ponge" in 1974, "Lyotard" in 1982. I don't have to say any more about that for you to be able, not so much to measure, for it is immeasurable, but rather to sense the immensity of my gratitude.

1.The adverbial fragment *depuis le temps*, which is not usually used as such in French, is repeated throughout the text. The relative form, *depuis le temps que*, has the sense of "for so long now." Below, I have used either that formulation or "since so long ago" except where Derrida's repetitions allow for the contrived phrase "since time." In all cases the reader should bear in mind Derrida's reference to the mythological and philosophical "prehistory" of conceptualizations of the animal that he is calling into question.—TRANS.

Everything I will venture to say today will be, once more, in order to express my thanks, in order to say, "thanks to this place, to those who greet us here and to you." I experience my returns to Cerisy as a wonderful and intense story that has marked out almost my whole adult life, everything I have managed to think about it out loud. If ever the animal that I am were to take it upon itself to write an autobiography (whether intellectual or emotional), it would have to name Cerisy again and again, more than once and in more than one way—in the renown of the proper name and of metonymy.

As for this conference, the third in something like a series, it seemed to me unimaginable, even excluded in advance. Last time, in 1992, when Didier Cahen alluded to its possibility in the attic on the last evening, asking me what the theme of a third conference would be, I still remember dismissing such a hypothesis: "This guy is crazy," I exclaimed. He wasn't so crazy, but the whole idea remains, like everything that happens, and such is the condition for something to be able to happen, impossible to anticipate. It is only after the event, reading the titles of these three meetings ("Les Fins de l'homme," "Le Passage des frontières," "L'Animal autobiographique") with a feeling of uncanniness, that I perceived a sort of prescriptive arrangement, a preestablished if not harmonious order, a providential machine as Kant would say precisely concerning the animal, "als eine Maschine der Vorsehung," an obscure foresight, the process of a blind but sure prefiguration in the configuration: one and the same movement being outlined and seeking its end. "Les Fins de l'homme" (title chosen by Philippe Lacoue-Labarthe and Jean-Luc Nancy without asking for my input, and I didn't ask to give it, although the title was also that of one of my texts), "Le Passage des frontières" and "L'Animal autobiographique" (titles that I myself proposed to Marie-Louise and to our hosts at Cerisy): later I began to hear in them, in these three kick-offs, what no one, least of all myself, had ever calculated, and what no one would be able to reappropriate, namely the outline or the temptation of a single phrase, a phrase offering more to follow [qui se donnerait à suivre].

It follows, itself; it follows itself. It could say "I am," "I follow," "I follow myself," "I am (in following) myself." In being pursued this way, consequentially, three times or in three rhythms, it would describe something like the course of a three-act play or the three movements of a syllogistic concerto, a displacement that becomes a *suite*, a result in a single word.

If I am to follow this suite [si je suis cette suite], and everything in what I am about to say will lead back to the question of what "to follow" or "to pursue" means, as well as "to be after," back to the question of what I do when "I am" or "I follow," when I say "*Je suis*," if I am to follow this suite then, I move from "the ends of man," that is the confines of man, to "the crossing of borders" between man and animal. Crossing borders or the ends of man I come or surrender to the animal—to the animal in itself, to the animal in me and the animal at unease with itself, to the man about which Nietzsche said (I no longer remember where) something to the effect that it was an as yet undetermined animal, an animal lacking in itself. Nietzsche also said, at the very beginning of the second treatise of *The Genealogy of Morals*, that man is a promising animal, by which he meant, underlining those words, an animal that is permitted to make promises (*das versprechen darf*). Nature is said to have given itself the task of raising, bringing up, domesticating and "disciplining" (*heranzüchten*) this animal that promises.

Since time, since so long ago, hence since all of time and for what remains of it to come we would therefore be in passage toward surrendering to the promise of that animal at unease with itself.

Since time, therefore.

Since so long ago, can we say that the animal has been looking at us?[2]

What animal? The other.

I often ask myself, just to see, *who I am*—and who I am (following) at the moment when, caught naked, in silence, by the gaze of an animal, for example the eyes of a cat, I have trouble, yes, a bad time[3] overcoming my embarrassment.

Whence this malaise?

I have trouble repressing a reflex dictated by immodesty. Trouble keeping silent within me a protest against the indecency. Against the impropriety that comes of finding oneself naked, one's sex exposed, stark naked before a cat that looks at you without moving, just to see. The impropriety [*malséance*] of a certain animal nude before the other animal, from that point on one might call it a kind of *animalséance*: the single, incomparable and original experience of the impropriety that would come from appearing in truth naked, in front of the insistent gaze of the animal, a benevolent or pitiless gaze, surprised or cognizant. The

2. "Que l'animal nous regarde": also "that the animal has been our concern."—TRANS.

3. "J'ai du mal": this colloquial expression also evokes the sense of evil or a curse. Here and below Derrida implies a recasting of the Genesis myth whereby it is an animal that brings man to consciousness of his nakedness and of good and evil rather than being the cause (via woman) of his fall.—TRANS.

gaze of a seer, visionary, or extra-lucid blind person. It is as if I were
ashamed, therefore, naked in front of this cat, but also ashamed for being ashamed. A reflected shame, the mirror of a shame ashamed of itself,
a shame that is at the same time specular, unjustifiable, and unable to
be admitted to. At the optical center of this reflection would appear this
thing—and in my eyes the focus of this incomparable experience—that
is called nudity. And about which it is believed that it is proper to man,
that is to say foreign to animals, naked as they are, or so it is thought,
without the slightest inkling of being so.

Ashamed of what and naked before whom? Why let oneself be overcome with shame? And why this shame that blushes for being ashamed?
Especially, I should make clear, if the cat observes me frontally naked,
face to face, and if I am naked faced with the cat's eyes looking at me
as it were from head to toe, just *to see*, not hesitating to concentrate its
vision—in order to see, with a view to seeing—in the direction of my
sex. *To see*, without going to see, without touching yet, and without bit-
ing, although that threat remains on its lips or on the tip of the tongue.
Something happens there that shouldn't take place—like everything that
happens in the end, a lapsus, a fall, a failure, a fault, a symptom (and
symptom, as you know, also means "fall": case, unfortunate event, coincidence, what falls due [*échéance*], mishap). It is as if, at that instant,
I had said or were going to say the forbidden, something that shouldn't
be said. As if I were to admit what cannot be admitted in a symptom
and, as one says, wanted to bite my tongue.

Ashamed of what and before whom? Ashamed of being as naked
as an animal [*bête*]. It is generally thought, although none of the philosophers I am about to examine actually mention it,[4] that the property
unique to animals and what in the final analysis distinguishes them from
man, is their being naked without knowing it. Not being naked therefore, not having knowledge of their nudity, in short without consciousness of good and evil.

From that point on, naked without knowing it, animals would not,
in truth, be naked.

They wouldn't be naked because they are naked. In principle, with
the exception of man, no animal has ever thought to dress itself. Clothing would be proper to man, one of the "properties" of man. Dressing

4. Later the same day, and on the next day, this introduction was followed by four
sessions during which I proposed readings of Descartes, Kant, Heidegger, Lévinas, and
Lacan. Those interpretations, as close and patient as possible, were designed to test the
working hypotheses that I am outlining here, on the threshold of a work in progress.

oneself would be inseparable from all the other forms of what is proper to man, even if one talks about it less than speech or reason, the *logos*, history, laughing, mourning, burial, the gift, and so on. (The list of properties unique to man always forms a configuration, from the first moment. For that reason, it can never be limited to a single trait and it is never closed; structurally speaking it can attract a nonfinite number of other concepts, beginning with the concept of a concept.)

The animal, therefore, is not naked because it is naked. It doesn't feel its own nudity. There is no nudity "in nature." There is only the sentiment, the affect, the (conscious or unconscious) experience of existing in nakedness. Because it *is* naked, without *existing* in nakedness, the animal neither feels nor sees itself naked. And it therefore is not naked. At least that is what is thought. For man it would be the opposite, and clothing derives from technics. We would therefore have to think shame and technicity together, as the same "subject." And evil and history, and work, and so many other things that go along with it. Man would be the only one to have invented a garment to cover his sex. He would only be a man to the extent that he was able to be naked, that is to say to be ashamed, to know himself to be ashamed because he is no longer naked. And knowing *himself* would mean knowing himself to be ashamed. On the other hand, because the animal is naked without consciousness of being naked, modesty would remain as foreign to it as would immodesty. As would the knowledge of self that is involved in that.

What is shame if one can be modest only by remaining immodest, and vice versa. Man could never become naked again because he has the sense of nakedness, that is to say of modesty or shame. The animal would be *in* nonnudity because it is nude, and man *in* nudity to the extent that he is no longer nude. There we encounter a difference, a time or *contretemps* between two *nudities without nudity*. This contretemps has only just begun doing us harm [*mal*], in the area of the science of good and evil.

Before the cat that looks at me naked, would I be ashamed *like* an animal that no longer has the sense of nudity? Or on the contrary, *like* a man who retains the sense of his nudity? Who am I therefore? Who is it that I am (following)? Whom should this be asked of if not of the other? And perhaps of the cat itself?

I must make it clear from the start, the cat I am talking about is a real cat, truly, believe me, *a little cat*. It isn't the *figure* of a cat. It doesn't silently enter the room as an allegory for all the cats on the earth, the felines that traverse myths and religions, literature and fables. There are so many of them. The cat I am talking about does not belong to Kafka's vast zoopoetics, something that nevertheless solicits attention, endlessly and from a novel perspective. Nor is the cat that looks at me, and to which I seem—but don't count on it—to be dedicating a negative zoo-theology, Hoffmann's or Kofman's cat Murr, although along with me it uses this occasion to salute the magnificent and inexhaustible book that Sarah Kofman devotes to it, namely *Autobiogriffures*, whose title resonates so well with that of this conference. That book keeps vigil over this conference and asks to be continually quoted or reread.

An animal looks at me. What should I think of this sentence? The cat that looks at me naked and that is *truly a little cat, this* cat I am talking about, which is also a female, isn't Montaigne's cat either, the one he nevertheless calls "my [pussy]cat" [*ma chatte*] in his *Apology for Raymond Sebond*.[5] You will recognize that as one of the greatest pre- or anti-Cartesian texts on the animal. Later we will pay attention to a certain evolution from Montaigne to Descartes, an event that is obscure and difficult to assign a date to, to identify even, between two configurations for which these proper names are metonymies. Montaigne makes fun of "man's impudence with regard to the beasts," of the "presumption" and "imagination" shown by man when he claims to assign them or refuse them certain faculties (*A*, pp. 331, 330). Contrary to that he deems it necessary to recognize in animals a "facility" in forming letters and syllables. This capacity, Montaigne confidently assures us, "testifies that they have an inward power of reason which makes them so teachable and determined to learn" (*A*, p. 340). Taking man to task for "carv[ing] out their shares to his fellows and companions the animals,

5. Michel de Montaigne, *Apology for Raymond Sebond*, in *Essays*, in *The Complete Works of Montaigne*, trans. Donald M. Frame (Stanford, Calif., 1957), bk. 2, chap. 12, p. 331; hereafter abbreviated *A*. The *Apology* needs to be examined very closely, especially to the extent that Montaigne doesn't just revive, in its luxuriant richness, a tradition that attributes much to the animal, beginning with a type of language. Most pertinent in this respect, marking a difference from the modern (Cartesian or post-Cartesian) form of a hegemonic tradition is the moment where Montaigne recognizes in the animal more than a right to communication, to the sign, to language as sign (something Descartes will not deny), namely, *a capacity to respond*. For example:

It is not credible that Nature has denied us this resource that she has given to many other animals: for what is it but speech, this faculty we see in them of complaining, rejoicing, calling to each other for help, inviting each other to love, as they do by the use of their voice? How could they not speak to one another? They certainly speak to us, and we to them. In how many ways do we not speak to our dogs? *And they answer us.* We talk to them in another language, with other names, than to birds, hogs, oxen, horses; and we change the idiom according to the species.

And following a quotation from Dante concerning the ant: "It seems that Lactantius attributes to beasts not only speech but also laughter" (*A*, p. 335; my italics).

and distribut[ing] among them such portions of faculties and powers as he sees fit," he asks, and the question refers from here on not to the animal but to the naive assurance of man:

> How does he know, by the force of his intelligence, the secret internal stirrings of animals? By what comparison between them and us does he infer the stupidity that he attributes to them?
>
> When I play with my cat [*ma chatte*], who knows if I am not a pastime to her more than she is to me? . . .
>
> The 1595 edition adds: "We entertain each other with reciprocal monkey tricks. If I have my time to begin or to refuse, so has she hers." [*A*, p. 331]

Nor does the cat that looks at me naked, she and no other, the one *I am talking about here*, belong, although we are getting warmer, to Baudelaire's family of cats,[6] or Rilke's,[7] or Buber's.[8] Literally speaking

6. *The Cat* is, as we well know, the title of two poems, but only the first of those directly addresses its subject in the singular, familiar form ("Viens, mon beau chat"), before recognizing in it the figure of "the woman I love" [*ma femme*]. Baudelaire even names the cat's gaze ("the image of the woman I love rises before me: her gaze, like yours, dear creature" ("Je vois ma femme en esprit. Son regard, / Comme le tien, aimable bête") and "When my eyes are drawn . . . towards my beloved cat . . . and find I am looking into myself" ("Quand mes yeux, vers ce chat que j'aime / . . . Et que je regarde en moi-même); and its voice ("To utter the longest of sentences it has no need of words" ("Pour dire les plus longues phrases, / Elle n'a pas besoin de mots") (Charles Baudelaire, "Le Chat" and "Le Chat," *Les Fleurs du mal*, in *The Complete Verse of Baudelaire*, trans. and ed. Francis Scarfe, 2 vols. [London, 1986], 1:98, 122, 121).

7. See Rainer Maria Rilke, "Schwarze Katze," in *Neue Gedichte / New Poems*, trans. Stephen Cohn (Manchester, 1992), pp. 202–3. On another occasion I will have to try to read this poem that I have rediscovered thanks to Werner Hamacher. The poem is dedicated, if that is the word, to "your gaze" ("dein Blick") and to a specter ("ein Gespenst")—those are its first words; one could set it into play with the poem he signs concerning "The Panther"; see pp. 60–61 (which again begins by naming the gaze [his gaze this time: "Sein Blick" are the first words])—rediscovered thanks to Richard Macksey, who has also translated it into English. Since the conference at Cerisy, cat lovers and friends the world over have been giving me cats like this. This would also be the moment to salute Jean-Claude Lebensztejn's forthcoming masterpiece entitled *Miaulique* (*Fantaisie Chromatique*).

A propos, why does one say in French "has the cat got your tongue" ("donner sa langue au chat") to mean that one has thrown in the towel?

8. "An animal's eyes have the power to speak a great language. . . . Sometimes I look into a cat's eyes" (Martin Buber, *I and Thou*, trans. Ronald Gregor Smith [New York, 1958], pp. 96–97). Buber also speaks of "the capacity to turn its glance to us." "The beginning of this cat's glance, lighting up under the touch of my glance, indisputably questioned me: 'Is it possible that you think of me? . . . Do I really exist?' . . . ('I' here is a transcription for a word, that we do not have, denoting self without the ego)" (p. 97).

at least, these poets' and philosophers' cats don't speak. "My" pussycat (but a pussycat never belongs) is not even the one *who speaks* in *Alice in Wonderland*. Of course, if you insist at all costs on suspecting me of perversity—always a possibility—you are free to understand or receive the emphasis I just made regarding "really a little cat" as a quote from chapter 11 of *Through the Looking Glass*. Entitled "Waking," this penultimate chapter consists of a single sentence: "—and it really *was* a kitten, after all"; or as one French translation has it: "and, after all, it really was a little black pussy cat" ["et, finalement, c'était bel et bien une petite chatte noire"].[9]

Although time prevents it, I would of course have liked to inscribe my whole talk within a reading of Lewis Carroll. In fact you can't be certain that I am not doing that, for better or for worse, silently, unconsciously, or without your knowing. You can't be certain that I didn't already do it one day when, ten years ago, I let speak or let pass a little hedgehog, a suckling hedgehog [*un nourrisson hérisson*] perhaps, before the question "What Is Poetry?" For thinking concerning the animal, if there is such a thing, derives from poetry. There you have a hypothesis: it is what philosophy has, essentially, had to deprive itself of. That is the difference between philosophical knowledge and poetic thinking. The hedgehog of "What Is Poetry?" not only inherited a piece of my name, it also responded, in its own way, to the appeal of Alice's hedgehog. Remember the croquet ground where the "balls were live hedgehogs" ("The Queen's Croquet-Ground"). Alice wanted to give the hedgehog a blow with the head of the flamingo she held under her arm, and "it *would* twist itself round and look up in her face," until she burst out laughing.[10]

How can an animal look you in the face? That will be one of our concerns. Alice noticed next that "the hedgehog had unrolled itself, and was in the act of crawling away: besides all this, there was generally a ridge or a furrow in the way wherever she wanted to send the hedgehog to" (*AW*, p. 90). It was a field on which "the players all played at once, without waiting for turns, quarreling all the while, and fighting for the hedgehogs" (*AW*, p. 91).

We will be all the more silently attracted to *Through the Looking*

9. Lewis Carroll, *Through the Looking Glass*, in *The Complete Works of Lewis Carroll* (New York, 1936), p. 268. Derrida used Lewis Carroll, *"Les Adventures d'Alice au pays des merveilles" et "Ce qu'Alice trouva de l'autre côté du miroir,"* trans. Jacques Papy, ed. Jean Gattegno (Paris, 1994).—TRANS.

10. Carroll, *Alice's Adventures in Wonderland*, in *The Complete Works of Lewis Carroll*, pp. 89, 90; hereafter abbreviated *AW*.—TRANS.

Glass given that we will have to deal with a type of *mirror stage*—and to ask certain questions of it, from the point of view of the animal, precisely.

But if my real cat is not Alice's little cat (certain translations say *le petit chat* for "kitten," or *une petite chatte noire*), it is certainly not because I am going to hurriedly conclude upon wakening, as Alice did, that one cannot speak with a cat on the pretext that it doesn't reply or that it always replies the same thing. For everything that I am about to confide to you no doubt comes back to asking you to *respond* to me, you, to me, reply to me concerning what it is to *respond*. If you can. The said question of the said animal in its entirety comes down to knowing not whether the animal speaks but whether one can know what *respond* means. And how to distinguish a response from a reaction. In this respect we must keep in mind Alice's very Cartesian statement at the end:

> It is a very inconvenient habit of kittens (Alice had once made the remark) that, whatever you say to them, they *always* purr. "If they would only purr for 'yes,' and mew for 'no,' or any rule of that sort," she had said, "so that one could keep up a conversation! But how *can* you talk with a person if they *always* say the same thing?"
>
> On this occasion the kitten only purred: and it was impossible to guess whether it meant "yes" or "no."[11]

You can speak to an animal, to the cat said to be *real* inasmuch as it is an animal, but it doesn't reply, not really, not ever, that is what Alice concludes. Exactly like Descartes as we shall later observe.

The letter counts, as does the *question* of the animal. The question of the animal response often has as its stakes the letter, the literality of a word, sometimes what the word *word* means literally. For example, if the word *respond* appears twice in all the translations of Carroll that I consulted, it doesn't correspond to any word as such in the English original. It is probably implied without being stated and this is surely a matter of economy. Where the translation says, without underlining the "always," *quoiqu'on leur dise, elles ronronnent toujours pour vous répondre*, the original simply says "whatever you say to them, they *always* purr." And where the translation says, without underlining the allusion to *pouvoir* ("can"), *Mais comment peut-on parler avec*

---

11. Carroll, *Through the Looking Glass*, p. 269.—Trans.

quelqu'un qui répond *toujours pareil?* Carroll himself writes, "But how *can* you talk with a person if they *always* say the same thing?"

That said, the sense of *response* seems to be implicit here; one can always maintain that the difference between the presence and absence of the word *response* doesn't count. Perhaps. Perhaps, on the contrary, one should take the matter very seriously, but we will come to that.

In any case, isn't Alice's incredulity rather incredible? She seems, at this moment at least, to believe that one can in fact discern and decide between a human "yes" and "no." She seems confident that when it comes to man it is possible to guess whether yes or no. Let us not forget that the Cheshire Cat had told her, in the course of a scene that deserves a long meditation: "'We're all mad here. I'm mad. You're mad'" (*AW*, p. 72). After that he undertakes to demonstrate to her this collective folly. It is the moment of a simulacrum of discussion, but which comes to grief as they are unable to agree on the sense of the words, on what a *word* means, and in the end no doubt, on what *word*, what the term *word* could ever mean. "'Call it what you like,'" the Cat ends up saying concerning the difference between growling and purring, before announcing that he will be present at the Queen's croquet game, where my poor hedgehogs will be badly treated [*mis à mal*] (*AW*, p. 72).

No, no, my cat, the cat that looks at me in my bedroom or in the bathroom, this cat that is perhaps not "my cat" or "my pussycat," does not appear here as representative, or ambassador, carrying the immense symbolic responsibility with which our culture has always charged the feline race, from La Fontaine to Tieck (author of *Puss in Boots*), from Baudelaire to Rilke, Buber and many others. If I say "it is a real cat" that sees me naked, it is in order to mark its unsubstitutable singularity. When it responds in its name (whatever *respond* means, and that will be our question), it doesn't do so as the exemplar of a species called cat, even less so of an animal genus or realm. It is true that I identify it as a male or female cat. But even before that identification, I see it as *this* irreplaceable living being that one day enters my space, enters this place where it can encounter me, see me, even see me naked. Nothing can ever take away from me the certainty that what we have here is an existence that refuses to be conceptualized. And a mortal existence, for from the moment that it has a name, its name survives it. It signs its potential disappearance. Mine also, and this disappearance, from that moment to this, *fort/da*, is announced each time that, naked or not, one of us leaves the room.

But I must also accentuate the fact that this shame that is ashamed of itself is more intense when I am not alone with the cat in the room.

For then I am no longer sure before whom I am so numbed with shame. In fact, is one ever alone with a cat? Or with anyone at all? Is this cat a third person? Or an other in a face-to-face duel? We will return to these questions later. In such moments, on the edge of the thing, in the imminence of the best or the worst, when anything can happen, where I can die with shame or pleasure, I no longer know in whose or in what direction to throw myself. Rather than chasing it away, chasing the cat away, I am in a hurry, yes, in a hurry to have it appear otherwise. I hasten to cover the obscenity of the event, in short to cover myself. One thought alone keeps me spellbound: dress myself, even a little, or, which amounts to the same thing, run away—as if I were chasing[12] myself out of the room—bite myself, bite my tongue for example at the very moment that I ask myself, Who? But, *Who* then? For I no longer know who I am (following) or who it is I am chasing, who is following me or hunting me. Who comes before and who is after whom? I no longer know where my head is. Madness: "'We're all mad here. I'm mad. You're mad.'" I no longer know how to respond, or even to respond to the question that impels me or asks me who I am (following) or after whom I am (following) and the way I am running.

To follow and *to be after* will not only be the question and the question of what we call the animal. We shall discover further along the question of the question, that which begins by wondering what *to respond* means, and whether an animal (but which one?) ever replies in its own name. And by wondering whether one can answer for what "I am (following)" means when that seems to necessitate an "I am inasmuch as I am *after* [*après*] the animal" or "I am inasmuch as I am *alongside* [*auprès*] the animal."

Being *after*, being *alongside*, being *near* [*près*] would appear as different modes of being, indeed of *being-with*. With the animal. But, in spite of appearances, it isn't certain that these modes of being come to modify a preestablished being, even less a primitive "I am." In any case they express a certain order of the being-huddled-together [*être-serré*] (which is what the etymological root, *pressu*, indicates, whence are derived the words *près*, *auprès*, *après*), the being-pressed, the being-with as being strictly attached, bound, enchained, being-under-pressure, compressed, impressed, repressed, pressed-against according to the stronger or weaker stricture of what always remains pressing. In what sense of the neighbor [*prochain*] (which is not necessarily that of a biblical or Greco-Latin tradition) should I say that I am close or near to the

---

12. "Chasser": also "to hunt."—TRANS.

animal and that I am (following) it, and in what type or order of pressure? Being-with it in the sense of being-close-to-it? Being-alongside-it? Being-after-it? *Being-after-it* in the sense of the hunt, training, or taming, or *being-after-it* in the sense of a succession or inheritance? In all cases, if I am (following) *after* it, the animal therefore comes before me, earlier than me (*früher* is Kant's word regarding the animal, and Kant will later be called as a witness). The animal is there before me, there close to me, there in front of me—I who am (following) after it. And also, therefore, since it is before me, it is behind me. It surrounds me. And from the vantage of this being-there-before-me it can allow itself to be looked at, no doubt, but also—something that philosophy perhaps forgets, perhaps being this calculated forgetting itself—it can look at me. It has its point of view regarding me. The point of view of the absolute other, and nothing will have ever done more to make me think through this absolute alterity of the neighbor than these moments when I see myself seen naked under the gaze of a cat.

What stakes are raised by these questions? One doesn't need to be an expert to foresee that they involve thinking about what is meant by living, speaking, dying, being and world as in being-in-the-world or being towards the world, or being-with, being-before, being-behind, being-after, being and following, being followed or being following, there where *I am*, in one way or another, but unimpeachably, *near* what they call the animal. It is too late to deny it, it will have been there before me who is (following) after it. *After* and *near* what they call the animal and *with* it—whether we want it or not and whatever we do about it.

I must once more return to the malaise of this scene. I ask for your forbearance. I will do all I can to prevent its being presented as a primal scene: this deranged theatrics of the *wholly other that they call animal, for example, a cat.* Yes, the wholly other, more other than any other that *they* call an animal, for example a cat, when it looks at me naked, at the instant when I introduce myself, present myself to it—or, earlier, at that strange moment when, before the event, before even wanting it or knowing it myself, I am passively presented to it as naked, seen and seen naked, before even seeing *myself* seen by a cat. Before even seeing myself or knowing myself seen naked. I am presented to it before even introducing myself. Nudity is nothing other than that passivity, the involuntary exhibition of the self. Nudity gets stripped to bare necessity only in that frontal exhibition, in that face-to-face. Here, faced with a cat of one *or* the other sex, or of one *and* the other sex. And faced with a cat that continues to see me, to watch me leave when I turn my back on it, a cat that, from that moment on, because I no longer see it seeing me still, from behind, I thus risk forgetting.

I have just attributed passivity to nudity. We could nickname this denuded passivity with a term that will come back more than once, from different places and in different registers, namely, *the passion of the animal, my* passion *of* the animal, my passion of the animal other: seeing oneself seen naked under a gaze that is vacant to the extent of being bottomless, at the same time innocent and cruel perhaps, perhaps sensitive and impassive, good and bad, uninterpretable, unreadable, undecidable, abyssal and secret. Wholly other, like the (every) other that is (every bit) other found in such intolerable proximity that I do not as yet feel I am justified or qualified to call it my fellow, even less my brother. For we shall have to ask ourselves, inevitably, what happens to the fraternity of brothers when an animal enters the scene. Or, conversely, what happens to the animal when one brother comes after the other, when Abel is *after* Cain who is *after* Abel. Or when a son is *after* his father. What happens to animals, surrogate or not, to the ass and ram on Mount Moriah?

What does this bottomless gaze offer to my sight [*donne à voir*]? What does it "say" to me, demonstrating quite simply the naked truth of every gaze, given that that truth *allows me to see and be seen* through the eyes of the other, in the *seeing* and not just *seen* eyes of the other? I am here thinking of those seeing eyes, those eyes of a seer whose color must at the same time be *seen and forgotten*. In looking at the gaze of the other, Lévinas says, one must forget the color of his eyes, in other words see the gaze, the face that gazes before seeing the visible eyes of the other. But when he reminds us that the "best way of meeting the Other is not even to notice the color of his eyes,"[13] he is speaking of man, of one's fellow as man, kindred, brother; he thinks of the other man and this, for us, will later be revealed as a matter for serious concern.

As with every bottomless gaze, as with the eyes of the other, the gaze called animal offers to my sight the abyssal limit of the human: the inhuman or the ahuman, the ends of man, that is to say the bordercrossing from which vantage man dares to announce himself to himself, thereby calling himself by the name that he believes he gives himself. And in these moments of nakedness, under the gaze of the animal, everything can happen to me, I am like a child ready for the apocalypse, *I am (following) the apocalypse itself*, that is to say the ultimate and first event

---

13. Emmanuel Levinas, *Ethics and Infinity: Conversations with Philippe Nemo,* trans. Richard A. Cohen (1982; Pittsburgh, 1985), p. 85.

of the end, the unveiling and the verdict. I am (following) it, the apocalypse, I identify with it by running behind it, after it, after its whole
zoo-logy. When the instant of extreme passion passes, and I find peace
again, then I can relax and speak of the beasts of the Apocalypse, visit
them in the museum, see them in a painting (but for the Greeks zoogra-
phy referred to the portraiture of the living in general and not just the
painting of animals); I can visit them at the zoo, read about then in the
Bible, or speak about them as in a book.

If I began by saying, "the wholly other they *call* the 'animal,' and for
example a 'cat,'" if I underlined the call [*appel*] and added quotation
marks, it was to do more than announce a problem that will henceforth
never leave us, that of appellation—and of the *response* to a call.

Before pursuing things in that direction, let me confide in you the
hypothesis that crossed my mind the first time my gaze met that of a cat-
pussycat that seemed to be imploring me, asking me clearly to open the
door for it to go out, as she did, without waiting, as she often does, for
example when she first follows me into the bathroom then immediately
regrets her decision. It is moreover a scene that is repeated every morning. The cat follows me when I wake up, into the bathroom, asking for
her breakfast, but she demands to be let out of that very room as soon
as it (or she) sees me naked, ready for everything and resolved to make
her wait. However, when I am found naked under the gaze of what they
call the animal, a fictitious tableau is played out in my imagination, a
sort of classification after Linnaeus, a taxonomy of the *point of view of
animals*. Other than the difference mentioned earlier between poem and
philosopheme, one can only find, at bottom, two types of discourse, two
positions of knowledge, two grand forms of theoretical or philosophical
treatise regarding the animal. What distinguishes them is obviously the
place, indeed the body of their signatories, that is to say the trace that
that signature leaves in a corpus and in a properly scientific, theoretical
or philosophical thematics. In the first place there are those texts signed
by people who have no doubt seen, observed, analyzed, reflected on the
animal, but who have never been *seen seen* by the animal. Their gaze
has never intersected with that of an animal directed at them (forget
about their being naked). If, indeed, they did happen to be seen seen
furtively by the animal one day, they took no (thematic, theoretical, or
philosophical) account of it. They neither wanted nor had the capacity
to draw any systematic consequence from the fact that an animal could,
facing them, look at them, clothed or naked, and in a word, without a
word, *address them*. They have taken no account of the fact that what
they call animal could *look at* them and *address* them from down there,

from a wholly other origin. That category of discourse, texts, and signatories (those who have never been seen seen by an animal that addressed them) is by far the most frequent. It is probably what brings together *all* philosophers and all theoreticians *as such*. At least those of a certain *epoch*, let's say from Descartes to the present, but I will say later why the word "epoch" and even this historicism leaves me quite uneasy or dissatisfied. Clearly all those (all those males but not all those females, and that difference is not insignificant here) whom I will later situate in order to back up my thesis, arranging them within the same configuration, for example Descartes, Kant, Heidegger, Lacan and Levinas, belong to this quasi-epochal category. Their discourses are sound and profound, but everything goes on as if they themselves had never been looked at, and especially not naked, by an animal that addressed them. At least everything goes on as though this troubling experience had not been theoretically registered, supposing that they had experienced it at all, at the precise moment when they made of the animal a *theorem*, something seen and not seeing. The experience of the seeing animal, of the animal that looks at them, has not been taken into account in the philosophical or theoretical architecture of their discourse. In sum they have denied it as much as misunderstood it. Henceforth we can do little more than turn around this immense disavowal whose logic traverses the whole history of humanity, and not only that of the quasi-epochal configuration I just mentioned. It is as if the men representing this configuration had seen without being seen, seen the animal without being seen by it, without being seen seen by it; without being seen seen naked by someone who, from the basis of a life called animal, and not only by means of the gaze, would have obliged them to recognize, at the moment of address, that this was their affair, their lookout [*que cela les regardait*].

But since I don't believe, at bottom, that it has never happened to them, or that it has not in some way been signified, figured, or metonymized, more or less secretly, in the gestures of their discourse, the symptom of this disavowal remains to be deciphered. This figure could not be the figure of just one disavowal among others. It institutes what is proper to man, the relation to itself of a humanity that is above all careful to guard, and jealous of, what is proper to it.

As for the other category of discourse, found among those whose signatories are first and foremost poets or prophets, in the situation of poetry or prophecy, those men and women who admit taking upon themselves the address of an animal that addresses them, before even having the time or the power to take themselves off [*s'y dérober*], to take themselves off with clothes off or in a bathrobe, I know of no *statutory representative* of it, that is to say no subject who does so as theoretical, philosophical, or juridical man, or even as citizen. I have found no such representative, but it is in that very place that I find myself, here and now, in the process of searching.

That is the track I am following, the track I am ferreting out [*la piste que je dépiste*], following the traces of this "wholly other they *call* 'animal,' for example 'cat.' "

Why rename that appellation? Why say "the wholly other they *call* 'animal,' for example 'cat'?" In order to recall a scene of name-calling, beginning at the beginning, namely in Genesis—and at least a type of new beginning, a second beginning in what is distinguished in Bereshit as the *second* narrative. For one must indeed specify that that story is a second "Heading" ("*Entête*" in Chouraqui's translation).[14] The man who, in that rendering, calls the animals by name, is not only Adam, the man of the earth, the husbandman [*glébeux*]. He is also Ish preceding Ishah, man before woman. It is the man Ish, still alone, who gives names to the animals created before him: "The husbandman cried out the name of each beast," one translation (Chouraqui) says; another (Dhormes): "Man called all the animals by their names" (Gen. 2:20).

Let me repeat: it is only recorded thus in the *second* narrative. If one believes what is called the *first* narrative, God creates man in his image but he brings male and female into the world at the same time. Naming will thus have been the fact of man as a couple, if it can be put that way. The original naming of the animals does not take place in the first version. It isn't the man-woman of the first version but man *alone* and *before* woman who, in that second version, gives their names, his names, to the animals. On the other hand it is said in the first version that the husbandman, created as God's replica, and created male-female, man-woman, immediately receives the order to subject the animals to him. In order to obey he is required to mark his ascendancy, his domination over them, indeed his power to tame them. Having created the living animals on the fifth day (the beasts, that is to say animals for domestication, birds, fish, reptiles and wild beasts), and having blessed them,

> Elohim said: "Let us make man in our image, in our likeness! Let them [note the sudden move to the plural] *have authority* [my italics] over the fish of the sea and the birds of the heavens,

14. In this section Derrida consistently compares two authoritative French translations of Genesis (Bereshit), those by Chouraqui and Dhormes (Pléiade). My transliterations lose some of the subtleties. For comparisons readers may consult the King James version, the Jerusalem Bible, or *The JPS Torah Commentary: Genesis*, trans. Jewish Publication Society, ed. Nahum M. Sarna (Philadelphia, 1989).

over the cattle, over all the wild beasts and reptiles that crawl
upon the earth!" Elohim therefore created man in his image, in
the image of Elohim he created him. Male and female he created
them. Elohim blessed them and said, "Be fruitful and multiply,
fill the earth and subdue it, *have authority* [my italics again]
over the fish of the sea and the birds of the heavens, over every
living thing that moves on the earth." [Gen. 1:26–28; trans.
Dhormes][15]

Elohim said: "We will make Adam the husbandman—
As our replica, in our likeness.
They will *subject* [my italics] the fish of the sea, the
flying creatures of the heavens,
The beasts, the whole earth, every reptile that crawls upon
the earth." Elohim created the husbandman as his replica,
As a replica of Elohim he created him,
Male and female he created them.
Elohim blessed them. Elohim said to them:
"Be fruitful, multiply, fill the earth, conquer it.
Subject [my italics again] the fish of the sea, the flying
creatures of the heavens,
Every living thing that crawls on the earth." [Gen. 1:26–28;
    trans. Chouraqui][16]

That is the first narrative. God commands man-woman to command
the animals, but not yet to name them. What happens next, in the second narrative? There occurs something, a single and double thing, twice
at the same time, something that, it seems to me, gets little notice in most
readings of this Genesis that is infinite in its second breath.

15. Elohim dit: "Faisons l'homme à notre image, à notre ressemblance! Qu'ils aient
autorité sur les poissons de la mer et sur les oiseaux des cieux, sur les bestiaux, sur
toutes les bêtes sauvages et sur tous les reptiles qui rampent sur la terre!" Elohim créa
donc l'homme à son image, à l'image d'Elohim il le créa. Il les créa homme et femelle.
Elohim les bénit et Elohim leur dit: "Fructifiez et multipliez-vous, remplissez la terre
et soumettez-la, ayez autorité sur les poissons de la mer et sur les oiseaux des cieux,
sur tout vivant qui remue sur la terre!"—Trans.

16. Elohim dit: "Nous ferons Adâm-le Glébeux— / A notre replique, selon notre ressemblance. / Ils assujettiront le poisson de la mer, le volatile des ciels, / la bête, toute
la terre, tout reptile qui rampe sur la terre." / Elohim créa le glébeux à sa réplique, / A
la réplique d'Elohim, il les crée, / mâle et femelle, il les crée. / Elohim les bénit. Elohim
leur dit : / "Fructifiez, multipliez, emplissez la terre, conquérez-la. / Assujettissez le
poisson de la mer, le volatile des ciels, / tout vivant qui rampe sur la terre."—Trans.

On the one hand, the naming of the animals is performed *at one and the same time*, before the creation of Ishah, the female part of man, *and*, as a result, before they perceive themselves to be naked; and they are at first naked without shame ("The two of them are naked, the husbandman and his wife; they don't blanch on account of it.")[17] After a certain serpent—one we shall return to—comes by, they will perceive themselves to be naked, and not without shame.

On the other hand, and this is especially important, the public announcing of names remains *at one and the same time* free *and* overseen, under surveillance, under the gaze of Jehovah who does not for all that intervene. He lets Adam, he lets man, man alone, Ish without Ishah, the woman, freely call out the names. He lets him go about naming alone. But he is waiting in the wings, watching over this man alone with a mixture of curiosity and authority. God observes: Adam is observed, within sight, he names under observation. In Chouraqui's translation: "He has them come towards the husbandman *in order to see* what he will call out to them" (Gen. 2:19).[18] He has them come forward, he summons them, the animals that, according to the first narrative, he had created—and I firmly underline this factor that is fundamental to what concerns us—he summons them in order to "subject" (Chouraqui) them to man's command, in order to place them under man's "authority" (Dhormes). More precisely, he has created man in his likeness *so that* man will *subject, tame, dominate, train,* or *domesticate* the animals born before him and assert his authority over them. God destines the animals to an experience of the power of man, *in order to see* the power of man in action, in order to see the power of man at work, in order to see man take power over all the other living beings. Chouraqui: "He has them come towards the husbandman *in order to see* what he will call out to them"; Dhormes: "He brings them to man *in order to see* what he will call them."[19] The "in order to see" that I have underlined twice seems full of meaning. It is the same expression in both translations. God gives Ish alone the freedom to name the animals, granted, and that represents at the same time his sovereignty and his loneliness. However, everything seems to happen as though God still wanted to oversee, keep vigil, maintain his right of inspection over the names that were about to echo out and by means of which Ish, Ish all alone, Ish still without woman, was going to get the upper hand with respect to

---

17. "Les deux sont nus, le glébeux et sa femme : ils n'en blêmissent pas."—TRANS.
18. "Il les fait venir vers le glébeux pour voir ce qu'il leur criera."—TRANS.
19. "Ils les amena vers l'homme pour voir comment il les appellerait."—TRANS.

the animals. God wanted to oversee but also abandon himself to his curiosity, even allow himself to be surprised and outflanked by the radical novelty of what was going to occur, by this irreversible, welcome or unwelcome event of naming whereby Ish would begin to see them and name them without allowing himself to be seen or named by them. God lets him, Ish, speak on his own, call out on his own, call out and nominate, call out and name, as if he were able to say, "I name," "I call." God lets Ish call the other living things all on his own, give them their names in his own name, these animals that are older and younger than him, these living things that came into the world before him but were named after him, on his initiative according to the second narrative. In both cases, man is in both senses of the word *after* the animal. He follows him. This "after," that determines a sequence, a consequence, or a persecution, is not in time, nor is it temporal; it is the very genesis of time.

God thus lets Ish do the calling of his own accord, he accords him the right to give them names in his own name—but just in order to see. This "in order to see" marks at the same time the infinite right of inspection of an all powerful God *and* the finitude of a God who doesn't know what is going to happen to him with language. And with names. In short, God doesn't yet know what he really wants; this is the finitude of a God who doesn't know what he wants with respect to the animal, that is to say with respect to the life of the living as such, a God who sees something coming without seeing it coming, a God who will say "*I am that I am*" without knowing what he is going to see when a poet enters the scene to give his name to living things. This powerful yet deprived "in order to see" that is God's, the first stroke of time, before time, God's exposure to surprise, to the event of what is going to occur between man and animal, this time before time has always made me dizzy. As if someone said, in the form of a promise or a threat, "you'll see what you'll see" without knowing what was going to end up happening. It is the dizziness one feels before the abyss opened by this stupid ruse, this feigned feint, what I have been feeling for so long [*depuis le temps*] whenever I run away from an animal that looks at me naked. I often wonder whether this vertigo before the abyss of such an "in order to see" deep in the eyes of God is not the same as that which takes hold of me when I feel so naked in front of a cat, facing it, and when, meeting its gaze I hear the cat or God ask itself, ask *me*: is he going to call me, is he going to address me? What is he going to call me, this naked man, before I give him woman, before I lend her to him in giving her to him, before I give her to him or before he gives her to himself by taking upon himself, from under him, from at his side [*à ses côtés*]? Or even from his rib [*de sa côte*]?

Since time.

For so long now it is as if the cat had been recalling itself and recalling that, recalling me and reminding me of this awful tale of Genesis, without breathing a word. Who was born first, before the names? Which one saw the other come to this place so long ago? Who will have been the first occupant, and thus the master? Who the subject? Who has remained the despot, for so long now?

Things would be too simple altogether, the anthropo-theomorphic reappropriation would already have begun, there would even be the risk that domestication has already come into effect if I were to give in to my own melancholy. If, in order to hear it in myself, I were to undertake to overinterpret what the cat might be saying to me, in its own way, what it might be suggesting or simply signifying in a language of mute traces, that is to say without any words. If, in a word, I assigned to it the words it has no need of, as is said of the cat's "voice" in Baudelaire ("To utter the longest of sentences it has no need of words").

But in forbidding myself thus to assign, interpret or project, must I conversely give in to the other violence or stupidity [*bêtise*], that which would consist in suspending one's compassion and in depriving the animal of every power of manifestation, of the desire to manifest *to me* anything at all, and even to manifest to me in some way *its* experience of *my* language, of *my* words and of *my* nudity?

From the vantage of that time when the animals were named, *before original sin*, I will mark, for the moment, still in the guise of an epigraph, the following reservation: the questions I am posing, my having confessed to feeling disarmed before a small mute living being, and my avowed desire to escape the alternative of a projection that appropriates and an interruption that excludes, all that might lead one to guess that I am not ready to interpret or experience the gaze that a cat fixes, without a word, on my nakedness, *in the negative*, if I can put it that way, as Benjamin suggests doing within a certain tradition that we must speak of later. In fact that tradition assigns to nature and to the animality named by Adam a sort of "'deep sadness'" (*Traurigkeit*).[20] Such a melancholic

20. Walter Benjamin, "On Language as Such and on the Language of Man ["Über die Sprache überhaupt und über die Sprache des Menschen"] (1916), trans. Edmund Jephcott, vol. 1 of *Selected Writings*, trans. Lloyd Spencer et al., ed. Marcus Bullock and Michael W. Jennings (Cambridge, Mass., 1996), p. 72.

mourning would reflect an impossible resignation, as if protesting in silence against the unacceptable fatality of that very silence: the fact of being condemned to muteness (*Stummheit*) and to the absence of language (*Sprachlosigkeit*), to stupor also, to that *Benommenheit* that Heidegger speaks of and that he defines, in a text that I would later like to read closely, as the essence of animality (*Das Wesen der Tierheit*). *Benommenheit* is a mute stupor, stupefaction, or daze. A new translation uses the word *absorption* [*accaparement*] in order to attenuate somewhat euphemistically the potential violence of this qualification but also in order to render the sense of a type of encircling (*Umring*) within which the animal, as *alogon*, finds itself, according to Heidegger, deprived of access in its very opening to the being of the entity as such, to being as such, to the "as such" of what is. It is true that, according to Benjamin, the sadness, mourning, and melancholy (*Traurigkeit*) of nature and of animality are born out of this muteness (*Stummheit, Sprachlosigkeit*), but also out of and by means of the wound without a name: that of having *been given a name*. Finding oneself deprived of language, one loses the power to name, to name oneself, indeed to *respond* to one's name. (As if man didn't also receive his name and his names!)

The sentiment of this deprivation, of this impoverishment, of this lack would thus be the great sorrow of nature (*das grosse Leid der Natur*). It is in the hope of requiting that, of redemption (*Erlösung*) from that suffering, that humans live and speak in nature—humans in general and not only poets, as Benjamin makes clear. More interestingly, this putative sadness doesn't just derive from the inability to speak (*Sprachlosigkeit*) and from muteness, from an aphasic inability or stupefaction that prevents the use of words. If this putative sadness gives rise to a lament, if nature laments, expressing a mute but audible lament through the sensuous breath and rustling of plants, it is because the terms have to be inverted. Benjamin suggests as much. There must be a reversal, an *Umkehrung* in the essence of nature. Following the hypothesis of this reversing reversal, nature (and animality within it) isn't sad because it is mute (*weil sie stummist*). On the contrary, it is nature's sadness or mourning that renders it mute and aphasic, that leaves it without words (*Die Traurigkeit der Natur macht sie verstummen*). For what, for so long now, has been making it sad and as a result has deprived the mourner of words, what forbids words, is not the muteness and experience of a powerlessness, an inability to name; it is in the first place the fact of *receiving one's name*. This is a startling intuition. Benjamin says that even when the one who names is equal to the gods, happy and well-blessed, being named (*bennant zu sein*) or seeing oneself given one's proper name is something like being invaded by sadness, it is sadness *itself* (a sadness whose origin would therefore always be this passivity of being named, this impossibility of reappropriating one's own name), or at least a sort of obscure foreshadowing of sadness. One should rather say *a foreshadowing of mourning (eine Ahnung von Trauer)*. A foreshadowing of mourning because it seems to me that every case of naming involves announcing a death to come in the surviving of a ghost, the longevity of a name that survives whoever carries that name. Whoever receives a name feels mortal or dying precisely because the name seeks to save him, to call him and thus assure his survival. Being called, hearing oneself being named, receiving a name for the first time involves something like the knowledge of being mortal and even the feeling that one is dying. Already dead by virtue of being promised to death: dying. (How could one, I ask in passing, thus refuse the animal access to the experience of death as such by depriving it of nomination?) But as I was suggesting just now, I am not (following) Benjamin when I find myself naked under the gaze of the animal; I am not ready to follow him in his wonderful meditation written right in the middle of the First World War, in 1916.

Why not? Among other reasons because such a meditation lays out this whole scene of a grieving aphasia within the time frame of redemption, that is to say after the fall and after original sin (*nach dem Sündenfall*). It would thus take place *since the time* of the fall. I situate this time of the fall at the purposive intersection of two traditions because in the Genesis tale as much as in the myth of Prometheus (let's remember the *Protagoras* and the moment when Prometheus steals fire, that is to say the arts and technics, in order to make up for the forgetfulness or tardiness of Epimetheus who had perfectly equipped all breeds of animal but left "man naked [*gymnon*]," without shoes, covering, or arms), it is paradoxically on the basis of a fault or failing in man that the latter will be made a subject who is master of nature and of the animal. From within the pit of that lack, an eminent lack, a quite different lack from that he assigns to the animal, man installs or claims in a single movement *what is proper to him* (the peculiarity of a man whose property it is not to have anything that is exclusively his) and his *superiority* over what is called animal life. This last superiority, infinite and par excellence, has as its property the fact of being at one and the same time *unconditional* and *sacrificial*.

That would be the law of an imperturbable logic, both Promethean and Adamic, both Greek and Abrahamic (Judaic, Christian, and Islamic). Its invariance hasn't stopped being verified all the way to our modernity. Yet I have been wanting to bring myself back to my nudity before the cat, since so long ago, since a previous time, in the Genesis tale, since the time when Adam, alias Ish, called out the animals' names *before* the fall, still naked but before being ashamed of his nudity.

I am thus speaking from within that time frame [*depuis ce temps*]. My passion for the animal is awakened at that age. I admitted just now to being ashamed of being ashamed. I could therefore be surprised by my uneasiness, my shame at being ashamed, naked before the animal or animals, only by taking myself back to a time before the fall, before shame and the shame of being ashamed. Before evil and before all ills. Can one speak of the animal? Can one approach the animal? Can one from the vantage of the animal see oneself being looked at naked? From the vantage of the animal before evil [*le mal*] and before all ills [*les maux*]?

I am trying to speak to you from within that time frame, of myself in particular, in private or in public, but of myself in particular. That time frame would also be that which, in principle, supposing it were possible, separates autobiography from confession. Autobiography becomes confession when the discourse on the self does not dissociate truth from an avowal, thus from a fault, an evil, an ill. And first and foremost from a truth that would be due, a debt in truth that needs to be paid off. Why *would one owe* truth? Why would it belong to the essence of truth to be due, and nude? And therefore confessed? Why this duty to pay off truth if hiding the truth, feigning truth, feigning also to hide, feigning to hide oneself or hide the truth, were not already the experience of evil and of ill, of a potential fault, of a culpability, of a sufferance, of a debt—of a deceiving and a lie.

How and why would truth be due? And how and why caught, surprised from the first instant in a logic of debt and owing? Why would truth be what is due, that is to say owed to veracity, to the revealing of oneself, to the truth of self as sincerity? Is there, and in particular in the history of discourse, indeed of the becoming-literature of discourse, an ancient form of autobiography immune from confession, an account of the self free from any sense of confession? And thus from all redemptive language, within the horizon of salvation as a requiting? Has there been, since so long ago, a place and a meaning for autobiography before original sin and before the religions of the book? Autobiography and memoir before Christianity, especially, before the Christian institutions of confession? That has been in doubt for so long now, and a reading of the prodigious *Confessions* of European history such as have formed our culture of subjectivity from Augustine to Rousseau, would not be about to dispel that doubt.

Between Augustine and Rousseau, within the same indisputable filiation, within the evolving history of the *ego cogito ergo sum*, stands Descartes. He waits for us with his animal-machines. I presume that he won't interrupt the lineage that, for so long now, has tied the autobiographical genre to the institution of confession.

Since that time, since time: that means since the time that has passed, but also since the time before time. Since time, that is to say since a time when there was not yet time, when time hadn't elapsed, if that is possible, before the verdict, the reckoning or the fall.

Although I must put off until later a patient reading and interpretation of the systematic and rich text that, in 1929–30, following *Being and Time*, Heidegger devoted to the animal, I note the following in anticipation of it here, having just spoken of time before time: one of the rare times, perhaps the only time (that needs checking) that Heidegger names the animal in *Being and Time*, a text that is also in its own way a treatise that seeks to be non-Christian, concerning a certain fall of the *Dasein*, it is in order to admit to a difficulty that will be saved for later (my hypothesis is this: whatever is put off until later will probably be put off for ever; later here signifies never). What is that difficulty? That of knowing if the animal *has time*, if it is "constituted by some kind of 'time.'" According to Heidegger that "remains a problem [*bleibt ein Problem*]":

> It remains a problem in itself [or for itself, *bleibt ein Problem für sich*: remains an original problem, separate, to be treated separately] to define ontologically the way in which the senses can be *stimulated* or *touched* in something that merely has life [*in einem Nur-Lebenden*], and how and where the Being of animals [*das Sein der Tiere*], for instance [*zum Beispiel*], is constituted by some kind of "time."[21]

The being of animals is only an example (*zum Beispiel*). But for Heidegger it is a trustworthy example of what he calls *Nur-lebenden*, that which is living but no more, life in its pure and simple state. I think I understand what that means, this "nothing more (*nur*)"; I can understand it on the surface, in terms of what it means, but at the same time I understand nothing. I will always ask myself whether this fiction, this simulacrum, this myth, this legend, this phantasm of what is offered as

---

21. Martin Heidegger, *Being and Time*, trans. John Macquarrie and Edward Robinson (New York, 1962), p. 396.

a pure concept (life in its pure state—Benjamin also has confidence in what can probably be no more than a pseudo-concept) is not precisely pure philosophy become a symptom of the history that concerns us here. Isn't that history the one that man tells himself, the history of the philosophical animal, of the animal for the man-philosopher? Is it a coincidence that the sentence is the last one preceding a chapter entitled *Die Zeitlichkeit des Verfallens* (the temporality of reckoning, fall, or decay)?

I suggested just now that for certain of us perhaps, for those who welcome us here, for those who have gratified me by coming back once more, this chateau has remained for me, for so long now, a place of friendship but also of haunting [*de l'amitié hantée*]. For nearly forty years. Indeed, friendship that is haunted, shadows of faces, furtive silhouettes of certain presences, movements, footsteps, music, words that come to life in my memory, on the terraces around us, among the trees, beside the lake and in all the rooms of this mansion, beginning with this room. I enjoy more and more the taste of this memory that is at the same time tender, joyful, and melancholy, a memory, then, that likes to give itself over to the return of ghosts, many of whom are happily still living and, in some cases, present here. Others, alas, have died since that time, but they remain for me, just as when they were alive, close and present friends: Toyosaki Koitchi, Francis Ponge, Gilles Deleuze, Sarah Kofman. From here I can see them see and hear us.

However, if I am to believe my memory that has thus been invaded by memories, for so long now, a memory that is almost hallucinated, I find myself about to embark upon the most *chimerical* discourse that I have probably ever attempted, or that has ever tempted me in this chateau.

We thus confront the scene of the chimera, the temptation of or attempt at a chimera in this haunted chateau. Is it an animal, this chimera, an animal that can be defined as one, and only one? Is it more than or other than an animal? Or, as one often says of the chimera, more than one animal in one?

The animal, what a word!

The animal is a word, it is an appellation that men have instituted, a name they have given themselves the right and the authority to give to another living creature [*à l'autre vivant*].

At the point at which we find ourselves, even before I get involved, or try to drag you after me or in pursuit of me upon an itinerary that some of you will no doubt find tortuous, labyrinthine, even aberrant, leading us astray from lure to lure, I will attempt the operation of disarmament that consists in *posing* what one could call some hypotheses in view of theses; posing them simply, naked, frontally, as directly as possible, *pose* them as I said, by no means in the way one indulgently poses in front of a spectator, a painter of portraits, or a camera, but "pose" in the sense of situating a series of "positions."

First hypothesis: for about two centuries, intensely and by means of an alarming rate of acceleration, for we no longer even have a clock or a chronological measure of it, we, we who call ourselves men or humans, we who recognize ourselves in that name, have been involved in an unprecedented transformation. This mutation affects the experience of what we continue to call imperturbably, as if there were nothing wrong with it, the animal and/or animals. I intend to stake a lot, or play a lot on the flexible separation of this *and/or*. This new situation can be determined only on the basis of a very ancient one. We must continuously move along this coming and going between the oldest and what comes of the exchange among the new, the "again," and the "anew" of a repetition. Far from appearing, simply, within what we continue to call the world, history, life, and so on, this unheard of relation to the animal or to animals is so new that it should oblige us to worry all those concepts, more than just problematize them. That is why I would hesitate to say that we are *living through* that (if one can still confidently call *life* the experience whose limits tremble at the bordercrossings between *bios* and *zoē*, the biological, zoological, and anthropological, as between life and death, life and technology, life and history, and so on). I would therefore hesitate just as much to say that we are living through a historical turning point. The figure of the turning point implies a rupture or an instantaneous mutation for which the model or the figure remains genetic, biological, or zoological, and which therefore remains, precisely, to be questioned. As for history, historicity, even historicality, those motifs belong precisely—as we shall see in detail—to *this* auto-definition, *this* auto-apprehension, *this* auto-situation of man or of the human *Dasein* with respect to what is living and with respect to animal life; they belong to this auto-biography of man that I wish to call into question today.

Since all these words, in particular "history," belong in a constitutive manner to the language, interests, and lures of this autobiography, we should not be overhasty in giving them credence or in confirming their pseudo-evidence. I will therefore not be speaking of an historical turning point in order to name a transformation in process, an alteration that is at the same time more serious and less recognizable than a turning point in the relation to the animal, in the being-with shared by man and by what man calls the animal: the *being* of what calls itself man or the *Dasein with* what he himself calls, or what we ourselves call, what we still dare, provisionally, to name in general but in the singular, *the animal.* However one names or interprets this alteration, no one could deny that it has been accelerating, intensifying, no longer knowing where it is going, for about two centuries, at an incalculable rate and level.

Given this indetermination, the fact that it is left hanging, why should I say, as I have more than once, "for about two centuries," as though such a point of reference were rigorously possible in speaking of a process that is no doubt as old as man, as old as what he calls his world, his knowledge, his history and his technology? Well, in order to recall, for convenience to begin with and without laying claim to being exact, certain preexisting indices that allow us to be heard and understood and to say "us" here today. Limiting ourselves to the most imposing of these indices we can refer to those that go well beyond the animal sacrifices of the Bible or of ancient Greece, well beyond the hecatombs (sacrifices of one hundred cattle, with all the metaphors that that expression has since been charged with), beyond the hunting, fishing, domestication, training, or traditional exploitation of animal energy (transport, plowing, draught animals, the horse, ox, reindeer, and so on, and then the guard dog, small-scale butchering, and then animal experiments, and so on). It is all too evident that in the course of the last two centuries these traditional forms of treatment of the animal have been turned upside down by the joint developments of zoological, ethological, biological, and genetic *forms of knowledge* and the always inseparable *techniques* of intervention with respect to their object, the transformation of the actual object, its milieu, its world, namely, the living animal. This has occurred by means of farming and regimentalization at a demographic level unknown in the past, by means of genetic experimentation, the industrialization of what can be called the production for consumption of animal meat, artificial insemination on a massive scale, more and more audacious manipulations of the genome, the reduction of the animal not only to production and overactive reproduction (hormones, genetic crossbreeding, cloning, and so on) of meat for consumption but also of all sorts of other end products, and all of that in the service of a certain being and the so-called human well-being of man.

All that is well known; we have no need to dwell on it. However one interprets it, whatever practical, technical, scientific, juridical, ethical, or political consequence one draws from it, no one can deny this event any more, no one can deny the *unprecedented* proportions of this subjection of the animal. Such a subjection, whose history we are attempting to interpret, can be called violence in the most morally neutral sense of the term and even includes a certain interventionist violence that is practiced, as in some very minor and in no way dominant cases, let us never forget, in the service of and for the protection of the animal, most often the human animal. Neither can one seriously deny the disavowal that this involves. No one can deny seriously, or for very long, that men do all they can in order to dissimulate this cruelty or to hide it from themselves, in order to organize on a global scale the forgetting or misunderstanding of this violence that some would compare to the worst cases of genocide (there are also animal genocides: the number of species endangered because of man takes one's breath away). One should neither abuse the figure of genocide nor consider it explained away. For it gets more complicated here: the annihilation of certain species is indeed in process, but it is occurring through the organization and exploitation of an artificial, infernal, virtually interminable survival, in conditions that previous generations would have judged monstrous, outside of every supposed norm of a life proper to animals that are thus exterminated by means of their continued existence or even their overpopulation. As if, for example, instead of throwing people into ovens or gas chambers (let's say Nazi) doctors and geneticists had decided to organize the overproduction and overgeneration of Jews, gypsies, and homosexuals by means of artificial insemination, so that, being more numerous and better fed, they could be destined in always increasing numbers for the same hell, that of the imposition of genetic experimentation or extermination by gas or by fire. In the same abattoirs. I don't wish to abuse the ease with which one can overload with pathos the self-evidences I am drawing attention to here. Everybody knows what terrifying and intolerable pictures a realist painting could give to the industrial, mechanical, chemical, hormonal, and genetic violence to which man has been submitting animal life for the past two centuries. Everybody knows what the production, breeding, transport, and slaughter of these animals has become. Instead of thrusting these images in your faces or awakening them in your memory, something that would be both too easy and endless, let me simply say a word about this "pathos." If these images are "pathetic," if they evoke sympathy, it is also because they "pathetically" open the immense question of pathos and the pathological, precisely, that is, of suffering, pity, and compassion; and the place that has to be accorded to the interpretation of this compassion, to the sharing of this suffering among the living, to the law, ethics, and politics that must be brought to bear upon this experience of compassion. For what has been happening now for two centuries involves a new experience of this compassion. In response to the irresistible but unacknowledged unleashing and the organized disavowal of this torture, voices are raised—minority, weak, marginal voices, little assured of their discourse, of their right to discourse and of the enactment of their discourse within the law, as a declaration of rights—in order to protest, in order to appeal (we'll return to this) to what is still presented in such a problematic way as *animal rights*, in order to awaken us to our responsibilities and our obligations with respect to the living in general, and precisely to this fundamental compassion that, were we to take it seriously, would have to change even the very basis (and that basis is what I wish to discuss today) of the philosophical problematic of the animal.

It is in thinking of the source and ends of this compassion that about two centuries ago someone like Bentham, as is well known, proposed changing the very form of the question regarding the animal that dominated discourse within the tradition, in the language of both the most refined philosophical argument and everyday acceptation and common sense. Bentham said something like this: the question is not to know whether the animal can think, reason, or talk, something we still pretend to be asking ourselves. (From Aristotle to Descartes, from Descartes, especially, to Heidegger, Lévinas, and Lacan, this question determines so many others concerning *power* or *capability* [*pouvoirs*] and *attributes* [*avoirs*]: being able, having the power to give, to die, to bury one's dead, to dress, to work, to invent a technique, and so on, a power that consists in having such and such a faculty, thus such and such a power, as an essential attribute). Thus the question will not be to know whether animals are of the type *zōon logon echon*, whether they *can* speak or reason thanks to that *capacity* or that *attribute* implied in the *logos*, the can-have [*pouvoir-avoir*] of the *logos*, the aptitude for the *logos* (and logocentrism is first of all a thesis regarding the animal, the animal deprived of the *logos*, deprived of the *can-have-the-logos*: this is the thesis, position, or presupposition maintained from Aristotle to Heidegger, from Descartes to Kant, Lévinas and Lacan). The *first* and *decisive* question will rather be to know whether animals *can suffer*.

"Can they suffer?" asks Bentham simply yet so profoundly.

Once its protocol is established, the form of this question changes everything. It no longer simply concerns the *logos*, the disposition and whole configuration of the *logos*, having it or not, nor does it concern more radically a *dynamis* or *hexis*, this having or manner of being, this *habitus* that one calls a faculty or "power," this can-have or the power one possesses (as in the power to reason, to speak, and everything that that implies). The question is disturbed by a certain *passivity*. It bears witness, manifesting already, as question, the response that testifies to a sufferance, a passion, a not-being-able. The word *can* [*pouvoir*] changes sense and sign here once one asks "can they suffer?" The word wavers henceforth. As soon as such a question is posed what counts is not only the idea of a transitivity or activity (being able to speak, to reason, and so on); the important thing is rather what impels it towards self-contradiction, something we will later relate back to auto-biography. "Can they suffer?" amounts to asking "can they *not be able*?" And what of this inability [*impouvoir*]? What of the vulnerability felt on the basis of this inability? What is this nonpower at the heart of power? What is its quality or modality? How should one account for it? What right should be accorded it? To what extent does it concern us? Being able to suffer is no longer a power, it is a possibility without power, a possibility of the impossible. Mortality resides there, as the most radical means of thinking the finitude that we share with animals, the mortality that belongs to the very finitude of life, to the experience of compassion, to the possibility of sharing the possibility of this nonpower, the possibility of this impossibility, the anguish of this vulnerability and the vulnerability of this anguish.

With this question—"can they suffer?"—we are not standing on the rock of indubitable certainty, the foundation of every assurance that one could, for example, look for in the *cogito*, in *Je pense donc je suis*. But from another perspective we are here putting our trust in an instance that is just as radical, however different it may be, namely, what is undeniable. No one can deny the suffering, fear or panic, the terror or fright that humans witness in certain animals. (Descartes himself was not able to claim that animals were insensitive to suffering.) Some will still try—this is something else we will come to—to contest the right to call that *suffering* or *anguish*, words or concepts that they would still reserve for man and for the *Dasein* in the freedom of its being-towards-death. We will have reason to problematize that discourse later. But for the moment let us note the following: the response to the question "can they suffer?" leaves no doubt. In fact it has never left any room for doubt; that is why the experience that we have of it is not even indubitable; it precedes the indubitable, it is older than it. No doubt either, then, for the possibility of our giving vent to a surge of compassion, even if it is then misunderstood, repressed, or denied, held in respect. Before the *undeniable* of this response (yes, they suffer, like us who suffer for them and with them), before this response that precedes all other questions, the problematic changes ground and base. Perhaps it loses all security, but in any case it no longer rests on the old, supposedly natural (its ground) or historic and *artifactual* (its base) foundation. The two centuries I have been referring to somewhat approximately in order to situate the present in terms of this tradition have been those of an unequal struggle, a war being waged, the unequal forces of which could one day be reversed, between those who violate not only animal life but even and also this sentiment of compassion and, on the other hand, those who appeal to an irrefutable testimony to this pity.

War is waged over the matter of pity. This war probably has no age but, and here is my hypothesis, it is passing through a critical phase. We are passing through that phase and it passes through us. To think the war we find ourselves waging is not only a duty, a responsibility, an obligation, it is also a necessity, a constraint that, like it or not, directly or indirectly, everyone is held to. Henceforth and more than ever. And I say "to think" this war, because I believe it concerns what we call "thinking." The animal looks at us, and we are naked before it. Thinking perhaps begins there.

Here now, in view of another thesis, is the *second hypothesis* that I think must be deduced without hesitation. It concerns or puts into effect another logic of the limit. I will thus be tempted to inscribe the subject of this thesis in the series of three conferences that, beginning with "Les Fins de l'homme" and followed by "Le Passage des frontières," have been devoted to a properly *transgressal* if not transgressive experience of *limitrophy*. Let's allow that word to have both a general and strict sense: what abuts onto limits but also what feeds, is fed, is cared for, raised, and trained, what is cultivated on the edges of a limit. In the semantics of *trephō, trophē*, or *trophos*, we should be able to find everything we need to speak about what we should be speaking about in the course of these ten days devoted to the autobiographical animal: feeding, food, nursing, breeding, offspring, education, care and keeping of animals, training, upbringing, culture, living and allowing to live by giving to live, be fed, and grown, autobiographically. *Limitrophy* is therefore my subject. Not just because it will concern what sprouts or grows at the limit, around the limit, by maintaining the limit, but also what *feeds the limit*, generates it, raises it, and complicates it. Whatever I will say is designed, certainly not to efface the limit, but to multiply its figures, to complicate, thicken, delinearize, fold, and divide the line precisely by making it increase and multiply. Moreover, the supposed first or literal sense of *trephō* is just that: transform by thickening, for example, in curdling milk. So it will in no way mean questioning, even in the slightest, the limit about which we have had a stomachful, the

limit between Man with a capital M and Animal with a capital A. It
will not be a matter of attacking frontally or antithetically the thesis
of philosophical or common sense on the basis of which has been built
the relation to the self, the presentation of the self of human life, the
autobiography of the human species, the whole history of the self that
man recounts to himself, that is to say the thesis of a limit as rupture
or abyss between those who say "we men," "I, a man," and what this
man among men who say "we," what he *calls* the animal or animals. I
won't take it upon myself for a single moment to contest that thesis, nor
the rupture or abyss between this "I-we" and what we *call* animals. To
suppose that I, or anyone else for that matter, could ignore that rupture,
indeed that abyss, would mean first of all blinding oneself to so much
contrary evidence; and, as far as my own modest case is concerned,
it would mean forgetting all the signs that I have sought to give, tirelessly, of my attention to difference, to differences, to heterogeneities
and abyssal ruptures as against the homogeneous and the continuous. I
have thus never believed in some homogeneous continuity between what
calls *itself* man and what *he* calls the animal. I am not about to begin
to do so now. That would be worse than sleepwalking, it would simply
be too asinine [*bête*].[22] To suppose such a stupid memory lapse or to
take to task such a naive misapprehension of this abyssal rupture would
mean, more seriously still, venturing to say almost anything at all for the
cause, for whatever cause or interest that no longer had anything to do
with what we claimed to want to talk about. When that cause or interest
begins to profit from what it simplistically suspects to be a biologistic
continuism, whose sinister connotations we are well aware of, or more
generally to profit from what is suspected as a geneticism that one might
wish to associate with this scatterbrained accusation of continuism, the
undertaking in any case becomes so aberrant that it neither calls for nor,
it seems to me, deserves any direct discussion on my part. Everything
I have suggested so far and every argument I will put forward today
stands overwhelmingly in opposition to the blunt instrument that such
an allegation represents.

   For there is no interest to be found in a discussion of a supposed
discontinuity, rupture, or even abyss between those who call themselves
men and what so-called men, those who name themselves men, call the

22. In modern French the noun, *une bête*, is normally used to mean "animal" with
a slightly familiar sense; as adjective *bête* means stupid. *Une bêtise*, which I have taken
the liberty of translating below with the neologism *asinanity*, means a "stupid mistake"
or "idiocy."—TRANS.

animal. Everybody agrees on this, discussion is closed in advance, one would have to be more asinine than any beast [*plus bête que les bêtes*] to think otherwise. Even animals know that (ask Abraham's ass or ram or the living beasts that Abel offered to God; they know what is about to happen to them when man says, "Here I am" to God, then consent to sacrifice themselves, to sacrifice their sacrifice or to forgive themselves). The discussion is worth undertaking once it is a matter of determining the number, form, sense, or structure, the foliated consistency of this abyssal limit, these edges, this plural and repeatedly folded frontier. The discussion becomes interesting once, instead of asking whether or not there is a discontinuous limit, one attempts to think what a limit becomes once it is abyssal, once the frontier no longer forms a single indivisible line but more than one internally divided line, once, as a result, it can no longer be traced, objectified, or counted as single and indivisible. What are the edges of a limit that grows and multiplies by feeding on an abyss? Here is my thesis in three paragraphs:

1. This abyssal rupture doesn't describe two edges, a unilinear and indivisible line having two edges, Man and Animal in general.

2. The multiple and heterogeneous border of this abyssal rupture has a history. Both macroscopic and microscopic and far from being closed, that history is now passing through the most unusual phase in which we find ourselves and for which there is no scale. Indeed, one can only speak here of history, of an historic moment or phase, from one of the supposed edges of the said rupture, the edge of an anthropocentric subjectivity that is recounted or allows a history to be recounted about it, autobiographically, the history of its life, and that it therefore calls *History*.

3. Beyond the edge of the *so-called* human, beyond it but by no means on a single opposing side, rather than "the Animal" or "Animal Life," there is already a heterogeneous multiplicity of the living, or more precisely (since to say "the living" is already to say too much or not enough) a multiplicity of organizations of relations between living and dead, relations of organization or lack of organization among realms that are more and more difficult to dissociate by means of the figures of the organic and inorganic, of life and/or death. These relations are at once close and abyssal, and they can never be totally objectified. They do not leave room for any simple exteriority of one term with respect to another. It follows from that that one will never have the right to take animals to be the species of a kind that would be named the Animal, or animal in general. Whenever "one" says, "the Animal," each time a philosopher, or anyone else says, "the Animal" in the singular and without

further ado, claiming thus to designate every living thing that is held not to be man (man as *rational animal*, man as political animal, speaking animal, *zōon logon echon*, man who says "I" and takes himself to be the subject of a statement that he proffers on the subject of the said animal, and so on), each time the subject of that statement, this "one," this "I" does that he utters an *asinanity* [*bêtise*]. He avows without avowing it, he declares, just as a disease is declared by means of a symptom, he offers up for diagnosis the statement "I am uttering an *asinanity*." And this "I am uttering an *asinanity*" should confirm not only the animality that he is disavowing but his complicit, continued and organized involvement in a veritable war of the species.

Such are my hypotheses in view of theses on the animal, on animals, on the word *animal* or *animals*.

Yes, *animal*, what a word!

Animal is a word that men have given themselves the right to give. These humans are found giving it to themselves, this word, but as if they had received it as an inheritance. They have given themselves the word in order to corral a large number of living beings within a single concept: "the Animal," they say. And they have given themselves this word, at the same time according themselves, reserving for them, for humans, the right to the word, the name, the verb, the attribute, to a language of words, in short to the very thing that the others in question would be deprived of, those that are corralled within the grand territory of the beasts: the Animal. All the philosophers we will investigate (from Aristotle to Lacan, and including Descartes, Kant, Heidegger, and Levinas), all of them say the same thing: the animal is without language. Or more precisely unable to respond, to respond with a response that could be precisely and rigorously distinguished from a reaction, the animal is without the right and power to "respond" and hence without many other things that would be the property of man.

Men would be first and foremost those living creatures who have given themselves the word that enables them to speak of the animal with a single voice and to designate it as the single being that remains without a response, without a word with which to respond.

That wrong was committed long ago and with long-term consequences. It derives from this word or rather it comes together in this word *animal* that men have given themselves at the origin of humanity and that they have given themselves in order to identify themselves, in order to recognize themselves, with a view to being what they say they are, namely men, capable of replying and responding in the name of men.

I would like to try and speak of a certain wrong or evil that derives from this word, to begin with by stammering some chimerical aphorisms.

The animal that I am (following), does it speak?

That is an intact question, virginal, new, still to come, a completely naked question.

For language is like the rest, it is not enough to speak of it.

From the moment of this first question one should be able to sniff the trace of the fact that this animal seems to speak French here and is no less asinine for it. "The animal that I am (following), does it speak?" This address could be a feint, like the switch from "I" to "it." The question could be the ruse or stratagem of a rhetorical question, one that would already be assured of a response. The question will shortly be very much that of the response, and no doubt I shall try to imply that one cannot treat the supposed animality of the animal without treating the question of the response and of what *responding* means. And what *erasing* means. Even those who, from Descartes to Lacan, have conceded to the said animal some aptitude for signs and for communication have always denied it the power to *respond*—to *pretend*, to *lie*, to *cover its tracks* or *erase* its own traces.

But whether it is fictive or not, when I ask "the animal that I am, does it speak?" that same question seems at that moment to be signed, sealed by someone.

What does it seal? What claim does it make? Pretense or not, what does it seem to translate?

What this animal is, what it will have been, what it would, would like to, or could be, is perhaps what I am following.

But saying that is *what I am (following)* [*que je le suis*] in French, in this and in no other language, amounts less to claiming some national idiom than to recalling an irreducible ambiguity about which we shall have more to say: an animal's signature might yet be able to erase or cover its traces. Or allow it to be erased, rather, be unable to prevent its being erased. And this possibility, that of tracing, effacing, or scrambling its signature, allowing it to be lost, would then have serious consequences. Having or not having traces at one's disposal so as to be in a position to cover or erase them, in such a manner as, it is said, some can (man, for example) and some cannot do (the animal, for example, according to Lacan), does not perhaps constitute a reliable alternative defined by an indivisible limit. We will have reason to go back over these steps and tracks. The fact that a trace can always be erased, and forever, in no way means—and this is a critical difference—that someone, man *or* animal, *can of his own accord* erase his traces.

It is a question of words, therefore. For I am not sure that what I am going to set about saying to you amounts to anything more ambitious than an exploration of language in the course of a sort of chimerical experimental exercise or the testing of a testimony. Just to see. We can act as though I was simply trying to analyze a number of discursive modalities or usages—in order to put them to the test and to see, to keep an eye out for what will come of it—that *they* (I insist on this "they"), what *humans* do with certain words, but also, and for some time yet, to track, to sniff, to trail, and to follow some of the reasons they adduce for the very confident usage they make, and which for the moment we are making together, of words such as, therefore, *animal* and *I*.

A critical uneasiness will persist; in fact a bone of contention will be incessantly repeated throughout everything that I wish to develop. It would be aimed in the first place, once again, at the usage, in the singular, of a notion as general as "the Animal," as if all nonhuman living things could be grouped without the common sense of this "commonplace," the Animal, whatever the abyssal differences and structural limits that separate, in the very essence of their being, all "animals," a name that we would therefore be advised, to begin with, to keep within quotation marks. Confined within this catch-all concept, within this vast encampment of the animal, in this general singular, within the strict enclosure of this definite article ("the Animal" and not "animals"), as in a virgin forest, a zoo, a hunting or fishing ground, a paddock or an abattoir, a space of domestication, are *all the living things* that man does not recognize as his fellows, his neighbors, or his brothers. And that is so in spite of the infinite space that separates the lizard from the dog, the protozoon from the dolphin, the shark from the lamb, the parrot from the chimpanzee, the camel from the eagle, the squirrel from the tiger or the elephant from the cat, the ant from the silkworm or the hedgehog from the echidna. I interrupt my nomenclature and call Noah to help insure that no one gets left on the ark.

Since this has come down to sketching out a taxonomy, excuse me the immodesty of a further confession. It won't be *oto*biographical, like that I tried on another occasion in respect of a Nietzschean ear, although he, like Kafka, knows his stuff better than most others when it comes to animals. Instead it will be *zoo*tobiographical. This zoo-auto-bio-bibliography will be brief. I allow myself or constrain myself to this indulgence precisely for mnemonic effect, in the name of the name of our meeting, "L'Animal autobiographique." I will indulge in it before dealing in a different mode with what ties the history of the "I am," the autobiographical and autodeictic relation to the self as "I," to the history of "the Animal," the human concept of the animal. Since today I would like to run ahead of myself and sketch out other steps in moving forward, that is to say in stepping out without too much retrospection and without looking twice, I will not go back over arguments of a theoretical or philosophical kind, or in what we can call a deconstructive style, arguments that for a very long time, since I began writing in fact, I have sought to dedicate to the question of the living and of the living animal. For me that will always have been the most important and decisive question. I have addressed it a thousand times, either directly or obliquely, by means of readings of *all* the philosophers I have taken an interest in, beginning with Husserl and the concepts of the *rational animal*, of life or transcendental instinct that are found at the heart of phenomenology (but, paradoxically, when it comes to the animal, Husserl, like Hegel, is not the most "Cartesian" of the philosophers I shall later speak of). Still, short of outlining a philosophical autobiography, short of retracing my steps along the paths of philosophy, I could have, or perhaps should have undertaken an anamnesic interpretation of all *my* animals. They certainly do not form a family, but they are the critters [*bêtes*] that I have been (following) from the start, for decades and from conference to conference. I will not do that, out of modesty or discretion, and because there are too many of them, it would be interminable and seen as indecorous in this august setting. But I do think I need to open other paths, two perhaps, for whomever might wish, retrospectively, to follow such an exploration. I shall do so briefly, limiting myself strictly to the theme of our conference.

On the one hand, my animal figures multiply, gain in insistence and visibility, become active, swarm, mobilize, and get motivated, move and become moved all the more as my texts become more explicitly autobiographical, are more often uttered in the first person.

I just said "animal figures." These animals are without doubt something other than figures or characters in a fable. For as I see it, one of the most visible metamorphoses of the figural, and precisely of the animal figure, would perhaps be found, in my case, in "White Mythology." Indeed, that essay follows the movement of tropes and of rhetoric, the explanation of concept by means of metaphor, by prowling around animal language, between an Aristotle who deprives the animal of language and word and *mimesis*, and a Nietzsche who, if it can be said, "reanimalizes" the genealogy of the concept. The one who parodied *Ecce Homo* tries to teach us to laugh again by plotting, as it were, to let loose all the animals within philosophy. To laugh and to cry, for, as you know, he was mad enough to cry for an animal, under the gaze of, or cheek to cheek with a horse. Sometimes I think I see him call that horse as a witness, and primarily, in order to call it as a witness to his compassion, I think I see him take its head in his hands.

Animals are my concern. Whether in the form of a figure or not.[23] They multiply, lunging more and more wildly in my face in proportion as my texts seem to become autobiographical, or so one would have me believe.

It is obvious. Even a little too obvious were we to begin, say, at the end, the end of "A Silkworm of One's Own," published in 1998.[24] Already, in the iconography of "Socrates and Plato" at the Bodleian Library, the animals emerge from page after page, says the signatory of a postcard from July 1979, "like *squirrels*," "squirrels" "in a forest." As for the *monkey* of "Heidegger's Hand," he takes, he grasps, but he will not give, or greet, and especially not think according to Master Heidegger. The *hedgehog* of "What Is Poetry?" letter written in the first person, bears in its quills, among other things, the heritage of a piece of my name. Which is signed "Fourmis" ["*Ants*"] in *Lectures de la différence sexuelle*.

For, *on the other hand*, I note in passing, almost all these animals are welcomed, in a more and more deliberate manner, on the threshold of sexual difference. More precisely of sexual differences, that is to say what for the most part is kept under wraps in almost all of the grand philosophical-type treatises on the animality of the animal. This opening, on the threshold of sexual differences, was the very track left by the hedgehog or ant, but more than that, in the most recent text, where it is precisely a matter of nakedness, with or without a veil, I was interested in the thinking of what is naked, as it is said, like a worm,[25] "A Silkworm of One's Own." From beginning to end that three-part journal talks of the ambiguity of the sexual experience at its birth. It deals with veils of modesty and truth, at the same time recalls one of the zootobiographical origins of my bestiary. After noting that "it was impossible to discern a sexual organ," the child recalls:

23. "Les animaux me regardent. Avec ou sans figure, justement": thus also, "Animals look at me. With or without a face, precisely."—TRANS.

24. See Derrida, "Un Ver à soie," in Hélène Cixous and Derrida, *Voiles* (Paris, 1998), pp. 23–85.

25. "Nu comme un vers": compare Chaucer, "naked as a worm"; modern, "naked as a jaybird" (*Oxford English Dictionary*, s.v. "naked").

There was indeed something like a brown mouth but you could not recognize in it the orifice you had to imagine to be at the origin of their silk, this milk become thread, this filament extending their body and remaining attached to it for a certain length of time: the extruded saliva of a very fine sperm, lustrous, shiny, the miracle of a female ejaculation which would catch the light and which I drank in with my eyes. . . . The self-displacement of this little fantasy of a penis, was it erection or detumescence? I would observe the invisible progress of the weaving, a little as though I was about to stumble on the secret of a marvel, the secret of this secret over there, at the infinite distance of the animal, of this little innocent member, so foreign yet so close in its incalculable estrangement.

Later, the child continues:

the spinning of its threads [or "sons"] or daughters—beyond any sexual difference or rather any duality of the sexes, and even beyond any coupling. In the beginning, there was the worm which was and was not a sex, the child could see it clearly, a sex perhaps but then which one? His bestiary was starting up.[26]

There is a rhythmic difference between erection and detumescence. It is no doubt at the heart of what concerns us here, namely, a sentiment of shame related to standing upright—hence with respect to erection in general and not only phallic surrection—and to the face-to-face. Let us leave that remark—notably the role played by sexual difference in the matter of shame—to be followed up on or discussed later: why would a man be at the same time *more and less* modest than a woman? What must shame be in terms of this *"at the same time"* of the *"more or less?"*

In calling up still more of my animal texts of yesterday or the day before, I take my cue from the title of our program. Indeed that title obliges us to cross the animal with autobiography. I therefore admit to my old obsession with a personal and somewhat paradisaic bestiary. It came to the fore very early on: the crazy project of constituting everything I have thought or written within a zoosphere, the dream of an absolute hospitality and an infinite appropriation. How to welcome or

26. Derrida, "A Silkworm of One's Own," trans. Geoffrey Bennington, *Oxford Literary Review* 18, nos. 1–2 (1996): 49, 50; trans. mod.

liberate so many animal-words [*animots*]²⁷ *chez moi*? In me, for me, like me? It would have amounted at the same time to something more and less than a bestiary. Above all, it would be necessary to avoid fables. We know the history of fabulation and how it remains an anthropomorphic taming, a moralizing subjection, a domestication. Always a discourse *of* man, on man, indeed on the animality of man, but for and as man.

Rather than developing that fabulous bestiary I gave myself a horde of animals within the forest of my own signs and the memoirs of my memory. I was no doubt thinking about such a company well before the visitation of the innumerable critters that now overpopulate my texts. Well before the ant, the hedgehog, or the silkworm; well before the spider, bee, or snakes of "Freud and the Scene of Writing" or of "White Mythology"; well before the wolves of the *Wolfman* in "Fors"; well before the horse of *Spurs* and especially before Kant's horse, about which it is said, in "Parergon," concerning his theory of free and dependent beauty, that unlike birds or crustaceans, it is "bothersome" (the theory is straitjacketed by this horse, whether one takes it to be wild or broken in, exploited, tamed, "finalized" by man, by the subject of aesthetic and teleological judgements; relayed through the jennet [*genet*], the Spanish horse that runs through the middle of *Glas*, the horse from "Parergon" is moreover compared to the steer, the sheep, the pig and the ass; there was also a quite different ass, the ass of multiple references to the *Ja Ja* of affirmation following the traces of Zarathustra); well before the mole from I forget where, *Specters of Marx* I think; well before Florian's hare and Kant's black swan in *Politics of Friendship*, but also before those I secretly call "my friends the birds" of Laguna Beach in "Circumfession," where I also bring back on stage certain white hens sacrificed in the *Pardès* on the Day of Atonement of my Algerian childhood; and still yet before the fish of "+R" in *The Truth in Painting* that plays upon "I" by means of the *Ich* of *Ichtus*, of Ish and Ishah, crossed with Khi by means of a chiasmus, and with a certain *Chi-mère* whose name decomposes in *Glas*, where a certain eagle soars over the two columns; well before the dead-alive viruses, undecidably between life and death, between animal and vegetal, that come back from everywhere to haunt and obsess my writing; well before the reminder of all of Nietzsche's animals in *Spurs* but also in "Otobiographies," including a certain "hypocritical dog"

27. This portmanteau neologism, combining "animal" and "word," is pronounced, in the singular or the plural, the same way as the plural of "animal." With its singular article and plural-sounding ending, it jars in oral French. See Derrida's discussion below.—TRANS.

(the Church) and the ears of a "phonograph dog"; well before Ponge's
zooliterature in *Signsponge* (the swallow, the shrimp, the oyster); well
before the sponge itself, that marine zoophyte that is wrongly held to
be a plant, and about which I spoke in this very place, but which had
also passed through my work earlier, again in "White Mythology," in
relation to what Bachelard identified by the name of the "metaphysics
of the sponge."[28] But since I wish ultimately to return at length to the
treatment of the animal in Heidegger, permit me to create a special place
in this short taxonomy in the form of a reminder [*pense-bête*], for a
note that appears in brackets. It is from *Of Spirit*. That short text deals
abundantly and directly with the Heideggerian concept of the animal
as "poor in world" (*weltarm*), something I wish to analyze tomorrow,
looking closely at the seminar of 1929–30. The note in brackets in my
text does not appear to relate to the development of the problematic
of the animal. It brings to the fore the "gnawing, ruminant, and silent
voracity of . . . an animal-machine and its implacable logic." But there
is only the resemblance of an animal-machine, Cartesian or otherwise.
It is an animal of reading and rewriting. It will be at work in all the
tracks we are heading down here, announcing them and ferreting them
out in advance:

> [Pause for a moment: to dream of the face the Heideggerian
> corpus would put on the day when, with all the application
> and consistency required, the operations prescribed by him at
> one moment or another would indeed have been carried out:
> "avoid" the word "spirit," at the very least place it in quotation
> marks, then cross through all the names referring to the world
> whenever one is speaking of something which, like the animal,
> has no *Dasein*, and therefore no or only a little world, then
> place the word "Being" everywhere under a cross, and finally
> cross through without a cross all the question marks when it's
> a question of language, i.e., indirectly, of everything, etc. One
> can imagine the surface of the text given over to the gnawing,
> ruminant, and silent voracity of such an animal-machine and
> its implacable "logic." This would not only be simply "without
> spirit," but the face (figure) of evil. The perverse reading of Hei-
> degger. End of pause.][29]

28. Gaston Bachelard, *La Formation de l'esprit scientifique* (Paris, 1972), p. 79.
29. Derrida, *Of Spirit: Heidegger and the Question*, trans. Bennington and Rachel
Bowlby (Chicago, 1989), p. 134; trans. mod. Would the language Heidegger uses, a lan-

This animal-machine has a family resemblance with the virus that obsesses, not to say invades everything I write. Neither animal nor nonanimal, organic or inorganic, living or dead, this potential invader is *like* a computer virus. It is lodged in a processor of writing, reading and interpretation. But, if I may note this in generous anticipation of what is to follow, it would be an animal that is capable of deleting (thus of erasing a trace, something Lacan thinks the animal is incapable of). This quasi-animal would no longer have to relate itself to being *as such* (something Heidegger thinks the animal is incapable of) since it would take account of the need to strike out "being." But, as a result, in striking out "being" and taking itself beyond or on this side of the question (and hence of the response) is it something completely other than a species of animal? Yet another question to be followed up on.

We are following, we follow ourselves. I shall not impose upon you a complete exposition of this theory of *animots* that I am (following) or that follow me everywhere and the memory of which seems to me inexhaustible. Far from resembling Noah's ark it would be more like a circus, with an animal trainer having his sad subjects, bent low, file past. The multiple *animot* would still suffer from always having its master on its back. It would have it up to the neck [*en aurait plein le dos*] with being thus domesticated, broken in, trained, docile, disciplined, tamed. Instead of recalling the menagerie that some who badmouth me might characterize as my autobibliography, I shall simply recall the idea, or rather the troubling stakes of a philosophical bestiary, of a bestiary at the origin of philosophy. It was not by chance that it first imposed itself in the region of an undecidable *pharmakon*. Concerning the Socratic irony that "precipitates out one *pharmakon* by bringing it in contact with another *pharmakon*," that is to say "reverses the *pharmakon*'s powers and turns its surface over," I tried (in 1968, that is thirty years ago) to imagine what the program of a Socratic bestiary on the eve of philosophy might be, and more precisely (I note in the context of Descartes) how that would appear in a place where the demonic, the cun-

---

guage "without" question, without question mark, this language "before" the question, this language of the *Zusage* (acquiescence, affirmation, agreement, and so on), therefore be a language without a response? a "moment" of language that is in its essence released from all relation to an expected response? But if one links the concept of the animal, as they all do from Descartes to Heidegger, from Kant to Lévinas and Lacan, to the double im-possibility, the double incapacity of question and response, is it because the "moment," the instance and possibility of the *Zusage* belong to an "experience" of language about which one could say that, even if it is not in itself "animal," is not lacking in the "animal"? That would be enough to destabilize a whole tradition, to deprive it of its fundamental argument.

ning, indeed the evil genius has some affinity with the animal: a malign and hence perverse beast, at one and the same time innocent, crafty, and evil. Keeping myself to the program, let me refer to the note that made explicit, right in the middle, in the very center, in the binding between the two parts of "Plato's Pharmacy," this alternating border crossing:

> Alternately and/or all at once, the Socratic *pharmakon* petrifies and vivifies, anesthetizes and sensitizes, appeases and anguishes. Socrates is a benumbing stingray but also an animal that needles [this is a reference to well-known texts]: we recall the bee in the *Phaedo* (91c); later we will open the *Apology* at the point where Socrates compares himself precisely to a gadfly. This whole Socratic configuration thus composes a bestiary. [Of course, since this is a matter of animal figures in Socrates' presentation of the self, the question is indeed that of Socrates as autobiographical "animal."] Is it surprising that the demonic inscribes itself in a bestiary? It is on the basis of this zoo-pharmaceutical ambivalence and of that other Socratic *analogy* that the contours of the *anthropos* are determined.[30]

At the risk of being mistaken and of having one day to make honorable amends (which I would willingly accept to do), I will venture to say that never, on the part of any great philosopher from Plato to Heidegger, or anyone at all who takes on, *as a philosophical question in and of itself*, the question called that of the animal and of the limit between the animal and the human, have I noticed a protestation *of principle*, and especially a protestation of consequence against the general singular that is *the animal*. Nor against the general singular of an animal whose sexuality is as a matter of principle left undifferentiated—or neutralized, not to say castrated. Such an omission is not without connection to many others that form either its premise or its consequence. This philosophical or metaphysical datum has never been required to change philosophically speaking. I indeed said "philosophical" (or "metaphysical") datum for the gesture seems to me to constitute philosophy as such, the philosopheme itself. Not that all philosophers agree on the definition of *the* limit separating man in general from the animal in general (although this is an area that is most conducive to consensus and is no doubt where we find the dominant form of consensus on the matter). But in spite of that, through and beyond all their disagreements, philosophers have

30. Derrida, *Dissemination*, trans. Barbara Johnson (Chicago, 1981), p. 119 n. 52.

always judged and *all* philosophers have judged that limit to be single and indivisible, considering that on the other side of that limit there is an immense group, a single and fundamentally homogeneous set that one has the right, the theoretical or philosophical right, to distinguish and mark as opposite, namely, the set of the Animal in general, the animal spoken of in the general singular. It applies to the whole animal realm with the exception of the human. Philosophical right thus presents itself as that of "common sense." This agreement concerning philosophical sense and common sense that allows one to speak blithely of the Animal in the general singular is perhaps one of the greatest, and most symptomatic idiocies [*bêtises*] of those who call themselves humans. We shall perhaps speak of *bêtise* and of bestiality later, as that from which beasts are in any case exempt by definition. One cannot speak—moreover, it has never been done—of the *bêtise* or bestiality of an animal. It would be an anthropomorphic projection of something that remains reserved to man, as the single assurance finally, and the single risk, of what is "proper to man." One can ask why the ultimate fallback of what is proper to man, if there is such a thing, a property that could never in any case be attributed to the animal or to God, thus comes to be named *bêtise* or bestiality.

Interpretive decisions (in all their metaphysical, ethical, juridical, and political consequences) thus depend on what is presupposed by the general singular of this word *Animal*. I was tempted, at a given moment, in order to indicate the direction of my thinking, not just to keep this word within quotation marks, as if it were a citation to be analyzed, but without further ado to change the word, indicating clearly thereby that it is indeed a matter of a word, only a word, the word *animal* [*du mot "animal"*], and to forge another word in the singular, at the same time close but radically foreign, a chimerical word that sounded as though it contravened the laws of the French language, *l'animot*.

Ecce animot. Neither a species nor a gender nor an individual, it is an irreducible living multiplicity of mortals, and rather than a double clone or a portmanteau word, a sort of monstrous hybrid, a chimera waiting to be put to death by its Bellerophon.

Who or what was the Chimaera?

Chimaera was, as we know, the name of a flame-spitting monster. Her monstrousness derived precisely from the multiplicity of animals, of the *animot* in her (head and chest of a lion, entrails of a goat, tail of a dragon). Chimaera of Lycia was the offspring of Typhon and Echidne. As a common noun *echidna* means serpent, more precisely a viper and sometimes, figuratively, a treacherous woman, a serpent that one cannot charm or make stand up by playing a flute. Echidna is also the name that is given to a very special animal found only in Australia and New Guinea. This mammal lays eggs, something quite rare. Here we have an oviparous mammal that is also an insectivore and a monotreme. It only has one hole (*mono-trema*) for all the necessary purposes, urinary tract, rectum, and genitals. It is generally agreed that the echidna resembles a hedgehog. Along with the platypus the five species of echidna make up the family of monotremes.

As the child of Typhon and Echidne, Chimaera interests me therefore because chimerical will be my address,[31] and I will gradually explain the reasons for it. In the first place it concerns my old and ambivalent attachment to the figure of Bellerophon who puts Chimaera to death. He deserves a ten-day conference on him alone. He represents, as is well known, the figure of the hunter. He follows. He is he who follows. He follows and persecutes the beast. He would say: I am (following), I pursue, I track, overcome, and tame the animal. Before Chimaera the animal in question was at first Pegasus, whom he held by the bit, a "golden bit given to him by Athene." Holding him by the bit he makes him dance; he orders him to do some dance steps. I underline in passing this allusion to the choreography of the animal in order to announce that, much later, we will encounter a certain animal danceness[32] from the pen of Lacan. Pegasus, archetypal horse, son of Poseidon and the Gorgon is therefore the half-brother of Bellerophon himself who, descending thus from the same god as Pegasus, ends up following and taming a sort of brother, an other self: I am half (following) my brother, it is as if he says, I am (following) my other and I have the better of him, I hold him by the bit. What does one do in holding one's other by the bit? When one holds one's brother or half brother by the bit?

There was also the matter of a dead animal between Cain and Abel. And of a tamed, raised, and sacrificed animal. Cain, the older brother, the agricultural worker, therefore the sedentary one, submits to having his offering of the fruits of the earth refused by a God who prefers, as an oblation, the first-born cattle of Abel, the rancher.

---

31. "Chimérique sera mon adresse": compare above, "*Limitrophy* is therefore my subject," and below, "the truth of modesty will, in the end, be our subject." Derrida is alluding to two previous Cerisy lectures, that on Ponge in 1975, where he asserted "'Francis Ponge will be my thing,'" and that on Nietzsche in 1972, where he stated "Woman will be my subject" (Derrida, *Signéponge/Signsponge*, trans. Richard Rand [New York, 1984], p. 10; see also Derrida, *Spurs/Eperons*, trans. Barbara Harlow [Chicago, 1978], pp. 36–37).—TRANS.

32. *Dansité*, another neologism, pronounced the same as *densité* (density).—TRANS.

God prefers the sacrifice of the very animal that he has let Adam name—*in order to see*. As if between the taming desired by God and the sacrifice of the animal preferred by God the invention of names, the freedom accorded Adam or Ish to name the animals, was only a stage "*in order to see*," in view of providing sacrificial flesh for offering to that God. One could say, too hastily no doubt, that giving a name would be a means of sacrificing the living to God. The fratricide that results from it is marked as a sort of second original sin, in this case twice linked to blood, since the murder of Abel follows—as its consequence—the sacrifice of the animal that that same Abel had taken it upon himself to offer to God. What I am here venturing to call the second original sin is thus all the more linked to an apparition of the animal, as in the episode of the serpent, but this time it seems more serious and more consequential.

On the one hand, in fact, Cain admits to an *excessive* fault: he kills his brother after failing to sacrifice an animal to God. This fault seems to him unpardonable, not simply wrong but excessively culpable, *too grave*. But isn't a wrongdoing always excessive, in its very essence? As a form of default in the face of the imperative [*le défaut devant le "il faut"*]? "Cain said to Jehovah: 'My fault is too great to bear'" (Gen. 4:13; trans. Dhormes). "My wrong is too great to carry" (Gen. 4:13; trans. Chouraqui).[33]

This excess will be paid for in two ways: by his flight, of course, for Cain is said to be "hunted," "expelled," tracked, persecuted ("you have expelled me," "you have chased me out," Cain says to God); but also by means of the flight of the one who feels pursued, by the shameful hiding of himself, by the veil of yet another nakedness, by the avowal of that veil ("I will hide myself from before you. I will be a fugitive and flee on earth and it will come to pass that whoever happens upon me will kill me" [Gen. 4:14; trans. Dhormes]; "I will veil myself before you. I will move and wander throughout the earth and whoever finds me will kill me" [Gen. 4:14; trans. Chouraqui]).[34] There is thus a crime, shame, distancing, the retreat of the criminal. He is at the same time put to flight and hunted but also condemned to shame and dissimulation. He must hide his nakedness under a veil. A little as though it followed a second original sin this ordeal follows the murder of a brother, it is true, but it also follows the test to which he has been put by a God who prefers the

33. "Caïn dit à Iahvé: 'Ma faute est trop grande pour que je la porte!'" "'Mon tort est trop grand pour être porté.'"

34. "Je me cacherai de devant toi. Je serai fugitif et fuyard sur la terre et il arrivera que quiconque me rencontrera me tuera" (Dhormes). "Je me voilerai face à toi. Je serai mouvant, errant sur terre: / et c'est qui me trouvera me tuera" (Chouraqui).

animal offering of Abel. For God had put Cain to the test by organizing a sort of temptation. He had set a trap for him. Jehovah's language
is indeed that of a hunter. As if he were going after a nomad shepherd
farmer, such as Abel, "herder of cattle" [*pâtre d'ovins*], or "shepherd
of small animals" [*pasteur de petit bétail*], as opposed to the sedentary
agriculturist, the "cultivator of the ground" [*cultivateur du sol*], "the
servant of the glebe" [*serviteur de la glèbe*] that was Cain who made his
offering from the "fruits of the earth" or of the "glebe." Having refused
Cain's vegetable offering, preferring Abel's animal offering, God had
exhorted a discouraged Cain not to lose face, in short to be careful not
to fall into sin, not to fall victim to the wrongdoing that was waiting for
him around the corner. He encouraged him to avoid the trap of temptation and to once more tame, dominate, govern:

> So Jehovah said to Cain: "Why do you feel anger and why is
> your visage downfallen? If you act well, will you not pick your-
> self up? If you do not act well Sin *lurks* at your door [I underline
> this word *lurks* (*est tapi*), referring to sin, like an animal lying
> in wait in the shadow, waiting for its prey to fall into the trap,
> a victim prey to temptation, a bait or lure]: its force is coming
> towards you but have dominion over it." [Gen. 4:6–7; trans.
> Dhormes][35]

The word *lurk* also appears in the otherwise very different Chouraqui
translation: " . . . at the opening fault lurks; its passion comes towards
you. Govern it" (Gen. 4:7).[36] By killing his brother Cain falls into the
trap; he becomes prey to the evil *lurking* in the shadow like an animal.

However, *on the other hand*, the paradoxes of this manhunt follow
one after the other as a series of experimental ordeals: "in order to see."
Having fallen into the trap and killed Abel, Cain covers himself with
shame and flees, wandering, hunted, tracked in turn like an animal. God
then promises this human animal protection and vengeance. *As if* God
had repented. *As if* he were ashamed or had admitted having preferred
the animal sacrifice. *As if* in this way he were confessing and admitting
remorse concerning the animal. (This moment of "repentance," of "re-
traction," "going back on oneself"—there is an immense problem of

35. "Alors Iahvé dit à Caïn: 'Pourquoi éprouves-tu de la colère et pourquoi ton vis-
age est abattu? Si tu agis bien, ne te relèveras-tu?
   Que si tu n'agis pas bien le Péché est tapi à ta porte : son élan est vers toi, mais toi,
domine-le!'"—Trans.
   36. "À l'ouverture la faute est tapie ; à toi sa passion. Toi, gouverne-la."—Trans.

translation here, unlimited stakes in the semantics that I leave aside for the moment—is not the only such moment; there is at least one other at the time of the Flood, another animal story.)[37] So God promises seven vengeances, no more, no less. He vows to take revenge seven times on anyone who kills Cain, that is to say the murderer of his brother, he who, after this second original sin has covered the nakedness of his face, the face that he has lost before Him.

This double insistence upon nudity, fault, and default at the origin of human history and within sight or perspective of the animal cannot not be associated once more with the myth of Epimetheus and Prometheus: first, man receives fire and technology to compensate for his nakedness, but not yet the art of politics; then, from Hermes this time, he receives shame or honor, and justice (*aidos* and *dikē*), which will permit him to bring harmony and the bonds of friendship (*desmoi philias*) into the city (*polis*).

In bringing Genesis into relation with the Greek myths once more, still within sight and perspective of the animal, of fault and of nakedness, I am not speculating on any hypothesis derived from comparative history or the structural analysis of myth. These narratives remain heterogeneous in status and origin. Moreover I don't hold them to be causes or origins of anything whatsoever. Nor verities or verdicts. Simply and at least I hold them to be two symptomatic translations whose internal necessity is confirmed all the more by the fact that certain characteristics partially overlap from one translation to the other. But translation of what?

Well, let us say of a certain "state," a certain situation—of the process, world, and life obtaining among these mortal living things that are the animal species, those other "animals" and humans. Its analogous or common traits are all the more dominant given that their formalization, that to which we are devoting ourselves here, will allow us to see appear in every discourse concerning the animal, and notably in the Western philosophical discourse, the same dominant, the same recurrence of a schema that is in truth invariable. What is that? The following: what is proper to man, his superiority over and subjugation of the animal, his

37. Genesis 6:6: "Jehovah repented for having put man on the earth" . . . "I repent for having made them" ("Iahvé se repentit d'avoir fait l'homme sur la terre. . . . Je me repens de les avoir faits [Gen. 6:6; Dhormes]). Chouraqui uses the verb *regretter* ("to regret, be sorry"). The King James version says, "It repenteth the Lord. . . . It repenteth me." I insist on what is almost remorse, for it immediately precedes Noah's ark and the new covenant; this time it is *all the living* that will accompany Noah. I will return to this.

very becoming-subject, his historicity, his emergence out of nature, his sociality, his access to knowledge and technics, all that, everything (in a nonfinite number of predicates) that is proper to man would derive from this originary fault, indeed from this default in propriety, what is proper to man as default in propriety—and from the imperative [*il faut*] that finds in it its development and resilience. I will try to show this better later, from Aristotle to Heidegger, from Descartes to Kant, from Lévinas to Lacan.

Let us return to Bellerophon. He didn't trouble me only because he gained the upper hand with respect to his animal brother or half-brother (Pegasus), nor only because he vanquished Chimaera and so confirmed his mastery as hunter-tamer. Rather, all of Bellerophon's exploits can be deciphered *from top to bottom* as a history of modesty, of shame, of reticence, of honor to the extent that he is linked to modest decency (*aischune* this time and not just *aidon*). That allows us to make explicit in advance the fact that the truth of modesty will, in the end, be our subject. The ordeals that constitute the story of Bellerophon are well known. They are all destined to put to the test his sense of modesty. Because he has resisted the shameless advances of Stheneboea, the wife of his host, Proetus, king of Argos; because he is accused by that shameless woman, also called Antea, of having seduced her or of having taken her with violence during the hunt, he is condemned to death by her husband. But, out of respect for the laws of hospitality, the latter cannot himself put his rival to death. He therefore sends to his father-in-law, king of Lycia, this Bellerophon bearing a letter that, instead of recommending him to his future host, prescribes his execution (this is already the story of Hamlet sent to England by his father-in-law who entrusts to him a letter that is a death sentence. Hamlet escapes the trap. I make this allusion to Hamlet in order to recall in passing that that play is an extraordinary zoology: its animal figures are innumerable, which is somewhat the case all through Shakespeare—more to follow). Bellerophon thus carries with him, without knowing it, a verdict in the form of a letter of death whose truth escapes him. He becomes its unconscious purveyor [*facteur*]. But his second host begins sheltering the postman before unsealing the letter; he is therefore obliged in turn, as if held by a potential bit, to respect the laws of hospitality and so defer the execution of the sentence. Instead he submits Bellerophon to a new series of hunting, war, and combat exploits. It is in that context that the hunt of the Chimaera takes place. The Chimaera was said to be "invincible," of a divine race and in no way human (*theion genos, oud'anthrōpon* says the *Iliad* in Book VI, line 180): a lion in front, a serpent behind, a goat in the middle, its breath spouting frightening bursts of flame (*chimaira, deinon apopneiousa puros menos aithomenoio*).

As we shall understand, that is not how Descartes describes the Chimaera whose existence is excluded at the moment of "I think therefore I am" in part four of *Discourse on the Method* ("we can distinctly imagine a lion's head on a goat's body without having to conclude from this that a chimera exists in the world.")[38]

What is this "world?" We will later ask what "world" means? In passing we can consider whether we should take seriously the fact that in his description of the Chimaera Descartes forgets the serpent. Like Homer he names the lion and goat, but he forgets the serpent, that is to say the behind. The serpent (*drakōn*, dragon) is the animal's behind, the part that is at the same time the most fabulous, the most chimerical, like the dragon, and also the most cunning: the cunning genius of the animal, the evil genius as animal perhaps. A question concerning the serpent, therefore, concerning evil and shame.

The final episode is not recounted by Homer but by Plutarch. It again puts Bellerophon to the test of nakedness. It is the seventh and last test. Once more Bellerophon falls prey, if I might suggest, to women. In a movement of shame or of modesty (*hyp'aischunēs*) before women he backs down from his outrage at the hounding persecution that he is victim to, perpetrated by his brother-in-law Iobates. Having decided to destroy the city with the help of Poseidon, his father, he advances on it followed by a wave that threatens to engulf everything. But the women come on to him, offering themselves to him shamelessly. Their behavior is doubly indecent for they expose themselves in all their nakedness and they offer their bodies, prostituting themselves, for sale. They try to seduce him in exchange for being saved. Faced with this pornography Bellerophon weakens. He doesn't give in to their shameless advances, quite the contrary; he gives in to the impulse of his own shame and backs down before the immodesty of these women. He pulls back, retreats in shame (*hyp'aischunēs*) faced with the shameful conduct of these women. So the wave recedes and the city is saved. This movement of shame, this reticence, this inhibition, this retreat, this reversal is, no doubt, like the immunizing drive, the protection of the immune, of the sacred (*heilig*), of the holy, of the separate (*kadosh*) that is the very origin of the religious, of religious scruple. I have tried to devote several essays to analyzing that, relating it to what Heidegger calls *Verhaltenheit*, restraint, in

38. René Descartes, *The Philosophical Writings of Descartes*, trans. John Cottingham, Robert Stoothoff, and Dugald Murdoch, 2 vols. (Cambridge, 1985), 1:131.

his *Beiträge zur Philosophie*. As I tried to do in "Faith and Knowledge" where I sought to account for all the paradoxes of the auto-immune, I might have been tempted today had I the time, which I don't, to bring into focus once more this terrible (and always possible) perversion by means of which the immune becomes auto-immunizing, finding there some analogical or virtual relation with auto-biography.[39]

Autobiography, the writing of the self as living, the trace of the living for itself, being for itself, the auto-affection or auto-infection as memory or archive of the living would be an immunizing movement (a movement of safety, of salvage and salvation of the safe, the holy, the immune, the indemnified, of virginal and intact nudity), but an immunizing movement that is always threatened with becoming auto-immunizing, as is every *autos*, every ipseity, every automatic, automobile, autonomous, auto-referential movement. Nothing risks becoming more poisonous than an autobiography, poisonous for itself in the first place, auto-infectious for the presumed signatory who is so auto-affected.

Ecce animot—that is what I was saying before this long digression. In order not to damage French ears too sensitive to spelling and grammar I won't repeat the word *animot* too often. I'll do it several times but each time that, henceforth, I say the animal [*l'animal*] or the animals [*animaux*] I'll be asking you to silently substitute *animot* for what you hear. By means of the chimera of this singular word, the *animot*, I bring together three heterogeneous elements within a single verbal body.

1. I would like to have the plural of animals heard in the singular. There is no animal in the general singular, separated from man by a single indivisible limit. We have to envisage the existence of "living creatures" whose plurality cannot be assembled within the single figure of an animality that is simply opposed to humanity. This does not of course mean ignoring or effacing everything that separates humankind from the other animals, creating a single large set, a single great, fundamentally homogeneous and continuous family tree going from the *animot* to the *homo* (*faber, sapiens*, or whatever else). That would be an *asinanity*, even more so to suspect anyone here of doing just that. I won't therefore devote another second to the double stupidity of that suspicion, even if, alas, it is quite widespread. I repeat that it is rather a matter of taking into account a multiplicity of heterogeneous structures

39. See Derrida, "Faith and Knowledge: The Two Sources of 'Religion' at the Limits of Reason Alone," trans. Sam Weber, in *Religion*, trans. David Webb, Weber, and Jason Gaiger, ed. Derrida and Gianni Vattimo (Stanford, Calif., 1998), pp. 42–47.

and limits. Among nonhumans and separate from nonhumans there is an immense multiplicity of other living things that cannot in any way be homogenized, except by means of violence and willful ignorance, within the category of what is called the animal or animality in general. From the outset there are animals and, let's say, *l'animot*. The confusion of all nonhuman living creatures within the general and common category of the animal is not simply a sin against rigorous thinking, vigilance, lucidity, or empirical authority; it is also a crime. Not a crime against animality precisely, but a crime of the first order against the animals, against animals. Do we agree to presume that every murder, every transgression of the commandment "Thou shalt not kill" concerns only man (a question to come) and that in sum there are only crimes "against humanity?"

2. The suffix *mot* in *l'animot* should bring us back to the word, namely, to the word named a noun [*nommé nom*]. It opens onto the referential experience of the thing *as such*, as what it is in its being, and therefore to the reference point by means of which one has always sought to draw the limit, the unique and indivisible limit held to separate man from animal, namely the word, the nominal language of the word, the voice that names and that names the thing *as such*, such as it appears in its being (as in the Heideggerian moment in the demonstration that we are coming to). The animal would in the last instance be deprived of the word, of the word that one names a noun or name.

3. It would not be a matter of "giving speech back" to animals but perhaps of acceding to a thinking, however fabulous and chimerical it might be, that thinks the absence of the name and of the word otherwise, as something other than a privation.

Ecce animot, that is the announcement of which I am (following) something like the trace, assuming the title of an autobiographical animal, in the form of a risky, fabulous, or chimerical response to the question "But me, who am I?" that I have bet on treating as that of the autobiographical animal. Assuming that title, which is itself somewhat chimerical, might surprise you. It brings together *two times two* alliances, as unexpected as they are irrefutable.

On the one hand, the title gives rise to the thought, in the informal form of a playful conversation, a suggestion that would take witty advantage of idiom, that quite simply there are those among humans, writers, and philosophers whose character implies a taste for autobiography, the irresistible sense of or desire for autobiography. One would say, "(s)he's an autobiographical animal," in the same way that one says, "(s)he's a theatrical animal, a competitive animal, a political animal," not in the sense that one has been able to define man as a political animal but in the sense of an individual who has the taste, talent, or compulsive obsession for politics: he who likes that, likes doing that, likes politics. And does it well. In that sense the autobiographical animal would be the sort of man or woman who, as a matter of character, chooses to indulge in or can't resist indulging in autobiographical confidences. He or she who works *in* autobiography. And in the history of literature or philosophy, if it can be suggested in such a summary manner, there are "autobiographical animals," more autobiographical than others, animals for autobiography: Montaigne more than Malherbe, similarly Rousseau, the lyrical and romantic poets, Proust and Gide, Virginia Woolf, Gertrude Stein, Celan, Bataille, Genet, Duras, Cixous; but also (the matter is structurally more rare and more complicated when it comes to philosophy) Augustine and Descartes more than Spinoza, Kierkegaard, playing with so many pseudonyms, more than Hegel, Nietzsche more than Marx. But because the matter is really too complicated (it is our theme after all) I prefer to end the list of examples there. With the problems it poses this connotation of the autobiographical animal must certainly remain present, even if tangential, to our reflections. It will weigh on them with its virtual weight.

But, *on the other hand*, I was not thinking of that usage of the expression "autobiographical animal" in the last instance and in order to get to some bottom of the matter, if there is such a thing. It happens that there exist, between the word *I* and the word *animal*, all sorts of significant connections. They are at the same time functional and referential, grammatical and semantic. Two general singulars to begin with: the *I* and the *animal* designate an indeterminate generality in the singular and by means of the definite article. The *I* is anybody at all; *I* am anybody at all and anybody at all must be able to say "I" to refer to herself, to his own singularity. Whosoever says "I" or apprehends or poses him- or herself as an "I" is a living animal. On the other hand, animality, the life of the living, to the extent that one claims to be able to distinguish it from the inorganic, from the purely inert or cadaverous physico-chemical, is generally defined as sensibility, irritability, and *auto-motricity*, a spontaneity that is given to movement, to organizing itself and affecting itself, marking, tracing, and affecting itself with traces of its self. This *auto-motricity* as auto-affection and relation to itself is the characteristic recognized as that of the living and of animality in general, even before one comes to consider the discursive thematic of an utterance or of an *ego cogito*, more so of a *cogito ergo sum*. But between this relation to the self (this Self, this ipseity) and the *I* of the "I think," there is, it would seem, an abyss.

The problems begin there, we suspect, and what problems they are! But they begin where one attributes to the essence of the living, to the animal in general, this aptitude *that it itself is*, this aptitude to being itself, and thus the aptitude to being capable of affecting itself, of its own movement, of affecting itself with traces of a living self, and thus of *autobiograparaphing* itself as it were. No one has ever denied the animal this capacity to track itself, to trace itself or retrace a path of itself. Indeed the most difficult problem lies in the fact that it has been refused the power to transform those traces into verbal language, to call to itself by means of discursive questions and responses, denied the power to efface its traces (which is what Lacan will do, and we will come back to everything that that implies). Let us set out again from this place of intersection between these two general singulars, the animal (*l'animot*) and the "I," the "I"s, the place where in a given language, French for example, an "I" says "I." Singularly and in general. It could be anyone at all, you or I. So what happens there? How can I say "I" and what do I do thereby? And in the first place, me, what am I (following) and who am I (following)?

"I": by saying "I" the signatory of an autobiography would claim to point himself out physically, introduce himself in the present [*se présenter au présent*] (*sui*-referential deictic) and in his totally naked truth. And in the naked truth, if there is such a thing, of his or her sexual difference, of all their sexual differences. By naming himself and responding in his own name he would be saying "I stake and engage my nudity without shame." One can well doubt whether this pledge, this wager, this desire or promise of nudity is possible. Nudity perhaps remains untenable. And can I finally show myself naked in the sight of what they call by the name of animal? Should I show myself naked when, concerning me, looking at me, is the living creature they call by the common, general and singular name of the animal? Henceforth I will reflect (on) the same question by introducing a mirror. I import a full-length mirror [*une psyché*] into the scene. Wherever some autobiographical play is being enacted there has to be a *psyché*, a mirror that reflects me naked from head to toe. The same question then becomes whether I should show myself but in the process see myself naked (that is reflect my image in a mirror) when, concerning me, looking at me, is this living creature, this cat that can find itself caught in the same mirror? Is there animal narcissism? But cannot this cat also be, deep within her eyes, my primary mirror?

The animal in general, what is it? What does that mean? Who is it? To what does that "it"[40] correspond? To whom? Who responds to whom? Who responds in and to the common, general and singular name of what they thus blithely call the "animal?" Who is it that responds? The reference made by this what or who regarding me in the name of the animal, what is said in the name of the animal when one appeals to the name of the animal, that is what needs to be exposed, in all its nudity, in the nudity or destitution of whoever, opening the page of an autobiography, says, "here I am."

"But as for me, who am I (following)?"

40. *Ça*, also "Id."—TRANS.